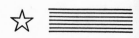

HOUGHTON MIFFLIN COMPANY · BOSTON

NEW YORK · ATLANTA · GENEVA, ILL. · DALLAS · PALO ALTO

DEMOCRACY, PLURALISM, and the SOCIAL STUDIES

Readings and Commentary

AN APPROACH TO CURRICULUM

DECISIONS IN THE SOCIAL STUDIES

Edited by James P. Shaver UTAH STATE UNIVERSITY

Harold Berlak WASHINGTON UNIVERSITY

Foreword

In American education today, one of the wide-open areas of controversy is the field of the social studies. Objectives, the role of values, the nature of social realities and the character of the thinking process are being re-examined. The question of what knowledge is of most worth is again being raised. The places of history and of the social sciences in the social studies curriculum are being vigorously debated. The quest is on for an adequate rationale for curricular decisions in the social studies. To the controversy and the quest, editors James P. Shaver and Harold Berlak contribute this book, *Democracy, Pluralism, and the Social Studies: Readings and Commentary*. Like the controversy, it is alive and provocative. Like the quest, it is thoughtful and probing. It raises questions, answers questions, and raises still more questions.

The readings gathered here deal with fundamental issues, alternatives, and ideas in social studies education. The selections themselves, written by committed scholars who do not pussyfoot, are almost certain to stir the thoughtful reader to agreement and disagreement, approbation and disapproval, delight and aggravation. Many sacred cows are prodded and many shibboleths are denied. Few are the viewpoints on the social studies which escape critical examination somewhere in the book.

The book is an ambitious enterprise which was well thought through by the two editors. The reader will find no random selections of readings here. The choices were carefully made and purposefully placed. The sections deal with

1) Objectives
2) Conceptions of the Society and the Social Studies Curriculum
3) History and the Social Studies
4) The Social Sciences and the Curriculum
5) Thinking About Thinking
6) Research in Social Studies Instruction

The editors enter into the examination of the central issues, too. Each of the six sections is prefaced by an editor's essay, itself provocative and probing, which extensively overviews the section through comments, introductions, criticisms, and questions concerning the selections which follow. The editors do not hesitate to examine the viewpoints of the authors they have selected. In addition, the editors enter into the debate by including selections by themselves and by a collaborator, Donald W. Oliver, which state the case for a rationale for decision making in the social studies which stresses the clarification of public issues.

Thus, the editors serve in this volume as both issue-raisers and protagonists. The reader emerges from his reading with a view of the range of ongoing controversies in the social studies and with an introduction to the editors' views of some desirable directions for the emerging social studies program. Yet these views are presented as one element among many in the total pattern of conflicting opinions of which the reader must take account. The reader is expected to be critical of the editors' views as well as the views of other contributors to the volume. In short, the reader is asked to use the method of intelligence throughout the entire book.

Democracy, Pluralism, and the Social Studies: Readings and Commentary is a significant contribution to the great debate on social studies teaching. Of the importance of the debate, one need only point out that desirable solutions to the problems of teaching social studies are vital to democratic citizenship in this nation.

William Van Til

Preface

This book of readings is the result of our experiences teaching courses on social studies curriculum and methods over the last few years. Both editors have gone through the process of attempting to select textbooks for such courses, and have found, with a couple of exceptions, that those available are sadly wanting. In general, the available texts tend to be repetitive of one another, and none is particularly provocative. They treat topics such as the history of the social studies, preparing units, lesson planning, and testing, routinely and superficially. There is little in them that would challenge the prospective teacher or curriculum developer to reflect deeply about the role of the social studies in this society, the significant choices that must be made in regard to content and method, or valid methods of assessing learning in the classroom. In short, available methods textbooks offer little that is likely to bring about a clearer, more seriously considered conception of the social studies curriculum.

There are some exceptions to this generalization. One is *Teaching High School Social Studies* by Maurice Hunt and Lawrence Metcalf (Harper, 1955). Rather than rehashing the old topics with slight refurbishing, the Hunt and Metcalf text attempts a bold, new look at the social studies. It suggests that social studies teaching should be organized around the consideration of certain societal problem areas that are ordinarily closed, i.e., not open to public discussion. The case is built for this approach, providing the student with an example of curriculum rationale building that goes beyond the trite treatment of how to plan a lesson.

For a methods course, the shortcoming of the Hunt and Metcalf text is that, because it is essentially an argument for one position, it is limited in scope. The student is not exposed to an adequate range of questions and positions for encouraging reflection about alternatives for the social studies curriculum. While making excellent supplementary reading, the defense of one position is not alone sufficient.

Teaching Public Issues in the High School by Donald W. Oliver and James P. Shaver (Houghton Mifflin, 1966) also provides a clear statement of a curricular position. In addition, it goes beyond Hunt and Metcalf by reporting the experimental use of a curriculum based on that position. But it does not, nor does it intend to, provide a broad treatment of the problems that the teacher faces in developing a specific rationale and curriculum.

The immediate response might be to suggest that we turn to books of readings for the social studies already available on the market. We have looked at these, and have a basic criticism. They seem to lack order — that is, selection and organization based on careful analysis of the areas to be considered in developing a rationale upon which to base social studies teaching. Moreover, they lean too heavily on current writings and on the writings of "social studies educators," ignoring scholars in the social sciences and other areas. They cover the waterfront, but without sufficient perception and depth.

As a consequence of our assessment of available books, both of us have used extensive reading lists rather than textbooks for our social studies methods courses. These have included selections from books, as well as journal articles. It became apparent during a discussion at an annual meeting of the National Council for the Social Studies that we had reacted to a common plight and had arrived at similar solutions. In fact, we found that our reading lists had much in common, although there were some significant variations. After some correspondence and further discussion, we decided that it might be of value if these readings were made available to students and instructors of the social studies methods course. We developed a perspective, which embodied our rationale for a book of readings and included some tentative selections, and fortunately, Houghton Mifflin saw merit in our proposal.

It was no accident that there was a great deal of similarity in the two editors' thinking about the current batch of social studies methods textbooks and collections of readings. We shared years as graduate students at the Harvard Graduate School of Education, working with Donald W. Oliver as our advisor and as a colleague on the curriculum project reported in *Teaching Public Issues in the High School*. We gained much from his provocative and often unconventional views of what social studies education should be about. Both of us profited from the atmosphere of free inquiry, controversy, creativity, and respect for the contributions of students and junior faculty that prevailed at the Graduate School of Education under the leadership of Francis Keppel and Judson T. Shaplin.

Of course, a book of readings, while requiring that the editors develop criteria, write introductory essays, organize the material, and try to make their rationale come through to the reader, basically depends upon the availability of quality readings. We would like to thank here the many authors and publishers who have allowed us to include their works. Each will be acknowledged at the beginning of the selections.

JAMES P. SHAVER AND HAROLD BERLAK

Contents

ix

6. Research in Social Studies Instruction

DEMOCRACY,
PLURALISM,
and the
SOCIAL STUDIES

Readings and Commentary

Introduction

Curriculum Decisions
in the Social Studies

When a democratic nation obligates all youth to spend the greater part of their daylight hours in school, the policies of that institution must be a matter for public debate. The school is not the only social institution which educates, but it is the only institution which is obligated to formulate and justify explicit educational policy. The most complex and controversial decisions an educator must make arise in formulating policy on what constitutes a wise educational program. He must decide what knowledge is of most worth to the young of the nation; in addition, he must decide how values are to be handled within the educational program, since the school, like other social institutions, inevitably shapes the feelings and values the young bring to adulthood.

Each curriculum is a response to the question of how the young should be educated. As with any policy, curriculum decisions can be subject to review. One may ask, What is the rationale for the decisions that were made, or if it is a new policy (a new curriculum), one may request that the bases for the decisions be made explicit so that they can be subjected to scrutiny.

The teacher as a key educational policy maker must base his curricular decisions on a careful rationale or argument — one laid out explicitly and in detail. The purpose of this volume is to raise issues and questions which will assist social studies teachers in carefully examining the reasoning lying behind their educational decisions. Although this book is not addressed to questions of wise educational policy in all subject areas, a number of the readings and the editors' introductory essays have bearing beyond the social studies.

As in other fields, there is a body of conventional wisdom concerning what should be taught in the social studies. Experienced and novice teachers often accept this conventional wisdom without questioning the justification for the traditional answers. Why, for instance, do we teach a chronologically organized American history course in the eleventh grade, and why does this course typically focus on the policies of presidential administrations and on the major wars? The point is not that American history should not be taught in the eleventh grade; rather, it is that the teacher should carefully explore the justification for this and all other courses. The search for justification must push back to *first* or *basic* questions. Answers such as "Every young person needs to know American history" are both superficial and non-responsive to the question of why a course is taught or why it is taught as it is. To examine the rationale for a course is to explore carefully and in detail the criteria which have been used for selecting content, sequence, and instructional strategy.

1

The examination or construction of a rationale for curricular decisions in the social studies is not an easy task. There are no simple formulas to be given to the teacher. What we have attempted to do in this volume is to identify several areas the educator must take into account in formulating or questioning his rationale. It is our position that the rationale for any given curricular decision is based on decisions in a number of related areas. By identifying these areas, explicating assumptions and formulating positions on the issues raised in each area, and seeking consistency and coherence among the positions, the teacher builds a basis for examining his teaching and the curricula proposed by others in order to detect weaknesses, contradictions, and absurdities of which he might otherwise not have been aware.

This volume identifies four areas to be considered in building a sound rationale for curricular decisions in the social studies. The four areas, which also serve as the basis for the organization of the book, are:

1. *Normative conceptions of the social world.* Ideas of *what is desirable* for man in society have an inevitable impact on the curriculum. Every educational program, whether it be within a free or a totalitarian society, is built on implicit or explicit notions about the "good man" and the "good society." If curriculum making is to be rational, the underlying normative assumptions or "values" must be laid bare and carefully scrutinized and reformulated. The way in which social values are handled within the curriculum will be based on implicit assumptions about what is good, if not on an explicitly formulated position.

2. *Empirical conceptions of the social world.* An educational program is not only predicated upon ideas of what is desirable, but also upon empirical or factual suppositions about what *is* and what *will be.* In other words, curricular aims are based in part upon the educator's conceptions of what the social, political, and economic system is and what it is becoming. If, as some contend, our society is becoming more depersonalized, increasingly specialized and complex, with political and social decisions becoming less comprehensible to the common man, then we must take this into account in forming a rationale for our educational programs. Whether the *content* of the curriculum will actually include any particular empirical proposition about the society is, however, another question. The curriculum maker may choose not to deal with all major social and economic changes, but he should not avoid any out of ignorance; rather, decisions regarding what to teach or what not to teach should be founded on sound educational grounds. How to characterize our society, as well as *if* and *how* formal curricula should treat issues related to social change, are major questions to be taken into account.

3. *The nature of social science and historical knowledge.* Any course in social studies requires that the teacher (or other curriculum developer) select and arrange for the learner materials which embody knowledge judged to be important. Any course or curriculum is an answer to the question posed by Herbert Spencer's essay, "What Knowledge is of Most Worth?" The answer to this question depends not only upon the educator's normative and empirical conceptions of society, but also upon his conception of the nature of knowledge itself. For instance, the degree to which the discipline of history is to be a central focus of a social studies program depends in part upon one's conception of historical knowledge and its limitations. The teacher selects material from

among those fields he views as the most relevant and valid for the educational goals he has in mind. He must reflect upon and develop some conception of the nature of social science and historical knowledge if he is to consciously and intelligently formulate a policy for selecting the knowledge that will be of most worth to his students.

4. *The nature of thinking.* Most educational programs aim to teach students to think. If this goal is to be more than a vaguely stated platitude, the teacher must have an explicit and viable concept of thinking. Thinking is the most complex and least understood of human endeavors, although assumptions about how it proceeds are implicit in the materials and teaching strategies built into a curriculum. In addition, any attempt to formulate a curriculum which presumes to teach thinking includes notions of what *good* thinking is. If an educator lacks a clearly articulated conception of *good* thinking, then it is unlikely that he will plan lessons or write materials which will encourage such thinking. A rationale must, therefore, include a consideration of how men think and of the characteristics of good thinking the curriculum is intended to shape.

The educator's views in each of the foregoing areas have a direct bearing on what he does in the classroom — the questions asked, the intellectual demands made, and the reading required of the students. In other words, the educator's views on these issues are not merely a matter of "philosophical" or "academic" interest. At the same time, it is obvious that social studies teachers have not always consciously reflected upon these elements of a rationale. Indeed, many teachers seem totally unaware of the empirical and normative conceptions of social reality, the conceptions of social science and history, and the conceptions of thought process that underlie their curricular choices. If this is the case, then these teachers will most certainly be unaware of the subtle and sometimes contradictory effects that these underlying conceptions have on their teaching.

How will this book raise issues in each of the four areas that have been outlined? The first section, "On Objectives," poses the question, What should be the objectives of social studies instruction? It should be noted, however, that a list of objectives is not the same as a rationale. A rationale provides the *reasons* for a particular set of objectives. Each of the subsequent sections, introduced with an essay by the editors, presents readings that suggest issues, ideas, and alternatives to assist the reader in constructing his rationale for social studies instruction. The intent is to assist in answering the questions posed by the first chapter on objectives. It will be obvious that the various sections are not independent. The concerns of the readings overlap and the issues raised are interrelated. For instance, conceptions of the desirable in society cannot usually be separated from conceptions of what is or what is not possible. And, the study of the nature of thinking may profit from an examination of how inquiry proceeds within history and the social science disciplines. However, the division of readings into four areas is intended to provide the reader with a structure or framework for his reflections about the social studies curriculum. It must be emphasized, however, that an educator's positions in each of the areas must be consistent with one another or his curriculum is likely to be confused or contradictory.

A Justification for Emphasizing Rationale in the Curriculum and Methods Course

This volume, which is intended for use in the social studies curriculum and methods course as well as by practicing teachers, may be seen as a proposal for a shift in the focus of many of the social studies curriculum and methods courses offered in university teacher training programs. It should be clear by this point that in our view this course should center on challenging the teacher to reflect upon and develop a rationale for his own curriculum. What is the justification for a heavier emphasis on rationale formulation in the social studies curriculum and methods course?

1. *Responsibility for Making Social Studies Curriculum Decisions.* Although the teacher is often *not* the official curriculum policy maker, it is the teacher who finally decides what is to be on the agenda when he faces his class — e.g., he decides what questions are to be asked, what the students are to read, and what issues will be focused upon. The crucial element in an educational program, after all, is what happens between teacher and student in a classroom day after day, not what is contained in a syllabus or an administrative directive. By default or intent, teachers have an extraordinarily high degree of latitude in making day-by-day instructional choices. Although experienced teachers know that they, not the various mimeographed and dittoed documents, determine the proceedings in the classroom, young teachers, expecting much direction and control, are often overwhelmed by their autonomy.

What of those who share the responsibility for shaping the curriculum? The principal is usually interested in the curriculum, but lacks the time, and often the competence, to play a major role in its determination. At best, he can only encourage curricular change. More commonly, his role is to guard against decisions that might lead to community disapproval or complaint. The district supervisors or curriculum directors who have direct responsibility for the curriculum have such heavy responsibilities that they must choose between spreading their efforts over too many classrooms or working intensively with a few teachers, often those having the most serious problems. Moreover, supervisors and curriculum coordinators are often generalists with little special training or competence in the social sciences or social studies curriculum.

The university professor might be an unofficial source of curricular decisions. However, most professors have little contact with the teacher once he leaves the university. And though university faculty may conduct in-service training or act as consultants to schools, professorial experiences are often so far removed from the elementary and secondary classroom that their recommendations miss the mark. When the professor does have something to contribute, his contact with teachers or school systems is usually too brief to have lasting impact. Even major curriculum projects sponsored by the U.S. Office of Education and other agencies depend upon the individual teacher for the translation of their products into classroom practice.

In short, it is the teacher who has the major impact on curriculum; if he fails, the curriculum fails.

2. *How the Teacher Exercises His Power.* Since the teacher has a great deal of *de facto* power over the curriculum, does he exercise it wisely and competently? Very often he does not! Often he relies on the conventional wisdom:

He emulates his former teachers as models of teaching behavior. He selects a textbook, or uses one already selected by someone else, and follows its organization and content, allowing the textbook author and publisher to determine much of the curriculum. Ironically, *no one* consciously makes many of the most interesting and significant decisions about the curriculum.

Even if a teacher is aware that he is not making carefully considered curricular decisions, he may still find it difficult to do so because of the great demands on his time and energy. Heavy teaching loads and the many routine non-teaching tasks make it exceedingly difficult for the teacher to engage in a careful examination of teaching objectives and in the development of appropriate teaching materials and strategies. And, too, the teacher often lacks the stimulation from concerned and active colleagues which is essential for remaining intellectually concerned and alert. Given, in addition, the fact that formal training at the university is rarely focused on the analysis of curricular decisions, it is not surprising that relatively few social studies teachers find time to examine their objectives and creatively reshape their curriculum.

The assumption underlying the selection of readings for this book is that the teacher is *the* vital link in the school's instructional program. It is our conviction that a major goal of teacher training programs should be to prepare the prospective social studies teacher to perform his curricular role explicitly and rationally. The entire college program, and especially the social studies methods course, should introduce the prospective teacher to the range of issues he should consider in making curriculum decisions in American elementary and secondary schools. Confrontation with these issues is obviously as important for experienced teachers and curriculum supervisors.

3. *The Teacher's General and Professional Education as Preparation to Make Curricular Decisions.* If teachers do, indeed, have primary responsibility for developing their courses, there probably should be systematic preparation for this role. Usually, however, neither the general or preprofessional education of prospective teachers is geared to this need.

General Education. A legitimate expectation is that general education programs, presumably intended to raise with the college student basic and significant questions about man and society, would stir the prospective teacher to question and explore educational priorities for social studies education. The detailed discussion of the shortcomings of general education in American universities is beyond the province of this essay.[1] However, many observers, including Bell, have noted that the general education movement in American colleges and universities is dead or in disarray. Whether general education courses ever did challenge the college student to reflect upon the purposes and goals of formal education in this society is a historical question which remains unanswered. We suspect that the answer is negative.[2] And today, with the increasing emphasis on specialization and vocationalism in the liberal arts college,

---

[1] For a review of three major general education programs and a new proposal, see Daniel Bell, *The Reforming of General Education* (Columbia University Press, 1966).

[2] We did examine a large volume which is intended for use in the Columbia University Contemporary Civilization Course, a part of the general education sequence. The book, *Man in Contemporary Society* (Columbia University Press, 1962), is a collection of essays dealing with issues and problems in contemporary society. Yet, within the 1226 pages, there is little which deals with education or the educative process.

it is likely that emphasis on educational issues in the liberal arts course is rare and is becoming more rare.

Professional Courses. If social studies teachers are ill-prepared by their general education courses to make basic curricular decisions, do they fare any better in their professional education programs? We have not made a comprehensive study of schools and faculties of education. However, our experiences in six institutions indicate that typically the systematic treatment of the basic questions relating to a rationale for the social studies is perfunctory.

Courses in psychological and sociological foundations do deal with areas which are central to making intelligent curricular decisions. For instance, the social milieu of the school and the psychological makeup of the student must be considered in determining the direction of any academic course. We have excluded a consideration of these factors from this volume not because they are unimportant, but because there are provisions for treating them in present teacher education curricula. It should be noted, however, that in the foundations courses, students are rarely challenged to apply behavioral science knowledge to the specific problems of making decisions about what and how to teach. Given the state of our psychological and sociological knowledge, it may be premature to press for this type of application. Whatever the reasons, social and psychological foundations courses do not often deal directly with the problem of building a rationale for curricular decisions.

Philosophy of education and historical foundations courses perhaps come the closest to confronting the basic areas in rationale formulation outlined above. These courses commonly focus on an examination of contemporary political and social issues in education and on the intellectual history of great educational thinkers. The latter may, in particular, suggest alternatives to the prospective teacher. But, because these courses must range over issues that are common to all of the school subjects (the physical sciences, the humanities, mathematics, and the social studies), a detailed analysis of special issues relating to the social studies is precluded. By virtue of the general nature of these courses, they do not often challenge the prospective teacher of the social studies (or any other specialized area) to consider alternative educational priorities in his special area of competence and relate these to the problems of determining teaching strategies and writing or selecting materials.

The Methods Course and Practice Teaching. In many professional fields, especially the more complex, there is an attempt to teach "basic principles," which presumably are general guidelines for the person in the performance of his professional role. For instance, there are courses in "principles of accounting" and in "principles of psychological" or "educational research." Along with the general principles, the novice in a number of fields is also taught, through course work or apprenticeship, the techniques which are basic to the performance of that role: the violinist, under the guidance of a master, learns to finger properly; the surgeon learns basic operating technique. For the prospective social studies teacher, the specialized methods course is often intended to teach the basic principles *and* the specific techniques for teaching history and the social sciences.

In our view, this effort is often futile and wasted. First, there are few principles of good teaching which can be taught with any confidence. Virtually all the principles of teaching stressed in methods textbooks are based on the writer's intuitions rather than on any systematic analysis or study of teaching and learning. The principles, more often than not, appear as over-generalized bromides or as quasi-self-evident propositions. Rather than focusing on principles, the methods course could focus on teaching techniques derived from a careful collection of the practical wisdom of successful experienced teachers. However, in our view, it is questionable whether technique can be taught in a formal course out of context of the classroom and without immediate opportunities for practice. Novices can undoubtedly learn technique better under the tutelage of an accomplished and patient master teacher during an apprenticeship.

In sum, the determination of what constitutes a good education is probably the single most perplexing and challenging question facing the social studies teacher. The issues that must be considered in order to deal intelligently with this question of priorities are rarely treated during the teacher's higher education, and the social studies curriculum and methods course is an appropriate place to open the inquiry.

The Social Sciences versus the Social Studies

Two terms, *social studies* and *social sciences*, already used in this introduction and throughout this volume, require some clarification. The definition of the *social sciences* as those scholarly disciplines concerned with the systematic, empirical study of man in his society is usually readily accepted. The term, *social studies*, however, is, in comparison, fraught with ambiguities in usage which often confound discussions of the curriculum. Some writers even insist naively that inadequacies in the teaching of the social studies, both in content and method, would be remedied if the term were abandoned and we spoke only of separate social science and history courses. Much of this dispute over the use of the terms *social studies* and *social sciences* is misdirected, since it avoids substantive questions of educational policy.

In fact, in the high school, the use of the term *social studies* is largely an empty convention. The courses taught are usually American history, world history, American problems, and a set of electives in the various social sciences. Regardless of the label, the courses remain the same. The question of their educational worth, which is the basic issue, can be discussed more profitably without becoming embroiled in a fruitless pursuit of *the* real meaning of *social studies*.

This is not to imply that the term *social studies* is meaningless. Indeed, it may be helpful to distinguish its several meanings. *Social studies*, as most frequently used in the educational literature, refers to the disciplines of the social sciences taken singly or collectively and simplified for pedagogical purposes. Thus, the meaning is reduced to "simplified social science."[3] A second meaning given to the term is as a general label for all the disciplines concerned with the

---

[3] This definition of the social studies was proposed by Edgar Wesley. See Wesley and Wronski, *Teaching Social Studies in the High Schools*, 5th ed. (Boston: Heath, 1964). This definition is frequently quoted and used by many other writers in social studies education.

study of man and society. The social sciences are *not* the only disciplines in which man in society is studied; man is a subject for study in some branches of the natural sciences, as well as the humanities and the arts.[4] Third, the social studies has been viewed as an educational program composed of social science and other concepts, but with an additional element: a focus on the examination of political-ethical issues in the society. Writers who use the term in this way would argue that the perspective of the social sciences taken collectively is not a sufficient basis for general education. The argument runs that adequate education for adult roles in a democracy entails the direct consideration of the ethical issues which confront men in society, and that this confrontation of ethical issues is not within the purview of most social science.[5] Fourth, the term *social studies* has been used somewhat amorphously to refer to *all* (curricular and non-curricular) activities of the school that are related to the socialization of youngsters in the society. This last meaning, which is more prevalent at the elementary school level, frequently muddles or ignores distinctions between systematic inquiry in any of the social sciences or the humanities. People who use *social studies* in this way prefer to talk as though the social studies were synonymous with social living. The traditional criteria for scholarship in the disciplines are generally taken to be irrelevant. This position has had a number of articulate defenders and has had, in the past, wide usage in the schools. It is important for the novice teacher to know that the term *social studies* may well conjure up in the minds of today's laymen this last definition.[6]

In this volume, we use the term *social studies* to refer to that portion of the school curriculum typically taken up by history or social science courses but intended as general education. According to this definition, an European history, economics, or combined social science course would be considered part of the social studies program if the major intent was to provide a program of general education. The justification of such courses must be based on an analysis of the requirements of citizenship in a free society. The readings in this volume are intended to provoke thought about our society and about alternative curriculum positions.

Curriculum and Instruction

Two other terms which play a central role in the discourse of this book should also be defined. The words *curriculum* and *instruction* are often used in educational parlance as if they referred to distinctly different aspects of the educa-

[4] A recent example of this usage of the term can be seen at the new University of Sussex in England, which includes a School of Social Studies. This school is composed of faculties in each of the disciplines engaging in the study of man — the physical and social sciences, and the arts and humanities.

[5] Oliver and Shaver, whose position is given in several places in this volume, take this view, as does Johnson in an article reprinted in Section 5.

[6] The social studies as synonymous with social living is frequently linked to Progressive Education and to John Dewey. While there may have been some in the Progressive movement who took this position, it is a mistake to identify Dewey and other giants of the Progressive era with this view. For an enlightening treatment of John Dewey's position on curriculum, see Arthur G. Wirth, *John Dewey as Educator* (New York: Wiley, 1966).

tional endeavor. That is, it is common to speak as if the curriculum existed separately and independently from the act of teaching or instruction. In numerous schools of education, for example, some courses are labeled *methods* or *instruction courses* and others, *curriculum courses*. The reason for this usage may be that historically *curriculum* has had several different meanings — each focused on the content of the course. The two most common meanings for curriculum have been: (1) the teaching materials used in a course, most frequently the textbook; and (2) the outline or syllabus for a course, that is, the guide to the content to be covered. On the other hand, *instruction* commonly has been used to refer to what the teacher does in the classroom.

The dichotomization of curriculum and instruction is unfortunate, since it leads to confused thinking about the improvement of teaching. It is a truism that what the teacher does in the classroom (i.e., how he teaches) is unavoidably intertwined with the content of the materials he uses. If the objectives of instruction are to be achieved, the teacher must adapt his methods to utilize properly the materials he has at hand. Conversely, if instruction is to reach the goals set, content must often be selected or written to meet the requirements of the method of instruction to be used.

That "content and method cannot be separated" is an old saw in teacher education, but the admonition to consciously adapt content and method to one another as a means to an instructional end is rarely taken seriously, partly because of the difficulty of doing so. In fact, little systematic evidence is available concerning what adaptations or combinations of method and content are most effective for accomplishing the various goals of social studies instruction.

As we have used the term in this volume, both content and method are included in the definition of curriculum, defined as *situations or activities arranged and brought into play by the teacher to effect student learning*. Instruction is nearly synonymous with curriculum by this definition, except that it emphasizes more strongly the behavior of the teacher in the classroom as he attempts to establish the desired learning situation. The process of curriculum development from this point of view must always include a consideration of what content to use, how it should be organized, and how it should be presented to students and used in classroom discourse.

It should be evident that the readings and commentary in this volume are concerned primarily with the problem of establishing an adequate rationale for the selection of course content and method. However, the final section of the book does treat briefly the empirical evidence from educational research that might help the teacher to select the content and method appropriate to his rationale.

The Challenge to the Social Studies Teacher

This volume does not provide many answers nor does it propose *the* rationale for the social studies program. The aim is more modest: It is to provide prospective and practicing teachers with a framework for approaching basic issues related to the formulation of an adequate rationale for the teaching of the social studies. With knowledge, intellectual stamina, and time, the teacher can continue to deal with the questions raised in this volume. If he does so, he will become increasingly able to define and clarify his own rationale and to implement his ideas successfully in the classroom. For some, we hope this volume will initiate a lifelong probe into significant curricular questions.

FURTHER READING

Beard, Charles A. *A Charter for the Social Sciences*. New York: Scribner's, 1932.

The specific recommendations in this report of the Commission on the Social Studies of the American Historical Association are dated. But Beard's discussion of the issues he argues must be taken into consideration in making curricular decisions remains one of the most significant theoretical and practical contributions to social studies education.

Bell, Daniel. *The Reforming of General Education*. New York: Columbia University Press, 1966.

A recent analysis of the problem of general education in the college written by a "one-man committee" whose charge was to pose reforms for the Columbia College undergraduate program. Although its brief treatment of the high school curriculum is not very interesting, the book includes a discussion of a number of the major issues which are central to making curricular decisions in the social sciences.

General Education in a Free Society. Cambridge, Mass.: Harvard University Press, 1945.

This famous "Red Book" is frequently mentioned in discussions of general education at the college level. It was prepared by a committee appointed by President Conant of Harvard to serve as the basis for revision of Harvard College undergraduate education. A substantial part of the volume is devoted to an analysis of general education at the high school level; the nature of society, the disciplines, and thinking are considered in relation to the high school and college curriculum.

Hook, Sidney. *Education for Modern Men*. New York: Knopf, 1963.

A contemporary re-statement of the Progressivist view and a literate reply to critics and writers who do not recognize the interconnections between education and the social and political system. Though its recommendations are directed mainly at the college, the issues raised are relevant to a consideration of the purposes of general education in the high school.

The Social Studies in General Education: A Report of the Progressive Education Association. New York: Appleton-Century-Crofts, 1940.

An old book, but a fine statement of a position now out of favor. It contains counter-arguments to the views of a number of contemporary writers on the nature and purposes of general education in the social sciences.

1

On Objectives

Our daydreaming may be without conscious purpose, and when we are preoccupied, our physical movements may seem aimless. However, for the most part behavior is purposeful. This is not to say that our conscious motives are always the real ones or that we are always fully cognizant of our reasons for acting. Nevertheless, most of our actions are intended to produce results that are deemed possible and desirable, whether or not we are fully aware of what we seek or our reasons for seeking it.

There are probably few situations in which purposeful behavior is stressed more frequently or emphatically than in teaching. The obvious intent of the teaching act is that it affect students, and a dominant theme of most teacher preparation programs is the necessity of specifying the anticipated outcomes in order to have guidelines for planning and carrying out instruction. Despite this emphasis, however, teachers often do not spell out their objectives. The teacher "knows" generally what he wants to do and so does not work out a specific statement of intent. As a consequence, his teaching is often guided unwittingly by the organization of the textbook he uses, by the instructional models he experienced in his own days as a student, or by other incidents in his distant or recent past. The failure to exercise judgment means that the teacher's objectives will often remain vague and unclear and that his day-by-day teaching will reflect the ambiguities and lack of clarity in his notions of what he is trying to accomplish.

The teacher has objectives, explicit or implied, for his day-by-day or week-by-week teaching and he also has long-range goals. The latter are his aims for the entire course or, perhaps, for the entire social studies curriculum. These long-range goals, which reflect the teacher's basic educational commitments, are also often vague and based on reasons that have not been carefully formulated. Each of us has fundamental views of the world — what we believe it is and should be — that guide our thinking and our behavior. Our educational goals and commitments are as much a part of this basic framework as any other aspect of our lives.

Charles Beard, in the first reading of this section, stresses the relationship between our fundamental views of the world and our teaching behavior. In the early 1930's, Beard served on the American Historical Association Commission on the Social Studies. He authored two of the Commission's volumes, *A Charter for the Social Sciences in the Schools* and *The Nature of the Social Sciences*. Despite the titles, the latter work presents the more perceptive analysis of the role of the social sciences vis-à-vis instructional goals for the social studies, and it is from that volume that the first reading is taken.

Beard begins by defining his use of the term *objectives* and, in doing so, he also sketches the Commission's position. His most important contribution, however, is an emphasis upon the critical role that the individual's "frame of social knowledge," i.e., his fundamental views of the world, plays in making the instructional decisions that are an inevitable part of teaching. Much of one's frame of reference lies below the level of consciousness, and Beard maintains that it is crucial, if educators are to make intellectually sound educational decisions, that they explicate and analyze the elements in their frames. These elements can then serve as a conscious basis for formulating a rationale by which curricular decisions can be justified.

It must be emphasized that the question is not whether we have deep-seated notions about what the world is or should be like, or whether these conceptions will have an impact upon our instructional choices. It is rather whether we will bring our frames of reference to the surface and examine them so that our choices can be conscious and rational. Such a process provides some guarantee that instruction will not be shaped by unreflected bias and whim; it can also provide the means of liberation from unconscious or irresolute reliance on decisions made by textbook authors and on patterns of instruction imbibed from previous experiences.

The effort to clarify and provide reasons for educational choices is not, then, in our view, merely an academic exercise. The purpose is to make teaching itself more adequate by providing a firmer basis for instructional decisions. In addition, having clarified his own frame of reference as it relates to goals of instruction should help to make the teacher more autonomous; he will be better able to make his own decisions and then defend them clearly and succinctly on the basis of a sound rationale.

The second article, by Donald W. Oliver, presents an exemplary attempt to make explicit the assumptions underlying a curricular position. Oliver develops his case by detailing his conception of the operation of our democratic society and then moving from this formulation to a clear statement of basic objectives for social studies instruction. He does not distinguish between the *social sciences* and *social studies*, but uses the terms interchangeably.

This selection is of particular value because the author begins by analyzing four other ventures in the justification of social studies content. In this way, he provides the reader with a brief historical resumé of past efforts, as well as with an indication of some of their deficiencies. This provides an excellent background for the next reading by Shirley Engle. He does not take a curricular position, but instead indicates some basic divisions in thinking about social studies objectives. Each prospective teacher undoubtedly has developed biases about the aims of social studies education through exposure during his own education to teaching based on at least one of the positions Engle discusses. His identification of various curricular positions and the points of difference among them raises a number of important issues. Also, the educational aims outlined by Engle can be found, at least implicitly, in a number of the readings in this volume in which curricular proposals are made.

Engle provides no answer to the question, What are the proper objectives for the social studies? He poses the issues and leaves their resolution to the individual curriculum builder and teacher.

In the final reading in the section, we return to Charles Beard and another selection from *The Nature of the Social Sciences*. This selection might well have been included in Section 5 on the social sciences and the social studies curriculum, because Beard discusses the nature of the social sciences, including their concerns, methods, and possible educational offerings. But he also deals with the relevance of the social sciences to the establishment of societal and educational objectives. With the current emphasis on the social sciences in the social studies program, what Beard has to say is perhaps more timely than it was in the 1930's. His admonitions about the limitations of empirical methods for determining the ends of either the society or its educational system raise a fundamental question. If the basic goals of the social studies are not to be derived from the social sciences, then from where are they to come? The remainder of this volume is intended to assist the reader in answering this question for himself and in formulating his own objectives and rationale.

The Intellectual Problem of Determining Objectives

Charles Beard

First of all what is a set of objectives? It is a scheme of purposes or ends to be attained by instruction. These purposes are individual and social, of necessity. They are individual because all instruction, even when carried on in the form of mass education, is directed to individuals, and the immediate results, whatever they may be, are to be found in the mind, spirit, and conduct of individuals. These purposes are also social, for the individual must live his life in society and certain social arrangements are indispensable to individual life. According to many schools of thought, some scheme of social arrangements is deemed so desirable and so supreme that the individual should be sacrificed for the attainment of the posited end. The individual is nothing; the State or society is everything — the sovereign consideration. That view of the matter, however, is not dominant in the United States; nor is it accepted by this Commission.

The position taken by the Commission, as set forth in the *Charter for the Social Sciences*, is that the fundamental purpose of instruction in the social studies is "the creation of rich, many-sided personalities, equipped with practical knowledge and inspired by ideals so that they can make their way and fulfil their mission in a changing society which is a part of a world complex." This is not a finding of exact science; it is a statement of an ethical ideal long inherent in Western thought: human beings are endowed with moral dignity, possess and present values in themselves, and cannot be used for purposes alien to humane ends. In the light of this assertion of values, a mechanistic society to which individuals are to be sacrificed, though conceivable, is a foe of ethics. This does not mean that the individual is considered as an abstraction moving in a social vacuum. The individual is born, lives, and works in a social environment, and the ethical ideal stated above requires for its fulfilment certain social and economic institutions which safeguard and assure the good or best life for the individual. In such a view there can be no individual aims or purposes apart from social relations; but society is not treated as an end in itself. While the instruction of individuals must be referred to a conception of the social relations in which individual life is to be lived, its supreme goal is not a fixed set of relations indifferent to human values. For this reason all those powers and qualities of the individual which it is the purpose of instruction to develop have a direct relation to the maintenance and development of social institutions which afford similar rights, duties, and privileges to other individuals.

A scheme of objectives, therefore, will set forth a conception of the good life for the individual and a conception of the social relations deemed indispensable to the good life, at a given time and place. For this Commission the time is now and the immediate future and the place is the United States. Such a scheme is a more or less idealized picture of individual life and society deemed desirable within the limits set by necessity. If it is to be effective and workable, it must embrace a knowledge of the necessities which will determine in part and condition in part the process of realization; it will include the inexorable — things that must be. Here the social sciences and their empirical method are instruments. It will also be an interpretation of what is possible and probable within the borders of necessities — existing and coming into being. In short, it will be an interpretation of what is taking place in community, state, nation, and wide world, and of the possibilities of controlling that development with reference to ideal ends. Here both the ethical and empirical findings of the social sciences are imperatives.

Given this statement of the problem involved in formulating objectives, it follows that the social sciences, as above described, are not in a position to make a blue print of objectives for the schools akin in nature to the blue print for a hydro-electric plant, which, if carried into execution, will guarantee positive results measurable in mathematical terms. The business is not so simple as that. Nevertheless, the social sciences can furnish knowledge, an insight into the processes of social thought, and a method indispensable to the operation of formulating workable objectives. They disclose, by examination and tabulation, the objectives which American society, acting through the public agencies of education and private associations, has already proclaimed. They present facts and organizations of knowledge and thought corresponding, with more or less accuracy, to the realities of American society and world relations, which must enter into the formulation of any workable scheme of objectives. They describe the general trends or tendencies of society which provide the only available indications for forecasting the necessities and probabilities of the future social situations in which children now in the schools will have to live their lives and discharge their obligations. They describe the ethical and esthetic ideals which furnish guidance in determining what is desirable within the limits of necessity, which may be potentially realized, in whole or in part, and which are bidding for the loyalty of coming generations. They describe qualities of human character that represent the ideal and are necessary to the maintenance and development of a society compatible with the realization of the ideal.

To the operation of thinking about and formulating objectives with the aid of contemporary knowledge, thought, and method, the social sciences also bring one conclusion of fundamental and inescapable significance which must preface the beginning of the operation: Every human being brought up in society inevitably has in mind a frame of social knowledge, ideas, and ideals — a more or less definite pattern of things deemed *necessary*, things deemed *possible*, and things deemed *desirable*; and to this frame or pattern, his thought and action will be more or less consciously referred. This frame may be large or small; it may embrace an immense store of knowledge or little knowledge; it may be well organized with respect to categories of social thought or confused and blurred in organization; and the ideal element in it may represent the highest or lowest aspirations of mankind. But frame there is in every human mind. This is known, if anything is known. If the fact be denied, if a large, clarified, and informed frame of purposes is rejected, is deliberately and ostentatiously put out at the front door of the mind, then small, provincial, local, class, group, or personal prejudices will come in at the rear door, occupy the background of the mind, and constitute the frame.[1] This conclusion of contemporary social thought applies to those who formulate objectives and curricula for the schools, to teachers who expound them, and to the writers of treatises on the social sciences. To repeat Cole's formula: no one can profess to know everything or to believe nothing, to possess the whole truth or to exercise no preferences in the selection, arrangement, and presentation of materials for thought and instruction with respect to particular truths.

Theoretically, to be sure, teachers of the social sciences might dump all things known in the social sciences before children pell mell and leave the children to "follow their own interests" in making pleasing, agreeable, or satisfactory selections from the heap of "facts." Practically no such operation is possible to the social sciences or to education when any large area of occurrences or experiences is under consideration. Since all things known cannot be placed before children in the school room, there must and will be, inevitably, a selection, and the selection will be made with reference to some frame of knowledge and values, more or less consciously established in the mind of the selector. If anything is known in the social sciences, this is known. With respect to the social studies in the United States, this frame of reference will be a picture of the American nation and the world of nations deemed real, possible, and desirable. The picture may be related to a past, present, or future order; it may be rigid or flexible; but it will be the determining and conditioning structure for the selection of objectives and facts of instruction. If the frame is too rigid it will prove unworkable in a changing and unpredictable world; if it is too loose it will afford no guidance for practical action. In the light of this finding of contemporary social thought, the ancient controversy between champions and opponents of "indoctrination" is resolved.

[1] Croce, "Politica in Nuce," *Die Dioskuren* (1924), p. 39.

In the light of the finding that some frame of reference, some conception of arrangements deemed real, possible, and desirable, will in fact control the selection and organization of materials in the social sciences — whether with respect to objectives and curriculum, or to great treatises in history, economics, politics or sociology — controversies over such intellectual operations as synthesis, integration, fusion, and correlation are also resolved. Contemporary social thought has surrendered the idea that an objective and empirical synthesis of social actuality and knowledge is forthcoming.[2] If possible to an infinite mind, it is impossible for finite minds. Any formulation of objectives, selection of materials, or organization of knowledge is controlled fundamentally by the frame of social reference, the picture of arrangements deemed real, possible, and desirable, existing in the mind of the formulator, selector, or organizer. That is what gives the appearance of unity to his system. And the validity of any such system depends upon the amount of accurate knowledge employed in constructing it and the success of the maker in forecasting the future on the basis of knowledge and insight, and in devising appropriate means of attaining ends desired. Constructing a workable scheme of objectives, curriculum, and materials is thus more complicated than putting together the pieces of a jig-saw puzzle cut out of a known and pre-existing unity.

It is within this setting of contemporary social knowledge and thought that specific criteria advanced for the establishment of objectives and selection of materials, such as the need-and-remedy or problem-and-solution criteria, must be considered. The initial formula, need or problem, involves more than an objective determination of objective facts. A social need or problem is not an objective condition like a burning house which obtrudes itself upon the view of all bystanders. It is not a phenomenon having weight, extension, and position. There are sections of the world where a man lying ill in a gutter or starving in a field presents no need or problem to passing pedestrians. A *need or problem is a conception which arises in connection with one's frame of reference*. It is a product of complex cultural evolution. It varies from place to place, age to age, class to class. The pressure for action in response to needs or problems actually recognized likewise varies. And where there is a general recognition of a social need or problem, there is likely to be a widespread difference of opinion over the remedy deemed desirable and to be applied, and often more or less disappointment over the failure of the social remedy to accomplish the solution or cure as projected.

[2] Kurt Riezler, "Idee und Interesse in der Politischen Geschichte," *Die Dioskuren* (1924); Croce, *History: Its Theory and Practice*; and Heussi, *Die Krisis des Historismus*.

The Selection of Content in the Social Studies

Donald W. Oliver

The Problem

Introduction. The problem of defining adequate criteria for the selection of social science content to be taught in the secondary school has become increasingly acute for at least two reasons. First; the methodology and accumulated substantive knowledge of the various social sciences have expanded tremendously in the last decade. A relatively new branch of social science, the behavioral sciences, has developed a methodology and an approach to human problems and society that is influencing disciplines such as political science and economics which have been traditionally historical. Second, with a growing emphasis on the belief that man might collectively control his own destiny if only he could cooperate with his fellow men, pressure to teach a direct morality of cooperation and brotherly love has become much greater. As a result of these two trends, the social science content taught in the public schools has been expanded to include principles of group understanding and group dynamics derived from the behavioral sciences as well as a broad ethic of collective responsibility.

Once the social science curriculum is consciously molded by the belief that direct morality should be taught via social science content — rather than the use of such content only to clarify moral issues — the door is open to an inevitable expansion of the social studies into ethical areas which have to be thought through clearly.

The Social Sciences as Disciplines and as General Education. Before presenting a review of some criteria for the selection of content in the social studies, a distinction should be made between the teaching of various social sciences as disciplines and the teaching of social sciences as subject-matter which, presumably, will contribute to the general intellectual competence of all the citizenry. We can illustrate this distinction with the following example. Suppose that a university scholar of the Jacksonian Period in American history is asked why he wishes to teach students the Jacksonian Period in American history. He might reply that it is because it happens to be his field of scholarly competence; and from a disciplinary point of view, need he answer more? His rationale for presenting some data and not other data bearing on the Jacksonian Period rests only on the assumption that a particular selection of data will represent a more accurate picture of the period. This historian might also include in his justifications of such content the hope that a spark of interest would be generated in his students (if it were not already there), and that after studying this content, the student might then pursue the subject of Jackson for the

Reprinted from the *Harvard Educational Review*, 1957, 27, pages 271–300, by permission of the *Harvard Educational Review* and the author.

17

sake of knowing — for scholarship alone. This justification asserts that the methodology and substantive knowledge of the various social science disciplines may be taught simply as an attempt to perpetuate scholarship. The same justification might hold for teaching large numbers of students introductory courses in the disciplines. Although only a small percentage of those introduced to a particular content area in such a course might actually enter training in a scholarly field, the procedure can certainly be defended on the basis of the difficulty of recruiting academic personnel who may make significant contributions to their own disciplines and to the culture as a whole.

The selection of specific content for general education is a more difficult problem. How does one justify choosing particular content areas and giving them priority over others? Trends in the present secondary school curriculum suggest that educators are seeking to solve the problem by introducing courses in which a wider and wider range of content is taught, e.g., the yearly extension of "United States History" courses to include contemporary events; and the current popularity of the courses commonly called "World Civilization," which literally cover recorded history from the first caveman to the last atom. Even if it is possible to teach such a course, there is still the problem of selecting particular content to put into the exhaustive chronological scheme. Perhaps teachers feel that because the chronology is complete, the selected content which parallels the chronology is also complete. This notion is, of course, absurd.

Assuming that it is impossible to teach the complete methodology and/or substantive content in any or all of the social sciences, and assuming that some information and understandings are in fact more valuable than others in educating citizens to exercise their social responsibilities, the problem of selecting specific content areas — and justifying this content — inevitably arises.

Some Major Attempts to Define and Justify
Social Studies Content

The problem of selecting and justifying social studies content in the secondary school is certainly not new. National committees of the American Historical Association, the National Education Association, and other scholarly organizations have periodically attacked the problem. We shall discuss four such attempts before presenting our own position with respect to this problem. The intention here is not so much to deal with the historical impact of the various reports as with an analysis of the philosophical difficulties that have become apparent in the short period of time that social scientists and educators have wrestled with them.

The four reports which we shall discuss are: The Report of the Committee of Seven of the American Historical Association published in 1899 (3); The Report of the Committee on the Social Studies of the Commission on the Reorganization of Secondary Education of the National Education Association, published in 1916 (7); The work carried out in the 1930's as part of the activities of the Commission on Social Studies of the American Historical Association; and the Preliminary Report of the Committee on Concepts and Values of the National Council for the Social Studies published in 1956 (5). The first two reports will be reviewed only briefly, and the last two in some detail. This is not because the first two have had any less effect upon social studies content in public education — probably the contrary is true — but rather because the most difficult problems of content selection did not seem to be fully appreciated until the work of Beard and his associates in the 1930's.

The report of the National Education Association published in 1916 represented a major change in thinking about the nature and purpose of social science education when contrasted with the 1899 report of the American Historical Association. The Committee of Seven apparently assumed that history was the only social science that could make a contribution to secondary education; that four years of history arranged chronologically was necessary; and that the appropriate techniques of teaching such content should consist mainly of feeding the learner codified historical literature and seeing to it that all the material was properly consumed. The National Education Association's report of 1916 showed certain striking reversals of this kind of thinking: it explicitly considered the frame of reference of the learner as important in the selection of materials; it dealt with history as only one of a number of social science disciplines capable of making a contribution to the secondary school student. It went so far as to suggest the institution of a "problems of democracy" course in the senior year of high school in which the student would ". . . study actual problems, or issues or conditions, as they occur in life, and in their several aspects, political, economic, and sociological." (7, p. 53) It is partly as a result of this committee's report that the term "social studies" gained respectability and came into common use.

Perhaps the most striking aspect of the 1916 report was its shift in the basis for justifying historical content. While in the 1896 report history was assumed to have a vague but generally beneficial effect upon the entire thinking process of the student, the 1916 report justified the teaching of history in terms of its immediate utilitarian value in understanding current and future problems. It is, perhaps, this shift in thinking about social studies objectives that raised the whole question of what is appropriate content for teaching. As long as there existed in the minds of educators a sacred body of historical knowledge, the only problem was rationalizing why it should be taught. Since 1916 this sacred body of knowledge has become less secure as other social sciences have risen to challenge the fruitfulness of the historical approach as a way of thinking about social issues; and history itself has assumed more and more the burden of becoming a social science rather than an impressionistic narration of the past. By 1916 the sanctity of historical literature had diminished to the point where educators (and some historians) refrained from prescribing a certain pat body of history as absolutely necessary for the education of the young. The "problems of democracy" course suggested by the 1916 report, which attempts to focus the findings from several social sciences upon concrete social problems, offered an alternative to the strictly chronological basis of content selection advocated by previous reports.

The most thorough and extended study of the teaching of social studies in the secondary school was undertaken in 1929 by the American Historical Association's Commission on the Social Studies. This group undertook surveys and research projects which resulted in no less than seventeen volumes published between 1932 and 1942. They made no recommendations for specific content at specific grade levels, but rather devoted considerably more energy to the careful formulation of objectives and the rationale for various types of content.

While the 1896 report assumed that history was "good for people" and proceeded to give reasons to support its belief; and while the 1916 report of the National Education Association turned an about-face by assuming that the good citizen is the objective of social studies instruction and then fumbled for appropriate content with which to build the good citizen; the Commission seemed to ask more basic questions: what is a good citizen? what is a good society?

The Commission's discussion proceeds logically from certain basic values to the learning outcomes that should be achieved to the particular content that should promote this learning.

Basic values are defined on two levels: societal and individual. With respect to individual values, the Commission states that the ". . . fundamental purpose of instruction in the social studies is 'the creation of rich, many-sided personalities, equipped with practical knowledge and inspired by ideals so that they can make their way and fulfill their mission in a changing society which is part of a world complex.' " (2, p. 178–179)

This individual ideal is to be accomplished within a general frame of reference which is ". . . a more or less idealized picture of individual life and society deemed desirable within the limits of necessity." (2, p. 179) The function of the frame of reference is further described as a "cultural guide to action, not fixed as the law of gravitation, but still a guide. It is both abstract and concrete. In its high unity it is a summation of relations built upon concrete situations and relations. Its base is the concrete situations and relations of life — personal, community, national and world." (2, p. 189)

The Commission, then, set forth two principles: the basic objective of social education in individual terms (the rich and many-sided personality), and the frame of reference in which such a personality is to be developed (a conception of society both desired and possible). The frame of reference is then translated into the specific social science knowledge required to achieve the desirable and possible society. The following excerpts from Beard's *The Nature of the Social Sciences* clearly state the Commission's argument.[1]

Any formulation of objectives, selection of materials, or organization of knowledge is controlled fundamentally by the frame of social reference, the picture of arrangements deemed real, possible, and desirable, existing in the mind of the formulator, selector, or organizer. That is what gives the appearance of unity to his system. And the validity of any such system depends upon the amount of accurate knowledge employed in constructing it and the success of the maker in forecasting the future on the basis of knowledge and insight, and in devising appropriate means of attaining ends desired. (2, p. 183)

[1] The position taken by the Commission with respect to objectives and the selection of content is either specifically authored by Beard, or quite obviously influenced by Beard's thinking. The final report of the Commission, *Conclusions and Recommendations*, contains a summarization of Beard's work for the Commission and is endorsed by eleven of the sixteen members of the Commission.

What fundamentals must the scheme of objectives as knowledge contain in order to conform to this frame of reference, this conception of contemporary social thought?

First, the most accurate picture of the total situation, general and detailed — its complex of related necessities, conditionalities, opportunities, interests, and ideas — the most accurate picture which is permissible to contemporary knowledge.

Second, the most accurate portrayal of movements and changes in this situation, general and detailed, including development, crises, revolutions, modifications, and experimentation. . . .

Given these fundamentals what will the scheme of objectives look like in actuality? Obviously, since the unitary frame of reference is the controlling consideration, controversies over the jurisdictions and boundaries of the social sciences cannot be taught at once, a beginning must be made with one or more aspects or manifestations of the actuality with which the respective social sciences are concerned; that is, with some economic, political, or cultural phase or manifestation of human life. (2, p. 189–190)

. . . what arrangement of the social sciences seems best calculated to realize the objectives of knowledge or information implicit in the frame of reference and the consequent curriculum? The following is proposed:

1. Geography. . . .
2. Economics. . . .
3. Cultural Sociology. . . .
4. Political Science. . . .
5. History. . . . (2, p. 191–192)

Knowledge for Beard, then, is a description of reality to guide social action for the purpose of more closely approximating the desired society envisioned by the individual or group. The hope of constructing a society to promote the "rich and many-sided personality" justifies the attainment of knowledge. And what knowledge is this? Geography, economics, cultural sociology, political science, and history; ironically, the same subject-oriented approach taken by the Committee of Seven.

The Commission's important contribution to the problem of defining objectives and content in the social studies was a recognition of the necessary ethical basis of social studies education. It presented the thesis that the validity of knowledge is relative to the scope of reality under consideration, and that when the scope is large, values of the observer will inevitably enter into the selection of those aspects of reality which are included in the historical narrative. Likewise when one is selecting those aspects of social reality which are to be presented in a formal educational setting, the values of the selector are a crucial consideration. The Commission's report further emphasized that when one selects and organizes data to be taught in the classroom, submerged or unconscious criteria will operate anyway. Some frame of reference, some value considerations are unavoidable:

Contemporary thought challenges the conception that the complete neutrality of empiricism is really applicable in the observation and description of *large areas of human affairs*. . . . In dealing with a large complex of occurrences and facts, the social scientist, being human and belonging to a definite age, nation, and group, brings to the "data" some frame of reference already in mind, and that frame will be some conceptions of ethics — good and evil, desirable and undesirable, praiseworthy and unworthy of praise. . . .

Hence it may be said that limits have been discovered to the applicability of the empirical method to social affairs and that efforts to push it beyond the boundaries of its applicability have precipitated a crisis in thought. Human beings are constantly confronted by the appearances of choices, small or fateful. Empiricism cannot tell them what they ought to do, even though it can often tell them what they must or must not do *if* they decide to gain certain ends. (2, p. 160–161)

Beard maintains that the only protection against committing major errors in one's own interpretation of social reality is for one to be self-conscious of his preconceptions about what he thinks that reality should be. The insight Beard had into the importance of values in shaping the individual's perception of raw empirical data is only now being fully appreciated as social psychologists probe the processes of selective perception and retention.

But Beard's handling of the problem of deducing specific areas of content from more general objectives reveals a curious gap in his thinking. His neat logical sequence from basic objectives (rich and many-sided personality) to a desirable and possible society (frame of reference) to specific content necessary to build that society suggests that a particular selection of content is somehow *not* arbitrary, but rather "possesses a certain scholarly authenticity." (2, p. 94) This selection is based on the best prediction that the social sciences can make about how to attain the desirable society. Beard thus assumes that once we know what is both real and possible (which social science *can* tell us), we can make intelligent decisions concerning the direction in which we *should* go.

The choice of ends involves both knowledge and thought — knowledge of what is possible and probable for the immediate future and thought about what is desirable. It thus involves a forecast of inevitable trends in human affairs and an assertion of values deemed attainable by choice and action within the broad lines laid down by the inexorable. For the educator it is nothing less than an interpretation of history that will be made and can be made in the coming years. (2, p. 162–163)

Using good prediction or "forecast of inevitable trends" as a criterion, Beard can say that some knowledge is more pertinent, more relevant than other knowledge when we are making a *particular prediction*. But after reaching this point, two difficulties present themselves. First, if the frame of reference defines the good society — and this frame grows out of a set of unconscious value judgments — what if there is not consensus in society (or even among educators and social scientists) concerning what the "good" society is? The second problem follows from the first. When there are a number of conflicting frames of reference, which particular set of social science propositions does the educator select to teach, or is there one set common to all frames of reference? In short, Beard's scheme requires the educator to set arbitrary limits upon his conception of possible alternatives society can consider at future choice points, and ignores the fact that the choices possible are determined by the common elements in the frames of reference of those groups and individuals who happen to be vocal or powerful when choice points are reached. That is, if the knowledge to be included in the curriculum is justified by predictions one makes about how to attain the good society, and the good society is constantly undergoing redefinition as various groups work for their own particular point of view, which frame of reference does one select as a guide to objectives and content?

Beard and the Commission side-step this problem by saying essentially that all of traditional content should be taught. Obviously, the educator cannot teach all content — as Beard himself admits, not because it is not desirable, but because it is not practicable. Thus the Commission's approach to defining criteria for the selection of content, while realistic in its frank acknowledgment of the limitations of empiricism, is aborted by its failure to give adequate weight to practical limitations of the formal educational setting.

In the twenty year period between the work of the Commission on the Social Studies of the American Historical Association and the Preliminary Report on Concepts and Values (5) of the National Council for the Social Studies, American society recovered from its worst depression in the process of waging its largest war, and entered upon a period of persisting international tensions. In such a series of national crises one would suspect that educators might revise their ideas of optimistic progressivism so eloquently proposed by Beard. The report of the National Council, however, reflects a faith in social progress that far outdoes Beard, but without Beard's qualifying phrase referring to a vision of society that is both desirable and *possible*.

The 1956 Report of the National Council for the Social Studies defines twelve themes which it phrases as goals or values, each of which is supposed to imply concepts and content. The title of the report itself is "A Guide to Content in the Social Studies." It was an effort to define very general areas of concern rather than specific guides to social studies content. In summary, the Themes are:

Theme 1. Reciprocal adjustment of man and nature.
Theme 2. The adaptation of individual and group ideas to an interdependent world.
Theme 3. Recognition of the dignity and worth of the individual.
Theme 4. The use of intelligence to improve human living . . . and . . . maintenance of the free marketplace for ideas and values.
Theme 5. The intelligent acceptance of individual responsibility for personal and general welfare.
Theme 6. Increasing the effectiveness of the family as a basic social institution.
Theme 7. The intelligent and responsible sharing of power in order to attain justice.
Theme 8. The wise allocation of scarce resources in order to bring about the widest material security.
Theme 9. Achievement of adequate horizons of loyalty . . . a sane and reasoned patriotism and a global humanitarianism.
Theme 10. Cooperation in the interest of peace and welfare . . . an increase in conference and conciliation, mediation and arbitration, seeking a consensus.
Theme 11. Achieving a balance between social stability and social change.
Theme 12. Widening and deepening the ability to live more richly. (5)

Perhaps the most interesting feature of these Themes is not that they achieved any new or striking intellectual breakthrough, but rather that there appears to be a retrogression to the days — *ante* Beard — when committees set up to determine educational objectives ignored or skimmed over important logical and ethical considerations, such as a statement of the relationship between values and empirical knowledge in the teaching process. In this respect the Themes seem to represent a fair sample of the level of thinking currently going on in the social studies, and thus deserve a more careful analysis.

One of the major difficulties with the Themes is that they indiscriminately mix moral dicta with social science directives. The moral implications of knowledge are in the mind of the knower. If the Themes are interpreted as values or moral directives, they leave little choice but to seek social science data that might bear out the "fact" that the values actually do imply "correct" conduct, e.g., if war is "bad," we demonstrate historically that war has never paid off.

In the first Theme, for instance, it is not clear what social science data could demonstrate. Is the goal that man *should* make a reciprocal adjustment to nature? If this is the case, what is the most appropriate adjustment? As the explication of the Theme indicates, man has made all kinds and all degrees of compromises with nature. We do not know for sure which of these compromises (or refusals to compromise) might be adaptive or deadly in the long run. (Cigarette smoking in our culture tends to relieve anxiety, but increases physical hazards, apparently.) The problem with respect to this particular Theme is whether social science knowledge is required simply to demonstrate the wide variety of adaptations man has made to his physical environment, or whether it is required also to point toward some optimum "reciprocal adjustment" of man and nature.

Theme two falls into a similar category. It says, in effect, that individual and group ideas should be adapted to an interdependent world. In further explanation of this point it states that "our best hope for physical health and a free society is to extend technology and education so that poverty and ignorance may be overcome." The implication is that "education" which overcomes "ignorance" will enable men to adapt their ideas to an interdependent world. Because of the evaluative overtones of the term "adaptation" it is again important to know whether the problem is simply to make the student aware of an interdependent world, or whether the social studies teacher is responsible for teaching the student specific ways of adjusting his ideas to the events of an interdependent world. If the latter is the case, we might ask whether there should be a common form of adjustment, whether individual students should be allowed to arrive at different types of adjustment, or whether some students should be allowed to oppose the whole idea of adjustment.

The Themes could have been improved considerably if value statements had been separated from social science theories and concepts, and both had been explicitly labeled. This is precisely what Beard had tried to do in his work on the Commission for the Social Studies of the American Historical Association. The Themes might have included a clear statement of fundamental values of the American Creed such as Myrdal presents in *An American Dilemma*. (6) These fundamental values could then be clearly distinguished from the conceptual tools of the social scientist, which, although they are extremely valuable to the social scientist, are not the basic ethical principles of our culture. The bias of the social scientist toward the value of his own conceptual tools should not lead him to believe that these tools are of the same import as the ethical principles which serve as a guide to the use of these tools in shaping our culture.

The vague but frequent use of the term "knowledge" constitutes a second difficulty in the interpretation of the Themes. Beard explicitly defines historical knowledge as a "collection of facts, verified, authenticated, and generally agreed upon." (2, p. 50) The Themes talk about schools having a "direct responsibility both to the dissemination of knowledge and its use, and to the maintenance of the free marketplace of ideas and values." (5, p. 212) Does this mean knowledge which has been validated by a disciplinary process? Does it mean speculation about empirical questions? Or does it mean "known" values?

A confusion of several conceptual levels of analysis arises from the failure to distinguish clearly among several possible definitions of knowledge. At one level there are statements about the basic moral values of society. At a second level is knowledge as the scholar sees it, which can be analyzed into several dimensions: methods of stating and testing hypotheses, predictable social phenomena, general bodies of theory, and conceptual tools for analyzing and understanding new data. At a third level are general run-of-the-mill beliefs — sometimes referred to as "common sense" — by which most of us guide our daily lives.

Obviously it is necessary to arrive at a definitive understanding of the validation processes of the social sciences before we can develop a clear conception of what the term "knowledge" means in the context of the Themes. As we have already indicated, clarifying the distinction between the social science disciplines — their methods, concepts, and findings — and ethical statements relating to their function and purpose is a necessary initial step that must be taken before one can develop meaningful criteria for the selection of content.

The failure of the Themes to deal with the relationship between knowledge and values, and their confounding of various types of knowledge, are related to an implicit but important set of assumptions endorsing the ultimate goodness of man and the perfectability of human societies. They fail to consider the possibility that fundamental problems which face man may be unending because of the nature of man himself. While we realize that the idea of man as a perpetually imperfect creature smacks of Old Testament theology, the fact that many philosophers and theologians deeply believe this at least suggests that the idea should not be ignored. Although the general notion of the perfectability of man and society is ingrained in our culture, it is subject to wide interpretation. It can mean, for instance either the opportunity for individual fulfillment or the fulfillment of the aspirations of a total culture. Such a distinction can be crucial in its implications for education. The former means that society allows each man to seek happiness and truth defined in personal terms; the latter means that ultimately there will be a recognizable common truth which "knowledge" or "intelligence" will identify for all men. Given the former assumption, human conflict becomes an inevitable fact of life. Men see truth and happiness differently and battle within the context of protected liberty. Given the latter assumption, conflict is only a temporary means of identifying the ultimate truth, which, when discovered, will mean that conflict itself — between man and nature, between man and government, between man and man — will become unnecessary, since all men will see truth in the same way.

The Themes appear to assert strongly the opinion that man has the ability to identify an ultimate truth, one that would eliminate conflict as a necessary ingredient of social living. The goals of man and nature are described by the Themes in such terms as "reciprocal adjustment," "adaptation," "liberty compatible with the rights of others," "superstition . . . not yet . . . routed," "a sturdy self-reliance coupled with an altruistic individualism," "a sane and reasoned patriotism, and a global humanitarianism," "greatest good for the greatest number," "balance between social stability and social change." All indicate, either explicitly or implicitly, a battle between conflicting forces to which some kind of verbal solution is given: either ultimate conquest of one force by another (the evil one losing, of course), or adjustment between two extremes. The philosophical question for each of these two types of solution automatically follows: (a) when one force must conquer another, how is man to know the devil from the god? and (b) when there is to be some adjustment between extremes, how are we to define moderation from extreme? The Themes implicitly assume that man can adequately distinguish moderation from extremism, and that he can distinguish between the devil and the god, hence, the potential solvability of all problems.

That man may be too puny a creature ever to assess the nature of the divine scheme — if there is one — or that he should ever be aware of his puniness and feel a deep humility before the awesome forces that surround and control him: these ideas are also a part of our cultural heritage, and perhaps should be considered when confronting the problem of selecting appropriate content in the social studies. Although the Themes make one feel that the requirements of man's happiness are a solvable riddle and present touching evidence of a tradition of American exuberance and optimism, we can not reasonably ignore the contrary possibility: that man is by nature fated to deal eternally with certain conflicts within himself and others. The notion of original sin, for instance, is contrary to the idea that there is an ultimate fulfillment for man on earth: man's life on earth necessarily involves trial and suffering. To reject such alternative interpretations of man and society by omission rather than making a direct case would appear to reflect an unfortunate blind spot in the thinking of modern social studies educators.

Beard and the Themes

We have now considered in some detail the approaches to selecting social studies content taken by the Commission of the Social Studies of the American Historical Association and the Committee on Concepts and Values of the National Council for the Social Studies. It is interesting to note the curious inability of the Committee of the National Council for the Social Studies to face a number of problems which had already been explored twenty years earlier by the Commission. It is especially surprising that this Committee did not consider important underlying assumptions of their scheme bearing on the definition and purpose of knowledge, and the distinction between knowledge and values. Also, their failure to talk about the problem of defining the "good" society is disappointing.

We might best illustrate the major distinction we feel exists between the approach of the American Historical Association's Commission and the Committee of the National Council for the Social Studies by presenting a statement by Beard from his treatment of competing philosophical schools:

If we examine narrowly the competing ideas of society which are offered by our time to those who concern themselves with civic instruction, we find that three emerge as the most persistent. The first is ideological: the present order is the best of all possible worlds and the business of learning is to rationalize the apparently predominating scheme of things. On close analysis this framework of philosophy dissolves into defense mechanisms historically inherited or practically developed by groups and interests in society primarily engaged in preserving particular forms and processes. The second is utopian — a conception of an ideal state, a scheme or perfection which if realized would become static; stemming from certain ideas emphasized by the first French Revolution it accepts the possibility of perfectionism here and now. The third tenacious social idea may be called progressive; it accepts neither perfectionism of current ideology nor the perfectionism of utopia, but is founded on the assumption that what we actually have to deal with in reality is a process, a changing order of things which carries along with it an ideological heritage, and bears within itself the possibilities of a more perfect order of things, never utopian and fixed, but always involving the perils of choice and the advantages of improvement. (1, p. 53–55)

The Themes appear to be plainly utopian, but in vague and general terms; there is a best of all possible worlds which cannot be described very precisely. Beard and the Commission are self-named progressives; things can be better, but the definition of better will be constantly shifting and changing, and just how far progress can go is an open question. In this comparison we might note that it is Beard's analysis that gives us an adequate conceptual scheme by which to understand better a contemporary group seeking to justify social studies content. The reasons that have led some modern educational thinkers to lose their taste for the tough-minded analytical thinking exhibited by Beard are possibly less important than the evidence that such philosophical retrogression has occurred.

A Tentative Approach to the Selection of Content in the Social Studies

Criticisms of the reports of the American Historical Association's Commission for the Social Studies and the National Council for the Social Studies' Committee on Concepts and Values may be summarized as follows: (1) there is a failure to consider adequately the question of the school's right to mold personal values of the student; (2) there is considerable confusion in the use of the term knowledge and in the relationship between knowledge and values; (3) there is a failure to take into account one of the major facts of American society — namely, the ferment and conflict over competing ideas and values most of which can be allowed because of a more basic creed of mutual tolerance; and (4) there is a failure to consider the difficulty of adequately describing American society, and the increasing problem which such a description will present to scholars because of the society's dynamic qualities.

We shall attempt to offer here an approach to the selection of content that will face some of these criticisms in an explicit manner. It should be stated that the criteria we are seeking for the selection and justification of content are not within the context of teaching the disciplines for the sake of recruiting and training scholars or knowledge for the sake of knowledge, but rather to justify knowledge and an approach to knowledge that will increase the student's ability to deal effectively with broad social issues which confront all citizens of our society.

A Basic Value of Society

Basic to our theme is a value judgment regarding the purpose of the institutional bulwarks of our society, i.e., the governmental functions in society, including formal education. This value judgment asserts that a citizen should have maximum freedom of individual choice in shaping his own destiny, in pursuing his own personal fulfillment. In other rather common but sacred terms this means that individual fulfillment is the end which all of the formal structure of society should serve. We do not intend to rationalize this value judgment; we are simply saying that this is a basic value in our society, and that we have selected it as the most important one to be protected and perpetuated.

This value judgment should be distinguished from Beard's "rich and many-sided personality" and the Themes' hope of "widening and deepening the ability to live more richly." So far as we are concerned, the individual can choose to be broad or specialized, sweet or sour, wide or thin, many-sided or single-sided. The basic value is simply that he have the *maximum opportunity to choose what he should be*.

There are undoubtedly a number of ways in which a society might organize itself to promote such a value. We are making the assumption here that in whatever way a society might organize itself to achieve this end, it will have one salient characteristic: a number of groups will exist which have differing value syndromes with respect to the basic societal problems that must be solved. That is, different behavioral solutions will have been developed by various groups to meet problems of socialization, e.g., aggression control, inhibition and channeling of physical drives, development of aesthetic tastes and creative expression. We are hypothesizing that in so far as there exists real freedom to choose among a variety of ways of life, there will be a multiplicity of groups to support solutions to the problems that all men must face in their dealings with the outer world. A society containing a multiplicity of groups has been denoted pluralistic, but perhaps a more accurate term would be "multi-value society."[2] This term implies not only the existence of sub-cultures, but also means that various sub-cultures may claim the mutual respect of one another.[3]

---

[2] As the term "value" is used here, it means the positive or negative feeling or affective response associated with a particular unit of behavior. This behavior can include perceiving the conduct of others as well as the perception of one's own conduct.

[3] We know that most societies have some degree of social stratification and that these strata tend to have different value syndromes. Our term "multi-value" indicates more than such a stratified society. It means that there are and should be groups in society who have reasonably equal cultural and economic bargaining power.

Given the existence of groups which hold quite different views toward the compromises man must make with his social and physical environment, two larger problems emerge: (a) defining the procedures by which interpersonal and intergroup conflict may be mediated; and (b) defining the common interests of the various groups which cement the society together. There must be some behavior which is valued by all members of society. We believe that working toward an adequate definition of the minimum degree of universal conformity necessary for the maintenance of society — a definition of personal liberty — is the continuous agonizing problem that faces any free society.

That these two problems — conflict-control and cohesion — will continuously recur is predicated on the assumption that when individuals are allowed wide latitude in making individual value choices, there will be inevitable disagreement over decisions that affect large segments of society and about which groups with various value-positions must reach some degree of consensus.[4] We maintain that this assumption of "inevitable conflict" can be bolstered by both psychological and historical evidence.

A Basic Problem of the Multi-Value Society — the Control of Conflict

We have made the assumption that a free society will tend inevitably to have severe conflicts over the definition of public policy because of the variety of choices made by individuals and groups about the conditions they perceive as leading to personal fulfillment as well as the variety of definitions of what types of fulfillment are desirable.

There are a number of possible ways that a society might approach these conflicts.[5] One is to assume that man is basically tolerant and that even though his values may be threatened by other individuals and groups, he can be trained to understand and "love" those who threaten his values. This approach is characterized by a faith in the ultimate educability of man; a faith that anti-social impulses can be trained out of man, or that he can be reared in such a way that there will be no desire for aggression.

A number of ideologies are based on this assumption, two familiar ones being Communism and Christianity. These ideologies assume an attainable truth regarding the definition of a "good" man and a "good" society, and further assume that when all men see this truth and act in accordance with it, they will have no need to be aggressive or intolerant.

Both ideologies agree that conflict is ultimately bad,[6] and both have prophets who have envisioned a society in which there was no conflict and need for conflict. This strategy might be called the sin and salvation approach. It asserts that there is conflict because man or society is sinful; but that there is hope that

[4] It might be argued, in fact, that the conflict assumption applies to all types of complex societies, but that only in a free society is the government's power to suppress public dissension deliberately kept within fairly narrow limits.

[5] The notion that man has some control over the mechanisms that determine the nature of his society is, of course, pretty well limited to Western thought. In this context, then, these generalizations are culture-bound and limited.

[6] Communism, however, believes that conflict and violence are necessary means to harmonious ends.

man and society can overcome this sin and arrive at an ultimate fulfillment of harmony and contentment. It looks upon conflict as a temporary state of society caused by the childhood of man.

A second approach to the problem of conflict is a rigidified or institutionalized variation of the sin and salvation approach presented above. It assumes that there is, here and now, a valid ideology of the "good life," and that there is no problem of seeking ultimate truth and then transforming society to meet the specifications. The problem is one of converting people to what is obviously the good life, the right conduct, the true values that all men should hold. The means by which this conversion is accomplished may be through peaceful missionaries or through ruthless tyranny, but the goal is the same: to narrow the varieties of conduct available in order to meet the specifications defined by a particular group as the "good life."[7]

A third approach to the problem of conflict is to accept as a fact that man is intellectually inadequate to define the ultimate truth, the ultimate criteria for the "good life." We feel that this approach is the one most consistent with a justification of the multi-value type society. The reason for allowing a variety of groups to exist and nourish what may be conflicting values is precisely that we cannot define with certainty the way to either "truth" or "happiness" for all men.

There are many implications of this approach. First, since there is no revealed truth, the formal institutions of society are obliged to protect people who hold to all types of value-syndromes or creeds. It means also that there is a constant battle among the various groups within society to maintain and assert their own value framework. The good society, then, is not one in which everyone behaves in the right way according to some commonly agreed upon definition; rather it is one in which individuals and groups in each new generation are allowed considerable latitude to develop their own standards and their own tastes. Human progress consists of increasingly long periods of non-violent co-existence of groups of free men who have chosen a variety of modes of conduct as exemplifying the "good life."

The Problem of Maintaining the Multi-Value Society in the Face of Opposing Social Processes

In terms of strategy for meeting conflict, we have outlined two alternative approaches. One assumes that for large areas of social conduct there should be agreement on common standards, and that the job of particular groups within society is to work toward establishing these same standards for all, i.e., creating a monopolistic, single-value society. (A teacher, within the framework of this assumption, would promote the values and biases of his particular group.) The second alternative assumes that institutional inventions or processes for enforcing mutual tolerance among various groups are the only areas in which there should be common standards. Starting from the premise that in order to maximize individual fulfillment it is good and even necessary to have a variety of

---

[7] So-called "modern education" which stresses life-adjustment seems to grow quite directly from approaches one and two, e.g., where cooperation is taught as a good in itself.

value positions represented in society, the latter strategy is obviously more consistent with our basic value.

However there are forces existing in any society which tend to work against the continuance of a multi-value framework. These forces, we believe, stem from the desire of men not only for freedom to define their personal fulfillment, but the coordinate desire for security and acceptance by others. The following theory of the origin and development of group processes which work out this problem of ambivalence over freedom and security will make explicit certain hypotheses about society that lead to our scheme of justification.

Multi-Value Equilibrium Hypotheses

Members of society identify with particular groups[8] which represent particular value positions. In socializing the child, these groups teach love and respect for ingroup members as well as suspicion and distrust of outgroup values and conduct. Various competing groups attempt to establish or secure their own values at the expense of other groups. Groups fight to maintain stability within their own value-framework, and in some cases, fight to impose their values upon others.

There is always the threat that any given group will become sufficiently skillful in structuring an appeal to other groups in terms of common values that it will rally enough support to enforce a single-value system on all society. The rewards for the dominant groups in such a society are obvious. Temporarily, at least, there would be maximum reinforcement of conduct consistent with a uniform code, and minimum threat from groups with competing values. There could be formal sanctions against resistance to this uniform code of conduct. Because of the high rewards that accrue to dominant groups in a monopolistic culture, there may well be an inevitable tendency for the more dominant groups to push toward this type of society.

However, a desire for immediate protection within the existing multi-value system somewhat tempers this push toward a monopolistic society. It is as if each major group had the long range strategy of establishing a monopolistic society with its own group values the dominant ones, but for tactical reasons must allow a temporary truce in order to gain time to "convert" or "destroy" groups with opposing or differing values. The strategy necessary in the free society, however, is to maintain a permanent truce and allow for continuous negotiations and peaceful conflict — permitting only verbal or symbolic aggression.

We may characterize this particular aspect of the pluralistic society by the term "multi-value equilibrium." That is, there is a balance between values held in common by all group members and the number of specific values held by the various groups within society. This balance is constantly shifting back and forth as various groups become more or less powerful in enforcing particular modes of conduct on all society. For example, the recent change in the salute to the flag to "one nation, *under* God" illustrates the increasing power of religious groups in enforcing conformity to a religious ritual.

[8] Family, clan, neighborhood, class.

Ambivalence Hypothesis

We are hypothesizing that groups have ambivalent feelings about the comparative worths of a multi-value society and a monopolistic society. Members of a group may desire a monopolistic society in which their own particular group is the main determiner and protector of standards. They may attempt to do this by building rigid status hierarchies, by defining "truth" and "law" and the givers of truth and law. They may try to establish what they consider to be permanent symbols of status: seals, mansions, split-level houses, union cards, leather jackets. But as the battle proceeds they must give lip-service to the notion of equality of all groups and all men, if for no other reason than their own protection.

This gives the multi-value society a strange appearance to the objective observer. He sees men everywhere arguing and debating the great issues of the day. Yet when he listens to the words he can often see no essential difference in what men are saying. Indeed, when he questions the debaters further, there is often little difference between the value statements to which they will subscribe. But a considerable difference exists in their underlying feelings about what specific conduct is good, and in the non-verbal behavior they exhibit.

This difference between what men say is right and what men actually do — Myrdal's American dilemma (6) — might be reinterpreted to mean that there are actually two sets of moral standards: one which applies to the conduct of a particular group at a particular time; and one which applies to all men in a society at any time. The more general societal standards are those uttered in public (and to social science interviewers). The specific group's values are those which are closer to the actual determination of conduct.[9] Instead of there being an inconsistency between what men believe and what men do, as Myrdal contends, there is an inconsistency between two sets of beliefs learned at different points in the history of the individual. One set of beliefs tends to be more often verbalized in public; the other, when the individual is in the privacy of the groups with which he associates. Thus it only appears as if there were an inconsistency between belief and conduct. The individual, then, constantly faces two problems — the problem of group conformity, and the problem of societal conformity. The lack of integration of the solutions to these two problems may be related to the heterogeneity of "American culture."

Dual Socialization Hypothesis

We have hypothesized that there is an inconsistency between two sets of belief systems: one which applies to all society; one which applies only to the particular groups with which an individual identifies his personal interests. We believe the explanation of this inconsistency lies in the existence of two processes of socialization in a multi-value society: one, which meets the standards of each particular group, is administered largely by the child-rearer; a second, which is required to meet the standards of the larger society, is carried out by

---

[9] This does not mean that men are slaves of group norms, but deviate from general societal norms at will. Deviance, of course, occurs at both levels.

a variety of social agencies — school, job, church, political party. The nature of standards promulgated in these two processes can be quite different. The family and clan probably determine the specific methods by which one learns to control such basic impulses as aggression and affection. These methods of control then generalize to provide the individual with a general orientation toward others — a style of behavior in interpersonal relations.

The second socialization process carried out by social agencies, of which the school is one, attempts to teach the individual to internalize love and tolerance for all groups in the society. This might be positively designated as "patriotism," and negatively as "conscience" or feelings of guilt over hostile reactions against other groups within society. The essential value which the larger society imposes on the individual is respect or, at least, tolerance for other people whose values and conduct differ from his own.

Here, we believe, is a source of constant friction between the individual or group and the formal agencies of the larger society. Society has set up certain agencies to protect individuals who deviate only from the transient norms of various groups. Society is also obligated to restrict forcefully the conduct of individuals or groups whose purpose it is to destroy the right of others to make individual value choices.

Theoretically, then, there is a sharp distinction between two types of deviance: deviance from a norm established by some group; and deviance from the fundamental value of the larger society which would consist of an invasion of another person's right to make his own conduct choices. In practice, this distinction is often agonizingly difficult to make. The thief or murderer is obviously violating the right of other individuals to make choices for themselves. The atheist or agnostic is clearly not injuring the rights of others to seek religious fulfillment in whatever way they please. But the militant pacifist, who actively teaches young men that military conscription is an invasion of freedom, presents a more difficult problem. Is he endangering the ability of the society to defend its integrity against forces that would subvert its fundamental tenet of basic tolerance?

The great achievements of our liberal democratic tradition, and the governmental institutions that have been built within that tradition, are those which deal with this problem of distinguishing group deviance from societal deviance. These achievements are impressive. They include: the explicit recognition of the two types of deviance; the notion that simply deviating from group norms is not enough to threaten the larger society and justify formal sanctions; the convention that people who formulate values independently must be protected from persecution; and the concrete procedures set up to determine who is violating arbitrary norms established by a group and who is violating the standard of basic tolerance. These procedures are embodied in such social inventions as the jury system, the separation of the court from the law-making branches of the government, and the establishment of a higher law or rule of law concept to inhibit the arbitrary exercise of power by any group having temporary control of the formal sanctions of government.

The elaborate nature of the institutionalized methods of handling deviance in our society suggests that it is not easy to accomplish the secondary socialization process which should prevent such deviance. This may be related to the fact that the initial socialization process is probably easier to carry out than the tolerance-building attempted by the larger society, for once a narrow set of family or clan values has been established, it may be almost impossible to teach individuals to consider the possibility that other legitimate value choices exist, even though we feel that the subjective consideration of this possibility is a necessary antecedent of basic tolerance.

An Interpretation of the Purpose of
Social Science Instruction

The goals outlined below, which determine the criteria for the selection of social studies content, are closely related to the basic values, assumptions, and hypotheses we have presented. For this reason we would like to summarize the major points already made.

We have stated that one of the pillars upon which our type of society rests is the right of individuals to make personal choices regarding appropriate conduct in seeking fulfillment. When this kind of freedom exists, we assume that there tends to be disagreement and conflict within society because different individuals (who are associated with different groups) see fulfillment and the conduct leading to this fulfillment in different terms. That is, while the existence of many groups tends to promote the right of individual choice, some groups will continuously resist mutual toleration of a variety of sub-cultures. Society's cyclical tendency to gravitate toward conformity of values of major groups, and then to react away from such conformity we have labeled "multi-value equilibrium." We have noted that the various groups might see the multi-value society as both good and bad — good in that it guarantees protection for each group when it happens to deviate from the standards set by a more powerful group; bad in that it will not allow any single group to bludgeon the rest of the society into conformity to a single-value system.

We then tried to relate the notion of group ambivalence toward the multi-value society to the idea of a dual socialization process. The family or clan is the conditioning agent for the individual's deepest personal values, which usually include an intolerance for members of outgroups. This intolerance is then counteracted by a second socialization process which attempts to provide wider societal cohesion through the promotion of mutual toleration of all groups within society.

From this general theoretical base we now propose to set forth a justification of content for social studies education. We want to emphasize our assumption that, before any instructional procedure can be used to carry out proposed objectives, the basic processes of socialization (the unconscious internalization of social values) have already taken place. The student already has a descriptive knowledge of his culture and has internalized the specific beliefs of his family or clan as well as some of the more general beliefs and values of the total society, e.g., liberty, equality, love of country.

When the student has reached this stage of development, we propose that the relationship between personal values, the general canons of tolerance of our society, and the determination of public policy for the regulation of human affairs be made the center of the social studies curriculum in the public school.

The basic core of content would consist of the study of existing and predicted conflicts caused by differing definitions and interpretations of the meaning of liberty, security, and public welfare.

Translating this into concrete educational goals, it means consciously and explicitly teaching the student to deal with the problem of defining liberty within the context of the total society. We feel that one of the essential requirements of this task is that the individual student be liberated from his own narrow value system to the point where he can see the relationship between his personal value judgments and those of other groups within society; to the point where he can see and feel sources of conflict within himself, and between himself and others; and to the point where he can handle these conflicts by predicting courses of action which will maximize the possibility of individual or group fulfillment as individuals and groups may define this fulfillment. Such prediction involves an understanding of one's own feelings and values and the feelings and values of other individuals and groups, as well as a descriptive knowledge of the general beliefs and artifacts of the society.

The object of teaching the skills that will allow the student to make reasonable predictions about methods of social control within a free society may be broken down into a number of very specific goals. It is important that one read these specific objectives in the context of the model of society and the description of the values and assumptions set forth above.

An Outline of Specific Objectives of Social Science Instruction in General Education[10]

I. Students should be taught to recognize and define areas of human conflict. The basic values of the student should be related to larger political and social issues to the point where the words and symbols which describe these issues became charged or affectively loaded for the student in the same way as the words which describe his own values. That is, the student should learn a vocabulary that is charged — either positively or negatively — for the whole society. There should be established a common language through which the individual can describe and feel general societal conflicts. We think the individual should understand to some extent (both intellectually and emotionally) the value positions of other groups which may oppose or support his own personal beliefs.

II. With reference to specific political and social issues, students should be taught to define alternative methods of regulating human affairs that are possible from the point of view of major value positions in society.
Once the student sees an area of social conflict and can feel the value positions of various groups having an interest in this issue, his problem is to offer alternative modes of regulation which are *possible* in the light of the value positions of the groups involved. That is, the student should be taught to state alternatives which encompass both his own value orientation and those of opposing groups.

10 This outline contains nothing about methods of teaching, but is concerned only with goals. However, in any specific statement of goals, approaches to the attainment of these goals are often implied.

III. With reference to specific social and political issues, students should be taught to make thoughtful predictions about the consequences of various alternative methods of regulating human affairs.

After the individual has considered possible alternative approaches to the regulation of human affairs, he should be taught to make considered predictions regarding the possible consequences of the various alternatives deemed possible, and to try to assess the degree of probability with which one might predict that these consequences will, in fact, occur. Predicting consequences of social action involves the procedures and methodology of the social sciences. This is the justification of "knowledge" or evidence: it sheds light upon the probability that a given consequence will occur as a result of a social action. Any approach to the regulation of human affairs designed to meet the demands of a specific issue can conceivably have both positive and negative consequences. These possible consequences are, in fact, hypotheses, and can be tested to some extent by such available social science procedures as:

a. The careful definition of rules of evidence which apply to the type of data under consideration.
b. The discrimination of what evidence may be pertinent, i.e., what evidence might logically bear upon a given hypothesis.
c. The maximum use of available evidence so as to make the best prediction — this means ignoring disciplinary boundaries and also using data outside the formal academic definitions of social science.
d. The determination of the limits of probability which apply to a given hypothesis.

In an effort to clarify our position, we might use as an illustration the conflict over distribution of goods and services to farm workers as opposed to industrial workers. The issue could be described as a conflict over the problem of unequal pay for equal work when such variables as ability and training are held constant. Assuming that many people will agree that hard-working farmers should not suffer severe economic losses, the problem becomes one of regulating human affairs in such a way as to prevent inequities. An infinite number of approaches to this problem are *theoretically* possible. The first task is to select for consideration only those alternatives that are possible with respect to the values of the groups involved. Second, possible consequences of these alternatives have to be predicted; and finally, an alternative must be selected and defended on the assumption that it has the largest number of beneficial, and the least number of deleterious, consequences from the point of view of the personal value system of the individual student. In the farm issue, for instance, government aid by direct subsidy might be one alternative, while drafting farmers into the army at a higher rate than industrial workers might be another. It may be that the second alternative is not *possible* considering the basic values of the various groups involved in the conflict. If the student decided that the first alternative was possible, some people might argue that it would result in a decrease in the initiative of farmers and thus injure their characters. This would then be a hypothesized consequence of the alternative of providing direct government subsidy, and could be tested by social science procedures.

The objective of social science education, according to this approach, is to introduce young people into the fire and controversy that rages within a free society over ways of regulating human affairs — ways that might presumably maximize the freedom of the individual to pursue his own fulfillment as each person defines that fulfillment. In such an introduction we would hope to provide the student with a way of approaching conflicts and controversies that is more "rational" than blind adherence to some ideology which happens to be consistent with those values learned during early socialization. "Rational" does not imply a denial of the importance of personal values (or emotionality) as forces to be considered in social decisions, but rather emphasizes the ability to see social problems explicitly as conflicting affective reactions by various groups and individuals.

This approach would mean a dramatic shift in the type of content now taught in the secondary school. Since the curriculum builder would begin by inquiring into the major areas of conflict — both those we perceive in current affairs and those which will probably occur in the future — there would be a strong emphasis upon the sociological, political, and economic disciplines as well as competent journalism; and there would be less reliance upon traditional historical literature. If the issue of a deflated farm income were used as a major conflict in public policy, and the problem was to predict the consequences of alternative modes of regulation, it is apparent that the disciplinary boundaries would necessarily break down. Similar problems have occurred in the course of history and various approaches have been taken: this would provide pertinent data. Other necessary information such as the existing attitudes and feelings of actual groups in conflict today and the voting patterns of Congressmen and agencies representing various pressure groups could be derived from current sources. In addition, some understanding of general principles of economics regarding the relationship between supply, demand, and prices as well as the way these factors are deliberately manipulated by organized groups would be important.

In considering such a problem, the basic criteria for the selection of content would be (a) whether the information would enable the student to conceptualize possible alternative modes of regulating human affairs with respect to this particular conflict; (b) whether the information would give some indication of the consequences of each alternative considered; and (c) whether it would permit us to say something about the probability that these consequences would, in fact, occur.

To use this approach would mean leaving out large areas of American history. But, as we have suggested, the traditional body of historical literature would continue to be presented to children in the early school years. This is part of what we have called the societal socialization process. By the time the student encountered our curriculum, he would have a descriptive knowledge of his own culture as well as some knowledge of other cultures. (Children living in the city of Boston would have some understanding of living conditions in rural Arkansas.) However, we would not call either the combined fact-myth-legend representation of history taught in most public schools or a purely descriptive account of immediate and distant cultural settings "social studies." Our justification for calling this approach "social studies" or "social science education" rests with our concern for predicting the consequences of alternative modes of social action. We feel that there is a crucial distinction between education as an unconscious internalization of the values and beliefs of the culture and an explicitly critical attempt to stand aside from these immediate values and beliefs and make objective predictions about how to control major conflicts in the regulation of human affairs. The substantive values with which the student would be indoctrinated in this approach would relate only to the idea of basic tolerance and to the social inventions and mechanisms that protect this tolerance.

Our approach is a combination of ethics and social science, with ethical considerations paramount because of the conscious attempt to teach students the analytical tools by which they may continuously redefine legitimate areas of personal liberty. We believe that it is the particular way we treat the relationship between ethics and empirical knowledge, between emotional and intellectual perceptions of social issues, that distinguishes this approach most clearly from the approaches to social science education discussed earlier in the paper, and from the traditional university conception of the teaching of social sciences as semi-related but independent disciplines.

A Consideration of Some Difficulties in the Social Conflict Approach to the Selection of Content

One of the greatest difficulties in any "problems approach" to the selection of content consists of the definition of "problem." If one is concerned with the teaching of conflict situations, how does he decide which of the multitude of conflicts among individuals and groups are most important to the survival of a multi-value society?

In answering this question, an initial step might be to describe various types or sources of conflict. For example, a distinction can be made between conflicts arising from disagreements over prediction and conflicts arising from disagreements over values themselves. The former can arise if there is a difference of opinion regarding the consequences predicted from one or more courses of action, e.g., a disagreement over whether the establishment of public housing for low-income families will increase or decrease their dependence upon welfare agencies. The latter can arise if all antagonists agree that certain consequences will result from public action, but disagree over whether the consequences are good or bad, e.g., all factions may agree that integration in the public schools will lead to less racial self-consciousness, but will not agree on whether this is good or bad.

This example of an analysis of social conflict simply indicates that it may be possible to describe, enumerate, and categorize major conflicts over public policy. However, our ability to distinguish among different types of conflict should not mislead us into thinking that there is no real problem in defining which specific conflict situations should be placed in the curriculum. Despite the obvious difficulties of selecting conflict situations, the problem seems manageable. It might well be possible for journalists, social scientists from a number of disciplines, and men of practical affairs to define the most crucial areas of conflict that can be anticipated, as well as those which are immediately upon us. It might also be possible for these same men to discuss which alternative courses of action seem possible as ways of dealing with the conflicts, as well as probable consequences of the various alternative approaches. The information which bears upon the pressing problems of the day — as decided upon by such a group of scholars and men of practical affairs — would then become the content selected for students in the classroom.[11] While the conflict selected might be changing constantly as a result both of the identification of emerging problems and of the increased social science knowledge, we anticipate that the core of conflict situations would remain fairly stable.

A second difficulty that must be faced by the conflict-problems approach to the selection of content concerns the question of how much the student must "know" — how much descriptive political and social experience he must have had before he can deal intelligently with major societal conflicts. No one would question the assumption that a student should know something about his culture before he arrives at our proposed curriculum. As to a definition of just what he should know, we have two very tentative suggestions, one of which has been indicated already. (1) In order to have a sense of cultural identity, the student should be familiar with the combination of fact-myth-legend he is now exposed to in history texts and social studies literature. (2) The student should have some realistic descriptive knowledge of the existing culture, including both the general and technical social science vocabulary required to talk about it. Since the current culture can be observed directly, perhaps the most effective way of teaching these constructs would be through demonstrations in the field. Most of the important terms and constructs used by the social scientists have observable referents. For instance, it is quite obvious that one can see concrete manifestations of such terms as "mass production," "slums," "mechanization of farms," "labor unions," and "social class." The problem of selecting content becomes acute only when one wishes to give order and interpretation to these terms.

The position we are taking here is that it is not necessary or useful to put such terms and constructs into an ordered interpretative narrative until the student is sufficiently mature to study the regulation of human affairs in the context of social conflict.

An issue that is closely related to the question of how much one must "know" before he studies current controversy is the relationship of history — as a discipline — to other sources of social knowledge. We realize that many educators are of the opinion that "no conscious advance, no worthy reform, can be secured without both a knowledge of the present and an appreciation of how forces have worked in the social and political organization of former times . . . — that historical-mindedness should be in some slight measure bred within [boys and girls], and that they should be given the habit, or the beginnings of a habit, of considering what has been, when they discuss what is or what should be." (3, p. 20) The general thesis is that without the tempering influence of history to give a broader perspective to the present, there is danger of great distortion

---

[11] This does not mean that the student would be required to memorize the list of conflicts, the alternative approaches, the possible consequences of each approach, and the data bearing on the probable occurrence of each consequence. The pedagogical strategy required to attain the objectives listed earlier is an empirical problem requiring careful research into the effect of specific content selections interacting with procedures for presenting this content.

in a picture of current social reality. So far as we know, there is little systematic evidence to back up this thesis. The notion that history tends to give one a broad and total perspective of current society presents only one side of the issue. History can also give one a narrow and biased view of current affairs. It all depends upon who has written the "history." History is not totality, but rather one artist's conception of what a limited selection of past events indicate might have happened. And the historian, by refusing to abandon the narrative form of summarization and generalization is so restricted in the number of events he can present that it is doubtful whether a valid picture can be painted within these limitations.

We would certainly not deny that the process of writing history — of carefully weighing the importance of past events and sifting and selecting such events for a narrative — may have desirable effects upon the writer.[12] But we do not teach students to write history, we teach them historical writings. If we were to teach students to write history, it would be impossible to teach them more than a small slice of chronology. We believe that there is a contradiction between teaching a wide scope of chronology through existing historical literature and teaching a discipline of mind that may come through one's attempt to validate and synthesize records of the past. If the scholarly canons are taught, this must be done within a narrow range of chronology.[13] Given the practical limitations of time within the formal educational setting, it may be impossible to do both. But is it defensible to teach the surface area of large volumes of the past without at some point providing the student with the intensive validation techniques of the historian? So far as our approach is concerned, we conceive of historical knowledge as one source of evidence out of many to be brought to bear upon immediate and pressing social conflicts.

A third difficulty of the conflict-problems approach discussed here is its essential negativism. There is the potential danger that such an approach might place too much emphasis upon the negative aspects of social organization and would not deal adequately with the positive traditions and institutions that also characterize our society. In considering this difficulty we would emphasize that included in the conflict-problems approach is the teaching of the institutional safeguards to personal liberty that have been developed within the tradition of Western Civilization. Perhaps the teaching of such safeguards to personal liberty would take on dramatic meaning as the student came to see the severe problems of controlling and mediating conflicts within a free society. This is not to deny that our approach does explicitly set out to describe in depth the disintegrative forces in the culture. It does this, however, in the hope of directing such forces so as to prevent major disruption to the institutions which protect a heritage of liberalism.

There is, of course, a more fundamental criticism of our approach which strikes at the heart of our assumption that tension and conflict are inevitable.

---

[12] Those who have advocated most adamantly that children study history have almost always been writers of history. Is it possible that they have confused the value of reading history with the very real benefit they feel from both reading *and* writing history?

[13] This is not to deny that a knowledge of the wide scope of the past may have heuristic value for the scholar as he searches through the records of the past within a restricted chronological area.

What right have we to establish an educational program which assumes from the beginning that a culture governed by love for others and sacrifice of self cannot be achieved through the conscious efforts of seers and educators? Our reply to such a question is that one cannot teach men to love without telling them what is worth loving — and except for the teaching of love for liberty and tolerance this is not possible in a system of public education established by a multi-value society. We cannot deny the possibility that the Christian vision or a similar model of society may eventually materialize on earth. The question is whether it is the responsibility of social education to teach such a vision. We think not. We feel, rather, that it is the responsibility of social education to teach a tradition established by the toughminded jurists of Rome and England; a tradition that involves a set of concrete institutions which protect our free way of life — which give man the right to be a Christian, an agnostic, or an atheist. We further assert that while the Christian vision embodies some of the noblest aspirations of mankind — as do many ideologies — it makes assumptions about the nature of man and the road to his fulfillment which are too narrow to be enforced in a free society. The teaching of harmony and love as totalitarian goods contradicts other possible, and very legitimate, interpretations of man's road to fulfillment.[14]

Conclusion

Our approach to the selection of content may be stated simply as one in which the central core of the curriculum would be the study of those human affairs fraught with conflict or tension which might threaten the integrity of a free society. We have pointed out that this does not preclude the teaching of the fact-myth-legend content usually referred to as "history" or "citizenship education" in the public schools. The type of social studies program proposed here is a tough-minded scientific approach which presents immediate and future conflict situations in the hope of inducing the student to utilize social processes and to make social predictions and decisions that will keep such conflicts within reasonable limits. This approach to social studies objectives, we feel, clearly recommends some specific content areas and indicates an explicit relationship between the basic values and assumptions with which we begin and the specific objectives and content with which we end. At this point we can see the necessity of careful research into whether learning outcomes defended here can be effected through a series of definable learning treatments. This research is now being carried forward by a number of investigators, including a group at Harvard.

Our severest critics — and this, of course, is only speculation — will consist mainly of two groups: those who wish to maintain historical literature as the bulwark of the social studies curriculum of the high school; and those who wish to teach, overtly or covertly, an ideology of love and harmony as solutions to the inevitable tensions and stresses within society. Our answer to these hypothetical critics will be a simple challenge: let them say what content should be

---

14 It seems to us quite reasonable to believe, for instance, that man's aggressive impulses must of necessity find expression, and should, therefore, not be considered altogether evil or destructive.

taught; let them justify it by means of a philosophical scheme that is consistent with the values and assumptions of a liberal democratic society. Most important, let them demonstrate that the content and the procedures by which it is presented do, in fact, lead to the changes in social behavior they believe are desirable. It is our conviction that American society is too pressed by existing and impending tensions to continue to rely upon pious hopes and emotional arguments in defense of teaching any subject matter that is so closely related to the preservation of our basic freedoms.

BIBLIOGRAPHY

1. Beard, Charles A. A Charter for the Social Sciences in the Schools. (Report of the Committee on the Social Studies of the American Historical Association, Part I) New York: Charles Scribner's Sons, 1932.
2. ——— The Nature of the Social Sciences. (Report of the Committee on the Social Studies of the American Historical Association, Part VII) New York: Charles Scribner's Sons, 1934.
3. Committee of Seven. The Study of History in the Schools: Report to the American Historical Association. New York: The MacMillan Company, 1899.
4. Conclusions and Recommendations of the Commission. (Report of the Committee on the Social Studies of the American Historical Association) New York: Charles Scribner's Sons, 1934.
5. McCutchen, S. P. "A Guide to Content in the Social Studies." Social Education, 20 (1956), 211–218.
6. Myrdal, Gunnar. An American Dilemma. New York: Harper and Brothers, Publishers, 1944.
7. "The Social Studies in Secondary Education." (Compiled by Arthur William Dunn) U.S. Bureau of Education Bulletin No. 28, 1916.

Objectives of the Social Studies

Shirley H. Engle

According to High (1962, p. 3) the aim of the social studies is to teach competent citizenship. That a claim so generally made and seemingly innocuous should produce dissent among the practitioners of the social studies indicates the wide disagreement which exists as to both the nature and the objectives of social studies instruction. Keller (1961, p. 60) dismisses as extravagant the claim made in a recent position paper of the National Association of Secondary-School Principals (1961, p. 2), prepared with the help of social studies specialists, which says in part, "Persons with a rich background in the social studies . . .

From Current Research in Social Studies, Bulletin of the School of Education, Indiana University, 1964, 40, pages 1–12, by permission of Indiana University and the author.

are able to recognize the struggle for freedom wherever it occurs and to detect, appraise, and overcome the enemies of freedom in whatever guise they appear." Instead, Keller (1961, p. 62) would make "no attempt to claim for history and the social sciences the exclusive task of making good citizens and of creating democratic attitudes." He adds, "What students should do in school is to study subjects and become acquainted with facts and ideas."

Social scientists blow first hot and then cold on the question of the relation of their respective disciplines to the problems of practical citizenship. As Herring (1958, p. 2) points out, "The problem of method in the social sciences . . . is best understood in relation to purpose. The more scientific the bent of the investigator, the less he is concerned with over-all social problems or broad dilemmas that invite speculative thinking." And again he says "social science knowledge can contribute, in some measure, toward the realization of the goals of government or religion or industry, but it cannot function as a rival or a substitute. Should social science be conceived in such terms, it would cease to be science; and, should social scientists contrive for such ends, they would find themselves becoming politicians, theologians, or entrepreneurs" (1958, p. 5). But later, in quite another vein, he says, "The basic objectives of the social scientists . . . is the objective of all men of good will, seeking the good life: it is to release the best of mind and spirit to realize human potentialities. The methodology of all learning is subordinate to the purposes sought and to be vital must be changing and developing. The plea is for pluralism of intellectual effort and shared respect for varied methods of inquiry and forms of knowledge. It is this universe of discourse that needs to be understood and appreciated by our fellow citizens as never before" (1958, p. 11).

Two basically different positions with respect to the nature and hence the objectives of the social studies are already obvious. To some the social studies are essentially the same as the social sciences. To others the social studies are concerned directly with developing the attributes of good citizens. Within each major position a variety of alternatives may be found, each predicting a somewhat different objective for social studies instruction. Efforts to reconcile these positions have not proved entirely successful. No one has really taken up the challenge to the social scientists thrown down by Lynd under the exciting title "Knowledge for What?" As Metcalf (1963, p. 6) says, confused and even contradictory aims for social studies instruction result.

The classic statement of the position which holds that the social studies are essentially the same as the social sciences is that of Edgar B. Wesley (1958, p. 3), "the social studies are the social sciences simplified for pedagogical purposes." While this definition has been quoted approvingly in almost every work on the social studies written in the last quarter century, it clearly falls short of the concept held by those who would make the development of the attributes of good citizens the central purpose of the social studies, as, for example, Metcalf (1963, p. 197), Engle (1960, p. 301), and Oliver (unpublished manuscript). Neither does Wesley's definition make it at all clear what, short of citizenship attributes, the outcomes of social studies instruction are to be. Is the student to become a minuscule social scientist and the classroom a reasonable facsimile of the social science laboratory, as Bruner (1962, p. 14) implies? Is the student to be engaged in some manner and to some degree in the same scholarly research in which the scholar is engaged, being concerned more, as Herring (1958, p. 2) has pointed out, with fact gathering and the quest for the concrete, the observable, the measurable, and the definable than with the solution of over-all social problems? Is the acquisition of the insights, skills and attitudes which constitute the separate methodologies of each of the social sciences, i.e., the method used by the historian, the sociologist, etc., to be an end of social studies instruction? Is the student to be involved as the discoverer or perchance rediscoverer of previously unrecognized relationships, as Bruner insists (1962, p. 20). Or, as is much more commonly held, is the student to become a consumer merely of the products of research in the several social sciences; i.e., is transmission of knowledge the end in view? While those who speak approvingly of Wesley's definition do not exclude explicitly the "involvement in discovery" suggested by Bruner (1962), Massialas (1963), and others, they frequently fall into ways of talking which belie this purpose. Thus Gross (1960, p. 1296), elaborating on Wesley's definition, allows that "the social studies are those studies that provide understandings of man's ways of living, of the basic needs of man, of the activities in which he engages to meet his needs, and of the institutions he has developed." This language clearly implies that the social studies is a body of predigested and organized knowledge ready to be transmitted to the learner. There is no suggestion of the tentative and approximate nature of whatever passes for knowledge in the social sciences at a given time; there is no suggestion of student participation in the process by which larger facts or more general conclusions are sorted out and validated from lesser facts and values; there is no mention of involving students in the act of discovering for themselves the general laws and commonalities of human society, in the sense recognized by Bruner (1962).

Many, possibly most, of those who accept Wesley's definition of the social studies do so in the narrow sense of a storehouse of knowledge, skills, and specific virtues, the presumed product of research in the social sciences, to be transmitted to students. The following list of aims for the field proposed originally by Carr and Wesley and reported by Gross (1960, p. 1298) as having remained the fairly fixed aims of the social studies, tends more to confuse than to clarify the issue:

1. To respect the rights and opinions of others
2. To be skillful in securing, sifting, evaluating, organizing, and presenting information
3. To assume social and civic responsibility
4. To act in accord with democratic principles and values
5. To become a judicious consumer
6. To understand principal economic, social, and political problems
7. To learn about vocational activities and opportunities
8. To understand the interdependence of peoples and groups
9. To become a happy member of a home
10. To make intelligent adjustments to change
11. To get along with individuals and groups
12. To use basic social studies skills
13. To exercise critical judgment
14. To understand and promote social progress.

If we may take Herring's interpretation (1958), cited above, as a fairly accurate description of the way in which social scientists regard their field, items 1, 3, 4, 5, 9, 10, 11 are clearly beyond the pale of the social sciences and move Carr and Wesley, and by implication most social studies teachers, since these are regarded as the fairly fixed objectives of the field, far into the camp of those who see citizenship education as the central concern of the social studies. This is hardly a contingency for which Wesley's definition provides. Neither is it at all clear even to the social scientist, let alone to those who teach the social studies, just how the content of the social sciences is translated into the kinds of behavior listed by Wesley. In fact, as indicated by Herring (1958, p. 9), many social scientists frankly disclaim any intent to affect moral purpose or normative judgment which is clearly involved in such items as 1 and 4 in the list above. Further, many of the items listed above, especially 13 and 14, are clearly general objectives of all education and could not, therefore, as implied by the definition, grow strictly out of the social sciences, as Metcalf has sagely pointed out (1963, p. 930).

Neither does the list, which presumably is consistent with Wesley's definition, give too much solace to those who hold with Bruner (1962) that involvement in the process of discovery and the attainment of skill in the methodologies of the several social sciences is the central aim of the social studies. Item 12 gives a nod in this direction, but it is not at all clear how the preponderant demands of the list for fixed knowledge and behavior patterns could be poured through so scant a funnel. One gets the impression that lip service only is being given to items like 12 and 13 and that there is no clear intent to substitute the slow and uncertain process of scientific inquiry for the transmission of knowledge and fixed attitudes.

But we are still not out of the forest into which Wesley's definition leads us. If knowledge is the important end of the social studies, what is to be taken as passing for knowledge? Is knowledge to be equated with having the facts in mind? If so, is the distinction to which Larrabee alludes (1945, p. 128) to be made between facts which refer merely to single events, largely without meaning until linked with other events in support of a more general proposition, and facts which refer to broad generalizations, theories, or ideas about human affairs. If the latter, how can one be said to really know or understand a more general fact unless he is also master of the myriad lesser facts which go to provide the grounds upon which the more general fact rests, as Massialas (1963, p. 186) has pointed out. The enterprise in which the social scientist is engaged is not merely that of amassing data but it involves much more importantly the interpretation of data; generalizing, speculating, hypothesizing, theorizing about relationships between events, and searching out the lesser and relevant facts to substantiate or repudiate the theory. To this which is the social sciences, the so-called social sciences simplified for pedagogical purposes has no clear resemblance. As Handlin (1957, 1962), Metcalf (1963, pp. 953–954) and others have pointed out, the simplification of the social sciences for pedagogical purposes requires, because of the increasingly great mass of material that must be covered, the progressive boiling down of the content to ever and even more general propositions which are presented as facts, on the authority of the scholar or textbook writer, without benefit or even a suggestion of the factual grounds, if indeed there be any, for holding the belief. Potter (1954, Part I) has brilliantly demonstrated how grievous can be the error in such procedure. What is more to the point here, the "simplification of the social studies for pedagogical purposes" may compound errors in knowledge without insuring that students will really attain what is possibly a more lasting objective of the social sciences, a readiness always to inquire and a skill in conducting the inquiry, objectives emphasized by Herring (1958), Bruner (1962), Metcalf (1963), and many others.

In sharp contrast to those who conceive of the social studies as essentially the same as the social sciences are those who see the social studies as directly concerned with developing the attributes of good citizens. There are three clearly discernible schools of thought within this group.

One would approach the problem of citizenship development through the restructuring and unification of the content of the social sciences to bring this content more directly to bear on the broad social problems of the society; hence the content of the social studies is conceived as unified, synthesized, and applied social science. Another sees the crux of the social studies in the process of decision making (frequently referred to as problem solving or reflective method) under the wholistic and practical circumstances which face the citizen; hence the content of the social studies is delimited to that data which is relevant to the problems which citizens confront and to the exercise of the process by which information (and perchance values) is brought to bear on these problems. Still a third school conceives the social studies as that content (including myth as well as fact) by which budding young citizens may be indoctrinated with the "right" beliefs and attitudes believed to be necessary for the unity of the nation and the loyalty of her citizens.

Prominently among those who see the social studies as a unified and applied social science is Paul Hanna and his associates at Stanford. Hanna (1962, p. 64), who also allows the on-going activities of the community and the responses of children to experience as sources of content in the social studies, summarizes his concept of the social studies as follows: "The contemporary professional education literature clearly reflects the acceptance of the nation that 'today we teach children — something' and that something is the resultant of a synthesis of content from all three sources built around generalizations drawn from the social sciences." Again Hanna (1963, pp. 191–192) refers to the desirability of a "unified, coordinated, wholistic study" of "men living in societies" particularly in the elementary school and adds "we believe the child is psychologically helped, when we start his systematic school study of men in groups by having him observe and generalize about total cultural patterns rather than concentrate on the separate social science threads pulled out of the cultural textile (as is done by scholars engaged in sophisticated and detailed analyses)."

From the content of six selected social sciences, Hanna and his students were able to identify and synthesize 3,005 generalized statements universally applicable . . . and relevant to all time or to a stated time about man past and/or present, engaging in a basic human activity and to categorize these statements under nine basic areas of human living (protecting and conserving life and resources; producing, exchanging, and consuming goods and services; transporting goods and people; communicating facts, ideas, and feelings; providing education; etc.) each of which cuts across or overarches the several social sciences and each of which corresponds roughly to an area in which persistent social problems may be found. What Hanna (1963, p. 193) refers to as the "grid of basic human activities," i.e., the various basic categories into which human activities fall each with its attendant set of generalizations, is somehow applied, though exactly how is never made clear, to the study at different grade levels of expanding communities of men, i.e., the family, the school, the neighborhood, etc.

Among others who conceive the social studies as a unified and applied social science is a Committee of the National Council for the Social Studies which proposes 14 basic themes, somewhat like Hanna's basic human activities, to serve as the framework of the entire social studies program (The Committee, 1957). As did Hanna, the Committee has identified a number of generalizations drawn from the content of the several social sciences and history which cluster about and tend to support each theme.

In somewhat like vein the State Central Committee on Social Studies of the California State Department of Education (1957) sought, with the aid of scholars in eight of the social sciences disciplines, to identify the generalization thought to be most important in each field, and to prepare a synthesized list of high order generalization (18 such were identified) which would serve to overarch and unify the entire social studies program in all subjects and at all grade levels.

Engle (1963) suggested nine basic ideas corresponding roughly to the principal areas of persistent social problems which should receive regular recurring emphasis in the social studies. As with the others, he did not make it completely clear how this grid of basic ideas and problems is to be worked into the social studies program at the level of grades, subjects, and topics.

Putting aside the knotty question of how a genuine synthesis of the several social sciences and history is to be effected in the curriculum, a question not yet satisfactorily dealt with in any of the studies cited, these studies have a significant bearing on aims of the social studies. Though not made explicit, the clearly implied aim of the social studies as conceived by Hanna and others is the possession of a set of important and valid beliefs or generalizations linked closely in some way to the areas of living in which human beings experience persistent social problems. Such an aim for the social studies has the great advantage of being specific; mastery of a specific generalization is the kind of aim one can easily get hold of, and the degree of achievement of such an aim can be reasonably well measured.

But seeing that each brick is carefully laid does not necessarily add up to a house. What is the nature of the house we are trying to build? Here those who would synthesize the social sciences are just as unclear as those who would simplify them for pedagogical purposes. How is mastery of a set of valid and important generalizations to be achieved? Are generalizations (and the reference here is to a high order of generalization) to be learned as facts on the authority of the scholar or textbook writer who is presumed to know the facts? If so, the same criticism may be leveled at this version of the social studies as was leveled earlier at the teaching of a simplified version of the social sciences. Or are generalizations to be derived and discovered from source materials as suggested by Bruner? The point is that a far different image of the end product, i.e., the citizen, emerges, depending upon which view is taken of the process by which knowledge, i.e., generalized beliefs about practical human affairs, is achieved. In the one case knowledge is taken as relatively fixed, something to be known; the end is the knowing student, one who has mastered all the correct answers. In the other, knowledge is taken as always changing, open continually to new interpretations as the circumstances of life change; the end in view is the student who knows how to achieve reasonably accurate conclusions at a given time now or in the future.

It is at this point that the school of thought which conceives the social studies as essentially the process of decision making under all of the practical circumstances which confront the citizen, launches its barb at the other schools of thought. Although they do not make it completely clear whether the perfection and habituation of an intelligent way of inquiry or a set of meaningful and tested generalization in relation to critical areas of controversy is the end of social studies instruction, Metcalf (1963) and his mentor Alan Griffin (1945) may be taken as the foremost proponents of the school which equates the social studies with the decision making process. For the sake of clarity it might be well at this point to draw a fine distinction between Metcalf's and Bruner's positions. Bruner, too, sees the process of inquiry and participation in discovery of general ideas as of central importance, but he seems to see these in the more restricted context of the separate social sciences, while Metcalf sees process as applied social science in the context of broad social problems.

Metcalf (1963, pp. 197–198) chides those who ascribe to the social studies long lists of impeccably general purposes which he says are usually operationally vague and poetic expressions shot through with contradictory and incompatible destinations. He suggests instead a single purpose which is "to help students examine reflectively issues in closed areas of American culture, i.e., in such areas as sex, economics, religion, race, and social class" (1963, p. 197). Engle (1960), Massialas (1963), and Oliver (unpublished manuscript) make common cause with Metcalf, though all of these clearly see the tested beliefs which the student achieves through the process of inquiry as complementary objectives of social studies instruction, and none would limit this approach to the study of critical or closed areas of American culture, seeing opportunities with Bruner for what Massialas calls the "creative encounter" in whatever is the content of history or the other social sciences at a given time (1963, p. 186).

Swift (1961, Ch. 11) and, in more general and somewhat like vein, Hullfish and Smith (1961) have spelled out the decision-making process operationally, i.e., what is involved in solving problems of *definition*, what is involved in solving problems of *explanation*, what is involved in solving problems of *valuing*; in short, how does one ground the generalizations about human affairs which he holds or may come to hold.

Ballinger (1963) and Massialas (1963) have called attention to the marked tendency in the social studies to neglect problems of value. As Oliver (unpublished manuscript) has pointed out, the problem of what to value or in a given situation what choice to make between values is at the crux of all social problems. Yet Ballinger (1963, pp. 200–201) found that only one of eleven authors of textbooks in social studies methods has anything substantial to say about teaching values. Only those who see the central concern of the social studies as decision making seem to be sensitive to the process of valuing as an end of social studies instruction, and these would sharply distinguish their objective from that of the school which would use the social studies to indoctrinate, deliberately stacking the cards in favor of particular values deemed "right" and against others considered "wrong." Instead, as Metcalf (1963, p. 201) suggests, the primary end is perfection of the process of inquiry into questions of value.

Uncomfortable bedfellows with Hanna, Metcalf, and others who see the social studies as concerned focally with citizenship education is a third group, which sees the role of the social studies as indoctrination. For a statement of this position one may turn to *Resolutions Adopted by the National Executive Committee of the American Legion* (1957). In agreement with Metcalf though not with Hanna, this group is centrally concerned with values. But in sharp contrast with Metcalf (1963), who sees perfection of the process of valuing as much or even more than values *per se* as an appropriate end of the social studies, this group looks upon values as being final and absolute, the right values to be accepted unquestionably from one's elders through the school. Facts, too, are treated as the unquestioned facts, the right facts, those everyone should know, serving as the rational for the right values, those that everyone should accept. The objective of the social studies is to teach the student what to value, not how to choose from among competing values.

Many, possibly most, teachers and many laymen, either by deliberate choice or perhaps unwittingly subscribe to this objective of social studies teaching. A few would limit such an approach to the formative years, being willing later after a proper set has been established to lay bare the facts of life. Extremists conceive the social studies as a closed body of facts and values, even unto college. Though such a position obviously removes the social studies from any very clear relationship to the social sciences, some social scientists, by declining in the name of science to deal with values and valuing, abdicate in the realm of values to those who would willingly indoctrinate.

During the period 1959–1963 covered by this summary, three more or less authoritative statements on aims of the social studies have appeared in the literature, that of the NCSS Committee on the Role of the Social Studies (1962), that of the NASSP Committee on Curriculum Planning and Development (1961), and that of Berelson (1962), which reputedly summarizes the thinking of the group of scholars from the several social science disciplines commissioned by the American Council of Learned Societies and National Council for the Social Studies to formulate basic objectives for the social studies (1962, Introduction). Though all agree in general terms that the development of desirable socio-civic and personal behavior is the ultimate goal of the social studies, the variety of means implied suggests no real agreement as to particular ends desired.

As with many earlier statements of social studies objectives, those of the Committees are open to widely varying interpretation and, if the language can be trusted, harbor within themselves inconsistent destinations. On the one hand, claims for the social studies seem hardly distinguishable from claims for all of general education. On the other, there is the denial of any one-to-one relationship between means and ends, an obvious error in logic. Thus the Committee of the National Council for the Social Studies (1962, p. 315) disclaims in the very beginning a relationship between means and ends saying "the term social studies implies no particular form of curriculum organization. It is applicable to curricula in which each course is derived for the most part from a single discipline as well as to curricula in which courses combine material from several disciplines." Thus, while the Committee seems to conceive of the social studies as broad enough to include Wesley and Hanna, it seemingly ignores or possibly misses entirely the real point of Bruner's work, the goal of which (the creative, reflective scholar) cannot be safely predicted as emanating from just any curricular organization which one may conceive of as coming from one quite as well as from another, which is exactly the point made by Metcalf and the "decision making" school. Further, the Committee lists numerous specific behavorial patterns, beliefs, and skills which, though in no way operationally stated, would be largely unacceptable as social studies objectives to the scholars whom Berelson represents.

In contrast to the Committee's effusiveness as to aims, Berelson, who purports to summarize the thinking of scholars in the social sciences, is much more reserved. According to Berelson, the scholars will accept "preparation for responsible citizenship" as the goal only if they can dictate the means, which is the presentation of each subject for its own intellectual sake in the spirit of the liberal arts. This, it is argued, is the "best preparation for responsible citizenship" (1962, p. 6). Thus, as indicated earlier, the scholar disassociates himself from a direct attack on the problem of citizenship education and, as Keller (1961, p. 60) has insisted he should, from the whole enterprise which others would equate with the social studies.

In neither of the committee statements or in Berelson's summary is implicit or operational recognition given to the "process of inquiry" or to "participation in discovery" or to "decision making" as a legitimate objective of the social studies. Whether this is because these authorities have missed the point of Bruner's work or whether, for commonsense reasons, they feel that it is impractical or even dangerous to involve children, as Metcalf would have us do, in the actual process of inquiring into social problems, especially during the tender years before an unquestioned foundation of fact and value has been acquired, this author has no way of knowing. It is rather the purpose of this paper to draw out the issue over objectives than to resolve this problem.

BIBLIOGRAPHY

Ballinger, Stanley E., "The Social Studies and Social Controversy," *School Review* 71:97–110, Spring, 1963.

Berelson, Bernard, "Introduction," in *The Social Studies and the Social Sciences*, A publication of the American Council of Learned Societies and the National Council for the Social Studies, Harcourt, Brace, and World, New York, 1962, 303 pp.

Bruner, Jerome S., *The Process of Education*, Harvard University Press, Cambridge, Mass., 1962, 92 pp.

California State Central Committee on Social Studies, *Building Curriculum in Social Studies for Public Schools of California*, California State Department of Education Bulletin, no. 26, The Department, Sacramento, 1957, 109 pp.

Carr, Edwin R., and Wesley, Edgar B., "Social Studies," in *Encyclopedia of Educational Research*, pp. 1213–1238, edited by Walter S. Monroe, The Macmillan Co., New York, 1950.

Engle, Shirley H., "Decision Making: The Heart of Social Studies Instruction," *Social Education* 24:301–304, 306, November, 1960.

"Thoughts in Regard to Revision," *Social Education* 27:182, April, 1963.

Griffin, Alan, *The Subject Matter Preparation of Teachers of History*, Unpublished dissertation, The Ohio State University, Columbus, 1942.

Gross, Richard B., "Social Studies," in *Encyclopedia of Educational Research*, pp. 1296–1319, edited by Charles W. Harris, The Macmillan Co., New York, 1960.

Hanna, Paul R., "Revising the Social Studies; What Is Needed," *Social Education* 27:190–196, April, 1963.

Hanna, Paul R., and Lee, John R., "Content in the Social Studies," in *Social Studies in Elementary Schools*, pp. 62–89, edited by John U. Michaelis, Thirty-second Yearbook, National Council for the Social Studies, Washington, D.C., 1962.

Handlin, Oscar, "Are the Colleges Killing Education," *Atlantic* 209:41–45, May, 1962.

"The Textbooks That Don't Teach," *Atlantic* 200:110–113, December, 1957.

Herring, Pendelton, "Toward an Understanding of Man," in *New Viewpoints in the Social Sciences*, pp. 1–19, edited by Roy A. Price, Twenty-eighth Yearbook, National Council for the Social Studies, Washington, D.C., 1958.

High, John, *Teaching Secondary School Social Studies*, John Wiley and Sons, Inc., New York, 1962, 481 pp.

Hullfish, H. Gordon, and Smith, Philip G., *Reflective Thinking: The Method of Education*, Dodd, Mead and Co., New York, 1961, 273 pp.

Keller, Charles R., "Needed: Revolution in the Social Studies," *Saturday Review* 24:60, September 16, 1961.

Larrabee, Harold A., *Reliable Knowledge*, Houghton Mifflin Co., Boston, 1945, 685 pp.

Lynd, Robert, *Knowledge for What?* Princeton University Press, Princeton, N.J., 1948, 268 pp.

Massialas, Byron G., "Revising the Social Studies: An Inquiry–Centered Approach," *Social Education* 27:185–189, April, 1963.

Metcalf, Lawrence E., "The Reflective Teacher," *Phi Delta Kappan* 44:17–21, October, 1962.

"Research on Teaching the Social Studies," in *Handbook of Research on Teaching*, pp. 929–965, edited by N. L. Gage, Rand McNally and Co., Chicago, 1963.

"Some Guidelines for Changing Social Education," *Social Education* 27:197–201, April, 1963.

National Association of Secondary-School Principals, "Social Studies in the Comprehensive Secondary School," *Bulletin of the National Association of Secondary School Principals* 45:1–17, September, 1961.

National Council for the Social Studies, Committee on the Role of the Social Studies, "The Role of the Social Studies," *Social Education* 20:315–318, 327, October, 1962.

National Education Association, National Council for the Social Studies, *A Guide to Content in the Social Studies*, Report of the Committee on Concepts and Values, The Council, Washington, D.C., 1957, 78 pp.

Potter, David M., *People of Plenty*, The University of Chicago Press, Chicago, 1954, 217 pp.

Resolutions Adopted by the National Executive Committee of the American Legion, The Committee, Register no. 23, November 20–26, 1957.

Swift, Leonard F., "Explanation," in *Language and Concepts in Education*, pp. 179–194, edited by B. Othanel Smith, and Robert H. Ennis, Rand McNally and Co., Chicago, 1961.

Wesley, Edgar B., and Wronski, Stanley P., *Teaching Social Studies in High Schools*, D. C. Heath and Co., Boston, 1958, 628 pp.

Conclusions Bearing on the Determination of Objectives

Charles Beard

What conclusions bearing on objectives and curriculum are to be drawn from ... [a] survey of the social sciences? They may be set forth briefly.

I. The social sciences are concerned with the actuality of society in development. In detail they describe particular situations and relations and movements in situations and relations. To borrow terms from physics, the social sciences deal with both statics and dynamics. Each of the social sciences treats of particular phases or manifestations of the same thing, namely, society in development; they are, therefore, not sharply separated sciences but are linked by the linkage of the actualities which form the subject matters of their observation and study.

II. The social sciences embrace great bodies of accurate knowledge pertaining to society and social relations in development — knowledge derived from direct observation of society and from the study of records. This knowledge distinguishes civilization from barbarism. All the arts, pure and applied, of economy, government, and social living rest on this knowledge. The wider, the deeper, the more accurate the knowledge, the more likely the success in any achievement projected, either public or private.

III. The literature of the social sciences may be, for convenience, divided into two classes, though they are not sharply separated in fact, namely, *empirical* and *ethical* or *normative* works.

Empirical literature, which is often meant when education is discussed by specialists in the United States, purports to be scientific, objective, and neutral as to choices, values, and decisions involving policy. By its very nature it is pre-

Reprinted with the permission of Charles Scribner's Sons from *The Nature of the Social Sciences*, pages 157–166 and 170–173, by Charles Beard. Copyright 1934 Charles Scribner's Sons; renewal copyright © 1962 William Beard.

cluded from making moral judgments, from declaring what *ought* to be done in given situations. Empirical treatises in the social sciences claim to employ the objective method of the real sciences. They profess to adopt the attitude of complete neutrality over against the data of the social sciences. They search for the laws of social operations and development, as the natural sciences search for the laws of physics or chemistry. Their avowed purpose is to discover and describe things as they have been and are, not as they should be. In doing this, they usually proceed, more or less, on the assumption that the principle of determinism, once regarded as applicable to physical phenomena, is also applicable to social phenomena. And thinkers who have carried the principle of determinism to its logical conclusion have contended that a complete, closed system of social science, akin to that of celestial mechanics in precision, could arise from the observation of social data, if the human mind were competent to the task and all the facts could be known in their proper setting.

On the assumption that their fundamental assumptions are valid, that social data are subject to laws akin to the laws of physics, and that the human mind, in dealing with human affairs, can be neutral, academic leaders in the social sciences have been operating for many years. Investigations have been made in every direction on the theory that when "the facts" are assembled, sorted, classified, and arranged, imperative laws, truths, and determinations will automatically and inexorably emerge. On this theory some have been bold enough to speak of "the science of education" or "the science of economics," disclosed or to be disclosed by fact-finding and arrangement — usually without inquiring what such a science would look like if it could be established.

The second type of literature in the social sciences, the ethical, includes works which openly declare values to be achieved, and advocate choices and lines of action. Into this class fall great works — the classics of the social sciences — Plato, Aristotle, Machiavelli, Hobbes, Locke, Rousseau, Wollstonecraft, Adam Smith, Hamilton, Madison, and Jay (*Federalist*), Comte, Marx, and Ruskin, for example. These writers do not profess the complete neutrality of empirical science. Consciously or unconsciously, they posit values to be realized in society, by action, individual and collective. These works are arguments for the adoption of policies deemed desirable as positive good or as better than prevailing policies. Such treatises do not ignore the hard facts with which empiricism works. On the contrary they are characterized by more or less exact knowledge of social realities and human nature. But they assert values — ethical and esthetic, render judgments on the basis of experience, knowledge, and insight, and advocate choices to be made in contingencies. And these values, judgments, and arguments have their origin and support in what may be called ethical conceptions, deep rooted in the human spirit.

IV. Contemporary thought in the social sciences is also deeply concerned with exploring the boundaries between empirical and ethical operations in the social sciences, and a large body of literature on this subject has been created, especially since the outbreak of the World War.[1] The conclusions of recent inquiries may be summarized.

1. Empiricism is a precious and indispensable instrument of the human mind for developing exact and accurate knowledge respecting all phases of

[1] See, for instance, Karl Heussi, *Die Krisis des Historismus* (1932).

human society and conduct. The neutral or judicial calm of empiricism is a civilizing force of the utmost value to society, particularly in time of crisis. Without the empirical method and knowledge empirically acquired, neither individual nor social life could continue.

2. There are many "areas" of social action to which the empirical method can be effectively applied and there are types of human activity so regular and repetitious that axioms, sometimes called "laws," may be derived from the study of them, but all such axioms are provisional in character and their continued validity depends upon the course of surrounding circumstances.

3. The total actuality of society in development, which is the concern of the social sciences, has not been brought within the formula of any "social law" or "laws," and contemporary thought is inclined to the view that the assumptions of physics are inapplicable to the whole range of human affairs. It has practically discarded the possibility of devising a system of social mechanics comparable to that of celestial mechanics.

4. Contemporary thought challenges the conception that the complete neutrality of empiricism is really applicable in the observation and description of *large areas of human affairs*. The thinker in the social sciences may be neutral in the presence of the question: What was the year of Abraham Lincoln's birth? But he cannot be absolutely neutral in fact when he attempts to answer the question: What was the character of Lincoln's administration? In dealing with a large complex of occurrences and facts, the social scientist, being human and belonging to a definite age, nation, and group, brings to the "data" some frame of reference already in his mind, and in that frame will be some conceptions of ethics — good and evil, desirable and undesirable, praiseworthy and unworthy of praise.

5. Hence it may be said that limits have been discovered to the applicability of the empirical method to social affairs and that efforts to push it beyond the boundaries of its applicability have precipitated a crisis in thought. Human beings are constantly confronted by the appearances of choices, small or fateful. Empiricism cannot tell them what they *ought* to do, even though it can often tell them what they must or must not do *if* they decide to gain certain ends.

Ethical considerations are, therefore, being openly restored to the social sciences, from which they were never excluded entirely, and ethical considerations as applied to society imply some ideal of good, better, or best social arrangements for the service of human life. This ideal is a unifying conception. It is a unity, not a fusion or integration of disparate items. This restoration of unifying ethical considerations is well exemplified in the "Review of Findings" which accompanies the Report of President Hoover's Committee on Social Trends (p. 154).

V. By its very nature (neutrality) empiricism is precluded from attempting to set objectives for instruction in the social sciences, for this operation is posited upon a declaration of values or preferences, within the limits of necessity. Since such objectives inherently involve the assertion of values to be attained, empiricism cannot pass judgment upon them without setting up values of its own, that is, violating its method. Nor can empiricism prepare any program of instruction in the social sciences. Such a program involves choices which the scientific method is powerless to make. Empiricism cannot write a manual on any social subject for instruction in the schools, because such a manual involves the *selection* of materials with reference to some utility or value on which empiricism cannot pass judgment without violating its rule of neutrality. It cannot even declare that the empirical method *ought* to be taught in the schools without referring to some advantages or ends to be attained, that is, again violating its rule of choiceless neutrality. In short, pure empiricism and education are contradictions.

If empiricism could conceivably set up by some as yet unknown process a completely purposeless and choiceless scheme of instruction in the social sciences, it would have to be indifferent to ultimate results considered in terms of human performances. With human results no science as such can be concerned. Mathematics may be employed to keep the books of a legitimate manufacturing establishment or the records of a gang of robbers. Physics may be employed in industry or burglary. Chemistry may be used in healing the sick or poisoning the food of a personal enemy. There is nothing in mathematics, physics, or chemistry which declares what uses ought to be made of their axioms and laws. The social sciences considered empirically are equally indifferent to results. A knowledge of party machinery may be made the basis of public service or corrupt operations in politics. Knowledge of economics may be employed to preserve the integrity of a bank or to loot it.

VI. Discovering in the social sciences that the ends of instruction are not fixed by empiricism and that choices are precluded by it, the formulators of objectives and curricula in the social sciences are thrown back upon ethical considerations: What are the good, better, or best ends that are possible of attainment by instruction in the social sciences? This seems to be inescapable. The choice of ends involves both knowledge and thought — knowledge of what is possible and probable for the immediate future and thought about what is desirable. It thus involves a forecast of inevitable trends in human affairs and an assertion of values deemed attainable by choice and action within the broad lines laid down by the inexorable. For the educator it is nothing less than an interpretation of history that will be made and can be made in the coming years. To this fundamental conclusion contemporary thought in the social sciences has led us. If it is complex and difficult in nature, that is no reason for seeking an avenue of escape through a false assumption of simplicity.

VII. If empirical science has been unable to create a closed science of society or education, it nevertheless presents to thought about objectives and curricula positive conclusions of undoubted imperative. If empiricism has not been able to create a science of society in all fulness and completeness, sovereignty has not been surrendered to intuitive guesses, valuations, and judgments. Because all is not known, it does not follow that nothing is known. Because it has not been proved that deterministic laws apply to the whole domain of social ideas and interests, it does not follow that they do not apply to any area of ideas and interests after appropriate assumptions are made. If fact-finding conducted without knowledge of past structures of thought and without reference to any conceptions of value or bench marks of posited significance is usually a fruitless diversion, we are not driven to the conclusion that intuitive judgments conceived in ignorance of facts and historic thought-structures can supply guidance to society. The shortcomings of empiricism do not impeach its validity as an instrument of inquiry and thought or in any way diminish the desirability of using it in dealing with all areas of human affairs to which it can be applied and with all the rigor that is possible to the human mind.

It may be instructive and comforting to recall, in this connection, that even the most exact sciences, when taken out of the artificial conditions of the laboratory and put to practical uses, also suffer from limitations in accurate calculations and forecasts as to results. In building a water works plant for a city, the hydraulic engineer finds it difficult to estimate with precision the amount of water that will actually be used, the growth of population in the near future, and the extent of the fire hazards likely to exist in the community. He must make wide allowances for a margin of error. The architect and engineer, unable to discover precisely the load which an office building may have to bear, must likewise leave room for unexpected contingencies. This in no way impugns the value or rigor of such sciences as far as they go, but indicates the hazards of calculation respecting the results of any procedure whenever human beings enter into the scene of operations — human beings whose activities and interrelations form the fundamental subject matter of the social sciences.

What then has the human mind, by applying as rigorously as possible the scientific method to the data of the social sciences, actually and positively accomplished?

1. Within its several areas of operation it has assembled large bodies of facts and arranged them more or less coherently in accordance with the observable outward relations which they represent. Take, for example, statistics on natural resources, population, marriages, births, deaths, and immigration.[2] These are bodies of facts assembled with the aid of the empirical method. They represent outward realities. However closely related to one another as realities they may be, they also present categories of thought to the human mind, as do physics and chemistry. It would, therefore, be unreal to present these facts all in one table without classification or distinction, for instance, giving first in the same column the number of acres of timber in the United States, second the number of marriages in France last year, third the number of emigrants from Rangoon to Ceylon, and so on. Employing the empirical method, the human mind has assembled large bodies of social facts with reference to relations. In doing this, it has employed engines of inquiry, verification, criticism, and authentication, which may be properly described as scientific in character.

2. With the aid of the empirical method, the human mind has also erected in each of the great divisions of social science a thought-structure which in broad outline at least appears to correspond with the actual structural arrangement of the objective data observed. By comparisons and criticisms akin to those used in the physical sciences, contemporary thought in social sciences has arrived at a belief in the realism of these thought-structures, although they cannot be given the precision of thought-structures in physics and chemistry. For example, when the economist places in the center of his thought the production, exchange, and distribution of commodities, he has empirical reasons for believing that they are essential to thinking about the subject, whether his purposeful or subjective tendency be individualist-liberal, socialist, fascist, or communist.

[2] They would not exist, however, if they had not been deemed valuable for some purpose.

In other words, all is not ideological or utopian in the erection of social thought-structures.

3. Still more recently the social sciences have been occupied with tendencies or "trends" in social affairs — in technical changes, in the organization of industry, labor, and agriculture, in the functions of government, in education, and all the other departments of life with which the social sciences deal. To some extent these changes may be listed in historical or chronological order and plotted in graphs. Thus changes and tendencies have become primary objects of study and consideration in the social sciences. Formal knowledge about society has become dynamic, and static conceptions of society have been demonstrated as unreal in nature and inefficient, if not dangerous, in applicability.

4. Employing the comparative and sifting method, contemporary social sciences have been drawing together, seeking to grasp the scheme of society entire, and to find empirical categories for the classification of social activities and phenomena — categories which are fundamental in themselves and permit of the evaluation of means in relation to ends. For convenience the term "processes" is borrowed from physics and biology to cover these essential categories — the biological process of continuing human life, processes of economic support, of government, of establishing social norms or rules of social living, and processes of defense against other societies, for example.[3]

5. Finally, the social sciences may legitimately claim that the method of empiricism now emphasized by them is indispensable to the discovery of necessities, probabilities, and possibilities in the social field and to the creation of social inventions designed to realize purposes and values arising in the human mind, by whatever processes, as yet inconceivable as deterministic sequences.

. . . .

Besides encountering in human affairs certain forms and processes to which systematization is given, the social sciences as empirical sciences also confront as realities changes or developments in forms and processes. Attempts have been made to explain these changes by determinism, by arranging chains of causation, but such attempts have not been successful on any considerable scale. It has also been argued that "problems" arise out of change, but it may also be argued that changes arise out of the appearance of problems in the human mind. The ancient issue whether deed or thought marked the beginning has not been settled and cannot be settled. What is well established, however, is that fact and idea evolve together in reciprocal relation. Interests and ideas run side by side through historical development. When they are in harmony there are no tensions in society, no problems. When, through either a development of ideas on one side or a movement of interests on the other side a tension arises, there appears a problem presenting what seem to be possibilities of choice, however limited and conditioned by social realities.

At this point empiricism in the social sciences is challenged by two considerations: what forms and directions will these changes take and what choices should be made in contingencies? It may, of course, choose to avoid them, for there is nothing in empiricism which of itself compels it, by value or logical necessity, to deal with anything. If, however, it pushes its inquiry as far as

[3] See Leon Marshall's volume on *The Process Approach to the Social Studies*.

possible toward the periphery of its subject matter, it must then examine and describe as accurately as possible these tensions of change and direction and the ideas of choice offered by human thought.

And when the social sciences discharge this obligation faithfully, they disclose the fundamental fact that the whole political system through which adjustments are made in the United States is founded upon the conception of a flexible frame of control and reference — the Constitution of the United States. Born of a tension, it assumes the perdurance of tensions and the possibility of adjusting them by inquiry, discussion, proposal, and decision within the borders of law. The values for such adjustments are furnished by the cultural heritage of the nation and the ideas evolving out of and added to that heritage. Empiricism discloses politics in fact as mainly composed of, and made dynamic by, the conflicts of special interests, with their accompanying ideas, and the art of politics as concerned with the control, suppression, and advancement of special interests, usually, it is claimed, in the name of the general interest. The extent to which the realities disclosed by empiricism can be taught as descriptions in any particular institution of learning depends not merely upon the truth of the matter; it depends in part upon the pressures which such interests exert on educational authorities.[5] In any case, educational statecraft, not empiricism, must decide this issue in setting up objectives and curricula for the schools.

Now we come to the second question raised by tensions and changes in society: What choices should be made in contingencies? Here the social sciences, working as descriptive sciences with existing and becoming reality, face, unequivocally, ideas of value and choice — argumentative systems of social philosophy based upon conceptions of desirable changes in the social order. At this occurrence empiricism breaks down absolutely. Bound to neutrality by its nature, it has nothing to say. It is impossible to discover by the fact-finding operation whether this or that change is desirable. Empiricism may disclose, within limits, whether a proposed change is possible, or to what extent it is possible, and the realities which condition its eventuation, but, given possibility or a degree of possibility, empiricism has no way of evaluating value without positing value or setting up a frame of value.

6. Nevertheless empiricism can present types of ethical and esthetic conception and interest — possibilities of choice and points of reference for the formulation of policy. It may, for example, present complete systems of thought and design showing efficiency in economy, beauty in town and country, and humaneness in life. It cannot present these as imperatives but as alternatives, as possibilities. By its own logic it is compelled to consider them if it extends its operations to the periphery of its domain. If called upon, it may proceed with scientific rigor to inquire what is possible as well as what is probable.

7. While empiricism cannot thus set objectives, it can discover the objectives which society, through lawmakers, school authorities, and other agencies, is projecting as the ends of education and can tabulate, classify, and organize them according to their congruities. It can indicate, with more or less accuracy, the ideas, interests, and methods calculated to realize these objectives in instruction itself, without being able to forecast their distant outcome in society itself. It

[5] Bessie L. Pierce, *Citizens' Organizations and the Civic Training of Youth.*

can state with a reasonable degree of assurance that the children now in the schools will in later years confront opportunities for choice and the necessity of acting on choices amid changes and contingencies, but it is not able closely and minutely to describe these opportunities, necessities, changes, and contingencies in advance.

In fine, contemporary knowledge in the social sciences has come back to the old formula for human life which Machiavelli summed up in three words: *necessità, fortuna, and virtù.* It cannot fix their boundaries absolutely or formulate their process in a differential equation, but it can make disclosures in each field. Under the head of necessity it can, with more or less precision, establish the general framework of determining and conditioning realities afforded now by Industrial Society, the Interventionist State, and Western Culture, including the climate of opinion composed of ideas. It can describe, without forecasting accurately for any length of time, the tensions which offer the appearances of choice and decision. It can throw light on the human being as a thinking, knowing, creating, achieving personality.

Beyond this it is impossible for the social sciences, in their present state, to go. They cannot foreclose on the future, foretell the exact conditions in which coming choices must be made, empirically prescribe the right choices, or be absolutely certain that instruction in their materials will mechanically produce just the results expected.

Such are the positive and negative "offerings" of the social sciences. They cannot create a science of education which will deliver imperatives to educators and relieve them of the hazards of purpose and choice. As empirical sciences, they can present systems, trends, probabilities, and alternatives, but they cannot declare purposes or make choices. What use the educator will make of their findings depends upon the prevailing ethics of education and not upon any "laws" of social science. They can speak only of conditionalities; they do not issue commands. They cannot declare ends; they are means to ends.

FURTHER READING FOR SECTION 1

Benjamin, Harold. *The Saber Tooth Curriculum.* New York: McGraw-Hill, 1939.
This very readable book is a provocative satire on the inflexibility of educational institutions. It suggests serious questions about the justification for much social studies instruction.

Bloom, Benjamin S. (ed.). *Taxonomy of Educational Objectives: Handbook I: Cognitive Domain.* New York: Longmans, Green, 1956; David R. Krathwohl, Benjamin S. Bloom, and Bertram B. Masia. *Taxonomy of Educational Objectives: Handbook II: Affective Domain.* New York: David McKay, 1964.
These handbooks were prepared to assist in the specification of objectives and tests to measure their attainment. Chapter 2 of *Handbook I* provides an excellent treatment of some considerations in framing educational objectives. Affective objectives, their neglect and formulation, are treated in a forthright manner in Chapters 2 and 3 of *Handbook II.*

Oliver, Donald W., and James P. Shaver. *Teaching Public Issues in the High School.* Boston: Houghton Mifflin, 1966.

Chapter 1 is a discussion of the problem of setting goals for the social studies in a democratic society. Chapters 2–4 explicate a rationale for the social studies curriculum.

Taba, Hilda, *Curriculum Development: Theory and Practice.* New York: Harcourt, Brace & World, 1962.

Chapter 13 presents an excellent analysis of the levels of generality on which objectives can be stated and the roles which objectives can and should play in curriculum development. Helpful guidelines for formulating objectives are also provided. Chapter 14 is a comprehensive discussion of the variety of objectives that might be sought in the classroom.

2

Conceptions of the Society and the
Social Studies Curriculum

Each of us, as noted by Charles Beard in Section 1, has a frame of knowledge and values about the social world which directs our behavior. This frame of reference may be explicit or implicit, contradictory and muddled or rigorously defined and carefully formulated. Whatever state the frame is in, the educational program, including the social studies curriculum, probably has helped shape it. Consciously or not, the teacher in the classroom teaches a set of attitudes and an array of ideas about the society, and his social frame of reference guides his selection of content and teaching strategies. The teacher may be totally unaware of or unconcerned with the conceptions of society that underly his curriculum, or he may be fully aware of them and deliberately attempt to alter his students' views. The effects on his students may be quite different from what he intended; however, the critical point is that the content and teaching strategies selected for a course by a teacher, a textbook publisher, a curriculum committee, or a curriculum development project presume certain notions about society, whether or not openly espoused and examined.

This introductory essay and the readings in this section are intended to assist the teacher in elaborating, clarifying, and then subjecting to critical analysis and reformulation the conception of the social world that underlies his curricular decisions. Bringing a frame of reference from the subconscious to a conscious level where it may be examined by reasonable men to expose its contradictions and questionable assumptions is exceedingly difficult. It is, perhaps, even more difficult to convince teachers that there is an implicit conception of the social world underlying their curricular choices.

Some people insist that they never teach attitudes toward social reality. One counter-argument to the position that an educational program has an underlying conception of the social world which invariably shapes the student's values, his knowledge, and his ability and inclination to use his intellect runs something like this: "Education in the western liberal tradition has the goal of freeing or liberating a man's intellect. Therefore, the school must not aim to shape people's beliefs and ideas. The attempt to select and specify for the student intellectual operations, values, and knowledge is tantamount to indoctrination. Such an education is perhaps appropriate for a totalitarian society, but not for a free society." We have stated this position as a somewhat oversimplified composite, but it is not a caricature; it has been put forth in a similar form by a number of responsible writers.[1] And it has wide enough acceptance to warrant brief treatment here.

[1] See, for example, Arthur Bestor, *The Restoration of Learning* (New York: Knopf, 1955); James Koerner (ed.), *The Case for Basic Education* (Boston: Little, Brown,

61

Suppose a teacher accepts the educational goal of "freeing man's intellect." Does this mean that he has thereby escaped making decisions about the values and knowledge his students should hold? To the contrary, "freeing man's intellect" clearly implies that the teacher is to develop persons who are *willing* to entertain different points of view and who are *willing* to deal with alternatives rationally. Both are attitudes of mind, or values, which have important implications for the student's view of society. The goal also suggests that the school develop in students the *ability* to cope with the world rationally, or in other words, that students must learn to make decisions by force of intellect rather than by emotion alone.

The teacher's curricular choices may affect the student's frame of reference even more subtly, however. As a case in point, let us examine some possible consequences for student and society which may follow from the way in which a teacher handles one part of a modern European history course. Any modern European history course, it can be assumed, will deal with events in Germany at the time of Hitler. The teacher has a number of choices as to what to include and how to approach the topic or events he includes. He can, for instance, ignore the topic of genocide altogether; or he can deal with the topic, but avoid making or eliciting any value judgments while to the best of his ability remaining impartial and descriptive; or he can solicit and help the students to question their own values.

Let us say the teacher chooses to avoid making or soliciting value judgments as to whether or not genocide should be condemned on moral grounds. In this case, his students will be studying probably one of the most systematic, bestial mass killings of all time without having their attention focused on the moral issues involved. Even though the teacher is attempting to avoid values, the student may be learning an evaluative orientation to human affairs. In this case, the orientation can probably be characterized as moral disengagement from the crises of our society. If this teacher deals with most moral issues in human history in a similar way, he has, perhaps unknowingly, taken a curriculum position that could have profound effects on his students' social views, and, indirectly, on the shape of the society they help build.

Political theorists have long recognized the effects the educational program may have on the society through intentional and unintentional influences on the values, attitudes, and knowledge of citizens. In the first selection in this section, Karl Friederich, as he examines the role of tradition in education, clarifies the intricate relationship between education and the social and political order. Mr. Friederich's argument should lay to rest the view that education can be "value free."

In sum, educators cannot escape judgments concerning the values, competencies, and knowledge that students should have. And these judgments indirectly or directly help shape what the social system is or may become. Stated differently, there is inevitably a frame of social knowledge or conception of the society imbedded in the teacher's choice of what and how he teaches. A 1934 report by the Commission on the Social Studies of the American Historical Association takes a similar position:

1959); Charles Keller, "Needed — Revolution in the Social Studies," *Saturday Review*, Sept. 16, 1961. pp. 60–62.

1. Education is a form of action on the part of some particular social group; it is not a species of contemplation removed from social life and relationships.

2. Education always expresses some social philosophy, either large or small, involves some choices with respect to social and individual action and well-being, and rests upon some moral conception.

3. Conceived in a large and clarified frame of reference, education is one of the highest forms of statesmanship: a positive and creative attack upon the problems generated by the movement of ideas and interests in society.[2]

In our view, every teacher and curriculum specialist has the obligation to make explicit the social philosophy which underlies his social studies curriculum. If this is not done, any analysis and criticism of the curriculum and its underlying assumptions is difficult, and there is grave risk that the assumptions themselves will be unclear, contradictory, naive, or otherwise inadequate. For as we have attempted to show, any confusion in frame of reference is not merely of academic interest; it will most likely be reflected in the classroom.

A second example may help to show why a careful examination of implicit frames of reference is essential. A modern example of confusion in social philosophy that has had considerable impact on the schools had its roots in the 1930's and 1940's. During that period, what we will call the "democratic process" view prevailed. Much of the literature in social studies education stressed what were called *democratic classroom experiences*, characterized by cooperation, teacher-pupil planning, committee work, and decision by majority vote. In methods textbooks of that period,[3] teaching was discussed in terms of an authoritarian versus a democratic style, with the latter clearly considered desirable. Primary social political values involved in this position, either explicitly or by implication, included "social harmony," "cooperation," and "literal majoritarianism"; it was maintained that men should work together cooperatively and live in harmony, making decisions by majority vote.

Here, then, is an example of an educational position tied to a notion of the desirable society and the good man. The weakness of the position is *not* that it attempted to relate educational policy and practice to a social theory; indeed this is its strength. The problem is that the theory itself is open to attack on a number of grounds. Two brief criticisms will illustrate our point.

First, we may question the emphasis upon literal majoritarianism as either an operative or desirable ideal of a modern democratic state. Some notion of majority rule may be a central and important value in our democracy, but its position as a societal norm is more subtle and complicated than the literal New England town meeting majority rule which was often the basis of classroom practice. In a modern state, the majority not only does not govern directly, but as more than one of the readings in this section notes, the majority rarely gives

[2] American Historical Association, *Report of the Commission on the Social Studies* (New York: Scribner's 1934), "Conclusions and Recommendations," page 30. Although the author of the report is not identified, there is reason to believe that it was Charles Beard.

[3] For an example of a recent textbook in which the point of view persists, see Maxine Dunfee and Helen Sal, *Social Studies Through Problem Solving* (New York: Holt, Rinehart & Winston, 1966).

its consent to major economic and political decisions. Moreover, majority rule cannot be considered the preeminent value of our society; otherwise, for example, genocide could be justified by a majority vote.

Second, the "democratic process" movement is also open to the criticism that *cooperation* and *harmony* were made almost synonymous with *democracy*. Clearly, our society is characterized by pluralism and dissent, and many commentators see these as at least as vital to a democracy as harmony or cooperation.[4]

These criticisms of the "democratic process" movement, while brief, are given to illustrate that analysis and criticism of social frames of reference are necessary and useful if we are to make rational decisions about the social studies curriculum. It is possible, though difficult, to ferret out and subject to analysis the views of the society implicit in a curricular position. If, however, these views are made explicit and defended rationally, there is greater chance that there will be intellectual integrity and clarity in what the teacher does in the classroom.

It is interesting that some recent writers, perhaps as a reaction to the democratic process movement's disturbing misinterpretations of democratic theory, have left their social philosophy entirely implicit. For instance, Jerome Bruner, one of the more prominent of present-day educational theorists, seems to take the position that the structure of the disciplines should shape the entire general education program.[5] He does not deal explicitly with the conception of society implicit in his recommendations, and it is difficult to piece together his views on social and educational priorities from his collections of essays and lectures, each addressed to a variety of issues. Nevertheless, one can be certain that there is an underlying, implicit conception (or conceptions) of the social world. This is indicated by, if nothing else, Bruner's dissatisfaction with past and current educational practice.

The Values of Democracy

The other readings in this section are divided into two sets, both of which are intended to clarify and provoke further questions about the teacher's social frame of reference. The first set includes pieces by Charles Frankel, Gunnar Myrdal, and Donald W. Oliver, selected to raise issues about the nature of the democratic value system and implications for the social studies curriculum.

The reading by Charles Frankel is a chapter from his book, *The Democratic Prospect*, which is devoted to an examination of the ideals of democracy and the prospects for an open society. In this chapter, Frankel clarifies some common misconceptions about democratic values and suggests four ideals that he believes are fundamental to the Western democratic tradition. Frankel is obviously not the last word on democratic values; however, his essay is included to suggest to the teacher the importance of a careful consideration of democratic values, as well as to suggest the complexity and range of issues raised when one attempts to make explicit a conception of society.

[4] For an interesting critique of some of our procedural institutions, see, M. Judd Harmon, *The Search For Consensus* (Faculty Association Honor Lecture, Utah State University, Logan, 1964).

[5] See, e.g., *The Process of Education* (Cambridge, Mass.: Harvard University Press, 1960), or *Toward a Theory of Instruction* (Harvard University Press, 1966).

The selection by Gunnar Myrdal is made up of three excerpts from his seminal study of the Negro in the United States, An American Dilemma. Here, Myrdal attempts to characterize the American value system — the American Creed — and to show how it is related to the actions of citizens. He points out the contradictions in the Creed that become troublesome as individuals apply it to specific situations, and he discusses the ways these contradictions are normally handled.

Myrdal is concerned primarily with the conflicts that occur between the more general values of the Creed and the valuations of particular groups or situations. However, it is also possible for the most general values of the American Creed to conflict. For instance, passage of "fair housing" legislation may be justified by reference to equality or equal opportunity; but opposition to such legislation may be justified in terms of such values as property rights and freedom of association. All are basic values of the American Creed. An adequate view of our society must take both types of conflicts into account.

In the third article, Oliver discusses the cohesion-diversity dilemma in a democracy and deals with its implications for the curriculum. The selection is included here because it is an attempt not only to clarify and defend a social philosophy but to move logically from the philosophy to criteria for the selection of content and, to some extent, instructional strategies.

Conceptions of Democracy: An Empirical Perspective

The decision concerning what and how to teach in social studies, we have said, requires that the teacher make moral judgments; these in turn imply a social frame of reference, or "social theory."[6] The term social frame of reference as used by Beard and as used here includes convictions about what is desirable, e.g., a conception of the good society, as well as beliefs about what the society is, can become, and is becoming. The first involves moral propositions, the last three are empirical. A simple example may clarify the distinction. If we assert that the purpose of social studies should be to teach students to deal with public issues rationally, at least two assumptions are made: first, that rationality is good and should be fostered by the schools; second, that rationality will be useful in dealing with political issues within our society. The first is a moral proposition in that it prescribes what ought to be done; the second is an empirical proposition about social reality.

In choosing what to teach, the teacher makes both types of assumptions — empirical assumptions about the operation of our social, political, and economic systems, and value assumptions. One does not have to search far to discover confused and contradictory conceptions of the good society implicit in

[6] At times we use conception of society and social frame of reference interchangeably with social theory. The terms social and political theory and social philosophy are ambiguous and have led to considerable debate among social scientists. The way we have used the terms social and political theory to mean somewhat the same as frame of social knowledge and conception of the society is closer to the classical conception of political theory rather than the meaning given to the term theory by modern behavioral scientists. Theory, to these scientists, refers to a set of systematically related propositions which may be subjected to direct or indirect empirical tests. Doubtless, they would not use the term theory when speaking of a loosely conjoined set of value and empirical statements, which is how we are using the term here.

social studies courses, nor need one look long to uncover social studies courses and texts which contain empirical conceptions of the social, political, and economic order that are at variance with reality.

The second set of essays in this section deals with *empirical* conceptions of the social, economic, and political order. The changes within our economic and political systems over the last quarter century have been so striking and in some cases so complete that there has not yet developed a vocabulary adequate to describe the changes. Fortunately, in the last few years, there has been an increasing number of incisive analyses of our social, economic, and political institutions and processes. These writings have clarified some of the most common and mistaken interpretations of our contemporary society.

It is commonplace to declare that the world is changing. But for teachers to know that the world is changing is not sufficient; they must comprehend some of the most significant changes so that at the very least they do not unknowingly perpetuate archaic interpretations of democratic institutions. For example, Kimball and McClellan have proposed that social relationships in America are undergoing radical and fundamental alterations.[7] The personal involvement of "Main Street," the source of social and economic status and the center of voluntary organizations in the nineteenth century, contrasts sharply with the anonymity of the contemporary shopping center and the character of present-day professional organizations. Kimball and McClellan contend that the disappearance of the nineteenth century type of community from our society has left us with dated concepts of political community. The need to redefine community is but one area of societal change demanding the attention of social studies teachers.

We have selected from among recent writings several which might cause the teacher to examine and perhaps revise his conceptions of the social and political world. These selections, of all those in this volume, are especially open to criticism. Although the writers chosen are, in our view, on the forefront of attempts to examine contemporary society, we could not present a cross section of writers or of the issues confronting modern America; the number of issues and writers is simply too great. Some of the issues and writers omitted may be more important than those included. However, we have attempted to include provocative pieces, clearly and concisely written, which would challenge several common assumptions about the way our political and economic systems operate. Our hope is that these writings will lead the reader to additional reading and to a further examination of his assumptions about our society and, consequently, to a more adequate consideration of the goals of social studies instruction.

The thread that runs through all these readings is that with the twentieth century has come a "new society," and many of the traditional formulations must be re-examined. The writers argue that long-standing conceptions of our economic system, of constitutional law and politics, of social relations, and of our international setting must be modified to fit the facts.

The first selection is taken from a publication of the Center for the Study of Democratic Institutions. The Center has, within the last several years, contributed a number of significant interpretations of American society. In this

[7] S. T. Kimball and J. E. McClellan, *Education and the New America* (New York: Random House, 1962), especially pages 186–211.

excerpt from "The Rise and Fall of Liberal Democracy," Harvey Wheeler presents a convincing case that "participational democracy," the dominant theme of modern Jeffersonian democracy, is dead. He concludes that "our times demand a development of new conceptions of legislation and new processes of deliberation . . . appropriate to the condition of bureaucratic cultures and adequate to the challenges of the scientific revolution."

From a different stance, A. A. Berle, in the next selection, argues that the Jeffersonian notion of "possessory property," carrying with it political and economic power, is no longer tenable. He argues that the corporate system, the successor, presents challenges to our political and economic institutions which are not generally recognized or adequately dealt with under present arrangements.

In the final reading, Robert L. Heilbroner sets contemporary society in an international context that contrasts sharply with that at our country's birth and during our expansionist period. Heilbroner's general theme is that, although the tide of history was for generations congenial to the American way of life on the international scene, it has now ebbed, and we must reappraise our values in the light of the changes confronting us. For instance, is traditional or nineteenth century capitalism, which Heilbroner argues no longer exists in our country, adequate for the emerging nations? The reader may well want to turn to Heilbroner's book, *The Future as History*, for an examination of the effects of science and atomic weaponry on contemporary society.

These selections do not begin to touch upon all the issues related to conceptions of our society which have bearing on the social studies curriculum. Perhaps the readings will alert the prospective or experienced teacher to an important aspect of his own frame of social knowledge that he must consider in formulating an adequate rationale for curricular choices.

Tradition and the Role of Education

Carl Joachim Friedrich

Any analysis of political life which stresses values and beliefs alongside of interests is bound to be concerned with tradition. For such values and beliefs must be transmitted in order to be fully operative. Any strictly temporary belief or value is bound to be of limited impact, except in periods of revolutionary upheaval.[1] There have been numerous occasions in the preceding chapters on

From *Man and His Government* by Carl Joachim Friedrich. Copyright © 1963 McGraw-Hill Book Company. Used by permission. pp. 613–615, 617–620, and 621–622.

[1] Accordingly, Max Radin defined tradition as "not a mere fact like an existing custom, nor a story that exhausts its significance in being told; it is an idea which expresses a value judgment. A certain way of acting is regarded as right; a certain order or arrangement is held desirable." ("Tradition" in *ESS*.) Cf. also Friedrich, a, 1953; I there noted, p. 42, that "tradition is essentially a romantic concept," and on p. 46 that "an argument from tradition is an argument from sentiment," and that these "sentiments . . . invest certain past events with a highly positive evaluation."

which reference has had to be made to tradition, notably in the discussion of ideas, myths, symbols and religion (Chapters 4 to 6), in that of authority and legitimacy (Chapters 12 and 13) and in the earlier chapters of Part IV. The difficulty in the past has been the tendency of political thinkers and theorists either to under- or to overestimate tradition, especially in the great controversies of revolutionary periods. Actually, tradition has been a continuous factor of great importance in politics, but one which has hindered and hurt as well as helped and supported the political community. Too much tradition ossifies a political order, while too little tradition dissolves it. *Anomie* was coined by the Greeks as a pejorative term to designate the latter situation when there is no *nomos*, no sacred custom and hence no basic law to guide men's actions, while the opposite fault has been castigated by revolutionary writers in terms appropriate to the particular order they were fighting without giving rise to a general term. It might be called *nomocracy*, to describe a state where everything is judged in terms of traditional values and beliefs, where the *nomos* has become the tyrant of the community and forestalls all forward movement. This was the state of affairs in the West at the time of the French and American revolutions; it was more recently the condition of many colonially administered countries. Statesmanship of the highest order will be required to guide them out of this condition into a balanced political order and not to allow them to fall into *anomie*.

In broadest analytical terms, tradition consists of any set of established values and beliefs which have persisted over several generations in a particular political community. It is thus the antithesis of ideology,* with which it is often unfortunately confused by those who identify any prevailing system of ideas with ideology (Chapter 4). Traditionalism is a self-conscious and deliberative insistence upon, or more especially a harking back to, such values and beliefs, often embodied in and symbolized by habits, customs, usages, and the like.[2] Thus traditionalism may become itself an ideology of reactionary cast, as has happened in the case of fascism and certain forms of nationalism.[3] This fact has tended to obstruct the recognizing of tradition as an ineluctable element of all community, and more particularly political community. It may cogently be

---

* *Editor's Note:* The reader should be familiar with Friedrich's use of the term *ideology* in order to comprehend this passage. In Chapter 4 (page 89) of *Man and His Government*, Friedrich provides the following clarification: "Ideologies are action-related systems of ideas. They typically contain a program and a strategy for its realization, and their essential function is to unite organizations which are built around them. It is confusing and fails to provide the opportunity for political analysis, to call any system of ideas an ideology, such as the philosophy of Aristotle or the theology of the Old Testament. Such systems of ideas *may* provide the *basis* for an ideology, but only after being related to action in a specific sense and for a specific situation. Ideologies are sets of ideas related to the existing political and social order and intended either to change it or to defend it. . . . The ideas an ideology contains are as such action-related and may or may not be very true and appropriate; what makes them "ideology" is their function in the body politic. . . ."

[2] Hoselitz, in his chapter in Braibanti and Spengler, 1961, undertakes systematically to subdivide tradition in terms of habits, usages, norms and ideologies (meaning beliefs), but I doubt the pertinence of this aspect of his otherwise valuable and balanced analysis. For an elaboration of the distinction between tradition and traditionalism, cf. also Shils, a, 1958; this distinction was already used, in a rather similar sense, in ESS.

[3] The failure to bring out this dimension mars the otherwise interesting attempt to treat nationalism as a rival ideology in Bowie et al., 1959, esp. pp. 8ff. and 51ff.

asked whether "it is reasonable to stipulate any traditionless society,"[4] and the question of the role of tradition can thus only be whether a political order is more or less traditional. Indeed rationality itself may well become a tradition, as it has in the modern West, and more particularly in America. One of the obstacles which reactionary attacks against the existing order encounter in the United States is due to this circumstance. An appeal to American traditions and more especially to the Constitution always involves such a plea in a reassertion of the rational values of a constitutional order and its liberties, such as free speech and other forms of self-expression.

A political tradition is more specifically a tradition concerning the political community, its values and beliefs, including the conduct of men as political persons. Political tradition defines how rule is conducted, and how those ruled behave toward the rulers, including their participation in the electing and controlling of them. Such tradition always is embodied in habits, customs, and norms which express the values and beliefs prevalent in a given community.[5] This undoubted context of political tradition has given rise to such notions as that the "agreement on fundamentals" is essential for any political order, or for some particular type. As we have shown there needs to be a certain measure of agreement and a patterning of values and beliefs, but this fact does not constitute an "agreement" on fundamentals. A measure of consensus there is in any functioning political order, but it may be structured in a highly pluralistic fashion.

. . . .

The term "tradition" has its ecclesiastical roots, as does so much of our political vocabulary. Tradition, in this religious sense, is "the delivering of a precious deposit, whose source is held to be divine, to a specially selected person."[9] But this is only one side of the picture. The other is the pliability of tradition. "In face of traditions become obsolete an appeal was made to other traditions, or to the Bible; where written testimony was uncertain or awanting [sic], recourse was had to tradition; that is, that was declared to be tradition which was not to be justified under another title."[10] The similarity here to be observed is to the process of arguing from precedent in the common law[11] and from ideology in

<hr/>

[4] Hoselitz, 1961, p. 84. The well-known "reified" alternatives of Weber's typology of authority-legitimacy (see above, Chaps. 12 and 13) and the related notion of Riesman's tradition-directed versus inner- and other-directed (as if tradition were not a factor in both inner- and other-directed conduct) illustrate the widespread propensity to treat tradition pejoratively and to juxtapose it, often by way of a dichotomy, to rational conduct. Hoselitz' paper rightly questions this propensity, as does Polanyi, 1958, pp. 53–54, 374–379, and *passim*. Cf. also Popper, 1957.

[5] It is not possible, as Radin would have us do, to exclude all customs from tradition (see above, fn. 1), though it is quite true that not all customs are part of tradition, except in a very general sense. A value or belief must be attached to them. If the particular custom or belief is maintained and based on no other value judgment than that it is a tradition, it becomes traditionalist. Hannah Arendt, 1957, pp. 9ff., in arguing that a particular tradition of political thought began with Plato and ended with Marx, is apt to generate a traditionalist reaction in those who like herself wish to recapture this particular tradition.

[9] Radin, in *ESS*, p. 63. His discussion is based upon Harnack, 1885 (English transl. Dover, 1961), vol. III, pp. 207ff., and *passim*.

[10] Harnack, 1961, pp. 207–208.

[11] K. N. Llewellyn, 1960; cf. above, Chap. 15.

totalitarian systems.[12] In all three cases, the politically crucial question is who possesses the authority to say what is true, that is, what is "tradition" or what is "law" or what is "idea." We are here face to face with a key aspect of authority; reasoning from tradition is considered a genuine elaboration by those who believe in the particular item alleged to be part of the tradition. Such tradition may be embodied in sacred texts, such as Magna Charta, the Constitution or the Declaration of Independence; or it may be found in writings and sayings of founders and fathers. Or it may be derived from the story of act and deed. It always involves authoritative interpretation.

Such authoritative interpretation occurs in all kinds of contexts, but its transmission to subsequent generations is more specifically the task of education. It may even be said that in a measure education, *paideia*, developed in response to this task as much as any other. Eventually, human groups typically crystallize their values in terms of an image of what man ought to be like — an idealized projection of all the relevant aspirations. The Greek *Kalso k'agathos* and the English gentleman embody such aspirational images. All education has, therefore, an eminently political function without which it becomes either purely technical or idle play. Education for education's sake is, like art for art's sake, the escapist slogan of a leisure class which has lost a sense of its dependence upon the political order for its survival.[13] Technical utility, as expounded by others, leaves the community without a sense of direction. In the political perspective, then, all education has the function of providing value perspectives through either the transmission of a tradition or the inculcation of an ideological position, or a combination of both. To put it thus is to see it politically as vitally related to cohesion and consensus in a political community. The transmission of a tradition may take place in the family and its intimate associations, as it has for most of mankind until now, or it may become more formally organized in school, church and university. The inculcation of an ideology, seen by traditionalists as the perversion of education into propaganda, typically calls for these more formally organized methods. But whether formal or informal, education is evidently of the highest importance for the maintenance of a community. By supporting the values and beliefs prevalent in a community, education provides the underpinning for an authority and legitimacy which as we have seen depend upon these values and beliefs. For it is in their terms that the reasoned elaboration of authoritative communications has to be cast, and the title to rule has to be argued. It is therefore no wonder that political philosophers and theorists have been interested in education since the days of Plato and Aristotle. Indeed, these thinkers only made explicit what had already become the settled conviction of most Greeks, partly as a result of Sophist teachings. A leading historian of ideas has shown the central position which the notion of *paideia* occupied in all Greek thought and culture,[14] and

---

[12] Friedrich and Brzezinski, 1956, chaps. 2–4; cf. above, Chap. 4.

[13] Cremin, 1960, and below.

[14] Jaeger, 1939–1944, *passim*. The title preserves the Greek term because "education" does not render it accurately. In the German original the title speaks of *Bildung*, which helps because the German *Bildung* more nearly corresponds to the Greek word which lies somewhere between education and culture, in the personal sense. Jaeger himself put it this way: "The ancients were persuaded that education and culture are not a formal art or an abstract theory, distinct from the objective historical structure of a nation's spiritual life. They held them to be embodied in literature. . . ." Vol. II, p. vi.

has traced the interrelationship with politics throughout. But as in so many matters, so in this recognition of the importance of education for politics, the Greeks brought into the full light of consciousness what was practiced and to some extent preached elsewhere. Confucius, for one, certainly had a vivid sense of the importance of education for politics, and his teachings were the cement which held the mighty Chinese community together for thousands of years.[15] Indeed, Chinese Confucianism contains perhaps the most imposing theory and practice of a political tradition transmitted by education of a fairly formalized sort.[16] It all revolved around the nearly untranslatable concept of *li*, which is *nomos*, mores, custom and manners all rolled into one, yet all focused upon the political order.

The only comparable political achievement is that of Judaism. The Jews succeeded in maintaining a community intact by a similar stress upon education as the mode of transmitting a tradition embodying communal values and beliefs for two millennia. The leader of the community, or rabbi, while also priest and judge, was and is centrally a teacher who by education and example upholds a tradition of faith and law.[17] In keeping with this tradition, Jesus also conceived his function as that of a teacher, and the conception of education thus became doubly rooted in the mind of Western man.

A broad conception of education is also suggested by the study of political order among "primitive," highly traditional societies. Largely informal, education as the process of transmitting a tradition occupies nonetheless a central place in the life of each man and woman. Its importance for the political order is very generally recognized, and anthropological writings are full of illustrations. Education for citizenship may be either formal or informal. Informal education is generally provided by the members of the extended family — parents, grandparents and elder siblings — or by the members of peer groups. Formal education occurs in particular contexts such as initiation ceremonies at puberty, schools, age-grade systems and evening story-telling sessions. Whether formal or informal, education in primitive societies is also intended to ensure the continued existence of the political order by inculcating its norms and values in its future members.[18] The use of these several methods is widely diversified, and by no means all these societies employ formal methods; such methods do, however, occur with sufficient frequency to permit us to consider them perfectly normal.[19] For these processes, the term "socialization" has in recent years been put forward with the intent of avoiding exclusive preoccupation with the formal and

---

Aristotle discusses this problem when stressing the importance of education for transmitting the ethos of a particular constitution.

[15] Fairbank, 1951, esp. part I.

[16] Max Weber, 1922–1923, vol. I, pp. 395ff.

[17] *Ibid.*, vol. III. Orlinsky, 1954, chap. 7.

[18] The tribes for which these statements have been checked are: Yahgan, Hausa, Rif, Amhara, Ifaluk, Fanti, Nupe, Tiv, Bemba, Mende, Ganda, Kikuyu, Nuer, Tikopia, Samoa, Alor, Ojibwa, Iroquois. Cf. specifically, Christensen, 1954, pp. 49, 97f.; Evans-Pritchard, 1951, p. 137; Firth, 1936, p. 148; Dubois, 1944, p. 62; Noon, 1949, p. 33; Spiro, 1949, pp. 99, 111; M. Mead, 1928; Messing, 1957, p. 438; Gusinde, 1937, p. 864; Richards, 1956, p. 128; Little, 1951, p. 121; Kenyatta, 1938, pp. 109–110; W. G. Smith, 1955, pp. 99–100; Coon, 1931, pp. 316–317; Nadel, 1942, p. 401; Mair, 1934, p. 66; Hilger, 1939, p. 100.

[19] See E. A. Weber, 1929, for an extended treatment of the practices in connection with initiation of the tribes covered, embedded in a rich comparative treatment.

rational aspects of education. Thus we read in a recent study that what is meant by socialization is "that all political systems tend to perpetuate their cultures and structures through time, and that they do this mainly by means of the socializing influences of the primary and secondary structures through which the young of the society pass in the process of maturation." "Political socialization is the process of induction into the political culture."[20] What is involved here is a learning process in the course of which the young *discover* what it takes to become a political person in the particular cultural setting which the order structures. Once the process is seen in this perspective, it becomes apparent that the transmission of a culture's values, beliefs and patterns of behavior is a "personalizing" as much as a "socializing" process. More broadly put, it is a "humanizing" process in the course of which the unformed infant becomes a human being. Hence the term "socialization" does not seem desirable, for several reasons related to the foregoing remarks. In the first place, it assumes that there exists a person apart from society who is then "socialized," that is, fitted into society, whereas actually the infant is at the outset begot by the society and in the process of becoming aware of the tradition (and/or ideology) of the society is "personalized," that is to say, put into a position to take his personal, individual place in the political (and social) order. Second, the term has a very different and highly emotive meaning in the political arena, and the inconvenience of one word referring to quite disparate referents should, when possible, be avoided. *Paideia*, in the Greek meaning, would actually be a very good term if it could be effectively popularized, but since this is unlikely the French-derived term "formation" would seem suitable. Formation suggests that the infant is being formed or shaped by all the different activities and situations which are involved in growing up and that he becomes an effective member of the political (and social) order. Values and beliefs are acquired, but since these are not a rigidly defined constellation of indisputable meaning, but subject to subtle differentiation and variation, the person in growing up chooses within reasonably defined and varying limits his own way of participation. The novel way is not excluded. Innovation, while frowned upon and made difficult by the inertia of tradition referred to above, is possible and keeps occurring as new and unexpected situations are encountered.[21]

· ·

The transmission of tradition is by no means only a matter of values. A great deal of tradition in the broad sense consists of knowledge. The proverbial three R's are tradition, but so is the vast storehouse of science and technology, of learning and the arts. If tradition is, however, restricted along the lines suggested earlier in this chapter, then education — formation — has to be understood as concerned not only with the transmission of tradition and/or ideology, but also with these ranges of knowledge and information. However, in the selection of what to transmit the traditional or ideological values intrude them-

[20] Almond, in Almond and Coleman, 1957, p. 27.

[21] On socialization, cf. Hyman, 1959. Almond and Coleman, 1959, pp. 26ff., adopt and apply the notion to the political. They seek to "combine" the intellectual tendencies, namely, the "rational, voluntarist theory of Enlightenment and liberalism" and the one "stemming from psychoanalytic theory" stressing "the unconscious and latent attitudes." This intent is laudable, but "socialization" is not a good term for fostering the "combination."

selves and become the basis for selecting "the more important." That is why in transitional periods controversies inevitably arise as to what should be taught. We hear again and again that the newly emerging nations prize education above all else. Thus we read in a recent comprehensive survey of Africa: "Nobody can travel in tropical Africa without soon being made aware of the importance attached by the African to learning. Ask a hundred literate men what they consider to be the greatest need of their people, and ninety will unhesitatingly reply 'education.' "[25] But what they mean by their reply is an acquisition of certain bodies of information, certain craft skills and technological know-how, rather than formation in deeper value terms. "If education be defined as the whole process by which one generation transmits its culture to the next, then there has been no lack of education in Africa," states the same writer.[26] In the political sphere, such skill and know-how is what is meant by "democracy," although the actual need may be much more for "bureaucracy" — the techniques of modern administration in the West. It is too often forgotten that both administrative and political techniques and behaviors are rooted in the traditional values of the West, and may not be transferable without them.

The same problem arises within a culture when radical transformations in its values and beliefs occur. Modern science rests upon certain values and beliefs without which it makes no coherent sense; scientists are "involved" in these values and beliefs and are personally committed to them.[27] If these values and beliefs are rejected, science is likely to wither on the vine. Though still remote, this possibility cannot be ruled out. The more strictly organizational and political beliefs and practices are even more obviously linked to specific convictions regarding values. If therefore these convictions decline or vanish, the organizational practices become feeble and corrupt (Chapter 33). Hence the inclination of rulers to stem the proclivity to such perversion by educational effort. It may happen, however, that the educational system itself produces the forces which corrode the values upon which the social order rests. A movement for educational "reform" may be profoundly justified by changes in the value pattern of one life sphere, yet may carry lethal implications for another and related one.

Ideals and Idols of Democracy

Charles Frankel

First and foremost, "democracy is a political term." It is a name for a particular set of conditions under which the right to coerce others is acquired and held. To be sure, there are many definitions of democracy, as many as there are

25 Kimble, 1959, chap. 16, p. 93. The author fully realizes that that "is not to say that all Africa is hungering for the white man's learning." *Ibid.*, p. 94.
26 Kimble, 1959, p. 94.
27 Polanyi, 1957, esp. pp. 299–324. Cf. above, Introd.

men with causes they want to coat with legitimacy. Democracy is defined as rule by law, as a society that makes the individual central, as government by the people, as government for the people. Many conceive it as a great process of turning history around, a lifting of the masses from their ancient condition. And there is a point to most of these definitions. By and large, democracy works towards such ends, though not unfailingly. But to try to pin down the meaning of democracy by talking about these products of democracy is like defining the game of bridge in terms of brainwork and pleasant evenings. The one incontrovertible sign of a democracy is the way in which it makes the sticky decisions that are the business of politics. In its primary meaning, democracy is a system in which men acquire the right to govern through a system of free and open competition for votes, and in which they make their decisions while under the pressure of outside groups whose right to put them under pressure they must protect.

Yet politics is only machinery. Elections, parties, political bosses, and pressure groups are the unmistakable signs of the existence of democracy, but they have obviously not been the reasons why democracy has excited men. Something else, a change in the character of their experience at a deeper and more intimate level, has been what democracy has seemed to promise them. It is traditional to speak of the ideals that are presupposed by a political system — a habit of thought at once flattering and misleading, since it suggests that men know what they are about when they commit themselves to a political system. It is more appropriate to judge a system by the character of the ideals and expectations it encourages men to hold, and by the degree to which it fulfills these expectations. It is time for us to turn, therefore, from the framework of democracy to the aspirations that give it its reason for being. What is all the shooting about? What is the democratic system an attempt to accomplish?

To ask these questions is to begin to find out why so many devoted partisans of the successful democracy we enjoy in the United States today are nevertheless disoriented and disturbed. For the democratic system depends on a population that has certain expectations, and encourages them to have these expectations. And changes of geological proportions in the social terrain on which we move have challenged these expectations.

The Democratic Bias

The way to begin, I think, is not with abstract ideals but with something simpler and more fundamental — a state of feeling and sentiment, an emotional posture. Beneath democratic ideals there is an elementary bias, an attitude that belongs to men who, without taking thought or giving reasons, look at the world in a certain way.

Our everyday use of the word "democratic" suggests what this attitude is. A man with democratic feelings habitually judges his fellows without regard to their rank or status. He looks on them as members of a single moral community in which all possess the same fundamental rights and obligations. He is suspicious of the sweeping social distinctions that place men in separate boxes. But he is also suspicious of universal formulas that place all men in the same box. He looks skeptically on any effort to define the good life for everyone. The ideal democrat is egalitarian not because he thinks all men are the same, but because he doubts, when the chips are down, that there is any single comprehensive standard of human excellence by which all men can be measured and compared. He is ready to assign all men the same rights without insisting that they all live by the same lights.

Democratic cultures, therefore, are normally the scene for a kind of moral drama, a recurrent contest between Babbitts and Bohemians, conformists and freebooters. There is a tension within them between gregariousness and a respect for privacy, between hostility towards the man who sets himself apart and admiration for achievement. Thirty years ago moral criticism in the United States was principally directed against unchecked individualism, particularly in the economic sphere. Today criticism is directed against a sentimental egalitarianism that denies the differences between individuals. By and large, indeed, there are two democratic traditions, not one. The Continental democratic tradition has in the main stressed the equality and fraternity of men — the falseness and injustice of class distinctions and racial barriers, the essential identity of all individuals as possessors of the same fundamental rights. The Anglo-Saxon tradition, in contrast, has stressed liberty — the intrinsic value of freedom of choice, the irreducible diversity of persons, temperaments, and talents for which a just society must find room. But the quarrel between these two traditions is a family quarrel. The belief that men are members of the same moral community and the belief that each man has his own singular good to pursue both represent the effort to escape the gravitational pull of a simple and stubborn human inclination — suspicion of the outsider, hostility towards the man who is different.

Far from being the expression of an aboriginal human preference, a democratic moral outlook is an instrument and symptom of the breakdown of the traditional moral codes which have divided men into members of the tribe and strangers, believers and unbelievers, U's and non-U's. Although democracy has been said to rest on the doctrine of natural rights, it is an acquired taste. The democratic outlook occurs only to those who have learned to look upon the existing lines between men as conventions, who want to redraw these lines, who think they may have some business on the other side of any line. And it is the attitude of men who have learned to take human diversity in stride, and who think that the man who sets himself up as a watchman over his neighbors is precisely the man who bears watching.

These are the twin attitudes — the belief in a moral community, the regard for individual difference and privacy — that generate the characteristic ideals of democracy. And there are many ways of describing these ideals. But if we examine the sources of our present anxieties, if we try to bring together the experiences that have led us to suspect that the democratic image and democratic realities do not fit together, certain central themes emerge. Political democracy may be conceived as an instrument for the construction of a civilization in which four ideals are pursued.

The Consent of the Governed

The first is the ideal of the consent of the governed. If the lines between men are to be softened, then the most irritating and dangerous line of all — that between those who command and those who obey — has to be redrawn.

It cannot be erased, but it has to be made emotionally and morally digestible. And this can be done, so democratic theory has held, only if government rests on the consent of the governed.

Yet the phrase "the consent of the governed" is not an easy one to unravel. If those who are governed always consented to the decisions of their rulers, there would be no need for government, for police and taxes and penal sanctions. And no actual government, after all, can be absolutely even-handed in the way it conducts its business. The beginning of political education might be said to lie in the recognition that there is no such thing as an entirely equitable law. Ordinances against walking on the grass fall more heavily on dog-owners than on those who keep goldfish for pets, and rules against smoking in elevators ask smokers to sacrifice themselves while allowing nonsmokers to enjoy the benefits without cost. Even the recognition of everybody's right to free speech creates difficulties, after all, for the man who treasures silence. With the best will in the world, government is inevitably a process that takes more from some and gives more to others. And democratic government is simply one technique for determining who the winners and who the losers in the political fray will be. "Government by consent" cannot be interpreted to mean that those who are governed necessarily agree with what their rulers decide to do. Nor can it mean that "the majority" agrees. For in a democracy the minority, too, is presumably governed by its consent.

But to speak of majorities and minorities and the inevitability of disagreements is to suggest what "government by consent" expresses. It expresses the hope for a society in which ordinary people can influence the actions their leaders take. This means that they can exercise some control over who their leaders will be. And it also means that they are required to obey only after having been actively consulted by those who issue the orders. Coercion is implicit in all forms of government, but democracy nevertheless promises a peculiar prize to the individual citizen. It promises him that he will be present, personally or through a representative, when decisions that concern him are made, and that he will have instruments at his disposal that will give his presence some force.

The inside story, the experienced substance, of government by consent is told, therefore, when we describe the distribution of power and opportunity in a society, when we look at the internal structure of the groups that take part in the political competition and at the people they represent and the powers they command. The ideal of government by consent, to be fully effective, demands a society in which individuals who want to do something about their condition can find the allies, money, and talent to help them. It requires a social system which places weapons at the disposal of the ordinary citizen that force his rulers to deal with him as a party to a bargain and not as a passive instrument of their own purposes. The promise of government by consent does not imply that the individual will ever inhabit a social order in which all gradations of power and prestige have been abolished and everyone enjoys precisely the same amount of influence and authority. But it is a promise whose fulfillment requires much more than just one vote to every man or legal guarantees of personal freedom.

Accordingly, if significant sections of the community are unorganized, or if their opinions and interests are not brought insistently to the attention of the decision-makers, government by consent is absent to that extent. Similarly, if those who are attempting to press their opinions and interests have no powers to reward or punish those who make the decisions, their consent becomes gratuitous. Again, if there is a sizable imbalance of power between contending groups, then the settlement that is reached is an imposed settlement and not a free bargain. And if individuals cannot make their voices heard in the groups that claim to represent them, then they are not active participants in the processes by which the decisions that affect them are reached. "Government by consent," in short, is a function of underlying social arrangements.

But if this is true, then one reason for our present uneasiness becomes plain. The fundamental social arrangements in which government by consent has traditionally been embodied have undergone a radical alteration. The ideal of government by consent defines one major area in which we are in trouble.

The Ideal of an Open Society

Closely connected to the ideal of government by consent is the ideal of an open society. "Democracy" designates at least this much — a social order that deliberately protects men and agencies whose function it is to criticize what exists and to indicate other possibilities. The ideal of the open society proposes that men live under arrangements all of which are open to question. It holds that loyalty should be given to a social order precisely because it permits this process of criticism to take place. It insists that the process should be public and that everyone is in principle qualified to take part in it. And finally, it assumes that criticism and judgment are the preludes to corrective action.

To want an open society is thus to reject the classic view that men ought to expect a radical disparity between their hopes and the facts. There is a quality of impatience in a democratic culture. It eats away at any interest its members may have in consolation prizes. And in a community in which the ideal of an open society is widely accepted, those who have power or special knowledge must respond to a new imperative in human affairs. They have to provide those who do not have as much power or knowledge with information about what they are doing; worse, they have to appear to listen when their audience reports its reactions. In an open society, messages flow in two directions — from followers to leaders as well as from leaders to followers.

Even more than the ideal of government by consent, such an ideal presupposes social arrangements which cannot be secured simply by guarantees of freedom of speech and thought. These are essential but not sufficient. For communication is a complicated process. It depends not only on having something to say and knowing how to say it, but on being able to find an audience, and one that can do something about the message it receives. Freedom of speech serves a useful purpose even if it does nothing more than give men the chance to release their feelings by sending sounds out into the air. But the ideal of an open society encourages men to expect that freedom of speech will have other uses as well. In order for it to have these other uses, however, access to the instruments of communication has to be open, audiences have to be available that are organized and have powers of action, and the various participants in the discussion have to know the things they ought to know in order to speak intelligently and usefully. A bill of rights, therefore, provides only the supporting skeleton for an open society. The practical conditions for making such a society work lie outside the area of legal formalities.

And this is why the ideal of an open society is now not simply a promise but a provocation to cynicism. For the structure of the communications industry, the character of the groups that take part in the public debate, and the very nature of the issues that must now be debated do not fit our traditional assumptions. To say that what we now possess is an open society is not false. But it is a statement that requires a certain exercise of the imagination.

Individual Autonomy

The ideals of government by consent and of an open society bring us to another ideal — the one that is at the center of the democratic vision of human possibility. This is the ideal of individual autonomy.

One way to understand the emotional and moral impact of democracy is to see that it encourages great numbers of men to hold an expectation which only a life of privilege has bred in the past. Like the members of hereditary aristocracies in other days, a contemporary citizen of the United States is likely to grow up with the feeling that he counts just because he is who he is. And if his family is respectable and his skin not too heavily pigmented, he will probably feel that he is entitled to lead a life that he has chosen and made for himself. This, to coin a fresh and youthful phrase, is "the American dream." And pushed far enough, it is also the American fantasy. Scott Fitzgerald drew the picture of the pluperfect American in the great Gatsby — the man who interpreted the American ideal of the self-made man so simply and literally that he made himself up, inventing his past, writing his own ticket of admission to the great world, and creating a personality for himself as he would create a character in a romance.

But this pipe dream, this fantasy of self-creation, of perfect control over one's own nature and the conditions of one's life, does not prove that democratic ideals are immoderate and adolescent in their essence. Every social order produces its own special form of mad dream. Medieval society existed to make the journey of the soul to God more possible, but it was forced to organize monasteries in order to tame and socialize the extremists who took this promise too simply and literally. There is a kind of extremism proper to every society. The source of the Gatsby fantasy lies in the special sort of promise that a democratic culture makes to its members. It promises them that they will have personal autonomy — that they will be able to make uncoerced choices in terms of standards they choose for themselves. That no man can be free to adopt any standards he chooses is evident. But the presumed point of democracy, the consequence which those who have believed in it have claimed that it has, is that it gives its citizens the chance, more generously than any other system, to find themselves and their own talents and tastes, and, within reason, to seek their own ideals.

Yet not only the extremists, the moral purists and the morally insatiable, are doubtful today that democracy has this consequence. The realistic and the modest are also disturbed. Personal autonomy, so far as most men are concerned, seems to have been moved to the fringes of contemporary life. The packaged arrangements that are offered for our work and play; the massive industries that exist to manufacture opinion and engineer consent; the interventions of the State; the growth of technology and bureaucracy; the complexities of organization and regulation; the sheer pressure of our existence together in a crowded society — if the dim view of our future that now prevails has any substance, all these have weakened the ideal of personal autonomy and left the conditions in which it thrives in disarray. If the moral vision of liberal democracy is to be renewed, the prospects of individual autonomy on the contemporary scene have to be re-examined.

The Ideal of Responsible Government

Finally, there is a fundamental ideal in democracy which does not belong to democracy alone, but to all efforts to connect politics with the life of reason. What is it that the Greek meant, Mr. Kitto has asked, when he called himself "free" and the barbarian a "slave"? "Politically it meant not necessarily that he governed himself — because oftener than not he didn't — but that however his polity was governed it respected his rights. State affairs were public affairs, not the private concern of a despot. He was ruled by Law, a known Law which respected justice. . . . Arbitrary government offended the Greek in his very soul." To avoid arbitrary government, to live under laws that have reasons behind them that reasonable men can accept — this is not all there is to the idea of democracy. But it is the hope that allies democratic politics to other enterprises of liberal civilization. One large element in what men have meant by "freedom" is not the absence of external restraints on their behavior, but simply the chance to live under restraints they find intelligible rather than senseless and demeaning.

Liberal democracy has given a specific interpretation to this ideal of rational government. Rational government has meant, above all, responsible government. A responsible government, like a responsible man, is one that knows its limits. It conducts its affairs in accordance with the rule of law and with respect for the fundamental rights of individuals. Secondly, it is responsive government — government that is alert to the legitimate wants and potentialities of those it governs. And finally, it is a government that must respond satisfactorily when it is asked to account for its decisions. By responsible government liberal democracy has not meant simply government by responsible men. It has meant a government embedded in a certain sort of social structure, a government that is accountable to a larger society.

This is the basic ideal that justifies the curious organization of liberal societies. They are "dual societies," societies deliberately arranged to be at conflict with themselves. In all societies there are groups outside the official government — clans, businesses, clubs, cliques, and gangs — that lay down rules which control the behavior of men; and these groups, in all societies, possess sanctions like excommunication, expulsion, economic penalties, or the withdrawal of privileges, by which they enforce obedience to their rules. But in a liberal society these private governments do not exist through the weakness or indifference of the State. They exist as a matter of policy. They are conceived as checks against arbitrary government by the State, instruments that compel those who alone have the legal authority to use force to think twice before they resort to force. The existence of such private governments, indeed, is not only a condition for responsible government by the State. It is the source of one of liberal democracy's outstanding problems. For these private governments are also governments, possessing coercive powers, and powers sanctioned and supported by the State. If they exist to control the State and to keep it accountable, they, too, need to be controlled and held accountable.

And this seems to be the difficulty. Despite the persistence of elections, an independent judiciary, and all the institutions of free social inquiry and criticism that characterize liberal democracy, the process of holding the public and private governments that rule us to some effective system of accountability seems to have become increasingly complicated and uncertain.

Setting Words Aright

Before we can turn to examine the problems that now beset these ideals, we have to look carefully at some of the words we use to describe the democratic political method. For we shall have to deal with these problems democratically; and our discontents, indeed, are the consequences of what we think to be democratic standards. Yet there are easy but confusing misconceptions which lead us to diagnose our ailments improperly and sometimes to confuse symptoms of democratic health with symptoms of disease. There is good reason for many of our present discontents; but some of them are the products of our own unexamined and faulty ideas about democracy. Let us pass a number of them in review as a first step in putting our political ideas in order.

Begin with the most obvious mistake of all. It is the notion that government by consent, participation by the governed in the making of public decisions, means referenda, plebiscites, direct appeal to the people at every turn — in brief, a kind of giant and continuing town meeting. The idea has deep roots in the Western tradition. It is an inheritance from the theory and practice of democracy in the Greek city-state and the Puritan congregations of the seventeenth century. And it is a conception that is implicit in much that Rousseau, the prophet of popular sovereignty, had to say about the nature of political freedom. But it is plain, once the idea is made explicit, that the model of a town meeting is inapplicable to the processes by which the government of a modern nation-state can or should carry on its business. It expresses the hope, and the still realistic hope, that between the State and the individual, and between the large organization and the indivdual, there will be smaller, more manageable associations which the individual can join, and which will offer him the experience of face-to-face cooperation in dealing with immediate problems. But when this hope is inflated many times over, when it is applied to a modern nation-state as a whole, it overlooks the sheer size of modern societies, the fact of factions, the need for professional leadership, and the advantages that are bound to accrue to the specialist who can give the political business his full-time attention.

Yet despite the quixotic character of this ideal, it is invoked more often than we think. It is not invoked to say what should be done, but it is tacitly invoked to condemn what is done. Thus, some serious critics of the American scene have offered the fact that there was no general public debate before the atom bomb was dropped on Hiroshima as evidence that democracy in the United States is more advertised than real. But such criticism does more than skirt the question whether a popular refendum — and, necessarily, a secret referendum — in the middle of a war was possible. It overlooks the implications of the fact that there was widespread discussion after the decision. It treats as a lapse from democracy the legal fact that those who made the decision had the Constitutional responsibility to do so, and were prohibited from passing this responsibility on to others. And not least, it appears to rest on the cheerful assumption that the decision of the electorate would have been more gentle and humane than the decision that was actually made. It is an undeniable fact that our existing system assigns extraordinary power to a relatively small number of men. But the fact is not surprising. It is true of all large societies and of most small ones. To condemn this state of affairs as a distortion of democracy is to wash out all important distinctions in a bath of indignation. It is to employ a concept of democracy that could have no possible applicability. A man may complain if he thinks the wrong people have great power. But some people are going to have such power.

More plausible notions than that of the town meeting, however, are also capable of causing misformulations of the issues. The apparently simple idea of "majority rule," for example, is full of pitfalls which become noticeable only after the idea has been held in the air for a moment and examined. The majority of those who vote surely do determine who wins. But that majority is not a cohesive social group that persists once the election is over. It is an abstraction, a creation of the electoral procedure itself. Once the vote is counted, it is replaced by more palpable entities like political parties, businesses, unions, and the inevitable individuals who take it upon themselves to speak for "the majority." And if the idea of a majority is elusive, the idea of majority rule is doubly so. For an electoral majority registers no single definite opinion on any question but that of the candidate who is preferred. And even this preference is governed by the alternatives presented. "The people's choice" need not be the man most preferred. He may only be less dispreferred than his opponent. In between elections, furthermore, the decisions made in a democracy are also influenced by the advice of administrative officers, the pressures of different groups, the necessities for compromise, the interpreted information about "public opinion" that comes to the decision-makers, and the simple and not-so-simple play of events. No political leader can say what his policy will be with regard to questions that no one has foreseen at the time of the election; and he cannot stop and turn to the electorate for its judgment when such questions arise.

This is not to say that elections have no influence over events. The announced programs of contending parties have more to do with the decisions a government makes than the cynics say. At the very least they tell the electorate where the candidate would like them to think his heart lies, and sometimes they tell the candidate, too. In the end "majority rule" has a meaning, but it is metaphorical rather than strictly literal. It describes a society in which the fact that there are elections exerts a general climatic influence on the decision-making process, requiring those who make the decisions to keep themselves aware of the reactions of ordinary citizens. It points to the fact that while decisions in a democracy may be made behind closed doors, there is always someone pounding at the doors. "Majority rule" is in this sense an arithmetical figure of speech describing a government that can be discussed, investigated, and scolded. And most important of all, "majority rule" points to a fundamental characteristic of democracy. Democracy is not exclusive rule by any minority.

In the American democratic system most of the organized groups in the community are able to make themselves heard in the elaborate process by which the decisions of government are finally made. The statement has to be read as it is written. It is the organized groups, not the unorganized ones, that make themselves heard; they make themselves heard mainly through their leaders; and we can only be reasonably sure that they make themselves heard, and not that what they say necessarily makes a difference. Still, such a process is one of extended competition among different interests, no one of which has a clearly secure position in the forefront, and every one of which has to fight for the approval of the bystander.

"Majority rule," in short, expresses the democratic attempt to give ordinary people a large measure of control over their leaders. It speaks for the effort to organize a society in such a way that it will not be dominated by any single center of power. And it describes the historical direction in which democratic governments, with slips and falls, but steadily over the long run, have come to serve the interests of ever larger sections of the nations they rule. But, strictly speaking, the phrase "majority rule" is a misnomer when applied to the democratic process. The proper phrase, as Robert Dahl has suggested, is rule by minorities. For every interest is in the minority when set against all the other interests with which it competes. It is cant, therefore, to condemn the victory of any interest in a democracy simply because it is a minority interest. There is no other kind.

This examination of what we can mean when we speak of "majority rule" leads us to an even more crucial idea in the lexicon of democracy — "representative government." The classic idea of representative government, and the idea that still forms our image of what democracy is or should be, is that of an electorate which chooses representatives who carry the popular will into effect. It is not an idea that stands up to scrutiny, and it causes unnecessary and debilitating anxieties and complaints when it is not scrutinized.

The first of the difficulties with the conventional belief that a democratic government exists simply to carry the views of the electorate into practice is that it rests on the concept of a "popular will." In large modern societies, political parties, the media of communication, voluntary organizations, and government itself act to define the questions to which the electorate addresses itself; they propose the alternatives between which the electorate makes its choice; they give the "popular will" its preoccupations, organization, and principal modes of expression. To assert under such conditions that "the people," or a majority of the people, have wholly self-engendered and precise demands to make on their leaders is to venture into the occult. And a second and even more serious difficulty with the theory that government should simply do what the citizens say is that it rests on an ideal that is clearly unrealistic — the ideal of the omnicompetent citizen, the man with a formed and informed opinion on all major issues.

The ideal is unrealistic not only because it demands a degree of omniscience which no citizen can have. It is also unrealistic because it overlooks a fact about human psychology. Few arguments are more difficult or dubious than those about the rationality or irrationality of the so-called "common man." But it is unnecessary to enter into such arguments. Imagine that all voters are reasonable and disciplined and have the necessary facts at their easy disposal. The views they hold about matters that are remote are formed under conditions that are significantly different just the same. For while the principle is not ironclad, a certain state of mind is generally a prerequisite to responsible judgment.

Normally, the individual making the judgment has to feel that the question under consideration is his personal business and that he will pay a personal price for giving the wrong answer. And this is the attitude that is bound to be attenuated in a contemporary polity. The housewife who has to decide whether the corner grocer is honest is under some compulsion to make a judgment that rests on more than a platitude about the honesty or dishonesty of all grocers. And besides, she has the inestimable advantage of being able to observe the grocer's behavior directly. These fundamental conditions do not hold in the relation of a contemporary citizen to his government. He may be concerned and informed, he may recognize the bearing that public issues have on his everyday life, but his identification with the issues is still mainly vicarious rather than direct.

This does not mean that education and public spirit have no bearing on the success of a democracy. It makes them more important, not less. If men are to make intelligent judgments about their leaders, they need a general understanding of the main drift of the issues, they need to have some shrewdness about the people they listen to, and they need to be able to tell the difference between sense and nonsense. And if democracy is unworkable, it is because the electorate cannot be counted on to have even these qualities. But the recognition of the difference between the two kinds of space in which men's minds move allows us to fix our sights more modestly and intelligently, and less discouragingly, on the proper objectives of democratic education and public spirit. Democratic government does not require an all-knowing electorate any more than any other system of government does. The theory of democracy that demands such an assumption is in error. Democratic government is simply a system in which the authority to govern is acquired through competition for the people's votes. The function of the electorate is to choose and remove a government. It is the function of the government to govern.

Nor is this a state of affairs that ought to be mourned. In the best of all possible worlds the ordinary citizen, we may hope, would still have his own work to do, and his own intimate and absorbing sphere of private experience and responsibility. The image of a society in which all men are wholly devoted to the great public business is worse than utopian. It is disagreeable.

But to point out that representative government means nothing more nor less than government chosen by free elections is not to finish the story. For the concept of a "free election" carries a whole baggage of notions with it. The liberal democratic tradition can be justly criticized for having frequently entertained an abstract and legalistic conception of representative government. Elections do not become free elections simply because legal safeguards may surround the exercise of the franchise. To speak of "representative government" is to presuppose the existence of appropriate social conditions as well. The distinction between a state of affairs in which an electorate is presented with actual alternatives and one in which it is only given the chance to acclaim the powers that be is fundamental. No reflections on the sociological conditions for free elections can erase that distinction. "Representative government," nevertheless, always refers to a relative state of affairs. Even mature liberal democracies never perfectly fulfill all the conditions that make government a representative process.

In estimating the degree to which elections are free and government is representative, the education, composition, and social circumstances of the electorate have to be taken into account. Will voters suffer ostracism if they support a particular slate? Is there an alternative in which a large number of them are vitally interested, but which has been excluded from the alternatives on which they vote? Has relevant information been systematically withheld from the electorate, or does any single agency monopolize all the important channels of information? Have representatives of all significant groups had a chance to formulate the issues under debate? The failure to raise such questions has been responsible for the fetishistic application of the principle of free elections to societies where the conditions for such elections are not present. It partly explains why the gospel of free elections has had less resonance in many parts of the world than liberal democrats habitually assume that it will.

For the conditions that make elections free and government representative include a cultural climate that is relatively open and tolerant; an electorate that understands the purpose of voting; broad participation in the organization of the election and in the formulation of party programs; a press that gives expression to enough crosscurrents of opinion to put any single interpretation of the facts under pressure to defend itself; and not least, a reasonably broad and balanced distribution of powers in the community, so that all important groups have a chance to get into the act. Indeed, the most important condition of representative government lies outside elections and the official representative institutions of democratic society. The decisive representative institutions of democracy are unofficial.

They are the political blocs and the pressure groups; it is these that carry most of the democratic mail. Representative government is of course a matter of elections, competitive party politics, public discussion, and civil liberties. But these are thin and precarious without the existence of social groups that make it probable that those who are going to be affected by a social decision will be seriously and honestly consulted by those who make the decision. That aspect of democracy which most regularly troubles its partisans — the open struggle among special interests — is precisely what marks democracy as a system resting on the consent of the governed. The politics of pressure groups is the essential feature of the politics of democracy. The only alternative to the politics of pressure groups is government that rules over isolated and rootless individuals who have no groups other than the government to protect them, and no autonomous social power of their own.

That is why a democratic system of government cannot promise what most other systems promise. It cannot promise to do away with the dirty business of politics and to melt all men together in love of God, country, or historical necessity. Politics is a democracy's official business, and not, as in other systems, an unofficial and hidden business. The basic instrument of the democratic citizen is the organized group with enough power and influence to command the attention of those who make the decisions. The basic instruments of democratic government are the bargain and the compromise. And the one unmistakable goal of all democratic governments, when they arrange their bargains and compromises, is to win the next election.

This is the context in which every discussion of planning and of the development of consistent policy in a democracy must be placed. It does not make planning or consistent policy impossible. But it gives the formation of plans and policies a quality of responsiveness — or, if one prefers, of opportunism — which is not so likely to be present in systems that do not have to worry about elections. To ask the living to sacrifice themselves for their grandchildren is easier in a dictatorship than in a democracy. And since it is not easy, in a world of accelerating changes, to predict the condition or desires of our grandchildren, this democratic state of affairs has some manifest virtues.

But it is for this reason too that democratic politics requires ideas. Unless men have some coherent conceptions of their existing condition, unless they can imagine the long direction in which they would like to move, the politics of the bargain, the politics of equilibrium, can be a deadly affair — unfocused, uninspired, and, for all its realism, unrealistic. It can settle down, not simply very close to the center, but to a dead center, quarreling over issues that are ghosts of the past and tinkering with problems that lie at the fringes of the questions that have to be faced. With reservations, that is the picture of American politics at present, at any rate so far as domestic politics are concerned. Were it not for the Russians, we could not be sure that we would have a purpose in life.

No doubt we can get rid of some misconceptions about democracy and, when we do, some of our discontents may be removed. But these are not the major reasons for our unmistakable dissatisfaction with things as they are. At bottom, our present uneasiness, our curiously embarrassed prosperity, is the consequence of the unfulfilled demands which democratic civilization itself has set in motion. The ideals of government by consent, of an open society, of individual autonomy, of responsible government, have become problems rather than promises, sources of disillusion rather than aspirations. For the social conditions on which they lean seem to have been subverted. Each of these ideals defines a major area in which image does not fit reality.*

* Editors' Note: Mr. Frankel, in subsequent chapters, discusses the sources of disillusion for each of the democratic ideals and assesses the prospects for these ideas in contemporary democratic society.

American Values and American Behavior: A Dilemma

Gunnar Myrdal

The Negro Problem as a Moral Issue

There is a "Negro problem" in the United States and most Americans are aware of it, although it assumes varying forms and intensity in different regions of the country and among diverse groups of the American people. Americans have to react to it, politically as citizens and, where there are Negroes present in the community, privately as neighbors.

To the great majority of white Americans the Negro problem has distinctly negative connotations. It suggests something difficult to settle and equally difficult to leave alone. It is embarrassing. It makes for moral uneasiness. The very presence of the Negro in America*; his fate in this country through slavery, Civil War and Reconstruction; his recent career and his present status; his accommodation; his protest and his aspiration; in fact his entire biological, historical and social existence as a participant American represent to the ordinary white man in the North as well as in the South an anomaly in the very structure of American society. To many, this takes on the proportion of a menace — biological, economic, social, cultural, and, at times, political. This anxiety may be mingled with a feeling of individual and collective guilt. A few see the problem as a challenge to statesmanship. To all it is a trouble.

These and many other mutually inconsistent attitudes are blended into none too logical a scheme which, in turn, may be quite inconsistent with the wider personal, moral, religious, and civic sentiments and ideas of the Americans. Now and then, even the least sophisticated individual becomes aware of his own confusion and the contradiction in his attitudes. Occasionally he may recognize, even if only for a moment, the incongruence of his state of mind and find it so intolerable that the whole organization of his moral precepts is shaken. But most people, most of the time, suppress such threats to their moral integrity together with all of the confusion, the ambiguity, and inconsistency which lurks in the basement of man's soul. This, however, is rarely accomplished without mental strain. Out of the strain comes a sense of uneasiness and awkwardness which always seems attached to the Negro problem.

The strain is increased in democratic America by the freedom left open — even in the South, to a considerable extent — for the advocates of the Negro, his rights and welfare. All "pro-Negro" forces in American society, whether

Abridgment of pp. xlv–xlix, 3–6, 1027–1031 *An American Dilemma* by Gunnar Myrdal, *et. al.* Copyright 1944 by Harper & Row, Publishers, Incorporated. Reprinted by permission of Harper & Row, Publishers.

* The word *America* will be used in this book as a synonym for continental United States.

86

organized or not, and irrespective of their wide differences in both strategy and tactics, sense that this is the situation. They all work on the national conscience. They all seek to fix everybody's attention on the suppressed moral conflict. No wonder that they are often regarded as public nuisances, or worse — even when they succeed in getting grudging concessions to Negro rights and welfare.

At this point it must be observed that America, relative to all the other branches of Western civilization, is moralistic and "moral-conscious." The ordinary American is the opposite of a cynic. He is on the average more of a believer and a defender of the faith in humanity than the rest of the Occidentals. It is a relatively important matter to him to be true to his own ideals and to carry them out in actual life. We recognize the American, wherever we meet him, as a practical idealist. Compared with members of other nations of Western civilization, the ordinary American is a rationalistic being, and there are close relations between his moralism and his rationalism. Even romanticism, transcendentalism, and mysticism tend to be, in the American culture, rational, pragmatic and optimistic. American civilization early acquired a flavor of enlightenment which has affected the ordinary American's whole personality and especially his conception of how ideas and ideals ought to "click" together. He has never developed that particular brand of tired mysticism and romanticism which find delight in the inextricable confusion in the order of things and in ineffectuality of the human mind. He finds such leanings intellectually perverse.

These generalizations might seem venturesome and questionable to the reflective American himself, who, naturally enough, has his attention directed more on the dissimilarities than on the similarities within his culture. What is common is usually not obvious, and it never becomes striking. But to the stranger it is obvious and even striking. In the social sciences, for instance, the American has, more courageously than anywhere else on the globe, started to measure, not only human intelligence, aptitudes, and personality traits, but moral leanings and the "goodness" of communities. This man is a rationalist; he wants intellectual order in his moral set-up; he wants to pursue his own inclinations into their hidden haunts; and he is likely to expose himself and his kind in a most undiplomatic manner.

In hasty strokes we are now depicting the essentials of the American *ethos*. This moralism and rationalism are to many of us — among them the author of this book — the glory of the nation, its youthful strength, perhaps the salvation of mankind. The analysis of this "American Creed" and its implications have an important place in our inquiry. While on the one hand, to such a moralistic and rationalistic being as the ordinary American, the Negro problem and his own confused and contradictory attitudes toward it must be disturbing; on the other hand, the very mass of unsettled problems in his heterogeneous and changing culture, and the inherited liberalistic trust that things will ultimately take care of themselves and get settled in one way or another, enable the ordinary American to live on happily, with recognized contradictions around him and within him, in a kind of bright fatalism which is unmatched in the rest of the Western world. This fatalism also belongs to the national *ethos*.

The American Negro problem is a problem in the heart of the American. It is there that the interracial tension has its focus. It is there that the decisive struggle goes on. This is the central viewpoint of this treatise. Though our study includes economic, social, and political race relations, at bottom our problem is the moral dilemma of the American — the conflict between his moral valuations on various levels of consciousness and generality. The "American Dilemma," referred to in the title of this book, is the ever-raging conflict between, on the one hand, the valuations preserved on the general plane which we shall call the "American Creed," where the American thinks, talks, and acts under the influence of high national and Christian precepts, and, on the other hand, the valuations on specific planes of individual and group living, where personal and local interests; economic, social, and sexual jealousies; considerations of community prestige and conformity; group prejudice against particular persons or types of people; and all sorts of miscellaneous wants, impulses, and habits dominate his outlook.

The American philosopher, John Dewey, whose immense influence is to be explained by his rare gift for projecting faithfully the aspirations and possibilities of the culture he was born into, in the maturity of age and wisdom has written a book on *Freedom and Culture*, in which he says:

> Anything that obscures the fundamentally moral nature of the social problem is harmful, no matter whether it proceeds from the side of physical or of psychological theory. Any doctrine that eliminates or even obscures the function of choice of values and enlistment of desires and emotions in behalf of those chosen weakens personal responsibility for judgment and for action. It thus helps create the attitudes that welcome and support the totalitarian state.[1]

We shall attempt to follow through Dewey's conception of what a social problem really is.

Valuations and Beliefs

The Negro problem in America would be of a different nature, and, indeed, would be simpler to handle scientifically, if the moral conflict raged only between valuations held by different persons and groups of persons. The essence of the moral situation is, however, that the conflicting valuations are also held by the same person. *The moral struggle goes on within people and not only between them. As people's valuations are conflicting, behavior normally becomes a moral compromise. There are no homogeneous "attitudes" behind human behavior but a mesh of struggling inclinations, interests, and ideals, some held conscious and some suppressed for long intervals but all active in bending behavior in their direction.*

The unity of a culture consists in the fact that all valuations are mutually shared in some degree. We shall find that even a poor and uneducated white person in some isolated and backward rural region in the Deep South, who is violently prejudiced against the Negro and intent upon depriving him of civic rights and human independence, has also a whole compartment in his valuation sphere housing the entire American Creed of liberty, equality, justice, and fair opportunity for everybody. He is actually also a good Christian and honestly devoted to the ideals of human brotherhood and the Golden Rule. And these more general valuations — more general in the sense that they refer to all human beings — are, to some extent, effective in shaping his behavior. Indeed, it would be impossible to understand why the Negro does not fare worse in some regions of America if it were not constantly kept in mind that behavior is the outcome of a compromise between valuations, among which the equalitarian ideal is one. At the other end, there are few liberals, even in New England, who have not a well-furnished compartment of race prejudice, even if it is usually suppressed from conscious attention. Even the American Negroes share in this community of valuations: they have eagerly imbibed the American Creed and the revolutionary Christian teaching of common brotherhood; under closer study, they usually reveal also that they hold something of the majority prejudice against their own kind and its characteristics.

The intensities and proportions in which these conflicting valuations are present vary considerably from one American to another, and within the same individual, from one situation to another. The cultural unity of the nation consists, however, in the fact that *most Americans have most valuations in common* though they are arranged differently in the sphere of valuations of different individuals and groups and bear different intensity coefficients. This cultural unity is the indispensable basis for discussion between persons and groups. It is the floor upon which the democratic process goes on.

In America as everywhere else people agree, as an abstract proposition, that *the more general valuations — those which refer to man as such and not to any particular group or temporary situation — are morally higher.* These valuations are also given the sanction of religion and national legislation. They are incorporated into the American Creed. The other valuations — which refer to various smaller groups of mankind or to particular occasions — are commonly referred to as "irrational" or "prejudiced," sometimes even by people who express and stress them. They are defended in terms of tradition, expediency or utility.

Trying to defend their behavior to others, and primarily to themselves, people will attempt to conceal the conflict between their different valuations of what is desirable and undesirable, right or wrong, by keeping away some valuations from awareness and by focusing attention on others. For the same opportune purpose, *people will twist and mutilate their beliefs of how social reality actually is.* In our study we encounter whole systems of firmly entrenched popular beliefs concerning the Negro and his relations to the larger society, which are bluntly false and which can only be understood when we remember the opportunistic *ad hoc* purposes they serve. These "popular theories," because of the rationalizing function they serve, are heavily loaded with emotions. But people also want to be rational. Scientific truth-seeking and education are slowly rectifying the beliefs and thereby also influencing the valuations. In a rationalistic civilization it is not only that the beliefs are shaped by the valuations, but also that the valuations depend upon the beliefs.

. . . .

American Ideals

Unity of Ideals and Diversity of Culture

It is a commonplace to point out the heterogeneity of the American nation and the swift succession of all sorts of changes in all its component parts and, as it often seems, in every conceivable direction. America is truly a shock to the stranger. The bewildering impression it gives of dissimilarity throughout and of chaotic unrest is indicated by the fact that few outside observers — and, indeed, few native Americans — have been able to avoid the intellectual escape of speaking about America as "paradoxical."

Still there is evidently a strong unity in this nation and a basic homogeneity and stability in its valuations. Americans of all national origins, classes, regions, creeds, and colors, have something in common: a social *ethos*, a political creed. It is difficult to avoid the judgment that this "American Creed" is the cement in the structure of this great and disparate nation.

When the American Creed is once detected, the cacophony becomes a melody. The further observation then becomes apparent: that America, compared to every other country in Western civilization, large or small, has the *most explicitly expressed* system of general ideals in reference to human interrelations. This body of ideals is more widely understood and appreciated than similar ideals are anywhere else. The American Creed is not merely — as in some other countries — the implicit background of the nation's political and judicial order as it functions. To be sure, the political creed of America is not very satisfactorily effectuated in actual social life. But as principles which *ought* to rule, the Creed has been made conscious to everyone in American society.

Sometimes one even gets the impression that there is a relation between the intense apprehension of high and uncompromising ideals and the spotty reality. One feels that it is, perhaps, the difficulty of giving reality to the *ethos* in this young and still somewhat unorganized nation — that it is the prevalence of "wrongs" in America, "wrongs" judged by the high standards of the national Creed — which helps make the ideals stand out so clearly. America is continuously struggling for its soul. These principles of social ethics have been hammered into easily remembered formulas. All means of intellectual communication are utilized to stamp them into everybody's mind. The schools teach them, the churches preach them. The courts pronounce their judicial decisions in their terms. They permeate editorials with a pattern of idealism so ingrained that the writers could scarcely free themselves from it even if they tried. They have fixed a custom of indulging in high-sounding generalities in all written or spoken addresses to the American public, otherwise so splendidly gifted for the matter-of-fact approach to things and problems. Even the stranger, when he has to appear before an American audience, feels this, if he is sensitive at all, and finds himself espousing the national Creed, as this is the only means by which a speaker can obtain human response from the people to whom he talks.

The Negro people in America are no exception to the national pattern. "It was a revelation to me to hear Negroes sometimes indulge in a glorification of American democracy in the same uncritical way as unsophisticated whites often do," relates the Dutch observer, Bertram Schrieke.² A Negro political scientist, Ralph Bunche, observes:

Every man in the street, white, black, red or yellow, knows that this is "the land of the free," the "land of opportunity," the "cradle of liberty," the "home of democracy," that the American flag symbolizes the "equality of all men" and guarantees to us all "the protection of life, liberty and property," freedom of speech, freedom of religion and racial tolerance.³

The present writer has made the same observation. The American Negroes know that they are a subordinated group experiencing, more than anybody else in the nation, the consequences of the fact that the Creed is not lived up to in America. Yet their faith in the Creed is not simply a means of pleading their unfulfilled rights. They, like the whites, are under the spell of the great national suggestion. With one part of themselves they actually believe, as do the whites, that the Creed is ruling America.

These ideals of the essential dignity of the individual human being, of the fundamental equality of all men, and of certain inalienable rights to freedom, justice, and a fair opportunity represent to the American people the essential meaning of the nation's early struggle for independence. In the clarity and intellectual boldness of the Enlightenment period these tenets were written into the Declaration of Independence, the Preamble of the Constitution, the Bill of Rights and into the constitutions of the several states. The ideals of the American Creed have thus become the highest law of the land. The Supreme Court pays its reverence to these general principles when it declares what is constitutional and what is not. They have been elaborated upon by all national leaders, thinkers and statesmen. America has had, throughout its history, a continuous discussion of the principles and implications of democracy, a discussion which, in every epoch, measured by any standard, remained high, not only quantitatively but also qualitatively. The flow of learned treatises and popular tracts on the subject has not ebbed, nor is it likely to do so. In all wars, including the present one, the American Creed has been the ideological foundation of national morale.

American Nationalism

The American Creed is identified with America's peculiar brand of nationalism, and it gives the common American his feeling of the historical mission of America in the world — a fact which just now becomes of global importance but which is also of highest significance for the particular problem studied in this book. The great national historian of the middle nineteenth century, George Bancroft, expressed this national feeling of pride and responsibility:

In the fulness of time a republic rose in the wilderness of America. Thousands of years had passed away before this child of the ages could be born. From whatever there was of good in the systems of the former centuries she drew her nourishment; the wrecks of the past were her warnings . . . The fame of this only daughter of freedom went out into all the lands of the earth; from her the human race drew hope.⁴

And Frederick J. Turner, who injected the naturalistic explanation into history that American democracy was a native-born product of the Western frontier, early in this century wrote in a similar vein:

Other nations have been rich and prosperous and powerful. But the United States has believed that it had an original contribution to make to the history of society by the production of a self-determining, self-restrained, intelligent democracy.[5]

Wilson's fourteen points and Roosevelt's four freedoms have more recently expressed to the world the boundless idealistic aspirations of this American Creed. For a century and more before the present epoch, when the oceans gave reality to the Monroe Doctrine, America at least applauded heartily every uprising of the people in any corner of the world. This was a tradition from America's own Revolution. The political revolutionaries of foreign countries were approved even by the conservatives in America. And America wanted generously to share its precious ideals and its happiness in enjoying a society ruled by its own people with all who would come here. James Truslow Adams tells us:

The American dream that has lured tens of millions of all nations to our shores in the past century has not been a dream of merely material plenty, though that has doubtless counted heavily. It has been much more than that. It has been a dream of being able to grow to fullest development as man and woman, unhampered by the barriers which had slowly been erected in older civilizations, unrepressed by social orders which had developed for the benefit of classes rather than for the simple human being of any and every class. And that dream has been realized more fully in actual life here than anywhere else, though very imperfectly even among ourselves.[6]

This is what the Western frontier country could say to the "East." And even the skeptic cannot help feeling that, perhaps, this youthful exuberant America has the destiny to do for the whole Old World what the frontier did to the old colonies. *American nationalism is permeated by the American Creed,* and therefore becomes international in its essence.

* * * * * * * * * * * * * * * * * * * *

Valuations and Beliefs

The Mechanism of Rationalization

People have ideas about how reality actually is, or was, and they have ideas about how it ought to be, or ought to have been. The former we call *"beliefs."* The latter we call *"valuations."* A person's beliefs, that is, his knowledge, can be objectively judged to be true or false and more or less complete. His valuations — that a social situation or relation is, or was, "just," "right," "fair," "desirable," or the opposite, in some degree of intensity or other — cannot be judged by such objective standards as science provides. In their *"opinions"* people express both their beliefs and their valuations. Usually people do not distinguish between what they think they know and what they like or dislike. There is a close psychological interrelation between the two types of ideas. In our civilization people want to be rational and objective in their beliefs. We have faith in science and are, in principle, prepared to change our beliefs according to its results. People also want to have "reasons" for the valuations they hold, and they usually express only those valuations for which they think they have "reasons." To serve as opinions, specific valuations are selected, are formulated in words and are motivated by acceptable "reasons." With the help of certain beliefs about reality, valuations are posited as parts of a general value order from which they are taken to be logical inferences. This value hierarchy has a simple or elaborate architecture, depending mainly upon the cultural level of a person. But independently of this, most persons want to present to their fellows — and to themselves — a trimmed and polished sphere of valuations, where honesty, logic, and consistency rule. For reasons which we shall discuss, most people's advertised opinions are, however, actually illogical and contain conflicting valuations bridged by skewed beliefs about social reality. In addition, they indicate very inadequately the behavior which can be expected, and they usually misrepresent its actual motivation.

The basic difficulty in the attempt to present a logical order of valuations is, of course, that those valuations actually are conflicting. When studying the way in which the valuations clash, and the personal and social results brought about by the conflicts, we shall, moreover, have to observe that the valuations simply cannot be treated as if they existed on the same plane. They refer to different levels of the moral personality. The moral precepts contained in the respective valuations correspond to different degrees of generality of moral judgment. Some valuations concern human beings in general; others concern Negroes or women or foreigners; still others concern a particular group of Negroes or an individual Negro. Some valuations have general and eternal validity; others have validity only for certain situations. In the Western culture people assume, as an abstract proposition, that the more general and timeless valuations are morally higher. We can, therefore, see that the motivation of valuations, already referred to, generally follows the pattern of trying to present the more specific valuations as inferences from the more general.

In the course of actual day-to-day living a person will be found to focus attention on the valuations of one particular plane of his moral personality and leave in the shadow, for the time being, the other planes with their often contradicting valuations. Most of the time the selection of this focus of evaluation is plainly opportunistic. The expressed valuations and beliefs brought forward as motives for specific action or inaction are selected in relation to the expediencies of the occasion. They are the "good" reasons rather than the "true" reasons; in short, they are "rationalizations."

The whole "sphere of valuations" — by which we mean the entire aggregate of a person's numerous and conflicting valuations, as well as their expressions in thought, speech, and behavior — is thus never present in conscious apperception. Some parts of it may even be constantly suppressed from awareness. But it would be a gross mistake to believe that the valuations temporarily kept in the shadow of subjective inattention — and the deeper-seated psychic inclinations and loyalties represented by them — are permanently silenced. Most of them rise to consciousness now and then as the focus of apperception changes in reaction to the flow of experiences and impulses. Even when submerged, they are not without influence on actual behavior. They ordinarily bend behavior somewhat in their direction; the reason for suppressing them from conscious attention is that, if obeyed, they would affect behavior even more. In this treatise, therefore, behavior is conceived of as being typically the outcome of a moral compromise of heterogeneous valuations, operating on various planes of generality and rising in varying degrees and at different occasions to the level of consciousness. To assume the existence of homogenous "attitudes" behind behavior would violate the facts, as we must well know from everyday introspection and from observation and reflection. It tends to conceal the moral conflicts which are the ultimate object of our study in this book.

The individual or the group whose behavior we are studying, moreover, does not act in moral isolation. He is not left alone to manage his rationalizations as he pleases, without interference from outside. His valuations will, instead, be questioned and disputed. Democracy is a "government by discussion," and so, in fact, are other forms of government, though to a lesser degree. Moral discussion goes on in all groups from the intimate family circle to the international conference table. Modern means of intellectual communication have increased the volume and the intensity of such moral interrelations.

When discussion takes the form of moral criticism by one person or group or another, it is not that the one claims to have certain valuations that the other does not have. It is rather an appeal to valuations which the other keeps in the shadow of inattention, but which are assumed, nevertheless, to be actually held in common. This assumption, that those with opposing opinions have valuations in common, is ordinarily correct. As we observed in the Introduction, cultural unity in America consists in the fact that most Americans have most valuations in common, though they are differently arranged and bear different intensity coefficients for different individuals and groups. This makes discussion possible and secures an understanding of, and a response to, criticism.

In this process of moral criticism which men make upon each other, the valuations on the higher and more general planes — referring to all human beings and not to specific small groups — are regularly invoked by one party or the other, simply because they are held in common among all groups in society, and also because of the supreme prestige they are traditionally awarded. By this democratic process of open discussion there is started a tendency which constantly forces a larger and larger part of the valuation sphere into conscious attention. More is made conscious than any single person or group would on his own initiative find it advantageous to bring forward at the particular moment. In passing, we might be allowed to remark that this effect — and in addition our common trust that the more general valuations actually represent a "higher" morality — is the principal reason why we, who are convinced democrats, hold that public discussion is purifying and that democracy itself provides a moral education of the people.

When thus even the momentarily inopportune valuations are brought to attention, an element of indecision and complication is inserted. A need will be felt by the person or group, whose inconsistencies in valuations are publicly exposed, to find a means of reconciling the inconsistencies. This can be accomplished by adjusting one of the conflicting pairs of valuations. If the valuation to be modified is on the less general plane, a greater moral harmony in the larger group is brought about. Specific attitudes and forms of behavior are then reconciled to the more general moral principles. If, on the other hand, an attempt is made to change or reinterpret valuations which are more general in scope and most of the time consciously shared with all other groups in society, the deviant group will see its moral conflict with other groups becoming increasingly explicit (that is, if the other groups are not themselves prepared to change their general valuations toward a moral compromise). This process might go on until discussion no longer becomes feasible. In the extreme case such a moral isolation, if the dissenting group is powerful enough, may break the peace and order of society and plunge a nation into civil war.

In the short-run day-to-day conflicts, usually no abrupt changes of valuations will occur. The need for reconciling conflicting valuations brought into the open through public discussion will, for the time being, only result in quasi-logical constructions. In the very nature of things, these constructions must be fantastic, as they represent an attempt to reconcile the illogicalities by logical reasoning.

The temptation will be strong to deny the very existence of a valuation conflict. This will sometimes bring in its wake grossly distorted notions about social reality. There is a sort of social ignorance which is most adequately explained as an attempt to avoid the twinges of conscience. It is, for instance, an experience of every social scientist, who has been working on problems of social policy and has taken some interest in people's reactions, that the strongest psychic resistance is aroused when an attempt is made to teach the better situated classes in a society about actual lower class standards of living and what causes them. This particular type of moral escapism works, sometimes with extraordinary effectiveness, in the American Negro problem.

The feeling of need for logical consistency within the hierarchy of moral valuations — and the embarrassed and sometimes distressed feeling that the moral order is shaky — is, in its modern intensity, a rather new phenomenon. With less mobility, less intellectual communication, and less public discussion, there was in previous generations less exposure of one another's valuation conflicts. The leeway for false beliefs, which makes rationalizations of valuations more perfect for their purpose, was also greater in an age when science was less developed and education less extensive. These historical differentials can be observed today within our own society among the different social layers with varying degrees of education and communication with the larger society, stretching all the way from the tradition-bound, inarticulate, quasi-folk-societies in isolated backward regions to the intellectuals of the cultural centers. When one moves from the former groups to the latter, the sphere of moral valuations becomes less rigid, more ambiguous and also more translucent. At the same time, the more general valuations increasingly gain power over the ones bound to traditional peculiarities of regions, classes, or other smaller groups. One of the surest generalizations is that society, in its entirety, is rapidly moving in the direction of the more general valuations. The speed stands in some relation to, and can be gauged by, geographical mobility, the development of intellectual communication, the decrease of illiteracy and the funds spent on education.

During this process of growing intellectualization, people's awareness of inconsistencies in their own spheres of valuations tends to be enhanced. At the same time — if moral cynicism does not spread, a possibility which we shall consider presently — they are increasingly reconditioned to demand consistency in their own valuations and, particularly, in those of other people. They learn to recognize and to avoid the use of illogicalities and misconceptions of social reality for overcoming the incongruities in their valuations. The impatient humanitarian might find this process exasperatingly slow, and the results meager. The perspective of decades and generations, however — providing moral catastrophes do not interrupt the growth process — yields a more optimistic impression.

We have already hinted at the fact that valuations are seldom overtly expressed except when they emerge in the course of a person's attempts to formulate his beliefs concerning the facts and their implication in relation to some section of social reality. Beliefs concerning the facts are the very building stones for the logical hierarchies of valuations into which a person tries to shape his opinions. When the valuations are conflicting, as they normally are, beliefs serve the rationalization function of bridging illogicalities. The beliefs are thus not only determined by available scientific knowledge in society and the efficacy of the means of its communication to various population groups but are regularly "biased," by which we mean that they are systematically twisted in the one direction which fits them best for purposes of rationalization.

There are in the Negro problem whole systems of popular beliefs concerning the Negro and his relations to the larger society which are crudely false and can only be understood in this light. These "popular theories," or ideologies, are themselves important data in our study, as they represent strategic social facts in the practical and political problems of race relations. A legitimate task of education is to attempt to correct popular beliefs by subjecting them to rigorous examination in the light of the factual evidence. This educational objective must be achieved in the face of the psychic resistance mobilized by the people who feel an urgent need to retain their biased beliefs in order to justify their way of life.

If this educational effort meets with success, the illogicalities involving valuations become exposed to the people who hold them. They are then pressed to change their valuations to some degree or other. For if popular beliefs depend upon valuations, as we have shown, the valuations also depend upon the beliefs in our civilization bent upon rationalism. When supporting beliefs are drawn away, people will have to readjust their value hierarchies and, eventually, their behavior. As the more general norms in our culture are given supreme moral sanction, this means — if we assume that this "valuation of the valuations" is upheld, and moral cynicism counteracted — that the valuations on a more specific level (often called "prejudices") will yield to them. This is the reason, and the only reason, why we generally assume that improved knowledge will make for "better" citizens. Facts by themselves do not improve anything.

NOTES

1. John Dewey, *Freedom and Culture* (1939), p. 172.
2. *Alien Americans* (1936), p. 149.
3. "Conceptions and Ideologies of the Negro Problem," unpublished manuscript prepared for this study (1940), p. 4.
4. "Memorial Address on the Life and Character of Abraham Lincoln" (1866), pp. 4 and 6.
5. Frederick Jackson Turner, *The Frontier in American History* (1921), pp. 281–282.
6. *Epic of America* (1931), p. 405.

Educating Citizens for Responsible Individualism, 1960–1980

Donald W. Oliver

Cultural Unity Versus Cultural Pluralism

In an eighth-grade classroom, Pete covertly slips a pencil down Roy's neck. Roy squeals, and the teacher steps in to reprimand Pete.

Jane raises her hand to state that a class meeting is needed because the girls' afternoon dance club is "leaving out" certain girls just to hurt their feelings. Jane maintains that this is unfair. The teacher refuses to discuss the subject, saying that it is up to the students to work out such a problem for themselves outside of class.

Later in the period, while the class is discussing labor unions and the struggle for collective-bargaining rights, Joe says that if the working-man is going to get a fair break, he is going to have to fight for it. The teacher closes off this line of discussion with a statement that we don't get things by fighting for them, but by working together and finding a common answer to a problem.

In this classroom, three students have expressed certain conscious or unconscious values. The teacher has made three decisions, all of which determine to some extent how these values will be expressed in the future. Whether the teacher likes it or not, he is a socializing agent. He teaches the student how he is to work out his problem as an individual and makes him aware of the extent to which he must consider a common group framework and common group norms in approaching his individual problems.

In "mass culture," socializing agents provide all members of the culture with one general or common solution for any particular cultural problem. Pete may not drop the pencil down Roy's neck. Here is the common solution to this problem. Uncontrolled physical aggression is not encouraged, although controlled aggression may be, as in football or boxing. In regard to the question of

From the 30th Yearbook of the National Council for the Social Studies, Franklin Patterson (editor), *Citizenship and a Free Society: Education for the Future*, 1960, pages 201–227. By permission of the National Council for the Social Studies and the author.

snobbishness in a peer group, the teacher indicates that she has no set answer and that the girls themselves are to search for the right solution. For the problem of labor relations, the teacher provides no specific solution, but he does close off one line of action, albeit in a rather vague and ill-defined way.

The basic issue of individualism versus mass culture as it confronts the public schools is not a simple matter of whether we are to take no stand with respect to socialization problems and have an "individualistic culture" or whether we are to provide common answers and have a "mass culture." It is not a matter of eccentrics versus robots. The issue is more complex. In what particular areas of thought and behavior are we going to provide common answers, enforcing these answers with sanctions; and in what areas are we going to leave freedom of choice? As the initial examples indicate, the areas involved run all the way from means of expressing aggression to broad political decisions.

There may well be a predominant set of values common to all Americans, as McCord* suggests in the preceding chapter. These values are, as McCord also indicates, many, varied, imprecise, and often conflicting. The present chapter tries to deal with the existing fact of variety in the American value system and at the same time to take into account the drive for conformity to a togetherness doctrine, about which McCord speculates.

One dilemma is basic to this issue. The more common values we accept and teach and the more often we express one accepted cultural response at a particular point of choice, the greater cohesion there probably will be within the culture. On the other hand, the greater the variety allowed in expressing answers to cultural problems, the wider will be the area for individual choice and individual freedom. McCord has defined areas of behavior and belief in which a large proportion of Americans seem to share common answers: togetherness, etc. To the extent that Americans actually hold these values, there is pressure not to choose alternative values. If most Americans value achievement, for example, it is more difficult for the individual to choose to be easygoing or "lazy." Teachers in a classroom are constantly making decisions which hang on one horn of this dilemma. No one denies that some conformity is necessary, both to prevent violent interference with human rights and to provide the culture with some sense of cohesion, unity, and common mission. The curious paradox is that the purpose for which this conformity is demanded is to protect individual freedom.

Enter the classroom again. The teacher asserts that the right way to solve problems between labor and management is through conciliation and mutual understanding. Joe insists that the basic method should be the naked use of power, strikes, and boycotts. The teacher tells Joe this is not the way to a peaceful, happy society. This is cave-man stuff.

If Joe has gumption enough — and wishes to risk a poor mark — he can push the point further. He can say, "As a citizen, I support the right of the big unions to push as hard as they can to get what they want. I am for a free economy." The teacher might then reply that there is a great difference between a responsible and selfish use of freedom.

In this situation, Joe's concept of freedom is quite different from that of his

* *Editors' Note:* William M. McCord, "Mass Culture and the Individual." In Franklin Patterson (editor), *Citizenship and a Free Society.* 30th Yearbook of the National Council for the Social Studies, 1960, pp. 185–200.

teacher. More important, the underlying purpose of freedom in this case for Joe is to better the lot of organized labor through any legal means. The underlying purpose of freedom for the teacher is to maintain harmony between powerful economic forces. Here, the teacher is not teaching Joe to love freedom; he is teaching Joe to value harmony as a particular interpretation of freedom.

Freedom must be translated into some substantive action one wishes to carry out before it has meaning. We value actions and beliefs as final goals; we value freedom only insofar as it allows us to express these actions and beliefs. Teachers are impelled to look for and to teach some sense of common mission. They probably tend more toward the cultural norms, and hence toward conformity, than they do toward diversity. Teachers are less inclined to teach children to cherish their own freedom of choice than they are to teach them to cherish the choice they have already made.

At some point the teacher must make a decision concerning the areas of human behavior for which he will provide specific answers; the areas of behavior about which he will simply raise questions; and the areas of behavior which he will deliberately ignore. When Joe suggests a particular approach to labor relations, the teacher can choose any one of these alternative responses to Joe's suggestion. He can say, "That's not within the province of this course. I simply teach the facts." He can say, "Your approach is wrong. It is too aggressive and conflict-ridden." He can say, "Support your position with good reasons and I shall respect it; otherwise, it is no good." With any teacher and in any content area of the social studies, questions of cultural commonality and of individualism inevitably arise. And always there is the inescapable dilemma: the need for diversity and variation which promote freedom of choice versus the need to control conflict and promote at least minimal societal cohesion.

The way in which groups within society generally approach this dilemma certainly conditions the teacher's outlook. A society with a rigid, totalitarian outlook will demand complete conformity. In a liberal society, such as ours, the demand for conformity to any particular dogma or rigidly defined set of behaviors is presumed to be minimal. Even in our society, however, the demand that we at least verbalize or publicly subscribe to some general tenets of the American Creed seems pressing. This inconsistency between freedom in private belief and action and conformity in public belief is, it will be suggested, the mechanism by which we promote simultaneously societal cohesion and private freedom.

The Unique American Solution to this Problem:
The Myth of Meaning

America has worked out a unique and creative solution to the problem of maintaining a large degree of individual freedom of choice while still providing a cohesive, integrative force within society. The solution is simple and ingenious. We act according to private beliefs, many of which are highly individualistic and rigid. Yet we think and speak publicly as if were all bound by a highly libertarian, equalitarian creed which we seriously and conscientiously pretend controls our actions. (In time of national crisis, we may even act according to this public creed.) The most distinctive feature of the public creed is its vagueness, its lack of precise definition. We must preserve the myth that

American ideals are translatable into a single set of concrete actions, but we must be certain that no *single* translation of our ideals does in fact crystallize.

The notion that the most powerful of American values are ill-defined and vague can be illustrated by McCord's description of American character. If we take any of the values he describes as characteristically American, we note the diversity of common meanings for those values. "Achievement" can mean making a million dollars and having a large number of servants do your work for you, or it can mean getting your hands dirty in "do it yourself" projects. Equality can mean anything from the assumption that we should all be looked upon and treated as human beings to the notion that everyone should have a split-level house and a two-car garage. Localism can mean anything from the importance of the local church or club to a belief that the Tenth Amendment takes precedence over the Fourteenth. Youth can mean anything from being young chronologically to "keeping yourself young," as McCord puts it.

This is not to say that these values have no substantive meaning. Achievement cannot mean inactivity; equality cannot mean a caste system. The important point is that any particular value label in the Creed has a broad connotative meaning which all of us can feel and verbalize. In its application to behavior, however, we tend to select from this broad meaning that part which corresponds with our own personal values and interests.

That this country's present trend is toward a restricted and rigid definition of one area of American values, the area of togetherness, is one of McCord's major points. We are being driven toward a highly uniform moral code that excludes large areas in which freedom of action was legitimate. The studies of college students' values compiled by Jacob[1] present evidence that a togetherness ideology is replacing the more individualistic notion that the citizen should settle his own fate through methods of his own choosing. The TV producers' great fear of offending any group even within the realm of creative work is further evidence of this trend. We may well be promoting the idea of tolerance and togetherness with such vehemence that it is crowding out positive action and belief which lead to alternative and legitimate moral commitments; for example, making money, the desire for power to control large numbers of people, and the like. The fact that a vaguely defined set of cultural values may preserve such alternatives and promote freedom and individuality seems little appreciated.

Many educators decry the disparity between the high ideals expressed in the American Creed and "spotty reality." In the thinking of these educators, the disparity between ideals to which people have a verbal commitment and their actions in the actual intercourse of life is a major problem. We are told that the mission of education is to make our ideals come to life. The 1954 Yearbook of the American Association of School Administrators summarizes this mission:

. . . knowledge by itself is not enough; . . . knowledge coupled with faith and loyalty is still not enough; . . . skill by itself or action by itself in conjunction with any of the others is not enough. Only when all four are

---

[1] Jacob, Philip E. *Changing Values in College: An Exploratory Study of the Impact of College Training.* New York: Harper & Brothers, 1957. 174 pp.

blended so that each supports the other do we have the kind of person that civic education seeks to produce.[2]

In a word, educators offer the dictum that our goal is to make American ideals reality. This statement carries with it an interesting contradiction already noted above. To make American ideals a reality is to translate broad, vague statements of liberty, equality, human dignity, achievement, and the like, into specific actions to be desired. Once this is done, ideology emerges, and education becomes the imposition of that ideology. The actual implementation of liberty and equality in terms of "action and skill" might well mean considerable losses in the very liberty we are trying to preserve.

In our fervor to implement the Creed, we tend to favor a personality type most consistent with immediate economic and political realities. Today, this happens to be the "tolerant personality" or the "democratic personality." The democratic personality has been given substantial definition and support as an antonym of the authoritarian, antidemocratic, or Fascist personality.[3] We now have measures of "authoritarianism" and "ethnocentrism." Clinical studies have been carried out to illustrate how rigidly and dogmatically the authoritarian thinks and acts. The "good guys" and the "bad guys" are labeled by more sophisticated educators as "nonauthoritarians" and "authoritarians," respectively. Our efforts to identify a cluster of personality traits which describe the bigot have deceived us into thinking that the other ends of the same dimensions are uniquely appropriate to describe those who subscribe to the Creed, especially the equalitarian-togetherness aspects of the Creed.

Some of the major principles of behavior supported by the togetherness school are:

1. Any kind of discrimination or segregation is to be prohibited. All categories of people are equal and should be treated equally. Demonstrable differences among groups are due to evils of the social system. Treat people alike, and they will act alike.
2. Interpersonal aggression, including verbal aggression, is to be strictly prohibited. We make war on poverty and disease and hatred, but we never say anything against people.
3. It is good to be "reasonable" at all costs. There is a high value placed on the well-modulated voice and the outward symbols of reasonableness.
4. There is a family-of-man doctrine, a notion that nationalism inhibits the fulfillment of the destiny of man. There must be equality, not only in this country, but literal equality of all men everywhere.

This has become the new "bill of rights."

A basic proposition underlying thinking concerning the "democratic personality" is the notion that we tolerate one another because we love one another, and we love one another because others are the same as we. It is a creed

[2] American Association of School Administrators. *Educating for American Citizenship.* Thirty-Second Yearbook. Washington, D.C.: The Association, a department of the National Education Association, 1954. p. 335.

[3] Adorno, Theodor W., and others. *The Authoritarian Personality* (Studies in Prejudice; American Jewish Committee Social Studies, Series 3). New York: Harper & Brothers, 1950 990 pp.

of universal togetherness and literal equality. In discussing anti-Semitism, Riesman comments on this creed:

. . . A friend of mine claims to have heard a radio jingle over a New York station, "He's no Jew, he's like you." I suspect him of satire. But if it didn't actually happen it might well have, given the notion of "defense" prevailing in many advertising minds. It is here that a mythical world is constructed in which Negroes and whites, Jews and non-Jews — and for that matter, men and women — are "really alike"; such differences as there still are, being expected to wither away like the Marxist state. On this level Jews fail to see that it is their very differences which may be both worthwhile and appealing. This insistence on denying differences, or on seeking to eradicate them, identifies "American" with "Americanization" — and insists that for people to be treated as equals they must have more than their humanity in common.

The chief quality I sense in discussion about Jews on this second level is piety, a kind of dreary piety, filled with platitudes about unity, amity, democracy, and so on. This piety, it seems to me, as it spreads throughout "official" culture, through our churches, schools, and many involuntary associations, has two consequences. On the one hand, in the obedient circles it tends to stultify observation and thought. On the other hand, it enables those rebellious souls who refuse to subscribe to it to appear as terribly dashing and bold and "militant."[4]

Citizenship education itself is moving toward a militant attempt to give literal meaning to "democracy" and the "democratic personality." The child is taught a whole mode of interpersonal behavior as part of his citizenship training. This school of thought, for example, is especially receptive to such institutions as the summer work camp where young people can "really live democracy." In this context, however, *democracy* refers to more than a set of political institutions designed to protect the right to be different. It is a general brotherhood doctrine translated specifically into harmonistic interpersonal relations.

This is a very obvious extension of the notion that educational goals should be defined behaviorally. It is much easier to "see" and to evaluate interpersonal and intergroup harmony than it is to observe the complex fruits of individual intellectual training. Quillen and Hanna can assert, for example, that a student is "co-operative" when he:

1. Works well with a group or committee.
2. Respects constituted authority.
3. Recognizes and carries out his share of responsibility.
4. Supports group and school activities.
5. Volunteers to bring in additional data or help in group projects.
6. Meets his obligations promptly and to the best of his ability.
7. Adjusts his interests to the best interests of the group.
8. Treats others and their ideas with respect and courtesy.[5]

---

[4] Riesman, David. *Individualism Reconsidered.* Glencoe, Illinois: The Free Press, 1954. p. 145–46.

[5] Quillen, I. James, and Hanna, Lavone. *Education for Social Competence.* Chicago: Scott, Foresman and Company, 1948. p. 55–56.

This tendency to shift our educational concern from the less easily defined intellectual verbal behavior to gross interpersonal behavior plays directly into the hands of the equalitarian literalist, who is very willing to define his objectives behaviorally and with a high degree of precision. It is easier to evaluate whether Johnny "gets along well with his peers" or whether he has a harmonistic attitude toward labor-management relations than it is to evaluate whether he can defend his behavior or attitudes with a valid argument. For who is to say what constitutes a valid argument?

The effort of some citizenship education programs to define correct interpersonal behavior in the classroom and in the summer work camp should not lead us to confuse these programs with others whose main objectives are to teach specific skills and responsibilities of citizenship — how to exercise the rights of free men. Teaching the student how to translate political convictions into political force is quite different from teaching the student how to "co-operate" or "get along" with fellow students.

Thus far three major points have been made:

1. The public school serving a free society faces the dilemma of whether to enforce particular dominant values of the society and promote cohesion or to stimulate students to behave in a more individualistic way that may coincide with other value systems learned outside of school.

2. The more general dominant American values have rich connotative meaning to most Americans, but are actually vague and ill-defined and thus give little specific direction to behavior.

3. Efforts to translate the values of the American Creed into "good" interpersonal behavior may be undesirable, because such efforts tend to interfere with individual freedom and heterogeneity, which we value above all in the liberal society.

Political-Process Values and Substantive Interpersonal Values

A sharp distinction should be made between two types of values: political-process values and substantive values. Probably the simplest way to state the distinction here is to quote the well-known sentence: "I disapprove of what you say, but I will defend to the death your right to say it." The attitude of the teacher toward conformity and individualism with respect to these two types of values could be quite different.

Political-process values, although they are constantly undergoing redefinition, are precisely defined at any point in time by the judicial system and are the foundation of our freedom. They include three important classes of rights:

1. Freedom of expression, including the important freedom to criticize the government

2. The right to evaluate and to judge governmental leaders from time to time and to alter or change policies by changing governmental leadership

3. The right to judicial due process before the government can exercise sanctions against the individual.

There is no suggestion that these values either are or should be ill defined. When a man standing on the stage of an auditorium makes a political speech to a large (and perhaps noisy) crowd, he should know as precisely as possible what legal risks he runs. Nor should teachers equivocate in teaching students the values which justify these political-process rights.

Substantive values are another matter. These values label people, actions, and objects as good or bad and indicate the specific "right" solutions to personal and community problems. For example, in debating whether racial or religious groups should be segregated in public education, it is hard to tell which of several solutions will be most consistent with the political-process values. Substantive values, on the other hand, could give a categorical answer: segregation is good, or segregation is bad.[6]

Teaching Values and Conformity in the Public School

We can now ask a more complex and realistic question regarding the dilemmas of unity versus diversity, cohesion versus conflict. To what extent can political-process values in themselves provide the necessary cohesion to hold a nation together? Is belief in free thought and speech, in representative government, and in due process sufficient to provide the unity for a large and complex nation? Is the teacher to feel that he can indoctrinate children only with political-process values, or is he justified in turning to equal-protection value judgments, or even to substantive values to provide this unity? The tremendous effort put forth by Americans to create a common public creed indicates our need at least to feel that we share substantive standards of conduct. We apparently want to feel that we have similar values: security, liberty, equality, fairness, youth, togetherness.

Yet, as McCord points out, within the fabric of American values are the tough-minded elements of achievement and vigilantism which often run quite counter to elements of equality and togetherness. The one generalization we can make about American values, perhaps, is that in terms of actual behavior and the private beliefs which rationalize this behavior, there is tremendous diversity. If the unity of this country necessarily requires a commitment to *specific* substantive values — whether they embody a 19th-century liberal ideology or a 20th-century togetherness — which must be translated into conduct, our nation would long since have rent itself to pieces.

Riesman has discussed this problem in the following terms:

The attempt to enforce such agreement on fundamental values seems to me to be a good way to bring on a civil war; and it is important to study those institutions in our society which allow society to function precisely in the face of profound disagreements on fundamentals. One of these institutions is, I suggest, the city bosses and their machines: these act as brokers among com-

---

[6] A transitional value somewhere between pure procedural values and substantive values is equal protection under the law. In order to make many kinds of laws, we have to categorize people into classes or groups. Laws treat people differently according to the class into which they are put. "Equality before the law" does not mean that each person is to be treated exactly the same way. It does mean that each person within a particular class of persons is to be treated impartially. A fundamental question, of course, is whether the value that dictates the classification is within the police powers of the state.

peting urban values, based as they are on religious, ethnic, regional, occupational, and other identifications. These bosses can trade a park in a middle-class section for a symbolically important Italian judgeship, and otherwise keep a tolerable peace by appropriate payoffs from the spoils of American productivity. The current attempt to unify the country against municipal patronage and bossism seems to me dangerous, because by enforcing an ideological unity on politics we threaten with extinction a few men, soaked in gravy we can well spare, who protect our ideological pluralism.[7]

Citizenship education programs which stress the importance of political-process rights have obvious value. Other programs which would solve community, national, or international problems by teaching or by implying that substantive-value differences are really due to some one's ignorance and that education will evitably result in a universal recognition of the mutuality of interests hold possibilities of danger. This implication was made in the AASA Yearbook, and the conclusion there is quite different from the one reached here:

> The Yearbook Commission upholds a broad concept of what constitutes a good program of citizenship education in the public schools. It recognizes that from the point of view of the political scientist citizenship education may be regarded as including only the education which deals with the individual citizen's relations with his government. Legal citizenship grows out of this individual-state relationship and in this sense education for citizenship can be regarded as concerned only with this relationship. Without denying the technical validity of such a concept, this Commission asserts that a broader concept would be more realistic when we are dealing with public-school education in citizenship. The general public to whom the schools are responsible thinks of citizenship education in broader terms and includes also education that contributes to the development of ability and willingness to carry on at a high level all the mutually helpful social relationships with others which democracy assumes should be characteristic of human life and living.[8]

From our point of view, the challenge for citizenship education is not in the realization of an educational system which will enforce a creed of "mutually helpful social relationships." Rather, it is in teaching the student to recognize differences in belief and value within our society which give it its basic characteristics of lively debate and free choice. A dual approach to citizenship training, to be discussed in the next section, hopefully may meet this challenge.

An Approach to Citizenship Education to Provide for Both Diversity and Conformity in the American Value System

In the first part of this chapter, a basic dilemma of the liberal, pluralistic society was discussed: the struggle between the societal need for unity, cohesion, and a sense of mission on the one hand, as against the individual need for

---

[7] Riesman, *op. cit.*, p. 18.
[8] American Association of School Administrators, *op. cit.*, p. 22.

diversity and freedom on the other. It is within this framework that the issue of mass culture and conformity has been considered.

A dual approach to citizenship education will now be considered which would not only allow for but encourage the expression of individual values, yet which would teach at least minimal conformity to certain areas of belief which foster social cohesion. The key to this approach is the theory that symbols of unity and cohesion can be taught on a very different level from the process of free inquiry which we commonly associate with individualism.

The first, or symbolic, level requires only that the student be taught to verbalize the general values in the American Creed and to experience a sense of identification with the nation that holds these values. Most of us acquire this sense of national identification very early in the elementary grades. We learn the legends[9] about Columbus, the Pilgrims, the Revolution, the Founding Fathers, the explorers of the West, and the Civil War. We learn that these events symbolize suffering and achievement, courage and killing, equality for all men, freedom for all men. Understanding and appreciating these legends requires no translation of the Creed into contemporary personal experience. There is a spontaneous projection of personal values into historical symbols, which give the Creed flesh and bones and reality. Understanding at this level is more emotional and symbolic than intellectual and literal.

The second or objective level of understanding is based on reasoned self-interest. It requires that the individual understand the system of government and law under which he lives, the broad concept of government by consent as well as supporting concepts that have been associated with it, such as federalism, checks and balances, an independent judiciary. This level involves a deeper understanding of the rationale for our particular system of government, including an understanding of the importance of applying one's own substantive values to the discussion and judgment of larger political, economic, and social issues; an awareness of the fact that one's own values influence decisions on political issues; and finally an awareness that both the right to have value commitments and the right to make choices which flow from them are only protected in so far as there is a political system which will ensure this protection.

The first level of understanding results in an emotional allegiance to a highly dramatic and personalized historical image of the nation; the second level results in enlightened self-interest within a multivalue society.

Teaching the First Level of Understanding

Teaching children to believe in the Creed without requiring that they translate it into a particular set of personal actions, as suggested above, may sound impossible. It can be done only by assuming that the individual can "understand" the world on more than one level of "reality." Myths, legends, symbols, the whole superstructure of religion, provide examples of truth at a level of consciousness in which scientific verification is not a relevant issue. Anthropologists, among others, call this level projective rather than objective reality.

The correctness of projective truth depends upon the extent to which the

9 The term "legend" is not to be confused with "fairy story." Legends are narratives having a basis in fact, but which tend to be colored by the basic ideals of the culture.

symbols that describe and explain reality serve both the internal emotional needs of individuals and the cohesive requirements of the society as a whole. Projective truths are set forth in order to allow people to translate their own internal needs, frustrations, aggressions, and sexual impulses into symbols which can transcend petty hedonism and which can be seen and understood by the culture as a whole. These symbols can then bind the culture together through apparently common methods of handling the problems of socialization and survival which everyone in society faces.

Teaching projective truth or projective conformity tends to develop an historical image of greatness in our children. This image of greatness focuses upon the problem of cultural integration and probably could best be taught in the elementary school. It does not demand that children act out a creed of literal equality and interpersonal harmony, as do some citizenship education programs. Rather, it instills cultural cohesion at the symbolic or projective level and allows the whole gamut of human emotions to find expression: love, dependence, aggression, courage. In short, it builds an image of individual and cultural greatness. It further allows the individual to internalize selectively those facets of a symbol which are most consistent with his own temperament and values.

The content of a great-image curriculum should be a moving personalized narrative history of America, written by literary artists. Such a history would be punctuated by dramatic ceremonials that would emphasize the highlights of the narrative. Perhaps great-image teaching can best be explained with an illustration.

Two of the mysteries and problems with which any society must deal are courtship and death. Societies develop a variety of ways of handling these problems. The commonness of such experiences within a single culture undoubtedly has much to do with cultural integration and cohesion. Carl Sandburg describes these experiences in the Lincoln family in the following way:

A wagon one day late in 1817 brought into the Lincoln clearing their good Kentucky neighbors Tom and Betsy Sparrow and the odd quizzical seventeen-year-old Dennis Friend Hanks. For some years Dennis would be a chum of Abe's. . . . The Sparrows were to live in the Lincoln pole shed till they could locate land and settle. Hardly a year had passed, however, when Tom and Betsy Sparrow were taken down with the "milk sick," beginning with a whitish coat on the tongue, resulting, it was supposed, from cows eating white snakeroot or other growths that poisoned their milk. Tom and Betsy Sparrow died and were buried in September on a little hill in a clearing in the timbers nearby.

Soon after, there came to Nancy Hanks Lincoln that white coating of the tongue; her vitals burned; the tongue turned brownish; her feet and hands grew cold and colder, her pulse slow and slower. She knew she was dying, called for her children, and spoke to them her last dim choking words. Death came October 5, 1818, the banners of autumn flaming their crimsons over tall oaks and quiet maples. . . . The body of Nancy Hanks Lincoln lay in peace, the eyelids closed down in unbroken rest. . . . The children . . . tiptoed in, stood still, cried their tears of want and longing, whispered and heard only their own whispers answering. . . .

Tom Lincoln took a log . . . , and he and Dennis Hanks whipsawed it into planks, planed the planks smooth, and made . . . a box to bury the dead wife and mother in. Little Abe, with a jackknife, whittled pine-wood pegs. And while Dennis and Abe held the planks, Tom bored holes and stuck the whittled pegs through the holes. This was the coffin they carried next day to the little timber clearing nearby. . . .

So Nancy Hanks Lincoln died, 34 years old, a pioneer sacrifice, with memories of monotonous, endless everyday chores, . . . of blue wistful hills and a summer when the crab-apple blossoms flamed white and she carried a boy child into the world. . . .

Lonesome days came for Abe and Sarah in November [the next year] when their father went away, promising to come back. He headed for Elizabethtown, Kentucky, through woods and across the Ohio River, to the house of the widow Sarah Bush Johnston. They said he argued straight-out: "I have no wife and you no husband. I came a-purpose to marry you. I knowed you from a gal and you knowed me from a boy. I've no time to lose; and if you're willin' let it be done straight off." She answered, "I got a few little debts," gave him a list and he paid them; and they were married December 2, 1819.[10]

The elements of greatness that one can select from this particular passage are numerous. The selection can be made in terms of the special values of the individual reader. The tender-hearted romanticist can see the tiptoed footsteps, the tears of want and longing, the wistful hills, and the crab-apple blossoms. The more practical-minded may see the whipsawed planks and homemade coffin and the brief, frank courtship between Tom and Sarah. The passage contains elements of courage particularly characteristic of our pioneering culture. As obvious as the deeper symbolic message contained in the passage, moreover, is its stylistic quality: the concrete, dramatic narrative which could provide all children with a somewhat common conception of the American heritage.

The conflict between scientificism and the image-of-greatness idea may make this approach repugnant to some teachers in the elementary school who feel a responsibility for teaching a realistic view of contemporary culture. The question may be raised: Why not teach an explicit contract theory of society from the beginning? We give allegiance to society, and in return for this allegiance we get services and, to some extent, the protection of our liberties.

The most important reason for teaching the great image as a crucial initial step in citizenship training is the need to provide a common, concrete basis for our dynamic faith in a truly liberal society. Otherwise there is the real possibility that some men may never be trained to see the world beyond their own petty personal interests. We must commit our children so completely to a system of government which protects constructive nonconformity that day-by-day contact with the hazards and realities of the system will not tarnish the ideals for which the system stands.

The hope is that later these same children will gain a self-conscious awareness of their own values and a realization that the right to apply those values in daily conduct is only protected by the allegiance they give to the system of government and of law in which they live. For some, then, the earlier historical or projective concept of America will no longer be required. For some, reality

10 Sandburg, Carl. *Abraham Lincoln: The Prairie Years and The War Years* (One-Volume Edition, Copyright 1939 by Harcourt, Brace and Company, Inc.; copyright 1954 by Carl Sandburg). New York: Harcourt, Brace and Company, Inc., 1954, p. 11–12. Reprinted by permission of the publishers.

is not too rich a diet for idealism. Some will be able to see the limits of man's tolerance, his natural tendency toward prejudgment, the mutual suspicion among men that develops within a pluralistic, multivalue society. Within this context, they cannot help but feel a deep respect for the wisdom behind the basic political institutions on which this country is founded. The crucial question, of course, is how many persons are capable of actually understanding this view of reality. For those who cannot, better the projective image of greatness than a total lack of idealism.

The problem of cultural cohesion is difficult enough in a society of free men. It is even more difficult in a culture that idolizes scientific rationalism. It is suggested here that a "reality" of historical imagery symbolizing our own liberal tradition should be provided to children to lay the basis for cultural commonalty until or unless a deeper appreciation of liberty comes with the self-conscious awareness that a variety of personal values — especially substantive religious and political values — is important and requires political protection.

Teaching the Second Level of Understanding: A Jurisprudential Approach to Citizenship Education

A projective view of America based on dramatic narrative history has been discussed. A second, and perhaps a deeper, foundation of loyalty can be based on a much more objective model of American society.

Freedom inevitably involves controversy. In a society governed by principles of constitutionalism, this controversy is expressed not in physical violence or intimidation but in words. The object of political life is not coercion, but persuasion. As Justice Douglas has said, "The function of free speech under our system of government is to invite dispute."

Much of the dispute centers upon the establishment of man's power relationship to his government: the definition of his rights and the restrictions upon his liberties. There is continuous controversy and redefinition of the words which describe these liberties, as well as the words which justify their restriction. All should have a right to "equal opportunity," "security," "a decent standard of living," "justice," "freedom," and "progress." But the government may restrict these rights "to provide for the general health and welfare of the community," "to prevent crime and disorder," "to provide for the common defense," "to prevent individuals or groups from being exploited," and "to penalize lazy, stupid, or incompetent people." These are the kinds of words we use in our political discussions. The definition of these words which describe our rights and their restrictions evolves through open discussion and application to particular situations and to particular problems.

This process of interpretation and intelligent application of words is not easy. Different people apply different meanings to the same rights. A Negro, for example, may say that it is his basic right to eat in a restaurant with whites. Some white people may say it is their natural right to associate with whomever they please, and this does not include Negroes. The white owner of the restaurant may say he has a right to control who will eat in his restaurant. Both Negro and white claim it is their right to have freedom, but the word has a different meaning for the two groups.

Often one right seems to conflict with another. One man wants to be free to see that his children get a better start in life than he had. If he has enough money, he will hire special teachers to give them a good education and use his influence to see that they get good jobs. Another who has less money may say that his children deserve equal opportunity. He wants his children to have as good an education as anyone else and to have the same chance to find a good job. The freedom of one may interfere with the equal opportunity of another.

Although we probably never shall solve the problem of defining basic rights to the point of universal consensus, through the process of free debate we continually define and redefine these rights and carry them into public policy. Each time a law is passed or a judicial decision is made, that law or decision defines the rights of people. By encouraging individuals and groups to debate and to work out conflicting definitions of basic rights, we come to conform to, if not to accept, restrictions upon these rights. We rationalize these restrictions by asserting that the government must have certain "police powers" in order to protect health, morals, safety, and the welfare of the community.

One of the most important jobs of a citizen is to reflect upon what he thinks these rights mean when applied to particular public issues. The citizen must constantly act as a judge interpreting the words which describe general moral and legal principles to see whether public action, and hence restriction of liberty, is warranted in a particular situation.

The strategy for teaching such a model of American society might be to build a curriculum — call it a "jurisprudential curriculum" — which would focus upon the earnest use of free speech and open debate for the students to determine what is man's proper relationship to his government. The question would be: To what extent should the government protect or restrict basic rights. The debate should not be carried on in an atmosphere of academic calm, but rather in the midst of that heat and pressure which characterize fundamental societal disputes.

Such a curriculum would focus upon a series of related questions:

1. What is an adequate description of the objective situation which causes the dispute? This refers to empirical, testable questions, though the evidence at hand may, in fact, be scarce. For example, how many labor unions really are corrupt? Exactly what is the nature of the dishonest acts in which some labor leaders engage?

2. To what extent is the situation so pressing that the government can justifiably use its police powers to restrict personal liberty? Will whites and Negroes, for example, corrupt each other's cultures so that "separate but equal" is a reasonable standard for legislation?

3. To what extent do the rights which we wish to restrict by laws have constitutional guarantees?

4. To what extent do specific checks within the American constitutional system adequately reduce or unreasonably restrict governmental power?

The jurisprudential curriculum would clarify these questions by teaching specific skills and content directed at them. This content would include:

1. Concepts relating to the process of proof
   For example:

  a. distinction and relationships among definitional, empirical, and ethical problems
  b. the process of proof and use of evidence for these different kinds of problems
  c. distinction between inductive and deductive types of proof
2. Concepts relating to the American form of government
  a. constitutional checks and safeguards; e.g., rule of law, federalism, separation of powers, checks and balances, judicial review
  b. constitutional rights; e.g., free conscience and expression, substantive and procedural due process, equal protection under the law, property and contract rights
  c. rationale for police power; e.g., provide for the general health and welfare, prevent crime and disorder, provide for the common defense, protect groups or individuals from being exploited
3. Concepts and facts necessary to describe disputes or problem areas. Selection of facts depends largely on problem area being described. Concepts, however, might run across several problem areas. Concepts such as "culture" and "social class" would certainly apply to many problem areas.

The essential skill which would come out of this program is the application of the content characterized as critical thinking and concepts of constitutional theory to actual conflicts and disputes within a free society.

Here is an example of how one content area might be treated within the framework of the jurisprudential curriculum. An immediate and pressing issue in America is certainly the regulation of interracial and intercultural relations. One facet of this broader issue is the school desegregation problem. Returning to the four basic questions, they might be applied to this issue as follows:

1. What is the objective situation that creates the problem?
   For example:
   a. To what extent has differential legal treatment of Negroes and whites injured the Negro?
   b. To what extent are there intellectual, physical, and moral differences between the races that might justify differential educational treatment?
   There is no clear-cut, definitive answer to these questions. Conclusions regarding answers could only be reached intelligently if the student had passed through an active process of claim-testing.
2. Can the government justify the use of police powers to restrict liberty?
   For example:
   To what extent are the intellectual, health, and moral differences between the races sufficient to justify segregation in order to protect the health, safety, and morals of the whole community?
3. Are the rights taken away guaranteed by the Constitution?
   In this particular case, at least two areas of the Constitution apply to rights already being restricted: equal protection and due process. But this does not solve the problem. The issue is whether public safety is so acutely jeopardized that these rights should in fact be restricted.
4. To what extent do specific checks within the American constitutional system adequately reduce or unreasonably restrict governmental power?
   In this case, the fact is that the schools are controlled by the states, which also maintain they have police powers to segregate the races. The Federal Government has the responsibility for upholding and enforcing the rights

guaranteed under the Fifth and Fourteenth Amendments of the Constitution. There is an ambiguous division of power and authority between the Federal Government and the state governments which has never been — and probably never will be — completely clarified.

Figure I illustrates four problem-conflict areas and schematically indicates the rights, police powers, and constitutional restrictions that might be discussed within the content of jurisprudential teaching.

Selection of content is, of course, only half the job. Criteria must be developed to define content-style, and procedures designed to present the content effectively. Figure II is an outline of a teaching strategy that is presently under experimental evaluation in Concord, Massachusetts, in the Harvard Social Studies Project.

Styles of content and methods of presentation are briefly described below. There is nothing new or startling about the various styles of content and strategy of teaching presented here. All have been used before. The purpose in giving the description is to clarify ideas suggested above and to show that they are not simply abstract theory. They can be put into practice.

Content and Presentation for the Jurisprudential Approach

Narrative Texts. These include the historical background of a problem area, with some supporting evidence.

Drill Materials. Questions based on the text are presented to the student, who has before him multiple-choice answers, one of which he checks as being right. Immediately after each question, the student is shown the answer so that he can find out whether his initial response was correct. This has been found a highly efficient way of teaching the basic facts contained in the text.

Illustrative cases. These are dramatic, concrete stories based on fact used to illustrate or concretize concepts or situations which might not otherwise be understood. The term "poor working conditions," for example, can be illustrated with cases spelling out the experiences of people actually involved in such situations.

Dilemma Cases. Dilemma cases dramatize a basic conflict within the unit. The school desegregation issue contains such dilemmas as these: Should people's rights be supported even though public school standards may be disrupted or jeopardized? Should the will of the majority within a state be disregarded by the Federal Government in its interpretation of correct regulation of interracial relations?

The basic characteristic of the dilemma case is that it is fairly concrete, specific, and authentic. The desegregation of schools in Washington, D.C., is used, for example, as a case to illustrate the dilemma of maintaining the right of equal protection versus avoiding disruption of the standards of public schools.

The dilemma case is generally discussed within a Socratic framework; that is, the teacher identifies which horn of the dilemma expresses a "solution" of the problem for particular students and then presses the students to take into account the unpleasant legal or empirical consequences of this solution.

FIGURE 1 / Illustrative Selection of Content under Jurisprudential Approach

Broad Problem Area	Subtopic	Constitutional Rights	Rationale for Police Power	Constitutional Checks and Safeguards
1. Racial Conflict	school desegregation	equal protection	prevent violence	federalism — division of authority between state and national government
		due process	protect health and morals	separation of powers
2. Labor Conflict	collective bargaining	freedom of association	prevent violence	federalism
		property and contract rights	prevent exploitation	separation of powers
3. Business Competition	fair trade laws	contract rights	prevent dishonesty and exploitation	federalism
				separation of powers, (e.g., F.T.C. vs. courts)
4. Government Defense and Security	federal loyalty-security programs	free conscience	national defense and internal security	separation of powers
		due process		
		equal protection		

FIGURE 2 / Outline of Teaching Strategy

I. *Introduction to the Problem*

  A. Narrative text outlining nature of the problem

    1. Definition of technical terms and concepts

    2. History of the problem to the point of policy clash

    3. Discussion of major legal or governmental questions before time of policy clash

  B. Case Illustrations

    Dramatic, concrete illustrations of key concepts, e.g., monopoly, poor educational facilities, unemployment, collective bargaining

  C. Drill on highly probable claims and facts

II. *Analysis of Controversy*

  A. Discussion based on Dilemma cases

    1. One or two cases illustrating two sides of a value dilemma; use of analogy to illustrate same dilemma with other situations

    2. Purposes of discussion cases to illustrate value concepts, force use of clear definition, dramatize need for further evidence to prove explanations and generalizations

  B. Students analyze argumentative dialogue

  C. Students analyze persuasive documents

III. *Student-Run Discussions*

  Small groups are asked to discuss a specific case and to come to a decision regarding the policy in question

IV. *Writing a Brief*

  Student required to write a brief justifying personal policy decision

Argumentative Dialogues and Persuasive Documents. When the student has learned to handle dilemma situations in discussion, he is taught to analyze written materials that are very similar to controversial discussion. He is presented with argumentative dialogues (sometimes typescripts of class discussions) and with speeches or articles written for persuasive purposes. The advantage of using such materials is that the level of sophistication of argumentative strategy can be regulated by the teacher according to the ability and training of the students.

Case-Play. Group decision making is the critical situation which demands effective use of the skills and knowledge taught in the jurisprudential approach. There are many ways in which to set up a decision-making situation. The one suggested here is based on the case-play written so that students can take the parts of people representing various shades of opinion in their view of the problem being studied. In the play, only arguments are presented, no conclusions. The students are then asked to arrive at some conclusion through open discussion.

The Brief. Group decision making sets the stage for individual commitment. Making public decisions demands open defense of one's views. The student should also have an opportunity to commit himself to a decision without the pressure of the group. He can do this by writing a brief in which he presents a careful, reasoned defense of his position. Writing a brief requires an adequate school library containing documents relating to the issue under study.

The jurisprudential program may be illustrated further by a spot view of some class discussions which were taped and transcribed. The classes were composed of eighth-grade students in Bulkeley Junior High School, Concord, Massachusetts. The first two scripts are Socratic discussions based on dilemma cases in the desegregation issue. The fact that in both instances the teacher is prointegration should not mislead the reader into thinking that the teacher probes only those students holding the segregationist viewpoint.

Typescript One: Restriction of Negro Voting versus Equal Protection

TEACHER: Do you think police power can be used to restrict voting rights as well as educational rights, John?

JOHN: I think that the police power can go only a certain way, that constitutional rights of voting, maybe the Negroes should have them.

TEACHER: Negroes should have the right to vote, even though there may be all kinds of violence? We should send troops there and protect every individual's right to vote?

JOHN: I'm not saying that. I don't think it would get that far, that we would have to send troops.

TEACHER: If it did get that far?

JOHN: Probably, yes.

TEACHER: Suppose people called up Negroes who intended to vote and said, "If you vote tomorrow, you'll never see your kids again." Do you think we should send the FBI to investigate these intimidations?

JOHN: No.

TEACHER: Why not?

JOHN: Because there isn't going to be any real violence. If he does vote, the threat probably won't be carried out. If he doesn't, there won't be any violence anyway.

TEACHER: What if the threat is carried out? Obviously the person doesn't vote because he thinks it may be carried out.

JOHN·   If the threat is carried out, then I would send troops.

TEACHER: After the violence has taken place, then you send some one to stop it.
You don't go along with the notion that if there is an atmosphere of fear and intimidation that we should do something to change the atmosphere so that people will feel free to vote. We shouldn't do anything until there is actual violence?

JOHN: In the case of Negroes, yes.

TEACHER: Why?

JOHN: Because I don't want to give them the complete power to vote. This is taking a little of it away.

TEACHER: You want to deny some of the right to vote that you're willing to give to whites?

JOHN: Yes.

TEACHER: Why?

JOHN: Because I feel that Negroes are inferior to whites.

TEACHER: In what respect? Intellectually?

JOHN: In intelligence and health and crime rate.

TEACHER: Are you suggesting that if a person is tubercular or sick, you should deny him the right to vote?

JOHN: No.

TEACHER: If he is a Negro and he is sick, we don't let him vote?

JOHN: Let him vote, sure, but I think they are inferior because of these reasons. I'm not saying because of these reasons I'm not going to let him vote.

TEACHER: For what reasons aren't you going to let him vote?

JOHN: Because I think they are inferior because of these reasons.

TEACHER: If a person is unintelligent or stupid, we shouldn't let him vote?

JOHN: Yes.

TEACHER: I'll go along with that. Suppose we pass a law that says that any-one who is given a standard I.Q. test and scores below 80 is denied the right to vote. This may be within the police powers of the state. But many Negroes would qualify under this criterion; yet you're preventing them from voting.

JOHN: I'm not preventing them from voting. I'm just taking away a little bit of that right.

TEACHER: Exactly what part are you taking away?

Typescript Two: Which Majority Should Rule — A Problem of Federalism

TEACHER: What about the Southern whites — does the majority have the right to deny the minority certain rights? Who is the majority? In this country, prointegrationists are the majority, so we're forcing our feelings on the white minority. Do we have the right to do this? We're telling white Southerners that they have to give up an institution that has existed for the last 50 years because we think it is right. And you think this is all right?

JANE: I don't think it is. These people have a right to their customs and the way they have lived for all these years. It is not the job of the rest of the country to deny these people their rights. It wouldn't be right of the Southerners, for instance, to tell the Vermonters to drop their Vermont accent.

TEACHER: Why not?

JANE: Because they couldn't enforce this decision.

TEACHER: Why not? We have an executive department. Send in the troops.

JANE: It isn't their place to do this.

TEACHER: Why not? In a democracy, the majority rules.

JANE: They aren't the majority — Well, they are in this case, though.

TEACHER: Well, the majority of people in the country are integrationists.

JANE: I still don't think they have the right to take away these people's rights as they want.

TEACHER: Suppose it were a custom in this community not to let people whose name is Jane vote. You shouldn't be able to appeal to the rest of the country to make the people let you vote?

JANE: I might be able to appeal to the country, but I might not win my case.

TEACHER: You think voting is just a matter of popular custom. If it's a popular custom to prevent certain people from voting, O.K.?

JANE: No, it's not all right.

TEACHER: Why not?

JANE: Because it's a right guaranteed in the Constitution.

TEACHER: Now we can force our will on the minority as long as it's in the Constitution?

JANE: There's nothing in the Constitution that says segregation is illegal.

TEACHER: There's something in the Constitution that says we have to give everyone equal protection.

JANE: They have equal protection.

TEACHER: They don't have equal protection of the state school law. They get an inferior education.

JANE: In the case that we were reading, the Negroes didn't have an equal school. They had a better school.

BILL: But just the very idea of segregation makes segregated schools unequal, because the Negro feels inferior. That's the whole purpose of education, to build up your mind; and if you feel inferior in one school and superior in another school, then they aren't equal.

Typescript Three: Discussion Based on a Case-Play in Which Students Play School Board Members in a Southern Town

DORIS: I'd like to tell the people who say the Supreme Court does not have a right to tell us to integrate the schools: it is a fact that you're not giving the Negroes their constitutional rights. That's why they're telling you to integrate. It's not that they're trying to interfere with your school system, but the Negroes don't get their constitutional rights, their natural rights. The Supreme Court can rule on this.

JEAN: The Supreme Court has no right to tell us what to do, it's a state right; and I believe the schools are run right.

DORIS: But what about the constitutional rights, their natural rights? They're not getting an equal schooling.

JEAN: They have the same schools; they have good schools.

DORIS: They do not have good schools.

BILL: Right here it says integration harms the Negroes by making them feel inferior. It doesn't matter whether the schools are equal or not. Segregation always makes the children feel inferior —

JANE: I don't think the Supreme Court has any right to make any such decision or any such generalization. Our schools for the Negroes are better than the schools for the whites. You could reverse that and say that Negroes feel superior to the whites because they have better schools, at —

BILL: They say it doesn't matter what the facilities are. The whole idea that the schools are separate makes them unequal.

KAREN: I'm not trying to test anybody, but I think there is a way we can test this. What is this *inferior*? What does it mean? If we define that, it will be easier. Is it inferior not to have good schools, or is there another definition?

DORIS: I suggest we leave the inferiority feelings of the Negro out of this; but as to whether the Supreme Court has a right to rule, I think that's important in this discussion.

BILL: Well, it was granted the right to rule by the United States Constitution, to decide what the law means, and what the Fourteenth Amendment means to the school system. You may disagree whether the Supreme Court has a right to make the decision, but it's been made and been backed up, so I don't think we can argue about it.

CARL: Our problem is not to worry about the validity of the Supreme Court at all. The decision has been made, and we have to comply with it. It is questionable whether the Supreme Court had the power to do that. But the ruling has been made, and we must comply with the court decision.

MARK: But you can go along with segregation as long as you want until you get an entry case.

JOHN: We can go along with segregation for a long time now until an entry case.

CARL: You won't go along for a very long time before you get an entry case.

JOHN: How do you know?

CARL: I'm positive. It just makes sense.

JOHN: In this book, *The Deep South Says Never*, there are dozens of instances where there haven't been any entry cases. Negroes have tried to go to school, but because of economic pressure and various other means, they have completely given up their cause.

MARK: And besides, the Supreme Court is not the law of the land. The Constitution is. By disobeying the Supreme Court's ruling, we're obeying the Constitution. The Supreme Court's ruling is unconstitutional.

BILL: The Supreme Court is given the power under the Constitution to decide what the law means, and the way they interpret the law is the right way, automatically. You can't say, "Why do they interpret the law that way?"

JANE: Isn't it possible for people to make a mistake, even if they're Supreme Court judges?

BILL: I think we should just drop this idea that the Supreme Court decision is not valid, because they're backed by the government. They may make a mistake, you may not agree with them, but it's the ruling. I don't think we should argue about it.

DORIS: I agree with Bill. I don't see any point in arguing about it. We can't change it.

Long-Term Continuity in a Curriculum

The basic core of content, then, would consist of the study of persisting conflicts caused by differing definitions and interpretations of the meaning of liberty, equality, security, and public welfare. In short, the attempt to instill a reasoned, objective commitment to our society would be carried on through appealing to the zest for discussing great issues, not for a year (as in the standard problems of democracy course) but perhaps for three or six years in the students' secondary school career. Each great issue would not necessarily have to be "covered" once in such a curriculum. One issue could be dealt with from two to four times, each time in greater depth, each time building upon knowledge previously gained. The general problem of race relations, for example, might be treated through school desegregation at one time and through discrimination in housing at another.

There are two obvious criticisms of a sustained great-issues citizenship education program running from grade seven through grade 12. The first has to do with maturity. It is commonly asserted that students are too young to discuss great national issues, at least in junior high school. "Too young" usually has two meanings:

1. The boys and girls do not possess sufficient experience to understand the problems.
2. They should not be "exposed" to adult-type issues when they are not emotionally mature.

In answer to the "deficient experience" criticism, we might say that the most crucial "real life" experiences an individual has probably come at the end of his total formal education. Age alone may be a less important factor than the extent to which various experiences are made available through good teaching materials, such as films, cases, etc.

To the criticism that children of ages 12 to 16 are emotionally immature, the answer would be that this is not the case in many other cultures and it could probably be changed to some extent in our culture by education itself. Social maturity has been pushed from college to the junior high school. Why not intellectual maturity?

We give adolescents very few rewards for responsible concern over national issues. Is there any reason why young people cannot be considered intellectual adults at puberty and be dealt with accordingly? As it is, we shelter them from the intellectual responsibilities of analyzing the real problems of our culture until they are 17 or 18, the age at which the more immediate decisions of vocation and marriage are crowding in upon them. Why not use the six years of secondary school to instill a more permanent interest in public affairs?

A second criticism has to do with the claim that only history can give a total perspective on problems. An adequate answer to this criticism would require much discussion. Here it is sufficient to say that history as an exciting narrative, surrounding the symbols of greatness that provide common cultural experience, should be taught — and taught well — in the elementary school. History as a social science discipline should certainly be studied by students who are capable of dealing with large amounts of data extending over long time spans. History taught initially as a strictly factual, chronological basis on which to build an understanding of contemporary problems is probably an inefficient pedagogical strategy. The forgetting rate is too rapid.

A distinction, furthermore, should certainly be made between the jurisprudential approach suggested here and the teaching of the social sciences as accumulated knowledge and as disciplines. A jurisprudential citizenship education program is not an alternative way of learning history or any other social science discipline. These disciplines have their place in the curriculum, just as do the science disciplines. It is suggested, only, that the citizen's relationship to public disputes and to the problem of settling these disputes be made the basis of a different kind of curriculum, a curriculum which has long-term continuity and which focuses directly upon issues that all citizens are likely to face and about which they must eventually make important decisions.

A final point should be clarified and stressed, although it is implicit in much that has already been said. The jurisprudential approach, while it openly teaches the importance of basic procedural values, assumes that positions taken in a societal dispute are largely conditioned by personal values, with which the school has no business interfering. It thus builds an attitude toward government and a person's relationship to his government, but no attitude toward the specific disputes with which government must deal. It does, however, develop a disposition to deal with disputes in a critical, rationalistic way. It demands sound reasoning, but does not dictate what position is to be justified.

Whether such a constellation of learning outcomes can, in fact, be taught with the particular curriculum suggested here is a testable assumption. Harvard is now engaged in such a test and should have information bearing on the question before long. We feel very strongly that careful description and evaluation of instruction are necessary corrections for the kind of speculation and intuitive reasoning in which this chapter has indulged. It may be said, for example, that a program is designed to affect only procedural values, while in fact it may affect many substantive values or it may affect no values at all. To such questions, only careful, plodding research can indicate answers.

Conclusion

As teachers, we face the inevitable conflict over the extent to which we set ourselves up as "transmitters" of the dominant cultural values versus the extent to which we teach students to dissect and interpret the culture. Unquestionably in the teaching of free men we are obligated to teach interpretative skills. Because we owe allegiance to the ideals for which the state has established schools, we are obligated to transmit some stable view of the culture.

This chapter outlines a suggested approach to meet this dual obligation. It proposes to establish a firm foundation of projective models early in the child's life with dramatic narrative history. This will give him a concrete image of the courage, suffering, adventure, co-operation, and aggressive impulses from which modern America has sprung. Upon this foundation may be built a deep and reasoned concern for the broader problems which will affect his interests and freedoms; and a critical outlook toward the words, the institutions, and the principles which may enhance or damage those interests. A basic justification for this dual approach rests upon the assumption that, although liberty cannot be made a sacred value to all men, the nation and form of government which will support and protect that liberty can.

The Rise and Fall of Liberal Democracy

Harvey Wheeler

The economic institutions and practices that flourished during the nineteenth century possessed several distinctive features. It was generally true that no buyer, seller, or entrepreneur was large enough or powerful enough to be able, through his own actions alone, to control or influence the price for basic commodities. The buyers and sellers in the basic sectors of the economy were so numerous and so relatively equal that the prices registered by the markets could be regarded as resulting from the sum of numerous independent actions rather than as being determined by the transactions of the leading traders. This empirical condition coincided so well with the earlier assumptions of the great classical liberal economists that their nineteenth century disciples never doubted that laissez-faire was indeed true to the facts. Capitalism was an operational fact as well as a body of ideas. Of course, economic historians now point out that these conditions were never perfectly realized and that in actual practice there were always some exceptions. Nonetheless, this is a fair picture of what actually went on under the name of capitalism.

Capitalist economic theory went even further. It developed an explanation of how scarce values are allocated. The theory was that when a market was characterized by numerous buyers and sellers and when it was not possible for any buyer or seller to influence prices by his own actions, then prices would tend toward an equilibrium under which all commodities would find their optimum utilization and all factors of production, including labor, would be in full employment. The result was said to be the same as if all traders were in fact equal. It follows that without doing violence to either theory or practice one could claim that commodities were evaluated and distributed "democratically." The equal participation of all traders in the market was just as important to the idea of the free market as was the equal participation of all citizens in democratic politics. One could then speak of "consumer sovereignty," in contrast to the previous economic sovereignty of the State, and in the same sense that the citizen was sovereign in politics. There was an obvious, direct relationship between the realms of economics and politics.

Today there is a mounting body of evidence that our economic institutions no longer operate in accordance with these tenets of classical theory. This does not mean that we do not still have something we call the private ownership of property and something that we call the free enterprise system. All it means is that the market conditions that by and large existed in the nineteenth century exist no longer. Yet we continue to apply the name capitalism to these two different economic systems.

From *The Rise and Fall of Liberal Democracy*, an occasional paper published by The Center for the Study of Democratic Institutions, pages 10–26. By permission of The Center for the Study of Democratic Institutions, The Fund for the Republic, Inc.

There is nothing wrong with this as long as we know what we are saying. Unfortunately, most of us do not. Usually, when we try to make the term "capitalism" do for both economic systems, we fool ourselves into assuming that the earlier ideals are still being approximated, though perhaps in a different way. Names are like that. They denote things that exist but they also connote abstract definitions, and it is difficult to keep the two different uses from interfering with each other. The mere use of the term capitalism today implies that it is still useful to retain the nineteenth century description of economic reality as if it were applicable today. Moreover, retention of the name capitalism tends to carry with it unconscious public policy implications. We are led to assume that the aim of economic policy should be to recapture insofar as possible the conditions of the nineteenth century rather than to deal with our present economic system on its own terms. This is serious enough by itself. However, the theory as well as the practice of capitalism was in for a shock. This came as a result of a startling discovery made by J. M. Keynes.

Working on the level of pure economic theory, Keynes showed that even if an economy were actually to work according to the classical laissez-faire model, equilibration and full employment would not result automatically. The romanticized conditions of the nineteenth century could no longer be put forward as a goal for present-day emulation or approximation. Even in that century, in fact, Keynesian regulations and welfare state measures would have been needed to ensure equilibrium and full employment. So, laissez-faire was deficient in theory as well as in fact. All of this forced laissez-faire theorists to look back into the philosophic and behavioral assumptions implicit in their creed, and in the past few years there has been an outpouring of "explanations" of the "axiological" foundations of classical economic theory. Books by Hayek, Mises, Knight, Roepke, and so on are master works in this area. Others redoubled their efforts to perfect the analytical tools that had grown out of classical economic theory. In so doing they produced an intellectual revolution of their own, one that might someday far overshadow the Keynesian revolution.

Careful craftsmen set to work tightening the logic and perfecting the mathematics. Based upon rigid assumptions about the allocation of scarce values, great theoretical extensions and refinements of the classical approach have occurred. Paradoxically, they resulted in the separation of theory and practice. New theoretical systems have been developed that do not depend upon the empirical existence of "capitalist" operating conditions for their validity. They apply to any kind of competitive struggle for valuables, as for example in warfare or in diplomacy. Examples of these are found in Games theory and in linear programming. They in their turn have led to numerous mathematical refinements and to extensive applications in the fields of decision-making theory, information theory, and organization theory. One of the most familiar direct applications is known as the cost-effectiveness approach to decision-making. After being pioneered and perfected by economists and mathematicians at RAND, it was introduced by Secretary McNamara into the decision-making processes of the Defense Department. Refinement, further extension, and computerization yielded the "systems" approach. Recently these have been extended to many other government agencies.

The result has been the creation of new families of theory, theories that have direct and immediate applicability, and not just to those few areas of the economy in which nineteenth century laissez-faire conditions still exist. They are destined, paradoxically, to come into their own, not under private enterprise but under extensive governmental planning of extremely complex and widespread operations — what the nineteenth century would have called "socialism." The word today is almost as inapplicable to actual events as the word "capitalism." Both were nineteenth century conceptions. Both were founded on very special and very temporal relationships between labor and capital. Twentieth century economic conditions are not recognizable as either capitalism or socialism.

This brief restatement of the economic situation has been made to help develop an argument about politics. The argument is that in the realm of politics an analogous process has been taking place. There is a practical reason for making this argument. The remedy usually offered to alleviate the malfunctioning of the economic system is to submit it to political controls and regulations. But this would be a satisfactory solution only if the political system itself were free from grievous malfunctioning. If it is not, no political solution to economic problems is possible until the political system is rendered adequate to the task. The question of the adequacy of the political system is the point at issue here and it takes us back to our story of American democracy.

What have been the chief institutions of American democracy? Is it possible to choose a high point of their development? Any such choice involves some prior working definition of American democracy. It is customary to refer to Lincoln's famous prepositions: government by, for, and of the people. But to narrow the search to the element most characteristic of the American brand of democracy, it is necessary to emphasize the first preposition: government *by* the people. I call this "participational democracy." (It should be pointed out immediately that I will distinguish this later from contemporary doctrines of *participatory* democracy.) What precisely was American participational democracy?

When Americans worked at developing institutions for their democracy, they seemed to have believed in popular participation in its most overt and straightforward meaning. They held that it was both desirable and practicable to refer all of the problems of government and politics to the judgment of all of the people, and that this could be accomplished through a series of political and electoral institutions and devices. The traditional words used to describe American democracy would probably be progressivism and populism, and the date that marked the highest point of development of populism and progressivism would be just before World War I, probably 1912. In that year all three of the leading candidates for President were progressives. Moreover, it was also in 1912 that American socialism reached its highest point. (A higher total socialist vote was registered in the election of 1920 because of the intervening enfranchisement of women, but the percentage of socialist voters was never again as high as in 1912.)

Three events illustrate the maximum thrust of American progressivism. The first was the enfranchisement of women. Male prejudice finally succumbed to ideology. If each was to count as one and none to count for more than one, the restriction of the vote to males was clearly undemocratic. At least it was contrary to the American quest to achieve participational democracy.

Second was the Eighteenth Amendment. This curious experiment has been commented upon from almost every conceivable angle, but surely one of the most remarkable things about it was the radical democratic assumption that underlay it. Implicitly, Americans were saying that the sway of democracy was complete. Its processes were to be so efficacious that the most fundamental cultural practices — and those involving alcohol are almost as deeply rooted as those involving sex — could be regulated and disposed of through the democratically expressed will of the electorate.

The third event was World War I and the slogan under which America abandoned her century-old policy of isolation from European squabbles. There was never much doubt about the kind of democracy for which Americans wished to make the world safe. Not for French democracy; not for Italian democracy; not for German democracy. It was a war to save the world for American participational democracy. This theme seemed always uppermost in Wilson's mind. He even wanted to conduct the Paris Peace Conference "democratically." It was to feature open covenants openly arrived at. Wilson seemed to believe that the principles of the New England town meeting were directly applicable to international diplomacy. In the post-war political reconstruction of Europe America made it clear that participational democracy definitely was for export. We urged the new post-war states of Europe to adopt constitutions and party systems as near as possible to our own. As we watched them from a distance, we grew censorious if such political traditions failed to develop. Specifically, we expected them to institute American, or at the very least, British-type, two-party systems. Already, twenty-five years before Churchill's Iron Curtain speech, we had laid the ideological groundwork for our latest cold war crusade.

But what were the specific domestic institutions that characterized American participational democracy?

1

The dogma and the practice embodied in the phrase "local home rule" was enthroned. Americans thought it was a self-evident truth that the closer the instruments of government were to the people, the more democratic and the better they would be. It was believed that there was something inconsistent between authoritarianism and small self-governing communities, though most of the world's experience with authoritarianism had been on the scale of the tribe and the city-state. Moreover, Americans themselves, in the North as well as in the South, had lived contentedly in highly authoritarian, small-town, self-governing communities. Today, most specialized observers of the American political scene conclude that there is little reason for the continued existence of the county as a governmental unit, but few of them feel that it can be eliminated. The defense given for the county unit and for those other features of autonomous authority remaining within our towns is that to do away with them and consolidate governmental functions at some more distant point would be "undemocratic."

2

Federalism is defended today as a variant of the same argument. Senator Goldwater is only the latest of a long line of states' righters who have claimed it as the most crucial element in the defense of American democracy and the American way of life. Yet it is clear that the conditions of twentieth century political life have passed by our state and local units. The major problems confronting the inhabitants of our states can no longer be dealt with at that level. The private businesses and organizations that threaten the individual with economic and political eclipse are too large in size and scope for the states to handle. Everyone is aware of this, and yet the tenacity with which we cling to our belief in federalism is marvelous to observe. When we defend it, it is almost always in terms of participational democracy.

3

Another of the chief elements in the drive toward full participational democracy has been referred to already: the gradual extension of the franchise. Universal suffrage can be and is defended on many different scores. But in the United States it spread under the banner of government by the people. Restrictions on suffrage were inconsistent with the belief that the average American should participate in all problems of government at all levels. The first theoretical treatment of this tenet of American democracy came in Ostrogorski's famous survey of nascent political democracy. It was he who first pointed out the failings of participational democracy, but he shared the progressive ideal of devising institutions that would allow people to exercise rational political judgment through an active, individualistic concern with electoral and administrative issues and determine them through their vote. It was this same impulse that led a later theorist of American democracy, Abbott Lawrence Lowell, political scientist and president of Harvard, to make one of the logical extensions of this argument: The limitations on government that were incorporated in our Constitution were pre-democratic. They were the kinds of limits required by a people who had to fight off monarchical despotism. But once the people had achieved their full participational rights, such limitations were anachronistic and illogical. Cut them all away, said Lowell, and let democracy express itself completely.

Lowell and the theorists of his time were writing before intellectuals became preoccupied with the role of the irrational in human culture. Theorists today are living at the high point of the opposite tide. Democracy has always had its critics, even in America, but during the nineteenth century they were almost thoroughly discredited. No effective argument could be made against the notion that everything should be done to insure the fullest possible participation of every citizen in our electoral processes. Large and effective organizations like the League of Women Voters and powerful public relations campaigns to make voting stylish owe their existence to the persisting vitality of this dogma. But the logic of the irrationalist message runs the other way, and today there seems to be increasing fear that over-emphasis on electoral participation by the masses may actually magnify the political expression of irrationality. Anyone who gives even qualified assent to the irrationalist thesis must question the advisability of stimulating everyone to vote on every issue and candidate at every election. For what this does is to harvest the unthinking impulses of those who have little interest in and less knowledge about politics and elections. The result must be to accentuate, rather than to mitigate, the role of irrational forces in politics.

4

The direct election of representatives was provided for comparatively early in the history of our democracy. There seemed no answer to the argument that election of representatives by state legislatures interposed an undemocratic element between the voter and his representative. One may agree in general with the economic historian's charge that the state legislatures of our early history were élitist, property-centered organizations, the political machines of privilege. But what we exchanged them for was not a democracy without any machinery interposed between the voter and his representative, but rather the interposition of different political machinery with a different type of political and economic skew. Elite machine politics merely gave way to boss machine politics. Few argue that the transition from property-centered political machines to mass-voter political machines was a bad thing. On the other hand, it is not legitimate to portray this transition as if it were the liberation of the voter from political bondage to political freedom.

5

The democratization of suffrage was accompanied by the demand that as many as possible of the decisions of government be submitted to the electoral process. This issued in the long-ballot movement. Its explicit aim was to convert the electorate into a public employment office. Functions reaching as far down the administrative hierarchy as clerical and custodial jobs were submitted to voter selection. When towns and villages were small and simple, needing only a few officials, and when the citizens lived in close, face-to-face relationships, it was possible to defend the long-ballot movement. But with the growth of the city, the multiplication of offices to be filled by election, and the development of the urban political machine, the long ballot became the instrument for thwarting rather than eliciting mass political rationality. Politicians supplied electors with candidates selected for the ethnic connotation of their names. They juggled ballot positions, banking on proven patterns of voter fatigue and frustration. Voters reacted to interminable lists of candidates with confusion and eventual apathy. Today a reaction is in full swing and the short-ballot school is in ascendancy. According to this school of thought democracy is furthered in exactly the opposite way. One reduces to a minimum the number of candidates for whom the citizen must vote so that his attention may not be diverted by a confusing list of strangers.

This revision may be the sounder approach to "democracy" under the conditions of a mass society, but it is a direct contradiction of the participational democracy of our past. Though its purpose is to enable the voter to exercise more discriminating judgment, it does so by restricting the vote to a few top officials whose authority is correspondingly expanded. The logic is unassailable: Average voters cannot truly judge the merits of specialized experts or obscure functionaries. Even if they could, they would not. Their interests will be better served if they delegate responsibility for the choice of such people to a few top officials. But the soundness of the argument merely serves to underscore the extent to which the older tenets of self-governing participational democracy have been abandoned. Montesquieu, perhaps, could have understood democracy this way, but not Tocqueville — and certainly not Thomas Jefferson or Andrew Jackson.

Recently, the trend initiated by the short-ballot reform has been carried to its logical conclusion in the proposition that the evils of government, national and state, are traceable to the fact that the authority of the President and of the state governors is not commensurate with the increased functions that have been forced upon them. The solution is to increase executive authority further.

In the early days of the republic the idea of democracy was closely associated with the effort to limit executive discretion and to prevent the expansion of executive functions. Apologists for democracy echoed the belief of Paine, Jefferson, and Jackson that man by nature tended to seek power and to be corrupted by it. One of the primary aims of constitutions was to prevent the expansion of executive authority through the system of checks and balances. But the extent of the change in our conception of democracy is illustrated by the trend that has characterized the middle years of the twentieth century: All attention now concentrates on the need for a strong executive, or, rather, for a strong President. Everything else is overshadowed by his imperious image. Those who write of the eclipse of the states and their governors move on to suggest that this means a further expansion of the Presidency. The successive Hoover Commission reports recommended what political scientists had been long proposing: Give the President the authority and the staff assistance to accomplish his job. The cultivation and exercise of presidential power and the need to expand presidential discretion became the subjects of an outpouring of influential literature that America's democratic forebears would have regarded as completely un-American. Formal obeisance was still paid to the principle of checks and balances but actual efforts were directed at its abrogation. The only check needed would be provided by the popular plebiscite of the people expressed at quadrennial elections. There has been a world-wide movement toward plebiscitary as distinguished from participational democracy. To suggest that political responsibility be concentrated in the highest official approaches what ancient cultures labeled dictatorship. This is the point at which American democratic theory is today.

6

An additional indication of the extent of the reversal in our conception of the executive is the collapse of the referendum movement. The referendum had been designed to provide the people with the opportunity to engage directly in the legislative process, freeing them from reliance on intermediary elected representatives. The referendum is now either abandoned or regarded as an archaic survival that tends to elicit and accentuate mass emotional prejudices.

7

The recall of legislation was the other side of the referendum idea. It was feared that elected representatives might ignore their masters and legislate counter to the will of the people. Therefore, democracy would not be fully operative unless the people were given the power of recalling legislation their representatives had enacted. In theory an alert electorate would intervene whenever its wishes had been misjudged.

8

Not only the legislature but also the judiciary might develop anti-democratic tendencies. To counter this, the judges of the states, with rare exceptions, were made elective, a practice that never fails to astound foreigners. However, Americans now point out that there is no cause for concern. Electing judges has become a meaningless ritual like that acted out in the electoral college, for it is actually the state bar associations that determine who will run for judgeships. Thus we disclose the extent to which our earlier notion of participational democracy has been abrogated.

9

The direct primary is another institution motivated by participational zeal. It appeared in response to the development of machine politics, rigged nominating conventions, and corrupt elections. It was an effort to place the nominating process in the hands of the people and thwart the work of the bosses. Today the direct presidential primary is almost the only residue of the system with vitality. But this is largely because of the novel mass media implications it was recently found to contain. Given sufficient wealth and energy an outsider to machine politics could use the presidential primaries as an entry onto the national scene.

10

The capstone of the progressive drive toward the full realization of participational democracy was periodic constitutional revision. This was in accord with Jefferson's principle that governments tended automatically to grow away from the needs and wishes of the people. The remedy he proposed was a revolution every generation. We have not had Jefferson's revolutions, but we have had a tame substitute in the form of frequent conventions and commissions to revise state constitutions. Originally, the idea behind these conventions sprang from democratic and participational impulses. They were often the vehicle through which the tenets of participational democracy were institutionalized. However, in the twentieth century a sharp change has occurred. The constitutional reorganization movement is still strong, perhaps stronger than ever, but it has lost all of the participational and democratic character that gave it birth. Now, constitutional reorganizations are accomplished by appointed commissions composed of community leaders and experts rather than by popularly chosen delegates, and their purpose is to dismantle the archaic institutional remains of participational democracy. Their theme is to strengthen the executive, give him a larger staff and more authority over administrative agencies, and firm up his hand against legislators.

What are the theoretical assumptions underlying participational democracy?

1

There were assumptions that the average man was wise; he could find solutions to his and society's problems; he would participate actively in politics; and he was more incorruptible than those in authority.

2

Next was an implicit theory of common goals and how society should realize them. The better statement might be that participational democracy implied a theory of "anti-goals." For it was held that the best way to produce political goals was not through explicit governmental policies but as a cumulative result of the people having been freed to develop, institute, and express goals individually and autonomously. This was the political counterpart of the unseen hand of classical economic theory. It yielded a counterpart of economic competition in the form of pressure-group politics. This was radical pluralism at the deepest level. If society refuses to make explicit its values and goals, the right ones are sure to appear as a result of free men and institutions struggling against each other to achieve their own interests. Every conflicting interest and goal will somehow eventually be harmonized as organized groups battle it out in the legislative chambers and lobbies. Given this view, American political science, like other liberal institutions, reflected instead of prescribing, and its contribution to knowledge was the group theory of politics. The theory still dominates the academy.

3

Participational democracy also implied an assumption about recruitment and employment. The best way to get the public work done was to see that political offices were filled only by average Americans. The wisest governors would spring from and automatically reflect the wisdom of the people. This tenet became enshrined in the folklore of American politics as the Lincoln tradition of log cabin to White House. It was not long ago that politicians finally abandoned their belief that rich men were unsuitable candidates unless they had risen from humble origins.

4

Related to this was a proposition about public administration. It derived from the ongoing struggle against a succession of power élites. The American doctrine was that politics and government were intrinsically simple from an administrative point of view. Nothing would have to be done in government that was above the comprehension or the ability of the average American. This was an attack on the European tradition of a professional civil service or administrative class, which Americans believed to be tainted by aristocratic or élitist principles. It was held that the average American was the most "professional" possible administrator of all governmental functions. Though this first appeared under the Jacksonians as the "spoils system," it persisted as the chief element distinguishing the American civil service from all others that had ever existed in history.

5

This in turn implied a theory about decision-making. Decisions should not be made by government officials except as a last resort and even then subject to severe restrictions. The ideal was that all decisions should be made by the sovereign people organized politically. Every possible governmental decision should be voted upon. Only with the fullest possible popular participation in the decision-making process could government function properly.

6

People who believed this way obviously could not see any virtue in formal organization, or bureaucracy. Accordingly, the belief carried with it a theory of organization, or rather anti-organization, which amounted simply to the proposition that all formal organization was bad: "That government is best which governs least." Every effort was made to hamper or prevent the development of formal organization.

7

Not only were government and administration believed to be intrinsically simple: the realm of politics itself was also considered simple. Americans trusted a kind of democratic Providence to guarantee them that the culture and the world would not confront them with problems so complex as to require specialized theoretical ability to solve them. Ordinary human beings would always be able to meet their collective problems by using the innate abilities that sprang from within themselves.

8

This also involved an anarchistic assumption about formal education or ac-culturation. Men should not take collective thought or action for the over-all shape or direction of their culture, their social institutions, or their system of values. Certainly the government should not be concerned with the nature of the family system, the economic order, the religious system, the direction of science, and so on. Everything would be done best if nothing were done about it. The result was a political system that was supposed to produce the common good in an automatic and unguided fashion. It entailed negative government: faith in the operation and efficacy of a kind of residual anarchist harmony. The nature of man plus ingenious participational mechanisms would release man to develop his highest potential (and he would do so), while the government would be prevented from controlling any of society's cultural functions. This meant that the automaticity of the system was supposed to produce:

—Children well educated and made into good democratic citizens simply by leaving with each family the responsibility for controlling the acculturation process of its members.

—An economy efficient, equitable, and always tending to the public good.

—An officialdom staffed through the rotation of average citizens in and out of office, responsible to the people, and achieving the public good.

—A free flow of information through numerous private channels that would automatically discover the things the people ought to know and see that the appropriate information was available to them when it was needed.

—A country essentially isolated from the rest of the world and able to pursue its own interests without regard to the impact of those interests on others.

—Avoidance of the evils traditionally associated with European cities.

—Avoidance of the evils of aristocracy, oligarchy, and conspiratorial factions not in harmony with the public good.

—A country without an official religion and with constitutional provisions regarding religion that committed the several religions, if they wished to exist, to a democratic religious ideology and thus in effect to the ideology of Protestantism. Even American Catholicism adopted the ideology of Protestantism.

This has been a brief catalogue of the rise and fall of the tradition of participational democracy in America. It gives some indication of the extent of our forebears' commitment to the belief that the best possible government was one in which everything it did was referred to and controlled by the desires of the average citizen. The purpose of the catalogue is to dramatize the extent to which this view of American democracy can no longer be considered valid. This has nothing to do with the question of whether the governmental system that we do have is working well, or whether it is a good system. It may be a better and a more sophisticated form of democracy than that of the past. The only point is that during the nineteenth century America made a great commitment to a special, and indeed a historically unique, form of democracy. It backed its gamble with some of the most ingenious governmental and political institutions known to history. Today, these institutions of populism and progressivism have been all but dismantled. They appear embarrassingly Victorian in retrospect as intricate gingerbread like those monuments of Victorian architecture we are now busily tearing down.

However, it is harder to eliminate beliefs and institutions than it is buildings. We still carry the participational commitment in two ways. First, a few of the institutional arrangements we developed to facilitate democratic participation are still with us, though often atrophied or modified. The direct primary is the most prominent example. Second and more important is the fact that even though in one part of our minds we realize that our participational experiment has failed, and even though we sometimes ridicule it, nonetheless, as a nation, we still hold to it, myth though it is. Participational democracy is the only really distinctive contribution we have made to politics and we seem fearful of admitting its failure. When we state the basis of our opposition to communism, it is that communism does not provide for democracy as we have understood it and therefore is not a "true" democracy. But the democracy we foist on others is one we ourselves no longer have. Despite our inner knowledge that our own participational forms no longer work, we continue to base our cold war on the claim that the non-Western world should adopt these forms forthwith, and when we look at the political systems of the newer democracies in the under-developed areas of the world, one of our chief criticisms is that they are not sufficiently participational in our special Victorian sense.

Participational democracy failed, but nothing was put in its place. We give ourselves numerous reasons for not redesigning our democratic institutions de-spite how badly they work in comparison with their original purposes. We reiterate defensively that though they may not achieve what they were designed for, what they do accomplish is pretty good; besides, things would be worse if any fundamentally new approach to democracy were attempted. Our immedi-ate, visceral reaction to any current political issue continues to spring from an emotional commitment to participational democracy. We worry about the political apathy of the average voter. We disapprove of any public figure who does not announce his devotion to the innate political wisdom of the common man. We insist that the primary function of our elected representative is to reflect the desires of his constituency, their private interests rather than the dictates of the common good, and when we complain about him as a wheeler-dealer, we do not say that he is applying a corrupt view of democracy or of representation but that he is representing the desires of the wrong groups or is giving too much weight to certain groups over others. We assume that by keeping "his ear to the ground," by "not losing touch with the grass-roots," and by employing the most scientific public-opinion polling devices, our represen-tative can make the original goals of participational democracy realizable.

More grievous delusions than these are hard to imagine, for on none of the major issues of today's political problems can we look to the common man for a rational solution. The problems are too complex for his inevitably limited knowledge; the deeper issues involving prudence and wisdom never reach him. The contemporary picture of the American electorate is one of a vast amor-phous reservoir of mass political emotion. The state of this emotion can be tapped accurately by public-opinion polling devices. The reservoir itself can be manipulated by suitable emotional appeals channeled through the mass media. As an issue arises, each candidate jockeys for primacy in the opinion-formation process in an effort to see that the mass media reflect his own position. This cannot be achieved through rational appeals, and so it must be achieved emo-tionally. The method is to stigmatize as fearful, dangerous, and alien the posi-tion one opposes; to give emotional patriotic coloration to the position one supports; and to do everything possible to see that the mass media express this bias. If this happens, the post-audit opinion polls will successfully record these carefully instilled prejudices and policies. The successful candidate then triumphantly announces them as the rational democratic will of the people.

A more devastating degradation of the democratic dogma would be difficult to find, for what the process achieves is of course precisely the opposite of our democratic belief. It enhances the position of those willing to resort to this new style of mass-media demagoguery and works to the suppression of rationality in politics. The responsible candidate who wishes to present the issues rationally is faced with a cruel choice. He must choose between his personal integrity as a responsible democratic leader interested in enhancing the rationality of the political process and his conviction that the interests of the people can be served only if he emotionalizes the position he believes to be sound, inducing them to follow the course of reason by manipulative appeals to the irrational. To be a successful democratic leader he must, like his opponents, become a demagogue.

Every society must cope with certain problems adequately in order to exist. It must provide for the maintenance of the quantity and the quality of its members. It must supply their subsistence needs. It must see that the requisite jobs get done and are integrated together into a workable whole. It must maintain adequate relationships with its own immediate environment as well as to the external environment consisting of other similar social systems. It must have an adequate organization of its information-communications system.

It can be argued that these elements of a viable social system are no longer being provided for in this country. Even in the beginning acculturation took place only by accident. Our forefathers assumed that the conditions they knew would last forever. Their America was a Protestant culture. Their State assumed that their church would remain vital and that there would be no need to take thought for the civilizing of its members. Everything rested upon the devoutly Protestant family continuing forever vital. Today, however, our family system has become a small, isolated, non-religious unit responsible on its own for most of the acculturation that takes place in our society. It is no longer an adequate channel through which the values of the culture can be transmitted to the young. In relation to its past autonomous functions, the present family has become so small as to have lost all contact with the wisdom of the aged. It has become so mobile it has lost permanent organic connection with any community. As this has happened, the community itself has lost cultural, if not physical, permanency. The family has changed in its relationship to the church and has lost what acculturizing benefit the church might have provided. In doing this, the family has had the same influence on the church that it has had on the community, leading the church as an institution to assume a progressively smaller role in the acculturation process. The result is a system in which the members of the family grow up with only accidental contact with the essentials of civilized life. The American family has become an agency for the de-civilization of children rather than their civilization.

We have already seen how the mass media have undercut democratic processes. They have also destroyed the mutuality of communication upon which community depends. What information we get and what communication takes place must come through the channels of the mass media. Yet there is no way of taking organized concern for our total informational needs and comparing them with what we actually produce. It is curious what happens to "communication" in a vast mass-media system. The word communication implies mutuality and reciprocation. But this is precisely what is missing.

We are familiar with the notion that the citizen is not in direct contact with any crucial source of information. This is the nature of a mass medium; in being large enough and extensive enough to cover the mass of people, it must be distant from every person. The individual does not consume information from another "person" directly, but only from mass media "images" which have questionable status as "persons." For each functionary in the mass media must take concern, not for what he is as a person, but for his "image." What we see and hear are constructed "images." This is a point often made in discussions of the mass media. Yet there is another side to it as well. For not only is the recipient in contact with mass-media images rather than persons, the image projected by the mass media is itself in contact with "mass images" rather than with "the people," because the only way to know about the effect on the masses of a mass-media image is to construct a profile "image" of the audience. The result is that communication, in the reciprocal sense, is entirely lost. It is not merely a one-way image-to-person process that has resulted, an entirely new relationship of image-to-image has been created.

Our relationship to our environment — to the other social systems around us — is another area in which we are malfunctioning. We continue to conceive of our foreign relations in terms of a world of nation-states, and this seems to be reinforced by the quest for national autonomy by the world's underdeveloped areas. It is inevitable for us to assume that this new nationalism is similar to the old nineteenth century variety with which we are familiar. It is also inevitable for us to assume that the newly arising political systems are "nations" in the old mold. But the fact is that the nation-state is disappearing from the world. It is not the "nation" of Laos that is the locus of our problem in that region. It is not the Congo "nation" that is the locus of our problem in that region. It is not "nation-states" that are the containers in which our problems over Germany and China arise. The overriding world struggle taking place today is the struggle for the political rationalization of the world community as a whole. For our part, however, rather than meeting this challenge, we are devoting our energies to preventing it. A more quixotic view of the world we live in is hard to imagine.

A further tragedy in our approach to the social system we live in is found in our beliefs about science and knowledge. The traditional liberal tenet has been that "truth" is determined and will prosper automatically out of the competitive intellectual process of the free market in ideas. This was the contribution of the utilitarians, especially John Stuart Mill. But there is a serious question as to whether John Stuart Mill's free market in ideas ever really operated in the high fashion he hoped it would. Indeed, Mill himself was doubtful that it would be realized in practice. He feared that monopolies of opinion would develop in the intellectual market just as monopolies had in commodity markets. It was his fears rather than his hopes that were in tune with the future. In any event the question has now taken on different dimensions. Today we wonder about the extent to which we can remain dependent upon "free private science" — the extent to which undirected science will produce the knowledge we require at the time we need it. And if science and knowledge must be organized and directed, what do we make of the argument that science and truth cannot develop except in an atmosphere of freedom? The entire scientific history of the recent past draws this into question. The science of fascism was perverted and controlled in the most gruesome ways, apparently without being self-defeating and without debilitating Germany's scientific effort. If Russia's dictation of science is less atrocious than that of fascist Germany, it is more complete and more totalitarian. But, if anything, one is forced to conclude that, far from John Stuart Mill's belief, science appears to thrive under totalitarianism.

This is not to say that American science in the future will have to exhibit the totalitarian features of the dictatorships. On the contrary, if the Anglo-American experiences with the rule of law has any promise for development and application to new areas, the most crying need for its utilization would appear to be in the area of science and knowledge. The constitutionalization of science — scientific "freedom under law" — would appear to be possible as well as coherent with our best traditions. But when anything is brought under law, the happy anarchy of simpler times is forfeited, and this seems to be the prospect for constitutionalized science and knowledge. Whether this effort will succeed it nevertheless seems apparent that the aimless and undirected development of science as we have known it in the past is a luxury that can no longer be afforded.

The final topic relevant to the capacity of a social system to perform its requisite functions concerns subsistence — the economic system. The burden of the argument is the same. With economic institutions, as with other basic institutions, we have held too firmly to arrangements that may once have been workable but are not workable today. Not only are they "dysfunctional" but, in addition, the attempt to use them beyond their obsolescence brings about a special irrationality attributable directly to the features of our economic institutions that we once thought were most admirable. It is a case of grave, unintended consequences of an institution that developed under different and simpler conditions and that now operates so as to aggravate rather than to alleviate the conditions with which it was supposed to cope.

Capitalism in its early form had many "democratic" features. It disapproved of legal barriers to private, subsistence-providing endeavors. It provided that each man was "equal before the market." It made all of nature available "democratically" for complete private exploitation. Its "free" market, at least in theory, provided for consumer sovereignty.

Inasmuch as one of the primary goals of the society was to achieve a high standard of living for all, and inasmuch as capitalism provided a technology that (it could be argued) would produce affluence automatically, as if guided by an unseen hand, it appeared to follow that the "science" of capitalism (classical economic theory) was so directly attuned to the basic goals of the society that the science did not have to concern itself with goals at all. Indeed, economics went to the other extreme. It claimed to be goal-less. It was a self-proclaimed science of means, not ends. However, as many critics pointed out, it was a science in which the means led only to one end, the proliferation of creature comforts.

The fact that capitalism was so astoundingly successful created some new problems. One of these had to do with the very factor at which it had aimed, a high standard of living. For it happened in several areas that capitalist production and capitalist distribution did not remain in the status of equilibrium described in pre-Keynesian classical economic theory. "Poverty in the midst of plenty" was one of the most popular expressions for the problem that arose in the great depression. The fact that capitalism was "participationally democratic" and that, in conjunction with it, political institutions grew up that were also participationally democratic influenced the kinds of solutions adopted to conquer the depression. The solution that won grew out of the democratic nature of the political system rather than out of the democratic nature of the economic system. Rather than trusting to consumer sovereignty in the market sense we began to apply the principles of consumer sovereignty in the political sense.

Market-type participational democracy was still a factor, but it was involved in a negative rather than a positive way. If the economic system failed to equilibrate production potentials and available resources (labor included), then one evidence would be the disappearance of consumers from the market. When that happened, it fostered a *political* demand to get consumers back in the market, and the *political* solution was to provide jobs. The sovereign consumer now leaves the market-place and enters the polling booth to demand politically that there be enough jobs available so that he can participate in the potential affluence available from the productive system. The success of capitalism in one of its aspects (productive capacity) brought about the reversal of the role of the consumer.

This reversal occurred in conjunction with an associated reversal, which had to do with certain unintended consequences of capitalism. Under primitive capitalism such unintended consequences as occurred still seemed to have a direct relationship to the quest for subsistence goods. That is, one could always relate the existence of coal towns, railroad market centers, and other social results of having a railway system to the operation of the participational economic democracy of the free market. The economic way of stating this is that under primitive capitalism expenditure decisions are subsistence-oriented and therefore market-oriented. But under mature capitalism expenditure decisions lose the directness of their tie to subsistence and to the market. Public expenditures may become job-oriented rather than market-oriented. When participational democracy is exercised privately in the form of union activity or publicly in the political arena, the result may be governmental interventionist programs which are defended politically on the basis of the number and kinds of jobs they will provide rather than on the basis of market demand. Secondly, almost any capital investment program engaged in under mature capitalism may have extensive side-effects.

An example of this is the effect of capital investment in the automobile industry. Implicit in the way a mature capitalist economic system operates is the assumption that Detroit "ought" to be able to distribute all of the automobiles it is able to produce each year. The mere fact that eight or nine million automobiles can be produced is the "given." It follows from this that the rest of the system must accommodate itself to whatever is required to distribute nine million automobiles each year. Even though this is a ludicrous situation on its face, it contains several important unintended consequences. In order for Detroit to be able to sell nine million automobiles each year the purchasing power of consumers must be at a certain level. Moreover, streets, highways, freeways, and parking lots must be changed and expanded in perfect unison, as if they were the last stage of Detroit's assembly lines. This means that cities and suburbs must be of a certain type. Houses must have half as much room for cars as they do for people. Air pollution intensifies and with it the death rate from respiratory diseases rises. This is just the beginning. Sociologists have long argued that the chief determinant of contemporary American folkways is the auto. It expresses our dreams, it receives our affection, it exhausts our bank accounts, it influences our leisure, it becomes the living room of the young and the poor. Courtship and eroticism conform to its functional imperatives. In making individual purchases of personal automobiles Americans are engaging in actions that add up to a "decision" to have an auto-based culture. This was a "decision" that no one made. It is the other side of the "unseen hand." Ours is an economy that produces a chaotic cultural system automatically, "as if misguided by an unseen hand."

This problem becomes increasingly significant as capital investment moves farther from an immediate preoccupation with the current market. The more capital investment is put into pure research the more one can see that capital investment will provide unintended consequences. For example, a significant capital investment is now being made in space exploration. The technological solution to air travel at several times the speed of sound has long since been solved. Commercial airliners capable of mach 3, 4, or "n" speeds and flights from Los Angeles to London in one hour are on the production lines. The airlines are queueing up to get them. Does this mean that, like the hopeless victims of Nazi concentration camps, we will all be herded witlessly into a culture blanketed over with incessantly crashing shock waves of sonic booms? The Air Force is patiently acclimating us. Our preordained fate is to match our already intolerable levels of air pollution with nerve-wracking levels of aural pollution.

Who's in charge here? Whose interest is paramount? Has the public interest lost out for good? Is politics destined to become a lost art, like Egyptian embalming? All this, of course, implies several other things. It renders obsolete present air traffic control and terminal facilities. New ways of orienting cities, residential areas, and transportation systems will have to come. A considerable reorientation of our cultural system is implicit in the decision to invest heavily in space exploration and supersonic travel. Yet no one will ever be given the real "choice" if decision-making remains as it now is. No one will ever be able to "decide" whether or not we should have the kind of cultural system that mach "n" air travel implies. But that new cultural system will confront us anyway, "as if 'provided' by an unseen hand."

This is what is meant when it is said that the entire culture, like the economy before it, now seems to be drifting without a rudder. This is true, but the even deeper truth is that the type of decision now being made is different from that of the past. All basic decisions have become culture-transforming decisions, with the extent of the implicit transformation completely separated from the decision-making process that causes it. This change in the nature of decisions produces a situation in which nobody is responsible for the social costs — the cultural side-effects — of our basic decisions. The political assumption implicit in our present way of making decisions is that even if we pay no attention to the long-run effects of decisions whose chief effects *are* long-run, they will automatically be good. This is the new form that a contemporary Mandeville would have to give to his version of the Fable of the Bees.

Private vices could yield public virtues only when they were current economic decisions in an equilibrating market mechanism. When decisions have their chief implications in the distant future there is no way that an automatic equilibrating political or economic mechanism can convert a private vice into a public virtue. Traditional political and economic theory cannot hope to equilibrate present conditions. Under contemporary conditions the traditional conceptions can be retained only if it is valid to assume that the universe, in its long-run historical processes, contains a built-in providential harmony that will prove the wisdom of today's haphazard decisions generations hence.

The side-effects of basic decisions are not visible from the immediate nature of the decision itself. There is here a counterpart to a notion in economic theory known as the "multiplier effect." It is multiplier effects that we are choosing to "consume" when we acquiesce, for example, in a space exploration project. But this conception of popular sovereignty is so far removed from its original meaning as to make its application to today's conditions a farce.

This brings us back again to the problem of full employment. There is much talk of a "second industrial revolution," the possibility of substituting thinking machines for men under systems that automate human functions. This raises the possibility of increasing the number of unemployed at a time when we expect larger numbers to enter the labor force. It is said that by 1985 (1984 is sedulously avoided as a target year) it might even be possible to eliminate both "middle management" and the unskilled and semi-skilled components of the labor force. When this spectre is viewed in traditional terms it raises the problem of structural unemployment, except, that is, in time of war, when we hide from ourselves the malfunctioning of our economic system.

The neo-Keynesian has a simple answer to the problem of structural unemployment whenever peace forces him to face it. There is no hard evidence, he claims, that the rate of structural unemployment is increasing. There is no reason to believe that it will increase in the future. For economists can show that the human being possesses an unlimited propensity to consume. No matter how much money he has, the average man spends all of it and then some. There is no reason for economists to think that this will change. It follows that there is no reason to fear the advent of an "affluent" economy. All that is necessary is for people to become ever more satiated with proliferating goods and services.

The formula is simple. So long as people have incomes they will spend them, and as long as people spend incomes it is possible to arrange things so that there will be only temporary unemployment. By definition structural unemployment disappears like the little man who wasn't there. The economist says that the primary solution to whatever structural unemployment problem may arise must be the stimulation of the economy through indirect and fiscal means, so that "effective" demand is maintained. But this is merely converting a structural problem in economics into a structural problem in politics, either foreign politics in the form of wars or domestic politics in their fiscal counterpart. What this Keynesian solution amounts to is a series of political prescriptions for preserving the present economic machinery intact. Inasmuch as unemployment cannot be allowed, harmless facsimiles of it must be devised. This requires increasing amounts of featherbedding, reducing work weeks, and expanding paid vacation time. But basically the tested welfare-state fiscal and monetary devices will maintain effective demand and therefore proper employment levels.

Notice the change that has taken place: It is no longer the problem of defending an economic system because of the nobility of the goals it serves but, rather, the goal of preserving the system for its own sake. We are forced into adopting a fetishistic attitude toward the economic system. We do not now ask whether it is good for every American to consume the waste, the planned obsolescence, the gadgetry, the featherbedding, and the expanding consumption levels. We do not now ask whether it is in the public interest for us to "trade" on the economic assumption of the infinite propensity to consume. We do not now ask whether it is wise to exhaust our national resources as rapidly as possible. What we ask is merely that the system as a system be kept going, and we imply that we will "consume" the chaotic cultural system implicit in keeping the economy going through the political stimulation of "effective demand." This is the price we pay in order to prove there is no such thing as structural unemployment. This is how we convert structural unemployment into structural irrationality. The economy becomes irrational, and so we overcome it by making our politics equally irrational. A small but familiar illustration is found in the farm support program: paying farmers millions of dollars for not farming. This cannot last for long. It runs counter to the logic of the most massive cultural force of our day, the scientific revolution.

The prospect of the scientific revolution is sometimes described as the coming of the second industrial revolution. However, it is really an anti-industrial revolution. It is proceeding in the opposite direction from that of our political and economic systems and we all know it. We know that for the first time in history it is technologically possible for man to become released from slavery to his subsistence needs. We know that man is on the verge of being able to convert the economy as a whole into his technological helot. He can make his economic system do what he wishes it to do. For the first time in history man can release himself from the necessity of being purely an economic man. Our economists are not telling us how to realize this potential but how to forestall it. This irony is compounded by the fact that it is the most "liberal" of the economists, the neo-Keynesians, who are the most "reactionary." They are the ones who are bent on patching up the old order through highly increased rates of consumption of goods, services, and make-believe work. They help us pretend that the scientific revolution will never happen. They promise that we can continue living in the archaic economic world of the New Deal when the primary problem was how to create industrial employment rather than how to supersede it.

Today's neo-Keynesians are playing out a role in economics similar to that of the mass-media demagogues in politics. In politics there are serious problems to be solved if the world is to persist. The gravest and the most difficult is the problem of the cold war, how to live at peace in a semi-Communist world. The participational democratic forms that we retain facilitate the development of a demagoguery that prospers through its ability to intensify mass emotional fears and prejudices and thereby to forestall the acceptance of the rational prerequisites to peace.

Similarly, the Keynesian "solutions" to our economic problems amount to a form of economic demagoguery. Is it not strange that the greatest economic fear of the 1960's should be that man may be released from the necessity to labor for his creature comforts? Is it not even more strange that we should confront this "threat" by, in effect, revising upward each day our definition of minimal creature comforts, just so we can all keep ourselves at forced labor to provide them? What a situation for a new Voltaire! And yet it is from the economic analogue of participational democracy that this anomaly arises. The preservation of consumer sovereignty — both on its own terms and in its political transformation into the artificial multiplication of quasi-jobs — becomes the sovereignty of consumption for its own sake: economic gourmandism run wild.

The American civic tradition contained two primary components, one economic and the other political. Both were intimately related. They were mass economic affluence and participational democracy. The first is about to suffer the eclipse of accomplishment. The second suffers from exhaustion, the exhaustion of obsolete machinery overloaded with burdens far in excess of its capacity. The difficulty derives not from democracy as such, but from the special form of democracy that became identified with the American way: direct participational democracy. We have explored some of the reasons for the failure of participational democracy in America. The question that remains is whether its aims have become equally as obsolete as its methods.

In a description of the history of economic development, Walt W. Rostow in his book *The United States in the World Arena* has detected five stages of development. The fifth stage he calls "mass consumption." The implication is that there is no sixth stage. Of course, we have not yet exploited stage five for all it is worth. Serious inequities persist. President Johnson's Great Society is dedicated to their elimination. But what if he succeeds? What problems will we face then? If there is to be a stage six, it seems apparent that the world will inevitably move away from its concentration on creature comforts toward a new emphasis on culture comforts, on the cultivation of our cultural, rather than our kitchen, garden. These goals are not novel. They are the traditional goals of humanism. They are the only goals worthy of man. But we are at the point, both in economics and in politics, where our forms of decision-making prevent us from making those decisions which are obviously right and lead us to make decisions which are obviously wrong.

This has been the story of the rise and fall of American liberal democracy. In both economics and politics a similar group of institutions and a similar rationale appeared. Both relied upon individualistic participation. Both rested on an assumption that the activities of the individual would add up to collective wisdom working for the general interest. Today, however, in each case, we have mounting evidence that this is what is causing our problems. When we hear that our economic system is obsolete, what is really meant is that the individualistic decision-making and allocating device that was at its heart is obsolete. Similarly, when we read pessimistic discussions of American democracy, what is really meant is that the participational decision-making component that was at its heart is no longer adequate. The "solution" we devise in response to the observation that our economic system is dysfunctional is to recommend that it be politicized, that it be placed "under law." But the burden of our argument here is that the political order is suffering from essentially the same disorder as the economic order. If this is true, we can do nothing but compound our difficulties by politicizing the economic order unless we first resolve the ills of the political order.

Does this mean the abandonment of democracy? It is not an idle question. Liberal democracy reached its high point in the era of World War I and has been in steady decline ever since, even within the countries of its origin. It is no longer the governmental ideal at which newly arising nations aim. Even inside America, the most thoroughly democratic member of the Western family, the voices raised in criticism of democracy are growing louder and more frequent.

The American Right is goaded by the fear that the masses will use their political power in too stringent control of wealth and property. The suggested solution is to curb the electoral power of the people in some way so that private ownership of property and private control of business are made more secure. Traditionally the American Left has been undeviating in its support of radical democracy. The relentless drive that issued in the fullest possible extension of participational democracy came from the nineteenth century Left. Its leaders never doubted that the people were also leftists by nature. The overwhelming popularity of the New Deal seemed irrefutable evidence that this was so. It seemed to prove that the masses would and could exercise reason at the polls. The shock came after World War II. The same masses that had followed FDR to the Left turned about and followed Senator Joseph McCarthy to the Right. For a century the common man had been over-praised, now he was under-valued. But there were other developments that cast doubt on the validity of participational democracy. The issues of contemporary politics had become so complex that not even the average intellectual, much less the average man, was capable of resolving them.

American democracy matured in unison with the expansion, the growing wealth, and the increased complexity of the country. Problems of coordinating and organizing became more difficult at the same time that the spreading affluence of the society enabled the people to exercise a certain veto power. Under such conditions the consent of the people is a functional prerequisite to keeping the society operating smoothly. Throughout history democracy has been the most effective device for complex societies to coordinate the actions of masses of people performing a large variety of complex functions. But this quickly produces a dilemma. A complex society requires the participation of the people in the decision-making process, but popular participation in decision-making is possible only at relatively primitive levels of development and complexity. The participational feature of democracy becomes unworkable precisely at the point when complexity calls it forth and affluent masses demand it. The result is that the demand for participational democracy occurs for political reasons just at the time when it has been rendered dysfunctional for technological reasons. This has a further misfortune. The principle of democracy becomes so closely identified with the failings of participational devices that the critics of participational democracy are then able to discredit democracy itself and attribute to it the chief responsibility for the political failings of mass culture.

This is a grave error. For the fact remains that in addition to its other virtues democracy provides the best and most efficient way of motivating and coordinating the activities of people in complex societies. It seems true that no such society can persist unless it can discover the form of democracy appropriate to its needs. America has outlived the participational democracy of her fathers. She must quickly bring forth a new one. Many familiar beliefs and practices seem slated for replacement. Our times demand the development of new conceptions of legislation and new processes of deliberation. The theories of Jeremy Bentham and James Madison must be supplanted by new ones appropriate to the conditions of bureaucratic cultures and adequate to the challenges of the scientific revolution.

Are there any signs of such a development? Recently a new doctrine of democracy has appeared. It was developed initially by young people in their twenties but, despite its adamant youth-centered bias, leadership of the movement is exercised by those already in their thirties. The "Port Huron Statement" of the Students for a Democratic Society, now only four years old, has already assumed the status of a holy text. Its framers, meaning to turn their backs on the ideological squabbles of the 1930's, seized upon a few simple propositions. Their overriding devotion was given to what they called *participatory* democracy. This not only referred to anti-organization principles for conducting the business of the movement itself but also expressed a new approach to working with the unrepresented or dispossessed members of society. The Establishment, standing in the way of participatory democracy, is the announced enemy. There is no real difference between the Establishment liberals and the Establishment conservatives, between the civil and the corporate élites. Indeed, liberalism's unshakable hold on political and industrial power makes *it* the more formidable adversary. The solution? Organize the unrepresented, activate the poor and the Negroes, reconstitute the discontented, form a new coalition committed to the building of a new society dedicated to democracy, world order, and civil and economic justice.

With its eyes closed firmly to the precedents of political history the protest movement has produced a diagnosis and a prescription that recapitulates with uncanny fidelity the pattern that has characterized the spirit of American democracy since the time of Thomas Jefferson. Those who are in the habit of taking their ideological bearings from the European tradition complain that the contemporary protest movement lacks a class basis and is shy of an ideology. But just the opposite is true. Its resonance with what was described as the American class system is too obvious to require discussion. Its ideology could have been lifted from Tocqueville's *Democracy in America.*

Economic Power and the
Free Society

A. A. Berle, Jr.

The cycle of shift from individual possessory holdings into power systems, and from power systems back once more into possessory personal holdings, appears to be a kind of rhythm of history, especially in the West. As the feudal system merged into the king state, the revolutionary doctrine that there should be private property began to assert itself, reaching a high degree of philosophical justification in the middle of the Eighteenth Century when the French physiocrats declared that if a man was to be free, able to speak his own mind, depict his own thought and develop his own personality, he would have to have a base apart from one that was politically or ecclesiastically organized and controlled. The theory of private property as a part of freedom reached its culmination in the French Revolution and in the far slower and quieter industrial revolution in England.

No doubt the American system is the child of that revolution. Certainly the Jeffersonian ideal was a country in which everyone had private property, no one was very rich, no one was very poor. In order to make this system work, however, a companion theory was needed — that economics worked automatically. The self-interest of men levering against each other and controlling each other through competition resulted in a splendid ethical balance wheel, which was the open market. This leveled out inequalities, eliminated the inefficient and through competition prevented an undue concentration of power.

Adam Smith's *Wealth of Nations* consecrated the theory. Smith said that this strange animal "the corporation" could never be a major factor in economics because in it men worked for other men, and obviously no man would

From *Economic Power and the Free Society* published by The Center for the Study of Democratic Institutions. By permission of The Center for the Study of Democratic Institutions, The Fund for the Republic, Inc.

ever pay as much attention to other men's affairs as he would to his own. Therefore, such a collective enterprise could never play a major role in society. Its inefficiency would always be such that the workings of the market would eliminate it. Thus, the corporation was merely an agency of the state for specialized purposes, and those suspect.

At the convention which met to draw up the Constitution of the United States the proposal was made that the Federal government be given the power to incorporate. According to Madison's notes the answer was: No, a corporation prevented men from getting into action and this is a dangerous power. A corporation had not merely the privilege of existence but other privileges as well, or if it did not have them it could get them. As a result monopolies would arise and dominate the United States. This should not be allowed.

So the Federal government was specifically denied the power to create corporations. This was to be left to the states and it was assumed that they would not exercise this power or, if they did, would exercise it only as a means of carrying on government. This doctrine survived less than fifteen years. By 1791 the Federal government found it desirable to organize a corporation entitled the Bank of the United States, and in the 1819 Supreme Court case *McCulloch v. Maryland* Justice Marshall decided that the implied powers granted to the government of the United States included the power to form a corporation if it were apposite to the particular functions the government wished to perform. It is still true that the Federal government can create corporations only for governmental or quasi-governmental purposes; the states, on the other hand, have been allowed to create them as they would, and as our technology developed corporations began to proliferate to such an extent that by 1835 our great-grand-fathers felt that the situation called for a close look.

As we look back on their findings now, they made a surprisingly accurate prediction of the probable effects of an unlimited corporate life. (They were not so sound, perhaps, in their estimate as to whether it was desirable or undesirable.) For the next fifty years they used every known legal means to keep a corporation to a single defined and manageable enterprise. The corporation lawyer of the period spent most of his time on the law of *ultra vires*, which dealt with corporations that tried to transcend the limits that had been set out for them. These limits ordinarily were:

First, that they could only own a limited amount of property, frequently and especially only a limited amount of real property. The fear was they would start absorbing huge quantities of land.

Second, that they could indulge in only one type of business. If a corporation was organized to run a flour-mill, it had to run a flour-mill and nothing more.

Third, that they should last only for a defined period of time, twenty or thirty years or whatever the statutory limitation was.

Not infrequently there was a fourth limitation. This was that the corporation should be subject to continuous inspection. The courts could appoint a "visitor" — today he would be called an auditor. He was authorized to inspect and analyze the workings of a corporation and report to the judge, who, in turn, had an undefined power to say what should or should not be done.

A variety of other limitations were imposed from time to time, all of them representing attempts to prevent exactly what happened:

First, that a corporation would grow so large that its economic strength would vastly outweigh the strength of any individual enterprise.

Second, that it would be able to rove the country, if not the world, at will and do what it wished in terms of economic enterprise.

And third, that it would become a trust for perpetual accumulation; that its assets, in so far as they were not distributed by way of dividends, would be permitted to pile up to unlimited amounts.

These three results have come about, of course. Corporations did do, have done and are doing exactly what our forefathers worried about. Part of their fear stemmed from the belief that the corporation was only an artificial personality and therefore did not have a soul or a conscience. Lacking a conscience, it had no morals and was *prima facie* dangerous. This is why throughout our history society has attempted to control and constrict the corporation.

The rise of the large contemporary corporation — the giant as we know it today, the true collectivism — began with the railroad systems. There were other large corporations, but the railroad systems were the ones that posed the real problems. They were the first to demonstrate the shift in the private property system that came about when we began to realize that there was no real way of constricting a corporation whose business the community needed. If its economic functions were necessary to the welfare of the community, the law somehow had to recognize that fact, however backhandedly. If a railroad needed to go through to the Pacific coast, the law had to find some way around the fact that the corporate power did not let it go that far.

A diagram of what was happening to private property while this was going on would look something like this:

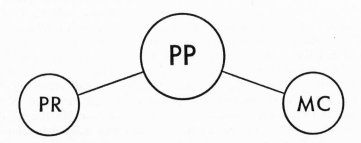

"PP" or possessory property is where it all began in about 1810 or 1820. This is our great-great-grandfather's farm or forge, which he had not only created but owned and operated. This was the assumed unit of property at the beginning, and even today we still talk in those terms. This possessory property becomes incorporated as an enterprise and is immediately split into two functions. At the left is one function — "PR" or "passive receptive." This is the receptive side of property, the shockholder's share. The shareholder cannot manage. Every corporation statute in the country says that the business of the corporation shall be managed by its directors, and almost every court has agreed that the director is not an agent of the stockholder and does not have to follow his instructions. So the right-hand side of the diagram is "MC" or managing and creating.

The business of stockholders is primarily to receive; the business of management is primarily to manage and create. In the early days, when corporations were still small, the stockholder powerfully influenced the director but today they are so far apart that the stockholder can hardly communicate with management even by megaphone. We go through the ancient forms and it is good that we do so, but everyone knows that a stockholders' meeting is a kind of ancient, meaningless ritual like some of the ceremonies that go on with the mace in the House of Lords. The "passive receptive" side of the corporation, in short, is functionless.

The "MC" side looks better at first glance. But in any large corporation the management group is actually as striated as it is possible to be. The president and the chairman of the board probably work together as the theoretically responsible officers, but they must operate through committees of officers — big officers, medium officers and little officers, all divided in as many different ways as the management experts can invent. While the top officers officially have the right to enter upon the property and do things, even though they are not able to own it, the fact is that they have had to sub-divide that right to such a degree that in practice the real possessor of a piece of property is the manager of the particular division or area of the property — and even he probably has to share his right with his plant manager if he's got one. This is possession without right, just as on the "passive receptive" side there is right without possession.

As things look now, this unbalance is about to be redressed. Whether it will be good redressing is another matter. Theoretically, management got its legitimacy by the fact that it represented the will of the shareholders. This was a kind of quasi-amateur democratic legitimacy. However, on examination, it was found that although the stockholders theoretically chose the management, in point of fact they were completely unable to do so. The management would send out a proxy naming three agents whom the stockholders appointed to cast their vote at a meeting. In older days the management often didn't even bother to say for what directors these proxies would cast their vote. Since the Securities and Exchange legislation, they have to do that, but the corporation secretary who sent out the proxies was the man who really determined what happened for all practical purposes in the power relationship. The president or the directors could fire him, of course, so he did what they told him to do. When the directors wished to renominate themselves or to add to their number or to fill a vacancy, they did it. This is still the method by which the directors in a great corporation are chosen. This is an automatic self-perpetuating oligarchy.

These are a string of bad words. There was at least one court case in which it was held that a self-perpetuating oligarchy was illegal. This was the famous case in which a life insurance company in New Jersey purchased control of a trust company by buying a majority of the shares. Thereafter it caused the trust company to purchase a majority of *its* shares. The result was an unbreakable ring. A New Jersey court said that this was illegal, created an oligarchy and was contrary to the theory of New Jersey corporation laws.

However, thereafter, somebody asked whether corporations really should be run democratically. Should this group or that group or the other group campaign against each other, offering inducements to shareholders to vote for them instead of the other group? Could corporations assimilate this kind of democratic government? There was no answer. In point of fact, the choice of management depends not on an assent of balanced interest but on expert judgment of technical ability with a companion judgment of honesty and character. As a result, for all practical purposes, management controls the corporation unless it is itself controlled by another oligarchy with enough shares to dominate the situation at all times.

There is a good deal of loose thinking about this. It is commonly believed that the holder of 20 per cent or 25 per cent of a corporation's stock can control that corporation. This was the inference in the recent du Pont-General Motors case. This is not true. It is true that with 20 per cent or 25 per cent of the stockholders' list of a large corporation *plus* control of the directors it can be done. But if the directors of General Motors decided not to vote with du Pont, it is very doubtful whether the du Pont interest is sufficient to be able to go out and get the other 30 per cent of General Motors stockholders which it would need. This is not pure theory. When a certain gentleman ran Standard Oil of Indiana he did various things that induced the so-called controlling group to want a change. They canvassed the board of directors and asked whether they would not fire the man. The directors said they would not. Thereupon the controlling group went to work to try to win the next election. Between their own and allied holdings they had slightly over 20 per cent of the stock. They did control in the end, and the man was fired. But they achieved it only by spending about $800,000 on a stockholders' campaign.

The control system in today's corporations, when it does not lie solely in the directors as in the American Telephone and Telegraph Company, lies in a combination of the directors of a so-called control bloc (a misnomer, incidentally) plus the directors themselves. For practical purposes, therefore, the control or power element in most large corporations rests in its group of directors and it is autonomous — or autonomous if taken together with a control bloc. And inheritance-tax distribution of stock being what it is, the trend is increasingly to management autonomy. This is a self-perpetuating oligarchy.

Meanwhile the next phase has been emerging. It will stay with us and it will be of some interest. This involves what are known as pension trusts — welfare funds and pension trust funds. A pension trust in most cases differs from an insurance trust in that it has an unlimited and indefinite obligation. It is there to pay pensions to X, Y and Z which shall be a fraction of the salaries X, Y and Z will have collected during the years of their tenure. The pension trust fund, if it is properly administered, has to think not merely of paying out a stated number of dollars in, say, 1980, as an insurance company does, but of having enough dollars to meet obligations later to be determined. No human being knows the future course of inflation of the dollar, prices, pay and so forth. Nevertheless, although the payment period may be twenty or thirty years away, the pension trusts must keep abreast of inflation at least as it affects pay.

This suggests, of course, that they must invest in equities, whereas, classically, trust funds invested in fixed obligations. This is the sharp difference between the kind of burden resting on an honorable pension trustee and on the directors of, say, the New York Life Insurance Company, whose business is to provide a stated number of dollars against stated contracts to pay those dollars with interest later on. The pension trust funds, therefore, belong among the stockholders in the "passive-receptive" column of our diagram because of their ownership of common stocks. The holdings of life insurance companies include less than 5 per cent in common-stock equities; in the pension trust funds equities are running close to 30 per cent of their assets and may be more. The total of pension trust funds at the moment is almost $31 billion. Roughly half of this is in the hands of insurance companies, which operate — perhaps erroneously — on the assumption that they have only another set of insurance policies. Ninety per cent of the remaining pension funds are in the hands of eight or nine New York banks, the largest single one being the pension trust fund of the American Telephone & Telegraph Company, which is about $2.2 billion so far and is operated by a committee through the Bankers Trust Company.

As a result of this broad-scale buying of equities the pension trusts are slowly "chewing up" control of those corporations which offer the best means of equity investment. These are voting equities. Thus far no attempt has been made to make use of this except in the case of the Sears Roebuck pension trust fund which undertook to buy Sears Roebuck stock and presumably now has a controlling interest in the company. As a result Sears Roebuck is socializing itself via its own pension trust fund, and is discovering that it is running into the same difficulty which a socialist or any other form of oligarchic government has — that it has self-contained control, and management is thus responsible to itself. Query: does it continue to have "legitimacy" when the only mandate it can refer to is its own?

The present $30 billion in the pension trusts of course is doomed to increase. These are compulsory savings and the funds must continue to accumulate. They now cover only about half of the non-farm labor force; they will undoubtedly soak up a considerable part of the balance before long, and must increase, particularly in view of the population rise. In addition, it will be another twenty or thirty years before this "levels off"; that is, before the payment from the funds begins to balance the incoming. The pension trust funds will perhaps level out at somewhere in the vicinity of $70 to $80 billion, probably increased by the coefficient of the increase in population or the increase in labor force within the population. This will mean that if the pension trusts continue to take the good equities as they have been doing, they may well have the prevailing control-stockholding position and the capacity to make it absolute. They will have, say, 20 per cent to 30 per cent of the good equity stocks and the capacity to increase that to 40 per cent or 50 per cent (45 per cent for practical purposes is a majority at any big stockholders' meeting).

With the rise of the pension trusts into the "passive-receptive" end of the corporation structure the old "passive-receptive" stockholder is gradually disappearing. At best he is, shall we say, a pensionnaire. The last vestige of his power to legitimate a management by a vote is in the hands of the pension trustees. He has an expectation arising out of the fact that he may have performed a certain number of years of acceptable work and fulfilled a certain number of other conditions. But does he have any property right in the pension trust? The courts say no. The power — what is left of it — lies in the trustees, or in those insurance companies which administer trusts.

When power is lodged in a particular group it has no choice except either to exercise it or to try to revolutionize the system. There is no way of avoiding power. If you take it and refuse to exercise it you suffer the fate of King Lear — the king who wanted to be king but did not want to be bothered. The trust funds admit they have it but they have thus far refused to use it. This situation cannot last very much longer. Somebody is bound to use that power, of necessity. Pension trusts are so concentrated that a relatively small amount in equities outbalances any number of scattered holdings.

The private property system in production, which began with our great-grandfather's farm and forge, has almost vanished in the vast area of American economy dominated by this system. Instead we have something which differs from the Russian or socialist system mainly in its philosophical content. Under a pure socialist or Communist system, in theory, every worker has an old-age pension at the end of his labors. We are developing the same thing by "socializing" property without a revolution. It is one of our more amazing achievements. Whether one likes it or not depends on one's philosophy.

Possessory private property in this area has been metamorphosed. In its place is a power pyramid. At the moment this is a management pyramid, but it is beginning to be balanced by a pyramid of men who have no possible property interest in the actual corpus but do have the power of choice — the pension trustees. These are naked power vehicles, with the "receptive" end so far dispersed that it cannot even be discerned. To make the joke complete, let us suppose that a pension trust liquidated itself tomorrow and satisfied its contract obligations. If it was a well-run trust, there would be a balance left over. That balance would very likely escheat to the state because there was no claimant to it left. In the most violently private-property-minded country in the world this is perhaps one of the most magnificent economic jests the world has seen.

None of this has come about as a result of the villainy of conspiring men. That might have been true in the free-wheeling corporation days of a hundred years ago, but it would be as ridiculous an assumption today as is the basic assumption of the Supreme Court decision in the recent du Pont case. This decision apparently assumed that because du Pont bought 23 per cent of General Motors forty years ago, perhaps hoping that it could control General Motors, du Pont still holds to the intention of exercising this control. Actually, there has been a kind of continual biological progression over the years. Change is part of the progression. Bigger enterprise was needed to satisfy the desires of the population. In addition, the techniques which made it possible to satisfy certain necessities made it *impossible* to rely only on the individual. Consequently, organization and power, not ownership, had to meet the resulting problems. The progression has been natural.

Today approximately 50 per cent of American manufacturing — that is everything other than financial and transportation — is held by about 150 corporations, reckoned, at least, by asset values. If finance and transportation are included, the total increases. If a rather larger group is taken, the statistics would probably show that about two-thirds of the economically productive assets of the United States, excluding agriculture, are owned by a group of not more than 500 corporations. This is actual asset ownership. (Some further statistical analysis is called for if financial corporations be included, for these, of course, double up. One of the largest and most plainly oligarchically controlled corporations in the United States, the Metropolitan Life Insurance Company, duplicates assets because it holds securities of other corporations.) But in terms of power, without regard to asset positions, not only do 500 corporations control two-thirds of the non-farm economy but within each of that 500 a still smaller group has the ultimate decision-making power. This is, I think, the highest concentration of economic power in recorded history. Since the United States carries on not quite half of the manufacturing production of the entire world today, these 500 groupings — each with its own little dominating pyramid within it — represent a concentration of power over economics which makes the medieval feudal system look like a Sunday School party. In sheer economic power this has gone far beyond anything we have yet seen.

We can talk about the various alleged legal controls which somehow or other, when the chips are down, neither control nor even seek to control. We can point out the fear of "monopoly" and "restraint of trade" and say that from time to time this fear has checked the process. True, our law has prevented any one of these power groups from becoming a monopoly, but it has not seriously prevented the concentration of power as power, though it has prevented certain ultimate results. The question is then: Why has concentrated economic power in America not got completely out of hand? Many of these corporations have budgets, and some of them have payrolls, which, with their customers, affect a greater number of people than most of the ninety-odd sovereign countries of the world. American Telephone & Telegraph, for example, based on combined population and wealth, would be somewhere around the thirteenth state of the union in terms of budget, and certainly larger than many of the countries of South America. Some of these corporations are units which can be thought of only in somewhat the way we have heretofore thought of nations.

Whether we like it or not, this is what has happened. As noted, it is not the product of evil-minded men. I believe that we must try to work with the system. The dangers are obvious. But history cannot usually be reversed. Until engineers and economic forces give us a way by which a man can manufacture an automobile in his back yard we will continue to have organizations the size of General Motors or Ford — as long as people want Chevrolets or Fords. We will have railroads the length of the Union Pacific as long as people want to go across the continent by railroad. In other words, until a combination of technique and organization can be invented permitting *individuals* to do the job, we are bound to try to make the best we can out of the situation. To my mind most of the results are rather surprisingly good.

This does not mean, however, that I am not afraid. I am. I believe it is the *content* of these systems rather than their *form* that matters. Their power can enslave us beyond present belief, or perhaps set us free beyond present imagination. The choice lies with the men who operate the pyramids, and with the men affected who can demand what they really want. Our Anglo-Saxon democratic liberties, after all, were beaten out, not against the framework of the personal possessory property regime, but against the background of two of the most brutal despotisms in Western history. Both the Angevin dynasty in Normandy and the Tudor dynasty in England were rank despotisms. The content of our democratic liberties from Magna Carta down was pumped in by extraneous moral processes. Our institutionalized liberties present the case of an institution conscripted into utility, rather than something that emerged full-armed from the head of Jove. It was probably better that way; the democracy of the Greeks did not work so very well.

We have to accept this power situation as, let us call it, a neutral mechanism subject to the control of the body politic as long as we *keep* it subject to that control. That control, I believe, will be essentially intellectual and philosophical, capable of being translated into legal rules when necessity arises. In that respect I make three points in summary:

1

The first is that whenever there is a question of power there is a question of legitimacy. As things stand now, these instrumentalities of tremendous power have the slenderest claim of legitimacy. This is probably a transitory period. They must find some claim of legitimacy, which also means finding a field of responsibility and a field of accountability. Legitimacy, responsibility and accountability are essential to any power system if it is to endure. They correspond to a deep human instinct. A man desires beyond anything else to have someone give him the accolade of "Well done, thou good and faithful servant," thereby risking the condemnation of "You have been no good — get out." If he has to say it to himself, or hear it from a string of people whom he himself has hired or controls, he is apt to die a cynical and embittered man.

The medieval feudal power system set the "lords spiritual" over and against the "lords temporal." These were the men of learning and of the church who in theory were able to say to the greatest power in the world: "You have committed a sin; therefore either you are excommunicate or you must mend your ways." The "lords temporal" could reply: "I can kill you." But the "lords spiritual" could retort: "Yes, that you can, but you cannot change the philosophical fact." In a sense this is the great lacuna in the economic power system today. In theory the stockholders can act as the "lords spiritual" through their vote. In fact they cannot, and they know they cannot. Are the pension trustees or their equivalent slowly emerging as the men who can? They had not thought so — nobody had thought so. They have been essentially a method of transmission of choice and not much else. We are looking for the kind of thing that C. Wright Mills in his recent book on the American power elite rightly said did not exist. He wrongly concluded, therefore, that the system was a mess, which it obviously is not. We are, if you choose, searching for the pyramid on the other side of our diagram. But every time we have had the chance to construct that kind of elite we seem to have abandoned it, and chucked in an administrator instead.

2

My second summary point is that the sheer power of invading personality is great and that a doctrine is already at work which plays a second joke on our constitutional system. The United States began by saying that its Federal government could not construct corporations and apparently by assuming that the states would not. Both have done so. It also said that corporations should be kept apart from governmental power. *De facto*, they have not been. We are now, in fact, beginning to converge on a doctrine which may well push right over the line when the next case comes up. This doctrine is that where a corporation has power to affect a great many lives (differing from the little enterprise which can be balanced out by the market) it should be subject to the same restraints under the Constitution that apply to an agency of the Federal or state government. In that case, the Bill of Rights and the Fourteenth and Fifteenth Amendments would apply. At the moment this is one jump ahead of current law. Yet it seems probable that this will be the next phase — just as we already have the constitutional doctrine that under the Fifth Amendment you may not by private contract prohibit a Negro from buying land.

3

My third point is destined to be in infinitely greater controversy, and I do not know what the end of the controversy will be. Great corporate power is exercised in relation to certain obligations:

1. It should supply the want in the area of its production. Where the community has come to rely on a corporation for steel, oil, automobiles or cigarettes, the corporation is obliged reasonably to meet that demand.
2. The price must not be considered extortionate. It must be "acceptable" — which doesn't necessarily mean fair or just.
3. It must provide at least some continuity of employment.
4. It must give a continuing attention to the technical progress of the art.

At every point in the individual history of large corporations there has been some moment of impact on the community when either the community felt the corporation was not fulfilling its obligations or, alternatively, the corporation realized it was up against a situation it could not handle. In every case the result has been either a friendly and orderly, or unfriendly and disorderly, hassle out of which a piece of planned economy emerged. Roughly two-thirds of American industry and much of American finance is now controlled by a formal or informal Federal industrial plan. Here are two illustrations at each end of the cycle.

The oil industry claims to be the most non-socialist, free-wheeling, private business that ever was. But the fact is that after many vicissitudes it sought control by, and is controlled by, various Acts of Congress. After orderly discussion certain laws were passed. Under these laws, first, the Bureau of Mines of the Department of Interior estimates the probable consumption month by month of gasoline and the chief oil products. Second, an interstate treaty exists among the oil-producing states, ratified by the Congress. Third, a Congressional Act makes it illegal to transport oil in interstate commerce which has been produced in excess of a state allowable. This legislation might break down if it were not for the fact that because there is a relatively concentrated system in the oil industry the refineries will not buy "non-certified" oil anyway. As a result, the big companies do not violate the Act; the little ones cannot; and the result is a planned oil economy by which supply is equated to demand and the oil industry from well to refinery to gas station is more or less geared to meet it.

Here is a disorderly example: Aluminum was manufactured by a monopoly which was ordered to be split up under an anti-trust decree. By a combination of administrative orders entirely without administrative rationale but all working toward the same end the Federal government used the aluminum plants it had created during World War II in order to set up two competitors to Alcoa. It likewise required Alcoa to sell its Aluminum of Canada shares. This was not enough by itself, so the government for a period of years handled its defense orders in such a way that the new companies had adequate assurance of a market until they could get properly under way. The policy still is to make certain that the new companies, which can stay in business only by being assured a reasonable market, will get the extent of market they need. There was a stockpiling arrangement at one time, followed later by the release of part of the stockpiled aluminum. In a wholly disorderly way which only the American system could ever conceive, there arose the equivalent of a *de facto* planned economy in aluminum. At the moment this industry now sails away, free-wheeling. But there is not the slightest doubt that if conditions required transition back into a planned economy it would happen.

These two illustrations could be multiplied. The point is merely that (a) through constitutionalization of the corporation some attention is being paid to the protection of the individual; and (b) through a slowly emerging, industry-by-industry, flexibly-planned economy, some protection of the community is coming about.

Obviously a system like this is just as good as the ideas and strength of the body politic behind it. The same system in the hands, for example, of a Latin American dictator could produce terrible oppression.

There is a gradually growing feeling that pension trusts, for example, must be controlled. A pension trust ring could be something to bind a man beyond belief. It could bind him to his job. He could not change it without losing a substantial part of his life savings. He might be controlled in all sorts of ways. We are beginning to think even that the pension trust right which cannot be transferred to some other pension trust is suspect.

As men think, so they are. We are really seeking now a body of doctrine which will control power. I close by returning to my first point, which related to the desperate search for a field of responsibility and accountability referent to some point of view outside the system: that is, to some modern "lords spiritual." I suggest that the real purpose of the Fund for the Republic's basic issues program is to supply exactly that.

The United States in International and Historical Perspective

Robert L. Heilbroner

The Awakening of the Colonial World

We have thus far been concerned with the effect which science in general and the new weapons technology in particular have had and will continue to have on our future. Now we must turn to the second of the great historic currents of our times. This is the revolutionary extension of popular political aspiration to the underdeveloped world.

At its roots the basic motivation of the contemporary revolution is a diffuse phenomenon. It is a movement of the "popular will" which springs from the awakening, in many millions of minds, of ideas of dignity, hope, ambition. But in the actualities of history we do not encounter it in such spiritual dress. Instead we meet it as an aspect of contemporary events with which we are very familiar under another guise — that of the increased turbulence of the "new" political areas of the world.

We need only to be reminded of a few instances of this characteristic "troublesomeness" of the underdeveloped nations. We find it in a movement away from constitutional government toward authoritarian and often militaristic regimes in many backward nations, including many of those nominally a part of the "Free World." We see it in the prevalence of local international tensions which result in an Indian-Pakistan rift, an Egyptian-Israeli war. We meet it again in the instability of governments which manifests itself in assassinations in Guatemala, Iraq; civil wars in Cuba, Indonesia; revolutionary turmoil in Algeria, riots in the Belgian Congo. And most important of all, we encounter it as an economic movement leftward which can be seen to some degree in nearly all the new nations.

It is difficult at first to connect this diversity of troubles with the rise and spread of the idea of political aspiration. And yet when we place these occurrences in an historic perspective, we can see that they have an integral connection with that revolution of expectations whose appearance in Europe in the eighteenth century contributed so much to our own changed attitude toward the future. Only, what is now happening is an extension of that essentially restricted revolution on a world-wide scale.

For we must realize that the seemingly vast industrial, political, and economic changes which ushered in modern history were in fact a series of events that directly affected only a tiny fraction of the world's population. Whole continents, entire cultures, vast societies were left aside in their course. Indeed, for the overwhelming majority of the world's people the revolution simply did not exist. Technologically, the bulk of the peoples on the Eurasian, Asiatic, African,

From pp. 75–96 of *The Future as History* by Robert L. Heilbroner. Copyright © 1959, 1960 by Robert L. Heilbroner. Reprinted by permission of Harper & Row, Publishers.

and South American land-masses remained in a pre-industrial and even a neolithic stage of development. Politically they continued to exist as a voiceless serfdom, which was generally the only condition of political existence they had ever known. Economically, although millions lay under the formal sovereignty of capitalist nations, only a fringe had any personal involvement in their Western ways of life.

For the last three centuries, in other words, there existed side by side two nearly separate worlds. One, mainly comprising the people of Europe and North America, was the beneficiary of the multiform revolution which had slowly come to maturity in its midst. The other, comprising the peoples of East and South, was its victim. For the contact between the two worlds, although restricted, was highly infectious. Indeed, it was toxic.

In part this was because the small and active European civilization often ruthlessly exploited the large and torpid Asiatic and African ones. Predatory as it was, however, this economic exploitation was perhaps the *least* destructive aspect of imperialism. In a sense it was only an intensified transplanting of an attitude toward labor which was also visible within the Western community. What was much more disastrous for the colonial world was that its economic penetration by the West came without any of the historic preparation that accompanied this development in Europe. Imperialism imposed on its colonies the raw economic drive of capitalism without the social and political underpinnings and protections which blunted that drive at home.

The result was in many ways a catastrophe for the colonial world. Into its primitive circulation of life a powerful and dangerous virus was injected with terrible effect. It turned millions of traditionally self-sufficient peasants into rubber-tappers, coffee-growers, tin-miners, tea-pickers — and then subjected this new agricultural and mining proletariat to the incomprehensible vagaries of world commodity fluctuations. It uprooted ancient laws and gave in exchange Western justice, whose ideas disrupted the local culture by striking at the roots of time-honored traditions and customs. It brought young men to the universities of Europe to learn the thought of the West, and then placed them in jail when they went home to preach it. Immense strides were made in orderly government, but it was government over and not of the people, and almost invariably concerned with preserving the prerogatives of feudal overlords rather than extending new privileges to the masses beneath them. Colonialism, even in its most missionary moments, never succeeded in seeing the "natives" as equals, and it usually simply took for granted their irremediable inferiority.

It is useless to lament this tragic chapter of the past, and still less useful to exaggerate its horrors. While colonialism was economically, socially, and politically disrupting and disturbing, one cannot forget that the way of life which it displaced was often brutally cruel and tyrannical. Nor can one ignore the gains which came with the penetration of the West: health and sanitation, transport and communication, law and order, and not least, the necessary stimulation to waken torpid peoples from their enslavement to the past.

But whereas the historic role of colonialism was a complex one, it is essential to recognize that the historic condition which produced it has now come to an end. The coexistence of two worlds, one active, one passive, is everywhere disappearing or has already vanished. With enormous rapidity the transformation of history which three centuries ago began to reorient the internal direction of Western man is now reorienting the face of man throughout the world. Attitudes of despair and futility, so deeply engrained that they manifested themselves not as frustration but as indifference, have given way to a new sense of impatience, desire, hope. The revolutionary concept of a meaningful future — of social progress — has finally penetrated to those vast areas of the world which until just recently existed silently and inertly alongside the ferment of the West. And with this change in attitude toward the future, there are being brought about not only the most rapid readjustments in world events, but — with the rising up of the new continents — the very inception of historic change on a truly world scale.

The Terrible Ascent

In its ultimate implications this is perhaps the most important revolution which mankind has ever experienced. Its eventual beneficiaries number more than a billion and a half human beings who are today the *misérables* of the earth.

Yet if their awakening from an agelong slumber marks the turning of a new page for humanity, it is also the commencement of a chapter of tragedy and sorrow. For the metamorphosis from poverty into decency will be a struggle of Herculean proportions and Sisyphian discouragement. Far from leading in a gradual progression toward enlightenment and well-being, it is almost certain to result at first in increased misery, violence, and unrest.

Typically a country which is now entering the mainstream of world history displays a schizophrenic attitude toward the world. In part it nurses its bitter memories of the past; in part it reaches for the future with a naïve enthusiasm. Hopefully and under good leadership, the latter attitude may come to predominate. But corresponding to this energizing shift of mind cannot come a commensurate mobilization of resources. What hinders the advance to the new future is not, so to speak, the lack of an automobile. It is not even the lack of shoes. It is the lack of a road.

Merely to highlight this terrible absence of the wherewithal for advance, let us contrast that most basic resource — power — in India and the United States. In India, in 1953, man and beast produced 65 per cent of all the nation's economic energy, and of the remaining 35 per cent of inanimately produced power almost three-quarters was secured by the burning of dung.[8] In the United States human and animal power together accounted for but one per cent of the nation's economic energy, and the use of primitive animal fuels was zero. As a consequence, India's total electric power supply was only about one-fiftieth of America's, and, on a per-capita basis, less than half of that. The total amount of electric power generated by India would not suffice to light up New York City.

To this typical and crippling lack of power — a lack which can be duplicated in industrial requirements of every description — must be added the further

[8] Wit and Clubok, "Atomic Power Development in India," *Social Research*, Autumn, 1958, p. 290.

handicap of an absence of the institutions needed for its repair. Nothing like a "capital market" to mobilize savings exists in most underdeveloped nations. Chronic shortages of foreign exchange restrict their import programs to a minimum. And perhaps most crippling of all is a lack of adequate *human* resources: workmen who can read and who understand the rhythms of industrial production, businessmen whose attitude toward business is to produce rather than to gouge, specialists of every variety, government officials who can transcend a tradition of bureaucratic indifference and petty graft. In a word, such societies tend to lack an "economic" population. They are made up of peasants rather than farmers, laborers rather than workers, peddlers and speculators rather than managers, sinecurists rather than government administrators. To be sure, this condition of economic backwardness varies considerably from, say, Mexico, to colonial Africa. But in general outline these maladies of underdevelopment are visible and vitiating in all.

Under these conditions there is only one way in which a massive and rapid economic advance can be begun, much less carried through. It must be done from the top. When men do not know what to do, when by habit they do the wrong things, when they do not understand the signals of the market place, or when this market place does not yet exist, then men must be told what to do. Every emergent nation, in beating its way to progress, must adopt a greater or lesser degree of centralized control over its economy, and the lower down on the scale is its starting point, the greater does that degree of control tend to be.

Thus we find a degree of collectivism vigorously espoused by nearly every underdeveloped nation — sometimes, as in Pakistan or Egypt, of a nationalist military complexion; sometimes, as with India, Indonesia, Ghana, of socialist leanings. No doubt the ideological preferences of their leaders play a role in this general collectivist orientation. Their bitter past experience with *laissez faire*, their disbelief in the willingness of the capitalist West, even now, to mount a really major effort of economic assistance, their susceptibility to Marxian optimism — all these factors play their roles. Yet at bottom the appeal of collectivism is not intellectual or emotional. It is functional.

For even if the backward nations wished to develop under the aegis of capitalism, capitalism is not so easily achieved. It rests on inner motivations, inner disciplines, on learned habits of economic "rationality" which cannot be inculcated into a peasant population overnight. In England it took generations before the uprooted yeomanry stopped burning down the factories they despised. In Prussia, Frederick the Great used to complain that his merchants were so timid and unventuresome that he had to drag them to their profits "by their noses and ears." Thus capitalism must grow up slowly, out of the experience of generations — and it is even doubtful in today's world if it would grow at all. Certainly it cannot be imposed, full-blown. But collectivism can. Peasants, moneylenders, petty bureaucrats can be told — ordered — to do what must be done. As a means of beginning the huge transformation of a society, an economic authoritarian command has every advantage over the incentives of enterprise.

Hence the very least that one can expect of the new economies is a powerful and prominent degree of central direction and control within a "free enterprise" milieu. But the logic of events does not stop with this arrangement. On the contrary, in the setting of underdevelopment, powerful forces are likely to press "mixed economies" in the direction of political and economic extremes.

For the enthusiasm of the initial awakening of a people soon outruns the reality of its sluggish progress. No matter how heroic the efforts of its regime, no underdeveloped nation can hope to make headway quickly. Indeed the fearsome possibility is that at first its condition may deteriorate. The early stages of the new industrialization will only add to the social dislocation which began under colonialism. The initial heavy investments will weigh upon rather than uplift the general population. Not least, the pressures of population growth, which are the main enemy of progress in nearly every underdeveloped land, will grow worse as broad health and sanitation measures take effect.

Thus the road to progress may well be more terrible than the roadless and mindless existence of the past. Nevertheless, once the great march has begun, it is no longer possible to turn back. The changes in the balance of the old static society cannot be undone. There is no choice but to tread the road to its conclusion — however long and agonizing the journey may be.

We need only think of the seventy-five to one hundred years which elapsed in Europe before industrialism began to make known its benefits, to understand the dismal prospect which stretches before every peasant nation, scratching its way up the cliff with its fingernails. In most of Asia, for example, the per-capita standard of living of the population is represented as "less than $100 a year." This is a standard which in fact defies numerical treatment: it means existence at the borderline of animal needs. If the pace of economic growth in Asia now continues at about its present rate, and if the Asiatic nations begin to control their population floods, it is possible that these per-capita "standards" may be boosted by 2 per cent a year. The peasants and city masses of the East can therefore look forward to the prospect that by the year 2000 their incomes may have reached a level of $200 a year. This is well below the level now "enjoyed" by a Portuguese peasant or by a farmer in the poverty-stricken lands of southern Italy. After forty years of immense labors, the result will still be abysmal poverty.

Thus economic development, in its agonizing slow pace, will not give rise to a glad acquiescence in the future and a sense of relief that progress is now on the march. On the contrary, every step forward is apt to worsen the mood of disaffection, to stir the fires of impatience. Economic development in its early stages is not a process of alleviating discontent. Initially it is the cause of deepening it.

The "Leap into Freedom"

Needless to say, all this lends a dark color to the outlook for a mild economic transition. High hopes, once aroused, are not so easily retired, and a government which does not satisfy the aspirations on which it rides into power will soon give way to another which will promise to do more.

This leads to two likely prospects. The first is the rise of authoritarian regimes in the underdeveloped nations. For the capacity for action of parliamentary governments is apt to prove inadequate to the heroic demands of rapid development. Parliamentary governments, even in those rare cases where they do not merely represent the privileged classes of peasant nations, naturally act to *slow down* the pace of social change by seeking to accommodate minority interests — a function which may be highly desirable once a level of tolerable social satisfaction has been reached, but hardly one which is apt to commend itself to a newly aroused and highly dissatisfied people.

Even in Western governments, built upon fairly stable social foundations, we have seen how vulnerable and weak are parliamentary regimes in times of stress, unless they produce their own "strong men" — as witness the cases of pre-Mussolini Italy and pre-Hitler Germany, of republican Spain and postwar France. Among the underdeveloped nations, bereft of any tradition of democratic compromise and cohesion, this tendency is a thousandfold multiplied. Thus we find the emergence of the soldier-ruler: in Pakistan, in Egypt, in China, in Burma, in Taiwan, in the succession of Latin-American junta governments. And while this array clearly reveals that not every authoritarian government is itself an agency for economic transformation, it stands to reason that, with the added stresses and strains of rapid development, the "attractions" of authority are made all the greater.

But the second prospect is even more sobering. It is the likelihood that the predominant authoritarianism will veer increasingly to the extreme Left.

For in their situations of genuine frustration, one lesson will not be lost upon the underdeveloped nations. This is the fact that two peasant countries in the twentieth century have succeeded in making the convulsive total social effort which alone seems capable of breaking through the thousand barriers of scarcity, ineptitude, indifference, inertia. These are the Soviet Union and now, even more impressively, China. It might be objected that the underdeveloped nations could also fasten their gaze on other nations, such as Western Germany or Japan, which have also recently shown startling rates of growth. But these are nations with their initial industrial "transformations" behind them. They began where the underdeveloped regions now seek to arrive. Russia to a considerable degree and China even more unmistakably began at scratch.

We are only beginning to appreciate the magnitude of the Chinese effort. Until recently we have been so repelled by the severity of the Chinese communist methods, with their Spartan communes, that we have overlooked what is the most significant fact about these methods. This is the attainment of what seems to be by far the largest rate of economic growth ever achieved by any peasant nation. According to the best estimates we now have (which discount China's own extravagant claims), China's per-capita output has been growing since 1952 at a rate of over 6 per cent a year.[9] This is a pace of advance which is between *double* and *triple* the rate of growth thus far achieved by India under non-collectivist conditions.

Meanwhile an equally startling performance has been evinced by the Soviet Union. Until the present decade of world history, the generally accepted para-

[9] A. Doak Barnett, *Communist Economic Strategy: The Rise of Mainland China* (National Planning Association, 1959), table 2. See also William V. Hollister, *Chinese Gross National Product and Social Accounts, 1950–1957* (Illinois, 1958); and Wilfred Malenbaum, "India and China: Contrasts in Development Performance," *American Economic Review,* June, 1959.

gon of economic progress was the United States. This is no longer true. Mr. Allen W. Dulles, comparing our performance with the Soviets, has noted:

Whereas Soviet gross national product was about 35 per cent of that of the United States in 1950 . . . by 1962 it may be about 50 per cent of our own. This means that the Soviet economy has been growing and is expected to grow through 1962 at a rate roughly twice that of the economy of the United States.[10]

To be sure, what strikes us in considering both instances of economic growth is the immense human price which has been paid for material progress. Russia's social agonies of development — the use of forced labor, the mass executions, the bludgeoning of the peasant into collectives and the Stakhanovist methods of securing industrial discipline — all these are well known. In the case of China, the human cost is even more nakedly revealed in the use of human labor as "capital." Essentially China has achieved its startling increases in output — in the case of food, a tripling of crops since 1949; in the case of steel, a sevenfold increase in the same period — by massively applying organized human effort in the same fashion and with the same huge end results as the Pharaohs used in constructing the pyramids.

Yet what seems to us to be a fearful exaction in terms of human suffering, political outrage, and slave labor conditions may not appear so intolerable to peoples who have always suffered, never known political freedom, and labored all their lives and all their histories as serfs. Human "price" is, after all, a matter of alternatives, and in the eyes of the underdeveloped peoples the alternatives do not allow for nice calculations of "comfort" and "austerity." Rather the choice is between a violent and often frightfully costly effort for a generation or two in the hope of freeing future generations from the yoke, or the patient endurance of a now bitterly resented misery for many generations while a more humane, but far slower, transformation is achieved.

There is no blinking the arduousness of this choice. Even existence at the very margin of life can be worsened by the extreme efforts of an all-out development drive, for people at the margin of existence can be driven over that margin into premature death. But this hideous price must be weighed against a continuation of the present state of affairs. In this truly anguishing choice, our own preferences for gradualism may well reflect nothing but our inability to appreciate the intolerable condition of life as it now exists in much of the world. Looking at the alternatives from below rather than from above, it is understandable that it may not be the *price* but the *promise* of rapid advance which exerts the more powerful sway. As the late John Foster Dulles has written: "We can talk eloquently about liberty and freedom, and about human rights and individual freedoms, and about the dignity and worth of the human personality, but most of our vocabulary derives from a period when our own society was individualistic. Consequently it has little meaning to those who live under conditions where individualism means early death."[11]

It would be both foolish and dangerous to maintain that all underdeveloped countries "must" sooner or later succumb to a rigorous communist collectivism

[10] *New York Times*, April 29, 1958.
[11] *War or Peace* (New York, 1950), p. 257.

in order to effect a major economic advance. Between one backward nation and another there are vast differences in needs, resolves, resources. One cannot easily generalize over a spectrum that includes such different cases as Brazil and Burma, Libya and Turkey. In many of the backward nations the critical determining factor may be the "historic force" of a commanding, but democratic and gradualist figure, such as a Nehru or a Muñoz Marin.

But honesty compels us to admit that Nehrus and Muñoz Marins are rare and still more rarely succeed one another, and that behind striking national differences is a common desire for advance which, once fanned, grows hotter and more impatient. Taking the long perspective of the decades ahead, it is difficult to ignore the relative "efficiency" of authoritarian over parliamentary regimes as a means of inaugurating growth, or the truly remarkable growth rates which, thus far at least, have only been attainable under the radical social reorganization of communist collectivism. Nor can one ignore the fact that property relations, as they now exist in many underdeveloped nations, often serve to impede the needed mobilization of resources even more than they facilitate it; and that the direction in which property institutions guide new capital may not be that which is most critically required for the future. All these facts must inevitably exert their gravitational pull on the course of events, and when we weigh their relative attractive powers it seems hard to doubt in which direction the compass needle of development will tend to sway.[12]

But it is not enough to come to a halt with this prospect for communism's expansion among the backward nations. In terms of anticipating the trends of world history, what is even more important for us to realize is that individual economic improvement, even at best, is not likely to come fast enough to satisfy the aspirations of the people. For in every underdeveloped nation, economic growth — with the exception of an increase in foodstuffs — is, at first, essentially a process of accumulating capital goods under forced draft, or alleviating as quickly as possible the crippling capital scarcity of the past. This necessarily means that the pace of *tangible* advance in the living standards of the masses is very slow, and nearly as imperceptible in communist nations with huge growth rates as in "mixed-economy" nations with smaller rates. Dams, reservoirs, roads, education, steel mills — all the basic necessities for advance — cannot be consumed, do not replace ragged clothes and hovels.

In this situation even the most sincerely motivated and efficient government is apt to find itself with an impatient and dissatisfied populace. Thus despite — or worse, because of — their all-out economic and social effort, fast-growing but still impoverished economies are likely to be impelled to seek incentives other than the self-sustaining impetus of economic improvement. These incentives may take the form of sheer compulsion, as has been the case in the communist states. But there is as well another means of mobilizing the stamina and morale needed to sustain the great ascent. This is the conscious direction of aspirations *away* from material ends, toward glory, conquest, or faith In a word, it is the employment of a fierce and often bellicose nationalism as a compensation for the inevitable disappointments of the early stages of economic growth.

[12] See also Sidney Hook, "Grim Report: Asia in Transition," *New York Times Magazine*, April 5, 1959.

We have seen the development of such a nationalism in virtually every nation which has begun the steep economic climb. In China as well as in Russia there has been recourse not only to a deliberately stimulated patriotism, but to the encouragement of smoldering grudges against colonialism and capitalism. In dictatorships of a more rightist leaning, such as Egypt, nationalistic incentives and diversions of a still cruder nature have been used: the reawakening of ancient loyalties and racialisms, the fanning of atavistic military and religious ambitions, the appeal, as in the days of heroic history, to the memories of the past.

It is probable that a degree of inflamed nationalism is an inseparable concomitant of forced economic development. The unfortunate result is that an era which could be a prelude to building for a great future runs the grave risk of becoming instead a period of heightened tensions and increased chances for the destruction even of present frail standards. The spread of high aspirations to the peoples whose conditions are now the least human on earth is a great and irreversible drama of our times, but during our lifetimes the drama promises to be as tragic as it may ultimately be ennobling.

What is likely to be the full impact on America of this challenge of economic development is a matter to which we shall return in our next chapter. But at this point, while we are reflecting on the nature of the history which is closing in upon and constricting our traditional optimistic plans, it may be useful to take one last view of the problem. For it is certain that the transition ahead will be ugly, and that the latent susceptibility to unrest and to political and economic extremism within the developing countries will exert tremendous and disturbing pressures on ourselves. What we would do well to remember in our consequent concern and likely irritation is that for many generations these submerged populations of the world suffered the impact of a Western dynamism whose purposes they did not understand and whose disruptions they could not control. Now they return their blows upon the West just as incomprehensibly and with just as staggering force. This is indeed a time of great trial for the West. But we must bear in mind that what is a closing-in of history for us, is an opening-out of history for most of the peoples of the world.

The Drift Away from Capitalism

Heretofore we have been concerned with the historic consequences of two great currents of world development: that of science in general and the atomic weaponry in particular, and that of the spread of popular aspirations, as it manifests itself in the revolutionary upthrust of the underdeveloped world. Now we must turn to a third current of world change which, as we shall see, derives much of its internal momentum from the trends we have already discussed. This third current is a basic change in the economic orientation of the world — a change we have already noted in the backward nations but which we can now deal with in generalized terms as affecting the advanced nations no less. It can be described as the collectivization of twentieth-century economic life.

Once again, however, it is well for us to approach this current of history in the concrete guise by which it makes itself visible and meaningful to us. And this immediate guise can be very simply stated. It is this: over the larger part of our history, we have faced a future in which our own form of economic organization, capitalism, was the triumphant and dominant form of economic and social organization in the world. This is no longer true. Today and over the foreseeable future, traditional capitalism throughout most of the world has been thrown on a defensive from which it is doubtful that it can ever recover. As a capitalist nation we are no longer riding with the global tides of economic evolution, but against them.

This is a transformation of contemporary history which is at one and the same time an indisputable reality of the recent past and a bitterly contested prospect for the future. Of all the transformations affecting the lineaments of the future, it is the one toward which we feel the greatest resistance and the least willingness to set ourselves at an intellectual remove. The result is that a trend of history which should be the object of dispassionate study and understanding, and which is of the greatest moment for our survival, becomes either ignored or seriously misinterpreted.

Let us begin by very briefly documenting the history of the transformation itself.

The nineteenth and early twentieth centuries, as we know, were the era of capitalist growth. Within a century of its first full bloom in the Industrial Revolution, capitalism had reached out to become the commanding economic structure of the Western world. Most of Europe, North America, Scandinavia, even the Antipodes, became market-oriented, profit-stimulated, industrially based economies. In all of them the acknowledged leadership of the social order was vested in the business world, whose purposes, values, and methods were broadly similar from one nation to the next. Meanwhile, as we have already seen, these countries in turn exerted their influence over a vast portion of the non-capitalist world — that is, over its unindustrialized areas. In the last thirty years of the nineteenth century alone, Britain, France, and Germany acquired domain over 125 million people and nine million square miles of territory.

By 1913 the conquest of capitalism appeared complete. It had either displaced, or was fast crowding out, the previous feudal economies. No other competitor of any degree of power even remotely appeared to challenge its pre-eminence. It is some testimony to the solidity of the capitalist system that until 1917 no major government in the world had ever been headed by a Labor Party, much less by a socialist regime of any description.

Yet this genuinely impressive accomplishment was now succeeded by a still more astonishing denouement. For the progressive success of capitalism over ten generations was to be undermined in less than two. In 1913 socialism was still the economic utopia of a dissident minority movement, without either the respectability of official government power, or the possession, however disreputable, of de facto power. Forty years later, in various guises, socialism as an economic reality had swept around the world. The Sino-Soviet enclave alone embraced a population twice as large as the whole capitalist world of 1913. Among the new nations emerging from the rapid break-up of the colonial portion of that world, virtually all bore the stamp of socialist orientation. More significant yet, within the erstwhile citadel of capitalism, nation after nation had defected from the ranks of orthodoxy. By 1959, in Australia, Belgium, Denmark, France, Germany, Iceland, Italy, Netherlands, New Zealand, Norway, Sweden, and the United Kingdom — all staunchly capitalist governments in 1913 — a so-called "Socialist" administration had at least once come into power; and in most of these nations it was either still in power or now headed the party of the Opposition. That this was a very different kind of "socialism" from the communist organization of society in the East was, of course, apparent. And yet even more than the spread of militant communism and of anticolonial revolutions, it was symptomatic of a basic and fundamental swing in the world's economic orientation. For it made apparent that *within* the capitalist powers themselves, the unquestioned supremacy of the old capitalist ideologies had been challenged by a new set of guiding ideas.

FURTHER READING FOR SECTION 2

Cox, Harvey. *The Secular City*. New York: Macmillan, 1966.

This theologican sees in the new mass urban technological society not the demise of an older and greater civilization but a vision of a greatly expanded and emancipated life.

Frankel, Charles. *The Democratic Prospect*. New York: Harper & Row, 1962. (Now available in a Colophon paperback edition.)

An assessment of the future of democracy in the light of some rather ominous social and economic developments. The volume is an antidote to the simplistic interpretations of the nature of the democratic state common in elementary and secondary school textbooks and in the writing of a number of professional educators.

Galbraith, John K. *The New Industrial State*. Boston: Houghton Mifflin, 1967.

A recent analysis of changes in the American economic system which has far-ranging implications for public — including educational — policies.

Heilbroner, Robert S. *The Future as History*. New York: Harper & Row, 1960.

Beginning with an analysis of historical forces which have shaped our expectations, Heilbroner proceeds to examine the challenges of the future. He finds that in many instances Americans do not, or are not willing to, recognize the significance of economic and political change.

Kornhauser, William. *The Politics of Mass Society*. New York: The Free Press, 1959.

A meticulous treatment of the empirical literature on the nature of contemporary society, vast in scope, and remarkably clear in presentation. Among other issues, he discusses the changing nature of voluntary organizations, and the problems of the "organization man," urbanization, and political alienation.

Miller, Arthur S. *Private Governments and Constitution*, an occasional paper published by the Center for the Study of Democratic Institutions, Santa Barbara, Calif., 1959.

This paper argues that the concentration of private power, political and economic, rivals, and in some instances exceeds, the power of the federal government itself. Miller challenges some of the more primitive views of modern politics and economics which are frequently expressed in curriculum guides published by school systems and state departments of education. The Center for the Study of Democratic Institutions also publishes other papers which express a diversity of opinion on the nature of contemporary society.

3

History and the Social Studies

It is common for social studies educators to speak as though the social sciences and history have equal status in the school program. However, if one looks at the course offerings required of all students, history continues to be predominant. Two years of American history, a year of world history, and from a semester to a year of local and state history are usually included in the required course of study from the seventh through the twelfth grades. In contrast, the various social sciences have a limited place in the curriculum. A semester or a year-long course in descriptive geography is often included at the junior high level; a civics course commonly taught in the ninth grade usually provides cursory contact with simplified political science in the form of topics such as "how a bill goes through Congress"; and problems of democracy courses commonly offered in the twelfth grade are supposed to rely on the social sciences, especially economics, sociology, and political science, to provide data for "understanding" public issues. In addition, the high school may offer elective social science courses outside the general education program.

The continued meager treatment may account in part for the emphasis on the social sciences in recent government- and foundation-sponsored curricular projects. The products of these projects may have a noticeable impact on social studies offerings in the near future. Certainly, as the products of the various curricular projects compete for time in the school program, the social studies teacher will be caught in the midst of controversy over priorities. Much of the debate will take place on the district level, as school systems wrestle with the problem of deciding what should be the over-all organization of their social studies programs. However, the individual teacher will face comparable problems if he attempts to decide expressly upon the orientation to be taken and the content to be relied upon in his courses. These decisions concerning the relative emphasis to be given history and the social sciences in the social studies curriculum should be based on a careful examination and analysis of the contributions each has to make to general education in a democracy.

As is often the case with confrontations between those who are strongly committed to their positions, arguments over the place of the social sciences and history in the curriculum tend to be cast in dichotomous terms — history versus the social sciences. The issues are, of course, not that simple. But the role assigned history and the social sciences in the curriculum will depend to a large extent upon the person's conception of each. The readings in this section and the next are intended to assist the reader in analyzing this important aspect of a rationale for decisions regarding the social studies curriculum.

One of the major issues in the social sciences vs. history debate revolves around the question of the nature of historical knowledge. Is it *objective*,

165

scientific knowledge? There are sound reasons for thinking that history is as scientific as the social sciences. Historians use systematic techniques of research in exploring the past; they also appear to have the same commitment to the tentativity of knowledge as do social scientists. Some historians are now using quantitative techniques usually associated with behavioral science. It has even been contended that history is the *queen of the social sciences* because, the argument runs, the historian synthesizes social science theory and data in re-creating the past. Yet many historians reject this characterization and feel a stronger identification with the humanities than with the social sciences. Indeed, there is sometimes a violent rejection of the canons of social science by historians, and an equally strong rejection by social scientists of historical data and methods.

It is commonly argued that history cannot be a social science because the historian cannot experiment, that is, control and manipulate variables, in his investigations. However, much social science research is not experimental. For example, the anthropologist and political scientist are rarely in a position to control variables (except statistically), and sociologists and psychologists carrying out longitudinal studies — as of juvenile delinquents, to cite a specific example — cannot experiment in the usual sense of the word.

Perhaps a more plausible explanation for the gulf between social scientists and historians lies in their differing attitudes toward reporting their findings. The historian sees written history as a literary presentation of descriptions, conclusions drawn from the data, and speculative generalizations. The dramatic narrative is a valued tradition in history. On the other hand, the social scientist normally avoids artistic recreation of his findings. Generally, he deliberately depersonalizes the reporting of his search for general explanations, relationships, and laws based on empirical investigation. When the social scientist chooses to use more connotative or expressive language in order to make the findings of his field palatable for general consumption, there is usually little doubt among his colleagues that he has abandoned his role as scientist. This leads to the often justifiable criticism that much social science writing is dreadfully dull, unnecessarily abstruse, and filled with jargon.

The historians' emphasis on literary expression does carry with it a host of hazards in establishing and communicating reliable knowledge. This, coupled with research problems unique to the investigation of the past, undoubtedly raises legitimate questions about the relative objectivity of historical knowledge. The readings in this section explore these questions. Though the immediate concern is with history, not with the social sciences, the two topics cannot be neatly separated. Teachers will be increasingly faced with arguments about the similarities and differences between historical and social science knowledge and the role each should play in the curriculum. The following selections have implications not only for one's conception of the nature of history, but for the validity of drawing distinctions between social science and history in the social studies curriculum.

Of what benefit might the study of history be in the schools? In the first reading in this section, Ray Allen Billington, Professor of History at Northwestern University, provides one historian's answer. This discussion of the value of studying American history was first published in *The Case for Basic Education,* edited by James Koerner. The book was intended to "define the nature and the need of education in certain basic subjects [including history], and to describe what grasp of these subjects a good student should have as he emerges from twelve years of public schooling."[1] *Good students* to Koerner are not only those in the top 20 per cent of the class. To the contrary, he has estimated that perhaps as many as 60 or 70 per cent of an "average" student-body could "profit from a solid curriculum,"[2] i.e., one based on "basic" academic subjects.

Billington has high hopes for the impact of history in the curriculum, and his views should not be dismissed lightly. In evaluating his claims, however, it is important to reflect on the nature of historical knowledge. Several of the readings following the one by Billington raise questions about the end product of the historian's studies. The reader should keep one question clearly in mind: If historical interpretation is as dependent upon the idiosyncracies of the man in his time as some writers (e.g., Becker in his selection) claim, is this not an argument for reducing the importance of history in the general education curriculum, if not for eliminating it completely?

The intial probe into the nature of historical knowledge is by C. Vann Woodward, Professor of History at Yale University, who briefly chronicles recent changes in historical interpretation. His article lays a framework for the following selections examining the nature of historical knowledge. The reader will find it difficult to check the validity of Woodward's claims about shifting emphases in history. However, the prospective or practicing social studies teacher may find it informative to re-read a few secondary school history textbooks to determine whether they reflect these recent shifts in interpretation. In fact, it might be helpful to inquire whether the texts even imply that history is under constant reinterpretation.

Following Woodward, Carl Becker asks the question, What is a historical fact? Becker, who was an esteemed historian and philosopher of history, wrote this essay in 1926, and it remains one of the more provocative statements on the nature of historical knowledge. Becker's treatment is much broader than the title indicates, for he maintains that *stating* historical facts cannot be separated from the *process of historical interpretation*. His view of the prospects for objectivity in history raises issues of special importance to the social studies curriculum, and the implications should be considered carefully, especially by those fond of asserting that "the facts speak for themselves."

Several issues related to historical synthesis are discussed next by Thomas C. Cochran, Professor of History at New York University. He criticizes the emphasis on the nation and, in particular, the succession of presidents, in historians' attempts to provide synthesis and structure in their writings about United States history. Cochran goes beyond criticism to suggest some difficulties in arriving at a new synthesis. In this context, he also notes the historian's general failure to utilize the social sciences as a source of data and theory.

To this point, the readings have suggested the difficulties of freeing historical scholarship from the biases of the writer, and of obtaining sufficient data to support the historian's generalizations and explanations. Ernest Nagel is not,

[1] James Koerner (ed.), *The Case for Basic Education* (Boston: Little, Brown, 1959), p. vii.
[2] *Ibid.*, pp. xi–xii.

however, pessimistic about the possibility of objectivity in history. A Professor of Philosophy at Columbia University who is well-known for his logical analyses of the scientific endeavor, Nagel considers several obstacles to historical objectivity. In doing so, he compares historical study to social science investigation and concludes that reasonably grounded explanations are not precluded by the historian's personal values or his position in a social milieu.

The reader must resolve for himself the vexing question of historical objectivity *vis à vis* history's place in the social studies. Arthur S. Bolster, Professor at the Harvard Graduate School of Education and also a long-time high school history teacher, attacks this question by comparing the claims made by historians for the value of history in the curriculum to their views of the usefulness of historical knowledge for understanding the present and predicting the future. Bolster, in analyzing the inadequacies of the curricular recommendations commonly made by historians, argues convincingly for the importance of explicitly formulated criteria to guide the selection of content and method.

The next two readings provide a critical appraisal of history textbooks. For, if there are difficulties in establishing historical truth, they are compounded many times in the process of distilling and compressing historians' findings into a textbook. Lawrence Metcalf, Professor of Education at the University of Illinois, treats briefly the problems created as history textbook authors are forced, as the years go by, to fit more and more into the same number of pages. His concern is with the superficial and inaccurate notions of explanation that students may acquire. Harold J. Noah, Carl E. Prince, and C. Russell Riggs deal more specifically with some of the historical accounts and explanations contained in textbooks. Their analysis, while particularly enlightening in the context of the preceding readings in this section, will not be comforting to those who would like to rely on textbooks as embodiments of historical truths to be learned by students.

Given the problems in historical knowledge and the common deficiencies in history books, what does the teacher do when faced with a history course to be taught using the textbook provided by the school district? Of course, there is no single answer to the question. Attempting to use original documents is one possible solution, and some history curriculum projects are predicated on the assumption that this approach will involve students in the process of historical inquiry. Materials are, however, no substitute for a probing student-teacher dialogue — although they may facilitate it.

What kinds of questions does one ask in leading students to probe behind textbook statements? The purpose of the concluding reading in this section is to provide exemplars that might be helpful in visualizing teaching alternatives. Written by Allan Griffin, who was for many years before his death an inspirational teacher at The Ohio State University, the excerpt suggests how the teacher might approach the task of getting students to formulate and test hypotheses, thus avoiding the usual emphasis on mere retention of data and generalizations. Involvement in the hypothesis-testing process suggested by Griffin might bring students to see historical statements in a new light and help them to comprehend some of the difficulties in establishing reliable historical knowledge.

It should be noted that this last selection presumes that history will continue to be a focus of teaching in the social studies. Griffin's examples are interesting and compelling, but they do not speak directly to the important questions about the nature of historical knowledge and the place of history in the general education program. Criteria for the selection of content, the time to be allotted history in the school program, and the relationship of history to the social sciences remain central issues in the attempt to build a rationale for social studies instruction.

The Case for American History

Ray Allen Billington

American history is to the people of the United States what memory is to an individual; with no knowledge of their past they would suffer from collective amnesia, groping blindly into the future without guideposts of precedence to shape their course. Only a thorough awareness of their heritage allows citizens to make their public decisions as they make their private ones: by reflecting on previous events rather than embarking on a plan of action that will carry them toward an unknown destination. A person without that understanding is "lost" in the same sense that a hunter may be lost in a deep forest; he knows where he is, but he does not know the relationship of the spot he occupies to the more familiar world he seeks. He is lost because he does not know the direction from which he came. Similarly Americans without a knowledge of their past are lost in the dimension of time. They are as powerless as the hunter to make decisions that will lead them toward safety. History is a compass that guides man into the future, and when the future is as troubled as that beyond our present horizons, such a compass is badly needed.[1]

From *The Case for Basic Education*, James D. Koerner (editor), by permission of Atlantic-Little, Brown and Co. Copyright, © 1959, by Council for Basic Education. Pp. 27–48.

[1] For aid in preparing this paper I am indebted to a number of American historians who were generous enough to respond to a form letter sent them during the summer of 1958. Some — notably W. T. Hutchinson of the University of Chicago, William Catton of Princeton University, Robert Miller of the University of North Carolina, Thomas Bonner of the University of Omaha, Irvin G. Wyllie of the University of Wisconsin, and Arthur Bestor of the University of Illinois — provided me with such extended and thoughtful answers to the questions under discussion that little remained for me to provide but a synthesis of their remarks. Others whose comments were scarcely less helpful were: O. Fritiof Ander of Augustana College, Lewis Atherton of the University of Missouri, Charles Barker of Johns Hopkins University, Nelson Blake of Syracuse University, John Blum of Yale University, Harold Briggs of Southern Illinois University, S. H. Brockunier of Wesleyan University, Ira V. Brown of Pennsylvania State University, John C. Caughey of the University of California at Los Angeles, Thomas C. Cochran of the University of Pennsylvania, Edwin C. Coddington of Lafayette College, Foster Rhea Dulles of Ohio State University, Brainerd Dyer of the University of California at Los Angeles, Gilbert Fite of the University of Oklahoma, Allen R. Foley of Dartmouth College, Bert J. Loewenberg of Sarah Lawrence College, Rayford Logan of Howard University, Rodman Paul of California Institute of Technology, Stow Persons of the University of Iowa, Carlton Qualey of Carlton College, Edwin C. Rozwenc of Amherst

I

The study of American history in our secondary schools will help train men and women capable of charting the nation's future course, just as it will enrich their lives and add immeasurably to their enjoyment in later years. It will do so by developing in today's youths valuable thought habits that will endure throughout their lifetimes, and by equipping them with the special knowledge needed to function as knowledgeable citizens of the Republic. As a mental discipline the study of American history (1) trains students in analytical and objective thinking, (2) broadens their horizons by adding the time dimension, and (3) introduces them to a knowledge of a variety of academic subjects that expand their vistas and increase their social usefulness.

That the study of history serves as a medium for cultivating valuable intellectual attitudes is obvious. The historical method as a mental discipline is useful far beyond the field of history, even for secondary school students. Through the study of the past they learn that human affairs can never be simple — that there are no pat heroes and villains, no "bads" and "goods," no simple cause and effect relationships, in human behavior. They realize instead that the social process is one of enormous complexity, and that man's conduct is often not only unpredictable but inexplicable. Once understood, this basic truth serves as a warning against precipitous conclusions on all subjects that defy superficial analysis. If a student emerges from his schooling with an awareness of history's underlying complexity, he will realize that large issues of all sorts seldom have a "right" or "wrong" answer, but must be appraised objectively in historical perspective. Such a lesson can be taught by the study of any subject dealing with society, but through none so effectively as American history. Already vaguely familiar to the high school student, the subject lends itself to secondary school instruction more readily than the other behavioral disciplines. And history, beyond all other subjects dealing with man's social behavior, stresses the need for objectivity in formulating judgments, the careful weighing of evidence, and the necessity for searching analysis before a final decision is reached. These are valuable mental traits in any situation.

No less important for the future functioning of knowledgeable citizens is the broadening influence of historical studies on the intellect. Most people live in a two-dimensional world as far as time is concerned; they are aware of the present and concerned with the future. To this the study of history adds a third dimension — that of time — that is essential for rational and objective thinking. Only an appreciation of the long view — of the historical dimension — allows mankind to think in depth. Only the study of past epochs and an understanding of their relationship to today's events brings the present into proper focus. American history is especially valuable in this respect, partly because it is easily comprehended by the student, but more because it provides an excellent laboratory for the analysis of a complex social evolution; the history of the United States proves that diverse peoples living in differing environments have

College, Charles Sellers of the University of California, James L. Sellers of the University of Nebraska, Donald Sheehan of Smith College, Wendell Stephenson of the University of Oregon, Richard Storr of the University of Chicago, Oscar O. Winther of Indiana University, and Harvey Wish of Western Reserve University.

been capable of producing one of the world's most effective industrialized societies without sacrificing individual liberty on the altar of efficiency. By grasping this story the student will be made aware of the infinite possibilities of the human experience, and will realize that society is, as it always has been, in a constant state of flux. He will also recognize the limitations of his own experience, and should achieve the humility that comes only with awareness of the complexity of mankind's behavior.

The study of history is not only an antidote to superficial thinking; it is also a successful introduction to other areas of learning. Occupying as it does an intermediate position between the humanities and the "social sciences," and employing both the qualitative approach of the humanist and the quantitative data of the behavioralist, it serves as a medium through which students can learn something of literature and the arts on the one hand, and politics, economics, and social behavior on the other. This is especially important because evidence indicates that American history is a "natural" course for students of high school age, appealing through its narrative presentation. College teachers report that students subjected to the "social studies" courses that have been substituted for historical studies in some schools develop lasting antipathies that lead them to avoid the further study not only of history but of economics and political science as well. Those trained in basic history courses show no such prejudices.

In the fostering of valuable mental attitudes, no substitutes concocted by the professional educationist have proven effective. The "social studies" course that he has fashioned from snippets of economics, political science, sociology, and history seeks to train good citizens by the group discussion of current topics, usually after only a hasty reading in contemporary documents and a still more hurried examination of precedents. This is both dangerous and unsound. It is dangerous because students are misled into believing that the problems they will face in later life can be solved by mere discussion or by consultation with others as ill-informed as they, without recourse to solid knowledge, logical analysis, or reliance on past experience. It is unsound because it is based on the assumption that knowledge should be acquired only incidentally as a means to a practical end; because it encourages the false belief that any modern problem can be comprehended without thorough familiarity with the long chain of historical events responsible for that problem; and because it encourages superficial thought and the formulation of snap judgments that are often false. The arrogance generated by the belief that logic alone can solve all the problems of human behavior hardly equips today's youth for the decision-making they will face in the future.

Historical studies, on the other hand, present students with a series of problems that must be solved by the careful sifting of evidence, the application of objective judgments, and the disinterested analysis of data. At the same time they provide those students with information that will allow them to formulate opinions on the basis of experience rather than prejudice. Who, for example, can comprehend the complexities of today's struggle over integration without familiarity with the history of slavery in the United States, the sectional conflicts of the 1830's and 1840's, the disruptive impact of the Kansas-Nebraska Act and the Dred Scott decision of the 1850's, the bloody horrors of civil war, the turmoil of reconstruction, and the reshuffling of the South's social order that occurred during the postwar era of industrialization? Equally important, the study of historical problems allows the student to test his conclusions against the actual solutions achieved by prior generations. More often than not he is able to see that his own judgments are wrong. Thus he is freed of the dangerous belief that solutions are easily achieved, or that the knowledge necessary for their resolution can be acquired without intensive effort. In a world where no one is omnipotent these are valuable attributes of the mind.

The tragic influence of these "social studies" courses, and of the poor or inadequate training in American history all too common in today's secondary schools, was revealed during the Korean War. Thousands of prisoners, subjected to modern psychological pressures by their Chinese Communist captors, failed to resist, partly because they had not the most rudimentary knowledge of their own governmental system or the democratic foundations on which it rests. One of their interrogators, a Chinese psychologist, penned an unanswerable argument for the study of American history when he wrote: "The American soldier has weak loyalties: to his family, his community, his country, his religion, and to his fellow soldier. . . . He is ignorant of social values, social conflicts, and tensions. There is little or no knowledge or understanding, even among American university graduates, of U.S. political history and philosophy; the federal, state, and community organizations; states and civil rights, freedoms, safeguards, and how these allegedly operate within his own decadent system."[2]

II

American history is more than invaluable mental exercise; it is a vitally necessary subject in the training of effective citizens for the Republic. Its role in this respect is fivefold: (1) It develops a sense of perspective that allows more intelligent political decision-making; (2) it creates a sense of identity with the past that deepens national loyalties; (3) it provides citizens with the practical knowledge necessary to function intelligently at the polls; (4) it endows them with a love for learning that continues to operate long after the schooling experience is over; and (5) it equips them with the information and tolerance necessary in a day when policy-making can no longer be viewed solely in national terms.

That the study of history endows its disciples with a valuable sense of perspective there can be no doubt. Familiarity with the past, covering as it does a long period of time and revealing a broad view of human nature, expands man's vistas, deepens his sympathies, and erases self-pity by showing him that his own generation is not alone in facing complex problems or challenging crises. By familiarizing us with past instances of heroism and past examples of wise leadership, history ennobles us, and quickens our faith in our heritage. By revealing the deficiencies of statesmen of former generations, it inclines us to be more tolerant toward the mistakes of today's leaders. By laying bare the record of man's slow struggle for liberty and security it convinces us of the inevitability

2 Quoted in Thomas N. Bonner, "Sputniks and the Educational Crisis in America," *Journal of Higher Education*, XXIX (April, 1958), 181.

of progress toward those goals, and inures us to the momentary setbacks caused by the rise of totalitarian systems. No one truly familiar with the history of the United States can adopt a defeatist attitude when facing the continuing crises of the Cold War, or surrender to doubt that democratic institutions will prevail. Only the study of history engenders such faith, and assures such hope for the future.

No less essential is the sense of identity with the past that is bred into any people by the study of its own history. This does not mean that schools should teach the Parson Weems style of superpatriotism. It does mean that the story of our heritage can foster in today's youth a fairly sophisticated understanding of the developments that have provided us with institutions, characteristics, and habits recognizably different from those of other peoples of the world. It does mean that the acquisition of this understanding will provide us and future generations with knowledge for the formulation of judgments essential to international understanding in the "one world" of the future. For until we understand ourselves, our own strength and weakness, our own virtues and defects, we can neither behave rationally toward other nations nor foster the deep-rooted loyalty to our country that will endow that behavior with forceful meaning. This sense of identity is especially important in a land fashioned from many regions and peopled by many races. Only by familiarizing ourselves with the many strands that have been woven into the warp and woof of American civilization can we cope with the domestic problems that disturb our peace and the international problems that threaten our existence.

In practical application, familiarity with the national heritage is essential to the continued success of the American Republic. A nation with democratic institutions *must* produce a reasonably educated citizenry if those institutions are to survive. Democracy is comparable to a modern car — it is costly to buy, expensive to maintain, and will not operate without constant attention, but the ease and security that it provides are worth every effort. Indifference is the most fatal disease endemic to representative government; no people can long govern a country when they vote blindly or not at all. Only when the study of history impresses on them the duties as well as the virtues of democracy will they realize this, and act accordingly. A schoolboy who proclaims that he will vote one way or another because "Dad always votes Republican," or "This part of the country always votes Democratic," is not only displaying his ignorance, but threatening the perpetuation of his heritage. Thomas Jefferson, who understood democracy as well as anyone in the eighteenth century and better than many in the twentieth, spoke not merely of rule by the people, but of rule by an informed, educated people. Knowledge of American history is a tool that transforms the voting booth into a sturdy foundation for democratic institutions.

Tomorrow's citizens will benefit from historical studies in a manner scarcely comprehensible to those of yesterday: as a profitable source of enjoyment during their ever-increasing leisure time. During the past decade automation has made such rapid advances that economists are already prophesying a twenty-hour week not many years hence; when this time arrives the useful utilization of the non-working hours will pose as many problems as earning a livelihood. In this situation, proper history teaching in the secondary schools will be more

than ever important, for a healthy percentage of those introduced to the plea-
sures of historical reading will discover a source of enjoyment that will enrich
their adult years. This has been amply demonstrated by the thousands of men
and women who, belatedly awakening to the realization that history is fun,
meet regularly in Civil War Round Tables or Westerners' Corrals to refight the
Battle of Gettysburg or argue interminably over Custer's tactics on the Little
Big Horn; it is similarly proven by the phenomenal success of *American Heritage* magazine. This is really not surprising. History, after all, is an art as
much as a science; writing it is an art, teaching it is an art, the resolution of a
research problem is something of an art insomuch as it requires proper instincts
as well as rigorous training. The enjoyment and appreciation of history are
directly comparable to those of looking at a painting, listening to a symphony, or
watching a play. All these media help mankind to understand the infinite
human spirit, and that is the ultimate aesthetic and emotional experience.

Finally, the study of our nation's history is essential not only for effective
American citizenship, but for world citizenship as well. Today and in the conceivable future the United States will face increasingly complex international
problems that must be intelligently solved through democratic processes if
nuclear extermination is to be avoided. These can be met only if Americans
possess a thorough understanding of their own national character, and of the
characters of the citizens of other lands that have been brought to our doorstep
by the revolutions in communication. No longer can we afford the luxury of
isolation; the historian of the Grant administration could tell his story without
mentioning the Franco-Prussian War, the Augustenberg crisis, and the Schles-
wig-Holstein controversy, but what future chronicler could describe the Eisen-
hower administration without dwelling on the Korean War, the Suez crisis, and
the controversy over West Berlin? Amidst the increasing complexity of modern
international affairs, a knowledge of the American past is ever more essential if
we are to behave as good neighbors and fulfill our role as agents of peace, for
only by understanding the historical evolution of the traits that distinguish us
as Americans can we manifest tolerance toward those possessing different characteristics. Nor does the world move so slowly that in times of danger we can
develop a "crash" program to train men for recurring emergencies; they must
be prepared and waiting. In today's troubled world ignorance and emotionalism
are instruments of national suicide; the balance wheel of history is needed to
keep us on the road to survival.

III

That the problems facing the United States today are deeply rooted in the
nation's past is made clear by even a rapid survey of its history. These problems, even those stemming from America's current role as a world power, are
often centuries old, and can be understood only against that background. No
hurried appraisal of recent decades will suffice to reveal the continuing interrelationship between the rest of the world and the United States since its
inception: the constant cultural transfusions that have enriched American life,
the capital imports and market demands that have partially governed its economic growth, the flow of immigrants that has hurried its elevation to world

status, and the diplomatic interplay during war and peace that has shaped its internal politics and hastened its emergence as a global power.

Neither past nor present problems can be understood, however, if the civilization of the United States is viewed simply as a transplanted version of European culture. When European nationals first ventured into the New World in the sixteenth and seventeenth centuries they encountered a unique environment destined to endow them with distinctive characteristics and institutions. The most striking feature of that environment was its man-land ratio; in the Old World men were many and land scarce, in the New, land was plentiful and men few. Such an atmosphere provided an opportunity for individual self-advancement unknown in crowded Europe, and with that opportunity came a demand that imported laws and customs standing in the way of progress should be discarded. Early American history can be understood primarily as the adaptation of European institutions and laws to the needs of an expanding social order where individual progress was all-important. Modern America must be viewed as a product of that evolution, just as the different attitudes of other nations can be appreciated only through an understanding of their differing backgrounds.

The interplay of the Old World heritage and the New World environment explains the success of England's colonizing efforts in contrast to those of her imperial rivals, France and Spain. Those nations, handicapped by autocratic rules, powerful established churches, and economies governed by feudal practices, so restricted their colonists that they could not take advantage of America's opportunities. Britain, however, entered the race for empire with a well-developed parliamentary theory that anticipated constitutional democracy, an emerging capitalistic philosophy fostered by a thriving commercial class, and a social structure sufficiently fluid to allow a greater degree of upward mobility than in more autocratic nations. These rudimentary institutional beginnings, combined with the inability of parliamentary monarchs to extend their absolutism beyond the seas, allowed British settlers freedom to modify laws and customs that restrained individual liberty. In Virginia, in Massachusetts Bay, and in later colonies, popularly elected legislatures were established, religious restrictions modified, archaic laws discarded, and feudal restraints on trade and manufacture ignored. The resulting civilization, allowing as it did for individual self-advancement, proved so attractive that the population multiplied, especially in the eighteenth century when major migrations of Germans and Scots-Irish occurred. By 1763 England's colonists were powerful enough to drive France from North America, and Spain from the region east of the Mississippi.

Britain's satisfaction over this victory was short-lived, for the very conditions that gave her colonies strength — a relatively fluid social order, political self-rule, and freedom of economic enterprise — predestined the American Revolution. Imbued with the idea of progress, and convinced that any interference with their natural liberties was tyranny, the Americans were quick to protest after 1763 when political and economic controls were tightened in an effort to restore unity to a dispersing empire. England lost its American colonies in 1776 because it failed to resolve the problem of reconciling the authority needed for effective rule with the liberty demanded by freeborn citizens. That same problem faced the new nation, and for a time threatened its speedy collapse. The first government, that under the Articles of Confederation, sacrificed authority for liberty and descended to near-anarchy; the second, symbolized by the Constitution of 1787 and its Bill of Rights, finally succeeded in achieving workable efficiency without infringing on popular freedoms. Yet each subsequent generation of Americans has refought that battle; even today the question of individual liberty versus governmental authority requires constant discussion and vigilance. No citizen unfamiliar with the long history of that question can act intelligently in its solution.

Scarcely had that problem been temporarily resolved than the new nation faced another of equal pertinence: how could the United States remain aloof from Europe's recurring conflicts? The wars that flamed in the wake of the French Revolution at first proved a boon to Americans, who fattened on profits from neutral trade or took advantage of English, French, and Spanish involvement in the struggle to secure favorable boundary adjustments and eventually the Louisiana Purchase. But participation in a war of global dimensions could never be partial. Inexorably the United States was drawn into the vortex of conflict. When it took up arms against England in 1812 it was following a pattern from which history has shown no deviation; from the seventeenth to the twentieth century America has entered every major struggle originating in Europe. The few modern Americans who still dream wistfully of isolation can learn much from this lesson.

The generation that emerged on the scene after the War of 1812 proved this to be the case, despite every intention to the contrary. The Monroe Doctrine of 1823 was designed to seal off the American continent from Europe's aggressors, but no mere declaration could curb the spirit of aggression on either side. Americans, convinced that their duty was the democratization of the world, continuously gave aid to European peoples struggling against tyranny, even at the risk of war; Europe's monarchs, as fearful of democracy as today's free world is of communism, persisted in meddling in hemisphere affairs as they had before. Then as now the sense of mission so strong on both sides of the Atlantic posed explosive problems: How far could the United States reconcile its desire to win self-government for all peoples with the limitations of its own strength and the horrors of war? How could it shrewdly gauge the future course of antagonist nations in determining its own line of action? Familiarity with the manner in which that generation solved these problems can guide today's statesmen and voters toward an honorable solution of their own.

No less timely than the external conflicts that plagued the United States during the first half of the nineteenth century were the internal divisions that led it along the road to war. These emerged when sectional economic specialization began after the War of 1812; as the Northeast devoted more and more of its energies to manufacturing, the South to plantation agriculture maintained by slave labor, and the West to small-scale farming, conflicts over legislative programs that would aid or harm each of these unique enterprises became increasingly bitter. These assumed more dangerous proportions when the emotional issue of abolitionism was injected during the 1830's and 1840's. As Northerners condemned slavery as a sin against God and man, and as Southerners rose to the defense of their peculiar institution, sectional feelings mounted to the explosion point. They erupted during the 1840's and 1850's as the nation realized its "manifest destiny" by expanding to the Pacific at the expense of

Mexico, then attempted to decide whether the Western territories should be slave or free. The Civil War that followed was fought over an issue as timely today as in 1861: the right of a minority to resist the will of the majority. Modern leaders concerned with regional differences arising from the integration controversy can help chart their course by the study of events leading to the irrepressible conflict.

The Civil War conjured into being other issues equally pertinent to today's United States. During the four years of fighting, the Americans began a significant transformation from a primarily agricultural people whose loyalties were local into an industrialized people committed to national consolidation and the supremacy of federal over local authority. This alteration posed a galaxy of vexing social and political questions. How could the people reshape their lives to benefit most from mechanization without allowing the machine to subordinate their individuality? How could they adjust to an impersonal urban environment without abandoning treasured personal relationships between men? How could they protect public morality when industrial titans possessed power that dwarfed that of emperors in the Old World? How could they adjust the economy to meet the needs of farmers and workers who were clamoring for a larger share of the wealth? How could they assimilate the millions upon millions of aliens attracted from Europe by the promise of jobs in the mushrooming factories? How could they adjust their foreign policy to the realities of a shrinking world where all men were increasingly interdependent? These were pressing problems, and most of them remain pressing problems today; familiarity with their origins will make their solution easier.

Before the people of that generation reached any solution, their troubles were compounded by the dawning realization that the nation's era of expansion was drawing to a close. With the continent settled and free lands in the West no longer beckoning the discontented, government leaders during the "Progressive Period" of the early twentieth century were brought face-to-face with a perplexing series of new questions. How could the economy continue to expand without periodic transfusions of freshly exploited natural wealth? How could men and women know security when escape to virgin frontiers was no longer possible? The imperialistic impulse that added domains beyond the seas was one answer to these problems; another was the inauguration of the "conservation" program designed to hoard the country's dwindling natural resources. More important was the revolution in political theory that cast the federal government in a positive role as guardian of its citizens' security. Theodore Roosevelt's "New Nationalism," Woodrow Wilson's "New Freedom," and Franklin D. Roosevelt's "New Deal," were all based on the assumption that society must provide security for its members when nature could no longer do so. Yet each step toward positive government action increased governmental controls, with a corresponding threat to popular liberties. In the early twentieth century, as in George Washington's time, the problem of reconciling liberty with authority plagued the United States, and its solution still is sought today.

The quest for an answer was further complicated in 1914 when Europe again plunged into war. Since that date the world has known no security, for the interludes between World War I, World War II, and the Cold War of today have brought no sense of enduring peace. In this continuing conflict the United States has inevitably been constantly involved, just as it was in the Napoleonic

Wars of a century and a half ago. The mobilization of resources necessary for this generations-long conflict has posed problems that our ancestors faced during the 1790's when the French menace seemed as foreboding as the Soviet menace does today: how to maintain adequate defenses without endangering the national economy, how to avoid bloodshed without retreating from positions based on sacred principles, how to guard against internal subversion without stifling popular liberties. History has no final answers for these problems or any others, for mankind's behavior is both variable and unpredictable, but today's citizens will be able to act more intelligently in their decision-making if they are familiar with the lessons it can teach.

IV

If familiarity with these broader and more timely aspects of the American heritage is to be transmitted to the next generation, the secondary school curriculum must be improved to provide students with both a better knowledge of United States history and a greater enthusiasm for its study than they possess today, and to offer them an elementary training in certain technical skills that will prove useful in all walks of life.

That the typical product of today's secondary schools is woefully deficient in his knowledge of American history is a sad but uncontradictable fact. Most have little or no time sense, are uncertain as to the sequence of past events, are unable to substantiate glib generalizations with factual information, and are prejudiced against a subject whose romantic glamour has been tarnished by poor instruction. Neither does the average high school graduate have any knowledge of how written history is derived from the history of actuality, or any awareness of the thrills of research, synthesis, and analysis. The poorer students have been bored, the better repelled, by a subject that seemed less worthy of their talents than courses in literature or science where they have been given some intellectual stimulus or at least the constructive atmosphere of a laboratory.

Certainly only an uncomfortably small percentage have a solid basic knowledge of the factual story of their nation's heritage. This knowledge is necessary because analysis and interpretation, in the discipline of history, are based on recorded events that are immutable in time and space. Historians emphasize chronology because the sequence of events is *the* clue to the understanding of both past and present. They insist that their pupils know important dates, not because those dates are significant in themselves, but because they are keys to a recognition and grouping of the various elements in the total situation. The university teacher of literature should not have to begin by teaching the ABC's, or the mathematician by convincing his pupils that 2 plus 2 equals 4. Nor should any student of secondary school American history complete his course without knowing such important dates as 1492, 1607, 1763, 1776, 1828, 1861, 1896, and 1929. He should not have to be told that the Mexican War preceded the Spanish-American War, or that George Washington did not deliver the Gettysburg Address. There are certain bare essentials in any discipline, and in history the chronological outline should be as familiar to students as the alphabet or the multiplication table.

All of this sounds like a dull exercise in memory, but this is not the case. If essential facts are presented to secondary school students as related, logical sequences in a predictable pattern, the exercise becomes less one of memory than of reason. That the Treaty of Paris of 1763 led to the Stamp Act, the Stamp Act to the Townshend Duties, the Townshend Duties to the Boston Tea Party, the Boston Tea Party to the Coercive Acts, the Coercive Acts to the First Continental Congress, and the First Continental Congress to the bloodshed at Lexington and Concord is as logical as a philosopher's exercise in deductive reasoning. Too often the victim of inadequate secondary school teaching is amazed to find that there is logic in the past; too often he reports that his teacher forced him to commit such reams of information to memory that he had forgotten every name and date within minutes after his final examination. Victims of such archaic methods of instruction are no more trained in history than another student who, after studying in a "life-adjustment oriented" school, remarked that he knew no facts but was thoroughly familiar with their significance. There is a middle ground between these extremes. This is achieved in the better university history courses, and should be in the secondary schools.

Important as this factual information is, it is meaningless unless the student has been taught something of the art of interpretation, analysis, and generalization. The secondary school graduate should have a rudimentary knowledge of the nature of historical causation, some elementary training in the methods of interpreting data, a sense of criticism, and a well-grounded awareness that the truth concerning human behavior can be realized only by weighing contradictory evidence as the basis for generalized conclusions. Once the student begins to understand these techniques, he will realize that his textbook has not spoken the last word, and that the world of historical studies is one of fascinating speculation in which half-truths alone are within the grasp of the scholar. These goals can be achieved if the secondary school teacher leads his more advanced students into the exciting realm of research and interpretation by assigning brief exercises in the analysis of documents that are readily available in printed collections.

Training such as this would accomplish another important purpose: it would help convince students that the study of history can be not only meaningful but fun. Once this is realized, enthusiasm for historical studies can never be quenched. Proper methods of instruction, while important, will not suffice to engender this in secondary school pupils, for an uninformed and uninterested instructor, parroting an over-factual textbook, would dim the interest of youth in sin itself. They must have teachers who are soundly trained in history rather than methodology, who regard the teaching of their country's past as a dedicated career, and who radiate such enthusiasm for learning that their students are inspired to follow in their footsteps. Until we stock our schools with such teachers and permit them to choose without interference their own teaching interests, the textbooks that they consider most suitable, and the course plan best adapted to their own techniques, all talk of improving American history instruction in the schools is futile. So long as would-be history teachers are forced to spend much of their training period in required education courses, meet rigid certification requirements unrelated to the subjects they will teach, and operate from a course plan handed down from on high, the enlistment of properly trained and adequately inspiring instructors will be impossible.

Properly trained secondary school graduates should be equipped with not only a basic fund of information, a rudimentary training in documentary interpretation, and a genuine enthusiasm for history; they should have been taught certain skills that would stand them in good stead in either college or the larger world. Students should emerge from high school history courses well enough versed in reading and writing to prepare a simple historical essay or paper; today most of even the better undergraduates have no knowledge of how to take notes on a book in the library, how to evaluate the material they gather, how to arrange it for logical presentation, and how to draw conclusions that will give meaning to the factual data they have collected. These are valuable mental exercises that can be employed in every walk of life. A similar training in basic exposition should be required of pupils in secondary school history courses by forcing them to take actual examinations rather than to dredge from their memories those snippets of information that are sufficient in themselves for the so-called "objective" tests favored by educationists. Proper training in answering essay questions, which test the student's understanding, his powers of selectivity, and his ability to organize intelligently, as well as his factual information, would go far toward equipping him for the logical analysis of problems that he will face in later life.

Finally, the well-prepared high school graduate should have been made to realize the interrelationship of all past events by taking courses that emphasize the chronological evolution of the social order rather than those employing the "unit" approach so universally used today. For reasons inexplicable to anyone with the slightest familiarity with history teaching, educationists have decreed that textbooks and course outlines should isolate specific aspects of man's behavior for separate study; a misguided student masters a "unit" in political history, followed by others in economic history, social history, and the like. The victim of this fragmentized method of instruction emerges with an awareness of a few threads of past behavior, but with no understanding of their complex intertwining, no awareness of the role of cause and effect, no sense of the social evolution that lends meaning and excitement to the study of the past. He has mastered some fragments of information, but he has learned little American history.

The curriculum changes that would achieve these laudable ends can never be realized until the American people alter their sense of values, for educationists who have perverted schooling into a pragmatic device for "life adjustment" are only responding to deep-rooted social pressures. The public must learn that history is not solely a key to the understanding of the present, but a liberal discipline that kindles the imagination, widens the individual's horizons, and stimulates the intellectual power that Bacon defined as the primary benefit of all learning. By studying national history we better understand ourselves and the forces responsible for our unique ideals and characteristics, and are thus equipped to explain and shape today's behavior. But this is the result, not the reason for historical study. When this has been realized by the people, and when they insist on secondary school teachers who have mastered their subject, are capable of radiating the enthusiasm that they feel for the study of the past, and can resist administrative pressures toward amorphous "social studies" courses embracing all contemporary social problems, the United States will be well along the road toward a proper respect for its heritage and the appreciation of true learning which will allow its democratic civilization to endure.

Our Past Isn't What It Used to Be

C. Vann Woodward

A decade or two is a brief span of time as history goes, but in the interpretation of history it can make a difference. Those who "learned" their American history before World War II or in the years immediately following would be in for some surprises were they to return to the old lecture halls today. The same professor might be holding forth. The names and dates and "facts" might sound familiar. But the old grad would soon become aware of new meanings attached to dates, altered significance given to names, and unfamiliar associations of "facts."

The changes are not primarily due to new information. It is true we have discovered, for example, that Alexander Hamilton was born a few years earlier than we thought, and we know more about the centuries of contact the white man had with the New World before Columbus. Important as they are, however, such discoveries do not account for the new look of American history. The difference arises mainly out of new readings of old evidence in the light of changed conditions by historians with new preoccupations, sensitivities, identifications, methods and moods.

Before trying to account for the changes in the historians it would be well to sample the changes in their interpretations. They are too numerous to list but most of them fall into one of four classes. One is an overhauling of historical reputations that has exalted some individuals, groups, or classes and lowered others in historical esteem and standing. A second is a general abandonment of the economic interpretation as an adequate or even acceptable account of historic movements. A third is an inclination to minimize or neglect the conflicts, contrasts, polarities, or antitheses in American history and to emphasize basic similarities, continuities and syntheses. A fourth tendency is to abandon the hunt for domestic villains to blame for our foreign wars.

The reshuffling of historical reputations can be illustrated on one level by what has happened to the prestige of the Puritans. Their stock has been going up since the 1930's but it has reached a new high in recent years. It has not been long since Puritans were pictured as a canting, bigoted, joy-killing lot of witch-burners. The revised picture is that of a humane, courageous, even pleasure-loving people with a passion for learning who are responsible for the choicest elements of our heritage. The transformation is the work of New England historians, but under their influence even Southerners strive to appreciate the sweet reasonableness of this breed.

The founding Fathers and Constitution framers, long under suspicion of unworthy motives and crafty designs, are the beneficiaries of another trend of reinterpretation that has appreciably improved their standing. The Abolitionists, who have suffered from an unfriendly historical press for many years, now tend to be revalued according to their own estimate. Their friends, the Radical Republicans, have lost their paranoidal scowl, dropped their economic motives, and glow with goodwill. Their strivings, now that the Second Reconstruction has gained momentum, are viewed in a new light. The lot of the Negro as slave, as freedman, and as underprivileged citizen is extensively reconsidered. The lowly immigrant, favorite scapegoat of Mugwump reformers (who have been slipping in status), has moved up in historical standing. Even the business tycoon of the Gilded Age, undefended since the 1920's, has found friends in the court of history.

In the meantime other groups have been declining in prestige. Conspicuous among the losers have been individuals, parties and movements traditionally identified with the popular cause or the common man against privilege and "the interests." Roger Williams of colonial Rhode Island and Nathaniel Bacon of colonial Virginia have lost their standing as precursors of democracy. More upsetting to traditional interpretations is the revisionist attack on Andrew Jackson and his party as authentic spokesman of the common man, whether western farmer or eastern worker, against the moneyed power and the aristocracy. Recent studies have increasingly narrowed the margin of difference between the supporters of Jackson and supporters of his opponents, denied the Old Hero a monopoly on equalitarian reform, and disclosed hankerings for privilege in his own camp. It has been seriously proposed that the whole concept of Jacksonian Democracy be abandoned.

Among more recent champions of the common man, the Populists and the Bryanite Democrats have suffered most from assault and battery by revisionists. Contending that Populists had been judged too leniently by indulgent liberals, their critics have focused attention instead on the delusions, myths and foibles of the Populists and charged them with responsibility for all manner of mischief, including racism, jingoism, mobbism, and anti-intellectualism. Some make them out to be the ancestors of fascism, and undergraduates are now heard to use "Populist" as a word of comparable opprobrium. The seamy side of the progressive movement has been subjected to a similar scrutiny and the exposure of such unlovely traits as blindness to minority rights and willful perpetration of racial injustice have disarranged the halo progressives once wore securely.

The old grad who returns for a refresher course in American history will soon become aware that something else is missing, something that was once quite prominent in lectures and textbooks: the economic interpretation. Little is made of it any more. The American Revolution, whether pictured as a fight for home rule or a fight over who would rule at home, was once interpreted as a struggle for material advantage motivated by economic grievance or hope of gain. The great debate over the framing and the adoption of the Federal Constitution, so it was once thought, hung primarily over conflicts of interest between the holders of two kinds of property called "personalty" and "realty." Party battles of the Jeffersonian and Jacksonian eras resounded with clashes between "agrarians" and "capitalists," debtors and creditors, hard money and soft, anti-monopolists and bankers. That was the way "progress" was achieved. The European peasant, weighing the decision to migrate to the New World, the pioneer spying out the West, and the abolitionist crusading against slavery, all responded consciously or unconsciously to the pocket nerve.

The classic conflict and greatest tragedy of American history was said to have had at the root of it an irrepressible incompatibility between an economy of plantations and farms at the South and an economy of commerce and industry at the North. In the historiography of our subsequent wars the economic interpretation has also played a conspicuous part.

More lately, however, historians have grown increasingly impatient with all simple and deterministic interpretations, economic determinism included. They tend to ask *who* rather than *what* was responsible for an event — which individuals, groups, votes, not what vast impersonal forces. With help from psychology and sociology they look for complexity rather than simplicity in human motivation. They pursue myth and symbol and the irrational with an interest once reserved for rational economic motives.

Another change that has taken some of the simplicity, as well as much of the drama and color out of the interpretation of American history has been the tendency to tone down the contrasts, to mute the clash of ideas, to soften the differences between classes, sections and interests, and to play up basic agreements and fundamental similarities. The boldness and vividness have faded from such standard polarities as Roundheads and Cavaliers, Jeffersonians and Hamiltonians, frontier and seaboard, labor and capital, liberal and conservative. We are often reminded that such tensions were always contained within a tacitly assumed consensus. The patriots of the Revolution were really conservatives, but they rebelled to conserve John Locke's liberalism. Jefferson is better remembered these days for saying, "We are all Federalists, we are all Republicans," than for endorsing a little rebellion now and then on the ground that "The tree of liberty must be refreshed from time to time with the blood of patriots and tyrants."

Under the influence of this mood, the old themes of social justice, protest, radicalism, utopianism and violence — all of which assume conflict — tend to be neglected. Interest in the come-outer, the hot-gospeller, the agitator (abolitionist excepted), and the prophets of revolution has waned.

A striking exception to the rule of muted contrasts and low moral voltage is some of the recent historiography of the Civil War and its background of sectional conflict. This does not include the prolific chroniclers of the Blue and Gray Gun Club, who tend to bury the hatchet of ideology on the hallowed battlegrounds these centennial years. But the political historians have dug up the hatchet again. Northerners complain that the Rebels have won the battle of books. Rejecting the concept of a "needless war" brought on by blunderers, and discarding the economic interpretation, which played down slavery, they have revived the moral interpretation and applied it sweepingly. They deny that there was an illiberal consensus of racism in 1860, unlimited by region or party, and define the Mason and Dixon Line as the boundary between right and wrong. Detachment is frowned upon. One is expected to choose sides, and history becomes the continuation of war by other means. As a consequence there is far less agreement over the interpretation of the Civil War today than there was a half century ago.

In the interpretation of later wars and their diplomatic history, on the other hand there is a growing tendency to let up on the search for villains and the passing of moral judgments. This is more in line with the prevailing revision of domestic history. For a long time it seemed to be assumed that when the United States went to war some mischief of a vaguely conspiratorial sort was afoot and that blame was to be assigned among certain domestic groups, interests, or high officials. The inquiry was carried out at home rather than abroad and it was likely to be conducted in a mood of cynicism and indignation.

Ernest R. May has divided diplomatic historians into the What-Went-Wrong School and the What-Happened School. The latter and newer school does not limit its investigation to American events but looks abroad and views developments from several angles. The studies of this school are likely to be more charitable to the intentions and efforts of American officials and less likely to spot a villain. Their findings have tended to improve the reputations for conduct of foreign affairs once assigned Presidents William McKinley, Theodore Roosevelt, Woodrow Wilson and Franklin D. Roosevelt.

All in all, the last fifteen years have witnessed the most sweeping reinterpretation of American history ever attempted in so brief a period. To account for it fully would require an intellectual history of the last two decades.

The old historians began the construction of their great synthesis toward the end of the last century and the beginning of the Progressive Era. Revival of the reform impulse in the 1930's renewed the appeal of some of their views, enhanced their influence, and prolonged their sway into an era where their ideas were less relevant. Outstanding leaders of the "Progressive" or "Pragmatic" school were Charles A. Beard, Carl Becker, Vernon Louis Parrington and Frederick Jackson Turner. Men of an intellectual stature that the new generation of historians has yet to equal, they were also great individualists about whom it is difficult and dangerous to generalize.

It is probably of some significance that all four men were from the Middle West and that, by and large, their identifications were with provincial, rural America and its values. They shared a deep belief in social progress, a faith in the common man, a sympathy for the underdog against privilege, and elaborate plans for reform. The history they wrote embodied these convictions. They were themselves conscious rebels against an older generation of "scientific" history, its stance of moral neutrality, and its conservative aloofness from practical affairs and social issues.

The Progressive school believed that history could be the handmaid of reform and that it should show how progress was advanced by conflict between forces of change and forces of reaction. They therefore stressed contrast, antithesis, and conflict, particularly conflict over economic issues, and they leaned to economic interpretations. Preoccupied with domestic problems, they neglected foreign comparisons and magnified internal differences. To divert public attention to foreign adventures was to evade the real business at hand.

In the light of the Atomic Age both the present and the past looked different. The path to social progress was dark and the old history did not light it. Many of the reforms had been accomplished. An economy of abundance replaced the economy of scarcity. Economic issues lost dramatic appeal. Change was feared, not sought. The common man had supported a variety of evil causes at home and abroad. His struggles had not invariably produced progress. His motives — many of them — were neither economic nor rational, and neither were those of his superiors. Growing awareness of foreign lands and their ways made social contrasts and ideological conflicts in American history seem mild by comparison. The great contrasts were between this country and others, not between fellow Americans. Homogeneity, compromise and continuity were the central themes.

Viewing the trend in reinterpreting our history, John Higham rightly observes that "A certain tameness and amiability have crept into our view of things" and complains of "the bland history" produced thereby. Not all the new history has been bland. No friend of the New Deal can complain of tameness in the leading books on that era, nor has blandness been a conspicuous fault of histories of racial minorities, academic freedom, and civil rights. Nor is it a characteristic of many fine new biographies. The unblandness of the civil war over the Civil War has been noted.

It must be admitted, however, that the typical product of the reinterpretation does not ring with a challenge to action, open vistas from the past into the future, nor present us with a new synthesis to replace the one rejected. The main results have been negative: rooting out untenable hypotheses, discrediting loose generalizations, breaking up outmoded categories, redefining terms. This work was needed and valuable. It clears the way for more positive contributions.

The reinterpretation is not finished. It will go on responding sometimes to fads and foibles, but fundamentally to the great thirst of our time for historical meaning. The historian will have all he can do in the way of reinterpretation to satisfy that thirst, to keep history meaningful, and to sustain the relevance of the past to the present.

What Are Historical Facts?*

Carl L. Becker

History is a venerable branch of knowledge, and the writing of history is an art of long standing. Everyone knows what history is, that is, everyone is familiar with the word, and has a confident notion of what it means. In general, history has to do with the thought and action of men and women who lived in past times. Everyone knows what the past is too. We all have a comforting

* This hitherto unpublished paper by the late Carl L. Becker was read at the 41st annual meeting of the American Historical Association at Rochester, New York, in December, 1926. It is printed here through the courtesy of the Cornell University Library.

From The Western Political Quarterly, 1955, Vol. VIII, pages 327–340. Reprinted by permission of the University of Utah, copyright owners.

sense that it lies behind us, like a stretch of uneven country we have crossed; and it is often difficult to avoid the notion that one could easily, by turning round, walk back into this country of the past. That, at all events, is what we commonly think of the historian as doing: he works in the past, he explores the past in order to find out what men did and thought in the past. His business is to discover and set forth the "facts" of history.

When anyone says "facts" we are all there. The word gives us a sense of stability. We know where we are when, as we say, we "get down to the facts" — as, for example, we know where we are when we get down to the facts of the structure of the atom, or the incredible movement of the electron as it jumps from one orbit to another. It is the same with history. Historians feel safe when dealing with the facts. We talk much about the "hard facts" and the "cold facts," about "not being able to get around the facts," and about the necessity of basing our narrative on a "solid foundation of fact." By virtue of talking in this way, the facts of history come in the end to seem something solid, something substantial like physical matter (I mean matter in the common sense, not matter defined as "a series of events in the ether"), something possessing definite shape, and clear persistent outline — like bricks or scantlings; so that we can easily picture the historian as he stumbles about in the past, stubbing his toe on the hard facts if he doesn't watch out. That is his affair of course, a danger he runs; for his business is to dig out the facts and pile them up for someone to use. Perhaps he may use them himself; but at all events he must arrange them conveniently so that someone — perhaps the sociologist or the economist — may easily carry them away for use in some structural enterprise.

Such (with no doubt a little, but not much, exaggeration to give point to the matter) are the common connotations of the words historical facts, as used by historians and other people. Now, when I meet a word with which I am entirely unfamiliar, I find it a good plan to look it up in the dictionary and find out what someone thinks it means. But when I have frequently to use words with which everyone is perfectly familiar — words like "cause" and "liberty" and "progress" and "government" — when I have to use words of this sort which everyone knows perfectly well, the wise thing to do is take a week off and think about them. The result is often astonishing; for as often as not I find that I have been talking about words instead of real things. Well, "historical fact" is such a word; and I suspect it would be worthwhile for us historians at least to think about this word more than we have done. For the moment therefore, leaving the historian moving about in the past piling up the cold facts, I wish to inquire whether the historical fact is really as hard and stable as it is often supposed to be.

And this inquiry I will throw into the form of three simple questions. I will ask the questions, I can't promise to answer them. The questions are: (1) What is the historical fact? (2) Where is the historical fact? (3) When is the historical fact? Mind I say *is* not *was*. I take it for granted that if we are interested in, let us say, the fact of the Magna Carta, we are interested in it for our own sake and not for its sake; and since we are living now and not 1215 we must be interested in the Magna Carta, if at all, for what it is and not for what it was.

First then, What is the historical fact? Let us take a simple fact, as simple as the historian often deals with, viz.: "In the year 49 B.C. Caesar crossed the

Rubicon." A familiar fact this is, known to all, and obviously of some importance since it is mentioned in every history of the great Caesar. But is this fact as simple as it sounds? Has it the clear, persistent outline which we commonly attribute to simple historical facts? When we say that Caesar crossed the Rubicon we do not of course mean that Caesar crossed it alone, but with his army. The Rubicon is a small river, and I don't know how long it took Caesar's army to cross it; but the crossing must surely have been accompanied by many acts and many words and many thoughts of many men. That is to say, a thousand and one lesser "facts" went to make up the one simple fact that Caesar crossed the Rubicon; and if we had someone, say James Joyce, to know and relate all these facts, it would no doubt require a book of 794 pages to present this one fact that Caesar crossed the Rubicon. Thus the simple fact turns out to be not a simple fact at all. It is the statement that is simple — a simple generalization of a thousand and one facts.

Well, anyhow Caesar crossed the Rubicon. But what of it? Many other people at other times crossed the Rubicon. Why charge it up to Caesar? Why for two thousand years has the world treasured this simple fact that in the year 49 B.C. Caesar crossed the Rubicon? What of it indeed? If I, as historian, have nothing to give you but this fact taken by itself with its clear outline, with no fringes or strings tied to it, I should have to say, if I were an honest man, why nothing of it, nothing at all. It may be a fact but it is nothing to us. The truth is, of course, that this simple fact *has* strings tied to it, and that is why it has been treasured for two thousand years. It is tied by these strings to innumerable other facts, so that it can't mean anything except by losing its clear outline. It can't mean anything except as it is absorbed into the complex web of circumstances which brought it into being. This complex web of circumstances was the series of events growing out of the relation of Caesar to Pompey, and the Roman Senate, and the Roman Republic, and all the people who had something to do with these. Caesar had been ordered by the Roman Senate to resign his command of the army in Gaul. He decided to disobey the Roman Senate. Instead of resigning his command, he marched on Rome, gained the mastery of the Republic, and at last, as we are told, bestrode the narrow world like a colossus. Well, the Rubicon happened to be the boundary between Gaul and Italy, so that by the act of crossing the Rubicon with his army Caesar's treason became an accomplished fact and the subsequent great events followed in due course. Apart from these great events and complicated relations, the crossing of the Rubicon means nothing, is not an historical fact properly speaking at all. In itself it is nothing for us; it becomes something for us, not in itself, but as a symbol of something else, a symbol standing for a long series of events which have to do with the most intangible and immaterial realities, viz.: the relation between Caesar and the millions of people of the Roman world.

Thus the simple historical fact turns out to be not a hard, cold something with clear outline, and measurable pressure, like a brick. It is so far as we can know it, only a *symbol*, a simple statement which is a generalization of a thousand and one simpler facts which we do not for the moment care to use, and this generalization itself we cannot use apart from the wider facts and generalizations which it symbolizes. And generally speaking, the more simple an historical fact is, the more clear and definite and provable it is, the less use it is to us in and for itself.

Less simple facts illustrate all this equally well, even better perhaps. For example, the fact that "Indulgences were sold in Germany in 1517." This fact can be proved down to the ground. No one doubts it. But taken by itself the fact is nothing, means nothing. It also is a generalization of a thousand and one facts, a thousand and one actions of innumerable sellers and buyers of indulgences all over Germany at many different times; and this also acquires significance and meaning only as it is related to other facts and wider generalizations.

But there are even more indefinite and impalpable facts than these. In the middle of the nineteenth century German historians (and others), studying the customs of the primitive German tribes, discovered a communal institution which they called the German or Teutonic Mark. The German Mark was the product of the historian's fertile imagination working on a few sentences in Caesar's *Gallic Wars* and a few passages in a book called *Germania* written by Tacitus, a disgruntled Roman who tried to get rid of a complex by idealizing the primitive Germans. The German Mark of the historians was largely a myth, corresponding to no reality. The German Mark is nevertheless an historical fact. The idea of the German Mark in the minds of the German historians is a fact in the intellectual history of the nineteenth century — and an important one too. All the elaborate notes I took in college on the German Mark I have therefore long since transferred to those filing cases which contain my notes on the nineteenth century; and there they now respose, side by side with notes on the Russian Mir, on Hegel's Philosophy of History, on the Positivism of August Comte, on Bentham's greatest good to the greatest number, on the economic theory of the British classical economists, and other illusions of that time.

What then is the historical fact? Far be it from me to define so illusive and intangible a thing! But provisionally I will say this: the historian may be interested in anything that has to do with the life of man in the past — any act or event, any emotion which men have expressed, any idea, true or false, which they have entertained. Very well, the historian is interested in some event of this sort. Yet he cannot deal directly with this event itself, since the event itself has disappeared. What he can deal with directly is a *statement about the event*. He deals in short not with the event, but with a statement which affirms *the fact that the event occurred*. When we really get down to the hard facts, what the historian is always dealing with is an *affirmation* — an affirmation of the fact that something is true. There is thus a distinction of capital importance to be made: the distinction between the ephemeral event which disappears, and the affirmation about the event which persists. For all practical purposes it is this affirmation about the event that constitutes for us the historical fact. If so the historical fact is not the past event, but a symbol which enables us to recreate it imaginatively. Of a symbol it is hardly worthwhile to say that it is cold or hard. It is dangerous to say even that it is true or false. The safest thing to say about a symbol is that it is more or less appropriate.

This brings me to the second question — Where is the historical fact? I will say at once, however brash it sounds, that the historical fact is in someone's mind or it is nowhere. To illustrate this statement I will take an event familiar to all. "Abraham Lincoln was assassinated in Ford's Theater in Washington on the 14th of April, 1865." That *was* an actual event, occurrence, fact at the moment of happening. But speaking now, in the year 1926, we say it *is* an historical fact. We don't say that it *was* an historical fact, for that would imply that it no longer is one. We say that it *was* an actual event, but *is* now an historical fact. The actual occurrence and the historical fact, however closely connected, are two different things. Very well, if the assassination of Lincoln is an historical fact, where is this fact now? Lincoln is not being assassinated now in Ford's Theater, or anywhere else (except perhaps in propagandist literature!). The actual occurrence, the event, has passed, is gone forever, never to be repeated, never to be again experienced or witnessed by any living person. Yet this is precisely the sort of thing the historian is concerned with — events, acts, thoughts, emotions that have forever vanished as actual occurrences. How can the historian deal with vanished realities? He can deal with them because these vanished realities give place to pale reflections, impalpable images or ideas of themselves, and these pale reflections, and impalpable images which cannot be touched or handled are all that is left of the actual occurrence. These are therefore what the historian deals with. These are his "material." He has to be satisfied with these, for the very good reason that he has nothing else. Well then, where are they — these pale reflections and impalpable images of the actual? Where are these facts? They are, as I said before, in his mind, or in somebody's mind, or they are nowhere.

Ah, but they are in the records, in the sources, I hear someone say. Yes, in a sense, they are in the sources. The historical fact of Lincoln's assassination is in the records — in contemporary newspapers, letters, diaries, etc. In a sense the fact is there, but in what sense? The records are after all only paper, over the surface of which ink has been distributed in certain patterns. And even these patterns were not made by the actual occurrence, the assassination of Lincoln. The patterns are themselves only "histories" of the event, made by someone who had in *his* mind an image or idea of Lincoln's assassination. Of course we, you and I, can, by looking at these inky patterns, form in *our* minds images or ideas more or less like those in the mind of the person who made the patterns. But if there were now no one in the world who could make any meaning out of the patterned records or sources, the fact of Lincoln's assassination would cease to be an historical fact. You might perhaps call it a dead fact; but a fact which is not only dead, but not known ever to have been alive, or even known to be now dead, is surely not much of a fact. At all events, the historical facts lying dead in the records can do nothing good or evil in the world. They become historical facts, capable of doing work, of making a difference, only when someone, you or I, brings them alive in our minds by means of pictures, images, or ideas of the actual occurrence. For this reason I say that the historical fact is in someone's mind, or it is nowhere, because when it is in no one's mind it lies in the records inert, incapable of making a difference in the world.

But perhaps you will say that the assassination of Lincoln has made a difference in the world, and that this difference is now effectively working, even if, for a moment, or an hour or a week, no one in the world has the image of the actual occurrence in mind. Quite obviously so, but why? Quite obviously because after the actual event people remembered it, and because ever since they have continued to remember it, by repeatedly forming images of it in their mind. If the people of the United States had been incapable of enduring memory, for example, like dogs (as I assume; not being a dog I can't be sure) would the assassination of Lincoln be now doing work in the world, making a difference? If everyone had forgotten the occurrence after forty-eight hours, what difference would the occurrence have made, then or since? It is precisely because people have long memories, and have constantly formed images in their minds of the assassination of Lincoln, that the universe contains the historical fact which persists as well as the actual event which does not persist. It is the persisting historical fact, rather than the ephemeral actual event, which makes a difference to us now; and the historical fact makes a difference only because it is, and so far as it is, in human minds.

Now for the third question — When is the historical fact? If you agree with what has been said (which is extremely doubtful) the answer seems simple enough. If the historical fact is present, imaginatively, in someone's mind, then it is now, a part of the present. But the word present is a slippery word, and the thing itself is worse than the word. The present is an indefinable point in time, gone before you can think it; the image or idea which I have now present in mind slips instantly into the past. But images or ideas of past events are often, perhaps always, inseparable from images or ideas of the future. Take an illustration. I awake this morning and among the things my memory drags in to enlighten or distress me is a vague notion that there was something I needed particularly to remember but cannot — a common experience surely. What is it that I needed to remember I cannot recall; but I can recall that I made a note of it in order to jog my memory. So I consult my little pocket memorandum book — a little Private Record Office which I carry about, filled with historical sources. I take out my memorandum book in order to do a little historical research; and there I find (Vol. I, p. 20) the dead historical fact — "Pay Smith's coal bill today: $1,016." The image of the memorandum book now drops out of mind, and is replaced by another image — an image of what? Why an image, an idea, a picture (call it what you will) made up of three things more or less inseparable. First the image of myself ordering coal from Smith last summer; second, the image of myself holding the idea in mind that I must pay the bill; third, the image of myself going down to Smith's office at four o'clock to pay it. The image is partly of things done in the past, and partly of things to be done in the future; but it is more or less all one image now present in mind.

Someone may ask, "Are you talking of history or of the ordinary ills of every day that men are heir to?" Well, perhaps Smith's coal bill is only my personal affair, of no concern to anyone else, except Smith to be sure. Take then another example. I am thinking of the Congress of Berlin, and that is without doubt history — the real thing. The historical facts of the Congress of Berlin I bring alive in memory, imaginatively. But I am making an image of the Congress of Berlin for a purpose; and indeed without a purpose no one would take the trouble to bring historical facts to mind. My purpose happens to be to convey this image of the Congress of Berlin to my class in History 42, in Room C, tomorrow afternoon at 3 o'clock. Now I find that inseparable from this image of the Congress of Berlin, which occurred in the past, are flitting images of myself conveying this image of the Congress of Berlin to my class tomorrow in Room C. I picture myself standing there monotonously talking, I hear the labored sentences painfully issuing forth, I picture the student's faces alert or bored as the case may be; so that images of this future event enter into the imagined picture of the Congress of Berlin, a past event; enter into it, coloring and shaping it too, to the end that the performance may do credit to me, or be intelligible to immature minds, or be compressed within the limits of fifty minutes, or to accomplish some other desired end. Well, this living historical fact, this mixed image of the coal bill or the Congress of Berlin — is it past, present, or future? I cannot say. Perhaps it moves with the velocity of light, and is timeless. At all events it is real history to me, which I hope to make convincing and real to Smith, or to the class in Room C.

I have now asked my three questions, and have made some remarks about them all. I don't know whether these remarks will strike you as quite beside the mark, or as merely obvious, or as novel. If there is any novelty in them, it arises, I think, from our inveterate habit of thinking of the world of history as part of the external world, and of historical facts as actual events. In truth the actual past is gone; and the world of history is an intangible world, re-created imaginatively, and present in our minds. If, as I think, this is true, then there are certain important implications growing out of it; and if you are not already exhausted I should like to touch upon a few of these implications. I will present them "firstly," "secondly," and so on, like the points of a sermon, without any attempt at coordination.

One implication is that by no possibility can the historian present in its entirety any actual event, even the simplest. You may think this a commonplace, and I do too; but still it needs to be often repeated because one of the fondest illusions of nineteenth century historians was that the historian, the "scientific" historian, would do just that: he would "present all the facts and let them speak for themselves." The historian would contribute nothing himself, except the sensitive plate of his mind, upon which the objective facts would register their own unimpeachable meaning. Nietzsche has described the nineteenth-century "objective man" with the acid precision of his inimitable phrases.

> The objective man is in truth a mirror. Accustomed to prostrating himself before something that wishes to be known, with such desires only as knowing implies, he waits until something comes and then expands himself sensitively, so that even the light footsteps and gliding past of spiritual beings may not be lost on his surface and film. Whatever personality he still possesses seems to him — disturbing; so much has he come to regard himself as the reflection of outward forms and events. Should one wish love and hatred from him, he will do what he can, and furnish what he can. But one must not be surprised if it should not be much. His mirroring and eternally self-polishing soul no longer knows how to affirm, no longer how to deny. . . . He is an instrument, but nothing in himself — *presque rien!*

The classical expression of this notion of the historian as instrument, is the famous statement attributed to Fustel de Coulanges. Half a century ago the French mind was reacting strongly against the romantic idea that political liberty was brought into Gaul by the primitive Germans; and Fustel was a leader in this reaction. One day he was lecturing to his students on early French institutions, and suddenly they broke into applause. "Gentlemen," said Fustel, "do not applaud. It is not I who speak, but history that speaks through me." And all the time this calm disinterested historian was endeavoring, with concentrated purpose, to prove that the damned Germans had nothing to do with French civilization. That of course was why the students applauded — and why Fustel told them that it was history that was speaking.

Well, for twenty years I have taken it for granted that no one could longer believe so preposterous an idea. But the notion continues to bob up regularly; and only the other day, riding on the train to the meeting of the Historical Association, Mr. A. J. Beveridge, eminent and honored historian, assured me dogmatically (it would be dogmatically) that the historian has nothing to do but "present all the facts and let them speak for themselves." And so I repeat, what I have been teaching for twenty years, that this notion is preposterous; first, because it is impossible to present all the facts; and second, because even if you could present all the facts the miserable things wouldn't say anything, would say just nothing at all.

Let us return to the simple fact: "Lincoln was assassinated in Ford's Theater, in Washington, April 14, 1865." This is not all the facts. It is, if you like, a *representation* of all the facts, and a representation that perhaps satisfies one historian. But another historian, for some reason, is not satisfied. He says: "On April 14, 1865, in Washington, Lincoln, sitting in a private box in Ford's Theater watching a play, was shot by John Wilkes Booth, who then jumped to the stage crying out, 'Sic semper tyrannis!'" That is a true affirmation about the event also. It represents, if you like, all the facts too. But its form and content (one and the same thing in literary discourse) is different, because it contains more of the facts than the other. Well, the point is that any number of affirmations (an infinite number if the sources were sufficient) could be made about the actual event, all true, all representing the event, but some containing more and some less of the factual aspects of the total event. But by no possibility can the historian make affirmations describing all of the facts — all of the acts, thoughts, emotions of all of the persons who contributed to the actual event in its entirety. One historian will therefore necessarily *choose* certain affirmations about the event, and relate them in a certain way, rejecting other affirmations and other ways of relating them. Another historian will necessarily make a different choice. Why? What is it that leads one historian to make, out of all the possible true affirmations about the given event, certain affirmations and not others? Why, the purpose he has in his mind will determine that. And so the purpose he has in mind will determine the precise meaning which he derives from the event. The event itself, the facts, do not say anything, do not impose any meaning. It is the historian who speaks, who imposes a meaning.

A second implication follows from this. It is that the historian cannot eliminate the personal equation. Of course, no one can; not even, I think, the natural scientist. The universe speaks to us only in response to our purposes; and even the most objective constructions, those, let us say, of the theoretical physicist, are not the sole possible constructions, but only such as are found most convenient for some human need or purpose. Nevertheless, the physicist can eliminate the personal equation to a greater extent, or at least in a different way, than the historian, because he deals, as the historian does not, with an external world directly. The physicist presides at the living event, the historian presides only at the inquest of its remains. If I were alone in the universe and gashed my finger on a sharp rock, I could never be certain that there was anything there but my consciousness of the rock and gashed finger. But if ten other men in precisely the same way gash their fingers on the same sharp rock, we can, by comparing impressions, infer that there is something there besides consciousness. There is an external world there. The physicist can gash his finger on the rock as many times as he likes, and get others to do it, until they are all certain of the facts. He can, as Eddington says, make pointer-readings of the behavior of the physical world as many times as he likes for a given phenomenon, until he and his colleagues are satisfied. When their minds all rest satisfied they have an explanation, what is called the truth. But suppose the physicist had to reach his conclusions from miscellaneous records, made by all sorts of people, of experiments that had been made in the past, each experiment made only once, and none of them capable of being repeated. The external world he would then have to deal with would be the records. That is the case of the historian. The only external world he has to deal with is the records. He can indeed look at the records as often as he likes, and he can get dozens of others to look at them: and some things, some "facts," can in this way be established and agreed upon, as, for example, the fact that the document known as the Declaration of Independence was voted on July 4, 1776. But the meaning and significance of this fact cannot be thus agreed upon, because the series of events in which it has a place cannot be enacted again and again, under varying conditions, in order to see what effect the variations would have. The historian has to judge the significance of the series of events from the one single performance, never to be repeated, and never, since the records are incomplete and imperfect, capable of being fully known or fully affirmed. Thus into the imagined facts and their meaning there enters the personal equation. The history of any event is never precisely the same thing to two different persons; and it is well known that every generation writes the same history in a new way, and puts upon it a new construction.

The reason why this is so — why the same series of vanished events is differently imagined in each succeeding generation — is that our imagined picture of the actual event is always determined by two things: (1) by the actual event itself insofar as we can know something about it; and (2) by our own present purposes, desires, prepossessions, and prejudices, all of which enter into the process of knowing it. The actual event contributes something to the imagined picture; but the mind that holds the imagined picture always contributes something too. This is why there is no more fascinating or illuminating phase of history than historiography — the history of history: the history, that is, of what successive generations have imagined the past to be like. It is impossible to understand the history of certain great events without knowing what the actors in those events themselves thought about history. For example, it helps immensely to understand why the leaders of the American and French Revolutions acted and thought as they did if we know what their idea of classical history was. They desired, to put it simply, to be virtuous republicans, and to act the part. Well, they were able to act the part of virtuous republicans much more effectively because they carried around in their heads an idea, or ideal if you prefer, of Greek republicanism and Roman virtue. But of course their own desire to be virtuous republicans had a great influence in making them think the Greek and Romans, whom they had been taught to admire by reading the classics in school, were virtuous republicans too. Their image of the present and future and their image of the classical past were inseparable, bound together — were really one and the same thing.

In this way the present influences our idea of the past, and our idea of the past influences the present. We are accustomed to say that "the present is the product of all the past"; and this is what is ordinarily meant by the historian's doctrine of "historical continuity." But it is only a half truth. It is equally true, and no mere paradox, to say that the past (our imagined picture of it) is the product of all the present. We build our conceptions of history partly out of our present needs and purposes. The past is a kind of screen upon which we project our vision of the future; and it is indeed a moving picture, borrowing much of its form and color from our fears and aspirations. The doctrine of historical continuity is badly in need of overhauling in the light of these suggestions; for that doctrine was itself one of those pictures which the early nineteenth century throw upon the screen of the past in order to quiet its deep-seated fears — fears occasioned by the French Revolution and the Napoleonic wars.

A third implication is that no one can profit by historical research, or not much, unless he does some for himself. Historical knowledge, however richly stored in books or in the minds of professors of history, is no good to me unless I have some of it. In this respect, historical research differs profoundly from research in the natural sciences, at least in some of them. For example, I know no physics, but I profit from physical researches every night by the simple act of pressing an electric light button. And everyone can profit in this way from researches in physics without knowing any physics, without knowing even that there is such a thing as physics. But with history it is different. Henry Ford, for example, can't profit from all the historical researches of two thousand years, because he knows so little history himself. By no pressing of any button can he flood the spare rooms of his mind with the light of human experience.

A fourth implication is more important than the others. It is that every normal person does know some history, a good deal in fact. Of course we often hear someone say: "I don't know any history; I wish I knew some history; I must improve my mind by learning some history." We know what is meant. This person means that he has never read any history books, or studied history in college; and so he thinks he knows no history. But it is precisely this conventional notion of history as something external to us, as a body of dull knowledge locked up in books, that obscures its real meaning. For, I repeat (it will bear repeating) every normal person — every man, woman, and child — does know some history, enough for his immediate purposes; otherwise he would be a lost soul indeed. I suppose myself, for example, to have awakened this morning with loss of memory. I am all right otherwise; but I can't remember anything that happened in the past. What is the result? The result is that I don't know who I am, where I am, where to go, or what to do. I can't attend to my duties at the university, I can't read this paper before the Research Club. In short, my present would be unintelligible and my future meaningless. Why? Why, because I had suddenly ceased to know any history. What happens when I wake up in the morning is that my memory reaches out into the past and gathers together those images of past events, of objects seen, of words spoken and of thoughts thought in the past, which are necessary to give me an ordered world to live in, necessary to orient me in my personal world. Well, this collection of images and ideas of things past is history, my command of living history, a series of images of the past which shifts and reforms at every moment of the day in response to the exigencies of my daily living. Every man has a knowledge of history in this sense, which is the only vital sense in which he can have a knowledge of history. Every man has some knowledge of past events, more or less accurate; knowledge enough, and accurate enough, for his purposes, or what he regards as such. How much and how accurate, will depend on the man and his purposes. Now, the point is that history in the formal sense, history as we commonly think of it, is only an extension of memory. Knowledge or history, insofar as it is living history and not dead knowledge locked up in notebooks, is only an enrichment of our minds with the multiplied images of events, places, peoples, ideas, emotions outside our personal experience, an enrichment of our experience by bringing into our minds memories of the experience of the community, the nation, the race. Its chief value, for the individual, is doubtless that it enables a man to orient himself in a larger world than the merely personal, has the effect for him of placing the petty and intolerable present in a longer perspective, thus enabling him to judge the acts and thoughts of men, his own included, on the basis of an experience less immediate and restricted.

A fifth implication is that the kind of history that has most influence upon the life of the community and the course of events is the history that common men carry around in their heads. It won't do to say that history has no influence upon the course of events because people refuse to read history books. Whether the general run of people read history books or not, they inevitably picture the past in some fashion or other, and this picture, however little it corresponds to the real past, helps to determine their ideas about politics and society. This is especially true in times of excitement, in critical times, in time of war above all. It is precisely in such times that they form (with the efficient help of official propaganda!) an idealized picture of the past, born of their emotions and desires working on fragmentary scraps of knowledge gathered, or rather flowing in upon them, from every conceivable source, reliable or not matters nothing. Doubtless the proper function of erudite historical research is to be forever correcting the common image of the past by bringing it to the test of reliable information. But the professional historian will never get his own chastened and corrected image of the past into common minds if no one reads his books. His books may be as solid as you like, but their social influence will be nil if people do not read them and not merely read them, but read them willingly and with understanding.

It is, indeed, not wholly the historian's fault that the mass of men will not read good history willingly and with understanding; but I think we should not be too complacent about it. The recent World War leaves us with little ground indeed for being complacent about anything; but certainly it furnishes us with no reason for supposing that historical research has much influence on the course of events. The nineteenth century is often called the age of Science, and it is often called the age of history. Both statements are correct enough. During the hundred years that passed between 1814 and 1914 an unprecedented and incredible amount of research was carried on, research into every field of history — minute, critical, exhaustive (and exhausting!) research. Our libraries are filled with this stored up knowledge of the past; and never before has there been at the disposal of society so much reliable knowledge of human experience. What influence has all this expert research had upon the social life of our time? Has it done anything to restrain the foolishness of politicians or to enhance the wisdom of statesmen? Has it done anything to enlighten the mass of the people, or to enable them to act with greater wisdom or in response to a more reasoned purpose? Very little surely, if anything. Certainly a hundred years of expert historical research did nothing to prevent the World War, the most futile exhibition of unreason, take it all in all, ever made by civilized society. Governments and peoples rushed into this war with undiminished stupidity, with unabated fanaticism, with unimpaired capacity for deceiving themselves and others. I do not say that historical research is to blame for the World War. I say that it had little or no influence upon it, one way or another.

It is interesting, although no necessary part of this paper, to contrast this negligible influence of historical research upon social life with the profound influence of scientific research. A hundred years of scientific research has transformed the conditions of life. How it has done this is known to all. By enabling men to control natural forces it has made life more comfortable and convenient, at least for the well-to-do. It has done much to prevent and cure disease, to alleviate pain and suffering. But its benefits are not unmixed. By accelerating the speed and pressure of life it has injected into it a nervous strain, a restlessness, a capacity for irritation and an impatience of restraint never before known. And this power which scientific research lays at the feet of society serves equally well all who can make use of it — the harbingers of death as well as of life. It was scientific research that made the war of 1914, which historical research did nothing to prevent, a world war. Because of scientific research it could be, and was, fought with more cruelty and ruthlessness, and on a grander scale, than any previous war; because of scientific research it became a systematic massed butchery such as no one had dreamed of, or supposed possible. I do not say that scientific research is to blame for the war; I say that it made it the ghastly thing it was, determined its extent and character. What I am pointing out is that scientific research has had a profound influence in changing the conditions of modern life, whereas historical research has had at best only a negligible influence. Whether the profound influence of the one has been of more or less benefit to humanity than the negligible influence of the other, I am unable to determine. Doubtless both the joys and frustrations of modern life, including those of the scholarly activities, may be all accommodated and reconciled within that wonderful idea of Progress which we all like to acclaim — none more so, surely, than historians and scientists.

The "Presidential Synthesis" in American History

Thomas C. Cochran

Fifty years of rapid growth in the social sciences have had surprisingly little effect on the general content and synthesis of American history. The main props of the synthetic structure, erected, more or less unconsciously, by such pioneers as Channing, Hart, McMaster, and Turner, are still securely in place. Although much new trim in the form of discussions of artistic and social movements has been added, the old skeleton of wars, presidential administrations, and the westward movement still holds the edifice together.

Examining the contents of the few interpretations of American history for the general reader or of recent college textbooks, including two first published in 1947, one is struck by the uniformity of the traditional synthesis. From the Constitution to the Civil War recent scholars have not strayed far from the paths trod by the turn-of-the-century pioneers. Jeffersonian and Jacksonian Democracy, the War of 1812, the Westward Movement, Territorial Expansion, and Sectional Conflict form a standard pattern. In the period between 1865 and 1896, then too recent for the pioneers to set in a definitive mold, the present synthesis offers somewhat more diversity. But the suspicion that the more varied treatment may also be due to the obvious inadequacy of national politics to serve as the thought-saving standby is supported by the resumption of the old pattern as soon as the presidency again becomes interesting. From Theodore Roosevelt on, presidential administrations and national political issues, including wars, again become the center of the narrative. For this reason I am going to refer to the standard pattern as the "presidential synthesis," realizing fully that the presidential chronology is not continuously adhered to, that many other themes are included, and that, in any case, such emphasis is only a superficial manifestation of more fundamental inadequacies.

Judged either by the complex of values and standards that may loosely be referred to as humanistic or by those of the social sciences, the presidential synthesis is a failure. It satisfies a follower of Toynbee, for example, but little better than it does the devotees of the dismal science. But, at present, I shall discuss only its inadequacy in dealing with the type of problems in modern society that most interest social scientists, or what may be termed from their point of view history's lack of social realism. To members of the disciplines that have to study the problems of industrial society, the basic data or trends with which the historian has traditionally dealt do not seem of the highest importance, and the studies themselves seem to the social scientist correspondingly futile. A consensus of the problems dealt with by social scientists would include such topics as the causes and conditions of economic growth or stagna-

From the *American Historical Review*, 1948, 53, pages 748–759, by permission of the American Historical Association and the author.

tion; the effect on enterprise of community approbation, competition, monopoly, and regulation; the social difficulties coming from great urban centers, new types of employment, and changing levels of opportunity; the psychological frustrations developing from urban insecurity, badly selected social goals and altered family relationships; and the origins and continuing support of social manners, attitudes, and beliefs. The rapid rise of such group problems has characterized the history of the last hundred and fifty years, but, needless to say, they are not the central feature of the presidential synthesis. Moreover, cursory study of general European history writing indicates that this weakness is not confined to the history of the United States.

How has this situation arisen? Why should an important intellectual discipline, occupying the time of many thousands of scholars, fail to keep pace with the spiritual and material problems of its civilization?

An obvious part of the answer lies in the fact that the writing of history is a time-honored and traditional occupation long antedating the modern emphasis on empirical method in the social sciences or present-day problems or source materials. The historical record prior to 1800 here or abroad is relatively scanty. The historian has to use the materials he can find rather than those that might best answer his questions. To begin with, these materials are largely governmental, and the fact that the modern syntheses were developed in a period of growing nationalism led to a still greater preoccupation with political sources. Historians, used to confining themselves to these old and easily available records for the earlier periods, failed to make use of new types of material as these became available in the later nineteenth century. The habits of the older historian, educated to a scarcity of records, perpetuated themselves amidst a later-day abundance. Statistical data, specialized periodicals, new types of correspondence, and the records of many organizations, profit-making or otherwise, were all relatively neglected, while the traditional sources were reinterpreted again and again.

This tendency has been noted or implied in various ways from the time of Buckle and Green in England and of the graduate seminars of the eighties in America. Yet, in spite of an increasing recognition of the importance and complexity of the elements in modern society that are but faintly reflected in national politics, no well-formulated rival synthesis is even contesting the sway of the presidential. No new texts and few other general histories have attempted to shatter the mold. No recognized "social science" synthesis of American history is challenging the traditional formula.[1]

The explanation of such a striking intellectual anachronism is bound to be subtle and complex, for if the antequated structure rested on one or two easily

[1] Guy Stanton Ford pointed out the need for such a synthesis over a decade ago in "Some Suggestions to American Historians," *American Historical Review*, XLIII (January, 1938), 267–68. High school textbooks, while reflecting the social scientific approach more than college, have not attempted any radical resynthesis. Henry B. Parkes, *The American Experience* (New York, 1947), while presenting an interpretation based on conflicting social ideologies, rather than the presidential synthesis, does not, in general, employ social science concepts or methods. Thomas C. Cochran and William Miller's *Age of Enterprise* (New York, 1942), offers a general synthesis, based on the social sciences, but puts specific emphasis on the role of business. See also Caroline F. Ware, ed., *The Cultural Approach to History* (New York, 1940).

recognized errors it could not have withstood the pressures of new generations of historians. A long list of causes must therefore be investigated, the absolute importance of any one of which is hard to evaluate, but all of which together seem largely responsible for the general failure of the historian of recent times.

The written record itself, particularly when buttressed with systematic documentation, exercises a tyranny that has been commented on frequently by students of the nature of language but often overlooked by scholars in other fields. The mere fact that a previous writer has organized his material and phraseology in a certain way creates a predisposition in its favor. The later writer can no longer respond entirely freshly to the original data; he may agree with or object to what has been said, but in either case his orbit of thought has been made to include the existing interpretation. A. M. Schlesinger, jr., and Joseph Dorfman, for example, may argue about the interpretation of "Jacksonian Democracy," but they both accept the traditional concept as central to the synthesis of the period. Charles A. Beard introduced new economic factors, but he employed them within the presidential synthesis. With its great quantities of traditional literature, and its lack of accepted conceptual tools for fresh theoretical analysis, history probably suffers more than any other discipline from the tyranny of written models.

In still another way, the inner compulsions of writing have ruled the historian. The traditional basis of history has been narrative. The "great" histories of the past such as Gibbon's *Decline and Fall*, Macaulay's *England*, or Motley's *Dutch Republic* have been exciting "stories." Furthermore, since historians like to have their books published, and are not averse to sales, the popular dramatic frame of reference has been used whenever possible. This general approach is often valid when applied to the actions of a single individual, but neither narrative nor popular drama is usually suited to the analysis of mass phenomena. While drama will still be found in the conflict and resolution of forces or in group challenge and response, this is likely to be drama on a non-popular abstract level. The historian has, of course, been aware of this dilemma, but, faced with the choice of retaining a false emphasis on colorful individuals and exciting events or of giving up the narrative style, he has clung as long as possible to storytelling and treasured most those source materials that permitted narration.[2]

By taking the written record that was easiest to use and most stirring from a sentimental or romantic standpoint, that is, the record of the federal government, the American historian prepared the way for one of the major misconceptions in American synthesis: the primary role of the central government in our historical development. While political scientists carefully pointed out that up to the First World War, at least, most of the normal governmental contacts of the citizen were with his state, and historians dwelt on the importance of sectionalism and state rights and joined with business leaders in emphasizing the laissez-faire doctrines that for a part of the nineteenth century kept government impotent and unimportant, the same men, influenced perhaps by nine-

---

[2] The time and energy that have been lavished on collecting and publishing even relatively unimportant letters of famous statesmen compared with that expended in trying to learn something of the communities in which they lived strikingly indicates the historians' leanings.

teenth century European training, persisted in writing a national history revolving around presidential administrations and constitutional law. In the early stages of the economic development of each region, government and politics were in truth of great importance, but government was that of the state and the politics revolved around such material questions as loans or subsidies to banking and transportation, practices of incorporation, and the degree of government ownership thought desirable. In a later stage of economic growth the states led the way in regulating business and economic activity in the public interest. In neither stage, prior to 1900, was the federal government of major importance except for the initial disposal of public land, adjustment of the tariff, and widely separated changes in banking policy. The sporadic transference of ultimate power from state to federal government by decisions of the Supreme Court and acts of Congress from the 1880's on, at first freed certain citizens from state controls without imposing effective federal ones. Not until the second decade of the twentieth century was the theoretical shift in power implemented by much effective federal action.

The realistic history of nineteenth and even early twentieth century politics, therefore, whether viewed from the standpoint of political parties or of the community, should be built around the states. This, of course, imposes an enormous burden on the historian. The situations in from thirteen to forty-eight states must be synthesized. Furthermore, the older state histories are inadequate as a basis for such synthesis. Scholars must first write new monographs on business and government in the states, and new cultural interpretations of state politics.[3] Indeed, at present, a general American history has to be more a series of suggestions of what needs to be known than a comprehensive analysis.

A somewhat similar obstacle in the path of the historian who approaches the problem of synthesis is the extent to which our existing knowledge of the past is based on the writings of a small group of cultural leaders. He will tend to see events not only through the eyes of men of more than average vigor, property, education, and intelligence but also in the light of the metaphors of those who wrote the most enduring and readable prose. The circle of possible deception is completed when the statements of such abnormal citizens are read back as typical of their class, section, or society as a whole, and the resulting analysis is used to explain still other situations. The brilliant John Taylor of Carolina was not the typical Southern planter, Susan B. Anthony's problems were not those of the average woman, nor was Herbert Croly a good representative of many phases of the progressive movement.

A major reason for this reliance on leaders is that historical data on average people and everyday situations is hard to find. What was the typical rural community of 1840 from the statistical standpoint? What were normal ideas among its average citizens? Until there are answers to such questions, generali-

[3] The Committee on Research in Economic History, of the Social Science Research Council, has sponsored studies of government in relation to economic life in the pre-Civil War period for four sample states. Oscar and Mary F. Handlin, *Commonwealth: Massachusetts, 1774–1861* (New York, 1947), and Louis Hartz, *Economic Policy and Democratic Thought: Pennsylvania, 1776–1860* (Cambridge, Mass., 1948), are the only ones that have been published.

THOMAS C. COCHRAN · 201

zations regarding the role of ideas in social change must rest on tenuous deductions.[4] Both quantitative and typical studies are sadly lacking. Some of these data can be assembled from better use of published and manuscript census reports, others will have to be examined by sampling methods, governed by proper statistical controls. The normal ideas of the average citizen in any time and place will have to be assembled from many indirect sources, such as the speeches of astute local politicians who, knowing what their constituents wanted to hear, mirrored public prejudices; the blurbs of discerning advertisers who sought in local papers to cater to public taste; and the letters of businessmen discussing public reactions that vitally concerned the future of their trade. Such materials are relatively hard to find and to use, but there are many indications of their widespread existence.[5]

Research in such sources immediately brings the scholar to a level of social relations deeper than that of conventional historic events, and exposes another major reason for the persistence of the presidential synthesis. As long as history consists of a series of important unique acts, thought to symbolize or cause change in society, a narrative account based on national happenings has a certain logic. But once the historian penetrates to the level of the social conditioning factors that produce people capable of such acts and tries to find the probability of the occurrence of any type of event, the acts themselves become a surface manifestation of more fundamental forces. While events are an indispensable part of the data of history, and even chance events, granting there are such, may have strong repercussions on their environment, the social science approach focuses attention on the aspects of the event that reveal the major drives of the culture rather than those that appear to be most colorful or unique. The latter elements, by definition not being representative of the general culture pattern, will presumably have only a limited effect or significance. Southern secession, for example, had its roots in cultural factors underlying such events as the tariffs, the acts of abolitionists, or territorial laws that seemed to produce the friction. These events are chiefly useful as clues to the nature of the basic differences between the sections. Similarly the American people in the early 1930's, facing a new cultural situation, displayed qualities of resignation not easily explicable on the basis of either the traditional or immediate events of their past.

Historical change on this level of basic social conditioning is, to be sure, a difficult, and, in the present stage of social science knowledge, a highly speculative study. Furthermore, the large quantities of material to be examined and the various types of special knowledge required often make group, rather than individual, research essential. The generally individualistic work habits of the historian, therefore, suggest another reason for the failure of historical scholarship in this area. But the topography of this field has been charted sufficiently

[4] See Theodore C. Blegen, *Grass Roots History* (Minneapolis, 1947).

[5] See Merle E. Curti, *The Roots of American Loyalty* (New York, 1946), Lewis E. Atherton, *The Pioneer Merchant in Mid-America* (Columbia, Mo., 1939), Thomas D. Clark, *Pills, Petticoats and Plows: The Southern Country Store* (Indianapolis, 1944), and Everett Dick, *The Dixie Frontier: A Social History of the Southern Frontier from the First Transmontane Beginnings to the Civil War* (New York, 1948), for use of such material.

to allow even individual historians to make rewarding sorties into its intricate terrain.[6]

In the space of an article one can suggest only a few of the many types of research that will help build a social science synthesis. As a beginning, it should be possible with patience and ingenuity to assemble the large number of career lines of different types of social leaders, essential for a picture of who succeeded in the society and how. Beside the pattern of how men succeeded in fact, should be further study, from qualitative sources such as private correspondence, of the alternative goals that influenced men's expectations.[7] How did their "level of expectation" from material or intellectual standpoints vary? What was the true "American dream"? Such considerations would lead not only to a higher level of generalization in our social history writing but to possible scientific comparisons between American and other cultures.

A more difficult excursion into the field of basic historical factors is the tracing of the changing character of family relations including both the relationships within the family circle and the aims and aspirations of the members of the family in their real and imaginary contacts with the outside world. Whether one uses a striking term like Kardiner and Linton's "basic personality"[8] or some time-honored word like "background" to cover the effects of familial conditioning, few scholars will deny the fundamental importance of this factor in shaping the course of civilization.[9] But the investigation of the precise reaction to change is difficult, calling for psychological and sociological knowledge seldom possessed by the historian, and hence the family does not appear as a factor on the level of historical events.[10] An additional deterrent to historical analysis is that there are many "American families" at any given period. The variation in conditioning between the family of a back-country mountaineer and a rural professional man, or a city slum dweller and a Fifth Avenue millionaire, may easily be greater than the variation between the Maori family and the Mari-

[6] For a number of suggestive articles, see *Conflicts of Power in Modern Culture*, a symposium edited by Lyman Bryson, Louis Finkelstein and R. M. MacIver (New York, 1947). Abram Kardiner with the collaboration of Ralph Linton, Cora Du Bois, and James West (pseud.), *The Psychological Frontiers of Society* (New York, 1945), and Talcott Parsons, *The Structure of Social Action* (New York, 1937), are examples of the type of social-psychological and sociological literature that merits the attention of all historians.

[7] See Frank W. Taussig and C. J. Joslyn, *American Business Leaders: A Study in Social Origins and Social Stratification* (New York, 1932). William Miller, in a study now in preparation, has assembled data on 350 business and political leaders of the decade 1900 to 1910. I have similar material for some 75 railroad executives of the period 1850 to 1890.

[8] Kardiner, *et al.*, p. viii.

[9] See, for example, Talcott Parsons, "Certain Primary Sources and Patterns of Aggression in the Social Structure of the Western World," in *Conflicts of Power in Modern Culture*, pp. 29–48.

[10] Arthur W. Calhoun in his *Social History of the American Family, from Colonial Times to the Present* (Cleveland, 1917–19), 3 vols., assembled a large mass of random material that has been rather uncritically drawn upon by historians. Sociologists studying the dynamics of the family have been more interested in the inner psychological tensions than in tracing historically the changing external pressures that altered the inner patterns. See, for example, Willard Waller, *The Family: A Dynamic Interpretation*, (New York, 1938).

copa.[11] As in current studies in cultural anthropology, such as *Plainville, U.S.A.* or the "Yankee City Series," half a dozen different types of families based on income and occupational levels must be studied.[12] The upper-class groups offer an abundance of data in the form of memoirs, letters, and contemporary comments;[13] the poorer groups, particularly before 1890, offer only a challenge to the investigator. But the scholar striving to check theories and hypotheses regarding the family against historical data, and no one not so motivated should essay the task, will doubtless find many clues that have been concealed from the "uneducated" eyes of the conventional historian. Perhaps some day it will be possible to guess wisely at the degree to which group aggressions, political radicalism, or instability in mass reactions were due to the stresses and strains of a family conditioning that became unsuited in varying degrees to the changes in surrounding society.

Looking at the situation more broadly, the new psychological problems of Western civilization by 1900 can be seen as the result of contrary types of conditioning: family and school conditioning in youth, based either here or abroad, on mores and folkways largely inherited from a preindustrial society; in maturity, conditioning in urban offices and factories, based on new mores and folkways that were evolving from the needs of business; and almost from birth to death, conditioning by pulpit, press, or other media of communication, based on a heterogeneous mixture of traditional and pragmatic doctrines.[14]

Shifting attention on this fundamental level from psychology to the rise of urban industrialism, the chief external pressure that upset existing family patterns, one enters a field where historians have done considerably more work but have in general subordinated their findings to the events of the presidential synthesis, and have failed, because of their disinterest in theory, to deal with many of the problems basic to urban sociology. Even A. M. Schlesinger, sr., who did much to start urban study among historians and whose general synthesis in the latter half of *Land of the Free* is one of the best, keeps the city in a relatively subordinate position.[15] Special sociological areas of first-rate importance, such as urban demography and its social consequences, are not properly considered in our general histories. The whole argument on this score might be summed up by saying that we have many "social" accounts of American historical data but few sociological interpretations.

In all this confusing historic picture of shifting ideas, folkways, and mores, of new family relationships and of growing urban problems, the massive physical

[11] The Maricopa are Southern Arizona Indians, the Maori are Polynesians. See also Clyde and F. R. Kluckhohn, "American Culture," in *Conflicts of Power in Modern Culture*, pp. 106–28.

[12] James West (pseud.), *Plainville, U.S.A.* (New York, 1945); W. L. Warner, ed., "Yankee City Series," I–IV (New Haven, 1941–47).

[13] By the biographer or historian these materials have been used chiefly to enrich and support narrative, but to the cultural anthropologist or psychologist they present clues to social and psychological patterns. Social scientists have made as little use of these historical materials as historians have of the techniques necessary to analyze them.

[14] See Thurman Arnold, *The Folklore of Capitalism* (New Haven, 1937); and also Elton Mayo, *The Human Problems of an Industrial Society* (New York, 1933).

[15] Homer C. Hockett and Arthur M. Schlesinger, *Land of the Free* (New York, 1944).

force producing change has been industrialism. Yet, judging from the presidential synthesis, the obvious fact that it was industrialism that moved us from the world of George Washington to that of the present day apparently needs still more emphasis. The spearhead of the multiple pressures of industrialization has been business, and businessmen have been of necessity the human agents who transmitted to society the physical changes born of science and industrial technology. The institutions of business, therefore, became the central mechanisms in shaping a new society and imposing industrial customs upon it. Before mid-century, the sensitive New England intellectuals were well aware of the change. "In America, out of doors, all seems a market," Emerson complained in 1844.

> . . . . I speak of those organs which can be presumed to speak in a popular sense. They recommend conventional virtues, whatever will earn and preserve property; always the capitalist; the college, the church, the hospital, the theatre, the hotel, the road, the ship of the capitalist — whatever goes to secure, adorn, enlarge these, is good, whatever jeopardizes any of these is damnable.[16]

From 1840 to 1860 the new impact of business and its urbanism upon American culture was perhaps greater relatively than in any other equal period, yet such forces appear only in the form of a few isolated phenomena in the presidential synthesis of the pre-Civil War era.

In the post-Civil War years the continuing cultural pressures of business, on which the Civil War had relatively little effect, are better recognized by our general historians. But a new difficulty now appears. Just as in the case of public opinion, the family, or urbanism, only the spectacular or exotic has been able to force its way into the traditional synthesis.[17] Our textbooks, for example, tell much of the resistance of certain farm groups to elevator and railroad practices but little of the growing force of business folkways and mores in the rural community.[18]

In this case the approach to a realistically balanced synthesis will be much easier than in those previously discussed. Business records of all types are becoming available in increasing quantities.[19] Monographic literature is steadily accumulating.[20] The general historian surveying this field, however, will find that while existing studies, in economics as well as in history, give much of the internal picture of the workings of business, the connections between business

---

[16] Ralph W. Emerson, *English Traits, Representative Men, and Other Essays* (New York, 1908), pp. 370, 371.

[17] See Thomas C. Cochran, "A Plan for the Study of Business Thinking," *Political Science Quarterly*, LXII (March, 1947), 82–90.

[18] See again, *Plainville, U.S.A.*; and also the extensive bibliography of older sociological studies of the rural community in Walter A. Terpenning, *Village and Open-Country Neighborhoods* (New York, 1931). Recent analyses such as Paul H. Landis, *Rural Life in Process* (New York, 1940), are still weak in tracing the gradual infiltration of business mores and folkways in the rural community.

[19] A National Business Records Management Center is now being organized by a committee of the Social Science Research Council.

[20] See "Harvard Studies in Business History," ed. by N. S. B. Gras (Cambridge, 1931—); and "New York University Business History Series," ed. by Thomas C. Cochran (New York, 1948—).

and society are not elaborated.[21] The business leader or entrepreneur, for example, was the arbiter not only of change within his company but also, to a large extent, of change in his community.[22] Since his money, and hence his approbation, was generally necessary for community welfare and improvement, he sat on the boards of the educational, charitable, political, and business institutions that dominated social habits and set social goals.[23] And necessarily, he carried into these other fields the habits formed by the needs of survival in business. He strove to make education, charity, politics, and social life "businesslike." Generations of historians have analyzed the thought of Clay, Webster, and Calhoun to extract every last vestige of social meaning, while Nathan Appleton, John Murray Forbes, and a host of other important business figures of the same period, awaiting their first social interpreters, do not appear in the presidential synthesis.

The modern corporation, a new social instrumentality developed primarily by business leaders, must also be given a much larger place in a social science synthesis. Here the problem is a very difficult one, challenging the scholar not so much from the standpoint of data or materials of research as from that of theory. The role of the corporation in modern society has never been adequately thought through by legal, social, or economic theorists. Noncorporeal, but quite real, the corporation, of both the profit and nonprofit variety, has established substates and subcommunities within our political and geographical divisions.[24] It has created both highly responsible and highly irresponsible entities with which all citizens are forced to deal, and under the jurisdiction of which most citizens spend a large part of their lives. The resultant problems of historical interpretation are too complex to discuss here, and have been in fact too complex for the wisdom of modern society, but complexity and difficulty are not valid excuses for historical neglect.

In summary, at the center of any social science synthesis, determining its topical and chronological divisions, should be the changes, whether material or

[21] See such studies of the current situation as Robert A. Gordon, *Business Leadership in the Large Corporation* (Washington, 1945); and Peter F. Drucker, *Concept of the Corporation* (New York, 1946). N. S. B. Gras, *Business and Capitalism* (New York, 1939) is a historical study of business organization. Some studies, such as Carl F. Tausch, *Professional and Business Ethics* (New York, 1926), and Max Radin, *The Manners and Morals of Business* (Indianapolis, 1939), deal with limited aspects of the relations of business to society.

[22] See Arthur H. Cole, "An Approach to the Study of Entrepreneurship," *Journal of Economic History*, VI, Supp. (1946), 1–15; Joseph A. Schumpeter, "The Creative Response in Economic History," *Journal of Economic History*, VII (November, 1947), 149–59, for general discussion of the socio-economic role of the business leader; and Thomas C. Cochran, "The Social History of the Corporation in the United States," in Ware, *The Cultural Approach to History* pp. 168–81, for discussion and bibliography on social aspects of business.

[23] See for example, H. P. Beck, *Men Who Control Our Universities* (New York, 1947), and Merle E. Curti, *The Social Ideas of American Educators* (New York, 1935) pp. 210–32.

[24] For discussion of the subcommunity or subgovernmental aspects of corporations, see A. M. Schlesinger, "Biography of a Nation of Joiners," *American Historical Review*, (October, 1944), 1–25; Guy Stanton Ford, *On and Off the Campus* (Minneapolis, 1938), pp. 149–51; and Stuart A. Daggett, *Chapters on the History of the Southern Pacific* (New York, 1922). For some suggestions of needed studies, see Charles A. Beard, "Corporations and Natural Rights," *Virginia Quarterly*, XII (July, 1936), 345 ff.

psychological, that have most affected, or threatened most to affect, such human conditioning factors as family life, physical living conditions, choice of occupations, sources of prestige, and social beliefs. While the historical analysis itself must, in our present stage of psychological knowledge, be concerned with concrete physical, political, or social changes or events, these should be assigned place and importance on the basis of their estimated relation to underlying social forces. The precise social effect of the rapid rise of the corporation from 1850 to 1873, for example, cannot be measured, but the social scientist is reasonably sure that it is of more importance than the presidential aspirations of Horatio Seymour.

For the period since the middle of the nineteenth century, the source material exists to make and ultimately to amplify a synthesis based on changes in major social forces.[25] While my personal bias leads me to believe that business and economic changes should be recognized as the most dynamic elements, further investigation may reveal alterations in family life or in social beliefs not stemming directly from business sources as more powerfully operative. But as long as the historian will equip himself with the knowledge necessary to probe these deeper levels, and approach the problems with the tools of theory and hypothesis, all social scientists must applaud the results as steps in the direction of historical realism.

Such a backbone of synthesis would not only sweep away the presidential structure but demolish most of the other familiar landmarks as well. War studied as a social institution would preserve its importance, but war as an arbitrary milestone for historical periodization would probably disappear. The Civil War, for example, that great divide of American historiography, viewed in the light of these long-run social criteria, shrinks in magnitude. Even in the deep South, the dramatic change in race and property relations brought on by the war will lose some of its importance when measured against a deeper background of the gradual social changes coming from the increase in middle-class farmers and industrial workers.[26] In any case, for nations as a whole, basic social change seems to come less cataclysmically than is indicated by wars or revolutions. Periodization should be recognized as wholly arbitrary and dependent upon the central focus of the synthesis employed. From the business and economic standpoints, for example, 1850 and 1885 are available points for periodization, the one symbolically marking the beginning of the rapid opening of a national industrial market, the latter roughly coinciding with the rise of a number of large semi-monopolistic business units and the beginning of federal regulation; but if the family or urbanism is made the central phenomena other dates might be selected.

For those historians who will mourn the passing of the historiographic sway of Jeffersonian and Jacksonian Democracy, the Era of Good Feeling, the Irrepressible Conflict, the Tragic Era, the Square Deal, the New Freedom, and the New Deal, there is the poor consolation that time must, in any case, doom the

[25] See, for example, the forthcoming handbook of historical statistics prepared by the United States Census Bureau in co-operation with a committee of the Social Science Research Council.

[26] See Herbert Weaver, *Mississippi Farmers, 1850–1860*, (Nashville, Tenn., 1945); and other studies directed by Frank Owsley at Vanderbilt University.

ancient subdivisions. When the United States is even two hundred years old instead of a hundred and fifty, it will no longer be possible to take up each presidential administration. Broader and less detailed syntheses will be demanded by the exigencies of space and time, and it will be up to the historian to choose whether he will avail himself of the aid offered by the social sciences or attempt an intuitive resynthesis of the type presented by Spengler or Toynbee.

The Logic of Historical Analysis

Ernest Nagel

It is a platitude that research in history as in other areas of science selects and abstracts from the concrete occurrences studied, and that however detailed a historical discourse may be it is never an exhaustive account of what actually happened. Curiously enough, it is the very selectivity of history that generates many of the broader questions relating to the nature of historical inquiry and is sometimes made the occasion for wholesale skepticism concerning the possibility of "objective" explanations in historical matters. Since a historian exercises selection in choosing problems for study, and also in his proposed solutions to them, it will be convenient to examine some of the relevant issues under these two heads.

1) Historians do not all concern themselves with the same things, and there are undoubtedly many past events that have received attention from no historian. Why does one historian occupy himself with ancient Greece, another with modern Germany, still another with the development of legal institutions in the American colonies, a fourth with the evolution of mathematical notation, and so on? Is there some general feature which differentiates those occurrences that are of concern to historians from those that are not? And, above all, is a historian prevented from giving a warranted or objective account of things because of his initial choice of a limited problem?

It is clear that there is no uniform answer to the first of these queries, for in historical inquiry as in other branches of science a variety of circumstances may determine what problems are to be investigated. It may be individual preference and endowment, controlled by education and the influence of teachers; it may be professional obligation or the desire for financial gain; it may be national pride, social pressure, or a sense of political mission. Historians of ideas have given some attention to this matter, and have uncovered interesting data concerning stimuli to specific investigations. But there is no prima facie reason to believe that, because a historical inquiry begins with a specific problem, or because there are causal determinants for his choice, a historian is in principle

From "Some Issues in the Logic of Historical Analysis," *The Scientific Monthly*, 1952, 74, pages 162–169, by permission of the American Association for the Advancement of Science and the author.

precluded — any more than is a natural scientist — from rendering an adequate account of the subjects he is investigating.

Many writers maintain, however, that the selectivity of history is peculiar in that the historian is inescapably concerned with "value-impregnated" subject matter. Thus, according to one influential view, an individual or process can be properly labeled as "historical" only if it is "irreplaceable," either because it uniquely embodies some universally accepted cultural value or because it is instrumental to the actualization of such a value. In consequence, the supposition that historical inquiry can ignore theoretical value relations is said by some writers to involve a self-deception,[2] whereas other commentators have concluded that unlike the physical sciences "history is violently personal," since "stars and molecules have no loves and hates, while men do."[3] There is, however, no basis for the claim that historical study is addressed exclusively to value-impregnated occurrences, unless indeed the word "history" is arbitrarily redefined so as to conform with the claim. For although undoubtedly much historical inquiry is concerned with events that may be so characterized, there are also many investigations commonly called "historical" that are not of this nature — for example, inquiries into the development of the stars, biological species, and much else. More generally, there appears to be no warrant for any of the various claims that the occurrences studied by historians are distinguished by some inherent differentiating feature from those that are not. Moreover, even when a historian is concerned with admittedly value-impregnated subject matter or with occurrences manifesting various passions, it by no means follows that he must himself share or judge those values or passions. It is an obvious blunder to suppose that only a fat cowherd can drive fat kine. It is an equally crude error to maintain that one cannot inquire into the conditions and consequences of values and evaluations without necessarily engaging in moral or aesthetic value judgments.

There is also the broad question whether historical inquiry is inevitably guilty of distorting the facts because it is addressed to limited problems and is concerned only with certain selected materials of the past. The supposition that it is entails the view that one cannot have competent knowledge of anything unless one knows everything, and is a corollary to the philosophic doctrine of the "internality" of all relations. It will suffice here to note that, were the doctrine sound, not only would every historical account ever written be condemned as a necessarily mutilated and distorted version of what has happened, but a similar valuation would have to be placed on all science, and indeed on all analytical discourse. In short, the fact that inquiry is selective because it originates in a specific and limited problem places the historian in no worse position than it does other scientists with respect to the possibility of achieving what is commonly characterized as objectively warranted knowledge.

2) Historical inquiry is selective not only in its starting point; it is also selective in proposing solutions to its problems. A variety of skeptical doubts about the possibility of an objective history has been expressed in consequence. One such expression takes the form that, in view of the inexhaustibly numer-

---

[2] H. Rickert, *Die Grenzen der naturwissenschaftlichen Begriffsbildung* (Tübingen: J. C. B. Mohr, 1921), p. 254.

[3] A. Nevins, *The Gateway to History* (New York: Appleton-Century, 1938), p. 29.

ous relations in which a given event stands to other events, no account can ever render the "full reality" of what has occurred. Accordingly, since every historical account covers only a few aspects of an occurrence and stops at some point in the past in tracing back its antecedents, every proposed explanation of that occurrence is said to bear the mark of arbitrariness and subjectivity. Part of this objection can be summarily dismissed with the reminder that it is never the task of any inquiry initiated by a specific problem to *reproduce* its subject matter, and that it would be a gratuitous performance were a historian in the pursuit of such a problem to formulate "all that has been said, done, and thought by human beings on the planet since humanity began its long career." Not only is the bare fact that inquiry is selective no valid ground for doubting the objectively warranted character of its conclusions; on the contrary, unless an inquiry were selective it would never come near to resolving the specific question by which it is generated.

However, the objection under discussion also rests on another misconception: it in effect assumes that since every causal condition for an event has its own causal conditions, the event is never properly explained unless the entire regressive series of the latter conditions are also explained. It has been maintained, for example, that

A Baptist sermon in Atlanta, if we seek to explain it, takes us back through the Protestant Reformation to Galilee — and far beyond in the dim origins of civilization. We can, if we choose, stop at any point along the line of relations, but that is an arbitrary act of will and does violence to the quest for truth in the matter.[4]

But is there any violence to the truth? Is B not a cause of A simply because C is a cause of B? When some future position of a planet is predicted with the help of gravitational theory and information about the initial condition of the solar system at some given time, is there ground for skepticism simply because the assumed initial conditions are in turn the outcome of previous ones? These are rhetorical questions, for the answers to all of them are obviously in the negative. Moreover, precisely what is the problem in connection with the Baptist sermon in Atlanta? Is it why a given individual delivered it at a stated time and occasion, or why he chose a particular text and theme, or why that occasion happened to arise, or why Baptists flourish in Atlanta, or why they developed as a Protestant sect, or why the Protestant Reformation occurred, or why Christianity arose in antiquity? These are all quite different questions, and an adequate answer for one of them is not even relevant as a proposed solution for the others. The supposition that, when a problem is made definite a regressive chain of answers must be sought if any one answer is to be objectively warranted, is patently self-contradictory. On the other hand, the fact that one problem may suggest another, and so lead to a possibly endless series of new inquiries, simply illustrates the progressive character of the scientific enterprise; that fact is no support for the claim that unless the series is terminated, every proposed solution to a given problem is necessarily a mutilation of the truth.

Skepticism concerning the possibility of objectively warranted explanations

[4] C. A. Beard, *The Discussion of Human Affairs* (New York: Macmillan, 1936), pp. 68–9.

in human history takes a more empirical turn when it bases its negations on the influence of personal and social bias upon such inquiry. The doubt embodied in the *aperçu* that history is written by the survivors is by no means a novelty; but in recent years it has been deepened and given a radical form by many sociologists of knowledge. According to some of them, all thought is conditioned and controlled by the "existential situation" in which it occurs; and, especially when thinking is directed to human affairs, the interpretation of observed facts, the selection of problems for inquiry and the methods employed for resolving them, and the standards of validity accepted are all functions of the thinker's unconscious value commitments and world outlook, his social position, and his political and class loyalties. Every cognitive claim concerning matters of vital human interest is therefore said to be valid only within the particular social setting in which it emerges; and the belief that it is possible to obtain explanations that are "true" for everyone, irrespective of his position in a given society, is declared to be part of the self-deception (or "ideology") of a culture.

There appear to be four distinct issues raised by this form of skepticism. In the first place, the choice of particular problems for study, especially inquiries into human affairs, is undoubtedly controlled by the character of a given culture, and sometimes by the status of the student in that culture. An investigation of traffic problems is not likely to be made in an agricultural society, and a man's interest in labor history may very well be causally related to his social position. But, as has already been seen, this form of selective activity on the part of an inquirer does not necessarily jeopardize the objectivity of his findings.

In the second place, no inquiry takes place in an intellectual vacuum, and every investigator approaches his task with information and guiding ideas derived in large measure from his culture. But it does not follow from this circumstance alone that the conscious and unconscious value commitments associated with the social status of an investigator inevitably influence his acceptance of one conclusion rather than another. The preconceptions he brings to the analysis of a given problem may be neutral to all differences in social values, even when that problem is concerned with human affairs. And, in point of fact, there are many questions in the social as well as in the natural sciences upon which there is complete agreement among students, despite their different social positions and loyalties.

It is undoubtedly the case, in the third place, that the standards of validity operative in an inquiry are *causally* related to other cultural traits, and that social status, class and national bias, and general world perspectives frequently influence what conclusions a man accepts. For example, the degree of precision currently demanded in experimental work is certainly not independent of the current state of technology; and a comparison of Southern and Northern histories of the period of reconstruction following the American Civil War makes amply clear the force of sectional and race bias. This is an area of study that has not yet been systematically exploited, although sociologists of knowledge have already illuminated the genesis of many ideas and the manner in which social pressures enforce their acceptance. In any event, biased thinking is a perennial challenge to the critical historian of human affairs; and research into the causal determinants of bias is of undoubted value for recognizing its occurrence and for mitigating if not always eliminating its influence. The very fact that biased thinking may be detected and its sources investigated shows that the case for objective explanations in history is not necessarily hopeless. Indeed, the assertion that a historian exhibits bias assumes that there is a distinction between biased and unbiased thinking, and that the bias can be identified — for otherwise the assertion would at best be simply futile namecalling. In consequence, it is possible, even if frequently difficult, to correct the bias and to obtain conclusions in better agreement with the evidence. Accordingly, if doubt concerning the objectivity of a historical explanation is based on considerations relating to the causal influence of various social factors upon the evaluation of evidence, it is often salutary and well taken; but it does not entail a wholesale skepticism concerning the possibility of such explanations.

This brings me to the final issue. It is sometimes argued that the social perspective of a student of human affairs is not only causally influential upon his inquiry, but is *logically* involved both in his standards of validity as well as in the meaning of his statements. And it is also maintained that one must therefore reject the thesis that "the genesis of a proposition is under all circumstances irrelevant to its truth."[5] On the other hand, the radical skepticism concerning objective explanations of human affairs that results is qualified by the further claim that a "relational" type of objectivity can nevertheless be achieved. Thus, students who share the same social perspective and employ the same conceptual and categorical apparatus will allegedly arrive at similar conclusions on any problem when the standards characteristic of their common perspective are correctly applied. And students operating within different social perspectives can attain objectivity in a "roundabout fashion" by construing their inevitable differences in the light of the differences in the structures of their perspectives.

There are, however, grave factual and dialectical difficulties in these several claims. There is no factual evidence to show that the "content and form" of statements, or the standards of validity employed, are *logically* determined by the social perspective of an inquirer. The facts commonly cited establish no more than some kind of causal dependence between these items. For example, the once much-publicized view that the "mentality" or logical operations of "primitive" social groups are different from those typical of European civilization — a difference that was once attributed to institutional differences in the societies compared — is now generally recognized to be without foundation. Moreover, even the most extreme proponents of the sociology of knowledge admit that there are many assertions (those usually mentioned come from mathematics and the natural sciences) which are neutral to differences in social perspective and whose genesis is irrelevant to their validity. Why cannot assertions about human affairs exhibit the same neutrality? If, as no one seems to doubt, the truth of the statement that two horses can in general pull a greater load than either horse alone is logically independent of the social status of the one who asserts it, what inherent social circumstance precludes such independence for the statement that two laborers can in general dig a ditch of given dimensions more quickly than either laborer working alone?

Second, what is the logical status of the claim that social perspectives enter essentially into the content and warrant of all assertions about human affairs?

[5] K. Mannheim, *Ideology and Utopia* (New York: Harcourt, Brace, 1936), p. 243.

Is the claim itself meaningful and valid only for those occupying a certain social status? In that case, its validity is narrowly self-limited, no student with a different social perspective can properly understand or evaluate it, and it must be dismissed as irrelevant by most inquirers into social questions. Or is the claim peculiarly exempt from what it asserts, so that its meaning and truth are not logically dependent upon the social status of those who assert it? In that case, then, there is at least one conclusion about human affairs which may be "objectively valid" in the usual sense of this phrase; and if there is one such conclusion, there is no clear reason why there may not be others.

Finally, the relational type of objectivity which the claim admits as attainable is nothing other than objectivity in the customary sense, which the claim appears to deny as possible. A translation formula which renders the "common denominator" of seemingly diverse conclusions stemming from differing social perspectives, cannot in turn be "situationally determined" in the sense under dispute. Indeed, the search for such formulas is but a well-known phase of theoretical research in all areas of inquiry. It is a search for objective invariants in numerically and qualitatively distinct processes; and when the quest is successful, as it often is, it terminates in laws of greater or less generality, with whose help what is relevant to the occurrence of an event or to the continuance of a process can be distinguished from what is not.

In brief, therefore, although the historian is undoubtedly selective in the conduct of his inquiries, and although personal and social bias frequently color his judgment and control what conclusions he accepts, none of these facts precludes the possibility of warranted explanations for the events he studies.

History, Historians, and the Secondary School Curriculum

Arthur S. Bolster, Jr.

Amid the ever-increasing literature on the secondary school curriculum recently appearing in the professional and popular press are found several essays on the social studies program by professors of history at major universities. Some of these scholars have concentrated on suggesting in what regard the present courses of study are inadequate;[1] some have gone further and proposed alternate content and methodology;[2] a few have been sufficiently concerned to

From the Harvard Educational Review, 1962, 32, pages 39–65, by permission of the Harvard Educational Review and the author.

[1] Cf. Arthur Bestor, The Restoration of Learning (New York: Knopf, 1955) especially chapters 10 and 28; Carlton J. H. Hayes, "European and World History" and Ray Allen Billington, "American History," in James D. Koerner (ed.), The Case for Basic Education (Boston: Little Brown, 1959), pp. 27–61.

[2] Cf. W. Burlie Brown, United States History: A Bridge to the World of Ideas, pamphlet published by the American Historical Association Service Center for Teachers of History.

take time to join their colleagues in the secondary school in the writing and teaching of revitalized courses in history.[3]

Regardless of their form, however, the public utterances of the professional historians have shown, not unexpectedly, a considerable uniformity. Since they have stemmed from similar basic assumptions about the nature and function of history, they have not only indicated alarm at the same qualities of the social studies program, but they have also suggested similar revisions. In the mind of the layman and the secondary school teacher the uniformity of the criticism has tended to add force to the arguments. Moreover, the generalizations with which the scholars have defended their reform proposals appear to have a simple logic that may well be seductive to history teacher and citizen alike. In any case, both the criticism and the proposed revision would seem to merit a more careful analysis than they have yet received.

Historical Background

The Committee of Seven

The post Korean War period is not the first in which historical scholars have become alarmed about the secondary school curriculum. The recent pronouncements are, in fact, a renaissance of active interest, for in the first two decades of the present century the content of the history courses in the nation's secondary schools was largely determined by the decrees of two committees of the American Historical Association. Of the two, the Committee of Seven, whose report appeared in 1899 and was reprinted nine times by 1915, was the more influential.[4] It prescribed the four-block program which dominated the teaching of history in the high school until after World War I.[5] History of the ancient and early medieval periods was to be taught in grade nine, medieval and modern European history since 800 A.D. in grade ten, English history in grade eleven, and American history and civil government in grade twelve. Nearly as influential on the content of the elementary school history program was the report of the Committee of Eight published in 1909 which advocated the chronological treatment of American history and a study of national and state governments as separate courses in grades seven and eight.[6]

The history curriculum of 1900 was undergirded with a carefully drawn rationale which validated the content. The Committee of Seven stressed citizenship education as the most important goal.

---

[3] For example Edwin Fenton and his colleagues at Carnegie Institute of Technology are conducting such a program in the Taylor-Allderdice High School in Pittsburgh, Pennsylvania.

[4] American Historical Association, *Report of the Committee of Seven* (Boston, 1915).

[5] My sampling of the courses of study of high schools published between 1900 and 1920 bears out this generalization. It is also supported by research reported in Rollo M. Tryon, *The Social Sciences as School Subjects* (New York: C. Scribner's, 1935), pp. 22ff., and by the data compiled by William G. Kimmel, *Instruction in the Social Studies*, Office of Education, Bulletin 1932, No. 17, monograph No. 21 (Washington, 1933).

[6] Grades seven and eight were part of the elementary school in most communities until the 1920's which witnessed the spread of the junior high school. American Historical Association, *Report of the Committee of Eight* (Boston, 1909).

The most essential result of secondary education is acquaintance with political and social environment, some appreciation of the nature of the state and society, some sense of the duties and responsibilities of citizenship. . . .[7]

This end was to be achieved by teaching the discipline of history which contained, by virtue of its traditional content and methodology, the learnings essential for competence in civic affairs. The Committee of Seven proclaimed that "the chief object of every experienced teacher is to get pupils to think properly after the method adopted in his particular line of work."[8] In the discipline of history the correct method of thinking was referred to as "historical mindedness."[9]

Historical mindedness should in some slight measure be bred with them [the students] and . . . they should be given the habit, or the beginnings of a habit of considering what has been when they discuss what is or what should be.[10]

History had two other virtues. It cultivated judgment by leading youth to deal with cause and effect, by teaching them how to acquire facts and arrange them logically, and by developing in them the scientific method of thinking.[11] Moreover, history imparted a sense of values. It led students to realize that what they saw about them was not eternal but transient, and that in the process of change "virtue must be militant if it is to be triumphant."[12]

Neither the influence of the Committee of Seven nor the content it recommended was surprising in terms of the social context in which the report appeared. In 1900 only about ten per cent of the nation's adolescents between fourteen and seventeen years of age were enrolled in school.[13] The high school was principally a college preparatory institution and it was logical to look to the university as the arbiter of content for the curriculum.[14] Moreover, quantification had not yet made its impact upon the social sciences, and history and government were the disciplines chiefly recognized as basic to the study of society. It was not difficult, in the relatively homogeneous community of 1900, to believe that the permanent values of mankind would emerge from a study of western history. In an age when social Darwinism motivated businessmen and Presidents, even scholars could understandably see in the story of western civilization the slow but steady progress toward a universally democratic world. That the scholar of history at the university was the person most qualified to prescribe the content of that portion of the secondary school curriculum dealing with man and society was thus patently obvious.

[7] Report of the Committee of Seven, p. 17.
[8] Ibid., p. 18.
[9] Ibid., p. 20.
[10] Ibid.
[11] Ibid., pp. 21–23.
[12] Ibid., p. 19.
[13] Bureau of the Census, Statistical Abstract of the United States, 1941 (Washington, 1941), table 127.
[14] The Committee of Seven was originally appointed "to consider the subject of history in the secondary school and to draw up a scheme of college entrance requirements in history." Report of the Committee of Seven, v.

These conditions were not to last, however. By the end of World War I a new social context provided the impetus under which the university historian's control was in large part surrendered. Of primary importance were changes in both the size and the nature of the student population of the secondary school. From a total of 518,251 in 1900, the year following the appearance of the Report of the Committee of Seven, the enrollment of the nation's public high schools jumped to 915,061 in 1910, 2,200,389 in 1920, 4,399,422 in 1930, and 6,601,444 in 1940.[15] In contrast to the ten per cent figure for 1900, eighty-two per cent of the nation's youth ages fourteen to seventeen were enrolled in school in 1950.[16] By mid-century the high school had changed from an essentially college preparatory institution to the modern comprehensive school. Simultaneously the nature of the content of collegiate fields dealing with man in organized society was broadening and diversifying. Alongside the traditional courses in history, government, and economics were appearing an increasing number of offerings in social sciences, anthropology, sociology, and statistics.[17] Furthermore, changes in the larger pattern of American life outside the school seemed to render the study of the history of western civilization and American government inadequate in themselves for fulfilling the purposes of citizenship education. In the more complex urban environment from which growing proportions of the high school population were drawn, new knowledges were increasingly necessary; knowledges so specialized and complex that the informal educative agencies — the home, the church, the shop — were unable to supply them. The need was most obvious in the technical information and skill demanded by industrial vocations, but it also reached into the civic and political area where, especially after the early thirties, the ever-extending power of government into economic and international affairs meant more perplexing issues for the voter to fathom; into economic relationships where the individual was submerged in ever more complex unions and corporations; into interpersonal relationships which the sheer closeness of urban life complicated and intensified. In such an environment it seemed increasingly doubtful that courses adequate to prepare students for advanced study at a liberal arts college were equally useful to youth terminating their formal training in high school. Courses in ancient, medieval, and European history, subjects far removed in space and time, appeared inappropriate for an adolescent about to take his place in the demanding urban present.

The effect of the new environment on the high school course of study was first conspicuously evident in the changed character of the reports of national professional organizations on the subject of curriculum. In 1913 the National Education Association which had originally requested the appointment of the Committee of Seven, set up a new group, the Commission on the Reorganization of Secondary Education. By 1918 this body was responsible for the publi-

[15] Bureau of the Census, *Statistical Abstract of the United States, 1955* (Washington, 1955), table 145.

[16] *Ibid.*, table 127.

[17] Cf. *Harvard University Catalogue* 1907–8 to 1930; Report of a Faculty Committee, *The Behavioral Sciences at Harvard* (privately printed, 1954), pp. 18–24; Catalogues of Columbia University, Delaware University, University of Georgia, Iowa State University, University of Michigan, University of California, Temple University, University of Texas, 1915–1940.

cation of seventeen documents, thirteen of which dealt with individual subject areas, and four with the more general matters of vocational guidance, physical education, moral values, and cardinal principles of education.[18]

The 1916 Commission

Both the composition of the subcommittee on social studies in the secondary school and the specific content of its report reflected what was happening to the influence of the university historian on the high school curriculum. In contrast to the Committee of Seven which was composed of six professors of history and a private school headmaster, the 1916 committee contained among its twenty-one members only two university professors of history.[19] Two other members were college teachers, one in home economics and one in rural sociology. The remaining were secondary school teachers and administrators or employees of government education departments. Clearly the report on the reorganization of the social studies was largely the work of a rapidly growing occupational group of professional educators who, though they would consult scholars in the individual disciplines on matters of course content, were neither by training nor commitment specialists in a traditional collegiate discipline, but rather were regarded as experts in school administration, instruction, and supervision.

The content which the committee suggested reflected the trend even more strikingly. Alternate programs were drawn up for grades seven, eight, and nine, which were now, because of administrative rearrangement, part of the new junior high school.[20] In place of American history and government which the Committee of Seven had prescribed for grade seven, the 1916 group proposed either a half-year of geography and a half-year of European history or a full year of European history correlated with geography. In either case civics of the local community was to be taught either as a separate study or integrated with the other subjects.[21] United States history and civics were to be retained in grade eight but they were to be closely coordinated so that the story of the growth of the "national community" would be seen as involving "all the elements of welfare."[22] In this grade geography was to be correlated with the United States history and civics. In place of ancient history in grade nine, a choice was again suggested: either a half-year of civics emphasizing state, national, and world interests, and a half-year of vocational and economic civics with history taught

[18] Bureau of Education, *Seven Cardinal Principles of Education*, Bulletin 1918, No. 35 (Washington, 1918); Bureau of Education, *The Social Studies in Secondary Education*, Bulletin 1916, No. 28 (Washington, 1916).

[19] The historians were William Mace of Syracuse and James Harvey Robinson of Columbia. Robinson had recently published his revisionary *The New History*: see James Harvey Robinson, *The New History: Essays Illustrating the Modern Historical Outlook* (New York: Macmillan, 1922 [first published March, 1912]). In an essay published in the *Proceedings* of the American Philosophical Society he had taken a firm stand in favor of rewriting history to shed new light on current issues: see James Harvey Robinson, "The New History," *Proceedings* of the American Philosophical Society, Vol. L (Philadelphia, Penn.: May-June, 1911), pp. 179–190.

[20] The Commission on the Reorganization of Secondary Education had recommended the junior high school movement highly. *Seven Cardinal Principles*, p. 18.

[21] *The Social Studies in Secondary Education*, pp. 15–20.

[22] *Ibid.*, pp. 21–22.

incidentally, or a full year of economic and vocational civics taught in conjunction with economic history.[23] For the high school (now grades ten, eleven, and twelve) a single sequence was proposed, paralleling the cycle offered in grades seven, eight, and nine.[24] Grade ten was to offer a survey of European history, half of which was to concentrate on "modern" Europe since 1700. Grade eleven would provide a study of American history since the end of the seventeenth century, and grade twelve a course in Problems of Democracy, stressing comprehension and analysis of contemporary social, political, and economic issues.[25]

The key to the difference between the proposals of the Committee of Seven and the 1916 Commission lay in their contrasting rationales. The distinction was not one of ends. Like their historian predecessors, the members of the Commission on the Reorganization of the Social Studies were unequivocal in their support of citizenship education. The aims of the social studies should be "an appreciation of the nature and laws of social life . . . a sense of responsibility of the individual as a member of social groups . . . the intelligence and will to participate effectively in the promotion of social well-being. More specifically social studies in the American high school should have as their conscious and constant purpose the cultivation of good citizenship."[26] But there was a fundamental difference in the means by which the 1916 group sought to accomplish its ends.

From the standpoint of the purpose of secondary education it is far less important that adolescent youth should acquire a comprehensive knowledge of any or all of the social sciences than it is that he should be given experience and practice in the observation of social phenomena as he encounters them; that he should be brought to understand that every social problem is many sided and complex; and that he should acquire the habit of forming social judgements only on the basis of dispassionate consideration of all the facts available. *This this committee believes can best be accomplished by dealing with actual situations as they occur and by drafting into service the materials of all the social sciences as occasion demands for a thorough understanding of the situations in question.*[27]

No longer, the committee proclaimed, should the focal point of the curriculum which deals with man and society be the discipline of history, because such a focus was inadequate to the key purpose of secondary education — enabling American youth to deal with the complex phenomena of modern society. Even where history courses were to remain as part of the curriculum, they should aim *not* at providing the student with the traditionally accepted knowledges and skills of an ancient and honorable discipline, but at understanding the vital

[23] *Ibid.,* pp. 15–25.

[24] The rationale for this repetition was apparently that in 1916 a great many youths still ended their formal education in the ninth grade. It was thus felt advisable to give them as thorough a survey of American institutions and problems as was possible at their age and repeat the program at greater depth and with greater analysis for those who did go on to high school. Bureau of Education, *The Public School System of San Francisco, California,* Bulletin 1917, No. 46 (Washington, 1917), p. 335.

[25] *The Social Studies in Secondary Education,* pp. 35, 52–56.

[26] *Ibid.,* pp. 9–10.

[27] *Ibid.,* p. 56. The italics are mine.

problems of the present world.[28] The change in orientation is clearly illustrated in the name the commission gave to the field of study. It was no longer *history*, but *social studies*.

We need not be centrally concerned here with the originality of the ideas expressed by the 1916 committee. Actually there is evidence that the recommendations were to a considerable extent patterned after practices already in existence in certain "advanced" city school systems, and there are some data to confirm the hypothesis that the communities influential in curriculum reform at least in the 1920's were not the fashionable middle class suburbs, but certain of the nation's large cities.[29] It would appear from this same data that the commission functioned more as a channel of communication for spreading changes already in progress than as the originator of a movement.

Of great importance to our present purpose, however, is an evaluation of the extent of the influence of the 1916 report, or at least of the kind of program it proposed. Several generalizations would seem to be supported by the data available on this subject. Generally speaking the courses of study which it advocated were the principal models followed in approximately a third of the nation's secondary schools in 1924 and by at least a majority of them in 1948.[30] Its most extensive influence was in the emerging junior high school where the present-centered rationale and the emphasis on community civics were widely adopted, and fusion or correlation of content was undertaken by approximately one fourth of the schools by 1930.[31] On the senior high school level a large number of schools adopted the Problems of Democracy course in the early 1930's. Elective twelfth grade courses in social science, economics, sociology, and less frequently psychology, were offered by many schools,[32] but by and large topical chronological courses in history have retained a dominant position in the high school social studies curriculum until the present day. Even within the history courses, however, the rationale represented by the commission was not without effect. Though the traditional form of the discipline has remained, the selection of content has been heavily influenced by its supposed contemporaneous importance.

At any rate it seems safe to state that rigorous courses in academic history are less frequently required of secondary school students today than was the

[28] *Ibid.*

[29] My own research into the published courses of such cities as Los Angeles, Indianapolis, Newark, Cincinnati, and Chicago bears out this contention. The Commission's report also claims to be based on "a definite trend in actual practice." *The Social Studies in Secondary Education*, p. 6.

[30] Edgar Dawson, "The History Inquiry," *Historical Outlook*, XV (June, 1942), 19. Tryon, *op. cit.*, pp. 20–21; U.S. Office of Education, "Offerings and Enrollments in High School Subjects," Chapter V, *Biennial Survey of Education*, 1948–50 (Washington, 1951), pp. 31–32.

[31] Tryon, *op. cit.*, pp. 229–237; Howard E. Wilson, *The Fusion of Social Studies in the Junior High Schools* ("Harvard Studies in Education," Vol. XXI; Cambridge, Mass.: Harvard University Press, 1933), Chapters 1 and 2; Kimmel, *op. cit.*, pp. 13–16.

[32] U.S. Office of Education, *Offerings and Registrations in High School Subjects*, Bulletin 1938, No. 6 (Washington, 1938), p. 16. Where the Problems of Democracy course was adopted the course in American history was moved to the eleventh grade, its most common location today. The World History course was apparently the product of administrative desire to save curriculum time by compressing ancient, medieval, and modern history into a single year's course.

case fifty years ago, and that the influence of the university professor of history on the secondary school curriculum is less strong now than it was then.[33] It is against this situation that the historians have directed their recent essays on curriculum and they should be seen within this historical framework.

Defining the Central Issue

It is not the function of this essay to evaluate the present social studies curriculum of the secondary school, but rather to analyze in some detail the changes in it which are being proposed by university professors of history who have expressed their views in writing. It would be helpful in defining the basic issues raised by the historians to summarize the general assumptions upon which they rest their arguments.

The basic tenet which underlies every criticism and proposed revision is that the discipline of history has unique characteristics which make its study indispensable to any individual who would be a competent member of contemporary democratic society. Since this is so, any valid analysis of the recent essays would seem to require us to consider two separate questions: (1) what purposes do the historian-critics see history as achieving in the secondary school? (2) what unique features of historical content and methodology do they claim fit it for the fulfillment of these purposes? To rephrase them as a single question, given the proposition that the human mind is incapable of conceiving of reality as a whole but must always organize its perceptions around certain concepts, what in the nature of history makes it peculiarly useful as a means of construing social reality?

The answers which the historian-critics have given to these questions are fundamentally those which were part of the rationale of the Committee of Seven. "Historical-mindedness" should be bred with our young people first, because only history allows man to examine social issues in the perspective of time; second, because the historical method involves the use of critical judgment in the drawing of conclusions and is therefore valuable training for the responsibilities of democratic citizenship; and third, because the study of the cultural heritage, particularly that of western civilization, increases the student's commitment to democratic values. Moreover, contemporary historians maintain that the usefulness of history in achieving these ends is not impaired by the great difference between the social contexts of 1960 and 1900. On the contrary, they contend that the quickened pace of change and the greater complexity of modern society make the study of history more important than ever and as vital for the terminal student as for the college-bound.[34]

Analysis of the Historians' Claims: (1)

There can be little quarrel with the assumption that among the disciplines oriented to a study of man and society only history attempts to construe reality across any considerable dimension of time. Nor can it reasonably be denied

---

[33] The conclusion would seem to be borne out by the apparent minimum influence of the 17 volume report of the American Historical Association's Commission on the Social Studies published in the 1930's.

[34] Cf. Brown, *op. cit.*, p. 6; Bestor, *op. cit.*, Chapters 19 and 21.

that human institutions are continually modified in response to new events and that the individual can be made aware of both continuity and change through a knowledge of past society. History, as Louis Namier points out, enables us to see what is and what is not typical of our own period in time.[35] It would thus seem logical to conclude that in so far as it is deemed important for members of society to have knowledge of what past institutions were like and how they differ from our own, to be aware of the change that has taken place in human society over any period of time, to that extent will some study of history be required in the public schools.

But having admitted this we have not solved, but rather created, a curriculum problem; that of selection of content. What is desirable that present-day citizens should know about past societies? Given the six thousand years of recorded history, the amount of description of the human past to which one *could* expose the oncoming generation is almost infinite. No matter what curriculum is constructed for six years of secondary schooling, the great mass of history must be omitted, and some means must be employed to separate what is to be included from what is to be excluded.

The Committee of Seven attempted to solve this problem by outlining in their four blocs the basic *minimum* knowledge of past society that any adequately educated citizen must possess. It prescribed a description of what the university historians deemed to be the major political and economic institutions and events in western civilization prior to 1900. It did not focus on the history of Asia or Africa, and it could include but a minimum of social history because not much in this area had been written by 1900. Nevertheless, the committee did feel that no part of its program could be omitted without a serious gap occurring in the student's knowledge. "The whole field gives a meaning to each portion that it cannot have by itself."[36]

The modern university historian faces this same problem of selection of content and though he has not explicitly indicated his solution, it can be inferred from his proposals that he employs the system used by the Committee of Seven — the prescription of minimum content adequate to a survey of all relevant past history. What he has failed to recognize, however, are the immense complications created for the curriculum maker by the phenomenal increase in historical knowledge since 1900.

Take, for example, the minimum knowledge which Carlton J. H. Hayes feels requisite to prevent American youth of 1960 from being "a lost generation, a generation isolated in time and space, a generation unstable and insecure."[37] Like the Committee of Seven, Professor Hayes would require a full year's course in ancient history, including deep enough coverage to secure an "appreciation" of the ancient empires of Egypt, Mesopotamia, China, India, and Persia, but centering on Greece and Rome. A second year he would devote to medieval and modern European history to 1750, and a third to European and world history from the mid-eighteenth century to the present day. A fourth year would be devoted to American history.[38]

---

[35] L. B. Namier, "History and Political Culture," in Fritz Richard Stern (ed.), *Varieties of History* (New York: Meridian Books, 1956), p. 372.

[36] *Report of the Committee of Seven*, p. 35.

[37] Hayes, *op. cit.*, p. 50.

[38] *Ibid.*, pp. 49–61.

At first glance such a program sounds reasonable, but if one juxtaposes Mr. Hayes's course of study with that recommended by his predecessors on the Committee of Seven, a basic difficulty becomes immediately evident. The new program includes all of the content of the older and a great deal more besides. If four full years of study were required to acquaint the student with the knowledge prescribed in the curriculum of 1900, how can the same amount of school time be adequate to the study of the same content plus a reasonable survey of all the key developments since 1900 together with significant information about the earlier period uncovered by modern historians?

Professor Hayes's solution is apparently to crowd each year with more material. The year's work which he recommends in European and world history since 1750 would include: "a running account of the major events of the period in Britain, France, Germany, Italy, Russia, the Balkans, etc. . . . the English and American Revolutions, the Great French Revolution, the Russian Bolshevik Revolution . . . the industrial revolution, with its bases in technology and science, with its spread from England to the European Continent and the United States and eventually throughout the world . . . a clear idea of the meaning of such terms as 'liberalism,' 'democracy,' 'socialism,' 'Marxism,' 'Communism' . . . historical study of Fascist Italy and Nazi Germany, and in greater detail of the U.S.S.R. and its satellite empire . . . basic knowledge of modern Japan, China, India, the Moslem countries, Latin America, the British Commonwealth [and their relation to] knowledge of modern Europe and the United States . . . acquaintance with internationalism as well as with nationalism and imperialism . . . the peace movements of the last century . . . the concert of Europe . . . the League of Nations, the United Nations, etc. . . ."[39] This course proposes, it is true, a lesser amount of knowledge than that presently doled out in the much-criticized world history course. It may thus alleviate but certainly does not obviate the primary reason for the latter's inadequacy. The only way to acquaint a student with such a vast amount of content in a single year's course is at a level of gross generalization, and if the purpose of the knowledge is to allow the student to orient himself in time and space, to know what is typical of his own generation and what is not, to be aware of change and continuity, there are two serious difficulties. The more gross the generalization (i.e., the more specific events are encompassed in a single historical concept) the less accurate it is as a description of past reality (i.e., the more specific exceptions there are to it) and therefore the less useful it is for orientation. And the more gross the generalization, the more abstract it is apt to be, and the less the student will be able to identify with it, that is, see it in terms of an event within his own realm of experience and thus comprehend it.

There are two alternatives to crowding each school year with more content. One is to take more time to cover the same amount of material, thus enabling more careful consideration of more specific events. The difficulty here is that there are other knowledges than historical ones which society deems it important for the school to pass on, and in an increasingly complex and technological culture their number is growing, as is their demand for curricular time relative

[39] *Ibid.*, pp. 58–59. The influence of the present international situation on Mr. Hayes's selection of content should be noted.

to history.[40] The other alternative is to practice more rigid selection — to limit the total amount of historical generalization which is deemed necessary to equip students adequately for social living. What is required in this case is not adding content to the already crowded curriculum of 1900 but finding justifiable means of limiting it still further.

It is here that the modern university historian-critic has been most remiss. He is either ignorant of, or has refused to face, an educational reality. It is very doubtful now, and it will be increasingly so as the future adds its share to recorded history, that it will be possible in six secondary school years to make meaningful to the average adolescent the major portion of the history of the world. A more rigorous selection of content will thus have to be practiced and this will require the construction of philosophically and pedagogically sound criteria by which choices of material may be made. Rather than attempting to summarize at a high level of generalization for the secondary school student the content conventionally covered in all the major courses in a collegiate history department (a process that may have been feasible in 1899 but is certainly not so in 1960), the modern university historian, if he desires to be of help to his secondary school colleagues, should devote his intellectual talent to the construction of these criteria.

Analysis of the Historians' Claims: (2)

The second major element in the rationale given by contemporary historians is the argument that the historical method involves the use of critical judgment in drawing conclusions on social issues and is therefore valuable training in democratic citizenship. This assumption, too, has been adopted from the Committee of Seven. If it can be validated, it would likely provide one criterion for the selection of content; that is, one could select that content best suited to train the student to use critical judgment in dealing with social issues. An analysis of the essays on curriculum being published by modern collegiate historians, however, indicates that before history can be used to teach critical judgment there are problems to be solved which are more complex than the authors of the essays have generally realized.

The Committee of Seven's case for history's value in enhancing the critical factor rested heavily on the now discredited theory of general mental discipline. History, they maintained, cultivates the judgment by developing the pupil's capacity to deal with cause and effect relationships,[41] by training him to gather and systematize ideas from many books thereby increasing his ability to make use of knowledge,[42] and by developing in him "the scientific habit of mind."[43] Modern historians, though they have abandoned the concept of mental gymnastics, rest their case heavily on the contention that the study of history acquaints the student with the historical process and that this process is basically

[40] This force has apparently been largely responsible for the increasing tendency to require less history study of modern high school students. The world history course was developed as an administrative device to save time for other subjects and even this course is less frequently required than was the case twenty years ago.
[41] Report of the Committee of Seven, pp. 7–21.
[42] Ibid., pp. 22–23.
[43] Ibid., p. 24.

the *same* process that should be used in critically analyzing any contemporary social situation. Both claims need modification.

Professor Brown's View

Let us take, for example, one attempt to construct an American history course which deals with historical process: *United States History: A Bridge to the World of Ideas*, written by W. Burlie Brown of Tulane University and widely circulated to secondary school teachers through the American Historical Association's Service Center for Teachers of History. Professor Brown in his introduction expresses his disappointment in visiting history classes in some forty American high schools at finding them all patterned after "what Arnold Toynbee has described as the 'one damn thing after another school of history'."[44] Present high school history courses, he notes, are just teaching students to memorize and regurgitate facts. Mr. Brown does not contend that solid knowledge of the facts of American history is unimportant. "One must know *what* happened before he can grapple with the problems of *how* and *why* it happened."[45] But he does want an effort made to do something more than just teach facts. With this in mind he has created a new high school course in American history, a job which he sees as being within the competence of only the university history instructor.[46]

Mr. Brown's course attempts to form a bridge between the simple narrative factual approach and the analytic approach to history which he develops with his classes at Tulane.[47] It is designed to require a full year's study and is divided into two sections. The first consists of seven topics arranged chronologically to cover the period from the founding of the English colonies in America to the end of the Civil War. The purpose of the first semester's work is not so much chronological coverage as to teach the student "the process of critical thought, historical understanding, the analytic method."[48] The topics are thus arranged to point up cause and effect relationships (e.g., "The Reasons for English Colonization of North America," "The Causes of the American Revolution"), and the teacher is to attempt to consider only three or at best four of the topics in the sixteen week semester.[49] The second half of the course deals with the process of historical synthesis — "the attempt to impose order upon a multiplicity of phenomena, a search for a kind of common denominator that will explain our contemporary civilization in most of its significant aspects."[50] Its purpose is to stress "the *relationship* among many forces and events, the *discovery of a pattern* of arrangement of these phenomena that makes them meaningful."[51] This part of the course consequently abandons the chronological narrative and organizes the data around a single theme, "the emergence of an urban-industrial way of life and the resulting dislocations, problems, and

[44] Brown, *op. cit.*, p. 3.
[45] *Ibid.*
[46] *Ibid.*
[47] *Ibid.*, p. 6.
[48] *Ibid.*, p. 7.
[49] *Ibid.*
[50] *Ibid.*
[51] *Ibid.*

changes that its advent brought to the practices, ideas, institutions and patterns of belief in the major areas of American life."[52]

Professor Brown's course represents a commendable example of the way in which justifiable criteria can be used to select content. He avoids the difficulties implicit in Professor Hayes's world history course by not trying to teach the major part of recognized content in his subject but rather by using a manageable portion of that content as the data for teaching the unique processes of the discipline. Presumably if the student can get from the course facility in the use of the processes, he can at any later time apply them to any historical content.

However, we must examine more closely the method by which he seeks to teach the two elements which he conceives as basic to the historical method — analysis and synthesis. In this connection Mr. Brown sees for the teacher a most active role. "He must lecture and conduct classroom discussions," for listening and note-taking is a very important intellectual exercise.[53] Furthermore, Professor Brown provides for both halves of the course a complete syllabus which "outlines each topic in detail, provides annotations that indicate direction and emphases to be given [to the content] and supplies a bibliography that will enable the teacher to go to the precise chapter and page of a large number of scholarly works selected from the vast literature on United States history to bolster his [the teacher's] *presentation*."[54] In short, the teacher is to teach historical analysis by pointing out to the student the analyses of contemporary scholars and to develop skills in historical synthesis by acquainting his pupils with *one* synthesis made by a professional historian of a selected number of events from the period from 1865 to the present.

It would seem at best problematical that such a technique will accomplish the ends intended for it. Indeed, excellent as the content of Professor Brown's course is (and I think it is superior in this regard even to the typical college survey of American history) it seems to differ from the run-of-the-mill high school courses he dislikes more in degree than in kind. Instead of being taught a simple chronological narrative, the student is now to be given a more sophisticated analytic view in the first semester, and a more elaborate synthesis in the second. In either case the student is being acquainted with the results of an historical process performed by someone else and I doubt if this will teach the critical judgment of the historian any more than memorizing Euclidean proofs, no matter how carefully laid out, teaches youngsters to think like geometricians.

Such a program may help young people to see our society within desirable perspectives. It may also teach the basic *structure* of history as a discipline.[55] But even if the objective of the course is limited to students' comprehension of analysis and synthesis as elements of historical structure, these elements must be emphasized *explicitly* in the classroom and not left *implicit* in the content itself. Understanding the nature of synthesis and analysis is far different from being able to perform the critical judgments necessary to use these processes.

[52] *Ibid.*, p. 34.
[53] *Ibid.*, p. 5.
[54] *Ibid.*, pp. 5–6. The italics are mine.
[55] For a psychologist's discussion of this objective of teaching cf. Jerome S. Bruner, *The Processes of Education* (Cambridge, Mass.: Harvard University Press, 1960), pp. 17–32.

The latter skills can be taught only by explaining to the student the specific steps in the processes and leading him to reach his own conclusions by their use.

It may be argued that such a practice requires having the students write their own history and that this is impractical in view of the average adolescent's lack of intellectual sophistication. The Committee of Seven, in fact, used this argument against the document-centered course sometimes found in the 1890's.[56] My own experience as a secondary school teacher would also lead me to predict that it will be necessary to limit the students' direct experience with historical method to smaller topics within a larger framework provided by the instructor. But this does not invalidate my major contention that the critical skills of the historian can only be effectively taught by having students use them directly.

Professor Bestor's View

Professor Arthur Bestor apparently bases his belief in history's value as citizenship education partly upon this same premise:

> The contribution that history can make to the discussion of contemporary affairs is not limited to the data it can furnish. Historians can assist in improving the *quality* [sic] as well as the content of public discussion if only they will point out more *explicitly* [my italics] than they have usually done the procedures upon which they rely for safeguarding the exercise of judgment against abuse and for testing its final results.[57]

Professor Bestor, like Professor Brown, conceives of the historian's task as either analysis or synthesis. The former process is apparently applied when he deals with single discrete historical episodes, that is, generalizations based upon a limited number of events. The method here is to examine the documents which previous historians have found crucial and then to check their generalizations against a large sample of other pertinent documents. As the historian continues to examine other evidence, "a more or less conclusive interpretation will have been taking provisional shape in his mind."[58] He must go on as long as feasible checking this interpretation in the light of new evidence, always guarding against his personal bias. "At some point, finally, he must make up his mind and put in final form the interpretation that appears to him to accord with the weight of all the evidence he has been able to examine."[59]

The process of synthesis is used when the historian, rather than dealing with interpretation of discrete episodes, is "treating the large and inclusive context of an event or when offering interpretations of broad scope."[60] In this case he is not writing after a painstaking treatment of a finite number of documents relating to a single event, but is selecting a small number of events from a myriad of happenings "to illustrate the play of historical forces as he sees and understands them."[61] Though the selectivity of evidence is different from that employed in the analytic procedure, the intellectual skill required to produce

---

[56] *Report of the Committee of Seven*, p. 23.
[57] Bestor, *op. cit.*, p. 437.
[58] *Ibid.*, p. 439.
[59] *Ibid.*
[60] *Ibid.*, p. 440.
[61] *Ibid.*, p. 441.

the final product is much the same, "setting forth, in all its complexity and with all the necessary critical reservations, his [the historian's] own final conception of the inclusive historical development with which he has concerned himself."[62]

Crucial in both processes are the "acts of judgment" which the historian performs in selecting, ordering, and assigning varying degrees of importance to the data upon which he relies for his interpretation.

What is called historical criticism or historical method is little else than the process of weighing and considering carried to a fairly high degree of refinement and subtlety.[63]

The establishment of this quality of "good judgment as a recognized ingredient of sound and serious thinking" is one of the great contributions of the teaching of history in the secondary school.[64]

We never learn from Professor Bestor precisely what this "act of judgment" is nor how it is performed. He explains with great firmness what it is *not*. It is not the process of quantifying one's data and determining a statistical mean of all the events and statements in a given space of time.[65] But what it *is* is never more specifically described than the process of making up one's mind after "an endless series of acts of judgment."[66]

Mr. Bestor has not analyzed the historian's craft with sufficient discrimination to isolate the various intellectual operations it encompasses. He has not carefully defined the methods used to authenticate data, conventionally referred to as internal and external criticism.[67] What is more important, he has also failed to distinguish between the two parts of the method used by the historian as scientist in arriving at his explanations, that of *forming* hypotheses, and that of *validating* hypotheses. The former, involving primarily an *intuition*, is indeed an "act of judgment" that resists exact description. The latter, involving the determination of the amount and direction of relationship postulated in the hypothesis (Mr. Bestor's "process of weighing"), is a much more precise "act of judgment" to which it might pay historians to consider applying statistical methodology rather than ridiculing it by misapplication as Professor Bestor has done.[68]

In any case, though the public school teacher may be willing to accept the claim that the intellectual processes which the historian uses in arriving at his construction of reality involve the use of critical judgment which can be applied to contemporary social issues, he will hardly be able to teach them to his stu-

---

[62] *Ibid.* Richard Hofstadter has distinguished these two roles of the historian differently and more accurately, I think, as the difference between writing an historical monograph and a traditional historical narrative. Richard Hofstadter, "History and the Social Sciences," Stern, *op. cit.*, pp. 359 ff.

[63] Bestor, *op. cit.*, p. 437.

[64] *Ibid.*, p. 452.

[65] *Ibid.*, pp. 441, 445–449. Professor Bestor's conception of the use of statistical verification is at best naive. No competent social scientist would ever argue that the most important generalization in a document could be discovered by counting the number of specific references to it in the document.

[66] *Ibid.*, p. 442.

[67] Cf. for such a description Homer C. Hockett, *The Critical Method in Historical Research and Writing* (New York: Macmillan, 1955), pp. 13–62.

[68] Cf. footnote 65.

dents unless he knows what they are. If the professional historians, therefore, are anxious to have the oncoming generation apply the historical process to present-day problems, they would be well-advised to devote more thought to a lucid explanation of its exact nature.

Professor Billington's View

Even if we assume, however, that the critical processes of the historian can be adequately defined, the assumption that history is uniquely adequate to the solution of current issues raises three problems. All are evident in Professor Ray Allen Billington's essay on "American History" in a volume entitled *The Case for Basic Education.*[69]

The first involves the method of approach to problems. Contemporary university historians frequently criticize the modern social studies curriculum because it falls prey to "the menace of excessive contemporaneity" in its attempt to equip students to deal with the problems of the world in which they live[70]; that is, the course of study overemphasizes the present and underemphasizes the past. The historical approach is more sound, to quote Professor Billington, because it adds the perspective of time and because today's problems "are deeply rooted in the . . . past [and] can be understood only against that background."[71]

There is in this argument, however, a potential contradiction. We may grant that adequate solutions to all contemporary problems require knowledge of their historical antecedents; nevertheless, if the *purpose* of our study of man and society is to help deal with *present-day* problems then pedagogically it would be most logical to start with present-day problems and not, as historical narratives do, at some professionally pre-determined point in the past. It is undoubtedly true that students cannot comprehend today's struggle over integration without some knowledge of the history of slavery in the United States, the sectional conflicts of the thirties, forties, and fifties, and the Civil War and reconstruction.[72] But if the central intent is to understand the integration issue, and if one is committed also to the scientific method, it is proper to start not with the history of Negro slavery but with a definition of the problem of integration today. Having isolated the elements of the problem, one would then proceed to gather evidence — historical, sociological, economic, ethnological — whatever is necessary to the generation and validation of relevant hypotheses.

The second difficulty in using history to aid in the solution of contemporary problems concerns the nature of historical content. Again Professor Billington's essay may be of help to us. "History, after all," he tells us, "is an art as much as a science; writing it is an art, teaching it is an art. . . ."[73] The appreciation of history he sees as "directly comparable . . . to looking at a painting, listening to a symphony, or watching a play." It involves "aesthetic and emotional experience."[74]

---

[69] Billington, *op. cit.*, pp. 27–48.
[70] Bestor, *op. cit.*, Chapter 10.
[71] Billington, *op. cit.*, p. 37.
[72] *Ibid.*, p. 31.
[73] *Ibid.*, p. 35.
[74] *Ibid.*, pp. 35–36.

This is on the whole a helpful distinction. History has evolved as a discipline over a long period of time and thus the qualities which define it have the force of tradition. The historian is a scientist in so far as part of his task is to determine explanations of past reality which are validated by specific evidence; he is an artist in so far as part of his task is to present his explanations within the context of a "living, human, story."[75] Such a definition of history, however, raises a potential liability of its use in solving contemporary problems: its description of past reality is subject to distortion by the traditional requirement that the historian "humanize" his presentation. This is not to say that there is no difference between reality and perceived reality, or that the generalizations of other sciences — natural or social — are unaffected by the "frame of reference" of the scientist who conceived them. It is to say that history as a traditional discipline, as well as facing the subjective limitations of any science, is peculiarly subject to "the tyranny of written models."[76] Professor Billington's essay furnishes an example. Having begun with the usual claim that history is valuable to secondary school students because it teaches them critical judgment and objectivity,[77] he summarizes in a later section a portion of the historical data necessary to understand one of the problems facing the United States today. (The italics in the passage are mine.)

The Monroe Doctrine of 1823 was designed to *seal off* the American continent from Europe's *aggressors*, but no mere declaration could *curb the spirit of aggression* on either side. Americans, convinced that their duty was the *democratization of the world*, continuously gave aid to European peoples *struggling against tyranny*, even at the risk of war; Europe's monarchs, as *fearful of democracy as today's free world is of communism*, persisted in *meddling* in hemisphere affairs as they had before. Then as now the *sense of mission* so strong on both sides of the Atlantic posed *explosive* problems: How far could the United States reconcile its desire to win self-government *for all peoples* with the limitations of its own strength and the *horrors of war*? How could it *shrewdly gauge* the future course of *antagonist* nations in determining its own line of action?[78]

One problem in applying the criterion of objectivity to this passage is the gross generalizations it contains. It would be unfair not to recognize the difficulties which limitations of space have placed upon Professor Billington. But more significant for our present purposes is the emotive tone of the language which he uses to enliven his narrative. The italicized phrases do indeed make his description vivid, even exciting. But what about the objectivity with which the study of history is to equip the younger generation to face today's complex issues? If unbiased critical judgment is the primary objective, it seems impossible that construing these past problems as Mr. Billington does here can, in

[75] The words are those of Paul Ward, former chairman of the Department of History at Carnegie Institute of Technology in his pamphlet *A Style of History for Beginners* (Washington, 1959), p. 15. The pamphlet was circulated to teachers of history by the American Historical Association's Service Center for Teachers of History.

[76] Thomas C. Cochran, "The 'Presidential Synthesis' in American History," *The American Historical Review*, LIII (July, 1948), 750.

[77] Billington, *op. cit.*, pp. 28, 31.

[78] *Ibid.*, p. 40.

his own words, "guide today's statesmen and voters toward an honorable solution of their own."[79]

Finally, any evaluation of the university historian's claim on the indispensability of history to the solving of contemporary problems must reckon with the question of the predictability value of history. If we claim that school children should be taught the record of the past chiefly as a *means* of solving current social problems, or at least a way of construing these problems so that they may be more easily solved, we mean that the problems are to be solved not at this instant, but in the future — tomorrow, next year, or, more logically, ten years from now when today's adolescent becomes a voter. This being so, we must also concede that historical knowledge will not help to solve these problems unless it has predictability value. Unless we agree that there is enough consistency in human behavior so that, knowing the results of man's actions in regard to a myriad of past conditions (what happened and why), we are in a better position to know how he should act in the present and the future, then we have no need for history in dealing with contemporary issues. If knowledge of how Rooseveltian New Nationalism and Wilsonian New Freedom attempted to preserve the balance between liberty and authority in our society is of any use in maintaining this balance today (as Mr. Billington says it is),[80] then it is because there is enough commonality in the problem and in the humans facing it so that knowledge of past involvements with the issue will allow us to predict in some helpful way the probable consequences of future behavior toward it. Any value of history as the "memory of the race" rests ultimately on its utility in prediction.[81]

Yet the professional historians who extol the value of their discipline in preparing students to face contemporary issues often are unwilling to claim that historical content is of any use as a basis for prediction. Professor Billington, for example, ends his discussion of the desirability of students knowing about the past attempts to solve the liberty versus authority dilemma with the following sentence:

> History has no final answers for these problems or any others, for mankind's behavior is both variable and unpredictable, but today's citizens will be able to act more intelligently in their decision-making if they are familiar with the lessons it can teach.[82]

The sentence contains an obvious contradiction. Either history has at least limited predictability value and therefore some lessons to teach or it has no predictability value, in which case it is useless as a guide to appropriate action on contemporary problems.

In summary, if the professional historian in his attempt to win more curricular consideration for his discipline in the secondary school is going to place any substantial reliance on its utility as a means of equipping the on-coming

[79] *Ibid.*
[80] *Ibid.*, p. 42.
[81] Historians, among them Professor Hayes, often use this precise metaphor in defending the social utility of their specialty. Cf. Hayes, *op. cit.*, p. 51.
[82] Billington, *op. cit.*, p. 43.

generation to deal with social issues, then he must present a more convincing case than he has yet been able to. He must strive to describe his methodology more precisely and demonstrate how it can be directly applied to current problems. He must frankly analyze the nature of his content field in order to evaluate it objectively. Finally, he may have to be willing to use his skill as a social scientist to predict what present problems are likely to remain crucial in the immediate future and center both his content and his methodology on their solution.

Analysis of the Historians' Claims: (3)

There remains a consideration of the third argument which is used to support the teaching of history in the public schools — that the study of the past, particularly of western culture, will increase the student's commitment to the basic values of our civilization. In the history of history as a school subject this has been its most frequently mentioned virtue. In the 19th century elementary school courses were largely devoted to this aim and they remain so in large part today. In defending its secondary school program the Committee of Seven considered the reaffirmation of militant virtue high on its list of criteria for citizenship education,[83] and the National Education Association's 1916 Commission on the Reorganization of the Social Studies assigned great importance to the creation of intelligent national loyalties.[84]

The rationales of the contemporary historians have frequently reiterated these arguments. Professor Hayes maintains that "particularly our schools should teach and inculcate in American youth a knowledge and appreciation of Western Civilization as a whole."[85] Professor Billington in his defense of a more thorough teaching of American history has been even more specific:

By familiarizing us with past instances of heroism and past examples of wise leadership, history ennobles us, and quickens our faith in our heritage. By revealing the deficiencies of statesmen of former generations, it inclines us to be more tolerant toward the mistakes of today's leaders. By laying bare the record of man's slow struggle for liberty and security it convinces us of the inevitability of progress toward those goals, and inures us to the momentary setbacks caused by the rise of totalitarian systems. No one truly familiar with the history of the United States can adopt a defeatist attitude when facing the continuing crises of the Cold War, or surrender to doubt that democratic institutions will prevail. Only the study of history engenders such faith and assures such hope for the future.[86]

The basic premise seems reasonable. Social cohesion is a requisite for the survival of any culture. Commitment of the masses of our people to at least the same central values is particularly necessary in a democracy which allows such tremendous diversity of value allegiance outside of the basic core. More-

[83] Report of the Committee of Seven, p. 19.
[84] The Social Studies in Secondary Education, pp. 9–10.
[85] Hayes, op. cit., p. 49.
[86] Billington, op. cit., p. 33.

over, in our own age when our society is threatened by a powerful external enemy it is unusually crucial that the oncoming generation have strong loyalty to the ideals which undergird our civilization.

Nor can it be doubted that history is a potentially effective way to create such loyalty. There is anthropological evidence that tales of folk heroes are means of effecting social cohesion. History itself — particularly that of the nations against whom we fought in World War II — confirms the power of the skillfully constructed chronicle in generating a sense of national purpose. The Soviet Union is apparently making efficient use of history to inculcate faith in Russian and Marxian ideals.[87]

Nevertheless, if we are to use history as a means of building allegiance to our cultural value system and simultaneously to employ it to teach critical judgment and to enable our children to deal objectively with contemporary problems, we face a difficulty which somehow must be reconciled. It can be illustrated strikingly by juxtaposing to Professor Billington's previously quoted statement (on the value of the study of the American past in quickening the student's faith in his national heritage) a declaration made earlier in the same essay on the subject of objectivity.

Through the study of the past they [the secondary school students] learn that human affairs can never be simple — that there are no pat heroes and villains, no "bads" and "goods," no simple cause and effect relationships, in human behavior. . . . If a student emerges from his schooling with an awareness of history's underlying complexity, he will realize that large issues of all sorts seldom have a "right" or "wrong" answer, but must be appraised objectively in historical perspective.[88]

Mr. Billington's apparent contradiction can be explained only by realizing that the two uses to which he proposes to put history are in some sense antithetical. In the first instance he is arguing for value inculcation. The study of history will show students the inevitability of progress toward democratic institutions. Why? Because a critical examination of historical evidence indicates that democratic societies are longer-lived than totalitarian societies? Because a greater proportion of the world's peoples live under democratic institutions today than one hundred years ago? Because non-democratic regimes can only be maintained by military force? It would be possible to arrange a historical narrative to substantiate these contentions, but it would also be possible to construct one to cast doubt upon them. It seems likely therefore that Mr. Billington is arguing for the use of history to show the *desirability* of democratic institutions, their *value, not their inevitability*. For if the history teacher desires to prove the value of democracy then he must select his data and write his generalizations with this end in mind. Though he may argue with logic for certain values, he cannot prove them by a scientific method because values are not scientifically provable.

[87] George S. Counts, *The Challenge of Soviet Education* (New York: McGraw-Hill, 1957), pp. 94–103. For a provocative interpretation of the role of the school in transmitting cultural heritage, cf. Ruth Benedict, "Transmitting our Democratic Heritage in the Schools," *American Journal of Sociology*, XLVIII (May, 1943), 722.

[88] Billington, *op. cit.*, p. 29.

Critical judgment, however, for which Professor Billington argues in the second instance, is a different matter. If by critical judgment is meant the scientific method, then it is crucial to realize that the only value accepted is the worth of the scientific procedure itself as a means of arriving at truth. Indeed, science begins in skepticism. No generalization is to be accepted unless the great preponderance of evidence clearly validates it (Mr. Billington's objectivity). Though in practice it is impossible, the ideal of the scientific method requires the scientist to select his data without reference to his personal value commitments.

For this reason the attempt to employ the same historical material to achieve the ends both of value commitment and of critical judgment creates a difficult curriculum problem. If history is to be used to promote faith in our unique heritage, our western political value system, then there are some generalizations which it is obviously pedagogically unsound to question. What Mr. Jefferson called "self-evident truths" had best be left self-evident. In fact the history teacher concerned chiefly with inculcating allegiance to these values could most efficiently achieve his goal by arranging his content in such a way as always to cast favorable light upon them: that is, the rationalization of certain values becomes the criterion for the careful selection of content, and the line between history and myth is blurred. If, on the other hand, the teacher is concerned about the use of historical content and method as an aid to teaching critical judgment, he must continually encourage skepticism. No truth should be accepted as self-evident, and Mr. Jefferson's whole philosophy should be subjected to a rigorous proof process.

A familiar content example may make the dilemma clear. How does the public school history teacher deal with Abraham Lincoln? Does he portray him as the exemplar of democratic humanism; the railsplitter and scrupulously fair backwoods lawyer; the humanitarian in the White House singularly dedicated to the rule of law; the Great Emancipator centrally concerned with human equality? Or does the teacher present Lincoln in Richard Hofstadter's terms as the "self-made myth": the shrewd man who deliberately built a public image of himself; the expedient candidate who in his quest for votes told a southern audience that the white race should be socially and politically superior to the negro; the chief executive who violated the lawful decisions of the Supreme Court and reluctantly freed the slaves more as a matter of military expedience than of moral rectitude?[89] Or does the teacher support neither interpretation, but merely raise the question what kind of man was Abraham Lincoln, introduce evidence on both sides, the speech on white superiority as well as the Gettysburg Address, *ex parte* Merryman as well as the Second Inaugural, and then say to the student, "make up your own mind, either way, but just be sure you use critical judgment."

There are ways of coping with this dilemma, but they are not without pedagogical difficulties. It is possible to use certain selected texts for value inculcation and confine critical judgment to different content or to plot one's teaching so that certain generalizations like the progress of democracy are not

---

[89] Richard Hofstadter, *The American Political Tradition and the Men Who Made It* New York: Knopf, 1948), pp. 92 ff.

open to criticism. Either process, however, would seem to violate the canons of scientific methodology. One may also follow what I take to be the presently favored procedure in the public schools, separate the two objectives by covering the material at two different times in the child's school career. Thus the current elementary school courses in American history are used to inculcate values, and critical analysis is reserved for high school or more often college. But there is considerable doubt that many high school courses can be expected to teach students to apply critical judgment to a significant number of historical generalizations, partly because of lack of availability of data with which to make such judgments and partly because of the insistence of pressure groups that certain viewpoints be maintained. Even if it were possible to convince a publisher, one can imagine the opposition of major patriotic organizations to allowing a textbook to raise the open-ended question, was Lincoln a great humanitarian or a self-made myth?

Nevertheless, the potential conflict between using history for critical judgment and history for imbuing loyalty to our cultural values is an issue to which some kind of resolution must be made if the teaching of social studies in the public school is to be substantially improved. It is thus an issue which the professional historian should not merely perpetuate by arguing at a high level of generality for both objectives simultaneously, but one to whose resolution he should turn his intellectual talent and effort.

Summary and Conclusions

What then can finally be said of the recent attempts of university historians to emulate their predecessors on the Committee of Seven and exert a salutary influence on the secondary school curriculum? If the essays reviewed in this critique are a valid sampling of professional opinion, they would seem to indicate the need for some specific words of caution.

First, if the contemporary historian is sincere in his desire to win for history a more careful and widespread treatment than it now receives in the curriculum, he should think and write more carefully about both its nature and its social utility. It is commendable, even essential, that scholars be deeply commited to their subject and desire others to share their enthusiasm. But scholars must beware that their ardor does not lead them to make loose claims for their speciality that do not stand the test of rational analysis. It is convincing for historians to proclaim that they are committed to history as are thousands of their fellow-men, that theirs is a discipline universally taught in colleges and one which millions of educated people have valued. But they risk doing their discipline a disservice if they rest their case on shallow generalizations: that no one who is unfamiliar with all major world developments since 4000 B.C. can be a competent citizen; or that a study of the past is uniquely and simultaneously able to produce lifelong commitment to certain values and consistent use of the skill of critical judgment.

Secondly, if university historians expect their thoughts on curriculum to elicit from those responsible for the secondary school the careful consideration they deserve, they must be willing to consider their subject within the context of the complicated curriculum problems facing the public educator today. They must be aware, for example, that in an increasingly complex culture, the public schools are being asked to pass on ever enlarging numbers of knowledges and skills which the community deems vital but which the other educational institutions are incompetent to teach; that the amount of knowledge it is possible to teach to young people is accruing with amazing rapidity; and that history is not the only branch of learning demanding more curricular attention.

Finally, if his suggestions are to be helpful to the social studies teacher, the university historian must seek to understand more accurately how the role of the secondary school teacher differs from his own. He must realize that a public school teacher is a public employee maintained in his position by all the people of the community to educate all of their children. This raises the familiar curriculum difficulty of having to teach students of varying abilities and interests — those who study because they *want* to, as well as those who attend class because they *have* to.[90] Equally important, the teacher's role as a *public* servant means that he is obligated to consider primarily the social utility of his subject. In the secondary school as in the college it is of vital pedagogical importance that the instructor be well-trained in his content field and personally committed to it. But for the public school teacher commitment and competence are not enough. He must also ask himself: what, in terms of society's goals, justifies my teaching this that I love?

It is this issue of the social utility of his discipline which is so difficult for the university scholar. It puts him in the uncomfortable and unusual position of trying to rationalize a branch of learning in terms of a higher goal. At the university the professor's position may be justified by his increasing the amount of knowledge in his field. But if he is to write about the public school curriculum he must push a step further. He cannot argue any knowledge, any discipline for its sake alone. He must join his secondary school colleague in coming to grips with the gnawing question: why *this* knowledge and *this* discipline?

It is a query he must approach with great caution, for the wrong kind of answer may nullify his contribution to the secondary school. On the one hand, he must find a response that is both specific and genuine. He must resist the temptation to utter generalizations so broad as to be meaningless. He must avoid the sham of disguising his personal commitment to history beneath a cloak of social platitudes. At the same time, he must guard the integrity of his discipline by not placing it in the service of some other end, thus depriving it of its effectiveness.

There is another crucial dimension which the university historian should recognize as distinguishing the secondary school teacher's role from his own, and that is the public school instructor's total involvement in the classroom. The high school history teacher cannot be an historian because he does not have time to be.[91] In the great majority of cases he must face a class five or six periods a day, five days per week — a total of thirty clock hours of teaching each five days. Added to this are the supervisory requirements in relation to extracurricular activities and the time necessary to read whatever he requires his

[90] Arthur Bestor has analyzed this problem in considerable detail. Bestor, *op. cit.*, Chapters 19 to 21.

[91] Professor Brown's visits to forty high schools apparently made him aware of this limitation. Cf. Brown, *op. cit.*, p. 6.

students to write. My own experience as a public school teacher convinced me that superior high school social studies teachers spend around fifty hours per week merely staying abreast of their teaching duties, and the majority of this time is used in energy-sapping direct personal contact with adolescents. There remains neither time nor strength for creative scholarship. Consequently there is an inevitable tendency to become further and further removed not only from new knowledge being unearthed within the subject-field but also from the intellectual process which distinguishes the discipline. The natural result is for the teaching to become largely the communication of historical generalizations — either those learned in the teacher's collegiate training, or those found in the textbook, or a combination thereof. Thus, to a great extent the conditions which dominate the American public secondary school make the achievement of any substantial intellectual objectives difficult if not impossible.

It is for this reason that the active interest of the university historians is desirable, perhaps even vital, to improvement of secondary school social studies curriculum. But if it is to be effective, it must be carefully and thoughtfully applied. The situation is far too complex to be altered by chauvinistic essays which merely repeat the ideas of the Committee of Seven. At minimum what is needed is a sympathetic understanding of the limitations which the public school environment places on the teacher and whatever influence the prestige of the university may exert to lessen them. More specifically the professional historian can be of service by producing realistic answers to the central curriculum problems: what historical content is it important for the oncoming generation to know and at the same time possible to teach them in the limited time available in the secondary school; what exactly is the historical process, should it be taught to adolescents, and if so, how; what means can be used to reconcile the conflict between history as value inculcation and the desired objectivity of social science?

Nothing short of the careful attention of the best historical scholarship is likely to have much influence.

History Textbooks and Explanation

Lawrence E. Metcalf

The pitfall of easy familiarity [with the past] originates to a considerable degree in the way textbooks in history are manufactured. The conditions surrounding textbook manufacturing practically guarantee that the textbook content will be conceptually empty at the same time that students, particularly the bright ones, will be led to believe that they are learning great and significant truths.

From "Research on Teaching the Social Studies," in N. L. Gage (editor), *Handbook of Research on Teaching*, Rand McNally & Company, 1963, pages 929–965. By permission of the American Educational Research Association and the author.

Over the years a standard content has been established in American and world history. An American history text that fails to mention the Emancipation Proclamation in both index and body runs the risk of losing customers among those who believe the book to be seriously incomplete because of this omission. But a book that is complete must also be up to date. If it fails to mention the more recent events, particularly those that have been admitted to the field of history since competing texts were published, it will lose customers among those who want a "new" or "modern" or "different" book. But a book that is complete and up-to-date must also be portable if it is to be used in schools that make use of a platoon system (in which two groups of pupils, called platoons, alternate in studying the tool subjects and in engaging in activities in special rooms) or homework, both of which require students to carry their books about. The requirement of portability places some general limit upon number of pages and weight.

The general requirement, then, of any textbook writer in the field of high school history is to write about more and more within roughly the same number of pages. Any modern tendency to make a book attractive and "teachable" by including charts, tables, pictures, and end-of-chapter teaching aids cuts into precious space. The only solution is for the writer to express himself in generalities, leaving out all the detail that would give these generalities meaning. He proceeds to violate a "law" laid down by William James who said that no one sees any further into a generalization than his knowledge of detail extends.

What does this practice of confronting students with other people's generalizations mean? How does it make students victims of the pitfall of easy familiarity? First, it must be recognized that a writer turns to generalities because he can use them as a kind of shorthand, a language that helps him to compress a great deal of information into a few words. Second, if he understands his own generalizations, it is because he possesses the information upon which they are based. Third, students won't understand what he is saying unless they also possess his information, and they seldom do. Fourth, they will be most aware of their ignorance only if the generalities are cast in technical language, the most effective of all shorthand. Fifth, history does not possess a technical language, such as is found in sociology or economics, but uses instead the abstractions of popular language. Because history uses a nontechnical language, students may feel that they are learning more than they are. Hence, they become victims of easy familiarity. The student in an economics course who is perplexed by the abstraction *marginal utility* may learn nothing. The student in history who reads the term *Manifest Destiny* may learn nothing but believe that he has learned something. A little analysis, which takes time and information, would help him learn the extent to which historical content is "true" as against the extent to which it is merely clever in its language and phrasing.

A knowledge of the kinds of explanatory sketches presented in textual materials is not available in the studies of bias listed by McPhie (1959), perhaps because the distinction between explanation and description was not a common one at the time most of these studies were made. We do not know at this time the extent to which explanations offered by social studies textbooks are descriptive, pseudo, teleological, or incomplete. Neither have studies been made of the logical or empirical adequacy of the explanations offered by textual materials. As pointed out below, Swift (1958) has suggested certain criteria for the evaluation of any explanation — the presence of lawlike statements, the testability of such statements, their truth, and finally, internal validity, that is, whether the statement describing or naming the event to be explained follows logically from the reasons stated in the major and minor premises.

One doctoral study has examined explanations in high school social studies textual material. Palmer (1960) studied 27 textbooks in world and American history to test the hypothesis that "high school history textbooks, by the explanations of social change they provide, contribute significantly to an understanding of the process of social change" (p. 187). His conception of an explanation was a broad one, not limited to Hempel's model or Swift's criteria. To test his hypothesis, he asked two questions: What is the nature of the explanations of social change which appear in high school history textbooks? and Do these explanations give promise of contributing significantly to the reader's understanding of the processes of social change?

Palmer used a jury to judge the adequacy of the explanations, rather than relying upon his own opinion alone. He found a high correlation between his and the jury's opinion. Only 5 of the 27 books, or 18 per cent, were rated as contributing significantly to the students' understanding of the process of social change. This percentage might well have been lower if Palmer had used the rigorously logical and empirical criteria implicit in Hempel's model. Of the books in his sample, 41 per cent were rated as contributing little or nothing to the readers' understanding of social change; 80 per cent were judged "inadequate" in their treatment of social change.

A study that reveals the theoretical inadequacies of textual material is more useful to teachers whose purpose is conceptual learning than are studies of bias in textbooks. A teacher of conceptual learning will approach biased or unbiased material in the same way; but the teacher who finds that the material lacks conceptual content, and emphasizes instead merely factual offerings, has a problem that may best be solved by not using that material at all except for reference purposes.

BIBLIOGRAPHY

Hempel, C. G. The function of general laws in history. In P. Gardiner (Ed.), Theories of history. Glencoe, Ill.: Free Press, 1959. Pp. 344–356.

McPhie, W. A comprehensive bibliographic guide to doctoral dissertations in social studies education. Research Committee, National Council for the Social Studies, 1959. (Unpublished)

Palmer, J. R. The treatment of social change in high school history textbooks. Unpublished doctoral dissertation, Univer. of Illinois, 1960.

Swift, L. F. The teaching of explanation in history. Paper read at Nat. Assoc. Coll. Teachers of Educ., Chicago, February, 1958.

History in High-School Textbooks

Harold J. Noah, Carl E. Prince,
and C. Russell Riggs

The aim of this paper (1) is to determine whether, by errors of omission or commission, the history of the United States, as presented in some current high-school history textbooks (2–12), is being distorted. Three periods of American history are examined: the Revolutionary period, the Civil War period, and the Cold War. Are our students being asked to accept stereotyped or chauvinistic accounts of events in American history that modern scholarship has often challenged and found wanting?

During the last half-century historical scholarship has produced some notably new and plausible reinterpretations of the people and the events of the Revolutionary period in American history. One important reinterpretation deals with the element of "internal revolution" in the War for Independence; another reappraises the "critical" nature of the Critical Period from 1781 to 1789; the third re-evaluation examines the accuracy of the "Legend of the Founding Fathers." To what extent do current high-school history textbooks take note of such twentieth-century historical scholarship? Do authors incorporate in their works new discoveries by and insights of modern historians?

J. F. Jameson published his work *The American Revolution Considered as a Social Movement* in 1926 (13). In this volume Jameson argued that the American Revolution, like all revolutions, embodied a social-class movement striving for democratic gains. That this movement was successful, Jameson asserted, was evidenced by many trends toward more democratic government during the years from 1763 to 1789. Despite the fact that the thesis is widely discussed and at least partially accepted by the most recent generation of historians, only two of the high-school history textbooks examined have sections dealing with the revolution as a social movement. Gavian and Hamm (5: 85–86) offer the best explanation of the "internal revolution." In a separately titled section the authors write that "many of the men who framed the new [state] constitutions had progressive ideas which conservative people of that time thought rather radical. Today we would merely call these ideas democratic." In *United States History* (6) the same authors also offer an adequate treatment. A less precise account is found in Bragdon and McCutchen (2: 65–66). The remainder of the textbooks either ignore the internal revolution or just touch on the results as if they were the natural and incidental by-products of the external War for Independence.

The textbooks that totally ignore the internal aspects of the American Revolution (apart from the usual Tory-patriot coverage) include the textbooks by Craven and Johnson (4); Hartman (9); McGuire and Portwood (10). Others touch on the internal revolution indirectly and inconclusively, without framing it as such. These textbooks treat internal change as a minor and fortuitous element of an external war. They include textbooks by Muzzey (11); Hamm (7); Harlow and Noyes (8). The textbooks that ignore the Jameson thesis imply that there is not even an intermediate approach to the question. The result is, inevitably, a unilateral version.

In 1888, John Fiske published *The Critical Period of American History, 1783-1789* (14). In this book, which Charles Beard said was written "without fear and without research" (15: xii), Fiske viewed the years from 1783 to 1789 as *the* "critical period" in American history. Fiske's criteria for the "critical period" include the assertion that a widespread depression gripped the United States in the 1780's. He also cited as evidence anarchy, disputes among states, and the failures of American foreign policy. While some of Fiske's claims are partially true, his book, like the textbooks which copied him, presents a single-faceted story, which has long since been extensively revised. This factor led Beard to make his famous criticism of Fiske's work. The latter was questioned as early as 1905, but it was not until 1950, when Merrill Jensen published his book *The New Nation*, that a thoroughgoing revision of Fiske took place (15).

Jensen found that the economic difficulties of the so-called critical period were no more vexatious than the difficulties that beset the nation during many later periods of depression. The picture painted by Fiske, Jensen wrote, "is one of stagnation, ineptitude, bankruptcy, corruption and disintegration. Such a picture is at worst false and at best grossly distorted" (15: xiii). Jensen's interpretation, which has been given historical currency, is based on his statement: "We have too long ignored the fact that thoroughly patriotic Americans during the 1780's did not believe there was chaos and emphatically denied that their supposed rescuers [constitutional reformers] were patriotic. The point is that there were patriots on both sides of the issue, but that they differed as to desirable goals for the new nation" (15: xiii). Many prominent historians have since been influenced by Jensen's appraisal of the Confederation and have, in their college textbooks, re-evaluated the 1780's in the light of it (16). Not so the high-school textbooks. Though more than a decade has passed, they have failed to introduce any reinterpretation of the Confederation period or even so much as hint at the possibility of a different explanation than the one provided.

Recent high-school textbooks that adhere wholly to the nineteenth-century Fiske theory and ignore entirely more recent scholarship on the subject of the Confederation include books by Bragdon and McCutchen (2); Harlow and Noyes (8); Muzzey (11). McGuire and Portwood offer a skimpy treatment (10: 188–95). Hartman even diagrams the fact that the Confederation was "breaking up" (9: 210). This textbook presents a classic example of a narrow, stereotyped, and inaccurate point of view. Another example with similar findings is Gavian and Hamm's *The American Story*, which opens the section of the Confederation with the words: "A time of weakness. The new republic was like a weak and sickly infant . . ." (5: 93). Though somewhat tempered, the story is essentially the same in the other Gavian and Hamm textbook (6). Only the book by Craven and Johnson admits that "business conditions were indeed bad, but not as bad as the merchants pictured them or as historians once thought" (4: 131). Unfortunately, the coverage of this textbook, like that of all the others, suffers from too many pictures and diagrams and too little space devoted to textual matter.

Since 1913, when Charles Beard published his *Economic Interpretation of the Constitution of the United States*, historians have been forced to take another look at our Founding Fathers (17). Beard questioned their motives and suggested that they were inspired as much by selfish economic interests as by their concern for the public good. Numerous historians have since successfully and rightly attacked Beard, but even his most recent and most devastating critics have not ruled out the possibility of some form of economic interpretation of the motives of the Founding Fathers.

Forrest McDonald's fine work destroys the Beard thesis as such but concludes that economic factors "were obviously of some weight" in the efforts of the Fathers (18: 401). He adds: "It is clear that the making of the Constitution cannot be rendered intelligible in terms of any single system of interpretation; that it is only through simultaneous application of several systems that sense can be made of the multitude of pertinent factors" (18: 401). This, in fact, is just what the high-school textbooks uniformly fail to do. Rather, they present long established, "patriotic" interpretations of the Founding Fathers.

Despite many studies of individual Fathers which cast doubt on the images of at least some of them as unselfish patriots, their unitary and common stereotypes have remained with remarkable persistence in the high-school textbooks. The Founding Fathers remain uniformly and without exception good and great men, disinterested promoters of the public welfare, sternly doing their duty to God and country.

A good example of the distorted legend of the Founding Fathers in high-school textbooks is the treatment accorded Robert Morris, known as the "financier of the Revolution." Although there has been considerable distortion of the images of most of the Fathers, Morris represents an extreme illustration. Such perversions of history emanate from the patriotic slants of nineteenth-century American historians, such as George Bancroft, James Ford Rhodes, and John Bach McMaster. Their biases have influenced current high-school textbooks, which skip over twentieth-century historiography. Morris, a member from Pennsylvania of the Constitutional Convention, is portrayed in the textbooks as one who sacrificed his own funds and thus lost his fortune in the War for Independence. He later again sacrificed personal considerations to reconstruct the finances of the nation during the Confederation as the Superintendent of Finance for the Confederation Government.

Many high-school textbooks indulge this stereotype. The textbook by Craven and Johnson is typical: "Only the splendid work of Robert Morris . . . enabled the young nation to keep afloat" (4: 111). Some books relate the apocryphal story of Morris, going from door to door in Philadelphia, begging money from his rich friends for General Washington. Textbooks that glorify Robert Morris include those by Hartman (9); Todd and Curti (12); McGuire and Portwood (10). Still others, rather than contradict recent scholarship, solve the problem by ignoring Morris entirely.

The work of recent historians such as Thomas C. Cochran (19) and Merrill Jensen casts some well-founded doubts on Morris' intent and activities. Jensen, in *The New Nation*, writes that it is a "myth that Robert Morris financed the American Revolution, a myth absurd if for no other reason than the fact that he did not take office until the Revolution was virtually over. Throughout the war he made money as an owner of privateers and as an international merchant, selling goods at high prices on both sides of the Atlantic. At the end of the Confederation . . . he still owed money to the United States. Here commentary [of contemporary newspapers] coincided with fact, for the books of the Treasury in 1790 showed him to be the government's largest individual debtor" (15: 57). Jensen adds: "From 1782 to 1784, Morris the Superintendent [of Finance of the Confederation] borrowed a total of about a million and a quarter dollars from Morris the Banker (15: 63). Morris speculated wildly on western lands, could not repay his fraudulent loans, and was sent to debtor's prison in the 1790's.

Yet the Morris legend lives on in many high-school textbooks. As we saw in the treatment of the periods of the Revolution and the Confederation, so here, too, in dealing with the framers of the Constitution, no reasonable alternative interpretation is apparent in the textbooks. The legend of the Founding Fathers, who could do no wrong, coming to the rescue of a sick and dying country, still pervades the high-school history textbooks. A monolithic and hence false interpretation of individual Founding Fathers is standard in this sensitive (and key) area of American history. The absence of contrast, when different interpretations are widely accepted, must mislead the student.

In dealing with the Civil War period, how do the high-school textbooks treat the origins of that war? Do they indicate that there is still considerable divergence among the most able scholars of the period about the significance and importance of the people and events that led up to the conflict? With one exception the answer must be no. Todd and Curti say that "the thoughtful historian does not attempt to give a short and simple explanation of the war between North and South. All he can safely do is to explain why northern extremists and southern extremists, a minority in each section, felt and acted as they did" (12: 379). Textbook after textbook suggests that the war just seemed to happen from the natural flow of events; these textbooks have no separate section dealing with the ultimate causes of the conflict (8: 305–309; 9: 410–15; 10: 373–78). Or the textbooks present one thesis that has suggested itself to a scholar of the period and indicate that this is the only explanation for what happened. Thus the book by Craven and Johnson essentially supports the Charles A. Beard thesis that the war was a result of a collision between two economic systems (4: 313). This is essentially the thesis that Beard developed (20). It has been elaborated and incorporated into the work of James G. Randall (21) and into the work of Avery O. Craven (22). In subsequent years, Craven, as evidenced by his book *The Growth of Southern Nationalism, 1848–1861* has somewhat modified his previous opinion (23). He no longer talks quite so much about a foolish generation of Americans who blundered into a needless war but spends most of his time examining the phenomena of southern nationalism. He still emphasizes the economic conflict between the two sides.

Muzzey (11: 285) relies solely on the thesis of Allan Nevins and Kenneth M. Stampp that slavery was the most important cause of the Civil War (24). The textbooks thus fail to introduce the students to the most fundamental historical technique, namely, the weighing and sifting of evidence, and the evaluation of conflicting points of view.

This criticism applies to the treatment of the election of 1860, to the constitutional problems occasioned by the Civil War, and to the figure of Abraham Lincoln. Nowhere do the textbooks make clear the tremendous complexity of the forces that were working toward the Republican presidential nomination of Abraham Lincoln in 1860 (2: 329; 5: 297; 6: 364; 10: 373–74; 11: 288), although the deals and the promises, part of the price that Lincoln had to pay to secure the nomination, are well known (25 and 26). As one recent historian wrote of Lincoln's nomination: "To believers in the hand of Providence in American History, the Chicago nomination must afford an amazing example of its mysterious ways. Midnight conferences of liquor-stimulated politicians, deals for jobs, local leaders pulling wires to save their state tickets, petty malice, and personal jealousies — a strange compound, and the man of destiny emerges" (26: 180). Could it be that the way in which Lincoln secured the nomination might not fit the image of Lincoln that the authors of these textbooks wish to project?

Nor is the nomination of Lincoln the only event of the 1860 election that is inadequately handled. Only two of the textbooks examined (7: 323; 11: 288) make the significant point that in the states that were later to make up the Confederacy, moderates won more votes than extremists, and in none of the textbooks is the fact made clear that Republicans actually lost ground in the congressional elections of 1860 as compared with the returns in 1858. It might be pointed out in passing that the book by McGuire and Portwood gives the erroneous impression that Lincoln actively campaigned in 1860. They say: "Lincoln makes plain in his speeches that his first interest is to save the Union" (10: 374–75). As is well known, Lincoln made no public speeches during the campaign (26: 181–82).

The period of Lincoln's war-dictatorship that lasted from April 15 to July 4, 1861 — a period when Lincoln ran the government alone, appropriated money, pledged the national credit, issued a proclamation blockading southern ports, called for men for the state militia and the armed forces of the United States, suspended the writ of habeas corpus, and ordered arbitrary military arrests (27) — is, if one brief statement is excepted, entirely omitted. Bragdon and McCutchen say, "During the three-month interval between the fall of Sumter and the opening of a special session of Congress in July, 1861, [Lincoln] performed actions normally reserved to Congress. He called out volunteers, expanded the army, and spent money that was not yet appropriated" (2: 350). Indeed, the whole problem of the Constitution and the Civil War is relegated to a back seat.

Bragdon and McCutchen's book gives a very brief picture of Lincoln's problems with the Copperheads, and it includes a slight discussion of Ex parte Milligan, 1866, though it ignores Ex parte Vallandigham. The authors conclude their discussion with the statement, "It is still a matter of dispute as to whether or not Lincoln was wise in exceeding his constitutional powers, but it is certain that he had no idea of trying to make himself a dictator in the modern sense. He made no attempt to reduce Congressmen to puppets, to interfere with free elections, or to rivet himself in power by building up a militaristic organization of his followers. 'The Constitution was stretched,' says the historian J. G. Randall, 'but not subverted' " (27: 350). Aside from this small discussion, the accuracy of which could be seriously questioned (the number of times federal troops interfered in "free" elections is legion), none of the textbooks examined deals with the constitutional questions raised by the war (28). It is true that the textbooks all have something to say about Lincoln's Emancipation Proclamation, but they do not deal with its constitutional ramifications. Again, many of the textbooks deal with the separation of West Virginia from Virginia, the denial of habeas corpus, or the arbitrary arrests, but do not relate them to the Constitution.

Very little is said about the important growth in the power of the federal government during the years of the Civil War. The battle waged between the government and the loyal state governments in the raising and organizing of troops is completely omitted.

Craven and Johnson say that the Civil War "determined, once and for all, the fact that we were a Federal Union and not a loose bundle of sovereign states" (4: 333). Gavian and Hamm in *United States History* say "that [at the end of the war] the Union was supreme over the individual states was no longer in doubt" (6: 386). Again, McGuire and Portwood say, "The war saved the Union. It settled the question of the right of a state to secede. Never since 1865 has any state suggested such a course of action" (10: 392); and Gavian and Hamm in *The American Story* say, "The questions of whether a state had the right to nullify a federal law or secede from the Union had been settled [by the Civil War]. The United States had become an 'indestructible Union of indestructible states'" (5: 319). Aside from these brief quotations the textbooks suggest nothing about the growth of federal power over state power during the war, and they say nothing whatever about the conflict between state and federal officials in the raising and equipping of the armies. In short, anything which might reflect adverse criticism on the Lincoln administration is suppressed. In fact, if one particular criticism of the treatment of the Civil War by the high-school textbooks is to be emphasized, it must be their failure to deal adequately with the towering figure of Abraham Lincoln.

Search as one will through the textbooks that are covered by this study, not a single serious criticism of any aspect of Lincoln's leadership is mentioned. The criticism of a historian such as Avery O. Craven in his *The Repressible Conflict* (22) to the effect that Lincoln by his silence between his election and his inauguration helped to precipitate the actions of the South is never mentioned. This thesis of Craven's is further elaborated in James G. Randall's *Lincoln the President* (29). The fact that Lincoln in his conduct of the war allowed certain violation of civil liberties, such as the suspension of habeas corpus and interference with elections, is mentioned only briefly in the textbooks. No textbooks subject Lincoln to the serious criticism found, for example, in Randall's *Constitutional Problems under Lincoln* (27).

Unwilling to criticize him, the textbooks are equally unable to appreciate him. None of them points out the agony of decision that was his. None tells of the suffering that he endured as the wholesale slaughter went on and on. None points out that here was one of the very few examples in world history of a man who was actually humbled by power and emerged all the greater because of it (30). Instead, students are presented with a conventional, stereotyped, father-figure portrait, more properly belonging to folklore than to history.

Finally, how do the high-school history textbooks deal with the period of the Cold War?

244 · history in high-school textbooks

All the textbooks examined deal objectively, if briefly, with Russian-American relations before the Bolshevik Revolution of 1917. Russian-American contacts in the nineteenth century were infrequent. It was often assumed — on rather exiguous evidence — that the two countries enjoyed friendly relations, perhaps because contacts were few. The purchase of Alaska is universally noted, but the sale of Alaska served Russian interests at the time and cannot be properly interpreted as evidence of good will between an avowedly democratic republic and the autocratic czarist government of Russia (31). The textbooks generally deal with the Alaskan boundary settlement between the United States and Russia as part of the background to the Monroe Doctrine (see Gavian and Hamm, *United States History* [6: 222, 226]; Muzzey [11: 202]; Bragdon and McCutchen [2: 233–34]). Russian approval of the Union cause during the Civil War receives mention in Bragdon and McCutchen (2: 372); Muzzey (11: 331); Gavian and Hamm, *United States History* (6: 398). What is noteworthy, in view of what is to follow, is that all these textbooks at least deal coolly, if briefly, with the major pre-1917 Russian-American contacts. It is the textbook treatment of the vitally significant Cold War years which falters under scrutiny.

The origins of the Cold War are generally placed in the Second World War, and this is quite acceptable. Bragdon and McCutchen write that "war-time cooperation with Russia presented the greatest difficulty" (2: 651) and "Roosevelt and his advisers left Yalta thinking that they had laid the foundations for a firm post-war understanding with Russia. But hardly was the ink dry on the Yalta agreement than friction arose over Russian unwillingness to allow freedom to the peoples 'liberated by her armies' " (2: 653). Gavian and Hamm, in *United States History*, write: "Even before the war ended there were signs of friction among the Allies. Russia remained neutral in the Far Eastern phase. . . . Russia also kept urging the opening of a second front in western Europe. As Russian armies advanced into Poland, Moscow announced that it would not recognize the pre-war boundaries of Poland . . ." (6: 773). Craven and Johnson's book also places the origins of the Cold War in the war-time period (4: 649). But Muzzey's work gives no indication of war-time stresses and strains (11); Harlow and Noyes's book barely hints at them (8: 735); Hartman's work puts the time of their appearance somewhat later: "Almost as soon as the war ended it became clear that it would be difficult for the U.S. and other former allies of Russia to cooperate with the Soviet rulers" (9: 656).

Where the textbooks best demonstrate their weakness is in their distortions of Soviet postwar policies and in their unquestioning placing on Russian shoulders the complete responsibility for the origins and subsequent development of the Cold War. Bragdon and McCutchen write: "The quarrel [between Russia and America] was not of our choosing. On the contrary, American diplomats and military men made large concessions to Russia, in the hope of continuing the wartime alliance" (2: 684). Gavian and Hamm in *United States History* write: "Although the Teheran Declaration said the three powers wanted to end 'tyranny and slavery, oppression and intolerance,' it soon became clear that Russia had imperialistic designs on Eastern Europe" (6: 739); and, again, the same textbook: "Yet the two governments might have got along peaceably except for the imperialist ambitions of the U.S.S.R. and its use of Communist parties throughout the world to promote revolution" (6: 773). Gavian and

Hamm, in *The American Story*, wrote: "The uncooperative attitude of the Soviet Union caused endless difficulties" (5: 667), and "Russian leaders preferred to keep the world in a state of unrest in order to promote the growth of communism" (5: 668). Hartman wrote: "The Western nations, in turn, distrusted the leaders of Communist Russia, bent as they were on the extension of their form of government to other parts of the world. As Russia greatly increased its armaments of various kinds, especially its air force, the Western nations became more concerned than ever before" (9: 656). The textbook by Harlow and Noyes, uniquely, recognizes the possibility that Russian suspicions of the West may have been real and compelling for the Russians, even if mistaken (8: 735).

There is general consensus that the Russians do not keep agreements, while Western nations do. Craven and Johnson wrote: "The Soviet Union had violated this pledge [made at the Yalta Conference] . . ." (4: 649). Harlow and Noyes wrote: "Western suspicions of the Soviet Union were increased by Russian actions in Eastern Europe. At the Yalta Conference in 1945, Stalin had agreed that free elections would be held after the war in the countries of Eastern Europe. But either the Russians had a peculiar definition of 'free elections,' or they just did not keep their word" (8: 735–36). Brown and Peltier wrote: "In a series of agreements made by President Roosevelt, Prime Minister Churchill and Premier Stalin, the Allies made plans for the orderly restoration of freedom wherever Hitler's armies had brought the Nazi tyranny" (3: 662). The textbook then goes on to list the occupation agreements for Germany, Austria, Berlin, and Vienna, and agreement of Soviet responsibility for Poland, Czechoslovakia, Rumania, Hungary, and Bulgaria: "One by one, the Soviet Union broke nearly all these agreements . . . the Austrian agreements were the only agreements not repudiated in one way or another by the Soviet Union" (3: 662). The books by Muzzey (11) and Bragdon and McCutchen (2) appear to keep clear of such recriminations.

The individual and cumulative effect of these viewpoints is to produce a sadly distorted interpretation of Soviet diplomacy and of the relations between the two global giants after 1945. No emphasis is placed on the essential historic continuity of Russian ambitions, which span the periods both before and after the Revolution of 1917. There is no recognition that Russia's historic ambitions in eastern Europe are not specifically Communist, but Russian as well, and that Communist Russia's encroachment in this area may be as valid (or invalid) diplomatically, culturally, and militarily as British interests in the Middle East and the United States' interest in the Western Hemisphere. One might conclude — and some historians have — that a "democratic" Russia, if it were strong, would have its eastern European ambitions, too. The readers of the textbooks are denied this important historical perspective (32).

The textbook by Brown and Peltier (3: 660) is the only one that recognizes the importance of understanding that the Soviet Union is guided by historic Russian ambitions as well as by Marxist dogma, but proceeds promptly to forget its own admirable injunction and analyzes Soviet foreign policy entirely in terms of ideology. The textbook by Craven and Johnson (4), the two textbooks by Gavian and Hamm (5, 6), the textbooks by Bragdon and McCutchen (2) and Muzzey (11) all ignore this interpretation. Hartman writes of the "trouble [which] soon developed between Russia and the Western nations. It became clear that Russia wished to establish Communism in countries beyond her national borders" (9: 677). Neither here nor elsewhere does the text advert to Moscow's century-old interest in securing a belt of "friendly" nations along the western frontier. Harlow and Noyes note that "it is not quite correct to say that Soviet forces 'took over' Eastern European countries from without. In every country there were native Communist Parties . . ." (8: 736). But here, too, there is no discussion of what motivated the Russians to wish to install "governments that were loyal to Moscow" (8: 736).

Other weaknesses follow from the original distortions. Although the mistakes, stupidities, and power-plays of the East are fully exposed, the mistakes, stupidities, and power-plays of the West tend to be omitted or played down. Compare, for example, the treatment of the U-2 incident with the treatment of Castro's policies in Cuba. On the U-2, Hartman says: "On May 1, shortly before the Paris Summit Conference, an American reconnaissance plane was shot down over Russia while photographing military bases without permission (9: 694). One might ask, parenthetically, just what do the last two words mean? Could the plane have gotten permission, if it had applied to the right Russian agency? Not merely is the language used the blandest possible, but the opportunity to explain the strengths and weaknesses of United States intelligence methods and policies is not taken.

One may compare this bland, neutrally toned reference to one of the West's mistakes with the language employed when the Communists are seen to be at fault. Muzzey, for example, notes: "The red hand of communism was likewise seen at work in Cuba where dictator Castro broke with the Catholic Church, confiscated all American owned properties, and openly boasted of military aid from Russia and China" (11: 673). What is one to make of the implication that breaking "with the Catholic Church" and confiscation "of all American owned properties" are sufficiently clear evidence of Communist inspiration? Could they not also be clear manifestations of nationalist sentiment? Were Martin Luther, Henry VIII, and the American Revolutionaries of 1776 Communists? Better arguments for indicting Castro as a Communist could be offered. Only the last of Muzzey's three reasons is valid in this context — a poor average for historical accuracy. One is driven to the conclusion that such passages use violence of language to gloss over deficiencies of careful thought and objectivity in presentation. As a result, students are not given sufficient information, objectively presented, to form valid bases for comparison between Western and Soviet methods.

Examples may be multiplied. Thus, the Berlin Blockade, the Communist revolution in Czechoslovakia, Soviet intervention in Hungary, are all given considerable notice, understandably in highly pejorative language. Much less attention is paid to the mistakes of United States policy in Latin America (for example, in Guatemala), to the Anglo-French attack on Egypt, and to Western support of reactionary leaders around the world, from Chiang Kai-shek to Salazar, from Franco to Trujillo. When these are discussed, the textbooks are careful to point out the compulsions that were forcing the West to act as it did, even though such actions may not meet ideal standards of international conduct.

Examples of this double literary standard are legion. One, from Muzzey, must suffice. The language used for describing the Suez "incident" of 1956 is exculpatory: Israel was "provoked by Arab border raids, blockade of their shipping, and threats of destruction. . . ." Britain and France "resolved to overthrow Nasser, protect their vital life line to Asia, and restore the balance of power in the Middle East" (11: 664). The discussion is cast in the blandest terms, with no mention of the world-wide condemnation of British and French policy. "Meanwhile," Muzzey's textbook continues with abrupt change of tone, "the Russians were brutally crushing the liberty-loving people of Hungary" (11: 664–65).

The books by Muzzey (11), Hartman (9), Craven and Johnson (4), Gavian and Hamm (5, 6) describe Soviet intervention to crush the Hungarian uprising. None of these books so much as mentions the role of the United States in intervention in Guatemala in 1954. Bragdon and McCutchen's book, however, offers a full description of the Guatemalan affair (2: 704) and also provides a frank analysis of the mistaken bases of United States policy in Latin America.

The textbooks examined leave the impression that Russian actions are sly, evilly motivated, and subversive, while Western moves represent honest, disinterested, and generous statesmanship. Nowhere is it even hinted at that responsible thinkers about the Cold War might hold the kind of view expressed by George F. Kennan in *Russia, the Atom and the West:* "The Russians are not always wrong, any more than we are always right. Our task, in any case, is to make up our minds independently" (33: 60).

The textbooks are highly ethnocentric. The world still looks very American as seen from the offices of the publishers of high-school history textbooks. A map in one textbook (2: 691) shows the Soviet Union, Eastern Europe, and China in pink; the United States and its outlying air bases in black; and the rest of the Western Hemisphere together with Western Europe, Turkey, Iran, Pakistan, Thailand, Laos, Cambodia, South Vietnam, the Philippine Islands, Taiwan, South Korea, and Japan in light green. All the other parts of the world are in neutral white. The pink parts of the map are labeled "Communist countries." The black part of the map is clearly labeled the "United States." The area in light green is labeled "Associated with the West." Does an Englishman or a Frenchman think he is only associated with the West? It is, perhaps, his clear understanding that he is the West.

Most devastatingly, the student is generally left with only one possible interpretation of the rise of communism in the twentieth century: that it is a conspiratorial movement, a world-wide, backstairs palace revolution, moving by stealth, beards, and bombs to accomplish its nefarious purposes. Rarely is the student apprised of the real strength of the Communist appeal. The book *The American Story* by Gavian and Hamm is a notable exception. It discusses the appeal of communism to "(1) those who have suffered much from war, (2) those living in economic misery, and (3) those who have endured great discrimination because of their color or religion." *The American Story* lists the following elements in the total Communist propaganda appeal "[The Soviet Union] told underprivileged peoples in non-Communist lands that they are the victims of capitalist exploitation. It claimed that under the Communist system all individuals could get shares of land and housing without discrimination on the basis of class, color, or religion. It argued that the personal liberties which democratic leaders talk about have no meaning for poor people. It taught that the Communist system would bring a higher standard of living and greater opportunities for education, recreation, and medical care. It stated also that a Communist revolution is sure to come in every country and that when all countries have adopted communism there will be no more war" (5: 660–61).

In the great debate between the two systems which goes forward across the world today, and in which our students must participate, textbooks leave them pitifully unwarned and unaware of the real strengths of communism. It is difficult to combat what one does not understand, and it is precisely this which, perhaps, constitutes the greatest danger in introducing propaganda into history textbooks. What is needed above all is an infusion into the textbooks of the type of scholarship represented by Isaac Deutscher (32), D. F. Fleming (34), George F. Kennan (33, 35), Frederick Schuman (36), and Max Beloff (37). In today's textbooks the absence of such influences is painfully apparent.

The world inhabited by the compilers of high-school history textbooks tends to be black and white, stereotyped, suitable for perpetuating the myths which pass for history, but unable to provide students with contrasting interpretations of events and policies.

This paper has examined three crucial periods in American history; the Revolutionary War period, the Civil War and the Cold War period. It is evident that reputable and widely used textbooks commit errors of omission or commission in their treatment of these periods. The fruits of historical scholarship are neglected, and single-strand interpretations are left unquestioned. This fault is strikingly evidenced when — probably quite unconsciously — textbooks are building wholly improbable stereotypes of, say, patriotic, unselfish Founding Fathers or of a god-like superstatesman, Abraham Lincoln. Discussion of Cold War tensions is conducted in terms of good guys and bad guys. The average high-school student is often reading not the results of careful historical research and evaluation, but propaganda. There are pitifully few attempts to present the point of view of the other parts of the world, Communist or neutralist, or to let the student judge for himself after reading a fair sample of the documents and pronunciamentos of the contending factions.

Because we in the West prize highly independent, critical thought in the attainment of truth, it is especially incumbent on us to make sure that our textbooks reflect this free tradition and do not distort history or invent historical "facts." It is a grave charge to make, but the conclusion is inescapable: under this treatment our students' minds tend to be closed, not widened. Students whose history reading is largely confined to the textbook (and there are many such) are subjected to a brain-washing as complete as it is dangerous. The burden placed on the teacher is thus grievously enlarged, and he is hindered in his task of enlightenment. The job of the teacher is not to reinforce the making of myths, which the organs of mass communications do only too well, but to acquaint the students with reality. In this high purpose, the high-school history textbooks, in the fields that this paper has examined, may be more of a hindrance than a help.

NOTES

Where more than one work appears in a note, the specific textual reference is the first work cited in that note.

1. This study is based on a conference held at the Madison Campus of Fairleigh Dickinson University, June 6, 1961, when three members of the faculty (the authors) presented papers that dealt with the way current high-school history textbooks treat the periods of the Revolutionary War, the Civil War, and the Cold War in American history. The conference was attended by seventy high-school history teachers in northern New Jersey and a number of educators from out of state.

2. Henry W. Bragdon and Samuel P. McCutchen. *History of a Free People.* New York: Macmillan Company, 1961.

3. Stuart G. Brown and Charles L. Peltier. *Government in Our Republic.* New York: Macmillan Company, 1960.

4. Avery O. Craven and Walter Johnson. *American History.* Boston: Ginn and Company, 1961.

5. Ruth W. Gavian and William A. Hamm. *The American Story.* Boston: D. C. Heath and Company, 1959.

6. Ruth W. Gavian and William A. Hamm. *United States History.* Boston: D. C. Heath and Company, 1960.

7. William A. Hamm. *From Colony to World Power.* Boston: D. C. Heath and Company, 1957.

8. Ralph W. Harlow and Herman M. Noyes. *Story of America.* New York: Holt, Rinehart and Winston, 1957.

9. Gertrude Hartman. *America, Land of Freedom.* New York: D. C. Heath and Company, 1961. (Educational consultant, Charles C. Ball; general consultant, Allan Nevins.)

10. Edna McGuire and Thomas B. Portwood. *Our Free Nation.* New York: Macmillan Company, 1959.

11. David Muzzey. *Our Country's History.* Boston: Ginn and Company, 1961.

12. Lewis P. Todd and Merle Curti. *Rise of the American Nation.* New York: Harcourt, Brace and Company, 1961.

13. J. Franklin Jameson. *The American Revolution Considered as a Social Movement.* Princeton, New Jersey: Princeton University Press, 1926.

Since the original publication many historians have accepted and incorporated Jameson's "internal revolution" into their treatments of the period. Especially notable in this respect is John Alden, *The American Revolution, 1775–1783* (New York: Harper and Brothers, 1954). In this book, which is a part of the widely accepted "New American Nation" series, one of Alden's main tasks is to offer the most acceptable historical interpretations of the Revolutionary period. Older works that reinforce the Jameson theory include Carl Becker, *History of Political Parties in the Province of New York, 1760–1776* (Madison: University of Wisconsin Press, 1909); Arthur M. Schlesinger, *The Colonial Merchants and the American Revolution* (New York: Frederick Ungar Publishing Company, 1918). More recent historians still accept a modified form of the Jameson thesis. Frederick Tolles, "The American Revolution Considered as a Social Movement: A Re-evaluation," *American Historical Review,* LX (October, 1954), 1–12, revises but accepts part of Jameson's work. Other recent studies that interpret the Revolution in part as a social-class internal revolution include Merrill Jensen, *The Articles of Confederation* (Madison: University of Wisconsin Press, 1940); John C. Miller, *Triumph of Freedom, 1775–1783* (Boston: Atlantic Monthly Press, 1948).

14. John Fiske. *The Critical Period of American History, 1783–1789.* Boston: Houghton Mifflin Company, 1888.

15. Merrill Jensen. *The New Nation, A History of the United States during the Confederation 1781–1789.* New York: Alfred A. Knopf, 1950.

    Earlier works differing with Fiske include A. C. McLaughlin, *Confederation and Constitution, 1783–1789* (Boston: Harper and Brothers, 1905), which offered an early revision of Fiske, and Charles Beard, *An Economic Interpretation of the Constitution of the United States* (New York: Macmillan Company, 1913). *The New Nation* is the recent standard interpretation.

16. Many historians agree at least in part with Jensen's reappraisal. For examples of the changing and changed approach to the period, see such college textbooks as Richard Hofstadter, William Miller, and Daniel Aaron, *The American Republic*, I, 214 ff. (Englewood Cliffs, New Jersey: Prentice-Hall, 1959); Dumas Malone and Basil Rauch, *Empire for Liberty: The Genesis and Growth of the United States of America*, I, 206 ff. (New York: Appleton-Century-Crofts, 1960); T. Harry Williams, Richard Current, and Frank Freidel, *A History of the United States*, I, 162 ff. (New York: Alfred A Knopf, 1959). *History of the United States*, I, 162 ff. (New York: Alfred A. Knopf, 1959). The latter textbook, indeed, explains that "actually the 1780's were years of hopeful striving rather than black despair, of economic recovery and not merely depression, of governmental progress under the Articles of Confederation despite temporary failures. Possibly the Articles with suitable revisions might still be serving as our twentieth-century frame of government, and serving reasonably well, if a group of determined and impatient men had not managed to bring about a drastic change in 1787–1788." A good summary of the conflicting viewpoints of the Confederation is Richard B. Morris, "The Confederation Period and the American Historian," *William and Mary Quarterly*, Series 3, XIII (April, 1956), 139–56. The article indicates that there is by no means the wide agreement on the "critical" nature of the Confederation implied in the high-school textbooks.

17. Charles Beard. *An Economic Interpretation of the Constitution of the United States.* New York: Macmillan Company, 1913.

18. Forrest McDonald. *We the People: The Economic Origins of the Constitution.* Chicago: University of Chicago Press, 1958.

    Another of Beard's major critics is Robert E. Brown, who wrote *Charles Beard and the Constitution, A Critical Analysis of "An Economic Interpretation of the Constitution"* (Princeton, New Jersey: Princeton University Press, 1956).

19. Thomas C. Cochran. *Basic History of American Business*, pp. 31–41. Princeton, New Jersey: D. Van Nostrand Company, 1959.

20. Charles A. Beard and Mary R. Beard. *The Rise of American Civilization.* New York: Macmillan, 1927–42. See especially Volume II, *passim.*

21. James G. Randall. *Civil War and Reconstruction.* Boston: D. C. Heath and Company, 1953.

22. Avery O. Craven. *The Repressible Conflict, 1830–1861.* Baton Rouge, Louisiana: Louisiana State University Press, 1939.

23. Avery O. Craven. *The Growth of Southern Nationalism, 1848–1861*. Baton Rouge, Louisiana: Louisiana State University Press, 1953.

24. See Allan Nevins, *The Emergence of Lincoln*, II, 468 (New York: Charles Scribner's Sons, 1950). See also Kenneth M. Stampp, *And the War Came: The North and the South and the Secession Crisis, 1860–1866*, pp. 1–2 (Baton Rouge, Louisiana: Louisiana State University Press, 1950).

25. William Baringer. *Lincoln's Rise to Power*. Boston: Little, Brown and Company, 1937.

26. Eugene H. Roseboom. *A History of Presidential Elections*, pp. 173–80. New York: Macmillan Company, 1957.

27. See James G. Randall's *Civil War and Reconstruction* (21) *passim*; also see the same author's *Constitutional Problems under Lincoln*, *passim* (Urbana, Illinois: University of Illinois Press, 1951).

28. Alfred H. Kelly and Winfred A. Harbison. *The American Constitution: Its Origins and Development*, pp. 407–49. New York: W. W. Norton and Company, 1948.

29. James G. Randall. *Lincoln the President: Springfield to Gettysburg*. New York: Dodd, Mead and Company, 1945–55. (Volume IV was completed by Richard N. Current after Randall's death.)

30. See, for example, the study of Lincoln in Richard Hofstadter's, *The American Political Tradition and the Men Who Made It* (New York: Alfred A. Knopf, 1948).

31. See Warren B. Walsh. *Russia and the Soviet Union*, pp. 481–82. Ann Arbor: University of Michigan, 1958.

32. Isaac Deutscher discusses the extent to which Soviet foreign policy in Eastern Europe has its roots in Russian history rather than in Marxist ideology. See his *Stalin: A Political Biographer*, pp. 530 ff. (New York: Oxford University Press, 1949); and the same author's essay "Two Revolutions," in *Russia in Transition, and Other Essays* (New York: Coward-McCann, 1957).

33. George F. Kennan. *Russia, the Atom and the West*. New York: Harper and Brothers, 1958.

34. D. F. Fleming. *The Cold War and Its Origins*. New York: Doubleday and Company, 1961. This book presents at length the unpopular thesis that responsibility for the origins and the continuation of the Cold War lies heavily on the West, and on the United States in particular.

35. George F. Kennan. *Russia and the West under Lenin and Stalin*. New York: Atlantic Monthly Press, 1961.

36. Frederick L. Schuman. *Soviet Politics, at Home and Abroad*. New York: Alfred A. Knopf, 1946 and 1953.

37. Max Beloff. *The Foreign Policy of Soviet Russia, 1929–1941*. New York: Oxford University Press, 1947–49.

Asking Questions in History

Alan F. Griffin

Let us suppose a world history classroom in which students have encountered, during the reading of an assignment, the statement used in [an earlier chapter] to illustrate the extreme of apparently useless information: "Alexander crossed the Hellespont with 35,000 men and began the series of conquests that quickly made him master of Darius' empire."

In the usual course of events, this statement would be "believed" in the limited sense of "not doubted," but nobody would be likely to care much one way or the other about it, except on the off chance that an examination question might call for its regurgitation. Nevertheless, for what it is worth, the students have seen the words and are able after a fashion to visualize some sort of event not inconsistent with them, which is about all the "knowledge of events" anyone ever does get out of a high school text-book.

Suppose, however, that the teacher raises the question, "Could that sentence be a misprint? Surely it doesn't sound reasonable that 35,000 troops could conquer a land containing many millions of people."

That much is enough to get the flow of student hypotheses started. "Maybe there weren't so many people in those days." Investigation will bear this out, but not in sufficient degree to explain Alexander's conquests. "Maybe his army increased as he went along." Investigation supports this also — at least, a student can readily find out that Alexander trained some 30,000 of his conquered subjects in Macedonian military techniques — but again the explanation is quantitatively inadequate. "Maybe the people had no weapons." But Macedonian weapons were not particularly complicated, as the student can easily discover. Vast numbers of people armed with only equipment for hunting, farm implements, clubs, and stones could make a fair showing against a small army. However, a new question could be introduced by the teacher, namely, "Why didn't Darius see to it that every household contained the simple weapons of his day?" Does anyone know why the people of Crete had no arms to combat the German invaders, boys and girls?

Sooner or later, someone will discover that the ordinary inhabitant of an Asiatic empire never took part in wars at all — that he apparently cared not at all who ruled over him. By the time a student has found out why, and has come to compare the passive hopelessness of the natives of Persia with the vigorous self-defence against Persia carried on by the Greek cities a century and a half earlier, and perhaps even to wonder what had enabled Alexander to conquer those same Greek cities, the comparison with the present scene will have become painfully obvious. The state of affairs in India, in Burma, in Egypt, in Malaya, will have become relevant to the idea under discussion,

From "A Philosophical Approach to the Subject-matter Preparation of Teachers of History," unpublished doctoral dissertation, The Ohio State University, 1942, pages 179–185 and 194–198. By permission of Eleanor F. Griffin.

which is no longer Alexander but rather the proposition, "People who believe that they have no stake in their government will not fight to maintain it." The sharp contrast of the Philippines will certainly be drawn, and the meaning of participation explored. The teacher will not, of course, be able to "move forward" in the text-book for many days, but if he sees the creation of a reflective atmosphere, such as has been roughly described, as the primary reason for having the book, he will not be disturbed.[1]

When, however, the class *does* return to the book, and plows ahead over its content, the central idea to which they have leaped, using Alexander as a springboard, is by no means left behind. When they encounter Pyrrhus of Epirus trying to conquer Italy with a small, well-trained force, and find him giving up in disgust because the defeat of one Roman army only meant that another would be sent against him, they may well be impelled to seek in the Roman way of life the qualities that made the common man ready to fight for his country, and to see more clearly than would otherwise have been possible how the slow rise of the common man toward equality and freedom made Rome great, and how the change of direction, resulting, at least in large part, from the accumulation of wealth in a few hands, the extension of slavery, and the growing poverty of the masses, destroyed the common man's commitment-through-participation and finally left Rome at the mercy of authoritarianism and naked force. They will be better able to understand, when they come to it, how the French Revolution made Carnot's *levee en masse* possible; and the Dutch loss of New Amsterdam will be the old story over again. They may come to understand more realistically the coolness of certain Negro groups to the war effort, and be able to think of sounder remedies than force. They may even come to question whether the threat to national safety of saboteurs and purveyors of sedition exceeds that created by the advocates of poll taxes and Jim Crowism. So far as the writer knows, that question is at the moment an open one.

Or suppose that the students read of how the terramare people brought with them into Italy from the Danube Valley (or Switzerland) a type of settlement built on piles, appropriate to lake-dwellers as a means of insuring safety, but somewhat incongruous on dry land. Was the practice a sheer habit, or had they come to identify safety and security with a method that had once, under utterly different conditions, provided it? Is the latter hypothesis consistent with what we know about history, and with the present day? Shall we turn back toward the Greeks, and the triglyphs on the Parthenon, which represented and resembled the ends of the wooden planks used in the days when temples were made of wood, and which were therefore necessary to a *real* temple, no matter how constructed? Or forward to General Braddock marching his red-coats against the French and their Indian allies in what was at any rate the *correct* formation for an honest-to-goodness army, under all possible conditions? And do we care to laugh — we who, knowing from bitter experience exactly how to operate an economy of scarcity, could do no better when at last we emerged into plenty than to plow under, burn, slaughter, destroy until scarcity had been regained and our cherished habits could work again? Can the terramare people top that one? And who recalls our smug certainty that war in Europe was

---

[1] Even the discovery by an alert youngster that most scholars fix the size of Alexander's army (at the Granicus) at 37,000 will not disturb him.

impossible because we had all the money and would virtuously refuse to lend them any? And so we are off after illustrations of the cultural lag; we are out to learn whether men have consistently loved their habits better than their dreams, their aspirations, their neighbors' welfare, and even the protection of their own lives. We shall look also for occasions when necessary transitions have been made; perhaps it is only in some areas that we persist in keeping on with obviously inept procedures. Has it *always* required a revolution to shake off the dead hand of tradition? Can we learn to loose its grip before the rigor mortis of reaction stiffens and tightens it?

The multiplication of examples is pointless. Enough has been said to indicate what is meant by the use of historical materials in reflection. The heart of the method is to point up an apparent conflict (e.g., the size of Alexander's army and the apparent magnitude of the forces against him, seen in the light of the student's prior experience with unequal numbers in combat) in such a way as to elicit explanatory hypotheses. Once that has been done, the testing of the hypotheses will call into action all relevant facts, historical or drawn from current situations, that anyone in the group knows or can dig up. It matters not at all whether we start with a fact encountered in an ordinary, prosaic history assignment, a unit topic, or a present-day problem, so long as we move at once toward the evocation of directing hypotheses which will order and arrange both the materials out of which we generated our initial question mark and an indefinitely large body of other materials employed to test our hypotheses.

The subject-matter which the teacher controls enables him to do three important things, namely:

(1) He is able to direct students who seek to ground hypotheses toward materials that will carry their thinking forward.

(2) He is able, at appropriate points, to "toss in" the precise bits of information necessary to give impetus to a student's examination of a hypothesis. He can challenge an idea that seems headed toward too ready acceptance, or support one worthy of consideration that is about to be dismissed as patently false.

(3) The fact that he can often adduce relevant information enables him without constraint to admit the lack of it. In this way he can strike a blow against the acceptance of authority as omniscient, and focus the reliance of the group, not upon the teacher's sure knowledge, but upon the method which he and they are both applying.

· ·

Let us suppose that a class is reading what the text-book has to say about the election of 1800. There will surely be something on the bitterness of the campaign, and on the horrible consequences predicted for the country if Jefferson, "a radical and an atheist," were elected.

A teacher may cut in here, in discussion, to raise the question, "Do you suppose these people — Dwight, for example — believed what they said? Or did they just make those things up for the election?" Groups will divide sharply on this question, some insisting that the sheer extravagance of the Federalist charges (the teacher may have to augment these, since texts often go easy at this point) reveals them as propaganda, while others insist that men like Adams and Hamilton would not deliberately be false to what they thought.

Now suppose that the teacher injects a new question: "If men really believe that the election of a given candidate will ruin the country, how far are they justified in going, out of sheer patriotism, to prevent his election?"

Some ideas will emerge here toward which the example of Hamilton's famous letter to Jay may be addressed. "Suppose, for the sake of argument, that Hamilton was perfectly sincere in believing that Jefferson's election would be disastrous. Now consider this: among the papers of John Jay (time out for "Who remembers Jay? What did he do?" etc.) was a letter from Hamilton, written just before this election of 1800. It asks Jay, as Governor of New York, to juggle the election laws (time out for, "Have you ever heard of that before? Tell about it. What's a 'gerrymander'? What happened recently to Congressman Eliot, of Massachusetts? etc.) in such a way as to insure a Federalist victory no matter what the people wanted (time out for "How could he do that?" discussion of electoral college, etc.). Now, then, what do you think of Hamilton's proposal? If he was trying to save his country from a horrible fate, wasn't he justified (time out for fairly heated forensics, largely ungrounded)?"

After a while, the teacher interjects, "Jay left a note on the envelope of that letter. It said, 'A proposal for party purposes which it would ill become me to consider.' How do you react to that?"

The point must be made clear that Jay agreed with Hamilton as to the character and extent of the disaster Jefferson's election would cause. It should also be made clear that the Federalists, being in power rather generally, could have followed Hamilton's suggestion with some success, and driven Jefferson's followers to submission or revolution as their only alternatives. Secondary school students probably cannot formulate the difference between Jay's outlook and Hamilton's, but they sense it readily and show some insight into its quality. They rarely condemn Hamilton out of hand, though; they seem to understand how loyalty to a set of fixed standards may compel that kind of behavior.

Other aspects of the same situation may be used in the same direction. Dwight was trying to save the country from the horrors of an atheist president. Has an atheist a right to run for president? Does the freedom of religion we are fighting for include the freedom to have no religion? Did Americans of the eighteenth century feel more friendly toward atheism than people do today? Why wouldn't Philadelphia permit a statue to Tom Paine? What kind of president did Jefferson turn out to be? What were the religious views of Benjamin Franklin? Of George Washington? (This last is perhaps *too* risky — if the youngsters find out, they'll probably bubble over in the wrong places. However, only the very diligent are likely to find out anything on this point until many years later.)

Some reference in this connection to the practice in many states of barring certain political parties from the ballot may also be related to the Hamilton-Jay business. The economic make-up of the Federalist party also has utility here, and a quick look back over Adams' administration, emphasizing the alien and sedition laws and Adams' immigration policy, will yield quantities of evidential material.

One may treat the election of 1800 in scholarly and thorough fashion without upsetting anyone and without doing more than skirt the edges of controversy. One may even promote a fair amount of thinking that way. But the intent to develop, through thinking, a frame of reference that *relies on* thinking, will make certain ideas and events seem almost to pop out of the pages of the text or out of our own remembered reading.

FURTHER READING FOR SECTION 3

Gardiner, Patrick. *Theories of History.* Glencoe, Ill.: The Free Press, 1959. Meyerhoff, Hans. *The Philosophy of History in Our Time.* Garden City, N.Y.: Doubleday, 1959. Stern, Fritz. *The Varieties of History.* Cleveland: Meridian Press, 1956.

These collections of writings on the philosophy of history and the nature of historical knowledge present conflicting points of view on the various perplexing issues regarding the nature and function of history. These are excellent compendiums for the student interested in historians' views of themselves as scholars and of their scholarly products.

Muller, Herbert J. *The Uses of the Past.* New York: Oxford University Press, 1957.

The personal confrontation by an historian with the meaning of history in the context of a study of former societies. Meant "to give perspective on the crisis of our own society," this book is an example of using history to paint bold, dramatic pictures. Its "uses of history" raise interesting questions.

White, Morton. *Foundations of Historical Knowledge.* New York: Harper & Row, 1965.

A readable treatment of issues in historical knowledge by a noted philosopher. White criticizes and analyzes the positions of a number of the writers who appear in the Meyerhoff and Gardiner collections mentioned above.

4

The Social Sciences and
the Curriculum

Man, perhaps in order to survive and perhaps for enjoyment, strives to order his social world. In seeking to provide this structure, we all develop ideas that categorize our experiences and we postulate relationships and explanations which we believe to be reasonable or useful. Such knowledge is "private" since there is usually little concern with whether it is usable or comprehensible to others. The social science disciplines, on the other hand, are committed to the development of public knowledge, "public" in two senses: (1) that it can be understood and used by others; and (2) that the classifications, interrelationships, and explanations devised by social scientists can be checked and examined by colleagues who apply accepted standards of logic and systematic research.

Each of the social sciences limits its scope of inquiry by defining an area or field of interest, and traditionally these fields have been political science, economics, sociology, anthropology, geography, and psychology.[1] Presumably, the social scientists in each of these fields share a body of knowledge, have an interest in similar questions, and abide by common rules of inquiry and discourse. Although the divisions sometimes entangle and obstruct the conduct of inquiry, the disciplines as presently constituted have contributed substantially to man's understanding of himself and his political, economic, and social milieu.

If a sound education is seen as one that will contribute to a person's capacity to know himself and to understand and cope with the social world, then it seems obvious that the social sciences must play an important role in the educational program, since the social sciences embody the most stable and reliable knowledge of social reality which we possess. The recommendation can be, and has been, made that the social studies curriculum should be devoted to teaching students the most recent and accurate findings of the social sciences, along with the understanding that what is known is tentative and inconclusive. The thesis of this section is that the determination of the place the social sciences should occupy in a general education program presents more difficult issues for the teacher than the foregoing recommendation suggests.

[1] Some would include history as a social science, but the question of history's relationship to the social sciences provokes lively debate among historians and social scientists. While we have no objection to classifying history as a social science, at least for the purpose of this discussion, we have chosen to treat history in a separate section of this volume, in part to draw the issues more sharply, and in part because of the special place that history occupies in the school curriculum.

257

The Aims of the Social Sciences and
the Goals of the Social Studies

A basic issue is, how helpful are the social sciences to the teacher in setting the basic goals of the curriculum? Stated differently, the question is, What are social scientists attempting to accomplish, and can they, in their role as social scientists, help the teacher determine the goals of his course? The answer to this question requires an examination of the aims of the social sciences.

One view is that social scientists, like their colleagues in the natural sciences, are searching for the principles, explanatory systems, and general theories which are assumed to be basic to science. Some social scientists are skeptical about the possibilities of arriving at general theories at the present stage of development of the social sciences, preferring to focus on the development of "middle level" theories and principles. Others argue that scholarly disciplines should emphasize description, classification, and the development of simple generalizations and relationships before attempting to arrive at more formal systems.[2] Regardless of differences on this point, the majority of contemporary social scientists are committed to the impartial and systematic collection of empirical data and to a rigorous process of making inferences. The conduct of inquiry must conform to the canons of "scientific method" shared by fellow social scientists. As several readings in Section 5 indicate, any attempt to characterize science or "scientific method" in a few words is hazardous. However, in the social sciences there is clearly a heavy emphasis on empirical research, and on quantification, coupled with a self-conscious effort to eliminate the effects of personal values on the outcome of research.

May the social scientist *in his role as scientist* make policy recommendations? If we accept the obvious proposition that policy recommendations invariably involve making value judgments, then we can see why many social scientists, especially the "behaviorists," resist making such recommendations. Many social scientists would argue that as scientists, they may say what *was*, what *is*, or what *is likely*, but not what *should be*. They regard values as one of the factors affecting human behavior, and thus as a variable to be studied in their efforts to explain and predict human affairs. But the social scientist's own personal value judgments are seen as impediments to his scholarship, to be eliminated from his deliberations so far as is possible.[3]

[2] For an interesting discussion of this issue, see H. L. Zetterberg, *On Theory and Verification in Sociology* (New York: Tressler Press, 1965).

[3] The role that the scientist's personal values should play in his research is often treated too simply by saying that the scientist removes his values from his work, or that *scientific* research is value-free. Such statements overlook the fact that the scientist must have certain commitments, beyond the desire for monetary gain or fame, if he is to continue his investigations, often in the face of frustration and obscurity. Bronowski states at least part of that commitment as follows:

"It is commonly said that science is ethically neutral, because its discoveries can be used for good or ill. This judgment confuses two meanings of the word *science:* the process of discovery, and what is discovered at the end of it. Of course what is discovered is neutral, whether it is Hooke's law, or a semiconductor, or the theory of evolution. But the long and dedicated activity of the men who made these discoveries was not neutral: it was firmly directed and strictly judged.

The social scientist who takes this position is put in an awkward position when he attempts to make recommendations as to what *should* be the focus and content of social studies in the schools. Beard, in an essay included in Section 1, points up this problem succinctly:

> By its very nature (neutrality) empiricism is precluded from attempting to set objectives for instruction in the social sciences, for this operation is posited upon a declaration of values or preferences, within the limits of necessity. Since such objectives inherently involve the assertion of values to be attained, empiricism cannot pass judgment upon them without setting up values of its own, that is, violating its method . . .

To use an example, an educator's decision to require that all high school students take a political science course that emphasizes how political decisions are made rests upon assumptions about what citizens should be like in our society. Empirical social science inquiry could conceivably tell us what behavior must be manifested by citizens of a particular type of political system in order for that system to function according to its norms. But empirical research cannot tell us which type of system, and therefore which type of citizen, should be desired.

In the first selection in this section, Philip M. Hauser, a sociologist, takes the position that there must be a complete separation of value judgments and social science in research *and* in teaching. If the integrity of the social sciences is to be preserved, Hauser argues, the direct consideration of policy questions must be kept independent of any attempt to teach the basic concepts of a social science discipline. If the schools are to deal with policy questions, according to Hauser, it should be done in separate "general education and/or humanities" courses.

Although Hauser's argument is probably easily accepted by the teachers of specialized university courses aimed at the training of scholars in the behavioral sciences, for the public school teacher his position raises a number of issues which cannot be easily brushed aside. For example, if we consider that *one* of the major reasons for studying the social sciences in the schools is to provide the student with a sound basis for making policy decisions, then a rigid division between "social science" and "general education" may make it less likely that this goal of general education can be achieved. How can we expect students to relate social science knowledge to policy questions as adults if, in school, we have insisted on strict separation? Indeed, the students may learn by implication that it is intellectually unsound to attempt to relate social science knowledge to policy decisions. Of course, the view that education should help students make wiser policy decisions may be rejected; but, then, what other rationale is there for teaching the social sciences to students who will never be social scientists? The second part of Hauser's essay is a concise summary of recent developments in the social sciences which may be helpful to social studies teachers whether or not they concur with his position on general education.

"In practicing science, we accept from the outset an end which is laid down for us. The end of science is to discover what is true about the world. The activity of science is directed to seek the truth, and it is judged by that criterion. We can practice science only if we value the truth." (J. Bronowski, *The Identity of Man* [Garden City, New York: The Natural History Press, 1965], pp. 99–100.)

Some social scientists hold a view contrary to Hauser's notion that it is desirable or necessary to detach "value" or policy questions from the social sciences. Especially within political science and history, there exists a tradition of direct concern with ethical issues. Peter Odegard, who may be regarded as a "traditionalist," argues in the second reading in this section that it is legitimate for social scientists to be concerned directly with policy questions. Although Odegard does not deal explicitly with the place of the social sciences in general education, it seems reasonable to infer that he would *not* draw the rigid distinction between general education and the social sciences that Hauser does.

The content and pedagogy selected for a course or for a total curriculum will be quite different, depending on whether Hauser's or Odegard's view is accepted. It will be helpful to the teacher, in considering the two positions, to focus on two questions: (1) What is the place of policy considerations in the social sciences? And (2) What is the place of policy issues in social science courses which are intended as general education? Both questions must be considered, but it is important to distinguish between them. Hauser is undoubtedly correct in criticizing the potpourri of value judgments and half-truths that are taught in the schools as "social studies." But does his analysis of the aims of social science research justify his proposal to separate social science and policy questions in the curriculum?

The Social Sciences as a Body of Substantive Knowledge and as a Way of Acquiring Knowledge

Social scientists are obviously seeking something more than a repertory of data. For example, the discipline of economics is not merely a collection of data about the economic system. Rather, economics embodies a specialized language, a set of concepts, relational propositions, and theories. The theories, which may be more or less abstract, attempt to systematize and unify the relational propositions, the concepts, and the data. The network of theory, generalizations, concepts, and data which a social scientist in any one area uses to conceptualize the social world has been called by some writers "substantive structure." Each social science discipline has a body of substantive structure (or, perhaps more accurately, structures, since at any given time there is more than one theory or set of concepts within a discipline). What is taught in the schools and what appears in social studies textbooks are often summaries or partial summaries of these substantive structures. For example, a sociology text may summarize one or more theories and an array of concepts, generalizations, and data which deal with "social class."

There are, however, obvious difficulties if we attempt to define the social science disciplines *only* in terms of the substantive structures. Social science knowledge, as has been noted, is built through a *process of inquiry* guided by canons of evidence and proof. In other words, the social sciences are not merely accumulations of substantive knowledge; they are also an accumulation of systematic ways of asking and answering questions. Thus, we can distinguish between the substantive structures of a discipline and the means or processes of inquiry used to build these structures. In his essay, Joseph Schwab clarifies the distinction between "substantive structures" and "syntactical structures" — the latter being akin to what we have called the "process of inquiry." His clarification of these terms is exceedingly important for the teacher because confusions will occur in the curriculum if the distinction is not understood. For example, social studies courses often unwittingly focus entirely on student mastery of substantive structures. Students normally learn generalizations and data related, for instance, to what caused the Civil War or descriptions of how the political system works. Schwab points out, however, that "unless we intend to treat all knowledge as literal, true dogma, and thereby treat students as mere passive, obedient servants of our current culture, we want our students to know concerning each body of knowledge learned, how sound, how dependable it is." According to Schwab's argument, social studies courses must treat the *syntactical* as well as the substantive structures of the social science disciplines. Schwab's proposal presents a number of theoretical problems which he considers in his essay.

There are also a number of practical problems. Most social science and history teachers are not well trained in the "syntax" of a discipline. Often, whatever knowledge they have of the process of inquiry is based on a formal "methods of social science" or a "historiography" course. Teachers may have *learned about* but rarely have *engaged in* any long-term social science inquiry of their own. As a consequence, they have very little applied knowledge of research concepts and strategies. If the argument for greater concern for process or syntax is a compelling one, then it seems obvious that the "content" of the social sciences cannot be restricted only to substantive structures. However, if students are to engage in a process of thinking somewhat like that used by the social scientist, teachers may well need far more specific, comprehensive, and working knowledge of the syntactical structures of one or more of the social science disciplines than they now generally possess.

The Changing Structures of the Social Sciences

Schwab also points out that the structures of a discipline (its theories, concepts, and generalizations) are not stable and enduring. They are under continuous revision, being replaced with more comprehensive and powerful conceptions. The substantive structures are especially subject to revision and discard, and this has important implications for the social studies. For example, suppose a teacher is teaching a course or portion of a course that deals with international relations. He selects a set of social science concepts that purportedly will assist his students in comprehending an international dispute. Let us say he chooses to employ, among others, the concept of "balance of power" as a useful political science concept. Balance of power, or any concept in the social sciences for that matter, has a limited life. Next year, two, or ten years from now, the concept may have been replaced and abandoned, either because more adequate concepts or theories have been devised or because the changing reality of politics among nations makes old concepts inapplicable. Yet the student, unless he learns otherwise, is condemned to using the outmoded concept to comprehend international relations.

We expect a great deal of disagreement over the structures of a discipline, particularly during its earlier stages of development. And within the social science disciplines, which are fairly recent in origin, we often find profound cleavages over what are the most promising and useful substantive and syntactical structures. The depth and range of controversies varies from discipline to discipline. For instance, in economics, there is far greater consensus over syntax than there is in psychology. How the teacher is to handle these differences is, of course, one of the most formidable questions he must face. And, the changing nature of social science concepts, plus the frequent lack of consensus within any one discipline, raises the basic question, What is the worth of social science knowledge in a general education program? It could be argued that if a major goal of education is to enable individuals to cope with the social and political world, then the student should be given more opportunities for practical experience and the teaching of formal conceptual knowledge should be curtailed or eliminated.

The essay by W. W. Charters, Jr. supports the contention that the concepts of the social sciences can be of enormous value to students. His argument is directed at demonstrating the value of social science concepts to the practicing school administrator. It is not difficult, however, to extend Charters' argument to general education in the secondary schools. It could be argued that many of the syntactical and substantive structures of the social sciences are useful (in Charters' sense) to men in comprehending their social world and devising solutions to social and political problems.

Even if we grant Charters' argument, however, there still remain at least two serious issues that arise, in part because of the differences between educating professionals for a specific role and the more complex problem of educating persons to confront the demands of the society at large. First, the professional may be sufficiently knowledgeable to recognize that all conceptualizations are tentative and have limits. The layman called upon to use a given conceptualization (e.g., balance of power) only on rare occasions may not be as keenly aware of its tentative nature. Second, deciding which social science conceptualizations shall be included in the general education of secondary school students is a far more difficult task than selecting a set of concepts that are to be used by a person in the performance of a specialized role. A school administrator has a far narrower range of problems to confront than does the active and concerned citizen. Thus, it is important that the social studies teacher develop a carefully considered, explicit rationale for general education to be used in selecting content from the broad range of social science and historical knowledge.

Do the Disciplines "Cover" the Entire Range of Human Activity?

A discussion of difficulties in utilizing the social sciences for the social studies curriculum must also include a consideration of their comprehensiveness. As has been noted earlier, academicians in a given social science discipline tend to limit their inquiries to a defined area, but the divisions among the disciplines are not as rigid as their labels imply. For example, political scientists sometimes ask questions that are not substantially different from those of sociologists; and, some historians do their research in ways similar to some economists or archaeologists. Nevertheless, no one discipline is broad enough to deal with the entire range of human activity. History, which is sometimes called the "queen," or the synthesizing, social science, is rarely concerned with the psychology of the individual or with the dynamics of the group. And sociologists rarely explore the historical antecedents of the phenomena they investigate.

This limited perspective of each social science discipline leads Earl Johnson, in his essay, "The Social Studies vs. the Social Sciences," to maintain that any *single* discipline is inappropriate as a basis for general education. He argues, as does Oliver[4] elsewhere in this volume, for a unified social studies course in order to achieve a more comprehensive view. But is it possible to synthesize the social sciences within the curriculum? Hauser argues that such syntheses are premature and unwise. Others argue that history is the unifying social science and should continue as the cornerstone of the curriculum. In any event, the results of attempts to effect a synthesis such as Johnson suggests have not been too encouraging to date. This, however, is no basis for rejecting his proposal.

Johnson, however, goes further than to attack the restrictive effect of individual disciplines. He suggests that even the perspective provided by *all* the social sciences taken collectively can be confining. To him, social studies is not merely a course in unified social science; rather, social studies courses must deal broadly with the questions of human value, and such questions are not the exclusive province of the social sciences. His recommendation for curriculum reorganization presents an interesting alternative view of how the social sciences can be employed in general education. It might be well for the reader to reexamine Johnson's position after reading C. I. Stevenson's essay in Section 5 which lays out some of the limitations of logic and empirical method for dealing with ethical issues.

Levels of Knowledge in the Social Sciences

It is clear that the social sciences provide knowledge at various levels of abstraction and specificity. There are, for instance, a number of comprehensive and abstract formulations, as well as accumulations of singular facts and simple generalizations, about our economic system. It is possible to classify and distinguish the various types of substantive and syntactical knowledge which have been accumulated by social scientists. A number of classification systems have been devised. For example, Benjamin Bloom and his associates, in *The Taxonomy of Educational Objectives*,[5] attempt to specify several levels of knowledge, as does Hilda Taba, in her book, *Curriculum Development: Theory and Practice*.[6]

In this section we have included a selection from Taba, who suggests four levels of knowledge: specific facts and processes; basic ideas; concepts; and thought systems. Of what practical significance for a teacher is it to draw such distinctions among the levels of social science knowledge? Does it matter whether the teacher knows whether he is dealing at the level of facts, concepts,

---

[4] See Donald W. Oliver, "The Selection of Content in the Social Sciences," Section 1.

[5] Benjamin Bloom (ed.), *Taxonomy of Educational Objectives: Cognitive Domain* (New York: David McKay, 1956), the section on "Knowledge," pp. 62–88.

[6] Hilda Taba, *Curriculum Development: Theory and Practice* (New York: Harcourt Brace & World, 1962).

or thought systems? The practical significance rests on the recognition that the specific mode of inquiry a social scientist employs in his research may differ according to the level of knowledge with which he is concerned. For instance, if the social scientist is attempting to devise or validate a theory to account for political revolutions in the modern world, his strategy will be different from what it would be if he were attempting to validate a piece of data about a given revolution. In a similar way, the teacher who is attempting to engage his students in social science inquiry must decide what mode of inquiry is appropriate to the level of social science knowledge being dealt with. Awareness of knowledge levels can also be helpful in choosing or writing materials to be used in teaching, as well as in devising teaching strategies appropriate to the materials.

In other words, the teacher must make curricular decisions for his course, and these decisions include choices of content, of material to present the content, and of teaching strategies. The teacher must decide what level or levels of knowledge to teach on a given day. Moreover, if he wants the student to become involved in "social science inquiry," the instructional strategy must be designed according to the syntax appropriate for the level of knowledge the teacher has chosen. The categories given by Taba, while wanting in some respects, provide the teacher with a scheme by which to approach these curricular decisions.

Citizenship Education and the Social Sciences

To this point, we have focused our attention on a number of general issues related to the social sciences and the school curriculum. However, anyone concerned with the curriculum in the social studies cannot ignore the obvious fact that the students who sit in the classrooms will take their place as citizens in a pluralistic society. If an educator takes the position that one of the goals of general education in the social studies is to provide students with the knowledge and skills necessary for an intelligent citizen, he must examine more carefully the potentials and limitations of social science knowledge in contributing to citizenship education. In the final article, Shaver and Oliver deal with a number of the issues raised in this introductory essay but they focus more directly on the relationship of the social sciences to citizenship education. They attempt to clarify several requirements of citizenship education and point to some of the confusions in discussions of both citizenship education and the social sciences. Their article underscores the difficulties in coming to facile conclusions concerning the role the social sciences can and should play in the social studies curriculum.

Social Science Research and the Curriculum

Philip M. Hauser

The relationship between research and the curriculum is a more complex one for the social than for the natural sciences. It is more complex for a number of reasons which should be stated at the outset and faced realistically in any consideration of the curriculum of tomorrow.

Problems of Social Sciences in the Curriculum

First, it is important to recognize that social science findings, unlike those of the natural sciences, generally include as objects of research, aspects of man, society, or culture in respect of which there are widespread, deep-rooted, sentimental, and emotional attitudes; and, frequently, also organized institutional interests prepared to resist any efforts to examine phenomena embodying values which they regard as "sacred" — values to which they are committed. The natural scientist, although he has had his troubles in the past, an observation documented by the mere mention of such names as Galileo or Tyco Brahe, is, in general, free to study what he pleases; and, within recently imposed security limits on some subjects, to report his findings with the expectation that they will be eagerly read both by an audience which seeks knowledge for its own sake and an audience which looks for the possibility of innovation, that is, technological advance. Society at large is receptive to natural science findings as harbingers of change in the form of technological advance. The American economy is in no small measure based on planned obsolescence which natural science findings help to effect; and society rewards the inventor. In such a context the flow of natural science research findings into the curriculum is a relatively smooth and uninterrupted one.

In contrast, the findings of social science research are likely to be resisted, and resented almost in proportion to the extent to which they may even suggest the prospect of social change. Studies of the United Nations and the Specialized Agencies may be branded as subversive and detrimental to Americanism; conclusions about the working of international trade may be regarded as dangerous to American industry or labor; findings on race differences and the dynamics of prejudice may be viewed with dismay as inimical to an established social order; and efforts to understand the behavior of juries may evoke Congressional prohibitions. Even though we can still remember the infamous Tennessee evolution trial, the Scopes case, it is the social science, and not the natural science, text books that are the targets of over-zealous defenders of the established order today.

In the debate about the inclusion of provision for support of the social sciences preliminary to the establishment of the National Science Foundation, the

From *The North Central Association Quarterly*, 1959, 33, pages 231–241, by permission of the North Central Association of Colleges and Secondary Schools and the author.

observation attributed to a Senator that this would be undesirable because there were already "too many short haired women and long haired men in the country" was by no means an isolated manifestation of the distrust and disrepute of the social sciences. Not only the social scientist but the educator who is responsive to social science findings, risks becoming suspect or risks open opposition by various organized groups, including the professional patriotic organizations, some religious bodies, and investigating committees of the Congress and the forty-eight State legislatures. In such a context the flow of social science findings into the curriculum is beset with many difficulties.

Second, the task of utilizing the findings of social science in school curricula is made more difficult than necessary by obstructions created by social scientists themselves. Social scientists have often tended to admix value judgment and policy formulation with research findings. This has been more true of some fields than of others. Especially given to normative considerations and policy recommendations have been political science; sub-fields of economics concerned with the business cycle and international trade; sub-fields of sociology interested in social problems; and more recently sub-fields of anthropology intrigued with "action anthropology."

This admixture of science and policy, recently formally merged into a new framework of the "policy sciences"[1] by a number of prominent scholars, is easily understood. It may be viewed as a transitional confusion arising from the absence, as yet, of an adequate body of well defined fields of "social engineering" — fields in addition to such established areas as law, social work, and personnel administration. But understanding the confusion does not make the task of introducing social science research findings into the curriculum any easier. For the curriculum committee, the teacher and the text book writer are still often faced with the *potpourri* of results of research confounded with normative judgments and policy views and recommendations which are admittedly not the result of research, but rather of value orientations — the predelictions and biases of the authors. This is not the place to elaborate the distinction between "social science" and "social engineering." But it is essential to the realistic consideration of the problem before us to observe that this is a distinction that, fortunately, is being increasingly recognized in social science; and that, as it becomes more honored in execution, will greatly facilitate the flow of social science research findings into those portions of school curricula that are reserved for social science.

A third problem in the introduction of social science research into curricula is generated, in part, by the over-enthusiasm in some educational quarters for "general education" and, in part, by the mistaken identification of the writings of non-fiction writers — journalists, *literati*, reformers, and social philosophers with social science. The desire of educators to provide a general education has, in my judgment, often led to premature efforts to synthesize and integrate social science knowledge — often in areas where it was non-existent. And the willingness of the fringe *literati*, and sometimes social scientists themselves, to reach a quick and unverified generalization has fed the burning appetite of general

[1] Lerner, Daniel and Lasswell, Harold D. (ed.), *The Policy Sciences: Recent Developments in Scope and Method*, Stanford, Stanford University Press, 1951.

educators. In consequence, much of what is labelled "social science" in general education today is a curious admixture of some social science research findings liberally sprinkled with large and variable doses of hasty and unwarranted generalizations. Ideal-type constructs designed as tools for research are treated as findings of research; hypotheses are transformed into conclusions; and "theories" include the plausible, the speculative, and the fanciful without benefit of empirical foundation. No one can deny the need for general education; but to be beguiled and mesmerized by the appeal of synthetic syntheses is not to be educated. An essential ingredient of a general education, too often missing, is the acknowledgement of ignorance where and when it exists.

Fourth, the findings of social science research appearing in the curriculum must be documented and validated as products of research. This is almost more important in the presentation of social science than of natural science findings, because social science concerns phenomena about which almost every person not only has some views, but also some "common sense" knowledge. Since the findings of social science are increasingly at variance with common sense, the superiority of scientific to common sense knowledge must be made clear. At this point the social sciences will undoubtedly continue to have a burden that the natural sciences fortunately escape. For physics findings on nuclear fission have no common sense counterparts with which to compete or which may impede their acceptance as valid knowledge. Particularly is this the case when a demonstration of fission can be presented to clinch the case.

In concluding these introductory observations I should like to be clear about two things to which I have referred. My references to normative judgments and policy formation and recommendations are not to be construed to mean that such material has no place in general education. On the contrary, they should undoubtedly have an important place in the curriculum — in ethics, religion, social philosophy, civics, or general survey courses, where they are recognized as such. My plea is that such materials not be confused with social science which they most assuredly are not. By properly identifying the normative as such, the student is put on notice that values are being presented that he must consider in the frame of his own value system. By keeping such value judgments out of the social sciences, or minimizing their inclusion, not only is the integrity of social science maintained, but the value judgments themselves are not given a false aura of validity by association with, or as presumed derivations of, "science."

Similarly, my impatience with premature and unwarranted generalization is not to be interpreted as intolerance with broad generalizations in an appropriate part of the curriculum. My point is that speculative generalizations should not be confused with social science, a confusion which, on the one hand, does injustice and damage to the social sciences; and on the other, tends to give to the generalizations an aura of validity which they do not possess.

What I am pleading for is that there be increased clarification among educators, as well as among social scientists, of social science as science — as distinguished from literature, polity, or philosophy. With such clarification I am convinced the findings of research in the social sciences would flow more readily and justifiedly into school curricula and serve a more useful and significant function in general education as well as in the education of the specialist.

Research Developments

With these observations in mind, what are the areas of research in the social sciences which hold promise for the curricula of tomorrow? First of all, with the increasing division of labor and specialization within the social sciences let me hasten to state that I cannot speak with equal competence for all of the social sciences. As a sociologist I can speak best for that field, but, even there, better for my own sub-field of interest — urbanism, demography, and human ecology. I shall attempt, however, to point to some of the more important research developments that hold promise for the curriculum of tomorrow in five of the social sciences — that is in addition to those in sociology, to research developments in social psychology, in economics, political science and cultural/social anthropology. My agreeing to this undertaking, I may say, was in no small measure based on the increasing availability of summaries of the state of these disciplines and research activities in them.[2]

In excluding history, education, and geography, I am assuming that the first two have a distinct status in the curriculum, the first usually through the humanities, and the second, through special facilities for training teachers to which it is not necessary to make special reference to educators; and that the latter is included as a natural science, except at those points where it converges with the interest of sociology in human ecology, namely, as manifest in human geography; and with economics as evident in economic geography.

In general, it should be recognized that with the possible exception of economics, research in the social sciences in any rigorous sense is a product of this century. Only relatively recently were the separate social sciences divorced from moral philosophy and global speculation, on the one hand, and reform movements or defense of the traditional order, on the other.[3] Each of the social sciences to which reference is made above has experienced its major develop-

---

[2] Foremost among these are the following which were heavily consulted in the preparation of this paper:

The UNESCO series, *Documentation in the Social Sciences*, especially:

Bendix, Reinhard and Lipset, Seymour M., *Political Sociology*, UNESCO, Paris, 1957.
Vining, Rutledge, *Economics in the United States of America*, UNESCO, Paris, 1956.
Waldo, Dwight, *Political Science in the United States of America*, UNESCO, Paris, 1956.
Zelterberg, Hans L. (ed.), *Sociology in the United States of America*, UNESCO, Paris, 1956.
Also the following:
Ellis, Howard S. (ed.), *A Survey of Contemporary Economics*, The American Economics Association, Blakiston Co., Philadelphia, 1948.
Gittler, Jos. B., *Review of Sociology: Analysis of a Decade*, Wiley and Sons, New York, 1957.
Hauser, P. M. and Duncan, O. D., *The Study of Population: An Inventory and Appraisal*, University of Chicago Press, Chicago, 1959.
Lindzey, Gardner (ed.), *Handbook of Social Psychology* (2 vols.), Addison-Wesley, Cambridge, Mass., 1954.
Tax, Sol, *et al.*, *An Appraisal of Anthropology Today*, University of Chicago Press, Chicago, 1953.
[3] Wirth, Louis, "The Social Sciences," in Curti, Merle, *American Scholarship in the Twentieth Century*, Harvard University Press, Cambridge, 1953.

ment since the turn of the century; and its empirical research development largely after the first quarter of this century.

During the past three decades significant developments have occurred which have affected the character of most of social science research. These include the diffusion of the natural science conceptions of method; development of special quantitative methods for social research, including the sample survey, in addition to the general developments in statistics; increasing specialization not only between the separate social sciences but, also, in sub-areas within them; and increasing inter-disciplinary and cross-disciplinary researches, partly in compensation for the increased specialization. Moreover, within the past decade technological developments which produced the electronic computer have opened up new vistas of opportunity for quantitative analysis in the years ahead. Finally, it must be recognized that there is a great unevenness in the extent to which rigorous research is being conducted both among the social sciences and within them in their various sub-fields. In consequence, it must follow that there will be unevenness in the manifestation of social science research findings in school curricula.

Sociology

Sociology has been sub-classified into three broad areas apart from general theory and method which cuts across the entire discipline. These three sub-fields are social organization, social psychology, and human ecology and demography.

Of these sub-fields social organization is by far the broadest, especially if it is envisaged as encompassing the various specialisms such as the sociology of religion, educational sociology, political sociology, industrial sociology, urban and rural sociology, and the like. In this sub-area of sociology, research has especially proliferated in recent years in such specific fields as social stratification; industrial sociology, including the sociology of work; political sociology; medical sociology; and a sub-field which cuts across social-psychological interests as well, the study of small groups.

By all means the most prolific and systematic research results are those accumulating in the study of the structure and dynamics of small groups — studies in social psychology as well as studies in social organization. Stimulated by ingenious methodological developments which have made it possible to quantify the various aspects of small group structure and dynamics including their population traits, characteristics of internal structure, and "syntality" traits (the characteristics of the behavior of the group as a whole), the effects of such variables as group size, the communication network, the nature of the group task, and the personalities of group members have been subjected to study with significant results. Moreover, the research in this area like that in the natural sciences is, through its additive character and replication, tending to become funded in a corpus of knowledge that may be expected to grow in a meaningful way.

Small group research, although satisfying in its rigor and cumulative character, is microcosmic and less exciting to those interested in the macrocosmic than the developments in political sociology. The task of political sociology has been defined as the comparison of the abstract and logical possibilities of decision-making, in the context of the status-structure of a society, with the actual decisions taken.[4] Research in this area, shared to some extent with political science, tends to be organized around class conflict and consensus, as one set of polarities; and bureaucracy and oligarchy, as another. Building on the insights and work of Max Weber and Robert Michels political sociologists are seeking to advance knowledge in their area of interest by means of more effective research methods than were available to the 19th and early 20th century students of these problems. Specific studies include those on voting, political participation, public opinion and attitudes, large scale organizations including "human relations" in industry, and leadership.

Small group research, political sociology, and social survey research are certainly the more lively and promising developments in research in social organization, but there is also a growing body of research materials in relatively new areas like industrial sociology, social stratification, and medical sociology, as well as the older ones of social pathology, marriage and the family, community study, and urban and rural sociology. Contributing to many sub-areas of social organization and to sociology in general have been the great advances in the use of the sample survey as means of research. Particularly worth observing and incorporating into the social science curriculum are the studies, as yet too few, which seek to test the hypotheses and theories of earlier thinkers and to reshape them as necessary on the basis of empirical observation.

Significant researches have been conducted in demography and human ecology which merit incorporation into the social science curricula. The research in these areas actually transcends the work in sociology, for the research in both demography[5] and human ecology[6] is cross-disciplinary in character.

In the area of "demↄgraphic analysis," demography conceived in a narrow sense,[7] some of the more significant studies include those using "cohort analysis" in the study of fertility, generation analysis of mortality, mortality in relation to morbidity, the estimation of current and future populations, studies of migration streams, and the analysis of labor force structure and dynamics. In the realm of "population studies" research into the relationship between population and other systems of variables, the more important research activities include the studies of fertility in relation to social and psychological factors, studies of population structure and change in relation to economic development, studies of the effects of migration, and studies of demographic factors on urbanization.

The field of human ecological research in sociology is one which overlaps with interest in human geography, location theory in economics, and general ecology in biology. Earlier studies in human ecology, confined largely to the mapping and description of phenomena in space, are being enriched by comparative researches employing functional-structural analytical methods and delving into the factors and processes producing the spatial and temporal patterns in society.

4 Bendix and Lipset, op. cit.
5 Hauser and Duncan, op. cit., Ch. I.
6 Duncan, O. D., "Human Ecology and Population Studies," in Hauser and Duncan, op. cit.
7 Hauser and Duncan, op. cit., Ch. I.

Studies in human ecology are greatly expanding knowledge about the metropolitan area as well as regional and functional units.

Research developments in social psychology will be separately considered in the section which follows, in which the developments in psychology as well as sociology are incorporated.

Social Psychology

The status of social psychology including research developments has been notably summarized by Gardner Lindzey.[8] It is on this comprehensive and excellent symposium that I have drawn largely in the materials which follow.

Contemporary research in social psychology may be better comprehended and interpreted in relation to the systematic framework from which it flows. Several such systematic frameworks exist. The first, representing the continuation of an old tradition, is the stimuli-response framework. In recent developments, however, including "contiguity theory" on the one hand, and "reinforcement theory" on the other, more explicit hypotheses than those of the past have been formulated and tested regarding human interaction. Second, the framework of cognitive theory concerned both with whether and how cognition, considered as a "centrally initiated process of representative external and internal events,"[9] plays a role in behavior. Third, the framework of psychoanalytic theory has increasingly become one of the themes of social psychological research. Fourth, "field theory," with the designation and concept drawn from developments in physics, produces research based on the assumption that the characteristics of an event are a function of its relations to a system of events of which it is an element. Fifth, the framework of "role theory" utilizes as its conceptual units "*role*, the unit of culture; *position*, the unit of society, and *self*, the unit of personality."[10]

Empirical research in social psychology was vastly expanded during the war and post-war periods, and has produced a relatively large fund of findings which continue to press for curriculum recognition. The studies have been characterized by advances in method including experimentation, attitude measurement, systematic observational techniques, sociometric measurements, systematic interviews, the social survey and a number of specific developments, mathematical and statistical, of great value in social psychological research.

Fields of research activity in social psychology include those in which the individual is studied in a social context, of which those of greatest interest may be studies of social motivation, perception, and socialization. Another focus of social psychological research is that represented by group psychology and processes and products of interaction. This area overlaps, of course, with the "small group" research to which reference was made above. Some of the more significant studies deal with group problem solving, social structure, mass phenomena, and leadership.

Important researches have also emerged from "applied social psychology" with significant findings for the social science curriculum, as well as that of

[8] Gardner Lindzey, *op. cit.*
[9] Scheerer, Martin, "Cognitive Theory," in Lindzey, *op. cit.*, p. 137.
[10] Sarbin, Theodore R., "Role Theory," in Lindzey, *ibid.*, p. 22.

general education. Among these are the studies of prejudice and technic relations, mass media of communication, industrial social psychology and the voting and political behavior representing a merger of interests with political science and political sociology.

Political Science

The consideration of research developments in political science was a relatively simple task because of the availability of *Political Science in the United States of America*.[11] Much of what follows is drawn from this UNESCO report.

Of the social sciences being considered, political science is probably the least advanced in its divorcement from its nineteenth century philosophical and value orientation. This is in part evidenced by the relatively great attention still paid to self-criticism, discussion of method, and debate about the place of values in the discipline.

On the other hand, there are a number of areas in political science in which increasingly effective empirical research is being conducted and impressive research findings are beginning to emerge. In general these are especially the areas where "behavioral science" imagery has penetrated and empirical research has achieved dominance over speculative thought. The areas which have been most affected by this development include, first of all, public opinion, voting and elections; but, also, although to a lesser extent, political parties, and pressure groups, international relations, and public administration. Studies in foreign and comparative government have been relatively little influenced by the development in behavioral science, while those concerned with public law, jurisprudence, and judicial affairs have been the least influenced.[12] The central foci of the behavioral approach to the study of politics have been "power," the "group," "decision-making," "political participation"; and lesser themes have involved the utilization of concepts such as "status," "role," "community," "elites," "symbols," and "communication." Comparative studies have also greatly increased in the postwar period.

Curiously enough, the acceleration of empirical research in political science has been accompanied by increasing concern with policy problems. The troubled postwar world has forced focus on the key issues of the day, the resolution of which may well mean the difference between extinction or survival. In combining the greater interest in empirical research with increased concern about contemporary political problems, sometimes in the same person (notably Lasswell), the political scientist is undoubtedly exacerbating the curriculum problem to which I referred above — the problem of distinguishing between social science research findings and their implications for policy, citizenship, or general education.

Much attention in political science is devoted to "theory," partly because of its close bond to nineteenth century political thought, and partly because "theory" as employed by the political scientist is, among other things, a vehicle for normative judgment and the transmission of value judgments. In the light of the position taken in my introductory remarks, much of what passes for "the-

---

11 Waldo, Dwight, *op. cit.*
12 Waldo, Dwight, *op. cit.*, p. 23.

ory" in political science may more appropriately appear in school curricula in the courses concerned with the consideration of "values," including courses in general education, than in courses labeled "social science." This is certainly true of such "theory" as that concerned with the debate about world political systems, e.g., democracy vs. communism; civil rights; and liberalism vs. conservatism. The debates themselves, and much of what is mistakenly labeled "theory" in them, are data for social science research which should not be confused with the product of such research.

In the specific sub-areas of political science in which research holds promise the following are perhaps the most noteworthy. In international relations especially interesting are the increasing number of studies of international organizations, especially those utilizing the "behavioral" approach. In foreign and comparative government the studies which are departing from the traditional consideration of structure and focusing more on process are especially germinal. The study of comparative government around such key concepts as "decision-making," "power," "ideology," and "political institutions" may provide new and fresh materials. The proliferation of "area studies" is another of the rapidly growing areas of political science. Necessarily cross-disciplinary "area studies" provide the political scientist with a useful focus and the resources of other social sciences in collaborative research. In the field of public administration earlier narrow research on specific problems of management has broadened to include the "behavioral science" approach on the one hand; and increased concern with policy matters on the other. Especially interesting may be the results of increased comparative studies in public administration. The most exciting of all of the expanded empirical research activity in political science is undoubtedly that, shared with sociology and social psychology, which is concerned with public opinion, voting behavior, politics, parties, and pressure groups. The results of the studies of these phenomena are earning an increasingly important place in the curriculum as social science, quite apart from their policy implications for the normative part of the curriculum.

Economics

Economics is the oldest and the best established of the social sciences under consideration in this paper. Yet it shares with political science a large admixture of normative considerations in its study of economic behavior.

Vining in his review and interpretation of research in economics for UNESCO, on which this section is in part based, uses as his point of departure the definition of an economic problem as "a problem of choice among alternatives."[13] In his delineation of three types of choice problems he provides on the one hand a frame for the review of research developments in economics, and on the other, a basis for separating the science from the normative aspects of economics. The three types of choice problems to which he refers are: one, the choice of a means to achieve a particular end; two, the choice by individuals of their ends; three, the choice by a group or society of constraints and regulations which are to be imposed on their individual actions. He succinctly describes

[13] Vining, Rutledge, op. cit., p. 9.

the third type of choice as necessitated by the second when the freedom of others to choose ends is also recognized. The second type of choice is interpreted as the subject matter of "classical" political economy.

The theoretical work of economists which has received the most attention in recent years has been that focusing on the first type of choice — the choice of means for a well defined end. In this realm the economist has been joined by the mathematician and statistician in developing theory and practice for decision-making. The developments in the "theory of games" and empirical researches employing this theory point to new areas of curriculum development. The studies in decision-making, developments in "operations research," and some aspects of the work in econometrics are especially noteworthy developments — developments with implications for the other social sciences which are also interested in decision-making as well as for economics.

Some of the research in econometrics and in decision-making is subjected to criticism by Vining because it confuses the means-ends problem with the problem of choosing ends — particularly those with social objectives of the type of concern to welfare economists. In elaborating on this confusion Vining is, in effect, also elaborating the desirability of separating the "scientific" from the "normative" in economics. The choice of constraints in the management of a society's affairs is not subject to solution by "theory of games" or linear programming. It involves value determinations, normative rather than instrumental judgments.

The great debate now in process about steps to be taken in respect of the present recession (1958) well illustrates the confusion between the choice of problems involved. For, although there is disagreement among economists about means by which a high level of economic activity is to be restored, it is evident that much of the disagreement reflects basic differences in values — more specifically basic differences in goals and in the choice of constraints. Economic research incorporated into social science curricula often requires careful screening to separate the normative from empirical research findings.

There has been a great increase in the flow of factual materials about the operation of the economy, largely from government sources, and, in consequence, a great acceleration in empirical research in economics in recent years.

Especially promising in contribution to the fund of social science knowledge are the increased number of empirical studies, including research in differential fluctuations and growth of economic activity, national income, industrial relations, labor, social security, international trade, prices, and agriculture. Recent research developments also are concerned with problems of economic development, arising from increased interest in the underdeveloped areas of the world; problems of location-theory; the interrelations of population and economic behavior; and, as a result of general developments in survey methodology, with family economic behavior including consumption, expenditures, savings and labor force participation. Finally, it should be noted that the empirical research in economics has probably, more than in any of the other major social science disciplines being considered, gone heavily quantitative, especially in the work of the econometricians and in the utilization of mathematical models in general. There can be little question that the mass of research findings becoming available in empirical economics will generate great pressure for curriculum changes in the years ahead.

Cultural/social anthropology.[14] Anthropology is in a federation of sub-fields with quite distinct specific interests — physical anthropology, archaelogy, linguistics, and cultural or social anthropology. Only the latter is considered here, because the other areas have perhaps closer affinities to the natural sciences or the humanities than to social science and because this assignment must be subject to some arbitrary restrictions. The availability of *An Appraisal of Anthropology Today*[15] has greatly facilitated the preparation of this section.

Cultural/social anthropology, as Kluckhohn has indicated, arises from "the investigation of regularities, variations and deviations in behavior."[16] Culture is used in two senses by the anthropologist: as "the logical construct in the mind of the anthropologist" and as "the norms internalized in individuals as manifested by patterned regularities in abstracted elements of their behavior." In these conceptions and their interrelation is found the basis for one of the most important research developments in social anthropology, namely, the study of the interrelations of culture, personality and behavior manifest in studies of "personality-in-culture," and of "cultural behavior."

The researches have demonstrated earlier general theses about the influence of culture on behavior. Not only are such behaviorisms as language, food habits, and etiquette largely a function of culture but, as the newer research is indicating, so also are many other aspects of behavior.[17] The influence of culture is being traced for example on such biological matters as tolerance to pain, rhythm of eating and evacuation, and psychosomatic disorders. Research also is being extended on the effect of culture on sexual behavior, motor habits, perception, cognition, affect, memory, abnormal behavior, evaluative behavior, child training behavior, and personality. As products of these types of investigation, knowledge has also been increased of universal behavior which transcends individual cultures.

Personality-in-culture studies have involved a shift in focus for the anthropologist from culture and society to the human personality. With the person as the center of the study of process the anthropologist has, in collaboration with psychologists, psychoanalysts and, to a lesser extent sociologists, thrown light both on the person as such, on "human nature," and on such processes as acculturation and social change.

Another type of study greatly stimulated by the exigencies of the war were investigations of "national character." Such research has, among other things, augmented comparative studies and given impetus to cross-disciplinary investigations.

Finally, note should be taken of "applied anthropology" as a major development during the war and post-war years. Applied or action anthropology, quite apart from its social engineering functions, is also being productive of research which merits attention.

While the above discussion refers largely to new research developments in social anthropology the work continues, of course, along more traditional lines as well.[18] Research activity has continued to add to knowledge about such

14 Tax *et al.*, *op. cit.*, pp. 218 ff.
15 *Ibid.*
16 Kluckhohn, Clyde, "Culture and Behavior," in Lindzey, *op. cit.*, p. 924.
17 *Ibid.*, p. 926.
18 Tax *et al.*, *op. cit.*

topics as social structure and social organization, sex and age grading, kinship and marriage, status and stratification, economic, political and ritual relations, social control, and social change. In the pursuit of his studies, however, the anthropologist is increasingly turning to contemporary, literate and advanced, as distinguished from primitive and pre-literate societies, as objects of study. In consequence, the distinction between the social anthropologist and the sociologist becomes more difficult.

Concluding Observations

The introduction of social science research findings into school curricula involves complex problems, in the main not shared by the natural sciences. These problems arise partly from the nature of social science subject matter; partly from the widespread confusion, even among educators and social scientists themselves, on the boundary lines between social science and non-fiction literary works on the one hand, and policy tracts on the other; and partly from the pressures created by the need for general education which has forced premature syntheses and generalization. Much of this confusion could be dissipated if the curriculum made provision for two distinct places for social science subject matter.

The first of the two places suggested should be courses labeled social science which are restricted to social science findings based on empirical research by professionally trained social scientists; and should exclude the non-fiction and policy literature, except perhaps as data for analysis not to be confused with the results of research. The second place is the general orientation course, or other courses properly labeled as courses in general education or ethics or religion or civics or citizenship or philosophy or literature; and not mislabeled as social science. Such a distinction I am convinced would have salutary consequences both for social science and for general education.

In the main body of the paper I have pointed, not comprehensively nor even in a balanced way, to some of the newer and more exciting areas in which research in the social sciences is most rapidly developing. In doing this I have necessarily been highly selective and have even excluded the consideration of entire disciplines including history, geography, and education. In pointing to newer areas of research, I have omitted adequate reference to a number of the more established areas which have produced and are still producing important research findings.

By comparison with the natural sciences the findings of the social sciences are as yet relatively immature and scanty. Yet, small as may be the fund of social science knowledge, it contains much more than society is prepared to accept and digest; and, in consequence, much more than has yet been incorporated into the curriculum of the schools, either as social science or as general education. For example, what is known about juvenile delinquency and crime, racial differences and similarities, inter-group relations and prejudice, group and collective behavior, the role of pressure groups and Madison Avenue in government, industrial relations, international trade, and international relations and organization far transcends common-sense knowledge, and could serve as a basis for modification of public policy and action. But for the reasons indicated above, such knowledge is more likely to be considered as subversive than to be used for the planning of social change. And indeed it is subversive in the sense that it may point to the need for modification which means change in established attitudes or behaviors. Perhaps enough research has not yet been done on methods for the transmission of social science knowledge to the school curriculum as well as to the public at large.

The teacher of social science, and especially the teacher of the policy implications of social science findings in general education, is caught in the conflicting roles of the teacher as "priest" and as "prophet."[19] In one role the social science teacher plays an important part in the transmission and conservation of the social heritage; and, in the other, he points to the paths of change. This posture of the social science teacher is, of course, shared with all of the other school functionaries who have a hand in the determination and administration of the curriculum.

In concluding these observations, it is perhaps unnecessary to point to still another development that may further obstruct rather than accelerate the flow of social science research into the curriculum. I refer, of course, to the amazing series of unprecedented *non sequiturs* in the history of education in the United States attributable to the near hysteria induced by Sputnik I.

One of the widespread reactions to the Russian intrusion into space was the erroneous conclusion that the Russians beat us to it because of the deficiencies of American education. More specifically, it has been contended that the Russian success was a demonstration of the inadequacy of natural science training in our secondary schools and colleges. While it may be true that more rigorous training in our secondary schools, colleges, and universities is desirable, certainly the need for such change was not demonstrated by Sputnik. The nature and intensity of the American reaction to Sputnik, however, carries in it the danger that the natural science curriculum will be greatly expanded at the expense of the curricula both of the humanities and of the social sciences. Should this occur another catastrophic *non sequitur* will have been writ large into the history of American education. For, it would seem that the danger that man may be unable to control his technological advances and the very fear of the implications of the Sputniks, the Explorers, and Vanguard may lead United States education to accelerate education for science and technology at the expense of education which may help in the control of its achievements.

[19] Johnson, Earl S., *Theory and Practice in the Social Studies*, Macmillan, New York, 1956, pp. 30 ff.

The Social Sciences in the
Twentieth Century

Peter Odegard

I might begin this paper with a dozen aphorisms to emphasize the importance of the social sciences. One or two will do. "Know thyself," said Alexander Pope, "presume not God to scan; the proper study of mankind is man."

Raymond Fosdick, for many years one of the great impresarios of social science research in America, once said, "We are discovering the right things in the wrong order . . . , we are learning how to control nations before we have learned how to control ourselves."

In like vein, President Franklin D. Roosevelt posed the central problem of 20th-century civilization when he said, "Today we are faced with the preëminent fact that if civilization is to survive, we must cultivate the science of human relations — the ability of all peoples, of all kinds, to live together and work together, in the same world, at peace."

And perhaps never before has the well-worn aphorism of H. G. Wells been so true — that "civilization is a race between education and catastrophe," and especially education in the social sciences.

I shall spare you further quotations from wise men, since nearly all point the same moral, namely, that the proper and most urgent study of mankind is man. And unless we are to accept a theory of determinism more extreme even than that of Thomas Hobbes, we shall have to assume that, in some measure at least, the fate and destiny of man are in his own hands. Even Karl Marx observed that "man makes his own history." It behooves us, therefore, to give more of our resources of matériel, time, and talent to the systematic study of man, as he goes about making history.

Since man, as we all know, is a social animal, the study of man includes the study of society. And since neither man nor society can be understood apart from the physical environment of soil, and sea, and sky, the systematic study of man will include the study of the human habitat — the planet earth and the universe of which it is a part. Viewed in this perspective, it isn't easy to set outer limits to the so-called social sciences which make man-in-society the central focus of their concern. The slightest reflection will indicate that as the oceans of the earth are one, so, too, is the universe of human knowledge. With all its specialized disciplines and forms of discourse, our knowledge of man and his environment is a seamless web. Follow any path you choose, and at some point it will converge on other paths that ultimately lead into that unified stream of life and thought that distinguishes the human condition.

As one moves outward from such disciplines as political science, sociology, and economics, for example, in one direction he encounters the humanities and

From *The Social Studies: Curriculum Proposals for the Future*, G. Wesley Sowards (editor), pages 17–40. Copyright © 1963 by the Board of Directors of the Leland Stanford Junior University. All Rights Reserved. Reprinted by permission of the publisher, Scott, Foresman and Company, Glenview, Illinois.

the fine arts, and in another, the natural sciences. Hovering uncertainly on one side in a kind of twilight zone between the humanities and the hard-core social sciences are such fields of study as law, history, archaeology, linguistics, and, of course, philosophy. And on the other side, standing between the social sciences and the hard-core natural sciences (physics, astronomy, and chemistry), one finds anthropology, psychology, medicine, biology, and, of course, geography. The boundary lines between these and the even more highly specialized sub-disciplines within them are hard to draw.

The natural sciences are concerned with the nature of the physical universe — i.e., with objects external to man — as someone has said, with objects that cannot talk back. When man is included within their universe of discourse, natural scientists — in this case, biologists — may regard him primarily as an organism without much regard for his individuality, personality, or social relations. Unfortunately, as we know, the living human organism, even when viewed strictly in terms of biology, biochemistry, or biophysics, is profoundly influenced not only by its internal structure and physiology but by its external environment, both physical and social, and not by that environment as an objective natural scientists sees it but as the human organism itself perceives it. As a popular medical aphorism has it, "it's not what man eats that causes ulcers; it's what's eating (i.e., bothering) him." The point is that to study man as an organism, apart from man as a thinking, perceiving, rationalizing person or as a social and political animal, is to arrive at partial truths at best. Hence, the biological study of man inevitably leads to the psychological, just as the psychological study of man is inextricably rooted in an understanding of the organism which biologists probe and ponder. For example, Sherrington's study, the *Integrative Action of the Nervous System*,[1] is as important for the psychologist as for the biologist. The ancient distinction between mind and body has become blurred, and these terms are no longer admissible for marking the proper limits of biology and psychology as scientific disciplines.

How fuzzy the lines of demarcation between the natural and the social sciences can be is illustrated by the remark of a Harvard psychologist in 1954. "Here [at Harvard]," he said, "the psychology department has psychology firmly in the camp of natural science . . . [but] there is a real question whether people working in clinical and social [psychology] should be regarded as natural scientists."[2] Similarly, many physical anthropologists prefer to be classified with the natural scientists although they concede that cultural anthropology can best be described as a social science. The same or similar arguments can be heard in other disciplines. Geographers, for example, moving in one direction, find themselves in bed with natural scientists like geologists, meteorologists, or soil scientists and in another direction, with economists, geographers, demographers, and students of geopolitics. Even the hard-core social sciences exhibit a similar ambivalence. In economics, econometricians sigh for the accolade of natural scientist, leaving the less glamorous title of social scientists to their institutional, classical, or historical brethren. In political science, the radical positivists and behaviorists like to be called hard-nosed scientists to distinguish themselves from those who continue to follow the classical patterns of political science laid

[1] Charles Scott Sherrington, *Integrative Action of the Nervous System* (New Haven: Yale University Press, 1906, 1947).
[2] The Behavioral Sciences at Harvard. Report of the Faculty Committee, 1954, p. 55.

down by the political philosophers (Aristotle and Plato, Machiavelli and Thomas Hobbes, John Stuart Mill and James Madison), the public lawyers (Edward Coke, William Blackstone, John Austin, E. J. S. Dicey, and Thomas Corwin), students of administration (such as Woodrow Wilson, John Dickinson, Leonard White, John Gaus, and Luther Gulick), writers on international relations (Hugo Grotius and E. von Vattell, John Bassett Moore, Grenville Clark, Philip Jessup, Frederick L. Schuman, and Hans Morgenthau).

Obviously these inter- and intradisciplinary distinctions cannot be attributed to differences in the subject matter with which they are concerned. Biologists, psychologists, anthropologists, sociologists, economists, political scientists, no less than historians and humanists, are concerned with man and the human condition. Even the hard-core natural sciences of physics and chemistry have relevance for the systematic study of man, not only when they become biophysics or biochemistry, but when as nuclear physics they threaten us with annihilation. Indeed, at some point and in varying degree, every branch of human knowledge comes to focus on man as an object of scientific or scholarly research. The progress of science and learning thus confirms the familiar aphorism that the "proper study of mankind is man."

What, then, are the grounds for these inter- and intra-disciplinary distinctions? Why do we hear on nearly every hand of tension and conflict, especially among those calling themselves social scientists? What is the meaning, validity, and significance of C. P. Snow's essay *The Two Cultures and the Scientific Revolution*?[3] Why is the so-called Community of Science and Scholarship ceasing to be a brotherhood (if indeed it ever was) to become a battleground? And what, if anything, can we do about it?

One basis for distinction and a common source of tension among scientists and scholars has been their methods of inquiry, observation, and analysis. The so-called Cartesian revolution of the 17th century has had its effect on the orientation and methodology of the social sciences as well as on those of mathematics and the natural sciences.

The novelty of Descartes' method lay in its rejection of the syllogistic method of deducing the particular from the universal. The proper method, said Descartes, was to "reduce involved and obscure propositions step by step to those that are simpler and then attempt to ascend to the knowledge of all others by precisely similar steps." Descartes' *Discourse on Method* (1637)[4] was followed and extended by positivists like Auguste Comte and empiricists like Bacon, Hobbes, Locke, Hume, J. S. Mill, and others, to create the basic framework for modern science.

The essence of scientific method, as Auguste Comte observed, is the subordination of imagination to observation, and he distinguished three major stages in man's intellectual development: (1) The *theological,* in which objects and events were attributed to supernatural causes; (2) The *metaphysical,* in which metaphysical or imaginary abstractions were confused with causes; (3) The *positive,* in which phenomena are explained only through observation, hypothesis, and experimentation. To this the empiricists added the principle that real

---

[3] C. P. Snow, *The Two Cultures and the Scientific Revolution.* The Rede Lectures, (Cambridge: Cambridge University, 1959).

[4] René Descartes, *Discourse on Method,* 1637 (New York: Everyman's Library, Dutton, 1912), pp. xiv–xv.

knowledge comes only from experience (i.e., sense perception from observation, description, classification, and analysis). Generalization, they argued, could never result in positive knowledge but only in greater or lesser degrees of probability.

Any discipline, whatever its subject matter, can become scientific only to the degree it conforms to these canons of scientific method. It is obvious that such methods can be more rigorously applied to so-called natural or physical phenomena than to man. It is not only that man has a will of his own and can talk back, but that, as man, he cannot be studied apart from other men and the society whose creatures and creators they are. Neither may they be studied under the kind of controlled laboratory conditions available in the study of the physical world. Hence, the materials available to the social scientist are likely to be fragmentary and uncontrolled; and he is compelled to rely on inferences, informed guesses, and his own imagination to a vastly greater extent than in the case of other scientists. Moreover, as Comte observed, since "society exists only where a general and collective action is exercised," a science of man cannot be built on the observation of individual instances but only on collective phenomena, the most difficult of all to identify and understand.

In studying man in society, the social scientist is under the additional handicap of being at the same time both the observer and the observed. All manner of dangers lurk in this situation — unconscious motives, stereotypes, value systems. We tend to see things not as they are but as we are, like the lady at a cocktail party who said to her husband, "Dear, don't you think you should stop drinking? Already your face is getting blurred." No one can read the literature of social science without noting how often hypotheses, generalizations, and abstractions are used, not as propositions to be tested, but either as truths to be demonstrated or as instruments of proof. Wishful thinking and rationalization are bound to afflict the social sciences and the humanities to a greater extent than they do other branches of science and scholarship.

Some of these hazards could be overcome by the development of more adequate instrumentation in the social sciences. The importance of instruments for the observation, measurement, and validation of phenomena in the development of modern science can scarcely be exaggerated. What would astronomy be without the telescope, meteorology without the barometer, biology without the microscope, medicine without the thermometer or X-ray, physics without the cyclotron, betatron, or a hundred other complex instruments and machines. In the social sciences, instruments for measuring reaction time, blood pressure, and intelligence and aptitude, the Skinner box, the radio carbon test for dating materials of ancient vintage, the paper ballot, and the voting machine—all have helped, but, by comparison with the natural sciences, social scientists have had to work, as it were, with their bare hands.

Denied both by the nature of their subject matter and their lack of instrumentation from extensive use of the controlled laboratory experiment, some social scientists have turned to model building, games theory, and simulation as a substitute. Extraordinarily complex models have been hypothesized and analyzed in what often resembles a vast game of mathematical charades.

Is it any wonder that, as Comte observed, "the sciences successively became positive in a natural order of sequence, that is to say, according to the degree of their remoteness from man. Thus, astronomy first, then physics, later chemistry, and in our own day [early 19th century], physiology, have been constituted as positive sciences."[5] Sociology (a term first used by Comte) and political science, he thought, could become positive sciences but they would be the last of all to develop.

Someone once said that there is just as much science in any discipline as there is mathematics in it. In any case, mathematics in one form or another has become the lingua franca of modern science. Hence, the use of mathematics, or at any rate some system of quantitative statement, has become the sign and symbol of the hard-nosed scientist. It is not surprising, therefore, that social scientists should strive to use mathematical or quantitative methods in their study of man and society. Statisticians, who in some form have been used by governments at least since the Domesday Survey of 1086, have become increasingly skillful and sophisticated. Improved methods of sampling, interviewing, coding, and analysis of statistical data have accordingly strengthened the scientific structure of the social sciences. Survey research centers, armed with modern data-processing equipment, have opened new windows upon many of the most difficult and complex problems of man and society. And they have made possible a vastly more rigorous empirical testing of many of our most cherished traditional concepts concerning human nature and human behavior. In the process, hard-nosed social scientists often find their hands stained with the slaughter of innumerable platitudes and clichés long cherished by the general public and by their older colleagues.

As a result they find themselves under attack not only from vested interests, ignoramuses, and politically ambitious educational administrators, but by those trained in the older traditions and methods of the social sciences. Thus, while we move toward unity in one direction, we encounter disunity and conflict in the other. Tension is exacerbated, on the one hand, by the traditionalists who castigate the new methodology as "thaumaturgy" and, on the other, by brash and bad-mannered young scholars who fancy themselves as pioneers on a new scientific frontier, being shot at from ambush and from behind by tribes of reactionary and redundant pedants. To the traditionalists, these young Turks appear as both arrogant and misguided; while to the self-styled "scientists" or "behaviorists," as they often call themselves, the traditionalists are simply an outmoded guild of fuzzy-minded taxonomists, mystical idealists, or at best pseudoscientists. In political science, at any rate, it is hard for the traditionalist to stand silent while quasi-literate, hard-nosed behaviorists patronize Aristotle and Plato, Machiavelli and Hobbes as well-meaning but mentally handicapped. It is equally difficult for serious young scholars striving for more rigorous standards of scientific observation and analysis to be told that nothing new has been discovered in social science since Aristotle.

When the methodological battlefront moves from these more or less personal vendettas to higher and more serious ground, more important issues are at stake. Among these issues is the alleged neglect by the new social science of the historical, institutional, legal, and philosophical problems and methods with which students of man and society have been concerned for at least 2000 years. The contemporary preoccupation with methodology, it is also argued, represents a

[5] Auguste Comte, *Early Essays on Social Philosophy* (London: 1911), p. 68.

"failure of nerve" — an escape into techniques to the neglect of substantive issues. "There comes a time," said a Harvard psychologist, quoting Freud, "when you ought to stop cleaning your glasses and take a look through them."[6]

This escapism is reflected in the passion for theoretical models, games theory, simulation, and other sterile statistical systems having little or no relation to life or reality. Excessive concern with such devices, it is said, can produce a new scholasticism in which Science or Scientism — immaculately conceived through mathematics — is worshiped rather than put to work on the difficult and dangerous problems of mankind. To reason from games and models to real-life situations, moreover, can be scientifically dubious and socially dangerous. On modest problems of limited scope and complexity, where the model or simulation can be tested by experience, the risks in such techniques are minimal. But when applied to problems of national, let alone international, scope or which involve complex patterns of motive and behavior, the value of these methods may be questioned. Speaking of the war-simulation tests at the Rand Corporation, Hilbert Schenck, Jr., of M.I.T., has said:

> What is remarkable to me is that the scientific and engineering communities . . . have displayed such blindness in their acceptance of the . . . scientific claims of the war-simulation gang — claims so unsupported by even the most rudimentary scientific controls as to belong in the class of the electric healing belt and seaweed tonics that restore vitality.[7]

If serious questions may be asked concerning the value of theoretical models and games theory, what about the use of quantitative methods in the study of man and society? To raise questions in this area is not to denigrate in any way the importance of mathematical and quantitative methods in the social sciences. The concept of a Gross National Product, not to mention other modes of quantitative analysis, have been major instruments in creating the science of economics. Moreover, as Marie Swabey has pointed out, the basis of all legitimate power in the modern democratic state is a quantitative one, based on the counting of votes. What we would all do without the statistical services of the Census Bureau and other government agencies had best be left to imagination. Every branch of social science has been enriched by quantitative studies. But when one moved from facts to values, from acts to thoughts and feelings, from means to ends, from process to policy, the uses of quantitative methods are less obvious. Yet so central are the problems of value or policy to the study of man and society that Professor Lasswell has suggested calling the social sciences policy sciences.

Where values are involved, rationalization competes with reason and interest with intelligence to make any strictly quantitative or scientific resolution of the issues involved extremely difficult. Policy propositions or value preferences are likely to be expressed in terms so vague and ambiguous as to preclude any very rigorously logical analysis. Such terms as *democracy, freedom, general welfare, equal protection under the law,* and even *education* invite controversy not only concerning the best means for achieving them but as to the meaning of the

---

[6] The Behavioral Sciences at Harvard. Report of the Faculty Committee; 1954, p. 56
[7] Hilbert Schenck, Jr., "Computing 'Ad Absurdum,' " *The Nation*, June 15, 1963.

terms themselves. Most so-called policy problems are of this order. Dealing with them, therefore, involves the social scientist in a continuous study of the logic of ambiguity. Only as ambiguity concerning values or policy is reduced or ignored is it possible to make extensive use of quantitative or, for that matter, rigorously scientific methods.

That is to say, as social scientists move from ends to means, from problems of policy to those of process or administration, the strictly scientific procedures available to them increase. To put the matter another way, the quantitative and experimental methods of the natural sciences become increasingly applicable in the study of man and society where human behavior can be standardized, routinized, and even mechanized to a point where ambiguity — i.e., individual discretion or freedom of choice — is either eliminated or strictly limited. Isn't this what is meant by the rationality of administration as distinguished from the nonrationality of politics? Isn't it also what is meant by the "rationalization" of a given industry, institution, or process?

It is not surprising, under these circumstances, that so-called hard-nosed social scientists — i.e., those that aspire to be grouped with the natural sciences — strive to avoid problems of policy and to concentrate on process. When they deal with value preferences at all, it is to measure their incidence, distribution, and intensity in a given population or the psychophysical characteristics of those who fall at different points on a given scale. Matters of this kind can be treated objectively, quantitatively, and scientifically. In this way the social scientist can avoid the fact-value syndrome that plagues his more traditionally oriented colleagues. He can describe himself as value-free and repeat with the late John B. Watson the admonition "feed me only on facts."

To the traditionalist with his strong humanistic bias, this value-free posture of the hard-nosed social scientist inspires grave misgivings. In this context, he argues, scientific objectivity may become a mask for impartiality or even indifference to the great moral, ethical, and political issues that both unite and divide mankind. Indifference to these issues of value and of policy and preoccupation with process and procedure operate, they say, to blind the social scientist to the really great problems of man and society and to focus his attention upon relatively unimportant issues. It is this moral or political astigmatism, say the traditionalists, that helps to explain the monumental accumulation of data, much of it trivial and transitory, the ponderous elaboration of platitudes, and the passionate quest for new vocabularies and new categories in the social or behavioral sciences. The result, they say, is the multiplication of pretentious semantic neologisms, useless even as scientific concepts and incomprehensible to everyone but their inventors. Familiarity with the new vocabulary, then, becomes a kind of status symbol among those who dedicate themselves to the new Eleusinian mysteries. This neutrality or indifference to value and policy, moreover, tends to trivialize social science and make it a more or less sophisticated servant of any power elite in the manipulation of human behavior regardless of goal or purpose.

The fact-value syndrome is but one cause of present discontent among scholars and scientists, especially among social scientists. Others arise from increasing specialization that has characterized the so-called Age of Analysis in which we live. The span of attention or at least of sustained interest among scholars and scientists has progressively narrowed. Yet it is only because scientists have been content to learn more and more about less and less that the world in general has learned more and more about everything. Without specialization, it is unlikely that the so-called knowledge explosion of our own generation could have occurred.

The age of science is not only an age of specialization, but, as Morton White has said, it is an age of analysis.[8] Analysis means to "unloose . . . , to dissolve . . . , to separate" anything, whether an object of the senses or of the intellect, into constituent parts or elements. In every branch of science, specialists have succeeded in pulling our world apart. The physical world has been reduced to smaller and smaller particles. So, indeed, has the world of man and society been reduced to an almost infinite number of cultures and subcultures, systems and subsystems, classes, groups, and interests forever clashing in a kind of Hobbesian state of nature. The individual is reduced to an impersonal psychoorganism, pushed this way and that, by forces beyond his ken or control — strictly according to Newton's Second Law — or he disappears altogether in the *role* or *roles* he is compelled to play in the great pageant of human life.

In this process of analysis, social scientists have laid such stress on measurable psychophysical forces at work both in the person and in his environment that the role of reason and of freedom to choose have had short shrift. The 18th-century model of the free, rational citizen has all but disappeared, and human behavior is increasingly conceived as nonrational and determined. When reason is admitted at all, it comes into our calculations only as a special kind of conditioned (i.e., determined) behavior or as an indeterminate variable not yet wholly understood.

Analysis, as I have said, means to dissolve, to disintegrate — not to integrate, and the progressive distintegration of the physical world and of man and society poses some difficult problems. One of these is the gap between appearance and reality. When John Doe is reduced to his basic elements and placed in neatly labeled bottles on a laboratory shelf, one is driven to ask where or what is the real John Doe? When the political community is reduced to a series (whether continuous or discontinuous) of systems and subsystems, each seeking to maintain its own inner equilibrium and to maximize its own interest, what happens to the community? When individual voters, doctors, lawyers, even professors become merely impersonal roles, moving like shadows in a cave or masks in a pageant, with differential arithmetic values, what happens to individual persons with their distinctive names and personalities? Are the rights and privileges, the goals and aspirations referred to in the literature of free societies attributes of real, living, individual men and women or of groups, or systems, or merely *roles* within systems?

Specialization and analysis thus pose still another problem, the establishment or reëstablishment of order, unity, and even meaning among otherwise disparate and meaningless particles of information. Otherwise we are left in a kind of nihilistic wilderness in which, as it were, "Ye shall know the facts and the facts shall be sufficient unto themselves." Analysis may clarify but it does not, as such, create knowledge. Knowledge comes not from more and more information about less and less but from the facts of life seen in some meaningful context. To meet this problem, social scientists, as I have said, strive constantly to

[8] Morton White, *The Age of Analysis* (Boston: Houghton Mifflin, 1955).

conceptualize, i.e., to find concepts which will restore some unity and meaning to the fragments of reality their analysis has revealed. The business cycle, imperfect, monopolistic or oligopolistic competition, national income and gross national product in economics; culture, status, stratification, role, social mobility, socialization in sociology; intelligence and aptitude, conditioned response, Gestalt, drive, anomie, id, superego and ego in psychology; bureaucracy, public opinion, decision-making, pressure politics, power elite, geopolitics, left, right, and center in political science are examples. Many others will occur to you.

New and useful concepts, however, are relatively few and far between. Most fruitful social science research has been concerned with the analysis of concepts long established and uncritically accepted. Concepts like capitalism, competition, laissez faire, the laws of supply and demand, value and price in economics; political power and influence, the state, sovereignty, pluralism, oligarchy, democracy, federalism, parliamentarism, balance of power, and national interest in political science are being subjected to more rigorous and systematic empirical study and analysis. In the process, social scientists have borrowed from one another and from the natural sciences such concepts as equilibrium or homeostasis, input, output, feedback, system, subsystem, even nuclear fission which have been put to new uses in the analysis of man and society.

Not the least of the problems created by this age of analysis with its attendant knowledge explosion and one that goes far to explain the tension and conflict within the world of science and scholarship is the problem of communication. The so-called gap between the natural sciences, the social sciences, and the humanities, to which C. P. Snow refers in his essay *The Two Cultures and the Scientific Revolution*,[9] is mainly due to a failure of communication. "I believe," says Snow, "the intellectual life of . . . western society is increasingly being split between two polar groups . . . : at one pole we have the literary intellectuals, . . . at the other, scientists."

Failure of communication, however, is found not only among the great branches of human knowledge but increasingly within them. To "keep up," I'm told, one would have to read 125 specialized periodicals in mathematics, 70 in psychology, and heaven knows how many in other disciplines. In addition to 100,000 government reports, there are nearly 500,000 papers each year in American technical journals, plus an estimated half million in other languages, 30 to 40 per cent of which, it is said, are trivial, repetitious, or redundant. The problem of retrieval from this avalanche of scientific literature has become so burdensome that "several industries follow a rule that if a research project costs less than $100,000, it is quicker and cheaper to work out the problem in the laboratory than to plow through the literature to find whether it already has been done." This duplication of work already done has been referred to as "rediscovering the wheel," a process that is perhaps more common in the social sciences than in the natural sciences. President Kennedy's Science Advisory Committee has only recently reported (January 10, 1963) that "science must be unified if it is to remain effective. . . ."[10]

[9] Snow, *op. cit.* See also F. R. Leavis, *Two Cultures?* (New York: Dutton, 1963), essay by Michael Yudkin, p. 51.
[10] *Science, Government, and Information.* Report of the President's Advisory Committee, 1963. (Washington, D.C.: U.S. Government Printing Office, 1963.) See also digest in *Current* Magazine, May 1963.

Science and technology can flourish only if each scientist interacts with his colleagues and his predecessors and only if every branch of science interacts with other branches of science. . . The ideas and data that are the substance of science . . . are embodied in the literature; only if the literature remains a unity can science itself be unified and viable. Yet because of the tremendous growth of the literature, there is danger of science fragmenting into a mass of repetitious findings, or worse, into conflicting specialties. This is the essence of the crisis in scientific and technical information.

The situation in the social sciences and even in the humanities is only slightly less complicated and ominous. "We are like soldiers," says Stuart Chase,[11] "lying in isolated foxholes without means of communication. . . . Yet the social sciences are concerned with the same critter — man, and the notion that we can abstract the economic or the psychological aspect of his behavior without regard to the rest is nonsense."[12] To solve this problem, the President's Science Advisory Committee suggests a centralized scientific depository — a kind of knowledge bank with an elaborate retrieval system to make any existing knowledge readily available. The committee also suggests that authors refrain from unnecessary publication. Universities and foundations could contribute to this end by easing the pressure of the "publish or perish" policy upon scholars and scientists. Equally important would be the rediscovery of some common goals for scientific research.

"Science for science' sake," no doubt, is as easily justified as "art for art's sake." But it is by no means clear that taxpayers who now provide the vast bulk of funds for scientific research will continue to do so simply to satisfy the curiosity of scientists. Nor are governments always likely to accept on faith the claims of scientists that what they do adds significantly to our knowledge of man and his universe. Already one hears mutterings in Congress about the well-nigh cosmic waste in space research and development. Outside the context of the cold war and without the rationalization of national defense, it is extremely doubtful that the tens of billions currently appropriated would be forthcoming. Can we find what William James would call a moral equivalent for war in seeking support for science and scholarship in our society? In the allocation of a nation's limited resources of manpower and materials, there are outer limits to the justifiable claims even of scientific research and development, especially when so much of it is repetitious and redundant. To provide for better communication among the various disciplines, the President's committee urges greater emphasis on the so-called "mission-discipline duality." That is to say, more interdisciplinary research upon common goals.

We are, in fact, confronted in all this with a central paradox of modern times. The very specialization and analysis that have been pulling man and his world apart have at the same time made men everywhere more interdependent. That

11 Stuart Chase, *The Proper Study of Mankind* (New York: Harper, 1948).
12 Roger Blough of the United States Steel Corporation in 1957 commented: "I have studied the economists' differing definitions of 'administered prices'; I have sought to comprehend that still-born concept called 'zone of relative price indifference'; I have struggled with that impossible paradox . . . 'monopolistic competition'; and pursuing my research even further into the semantic stratosphere of economic literature, I have encountered 'atomistic heteropoly' and 'differentiated polypoly.'" — *Steel and the Presidency*, 1962, by Grant McConnell. Copyright © 1963 by W. W. Norton & Company, Inc., New York.

each man is his brother's keeper is no longer a question but a condition. Disintegration through analysis has made integration not only inevitable but urgent if we are not to fly apart. Indeed the rediscovery of a sense of direction and purpose has become a matter of life and death for the human race. Central to this rediscovery is a continuous restudy of those basic concepts that lie at the core of human knowledge.

Concepts, like other things, come in many shapes and sizes and with varying degrees of significance. They also play different roles. Some merely seek to describe and define what *is*, some to outline what *ought* to be, and others to *predict* what will be or *could* be under certain circumstances. In general, contemporary hard-nosed social scientists, in their zeal to be value-free, eschew the use of concepts of what *ought* to be or even of what *might be*, if people were of a mind to have it so, in favor of concepts of *what is*. What this posture overlooks is that neutralism and indifference toward what *ought* to be not infrequently align the scientist with values and social forces least compatible with the freedom without which science itself cannot survive. Moreover, it tends to reduce the scientist to the role of technician and to sacrifice a philosopher's crown for a servant's cap.

It is obvious, of course, that a value-free science — a science without goal or purpose — becomes merely a form of random behavior which makes a mockery of the term. A scientist without values is like a fanatic who redoubles his effort after he has lost his aim. Nor is it enough to say that his values are merely methodological or procedural, concerned with means and not ends, except only the objective pursuit of truth. For truth wears many faces and, except as it is arbitrarily defined in terms of meter readings, can be as elusive as liberty, equality, and fraternity. Moreover, to discover what is true or false is not unrelated to the discovery of what is good or bad. A scientific concept can be true or false in the degree to which it corresponds to the norms or standards of science itself — i.e., to meter readings. So, too, it may be good or bad in the degree that it contributes to or corresponds with the basic needs and goals of human life. Unless science is merely random behavior or idle curiosity without purpose, it has a responsibility to discover and to serve these basic human needs.

This lays a special obligation on the social sciences because they are by definition concerned with man and society. So-called behavioral science, whether hard-nosed or soft-nosed, has no mandate to be indifferent to human goals or values. One of its major assumptions is that human behavior is goal-directed, and in striving for these goals, men choose among alternative modes of conduct. It assumes also that in choosing, they are conditioned not merely by the physical world and the pressures of appetite and instinct but by formal education in rational modes of thought and behavior. Rationally induced changes in human behavior thus become as reasonable, i.e., as scientific, as rationally induced changes in the physical environment. There is nothing unscientific in social scientists who seek to change those conditions of character and environment that impair man's ability to make rational choices among alternative modes of behavior.

There is nothing sentimental or sloppy in social scientists committed to the rational analysis and eradication of poverty, pestilence, and war, ignorance, fear, and hate. There is nothing unscientific in economists who are as much concerned with the components as with the size of our Gross National Product. Moreover, I suspect that integration of the social sciences and better lines of communication with the natural sciences will come as quickly through cooperation on problems of this kind as in conferences on scope and method.

Not less important is the task of social scientists, by precept and example, to encourage in every way possible and in every one they can reach a conscious and continuous reflection on the human condition and on alternative roads to the basic goals for which all men strive. This continuous and rational reflection on contemporary patterns of thought and behavior is but another definition of social ethics, without which men become but creatures of custom and habit, little better than beasts. Scientists are not immune from the responsibilities of other citizens. They need to be reminded that their attitudes of olympian indifference and skepticism toward moral and ethical problems in a society that has all but canonized the scientist can issue in apathy and cynicism among others; attitudes dangerous alike to science and a good society.

In a daring book called *Daedalus*, published forty years ago, J. B. S. Haldane said:

I think that the tendency of applied science is to magnify injustices until they become too intolerable to be borne. . . . I think [also] that moral progress is so difficult that any developments are to be welcomed which present it [i.e., moral progress] as the naked alternative to destruction, no matter how horrible may be the stimulus which is necessary before man will take the moral step in question.[13]

Have we now reached a point in history where the alternatives to moral and political progress are so horrible that we may at long last be willing to put forth the effort necessary to guide mankind into a more orderly and humane society? Unless we do so, we shall surely die.

Structure of the Disciplines: Meanings and Significances

Joseph J. Schwab

We embark here on an exploration of one of the most difficult of terrains: investigation of the nature, variety, and extent of human knowledge; and the attempt to determine what that nature, variety, and extent have to tell us about teaching and learning. My share of this task is a specialized one and a preliminary one. It is simply to map that terrain. Later papers will explore the land itself.

[13] J. B. S. Haldane, *Daedalus*. (New York: Dutton, 1924), p. 86.

From *The Structure of Knowledge and the Curriculum*, G. W. Ford and Lawrence Pugno (eds.), pages 6–30. By permission of Rand McNally & Company.

What is meant by the structure of the disciplines? It means three things, three distinct but related sets of problems. Let us take a foretaste of all three together without discriminating them by name.

It has been widely supposed that there are indubitable grounds for recognizing basically different orders of phenomena, each requiring a different discipline for its investigation because of the differences in the character of the phenomena.

There are many different views based on such a premise. For example, many philosophers have insisted on a fundamental distinction between living phenomena and non-living, thus generating the notion that there are two fundamentally different sciences, the biological and the physio-chemical. These two sciences were supposed to differ in method, in guiding conceptions, in the kind of knowledge produced, and in degree of certainty, differing to precisely the same extent that their subject matters were supposed to differ.

Another such view is generated by a distinction between man and nature, a distinction in which nature is conceived as bound by inexorable laws while men are in some sense and in some degree free. In this view, two major areas of investigation are again discriminated: on the one hand, science, concerned with the inexorable laws that nature presumably obeys; and on the other hand, a discipline in the neighborhood of ethics and politics, which would investigate the freedom that man has and the ways in which men make their choices.

There is also a view that emphasizes the vast difference between the generality of "natural" phenomena (i.e., their predictability, the tendency of "natural" things to behave or be the same in instance after instance) and the particularity of human events (the essentially unique and non-repeating character of acts notable in the behavior of man). Again, two widely different bodies of investigation and study are generated: science on the one hand and history on the other. Science, in this view, would seek the general laws that characterize the repeating behavior of natural things, while history would seek to determine the precise, unique events that characterized each life, each era, each civilization or culture that it studied. Hence, again, there would be two basically different curriculum components, differing in method, principle, and warrantability.

There have been similar separations of other disciplines, notably mathematics and logic. Mathematics was long ago seen to differ radically from other disciplines, including the sciences, in that its subject matter appeared to have no material existence. The objects of physical or biological enquiry could be seen, touched, smelled, tasted. The objects of mathematics could not. The plane, the line, the point, unity, number, etc. existed in some way which was not material or did not exist at all. This peculiarity of mathematical objects continues to be a puzzle. No one view of the nature of mathematics has been developed which is satisfactory to all concerned, though most moderns are agreed that mathematics differs radically from the other sciences.

Logic has been set apart because of its unique relationship to other disciplines rather than because of something peculiar about its subject matter. To one degree or another, all other disciplines test the reliability of their conclusions by appealing to canons of reasoning and of evidence which are developed in the first place by the discipline of logic. Since logic is responsible for developing these canons, it cannot itself use them to check its own work. Logic thus stands as a sort of "queen of the sciences," dictating their rules but having for itself rules of some other and puzzling sort. Unlike the case of mathematics, this peculiarity of logic is no longer universally recognized. In some quarters, for example, it is held that logic does no more than formulate the methods and the canons of reasoning and of evidence which other sciences have developed, used, and bear witness to by their effectiveness. In this view, logic is not so much the queen of the sciences as their handmaiden.

Let us continue our foretaste of the problems of the structures of the disciplines by noting a peculiarity of the distinctions we have described. The peculiarity is that the differences among phenomena which appear at one period in the history of the disciplines to be radical and self-evident may at a later date disappear or become inconsequential as bases for differentiating disciplines. Take, for example, the differentiation of biology from the physical-chemical sciences. In early times and through the eighteenth century, fundamental differences between the living and the non-living could not be evaded. The living thing was "self-moving"; no other object was. The living thing reproduced itself; the living thing developed, had a personal history which no non-living thing could duplicate. Then, in the middle to late nineteenth century, some of these differences ceased to be notable, others disappeared entirely from human recognition. In this altered climate, the physiologist Claude Bernard pleaded for a study of living things strictly in terms of physics and chemistry. Since then, such an approach to living things has been so fruitful that it is now safe to say that it will be only a brief time before we shall synthesize living molecules in the laboratory. In recent years a still further shift in outlook has taken place: we now hear pleas from some physicists that certain physical phenomena be treated in much the way that living things were investigated *before* Bernard.

A similar shift is visible on a smaller scale in the history of the science of mechanics. Three hundred years ago the behavior of celestial bodies (the planets and the stars) and the behavior of terrestrial bodies in motion (things rolling on the surface of the earth and things thrown or propelled through the air) appeared to be radically different. Terrestrial bodies inevitably came to rest and fell to earth; celestial bodies inevitably continued in their regular motion without stop. Then, with Newton, these differences, though still visible, became entirely unimportant.

In brief, what we see of and in things changes from epoch to epoch. Differences that once appeared to be radical are seen later to be illusory or trivial; then, at another period, some of these differences reappear in a new guise. What can account for such changes in what appears to be objectively perceived? The answer is most easily exemplified in the case of mechanics, where in our own day the once radical difference between terrestrial and celestial bodies continues to be treated as illusory.

Granted that this difference was an illusion, what made the illusion disappear? The answer is this: Newton conceived an idea called universal gravitation. In the light of this idea, it became desirable and possible to examine the motion of the celestial bodies (in Newton's case, the moon) in a new way. Specifically, it became desirable and possible to measure the changing directions and changing velocities of the moon in such a fashion that it could be described as continually falling toward earth, while, at the same time, continually moving in a straight line at an angle to its fall. Thus its continuous orbit of the earth could be understood as the resultant of these two motions. In the same way it became possible to conceive of a terrestrial missile as falling to earth and coming to rest there only because its initial velocity in a straight line was not great enough to carry it straight forward beyond the bend of the earth before its fall brought it into contact with the earth. One could then see that as the initial velocity of a missile became greater and greater, it would not only go farther before it fell to earth, but at some point the increased velocity would be so great that the fall of the missile would be compensated by the falling away of the spherical surface of the earth. Such a missile would then become a satellite of the earth precisely like the moon. In brief, a new conception dictating new studies and a new way to interpret the data exhibited the movement of celestial bodies as nothing more than an extreme case of the motions of familiar terrestrial bodies moving at lower velocities.

In general, two collections of phenomena appear to be vastly different because we have used separate and distinct bodies of conceptions in studying them and discovering knowledge about them. Each such body of conceptions dictates what data we think we should seek, what experiments to perform, and what to make of our data by way of knowledge. If widely different conceptions are used to guide enquiries on two different collections of phenomena, we end inevitably with bodies of knowledge which exhibit few similarities and many differences. It is through the limiting or distorting lenses of these bodies of knowledge that we look at things. Hence, if the lenses distort or limit in different ways, we see things as different. The differences we see disappear if, but only if, a new conception is given birth which permits the study of both collections of phenomena in one set of terms and therefore makes for unity where diversity existed before.

Before we discriminate the problems of the structure of the disciplines, let us take note of a *caveat*. It is this: the integration of previously separate bodies of knowledge by new and unifying conceptions should not blind us to the possibility that some of the differences we recognize among phenomena may be genuine; some differentiation of disciplines may be perennial. There really may be joints in nature, a forearm, then an elbow, and then an upper arm. Science, ethics, and aesthetics may indeed represent three widely variant objects of enquiry. The doctrine of the unity of science, which insists on a unification of all knowledge, is either a dogma or a hope but not a fact. There are no data from which to conclude decisively that eventually all the disciplines will become or should become one.

Now let us step back and identify in this foretaste of knowledge and knowledge-seeking the three major but related sets of problems which define the area called structure of the disciplines.

Recall first our brief review of efforts to discriminate life from non-life, science from history, and so on. These efforts illustrate the first problem of the structure of the disciplines. It is the problem of determining the membership and organization of the disciplines, of identifying the significantly different disciplines, and of locating their relations to one another.

This set of problems is illustrated by the following questions. Is mathematical knowledge significantly different from knowledge of physical things? If so, how are the behaviors of mathematical objects related to the behaviors of physical objects? That is, how must we account for the extraordinary usefulness of mathematics to the sciences? Is it because we impose mathematical forms on our observation of physical things, or is it because, in some mysterious way, the objects of the external world behave according to patterns that we discover through mathematical enquiry into our own intellects? Similarly, we might raise questions about practical knowledge and scientific or theoretical knowledge. Are they much the same or truly different? Is practical knowledge merely the application of science? Or does science take hold of ideal objects extrapolated from experience of things while practical knowledge must supply the bridge for return from scientific knowledge of such ideal objects to the actual and practicable? This set of problems may properly be called a problem of the structure of the disciplines, if we keep in mind that by the plural "disciplines" we refer to them collectively rather than distributively, while "structure" is singular and refers to the organization of the disciplines *inter se*.

The significance of this set of problems to education is obvious enough. To identify the disciplines that constitute contemporary knowledge and mastery of the world, is to identify the subject matter of education, the material that constitutes both its resources and its obligations. To locate the relations of these disciplines to one another is to determine what may be joined together for purposes of instruction and what should be held apart; these same relations will also weigh heavily in determining our decisions about the sequence of instruction, for it will tell us what must come before what, or what is most desirably placed first, or second, or third.

The second set of problems of the structure of the disciplines is exemplified by the tremendous role of the concept of universal gravitation in supplying us with a more nearly universal mechanics. A similar role is played by other conceptions in the attainment and formulation of all scientific knowledge. Embedded in the knowledge we have of the workings of the human body lies one or another concept of the nature of an organism, of the character of the parts of such an organism and how they relate to one another. Back of our knowledge of heredity lies a conception of particles behaving as do the terms in the expansion of a binominal to the second or higher powers. Back of our ability to make decisions in playing games lie similar conceptions. Again, the conceptions happen to be mathematical: the expansion of the binominal or a more complex mathematical structure derived by taking the expansion of the binominal to its limit. These mathematical conceptions provide us with a body of probability theory with which we play poker, determine tactics in battle, plan the production and sale of the products of our industries. Similarly, knowledge of human behavior, both individual and social, has arisen only as the men concerned with enquiry in psychology, sociology, and anthropology have developed conceptions that have enabled them to plan their researches.

In general then, enquiry has its origin in a conceptual structure, often mathematical, but not necessarily so. It is this conceptual structure through which we are able to formulate a telling question. It is through the telling question that we know what data to seek and what experiments to perform to get those data. Once the data are in hand, the same conceptual structure tells us how to interpret them, what to make of them by way of knowledge. Finally, the knowledge itself is formulated in the terms provided by the same conception. Thus we formulate and convey some of the knowledge we discover about the body in terms of organs and functions; we formulate and communicate our knowledge of atomic structure in terms of a concept of particles and waves; we formulate some of our knowledge of human personality in terms of psychic organs and their functions and other portions of it in terms of interpersonal relations.

In each science and in many arts such conceptual structures prevail. The second problem of the structure of the disciplines is to identify these structures and understand the powers and limits of the enquiries that take place under their guidance. Let us call this set of problems the problem of the *substantive* structures of each discipline.

Again, the significance of this problem of the structure of the disciplines to education is obvious enough — or at least one part of it is. For to know what structures underlie a given body of knowledge is to know what problems we shall face in imparting this knowledge. Perhaps the conceptual structure is no more complex than that involved in the discrimination of two classes of things by a single criterion, such as color or shape. In that case, we may suppose that little difficulty would be encountered in teaching this body of knowledge even to the very young. Perhaps the conceptual structure is more complex but so firmly embedded in common-sense knowledge of things that the child at some early, given age will already have encountered it and become familiar with it. In that case, we should, again, have little difficulty in imparting our knowledge, provided that we impart it at the right time in the development of the child in our culture. However, suppose the conceptual structure is both complex and largely unused in common-sense knowledge? This would be the case at the moment for the physical conception of a wave-like particle. In such a case, to locate and identify the conception is to locate and identify a difficult problem of instruction requiring much experiment and study.

A second curricular significance of the problem of the substantive structures of each discipline is less obvious. It concerns a peculiar consequence of the role of conceptual structures on our knowledge, a consequence little noted until recently. The dependence of knowledge on a conceptual structure means that any body of knowledge is likely to be of only temporary significance. For the knowledge which develops from the use of a given concept usually discloses new complexities of the subject matter which call forth new concepts. These new concepts in turn give rise to new bodies of enquiry and, therefore, to new and more complete bodies of knowledge stated in new terms. The significance of this ephemeral character of knowledge to education consists in the fact that it exhibits the desirability if not the necessity for so teaching what we teach that students understand that the knowledge we possess is not mere literal, factual truth but a kind of knowledge which is true in a more complex sense. This in turn means that we must clarify for students the role of concepts in making knowledge possible (and limiting its validity) and impart to them some idea of the particular concepts that underlie present knowledge of each subject matter, together with the reasons for the appropriateness of these concepts and some hint of their limitations.[1]

---

[1] See Joseph J. Schwab, "Enquiry, the Science Teacher, and the Educator," *School Review*, LXVIII (Summer 1960), for an elaboration of this point.

The third problem of the structure of the disciplines we shall call the problem of the *syntactical* structure of the disciplines. This problem is hidden in the fact that if different sciences pursue knowledge of their respective subject matters by means of different conceptual frames, it is very likely that there will be major differences between one discipline and another in the way and in the extent to which it can verify its knowledge. There is, then, the problem of determining for each discipline what it does by way of discovery and proof, what criteria it uses for measuring the quality of its data, how strictly it can apply canons of evidence, and in general, of determining the route or pathway by which the discipline moves from its raw data through a longer or shorter process of interpretation to its conclusion.

Again, certain obvious consequences to education accrue from such a study. For, unless we intend to treat all knowledge as literal, true dogma, and thereby treat students as mere passive, obedient servants of our current culture, we want our students to know, concerning each body of knowledge learned, how sound, how dependable it is.

In summary then, three different sets of problems constitute the general problem of the structure of the disciplines. First there is the problem of the organization of the disciplines: how many there are; what they are; and how they relate to one another. Second, there is the problem of the substantive conceptual structures used by each discipline. Third, there is the problem of the syntax of each discipline: what its canons of evidence and proof are and how well they can be applied. Let us turn now to a brief investigation of each of these problems.

The Problem of the Organization of the Disciplines

With the problem of the organization of the disciplines we must face at once one of the inevitable complexities of this terrain, the fact that it does not and cannot supply a single, authoritative answer to the question of what disciplines there are, how many there are, and how they are related to one another. The reason for this complexity is fairly obvious. The problem of organization is a problem of classification primarily. If we classify any group of complex things, we are faced with a wide choice of bases of classification. (Even with postage stamps, we could classify by country of origin, by color, by shape or size, or by some combination of two or more of these.) Disciplines are very complex, hence the diversity and variety of available modes of classification are great. Consequently, depending on what one emphasizes about the disciplines, one or another or still a third or a fifth or a tenth classification of them is generated.

Four bases of classification of disciplines have always demanded attention: (1) their subject matter, what they aim to investigate, or work upon; (2) their practitioners, what competences and habits are required to carry on their work; (3) their methods (syntax), and modes of enquiry by which the enquirer brings himself to bear on the subject matter; (4) their ends, the kinds of knowledge or other outcomes at which they aim. Let us, then, examine a few organizations of the disciplines which use one or more of these, choosing them for the light they may throw on current curriculum problems.

The basic organization of the sciences proposed by Aristotle is worth taking a brief look at nowadays because we have tended to forget what it emphasizes. In this organization, Aristotle made most use of the end or aim of the disciplines together with the character of the materials they work on, the subject matter. Using these two as bases of classification, Aristotle distinguished three major groups of disciplines, the names of which have survived even in our current common-sense knowledge of the disciplines — though the significance assigned them has altered or been lost. The three basic divisions are the *Theoretical*, the *Practical*, and the *Productive*.

The theoretical disciplines are those whose aim is to know. For Aristotle, "to know" meant to know indubitably. Therefore, the theoretical disciplines included only those whose subject matters exhibited such inexorable regularity that they could be considered proper objects of "knowing" enquiry. Aristotle thought there were three such "knowing" or theoretical disciplines: physics, mathematics, and metaphysics. Today, though we would be very doubtful about the possibility of indubitable knowledge, we would, nevertheless, recognize a group of "theoretical" disciplines whose aim was to know and whose subject matters were such that the knowledge these disciplines sought was as nearly stable as knowledge can be. We would include the physical and biological sciences in this group. We would include substantial portions of the social sciences. We would exclude metaphysics as doubtful indeed. We would exclude mathematics, not because it is doubtful, but because we would consider it very special.

The practical disciplines, for Aristotle, included those concerned with choice, decision, and action based on deliberate decision. Precisely because its aim was to do, and therefore to alter the course of things, its subject matter had to have the property that was exactly opposite to the property required for the theoretical sciences. The subject matters of the practical sciences by necessity, must be not inexorable in their behavior, but capable of alteration, not fixed and stable but changeable.

It is exceedingly important, if we are to appreciate the bearing of this Aristotelian classification on modern problems, that we realize that "deliberate action" meant for Aristotle actions undertaken for their *own sakes* and not actions undertaken merely as the necessary preliminaries to some other end. Such actions, undertaken for their own sakes, constitute, then, what we mean by "a good life." They are the activities that stem from and express the best of which each man is capable. The practical sciences were (and are) therefore, ethics and politics. For us in modern times, ethics and politics would include not only each individual effort to lead and examine a deliberate life and the governing the policymaking in high places, but also the difficult and terrifying business of being parents, of being teachers *deliberately* and not as automatons, and the responsible work of administration and policymaking at all levels, together with those parts of the social sciences which contribute to such activities. I need not add that of all the things the schools might do, they do least of this. A few nursery schools, a very few teachers at the elementary level, and some few men and women at the college level give thought and time and energy toward evoking in their students the competencies and habits that lead to the making of good choices and good decisions and help the person to act in ways commensurate with his decisions. But by and large, the time, the energy, and the resources of our public schools ignore the very existence of practical disciplines in the Aristotelian sense.

The productive disciplines in the Aristotelian scheme are what the work "productive" suggests. They are the disciplines devoted to *making*: the fine arts, the applied arts, engineering. In connection with the significance of the Aristotelian productive disciplines for modern curriculum problems, let us note a principal characteristic of the entire Aristotelian organization: it emphasizes the sharp differences among the three groups of disciplines. The theoretical disciplines, devoted to knowing, concern themselves with those aspects of things which are fixed, stable, enduring. Hence, the theoretical disciplines are concerned with precisely these aspects of things which we cannot alter by making or make use of by doing. The productive disciplines are concerned with what is malleable, capable of being changed. The practical disciplines are concerned with another sort of malleability of human character, its ability to deliberate on its future and (within limits) to do as it sees fit.

We, on the other hand, have tended to fall into the habit of treating all disciplines proper to the schools as if they were theoretical. We manage to maintain this preoccupation in the case of the practical disciplines by ignoring them. In the case of the productive disciplines, we ignore them in some cases and in others resort to the trick of treating them as if they were theoretical. Music appreciation is taught as if its purpose were to recognize obvious themes of symphonies or concertos and proudly announce the opus number and the composer's name. Performing music is taught as if the aim were merely to follow the notes and obey the teacher's instructions about the score. Literature is taught as if dramas and novels were windows looking out on life, or worse, as if, as in the case of music appreciation, the object of the game were to know choice tidbits about the character, the life, or the times of the author. Art is taught, like literature, as if its aim were to provide a true, a faithful photograph of life. Happily, the exceptions to these strictures are increasing. Music appreciation is more and more being taught as a mastery of those arts by which the ear and the mind creatively take in the form and content of music. Performing music is more and more being taught in such a way that the students learn the grounds by which to discover and select from alternative interpretations of the score. Poetry, literature, and drama are more and more the objects of the kind of scrutiny which permits their appreciation as works of art rather than as sources of vicarious experience. More and more teachers of art permit their students the freedom for creation which society has long since accorded the professional artist. Nevertheless, the theoretizing of the productive disciplines is still prevalent enough to render this warning relevant.

Let us turn to another organization of the sciences, notable in that one version of it is reborn with every undergraduate generation. This is Auguste Comte's positive hierarchy of the sciences. This scheme is based on the view that subject matter, and only subject matter, should provide the basis for classification. It takes the further view that subject matters should be ordered in terms of *their* subject matters; that is, Comte maintains that orders of phenomena can be discerned, each order consisting of members of the next lower order organized into more complex structures. Using this Chinese box conception of the world, Comte locates physical things as the simplest of all orders (presumably something like our modern fundamental particles). Chemicals come next, as consisting of physicals organized in a new way. Then come biologicals as still higher organizations of chemicals. Finally, at the top, come socials as organizations of biologicals. Thus the Comtian hierarchy of the sciences runs: physics, chemistry, biology, the social sciences. Then Comte adds one last factor. At the bottom of the entire structure he places another "science" — mathematics, mathematics conceived as a kind of natural logic governing the study of all the sciences above it.

Perhaps because of its simplicity and its tendency to be reborn in every generation, this particular organization of the disciplines has been one of the most tyrannical and unexamined curriculum principles in our time. It has dictated, I suspect, at least thirty-five per cent of all the sequences and orders of study of the sciences at the high school and college level in the country. The biologist tries to make his task easier by insisting that chemistry precede his subject field. In turn, the chemist demands that physics precede his. The physicist demands that mathematics precede physics. And each appeals to the Comtian hierarchy as the principal reason for his demand.

There is some justice in this view but there is injustice too. For it is quite possible to read the Comtian hierarchy the other way around. The inverted reading can, indeed, be done without departing from Comte's own principles, as Comte himself well knew. The principle in question requires that each science in the hierarchy shall be well developed before the one above it can be developed. Thus an adequate sociology must wait upon a thoroughly adequate biology; biology, in turn, cannot become complete until chemistry is complete, and so on. This *seems* to suggest that physics ought to be developed by a study simply of physical things, postponing chemistry until the study of physicals is complete; in the same way chemistry would be developed by a study of chemicals, postponing biology until the chemistry is complete. However, if we look closely at the basic Comtian principles, we realize that a complete, positive knowledge of the constituents and the organization of chemicals can be developed only if we have sought out and identified all the behaviors of which chemicals are capable. At this point arises the startling corollary that leads to an inverted reading of the Comtian hierarchy. For, clearly, if biologicals are organizations of chemicals, biologicals constitute the place in which some large array of chemical potentialities becomes real and can be seen. It follows, then, that a study of biologicals must precede any completion of chemistry; a study of socials must, in the same way, precede complete knowledge of biologicals, and so on.

The developments of science since the days of Comte most certainly bear out this reading of his hierarchy. Organic chemistry has developed only as we have studied the complex chemistry of the living organism. The behavior of the human individual has become better understood as we have studied human culture and society. The development by physicists of adequate theories of atomic structure rests upon knowledge of chemicals. Thus we see that it is just as plausible to read the Comtian hierarchy downward from sociology through biology, chemistry, and physics to mathematics, as it is to read it upward from mathematics to physics, to chemistry, to biology, and finally to social science.

We cannot, then, rest our arguments for mathematics as prerequisite to physics, physics prerequisite to chemistry, and so on, on the assumption that the upward reading of the Comtian hierarchy constitutes an unequivocal curriculum principle. Rather, we might well argue that bits and portions of each of these alleged prerequisites should be taught as the need arises during the study of the higher sciences. For example, physics might well be taught by examining the obvious behaviors of physical things up to the point where it becomes clear to student and teacher alike that further progress in the physics requires mastery of certain mathematical conceptions or operations. At this point, the class would turn to the mastery of the mathematics required by the physics under study. In the same way, the complex study of the microchemistry of the living cell would not be taught as a prerequisite to study of the organism and its larger parts and functions; rather, the visible behaviors of the organism, of its organ systems and gross organs might well come first, with the biochemical materials so placed as to be meaningful to the students as the physio-chemical basis for the behaviors already known.

The curriculum sequence of prerequisites based on the upward reading of the Comtian hierarchy (i.e., mathematics to physics to chemistry, etc.) is often referred to as the "logical order" of instruction. The fact that the Comtian hierarchy can be read plausibly in either direction requires us to realize, however, that the phrase "logical order" applied only to one of them is a special pleading. Either order is "logical." The upward order from mathematics to the social sciences we might well call the dogmatic order, i.e., the order that runs from the current explanation to that which is explained. The downward order from, say, biology to chemistry, we might call the order of enquiry, i.e., the order that runs from a display of phenomena calling for explanation to the explanation the science has developed. A curriculum choice between the order of enquiry and the dogmatic order cannot be made on subject-matter criteria alone. Rather, we must look to the capacities of our students, to knowledge of ways in which learning takes place, and to our objectives, what we hope our students will achieve, in order to make our decision.

The Problem of the Syntax
of the Disciplines

If all disciplines sought only to know and if the knowledge they sought were merely the simple facts, the syntax of the disciplines would be no problem. As we have seen, the disciplines are not this simple. Many are not, in the Aristotelian sense, theoretical at all: they seek ends that are not knowledge but something else — making, the appreciation of what is made, the arts and habits of deliberation, choice, and action. Those that are theoretical seek knowledge of different kinds (commensurate to their subject matters), hence use different methods and different canons of evidence and warrantability. For example, science seeks very general or even universal knowledge, while much history seeks the most detailed and particular knowledge. Each of these objects of enquiry poses problems peculiar to itself. Hence knowledge of each of them is sought in different ways. Even within the sciences there is much variability. Biologists find it necessary or desirable to seek knowledge in bits and pieces while physicists, at the other extreme, work hard to develop broad, comprehensive theories which embrace vast ranges of subject matter. The evidence that justifies the acceptance of an isolated bit of knowledge and the evidence that justifies the acceptance of a broad, comprehensive theory are of different sorts. There is a problem, therefore, of determining for each discipline or for small groups of disciplines what pathway of enquiry they use, what they mean by verified knowledge and how they go about this verification.

To illustrate this diversity, let us take three "things" that are asserted to exist and to have certain defining properties and behaviors. Let us take, first, an automobile, second, an electron, third, a neutrino. Let the three statements read as follows:

The automobile in front of the house is black.
The electron is a particle with a small mass and a negative electrical charge.
The neutrino is a particle with neither charge nor rest mass.

All three statements, let us suppose, are "true." That they are "true" in different senses becomes plain when we consider the following points. We say that the car in front of the house is black and say it with confidence on two bases. First, we look at the car and its neighborhood and report what we see. Second, we invite a colleague to look at the car and its neighborhood; we repeat the statement that reports what we saw; our colleague nods agreement. This, then, is a very simple syntax of discovery, requiring only a naive, private experience of the objects we propose to make statements about plus a transaction between ourself, another enquirer, and the same objects.

By contrast, the syntax that leads us to assert that the electron is a particle with a small mass and a negative electrical charge is far more complex. The statement most certainly does not rest on the fact that I have looked at an electron and that my colleague has also looked and nodded agreement. It cannot arise from such a syntax because the electron is not visible. It rests, rather, on a syntax that involves looking at quite different things, seeking agreement about them, and then adding two further steps. We note certain phenomena; others note the same; then we seek an *explanation* for what we have seen. For explanation we conceive the existence of a minute particle. To it, we assign precisely the mass and precisely the magnitude and kind of charge which would permit this particle — if it existed — to give rise to the phenomena we have observed. The two additional steps are hidden in the additional process of seeking explanation. First, we conceive of something that would account for the phenomena we are concerned about. However, we are not satisfied to use just any conception that will account for it. Rather, we demand that the conception fulfill a second condition: that it fit in with, be coherent with, the rest of the body of knowledge that constitutes our science. In the case of our electron we meet this condition by choosing a particular mass and a particular charge as its important properties. The choice of a particular mass ties our electron to the entire body of physical knowledge called gravitational dynamics. The assignment of a certain electrical charge ties our particle to our knowledge of electricity and its dynamical laws.

The assertion about the neutrino rests on still a third kind of syntactical structure. For not only are neutrinos invisible by definition but they have been assigned a *lack* of such properties as charge and rest mass which characterize the electron. The assigned lack of such properties means that in the ordinary course of events the behavior of neutrinos would have no detectable consequences, would give rise to no phenomena such as we observed and accounted for by positing the existence of the electron. Instead, the ground for positing the existence of the neutrino was roughly as follows: certain effects were found in a phenomenon called beta decay which appeared to be exceptions to certain of the so-called conservation laws, laws that formed part of the very foundation of the body of physical knowledge. One way to account for these beta decay phenomena would be to treat them as "disproofs" of these conservation laws. Another way would have been to treat the decay phenomena as exceptions to the conservation laws and then to dream up an ad hoc explanation for the exception. Physicists preferred, however (for reasons I shall not go into now), to keep the conservation laws intact and universal, and the only conceived alternative enabling them to retain these laws was to suppose the existence of a well-nigh undetectable particle that carried off the quantities whose disappearance would otherwise have called the conservation laws into question.

We have here, then, three different senses in which statements are said to be "true" or warranted, differences of sense not revealed by the statements themselves. The statements are all of the same form — the automobile is black, the neutrino is such and such, the electron is something else. Only the context, the structure of problem, evidence, inference, and interpretation which constitutes the syntax of discovery behind each statement, would reveal to us the different senses in which each is true.

The significance of this variety of modes of enquiry, of patterns of discovery and verification, lies in this: most statements of most disciplines are like the single words of a sentence. They take their most telling meanings, not from their dictionary sense, not from their sense in isolation, but from their context, their place in the syntax. The meaning of $F = MA$ or of free fall, of electron or neutrino, is understood properly only in the context of the enquiry that produced them.

This need for context of enquiry wherewith to make teaching and learning clear has been almost universally overlooked because of a singular failure in the subject-matter preparation of teachers. They have been permitted to assume, or, indeed, have been flatly told, that "induction" or "scientific method" stands for something simple, single, and well defined. Quite the contrary is true: "induction" is not the name for some single, definite process but merely an honorific word attached by various philosophers to whatever mode of enquiry they favor. To a few philosophers, "induction" means the process of simple enumeration of a large number of instances of something or other by which we try to discern what is common among them. In this view, the outcome of "induction" is "generalization." To other philosophers, "induction" means the analysis of phenomena into unit events and the attempt to find out which events invariably precede which others. To still others, "induction" means the attempt to conceive ideas, however remote they may be from the possibility of direct verification, which will "explain," "account for," "embrace," the largest possible variety of phenomena with the greatest economy.

The Problem of the Substantive Structures of the Disciplines

Let us first redevelop the idea of substantive structures and their role in enquiry as sketched in our introduction.

The fact that we propose to investigate a given subject is to admit that we are, in large part, ignorant of it. We may have some superficial knowledge: we may have dealt with the subject matter as part of our round of practical problems; but the very fact that we propose to investigate the subject means that we mistrust our knowledge or consider it entirely inadequate. Thus, enquiry begins in virtual ignorance. Ignorance however, cannot originate an enquiry. Subjects complex enough to demand enquiry are subjects that confound us by the great variety of characteristics, qualities, behaviors, and interactions they present to our view. This richness paralyzes enquiry, for it is far too much to handle all at once and, in our ignorance, we have no way of discerning the greater from the lesser fact; we cannot discriminate the facts that are most "telling" about our subject matter from those that are trivial. In short, if data are to be collected, we must have some sort of guide to relevance and irrelevance, importance and unimportance.

This role of guide to the enquiry is played by a conception borrowed or invented by the enquirer. These conceptions constitute the substantive structures of a discipline.

Let us take, as an example of a primitive beginning of enquiry, the situation that prevailed in the study of animal behavior some sixty years ago. Our knowledge of the behavior of small aquatic animals at that time was no greater than might have been possessed by an alert, small boy who had watched the darting of fish, the play of tadpoles, and the movements of insect larvae in the ponds and streams of his farm. What, then, should we investigate about these dartings, movements, and plays? Should we ask what needs they serve? Perhaps. Yet we do not even know that needs are involved. Shall we ask what purposes the animals have in mind? We do not know whether they have purposes or not. Shall we then try to discover the patterns of these motions, the order in which they occur? The trouble with this is that when a vast number of movements are involved, we must suppose, by analogy to ourselves, that they do not all belong together. Hence the over-all order of them would be meaningless. Yet we cannot discern each coherent sub-group of motions because we do not yet know either the beginnings ("wants," "needs," "stimuli") or their terminations ("goals," "needs satisfied," "terminal response").

This frustration of enquiry was resolved by appealing to the then popular view that all things, including living things, were no more than simple machines, the pattern of which was the simple one known to nineteenth-century physics. This idea of a simple machine was applied to the study of behavior by supposing that every movement through space of an animal was a response to some single, specific, stimulating factor in the environment. It was further supposed that each such stimulated response could be one of only two possible kinds — a movement toward the stimulus or a movement away from it. Such a movement was dubbed a "tropism," "taxis"; movements toward the stimulus being called positive, those away from the stimulus, negative.

This naive and now obsolete conception removed the frustration of enquiry by giving us questions to ask. We were to determine for each organism what stimuli it responded to and whether it responded in the positive or negative sense. These identified questions in turn determined the pattern of experiment. We were to place our aquatic organism in a tank of water, make sure that all physical stimuli but one were uniform throughout the tank, let one stimulus, light, for example, be of high intensity at one end of the tank and low intensity at the other, and then note, as our important datum, which way the animal went. Then our knowledge of animal behavior was to be summed up in a catalogue of negative and positive tropisms characteristic of each species investigated.

Similar naive conceptions enabled us to begin enquiry in other complex fields. Chemistry was able to make great advances in the study of the array of substances of the world by imposing on them the notion of "element." By "element" was meant a substance of ultimate simplicity, a substance made only of itself and incapable of being changed into another such simple substance. This conception dictated the questions to be asked of matter by chemists and the patterns of experiment. The fundamental question was: into what simpler substance can this substance be decomposed? Hence the patterns of experiment were analysis and synthesis. Similar "elements" were devised to guide our earliest enquiries into human personality. We conceived of each human person as consisting of a greater or lesser quantity of each of a number of "traits." Like the chemical elements, each such "trait" (such as courage, imagination, logical reasoning, assiduity) was supposed to be simple (made of no further sub-traits) and independent of all other traits.

The substantive principles chosen to guide enquiry are controlled by two opposing criteria. One of these I shall call reliability. Reliability requires that the guiding principle be free of vagueness and ambiguity, that the referents of its terms have unequivocal location and limit, and that the measurements or manipulations of these referents can be made precisely and can be repeated with uniform results. The substantive structures cited as examples above meet this criterion as well as could be expected.

They do not, however, satisfactorily fulfill the second criterion, which I shall call validity. Note the failure in each case which illustrates the lack of adequate validity. Animal behavior is reduced to a catalogue of independent responses to independently acting stimuli. Yet our knowledge of ourselves and of higher animals makes it highly unlikely that any animal's behavior will be a repertory of separate and independent responses to stimuli. It is much more likely (we suspect) that previous responses modify later ones and that the response to two stimuli presented simultaneously will *not* be the algebraic sum of the responses to each when presented separately. The idea of simple and independent traits, which enabled us to make a start on a study of human personality, is similarly questionable. It is entirely likely that traits are not independent at all but, rather, affect one another. Further, traits may not be fixed quantities but products of experience, changing as our experience grows and changes. Indeed, it may be that a much richer and more complete understanding of human personality could be achieved by doing away entirely with a notion of traits in any form. The notion of chemical element and compound in its most primitive form we may also suspect to be highly incomplete. It supposes that the properties of a compound arise simply by juxtaposition or union of two or more elements. Yet our experience in art, architecture, and engineering tells us that it is not only the constituents of a compound which confer properties on the compound but the organization of these constituents as well.

In short, the criterion of validity asks that the data we use be not only reliable but representative. It asks that the substantive structure that points to these data as the appropriate data of enquiry reflect as much as possible of the richness and complexity of the subject matter to which it is applied.

The existence of these two criteria is important to us because they lead to two characteristics of knowledge which, in turn, have important implications for curriculum. In the first place, the play of these two criteria confer on scientific knowledge a distinctly revisionary character. In the second place, in some sciences the same interplay leads to the concurrent development of a number of bodies of knowledge of the same subject matter.

The revisionary character of scientific knowledge accrues from the continuing assessment and modification of substantive structures. As investigations proceed under the guidance of an early, naive structure, we begin to detect inconsistencies in our data and disparities between our conclusions and the behavior of our subject. These inconsistencies and disparities help us identify the invalidities in our conception. Meanwhile, the naive structure has enabled us nevertheless to gain some knowledge of our subject and to sharpen our techniques for study. Our new knowledge of the subject, our improved techniques, and our sharpened awareness of inadequacies in our substantive structures enable us to conceive new structures more complex than the old, more adequate to the richness of the subject matter. With the advent of a new structure, the knowledge contained in the older conceptions, though "right" enough in its own terms, is rendered obsolete and replaced by a new formulation which puts old facts and new ones together in more revealing ways.

While different substantive structures tend to succeed one another in physics, chemistry, and biology, other disciplines are characterized by the concurrent utilization of several sets of structures. In the recent study of human personality, for example, two bodies of knowledge competed in the market place at the same time. One body of knowledge had been developed by conceiving personality, after the analogy of the body, as consisting of psychic organs. The other body of knowledge had been developed by conceiving of personalties as arising from the need of persons for one another, as developing, for better or for worse, out of the experience of self and of others. Personality, this body of knowledge held, is best described in terms of the various relations the self can establish with others.

Such a pluralism of substantive structures and of bodies of knowledge is characteristic of the social sciences generally and of many humane studies. There is more than one body of economic knowledge; different anthropologists and different sociologists tackle their problems in different terms and in different ways; different critics use widely different conceptions of the art object in the analysis and evaluation of drama, poetry, music, and painting.

The curricular significances of the revisionary character of knowledge and the plural character of knowledge are too numerous to develop fully here. Let us be satisfied with three.

In the first place, both characteristics point to the danger of a purely dogmatic, inculcative curriculum. If we dogmatically select one of several bodies of theory in a given field and dogmatically teach this as the truth about its subject matter, we shall create division and failure of communication among our citizens. Students of different school systems in different regions who are dogmatically taught different histories of crucial moments in our nation's development are an obvious case in point. It is no less divisive, however, if our future citizens are barred from sharing enjoyment of literature and the arts by having been the victims of different dogmas, or barred from understanding each other by having been inculcated with different dogmatic views of the roots of human action or the origins of culture and civilization. The alternative is to avoid indoctrination. We may, if we like, choose but one of several pluralities of bodies of knowledge. But if we do, let it be taught in such a way that the student learns what substantive structures gave rise to the chosen body of knowledge, what the strengths and limitations of these structures are, and what some of the alternative structures are which give rise to alternative bodies of knowledge.

The revisionary character of knowledge assumes curriculum significance because revisions now take place so rapidly that they will probably occur not once but several times in the lives of our students. If they have been taught their physics, chemistry, or biology dogmatically, their discovery that revision has occurred can lead only to bewilderment and disaffection. Again, the alternative is the teaching of scientific knowledge in the light of the enquiry that produced it. If students discover how one body of knowledge succeeds another, if they are aware of the substantive structures that underlie our current knowledge, if they are given a little freedom to speculate on the possible changes in structures which the future may bring, they will not only be prepared to meet future revisions with intelligence but will better understand the knowledge they are currently being taught.

Knowledge and Intelligent Behavior: A Framework for the Educative Process

W. W. Charters, Jr.

I would like to tell you about the position I have come to as I have tried to decide what I, a social scientist, am doing in the field of education. For a number of years now I have been thinking about how the social sciences can be useful to education and to the man of practical affairs. My teaching has forced

This paper, presented to the Philosophy of Education Society in St. Louis, Missouri, on April 5, 1966, is reprinted here by permission of the Philosophy of Education Society and the author.

me to it. I keep asking myself what I should be doing for the prospective teachers and administrators who sit in my classroom. It is possible that the same kind of questions would have occurred to me had I confined my teaching to the Liberal Arts college or had I been an elementary or secondary teacher. But ready-made answers regarding the value of liberal education and the goals of public education are available to persons following these pursuits, and I might never have had to grapple seriously with the questions on my own.

I suppose I should warn you that my views carry a distinct social science bias. In thinking through the bearing of the social sciences on the practice of education, I have tried to keep alert to empirical implications. I have attempted to phrase answers that would lead to specific operations with measurable inputs and outputs and, ultimately, testable propositions. The test I prefer to apply to my views is that of any explanatory theory — their productivity in extending dependable knowledge.

My thesis is a simple one. Let me state it in outline form first and then elaborate on it.

1. The human being approaches a problem situation, as he does any situation, by imposing on it sets of categories and conceptual schemes. It is by means of these that he "understands" the situation and formulates choices as to how he will behave. This holds for any person — adult, child, teacher, administrator, or what have you.

2. The successfully educated person is distinguished by the fact that he has available to him a wider array of conceptual schemes, each of which is more articulated, more rigorous, and more powerful, than those available to the uneducated person.

3. It is the business of science to construct, develop, and test systematically conceptual schemes and relations of wide generality. These become the explanatory theories of science. In the social sciences, where well substantiated theories are few and far between, the signal contribution is in the concepts themselves rather than in their known interconnections. The concepts of science are inclined to be explicit, operationally definable, internally consistent, and they are designed to penetrate beneath surface appearances. In short, they are powerful.

4. Each field of science abstracts from reality according to its own necessarily narrow purposes, and several fields may abstract different properties from the same concrete phenomena for their respective purposes of theory making. No field or combination of fields of science can comprehend the totality of the concrete, unique situation in which the man of practical affairs must act; nor, of course, can the actor himself. What appropriately chosen concepts of science can do for the actor is to provide him with a variety of perspectives from which to construe the problematic situation. The concept systems of the several fields supplement, in some cases supplant, the superficial and limited conceptual schemes the untutored person would otherwise employ to view his circumstances.

5. In the end, diagnosis of the problem situation and the formulation of choice requires the person to exercise his own free intelligence. Even a highly sophisticated social science cannot replace the application of intelligence in predicting the consequences of a concrete act in a concrete situation. It is the actor alone who can synthesize the various points of view he brings to bear,

incorporating in the synthesis idiosyncratic facts about the situation that escape the purview of science, and it is the actor alone who must take the critical step of decision.

To elaborate this thesis, I will begin with a brief excursion into some epistemological assumptions regarding the nature of reality and the nature of knowledge.

I

I begin with this assumption regarding realism: that there is a world out there to know but it is one that can never be known in anything even approximating its totality. The world is a never-ending, never-repeating procession of events, each infinitely complex, each concretely unique, and the events themselves essentially all of one piece. This undifferentiated flux is so fantastically rich that you and I, even with electron microscopes, cloud chambers, radio telescopes, infra-red photography, and radioactive isotope tracers, can never sense but a small fraction of it, let alone comprehend it *in toto*. Nothing is given except the fantastically variegated flux; anything that is made of it is a creation of the organism noticing and reflecting on it for its own purposes.

This may be an unnecessarily radical assumption for what follows, but I will stay with it until it gets me in trouble.

It is impossible for an organism, especially a complex one, to survive in a world that seems totally unpredictable. So he sets out to impose order on it. His first task is to invent attributes which, when applied to the variegated flux under his gaze, allow him to discern replications and regularities and permit him to construe similarities and differences. The attributes he conceives enable him to distinguish events and things. This is a task of pure abstraction, although not necessarily a very arduous one. It demands only that the organism attend to a very few things and ignore a great number of other things that could be noticed. By focusing his attention on the single feature of the absence or presence of light and forgetting momentarily all the other things that accompany the passage of time, for example, a person can come to the idea of distinguishing night and day.

Organisms distinguish features that hold significance for their survival — in the beginning, at least. The person need not have abstracted the attribute of absence or presence of light; there are innumerable others he might have chosen. But the night-day distinction is one that bears on his well-being. Consider a race of creatures insensitive to modest temperature variations, capable of seeing well enough in the dark to do what they need to do, and whose prey is no more elusive in the dark than in the light. Such a race might never find it useful to entertain a distinction between night and day, even though it were palpably present to a visitor from the human species.

Many distinctions that you and I draw are so pervasive in human experience that they seem to be inherent in reality and directly sensed without the intervention of cognition. Concepts like near versus far, smooth versus rough, or me versus you would seem to be given, not abstracted. That the distinctions are so universal, though, merely indicates that they hold universal significance for the species.

For most purposes of our everyday lives, you and I do not need especially elaborate sets of distinctions and concepts. We can usually cross streets safely or find meeting rooms successfully with a relatively small number of rough discriminations and calculations. Somewhat more complex sets of distinctions are required for coping with that unusually significant part of our world — other people. Other people are special nuisances because they are simultaneously trying to cope with us. They won't stand still. They keep changing and developing and reacting. We are normally forced to the position of endowing our friends and spouses with greater constancy in personality than is warranted, simply in order to interact with them. In any event, doping out, understanding, and predicting the variety of people with whom we must deal calls for more intricate conceptual systems than we need in meeting everyday problems with inanimate objects, like stuck windows or stains on a necktie. For a revealing exposition of the conceptual schemes used by ordinary people in trying to understand their fellows, I commend to you the book by a distinguished psychologist, Fritz Heider, *The Psychology of Interpersonal Relations*, written in 1958. Heider has made the study of common-sense psychology his life work, and this book sparked a major movement in the scientific investigation of interpersonal perceptions.

Despite the fact that our conceptions of the social world are more intricate than our conceptions of the physical world, it is still true that we can get by with crude, approximate conceptual schemes. By the time we are 15 or 20 years old, there are few social situations we encounter in our everyday affairs that we cannot comprehend sufficiently to satisfy our needs. This is partly due to the fact that our needs usually do not put much demand on our conceptions. Many of the things we seek from other people we can get, even while we misunderstand them. More often than we like to admit, there is neither the opportunity nor the necessity to refine or correct our views of the people around us.

II

In the process of developing my epistemological assumptions, I have moved rather far into the first point of my thesis. Let me approach it directly.

The point is that individuals, even young children, never meet situations in a totally naive fashion. The human being confronts the next moment of his life with reasonably stable, well-structured concepts and expectancies that allow him to bring order to what otherwise would be intolerable chaos. He construes the situation; he makes sense out of it the best he knows how. The concepts he applies are the ones that seem to have worked for him in the past in bringing him food, friends, fun, freedom from guilt, or other things he has sought. So long as they seem to work, these concepts usually remain unquestioned. As I have said, rarely is it necessary or possible to question them. Moreover, people typically go out of their way to arrange their worlds so that doubts about the validity of their views are not raised.

These enduring modes of perceiving and cognizing are what contemporary social psychologists mean, in part, by the term *attitude*. You may wonder at this. It may strike you that attitude means simply an inclination to be for or against something, to be favorable or unfavorable, pro or con. Indeed it did for the first 25 years of its history as a psychologically measurable attribute. In the last 15 years, though, social psychology has moved beyond this view to conceive of attitude as a multi-faceted attribute, consisting of cognitive systems as well as approach-avoidance tendencies.

One of the most exciting developments in social psychology has been the efforts to investigate and measure what people believe to be true about their world — their styles of cognition. The early studies of stereotypes were fore-runners. More recently there have been investigations of the attributes people use to classify their friends and acquaintances, of people's inclination to attribute causality to agents external to themselves, of differences in conceptions of time, and of the meanings people attach to common words. Psychological research is beginning to point up the wealth of differences in the ways people construe the situations they encounter. Research is also showing how diligently the individual is likely to labor to save the particular cognitive systems he has acquired over the years.

A fundamental ingredient in a person's cognitive system — you might say the building block of cognitions — is the concept. Concepts are the differentiations the person makes as he surveys events before him. They are the basic categories he employs. Often they correspond to words of language, and in fact there is some evidence that concepts coded into language are more likely to be exercised by the person than uncoded concepts. As the person discriminates and classifies aspects of the situation he finds himself in, so he affects the range of alternatives he will recognize. Powerful, well-differentiated conceptual schemes will yield more choices, and more effective courses of possible action, than superficial, poorly-differentiated conceptions. The concepts available to the man of practical affairs are significant determinants of intelligent behavior, and it is precisely their strengthening that education in our society is most fitted to accomplish.

III

The successfully educated person, I have suggested, is the one whose conceptual schemes are articulated, rigorous, and powerful. When a person uses a concept, it carries a number of meanings and sometimes a whole way of thought. Put differently, a concept invokes implicitly a network of other concepts and distinctions.

A classroom teacher, for example, who classifies a child as "bright" will assimilate to this concept a number of other ideas. Involved may be a set of conceptions about the IQ and intelligence testing, perhaps including a belief that tests do not always get at *true* intelligence. The concept may touch on ideas regarding how bright children get along with their peers and on a cause-effect relationship between brightness and classroom performance. It may invoke the idea that brightness is an immutable attribute of the child, imbedded through genetics somewhere in the child's cranium and potentially discoverable by physiologists as a clump of grey matter. Another classroom teacher, however, may assimilate quite different ideas to the concept of "brightness," ideas that have very different implications for diagnosis of problems and for possible courses of action.

Some concepts are weak, in the sense that they afford their users few alternatives for constructive action in problem situations. Concepts that revolve around surface appearances and accidental properties are weak in this sense. So are concepts that permit no refinement in the light of additional evidence — concepts that are categorically closed. Concepts that lead us to view the concrete case as *nothing more than* the properties we have abstracted to define the concept are equally fruitless. They carry what Whitehead calls the fallacy of misplaced concreteness. There are impoverished concepts and wealthy ones. Impoverished concepts are those which signify gross rather than fine discriminations and which articulate only vaguely and undependably with the net of additional concepts. The successfully educated person has at his command wealthy rather than impoverished concepts and, moreover, habitually puts them to use.

Beyond this, the educated person has available to him a *variety* of conceptual schemes which he can try out on a situation. No one of the schemes will give a perfect fit. It is impossible in principle. But some combination will yield increased understanding and wider scope of choice. Clearly, for a person to use concepts in this provisional way requires flexibility. A person whose thinking is highly concretistic is defeated from the start; his conceptual scheme permits of no alternatives. So an additional indicator of the successfully educated individual is the capacity to employ his conceptual schemes as tools — to try different ones until he finds some that work. This capacity, I am confident, does not come naturally but must be the object of deliberate training in the educative process.

IV

I am ready to turn to the third point of my thesis, having to do with the business of science, and especially social science. My concentration on the social sciences is deliberate. Problematic situations confronting the persons whose education I have thought most about — teachers and administrators — are almost universally issues of social relations and almost never issues of purely physical dimensions. I ignore the humanities for a different reason. While I am convinced that the arts and letters play a distinct and unique role in preparing people to construe their world more flexibly and fruitfully, I do not yet know how to describe the way in which they do so.

We can regard science as man's self-conscious, systematic extension of his effort to construe the situations of his world. The aim of science is to construct dependable explanatory theories covering selected events of the real world. Scientific concepts are abstractions from the flux of reality just as those of the ordinary man are . . . The products of science — the concepts and explanatory theories — differ only in degree from the cognitive systems of the layman.

Yet the scale of the difference is so great as to make it virtually a difference in kind. Much hinges on the fact that explanatory theories of science are explicit. They are public property and wide open to inspection for contradictions, superfluous assumptions, missing links of reasoning, and contrary evidence. Unlike the implicit, common-sense theories by which you and I act, the theories of science are regularly put to empirical test. If a theory is untestable, it is disdained. The tests are carried out in a way that will reveal which part of the theory is right and which part is wrong. The theory and its concepts are constantly questioned to the extent that the most creative minds of the age can question them. When a deeply imbedded concept like *phlogiston* no longer serves, it can be discarded when something better is offered. It is in the nature of science that its explanatory systems are subject to correction and elaboration; they beg to be corrected. In my view, all of this makes for a difference in kind. It is the natural result of converting implicit reasoning into public argument where all can reflect on it and where the argument can be put to empirical test.

Insofar as the social sciences are concerned, there are very few dependable theories and the few that exist cover an extremely limited range of phenomena. We cannot look to the social sciences for propositions that say, a given amount of Y will ensue from X under conditions A, B, and C. Nevertheless, the social sciences offer us fruitful concepts according to which we may seek to construe the situation. The concepts, I have said, deal with a small part of the unique, concrete case in which we must act, but they will probably be more powerful than those we ordinarily use. Their generality, for example, might elevate us above the particulars of the immediate circumstance and enable us to see things we otherwise would not have noted.

Take the case of a high school principal searching for a way out of a troublesome spot created, as he sees it, by that obstinate, cantankerous Mrs. Jones, 50 years in the second grade, and by his fresh, young superintendent so busy making up to the school board president that he does not care what happens to his principals. Suppose the principal could see his situation for a moment as an instance of role conflict, a concept of contemporary social science. It would induce him to see similarities between his own situation and the situations of industrial foremen, first sergeants, ministers caught up in a school desegregation crisis in the South, and maybe his own superintendent. It would attune him to the related concepts of role expectations, sanctions for non-conformity, reference groups, and the like. It might suggest that he explore the possibility that he has misperceived the expectations on him, a common condition contributing to role conflict. He might even ask himself if he is in one of those sub-types of role conflict that frees him to behave as he wishes rather than constrains his behavior.

Application of the concept does not, perforce, solve his problem; it provides no formula for action. It only offers a different perspective from which to construe his situation and, if he is lucky, to identify alternatives that might not have occurred to him. It is possible, too, that the concept would yield no ideas that he had not already considered by applying his untutored but perceptive conceptual schemes. In that event, he might turn to other concepts, such as *cognitive dissonance* or *repression*, to see what perspectives they might afford.

Between fields of science, and within the fields, different modes of abstraction are used to generate distinctive concepts and conceptual systems. Some systems envision processes and time sequences, while others envision structures and interrelationships. Some concepts imply genetic explanation, others a contemporaneous, field-of-forces explanation. Some abstract properties that vary only through great extensions of time or across great aggregates of individuals rather than between individuals. It is improper to say that one system is right and the others wrong; each abstracts differently according to its purposes. Kelly expressed the point well in considering the fields of psychology and physiology:

These realms have been given tentative boundaries based upon the presumed ranges of convenience of the psychological and the physiological construction systems, respectively. But many of the same facts can be construed within either system. Are those facts "psychological facts" or are they "physiological facts"? Where do they really belong? Who gets possession of them, the psychologist or the physiologist? While this may seem like a silly question, one has only to sit in certain interdisciplinary staff conferences to see it arise in the discussions between people of different professional guilds. Some individuals can get badly worked up over the protection of their exclusive rights to construe particular facts.

The answer is, of course, that the events upon which facts are based hold no institutional loyalties. They are in the public domain. The same event may be construed simultaneously and profitably within various disciplinary systems — physics, physiology, political science, or psychology.*

Conceptual systems within a field of social science may be as divergent as psychology and physiology. Within psychology, the schemes of Freudian psychology, of stimulus-response learning, and of the self are widely divergent in their perspectives. Indeed, there are often greater redundancies in the conceptual schemes between formally designated disciplines than within one.

VI

I have come to the conclusion of my thesis. When all is said and done, the responsibility for making wise choices rests in the only place it can — in the person who must act. The conceptual systems of the sciences can be made to converge on the actor to enlighten his understanding of the circumstances in which he finds himself and to free his intelligence from the constraints of ignorance and narrow perspective.

Education is admirably suited to the task of shaping views of the world — of illuminating conceptions of what things are like and how they work. Undertaking the job of influencing how people construe problem situations is a more modest and, I believe, realistic objective of education than in trying to instruct them in how to behave. The educator's challenge is to assess the weaknesses of the customary conceptual schemes and cognitive styles of the persons under his tutelage and design an educative process that will provide them with powerful concepts of considerable variety and relevant to the range of phenomena with which they must deal. The toughest challenges, though, are to assure that the schemes are employed habitually, not just academically, and to teach for flexibility, that is, to assure that they are used provisionally rather than finally. A significant reorganization of cognitive processes is the goal for which education must strive.

* Kelly, George A., *The Psychology of Personal Constructs*, New York: Norton, 1955, Vol. I, p. 10.

The Social Studies Versus the
Social Sciences

Earl S. Johnson

That an issue has arisen in the teaching of social knowledge in the secondary school which provokes an alternative as drastic as that stated in the title of this paper is, if taken literally, a symptom of deep intellectual confusion.

It is, in my view, a sad and tragic augury that we are now told by some that we must choose between the parent social science disciplines and the social studies. Such an "either-or" I categorically reject.

Let it be noted, however, that because I am against a return to the classic disciplines, now to be named high-school subjects and taught as such, I do not indorse a good deal of what now goes on under the aegis of the social studies. That term, as well as not a little teacher performance under it, has, not without considerable justification, been said to be "vague, murky, and too all-inclusive."

What the author of that indictment meant, in fine, I am not certain, but agreement, in whole or in part, with such a characterization does not, in my judgment, warrant the substitution of the separate and separated disciplines for the social studies. I look upon such a recommendation as a pedagogical *non sequitur*. A more sensible and more defensible alternative would be to cure the social studies of their vagueness, murkiness, and too all-inclusiveness, if on examination it may be established that they really are beset by these ills.

The invitation to return to the parent disciplines does, however, intrigue me. It reminds me of the quality of arguments posed by Hillaire Belloc in his *The Crisis in Civilization* which he would resolve by a return to the Middle Ages. Belloc's book bespeaks a nostalgia for some of "the good old days" — as does the invitation to return to the classic disciplines.

I might be willing to return to the disciplines if that were either possible or profitable. But the world in which the parent disciplines would be either possible or profitable as high-school subjects, and taught as such, we have not had for a very long time in this Republic: certainly not since the days of Andrew Jackson. Thomas Wolfe was right: "you can't go home again," for home is not what it was and we are not what we were.

But let me say what the two immediate origins of my present concern with the social studies are. The first I view, in part, with alarm, surprise, and dismay. It is Professor Charles Keller's article in the *Saturday Review* for September 16, 1961: "Needed — a Revolution in the Social Studies." The second is the volume, *The Social Studies and the Social Sciences*, done by an able and perceptive team of social science scholars under the joint auspices of the American Council of Learned Societies and the National Council for the Social Studies, and published in 1962 by Harcourt, Brace and World.

Reprinted from *The School Review*, 1963, vol. 71, pages 389–403 by permission of The University of Chicago Press. Copyright 1963 by the University of Chicago.

I find myself in hearty agreement with a great deal of Keller's diagnosis. It is with that part of his prognosis which I infer as the abandonment of the social studies in favor of a return to the disciplines with which I totally disagree. It is, in my view, a substitution of elegance for usefulness. The language on which I base my inference is this: "History and the social sciences are subjects with disciplines. . . . Subjects as such have disciplines that will help to develop students' minds . . . the study of history and the social sciences should begin in the fifth grade when they can be subjects with disciplines."

I should be ever so happy to learn that I had misread Keller, but in any case I do not wish to make a whipping boy of him. I find in his position, and *in his language*, a pathetic misunderstanding (or is it an *un-understanding?*) of the social world in which high-school students live and in certain pedagogical principles which permit teachers to deal, realistically, with that world.

The volume, *The Social Studies and the Social Sciences*, has put me deeply in debt to scholars who have refreshed my mind about the structure, substance, and methods of the several social science disciplines and made clear the bearing of their comprehensive and critical elaborations on the aims which we either have or ought to have served in our teaching of the social studies.

I find in this book a reasoned and temperate invitation for us to reflect on the need for revision, not the abandonment, of the social studies. Such upgrading or revision ought to be approached, as both Bernard Berelson in the "Introduction" and Lewis Paul Todd in the "Afterword" make clear, from the perspective of what aims we wish to achieve and what changes in the present organization and practice of the social studies would appear to be most appropriate to those aims.

I now intend, as you have already surmised, to bring under quite rigorous criticism the proposal that we abandon the social studies in favor of a return to the traditional disciplines. In this endeavor I swear an oath of good will whether or not, to anyone's satisfaction or dissatisfaction, I score a hit, a near-miss, or only waste my powder and shot and your time.

The issue is clear: It is the nature of a general education appropriate to the abilities of young people in the high school. The role of social knowledge in such an education at that level is to make its unique contribution to students becoming cultured persons. This requires their sensitive appreciation of the great adventure in which they live and will live and of which they are a part, their becoming knowledgeable about it and skilful in it, dedicated to it, and concerned to discover how they may make their own best contribution to it and, in doing so, come to the fullest and richest development of their intellectual and spiritual potentials which that dimension of experience allows. If you ask me to specify the chief aim which social knowledge should engender, I would answer: improvement in judgment about values.

To achieve such a generalized aim, with the many more definitive and operational aims in terms of which it might be realized, the traditional disciplines are inappropriate. They are inappropriate because they do not and cannot, taken singly or in any sequence, speak to or "fit" the student's "life-space" or "area of experience" — these, obviously, plural in number. These are situations of choice and personal judgment and all the phases of individual and collective life viewed from the perspectives of the related social processes about which Leon C. Marshall writes.[1]

It is in and by such thought-and-action configurations as these that high-school students and, for that matter, all of us live. We do not live either in or by the configurations or structures which, respectively, inclose the areas of the classic social science disciplines.

In this view, it is my position that none of the disciplines taken singly "give the student his world." Correlatively, none of the disciplines taken *seriatim* are adequate means to such an end. To suppose that an effective synthesis of the data and methods of the several disciplines might thus be brought about, with the result that operational meaning and significance would be given to students in such contexts, strikes me as fanciful as the view that history, conceived as "one damned fact after another," would give them a sense of the ethos or *Zeitgeist* of an historical epoch.

My argument thus far may be summarized in the comment that the experiences of human beings do not come wrapped in six or more packages, each bearing the label of, or containing only the substantive data of, one of the social science disciplines. Nor, to change the figure, can the meaning and significance of human life be known by experiences being submitted to a sum of analyses under any number of disciplines undertaking the task in sequence. When such a "sum of" or "in sequence" approach is espoused it is, I am quite sure, premised on the view that the student is able to take appropriate data from each of the disciplines as they pass in review and pattern them into operationally useful knowledge, germane to his "life-space" or "area of experience" as I have used those terms. There is little evidence that any but the most exceptionally brilliant students can affect such patterns of knowledge. It is for this reason that the teacher of the social studies is obligated to teach these patterns. Over forty years of teaching and working with young people in high school, college, and the graduate school convinces me of the wisdom of this view.

The position which I take in this matter traces to the abstract, partial, and fictional nature of the classic disciplines. That they differ among themselves in these respects is readily admitted. Economics is the most abstract, partial, and fictional, and probably sociology, at least as I conceive it, the least so. Geography would, in my view, fall into a class much less abstract and fictional (all disciplines are, in varying degrees, partial) and thus occupy a quite marginal place in the family of such disciplines. History falls completely outside the terms of reference which I am now using and enters, in no way, into the account I am now rendering. It constitutes a somewhat special case but can, in my judgment, be subject to the criteria on which I am insisting for the three disciplines which are my central concern, namely, economics, political science, and sociology, that is, the "policy sciences."

I am now obligated to say why I use the terms "life-space" and "area of experience" as my major datum and bench marks in the theory which I am sharing with you. I owe my use of, and my affinity for, these terms to Kurt Lewin and John Dewey, although I do not recall that Dewey ever used the latter term verbatim. (Lewin's use of the term "life-space" may be found in his *Resolving Social Conflicts*.) In *The Child and the Curriculum* Dewey remarks on the "need of restating into experience the subject-matter of the studies, or branches of learning." "It must," he writes, "be referred to the experience from which it has been abstracted. It needs to be psychologized, turned over, translated into the immediate and individual experiencing within which it had its origin and significance."[2] To this I add a brief extract from Dewey's *Democracy and Education:* "in the degree in which what is communicated cannot be organized into the existing experience of the learner, it becomes *mere* words . . . lacking in meaning."[3] It is my wont to insist that knowledge must be not only transmitted but also transmuted. This concern I find explicit in both of Dewey's observations.

To these remarks of Dewey I wish to add what I suppose might be called one of George Herbert Mead's most profound aphorisms, namely, that "thinking is not a field or realm which can be taken outside of its possible social uses." When, as Mead's student thirty-seven years ago, I heard him say this, I did not understand what he meant. Now that I have "had an experience" — indeed hundreds of experiences as a teacher — I understand.

But enough of theory; now to its practice. I now share with you my image of two teaching (really, teaching-learning) enterprises which will illustrate what I mean by my terms, "life-space" and "area of experience." The first is proposed for the freshman year; the second for the senior year.

Although titles are not very important, I have called the freshman course (designed for two semesters), "The Family and the Community." This is hardly an exciting title — even perhaps a trifle dull. But it covers two areas of experience with which I am concerned and in which ninth-graders are caught up and about which they are, many at least, mixed up.

The course takes its content, organization, and focus from the sociopsychological characteristics and status of high-school freshmen whose ages usually range from thirteen to fourteen — the first two years of the "teens." These two, and the early following years, are marked by emotional stress and strain, and the indecision and confusion which attend the early growing away from parental and familial controls. In these years boys and girls find themselves in a more or less rebellious state of mind toward their parents, as well as toward most rules except those of their own making.

This age group may be characterized as "transitional" or "marginal." Its members are in the process of seeking emancipation from parental controls, but they are not yet "at home" in the social world outside those controls. They have, to a greater or lesser degree, begun to reject parental controls but have not yet been *accepted by* nor *accepted* the control systems which are non-familial. (In a good many ways the non-familial world of control systems is not organized to either understand or help them make the transition.) Their acceptance *by* or *of* this new world of social rights and obligations will, of course, come about slowly in the process of their growing both up and out, that is, biologically and sociologically.

Hence the course is designed to give understanding of, and insight into, this transitional phase of growing up and out. It is rationalized in terms of the observation of the great Danish educator, churchman, and statesman, Bishop Gruntwig: "the only thing which can save this generation is the spectacle of its own condition." Thus the course would rest its case on understanding and insight, not on moral injunctions. It is the latter from which boys and girls of this age group are seeking emancipation. What they want and need is light on their status — their "own condition." From this will come the appropriate moral insights. If not, the school can do little to help them.

The transitional experience in which this age group is caught up lies between two poles, each of which symbolizes an idealized social situation — "ideal types," we call them. These poles may be designated as *family* and *public*.[4] To the ideal-type situation named *family* the following characteristics are assigned: status given, judgments accepted, intimate personal relations, and self-organization unconsciously achieved. To the ideal-type situation named *public* these characteristics are assigned: status earned, judgments self-made, impersonal relations, and self-organization consciously achieved.

The ultimate focus and purpose of this course would be to clarify the processes and problems associated with the students' transitions between these poles. The difficult part of the teacher's task would be to insure, as far as possible, that the students' sense of continuity with their familial world is maintained while, paradoxically, this same continuity is challenged, if not "broken" in many ways. Thus both continuity and discontinuity of students' self-conceptions, even their characters, are involved in the growing-*up* and growing-*out* experience which this enterprise is designed to analyze and clarify.

Helpful perspectives and insights on such a transition experience may be gained through cross-cultural and intercultural studies of two kinds. First, anthropological materials would provide an account of how this transition experience is met within primitive cultures. Such materials would treat with age and maturity groups and their corresponding statuses and roles. The strategy involved and intended would be that of an indirect and round-about approach to the situation which this age group faces in *its* culture. It is hoped that the students might thus come to see themselves in the mirror of a similar age group but in a simpler culture. Of special importance would be the study of *rites de passage*, the ceremonial observances at phases or "passages" from pre-teen to teen and post-teen years. Thus they might come to see the significance of such experiences as christening, confirmation, the taking of pledges or oaths of various kinds, "the first long pants," the first date, and the like. Second, historical materials would provide interesting accounts of the relations of parents and children in the American family at the turn of the century. Such materials would, one might hope, shed light on significant changes in the organization of family life, parent and child roles and statuses, the relation of the father's occupation to home life, the amount, kind, and ways of spending leisure time, that is, *en famille* or by age and sex groupings, and similar matters.

The focus of attention in these contrasting cultural settings would be the study of the relation between one's culture and the discipline, definition, and direction of native impulses — call it "original human nature." The nature of this relation might be even further clarified by comparing insect and human communities. Here the focus would fall on the difference between social organization based entirely on instinctive and hereditary factors and that based on these greatly modified by cultural factors.

Studies such as these would preface intensive and extensive studies of the modern family. These studies would be more difficult and more controversial.

No longer would the objectivity associated with the exotic-primitive and historical approaches be possible. But, if this age group is to understand its position vis-à-vis its own family life, such studies ought not to be foregone. They might well include a variety of types, for the American family is no cultural monolith. Among them are the following: the suburban family, the rural family, the slum family, and perhaps a typical southern-rural Negro family. It is anticipated that such studies would challenge the naïvete or smugness which often characterizes the attitudes of this age group.

Studies of the contemporary family would lead to inquiries into the nature of the relations which obtain now — and in the historical period just studied — between the family and the state which is the most formal and legal manifestation of "the public." Here the context would be provided by the difference between sentimental-kinship (*Gemeinschaft*) and utilitarian-territorial (*Gesellschaft*) types of social organization. This age group has just begun the transition from sentimental-kinship to utilitarian-territorial social contexts and types of social controls and is deeply involved in the difficulties of this transition. In them, as I have observed, it is caught up, and mixed up! (Needless to say that here, as well as in my remarks on the course for the senior year, I am using a kind and level of discourse which is designed for sophisticated readers, not for ninth- and twelfth-grade students. At those grade levels the language, like the subject matter, would have to make sense in the "life-space" or "area of experience" of the students.)

Such a polar and transitional view of the experiences of this age group would permit, even require, consideration of such concepts as these: love and justice, custom and law, status and contract, freedom and restraint, and private and public. Each pair would, obviously, require elaboration in terms and at the levels which would make sense to the students. Thus, in Dewey's terminology, their meaning would have to be "*psychologized*, turned over, translated into the immediate and individual experiencing within which [they] had their origin and significance."5

Thus *family* and *public* would become related in ways useful to those whose present life course newly and strangely runs between these poles. Correlative to the study of such pairs of concepts (and social situations) would go the study of situations and events which would permit practical understanding of such terms as leadership, policy, compromise, loyalty, propaganda, judgment, authority, and rights and obligations.

To the degree that the prosecution of such studies would involve acquaintance with the formal aspects of government, the study of its structures would always take second place to the study of its functions. Indeed these would be related as means to ends. "In the large," such structures and functions would be viewed as public rather than private agencies for social control. "Government," in all instances and perspectives, would be interpreted as "what some given policy-and-control-making and power-wielding group *does*, upon what *authority*, to what *welfare ends*, and subject to what kinds of *review* and popular *control*."

Among the specific aims of such an enterprise, the following may be named: to reveal to this age group some of the representative schemes of organization of the control patterns and processes in the non-familial world and how these affect the rights and obligations of all concerned; to show the inappropriateness and ineffectiveness of attempting to deal with secondary-group (i.e., public) situations with primary-group (i.e., familial) means and attitudes; to provide a view of "government" in wider and more useful ways than the typical "civics" book permits, that is, in its all too frequent legal-formal and constitutional approach; to reveal the difference between love as a motivating principle and justice as an organizing and power principle, as well as their appositive rather than opposite bearing on each other; to show that new and more "public" situations require new and different but no less demanding concepts of loyalty and dedication than those required in old and more "private" situations; to reveal that restraints may both increase and decrease freedom depending on their use; to show that the growth of the functions of the state is to be justified in terms of the greater security and dignity of persons and the community at large but only when such uses or ends can be shown actually to be their aim and consequence; and, in the service of such objectives as I have noted, to exploit to their maximum usefulness to the present experiences, individual and collective, of all those who "belong" to this age group.

A distinction which is implicit in the foregoing needs now to be made explicit. I speak of the difference between *method* and *technique* in teaching. By *method* I mean the teacher's scholarly knowledge, insight into its significance for those being taught, and skill in the means of critical inquiry. By *technique* I mean what the teacher does in order to adapt such scholarly knowledge, insight and skill to the subject matter so that those being taught will grow in knowledge, insight, and skill.

Now, a brief description of a course for the senior year. It is also conceived of as a two-semester enterprise; its title, "Social Knowledge and Social Policy."

It would seek to give students an understanding of the fact that social problems have their origin in conflicts in values. It would, perhaps, be intellectually the most rigorous and ethically the most penetrating course in the social studies curriculum. For this reason it is scheduled for the year by which students may be presumed to be ready for a learning experience of such a nature and be not too greatly upset by it.

It would seek to shed light on the nature of both private and public values and value systems, and the use and limitations of the tools of scientific inquiry in resolving value conflicts. The course content would consist of a selected few of the major problems of social policy which the Western world faces and will, in the foreseeable future, continue to face. It would seek, then, to deal with the present and the "shape of the future" rather than with what someone has called "disappearing difficulties."

Although some freedom might be given students to nominate the problems to be studied, the method of their analysis would permit no options. The range of problems should permit a sampling suggested in such as these: population and natural resources, the integrity of the family, unemployment (especially as it traces to technological factors), civil liberty, mental health, and peace.

The course would find its major context in the dual mores of our civilization: the *organizational* mores which the prevailing institutional apparatus and its values represent, and the *humanitarian* mores which are dedicated to bring about those changes in the organizational mores which would narrow the gap between our declared values and the service, both individual and institutional, which we render them.

Students would learn the nature of and the difference between three kinds of problems: (i) problems of effective means or problems of technology; (ii) problems of knowledge or the relation between variables; and (ii) problems of social policy, that is, the issue of what ought to be done.

The course would seek to make clear the difference between humanistic "oughts" and the facts of social reality as reliable knowledge, provided by the social science disciplines, reveals that difference. It would likewise seek to clarify the role of both persons and institutions in the onset, effects, and resolution of social problems and seek to make clear the pervasive nature of the "value problem," namely, the problem of discriminating between alternative value choices. In such a context it would undertake to expose the major fallacies entertained and practiced by those who hold to simple "answers" respecting both the cause and the resolution of social problems.

So conceived, the course would try to engender an abiding interest in social problem analysis; develop that unique balance between zeal, skill, dedication, and patience necessary for penetrating problem study and related social action; and develop critical awareness of society's need for more dedicated and knowledgeable persons, and more effective social institutions.

In such patterns as I have proposed, the course would draw upon and draw together materials and methods from the major social science disciplines. Thus social studies rather than the social disciplines would be shaped and taught. Students would be exposed to, and required to think with, the concepts primarily of economics, political science, and sociology and how these concepts complement one another in social inquiry.

The division of labor among these three disciplines would correspond to the distinctive tasks to which they address themselves: for economic analysis the relation of scarce means to unlimited wants or desires; for political analysis the problem of consensus, the process of achieving it and making it effective; and for sociological analysis the problem of elaborating the institutional forms as means through which past and present move to future in the lifetime of a society. Thus, the unity as well as the division of labor of the scholarly social disciplines would, I hope, be brought to student awareness and understanding.

An abundance of textual and fugitive materials is available for such an enterprise. But, because of the contemporary focus of the inquiries which would be advanced, firsthand experience in the community would be maximized.

Let me now submit for your reflective criticism the following commentary on the image of some social studies which I have sought to share with you. I have been careful not to confuse the scholar's form or structure of knowledge with the substance and method abstracted from it for the purposes in mind. In doing this I do not understand that I have depended any less on intellectually firm and reliable sources, even though I have not counseled that the "received" and classic disciplines be taught as such. I have sought to make values and their study integral parts of the enterprises and hence have not needed to devise some pedagogical *deus ex machina* to bring them on stage. I have, throughout, sought to "speak to the students' condition" by drawing on, and drawing together, the most reliable knowledge and skills available.

Whatever be the limitations of the theory and practice which I have shared with you, it represents a venture in general education, the road to which is synthesis. I wish now to share with you the most perceptive and boldest statement about synthesis which I know. I give you, too precious to be spoiled by my paraphrase, the language of Hoyt Hudson, late professor of humane letters at Stanford University:

The synthesizer lays himself open to attack from every quarter and by a variety of weapons. The specialist is safer, for he can be attacked only at a single point and by one sort of weapon. What the specialized critic overlooks is that his very safety is dangerous, so far as it depends on isolation, and that the synthetic thinker runs his hazards (of superficiality, of confusion, of categories, of false analogy) in the interest of a high cause — namely, the relief of man's estate. . . . It is surely not exorbitant to suggest that one goal — perhaps the highest — of any specialized group of thinkers should be the discovery of ideas and principles which may be added to man's common stock, with applications that transcend the field of their discovery. Hence, I am inclined to say, at the risk of sounding unscholarly, that a serious attempt to find effective relations among fields of study and knowledge is more praiseworthy than a denial, whether explicit in a statement or implicit in practice, that such relations exist. . . . No specialized mode of knowing, any mode short of the most full and most complete understanding possible, can be considered adequate — adequate either to the mind of man or to the problems of his life on earth.[6]

A test of synthesis has been proposed by Gordon B. Turner in his Foreword to *The Social Studies and the Social Sciences*. He asks, "Can the social studies program be designed simultaneously to provide knowledge about man and society and to make students aware of the general concepts and unity of social science?" I am sure such a program can and ask that my two-course patterns be tested by those very criteria.

REFERENCES

1. Leon C. Marshall and Rachael Goetz, *Curriculum Making in the Social Studies: The Social Process Approach* (New York: Charles Scribner's Sons, 1936).
2. John Dewey, *The Child and the Curriculum* (Chicago: University of Chicago Press, 1956), p. 22.
3. John Dewey, *Democracy and Education* (New York: Macmillan Co., 1916), p. 221.
4. See my *Theory and Practice of the Social Studies* (New York: Macmillan Co., 1956) for a discussion of these terms.
5. Dewey, *The Child and the Curriculum*, p. 22.
6. *Educating Liberally* (Stanford, Calif.: Stanford University Press, 1945), pp. 42–43.

The Levels of Content

Hilda Taba

Some of the confusion in the discussion of the function of subject matter in the curriculum and in the decisions flowing from this discussion can be prevented by a clearer analysis of what knowledge consists of and by clearer distinctions of the levels of content and the differences in functions that these levels may serve.

Specific Facts and Processes

One can view school subjects as consisting of knowledge on four different levels. One level is that of specific facts, descriptive ideas at a low level of abstraction, and specific processes and skills. Descriptions of the branches of government, of the characteristics of the digestive system, dates of events, specific rules of usage, and the computational processes in arithmetic and algebra belong in this category. It may be important to master some facts as facts, although it is not clear just what these may be in any given area. Agreements regarding what these fundamental facts are may also be more difficult to reach in some areas than in others. There are still disagreements as to which classics are worth reading by all students. The author's experience in looking for "landmark" events and facts in United States history revealed a disconcerting disagreement among historians both in the selection of these facts and in the degree of generality and specificity of the listings. A report on the discussions of scientists on what is important to learn in science points out that the only facts worth knowing are those that reconstruct a host of details when needed, such as basic scientific or mathematical formulas. Perhaps another kind are those that lure students onward, such as the discovery that metals bend when heated.

By and large the merits of mastering specific content and specific techniques are considered to be quite limited. This kind of knowledge is described as static, "dead end." Its mastery does not produce new ideas, does not lure the mind onward. Besides telling only part of a story of a discipline, the specific facts also have a pitifully short life even if remembered: they are highly obsolescent (*Bruner, 1960, pp.* 24–25). The "facts" of today easily become the "fiction" of tomorrow. White describes this danger of obsolescence in geography by commenting on the futility of introducing new units about any place that happens to be in the news. "In our earnest concern to prepare young people to live in an increasingly conflicted world, we are in danger of trying to teach them so many facts about the world as it was last year that we shall teach them little of the ways of thinking about the world that is becoming" (*White, 1958, pp. 63–71*).

From *Curriculum Development: Theory and Practice* by Hilda Taba, © 1962, by Harcourt, Brace & World, Inc. and reprinted with their permission.

This difficulty has been recognized by many educational writers and expressed in the use of the derogatory term "mere subject matter" when discussing the role of content in learning. Dewey described such knowledge as "dead baggage" well ahead of the more specific studies in learning and thinking which proved it. But many of Dewey's followers, failing to discriminate among the levels of knowledge, applied this view to all subject matter.

Specific facts, however, constitute the raw material for the development of ideas. Facts are "food for thought," the material from which to derive generalizations and insights and with which to make thinking precise. Therefore a careful choice of the details to study is as important as ever, and they need to be chosen selectively, to be related to and interpreted in the context of the ideas which they serve.

Because facts as such are only raw material from which to shape concepts and ideas, their role in the learning process is a fleeting one. They do not constitute the fundamentals in the sense that all students must master precisely the same content details. Nor should their mastery be the chief focus of instruction or of evaluation.

Basic Ideas

Basic ideas and principles represent another level of knowledge. The ideas about causal relationships between human culture and natural environment are of this sort. So are scientific laws and mathematical principles, the ideas stating relationships between nutrition and the metabolism of the human body, or ideas about how such factors as climate, soil, and natural resources produce unique constellations of a geographic environment.

Such ideas and principles constitute what currently is referred to as the "structure" of the subject: ideas which describe facts of generality, facts that, once understood, will explain many specific phenomena. Bruner uses as an illustration the principle of tropism, the idea that among simple organisms such a phenomenon as regulation of locomotion according to a built-in standard is a rule. There is a preferred level of illumination toward which these organisms orient, a preferred level of salinity, of temperature, and so on. The idea itself can be understood by studying some one phenomenon in detail, such as watching an inchworm climb a sheet of paper mounted on a board. When the board is straight, the animal walks straight; when the board is tilted 30°, the animal walks at an angle of 45°; when the board is tilted at 60° the animal walks at an angle of 75°. Evidently the inchworm "prefers" to travel uphill along an incline of 15°. Once understood, many other biological phenomena can be explained in the light of the idea of tropism. To understand "structure," then, means to learn how things are related (*Bruner, 1960, pp. 6–7*).

The idea that subject matter has structure and that understanding this structure should be the central objective in teaching is not entirely new. In the 1920's there were innumerable studies in social sciences searching for generalizations to guide and to unify the "unfortunate particularism" in this field (*Billings, 1929; Meltzer, 1925*). Marshall in his social-processes studies was seeking some unifying synthesizing approach to provide "greater unities of human experience" (*Marshall and Goetz, 1932*). In 1933 Parker, in dealing with the problem of distinguishing the descriptive facts of geography and the principles that explain things, admonished teachers that "pupils should be held responsible for independent use of familar ideas, but also be shown new ways in which geographic ideas would aid them in solving problems" (1933, pp. 73–177; see also Quillen and Hanna [1961, ch. 2] for an analysis of social concepts and generalizations).

Several yearbooks on teaching science have suggested that the teaching of science be organized around broad principles, because most facts serve as means to the end of gaining an understanding of concepts and principles, of inculcating scientific attitudes, and of providing skills in the use of scientific method (National Society for the Study of Education, 1947, chs. 2 and 3).

In mathematics such an approach is recent. Only in the last few years have mathematicians begun to examine the structure of their subject and to identify the basic principles which underlie and unify all aspects of mathematics: arithmetic, algebra, and geometry. But the recent programs in mathematics and science have gone further than simply to examine and enunciate these ideas. They have also begun to produce materials to make sure that the teaching of principles can become an actual fact (Keedy, 1959, pp. 157–88; Beberman, 1959, pp. 162–88).

The basic ideas give control over a wider range of subject matter, organize the relationships between facts, and thereby provide the context for insight and understanding. As the concept of tropism illustrates, these ideas and principles represent the kind of knowledge that is dynamic rather than dead-end, that can be applied to understanding a wide range of events, facts, phenomena, and problems and used to explain and to predict them. This type of knowledge frees the mind to explore more complex phenomena with some sense of excitement in discovery. A student can do much more with an understanding of "relations" as a general mathematical idea than by knowing only the specific aspects of mathematical relations, such as a coefficient. The idea that the existence of a physical frontier represented a stimulus to technological development and a safety valve for discontent helps interpret many single phenomena of American history, setting them into a pattern which is productive of reasoning and insight.

Such basic ideas are the fundamentals, in the sense that when carefully chosen, they represent the most necessary understandings about a subject or a field and thus constitute in a sense the core curriculum for everyone — something that every student would learn, even though in a different depth. . . . [T]hey may also be used as centers around which to organize the curriculum. It must be pointed out, however, that it may be difficult to reach agreement as to what constitutes basic ideas and principles for a given field. The experience of the California State Commission on Social Studies in obtaining a listing of general ideas around which to organize the social-studies curriculum in elementary and secondary schools suggests that agreement may be reached only on a level of such generality as to produce statements which have little meaning for curriculum guidance (California State Dept. of Education, 1957). This does not mean, however, that an identification of these basic ideas and generalizations is not a necessary step in enhancing the contribution of a field to learning.

Concepts

A third level of content is composed of what one might call concepts, such as the concept of democracy, of interdependence, of social change, or of the "set" in mathematics.

Concepts are complex systems of highly abstract ideas which can be built only by successive experiences in a variety of contexts. They cannot be isolated into specific units but must be woven into the whole fabric of the curriculum and examined over and over again in an ascending spiral. For example, a recent report on mathematics curriculum points out that the concept of a "set" can be advantageously used on all levels. It can be used to develop a number concept in elementary arithmetic, such as birds pictured on a page, or pencils in one's hand. The secondary level needs to explore the idea in a more abstract and formal way, such as applying the concept of "null set," which is empty of any elements, and of a universal set, which contains all elements under consideration (*National Council of the Teachers of Mathematics, 1959*). For an illustration of the idea of the "set" see *Rourke, (1958), p. 74.*

In a similar fashion, the concepts of multiple causation, of interdependence, or of democracy can be developed only if they run through a great deal of social science. From dealing in the first grade with interdependence of roles in the family and how its members help each other, one can progress in the twelfth grade to the notion of the economic and political interdependence of nations, a vastly more complex and abstract concept.

These types of concepts are usually in the background, and therefore are often relegated to incidental teaching. In a sound curriculum development they should constitute what some have called the "recurrent themes," the threads which run through the entire curriculum in a cumulative and over-arching fashion.

Thought Systems

The academic disciplines also represent thought systems and methods of inquiry. These thought systems are composed of propositions and concepts which direct the flow of inquiry and thought. Each discipline represented by a school subject presumably is organized around some such system of interlocking principles, concepts, and definitions. These systems direct the questions asked, the kind of answers sought, and the methods by which they are sought.

Presumably the most valuable contribution of a field of study lies in generating certain disciplined methods of forming questions, developing logical ways of relating ideas, and following a rational method of inquiry. Because the greatest need in the scientific age is for persons who can use their minds as well as their knowledge and who can apply their knowledge to new problems, systematic thought needs to be given to the ways and means by which the acquisition of knowledge simultaneously becomes also a method of inquiry and a method of thinking. For this reason, the problem of organizing the curriculum and teaching so that learning leads to disciplined thought is a critical issue of education today, especially on the secondary level.

BIBLIOGRAPHY

Beberman, M. "Improving High School Mathematics." *Educational Leadership*, 17 (Dec. 1959).

Billings, N. *A Determination of Generalizations Basic to the Social Studies Curriculum*. Baltimore. Warwick and York (1929).

Bruner, J. S. *The Process of Education*. Harvard University Press (1960).

California State Department of Education. *Building Curriculum in Social Studies for the Public Schools of California*. Bulletin, 26, No. 4, Sacramento, California (May 1957).

Keedy, M. L. "Mathematics in Junior High School." *Education Leadership*, 17 (December 1959).

Marshall, L. C., and R. M. Goetz. *Curriculum-Making in the Social Studies: A Social Process Approach*. Scribner (1936).

Meltzer, H. *Children's Social Concepts: A Study in Their Nature and Development*. No. 192. Teachers College, Columbia University. (1925).

National Council of the Teachers of Mathematics. "The Secondary Mathematics Curriculum." Report of the Secondary Curriculum Committee. *The Mathematics Teacher* (May 1959).

National Society for the Study of Education. *Science Education in American Schools*. Forty-sixth Yearbook, Pt. I. University of Chicago Press (1947).

Parker, E. P. "Basic Geographic Ideas." In National Society for the Study of Education, *The Teaching of Geography*. Thirty-second Yearbook. Bloomington, Indiana Public School Publishing Company (1933), Ch. 8.

Quillen, J., and L. Hanna. *Education for Social Competence*. Scott, Foresman (1961).

Rourke, R. E. K. "Some Implications of Twentieth Century Mathematics for High Schools." *Mathematics Teacher*, 51 (February 1958).

White, G. "The Changing Dimensions of the World Community." In F. S. Chase and H. A. Anderson (eds.), *The High School in a New Era*. University of Chicago Press (1959).

The Structure of the Social Sciences and Citizenship Education

James P. Shaver and Donald W. Oliver

After decades of relative inactivity, the number of curriculum development projects in the social studies has increased markedly since 1955. Previously, the social studies educator could speculate at his leisure about the appropriate content and sequence for the social studies program. Now, however, as federal money makes curricular work possible on a large scale and as new curricula

From the *Proceedings of the Utah Academy of Sciences, Arts, and Letters*, 1965, Volume 42, Part II, pages 311–318. By permission of the Utah Academy and the authors.

become available, perplexing questions about the rationale for and the substance of the social studies program take on a certain urgency.

As to rationale, one thing is clear on a general level. Social studies has long staked its claim — perhaps because of the lack of any other clear mandate — to a large portion of the school's responsibility for citizenship education. This concern was reflected in the Report of the American Historical Association's Committee of Seven in 1899,[1] even though it assumed that the teaching of history alone was sufficient to the task. The National Education Association's Committee on the Social Studies maintained the citizenship orientation in its 1916 report, but considered history as only one discipline with a contribution to make to the social studies program.[2] The work of the Commission on Social Studies of the American Historical Association[3] in the 1930's and of the National Council for the Social Studies' Committee on Concepts and Values[4] continued the emphasis.

Over the years, citizen education goals have been stated largely in terms of providing students with information and intellectual competencies necessary to participate rationally in the resolution of public issues. The basic premise has been that our form of government, call it a democracy or a republic, demands an intelligent, informed citizenry because individual citizens have an impact on important governmental decisions. Many have questioned the assumption that the electorate does have the power attributed to it by the citizenship education model.[5] There also have been grave doubts as to the effectiveness of the public school and its social studies program in promoting an informed, an intelligent, or a concerned citizenry.

The 1916 committee of the NEA not only postulated citizenship education as the central goal of social studies instruction, but proposed a sequence of courses for the secondary school. In general form, that sequence is familiar to all of us who have been schooled in America because it has provided the pattern for the social studies program for fifty years. With few variations, the geography, U.S. history, (sometimes state history), civics, world or ancient history, U.S. history, and problems of democracy sequence is followed with amazing uniformity throughout the country. Despite pronouncements of intent, however, history for history's sake has continued to dominate social studies teaching. Social studies content has borne little relation to stated citizenship objectives, unless one assumes that coverage of historical generalizations of doubtful validity[6] and commonly superficial background treatments of societal problems are

[1] Committee of Seven. *The Study of History in the Schools: Report to the American Historical Association.* New York: Macmillan, 1899.

[2] See, "The Social Studies in Secondary Education." (Compiled by Arthur William Dunn.) *U.S. Bureau of Education Bulletin* No. 28, 1916.

[3] See, e.g., Charles A. Beard. *A Charter for the Social Sciences in the Schools* (Report of the Committee on the Social Studies of the American Historical Association, Part I). New York: Scribner, 1934.

[4] Report of the NCSS Committee on Concepts and Values. *A Guide to Content in the Social Studies.* Washington, D.C.: National Council for the Social Studies, 1957.

[5] For example: C. Wright Mills. *The Power Elite.* New York: Oxford University Press, 1965; Fred M. Newmann. "Consent of the Governed and Citizenship Education in Modern America." *School Review*, 1963, 71, pp. 404–424.

[6] See: H. J. Noah, C. E. Prince, and D. R. Riggs. "History in High School Textbooks." *School Review*, 1962, 70, pp. 415–436. Also, F. R. Hartz. "Watered-Down American History." *High School Journal*, 1963, 46 pp. 175–178.

likely to affect the desired results. There is not much hope for the validity of this assumption on either logical or empirical grounds.

Structure Enters the Picture

It will be recalled that following the oft mentioned first sputnik, the initial flow of curriculum development funds from the national government was into the revamping of the science and mathematics curricula, supporting projects such as the Physical Science Study Committee (PSSC) and the School Mathematics Study Group (SMSG). The task was clear: Make secondary school science courses legitimate in terms of the conceptualization of their fields by competent scholars. Thus began an emphasis on use of the "structure" of a discipline as a basis for curriculum development.

Although others had utilized this approach previously, Bruner canonized the principle in The Process of Education.[7] The basic notion is that if the scholar analyzes the structure of his discipline, that is, makes clear the field of study, the substantive concepts used in thinking about the field, the methodological concepts used in studying or investigating the field, as well as the interrelationships among the various concepts, and this analysis is used as the basis for constructing the curriculum, two important educational results will follow: (1) The structure, in some legitimate form, can be taught to any age pupil; and (2) the relationships among concepts will be made more clear to the student, so that an unfolding of meaning will occur in moving through the curriculum and the concepts will be better learned and retained.

Structure and the Social Studies

With the involvement of scientists and mathematicians in secondary school curriculum development, two events occurred of great importance to the social studies. First, considerable success with the "structure approach" was reported in science and mathematics; and, second, social scientists, undoubtedly in part because of the availability of money, began to become involved in curriculum development for the elementary and secondary schools. With their considerable conscious striving to be "scientific" and considering the curricular successes claimed by their counterparts in the biological and physical sciences, it is not surprising that much of the curriculum work of social scientists has centered on using the structure of their scholarly fields as the basis for course construction.

There is no question but the increased involvement of social scientists in the development of public school curricula has been a most fortunate happening. The problems of curriculum development are so difficult and complex that the input of additional competencies can only be beneficial, especially as it encourages diversity in approaches to the curriculum and brings scholarly competence to a field too broad for any one teacher to master.

It is noteworthy that the entrance of the social scientist upon the scene has posed particular problems for the historian and, in particular, the history teacher in the secondary school. The dispute as to whether history belongs to

[7] Jerome S. Bruner. The Process of Education. Cambridge, Mass.: Harvard University Press, 1960.

the social sciences or the humanities is far from resolved. And, it is evident that to participate in the trend toward the analysis of structure[8] as a basis for the curriculum, history must be conceived of as basically a social science, with the historian's task the development of conceptual systems by which events can be ordered and related — or to put it another way, by which hypotheses can be developed and tested. Few historians or teachers of history are willing to adopt this view wholeheartedly.

Structure and Citizenship Education

The "structure" approach also raises crucial questions more directly related to citizenship education. The most basic one is simply, will a curricular sequence made up of courses based on the structure of the social sciences provide adequate citizenship education? Certainly the knowledge the social sciences have to offer about the behavior of individuals and groups has much to contribute to an informed citizenry. And, many would argue that the contributions the social sciences have to make to the decision-making process through their highly developed techniques for verifying knowledge are even more important. But, is the scientific frame too parochial a view of problem formulation and solution? Is the social scientist justified in imposing as the major ends of general education his commitments to inquiry and to the quest for knowledge within the highly specialized frameworks found in the work of those formally engaged in scholarship? The answer is clearly "yes" to the first question and "no" to the second.

In the first place, social scientists do not agree among themselves as to the essential concepts or the appropriate ordering and emphasis of concepts in their respective fields; nor do they agree on the possibility of a structure encompassing all of the social sciences. This lack of unanimity, while the essence of the academic pursuit, raises perplexing questions about which structures are to form the basis of the courses in the general education program. What criteria are to be used in selecting them? Or, is any structure appropriate as long as it has been carefully reasoned out by a recognized scholar? It is doubtful that many social scientists or educationists would respond affirmatively to the latter question.

Perhaps of more importance to those concerned with citizenship education, however, is the reasonable doubt as to whether the norms and intellectual styles preferred by scholars in their work are appropriate to the participant-citizen. While the vocabulary of the social scientist, especially that of the economist, is fast becoming a part of public discourse, there are serious questions about the extent to which the "layman" can transfer the social scientist's concepts and find them useful in the dialogue concerning public issues. Moreover, the social scientist himself has not made such clear and compelling contributions to clarifying or resolving public issues[9] as to suggest that his mode of thought should be adopted as *the* model to be used as the basis for citizenship education. To

---

[8] A report by Edwin Fenton and John Good indicates that this is currently the most popular basis for curriculum development in the social studies: "Project Social Studies: A Progress Report." *Social Education*, 1965, 29, pp. 206–208.

[9] Gunnar Myrdal's *An American Dilemma* (New York: Harper & Brothers, 1944), is a noteworthy successful attempt to clarify a public issue, but it is doubtful that his work has had any great effect on public thought.

what extent is Adams' poignant reaction to the academician's utility to the society in dealing with its crucial problems still pertinent today?

> The lecture room was futile enough, but the faculty room was worse. American society feared total wreck in the maelstrom of political and corporate administration, but it could not look for help to college dons. Adams knew, in that capacity, both Congressmen and professors, and he preferred Congressmen.[10]

It is possible that the narrowness of the scholar's intellectual frame may as often block as facilitate the perception of public issues. Gunnar Myrdal, in his classic study of the Negro in America,[11] notes a paradox that is both interesting and significant for the social studies educator; this is, that people often behave in specific situations in ways that seem to belie their general commitments to American ideals. For instance, a person who believes in the notion of full participation by citizens in a democracy may act to deny Negroes the right to vote. Myrdal's observation is keen and fits well with common and psychological knowledge about inconsistency in beliefs and behavior, but it does not go far enough when one is considering intellectual strategies for making decisions about public policy. Not only do specific values conflict with general ones, but general values conflict with one another when used as the basis for specific decisions. Civil rights laws have been supported in the name, for example, of equal opportunity; they have also been opposed in the name of private property rights and the right to local control.

It is rare that making policy about major issues does not involve this confrontation between basic values of our society.[12] How does social science methodology meet the citizen's need to determine appropriate ends or to choose between competing values? Charles Beard has an answer to this question in his treatise on the social sciences:

> Now we come to the second question raised by tensions and changes in society: What choices should be made in contingencies? Here the social sciences, working as descriptive sciences with existing and becoming reality, face, unequivocally, ideas of value and choice — argumentative systems of social philosophy based upon conceptions of desirable changes in the social order. At this occurrence empiricism breaks down absolutely. It is impossible to discover by the fact-finding operation whether this or that change is desirable. Empiricism may disclose within limits, whether a proposed change is possible, or to what extent it is possible, and the realities that condition its eventuation, but, given possibility or a degree of possibility, empiricism has no way of evaluating a value without positing value or setting up a frame of value.[13]

[10] Henry Adams. *The Education of Henry Adams.* New York: Random House, 1931, p. 307.

[11] Myrdal, *op. cit.*

[12] For a fuller development of this point, see: Donald W. Oliver and James P. Shaver. *The Analysis of Public Controversy: An Approach to Citizenship Education.* Report of Cooperative Research Project No. 551. Cambridge, Mass.: The Laboratory for Research in Instruction, Harvard Graduate School of Education, 1963 (mimeo.), Parts I and II. Also, Oliver and Shaver. *Teaching Public Issues in the High School.* Boston: Houghton Mifflin, 1966.

[13] Charles Beard. *The Nature of the Social Sciences.* New York: Scribner, 1934, pp. 171–172.

Beard's analysis is as valid today as it was in 1934; and he does not stand alone in his assessment. Many scholars (e.g., Stevenson, Hospers, Ewing and Russell[14]), while not in agreement on the specific process to be followed in making ethical decisions, agree with Beard that while the method of the scientist is in some measure useful in the process of ethical judgment, it is not sufficient alone.

It should be obvious that several different modes of endeavor and thought are relevant to a citizenship education curriculum that emphasizes confronting societal controversy. Identifying and synthesizing these modes into a curricular pattern is a major challenge to the social studies educator and other scholars who will work with him. Examples of alternative modes that might be considered are the poet-historian who helps to provide societal continuity and cohesion through his dramatic and poetic representations of past glories, the broad-ranging philosopher who raises questions about the criteria for intellectual truth and questions established standards of good and bad, the lawyer-statesman who is actively engaged in confronting the issues facing society, and the intelligent journalist whose concern is for the objective reporting of important contemporary events in historical and ethical perspective. Considering the attitudinal and temperamental as well as intellectual objectives of citizenship education, exclusive focus on the academic scholar as the model for an intelligent citizenry seems clearly inadequate.

What of the Student's Models?

There is another assumption that goes with the structure approach to curriculum building that is troublesome. A course based on structure seems to assume that the student comes into the classroom with his mind a *tabula rasa* so far as social theory is concerned. The educational task is to paint on the *tabula* the adequate framework for construing society. In reality, of course, the student comes to the classroom with his own social theory, as incomplete, fragmented, and otherwise inadequate as it may be. The task of the teacher is to help him explore and go beyond his present speculations about what makes people and societies function as they do. And the subject-matter of the social sciences is likely to have an impact on the student's thinking as it is related to his already existing concepts. The identification of crucial concepts for understanding society is a significant task. However, the extent to which the concepts are related to the student's existing frame of reference is a more likely basis for predicting the success of a social science course than is its faithfulness to some conception of structure in the scholarly field. To ignore the student, except as his interests and background can be utilized for "motivational" purposes in communicating the previously determined structure, is a dubious, if not haphazard and possibly disastrous, approach to curriculum building. But to accept the existence, relevance, and, to a considerable extent, the validity of the frame

14 Charles L. Stevenson. *Ethics and Language.* New Haven: Yale University Press, 1944, pp. 113–114; John Hospers. *An Introduction to Philosophical Analysis.* New York: Prentice–Hall, 1953, p. 494: E. C. Ewing. "Subjectivism and Naturalism in Ethics." In *Readings in Ethical Theory,* edited by W. E. Sellers and John Hospers. New York: Appleton-Century-Crofts, 1952, p. 120; Bertrand Russell, "The Elements of Ethics," in Sellers and Hospers, *ibid.,* p. 8.

of reference brought to class by the student is also to concede that the result of instruction cannot be a replication in the student's mind of the social scientist's model. The outcome will be instead an intellectual framework that is largely idiosyncratic to the individual student, but nevertheless valid for his own purposes of construing and relating to his social reality.

No Place for the Structure Notion?

If these reservations about the structure of the social sciences as a basis for general education in the social studies have some merit, is the idea of structure of no use to one concerned with the development of curricula for citizenship education? This depends to a large extent upon the concept of structure which one adopts. It is all too easy to fall into the error of talking about structure as if it were something inherent in nature, revealing itself as the scientist investigates his field. It is one thing to say that there is order in nature (including society as a "natural" setting for man), but quite another to say that the dividing of reality into segments for study — the basis for a discipline — reflects any natural order. The structure of a social science discipline is the result of man's efforts to study an arbitrarily defined field and of his analysis of the results of that study.

Looking at structure from this point of view raises a question of considerable importance to the social studies curriculum: Can a structure be created that provides a broader and more valid base for the general education curriculum than would the structure of social science disciplines? One alternative, as has been implied earlier in this paper, would be to focus on the making of decisions about public issues as *the* crucial element of citizenship behavior in a democracy.[15] Using a common threefold definition,[16] the structure would involve: (1) subject or field — making and affecting policy decisions in this society; (2) substantive concepts — those useful in describing and understanding the issues and the context in which decisions about them must be made; and, (3) syntactical, or methodological, concepts — those useful in arriving at rationally justified policy decisions. Obviously, the social sciences have much to contribute to the recognition and understanding of crucial issues, to the intellectual strategies adopted for determining desirable and possible policies, and to the procedures for affecting and implementing policy decisions. But so do ethics and logic; and, to the extent that certain commitments are prerequisite to functioning rationality, so do other humanities.

It may well be that even in the overall context of a curricular sequence based on the analysis of decision-making in a pluralistic-democratic society, social science concepts can be taught best with individual courses based on the structure of the individual social science disciplines. It is, however, difficult not to suspect that the motivational effects social scientists, including Jerome Bruner,

15 See Oliver and Shaver, *op. cit.*
16 Joseph J. Schwab. "The Concept of the Structure of a Discipline." *Educational Record*, 1962, 43, pp. 197–205. Also, Joseph J. Schwab. "Structure of the Disciplines: Meanings and Significances." In *The Structure of Knowledge and the Curriculum*, edited by G. W. Ford and Lawrence Pugno, Chicago: Rand McNally, 1964, pp. 6–30. [see above, pp. 289–305.]

assume their structured courses will have for restless and often non-intellectually inclined, if not anti-intellectual, children and adolescents is largely an unwarranted projection of the excitement and satisfaction they derive from their own investigations and models for construing reality. There is, moreover, some research evidence suggesting that concepts will be better retained and more readily transferred to the non-classroom public controversy setting if the relevance of the concepts to handling an array of issues important to the society and to the student is made clear. Perhaps courses based on structure could conclude with exercises in application of the social science concepts to public issues. This would, however, affront the "purist" social scientist who believes either that application automatically follows comprehension or that concern with application to citizenship problems contaminates the structure of the discipline. Some cyclical approach (not the present U.S. history course cycle of more of the same) might be used to introduce the student to the new dimensions of important public issues brought to light by the concepts introduced in each succeeding course. Possibly, however, the answer is a course sequence in which important concepts are introduced as relevant to crucial public issues, without individual social science (or ethics or logic) courses. The answers to the questions posed by such general proposals present the curriculum developer and researcher with problems of overwhelming complexity and difficulty.

Conclusion

It is patently clear, nevertheless, if one looks at the nature of the scientific endeavor with its limited intent, methodology, and subject-matter and contrasts this with the manifold demands of making rational decisions about public issues, that a citizenship education curriculum must be based on much more than the structure of the social sciences. At the same time, the current emphasis on building curricula based on the structure of disciplines is antithetical to citizenship education only if the intent is to have the general education social studies program made up exclusively of social science courses. If we can develop structures at a level above that of the individual course, such as a rationale derived from consideration of the elements in an adequate conceptual frame for making decisions about public issues, social science courses developed from the structure approach might well fit into the overall curriculum scheme.

However, alternatives to courses based on individual social sciences are available. Perhaps rather than worrying about the structures of their scholarly areas and whether these will be taught in some specified form in the public schools, social scientists could make a greater contribution to an intelligent citizenry by asking, as have the Anthropology Curriculum Study Project[17] and the Sociological Resources for Secondary School project,[18] what their areas of study can contribute to an understanding of the crucial issues facing our nation both internally and internationally. This, rather than the preservation of arbitrary intellectual domains, should be the central concern for citizenship education.

[17] Malcom C. Collier, Director. 5632 South Kimbark Avenue, Chicago, Illinois 60637.
[18] Robert A. Feldmesser, Director. Dartmouth College, Hanover, New Hampshire 03755.

334 · FURTHER READING

FURTHER READING FOR SECTION 4

Cohen, Morris, and Ernest Nagel. *An Introduction to Logic and Scientific Method.* New York: Harcourt, Brace & World, 1934.

An old but still useful and provocative treatment of the nature of scientific and logical thinking.

Handy, Rollo, and Paul Kurtz. *A Current Appraisal of the Behavioral Sciences.* Great Barrington, Mass.: Behavioral Research Council, 1964.

A summation of the current status of the newer and older behavioral sciences. Each chapter, devoted to a single behavioral science field, is organized into categories, e.g., "Working definition of the field"; "schools, methods, techniques"; "results achieved"; "contemporary controversy", etc. There is very little discussion or explanation of the issues, but the volume does give the layman an idea of the complexity and diversity of the social and behavioral sciences.

Kaplan, Abraham. *The Conduct of Inquiry.* San Francisco: Chandler, 1964.

A broad and readable treatment of a number of concepts and ideas which have recency in discussions of social studies curriculum, e.g., induction, deduction, discovery, inquiry. The distinctions the author draws among the types of social scientific laws are especially relevant to the question of what social science concepts should be taught and to what end.

Morrissett, Irving (ed.). *Concepts and Structure in the New Social Science Curricula.* West Lafayette, Ind.: Social Science Education Consortium, 1966.

A collection of papers and a summary of discussions from a conference attended by representatives of a number of social studies projects. The report reveals that surprisingly few of the projects have confronted the basic issue of why they intend to teach the "structure" of the disciplines. Papers by Herbert Feigl, James Shaver, Irving Sigel, and Michael Scriven are especially useful.

Rudner, Richard S. *Philosophy of Social Sciences.* Englewood Cliffs, N.J.: Prentice-Hall, 1966.

An abstract, technical treatment of epistemological problems and issues in the social sciences. Included are chapters on the nature of the social science theory and problems of objectivity. The selected bibliography includes a number of the more important technical philosophical works dealing with the nature of scientific knowledge.

Zettenberg, Hans L. *On Theory and Verification in Sociology,* 3rd ed. Totowa, N.J.: Bedminster Press, 1965.

A concise and lucid monograph, describing how one social science discipline constructs and verifies definitions, propositions, and theory. The treatment of the nature of and relationships between social science propositions and theory will be valuable to teachers who deal with social science data, propositions, and theories, yet are rarely aware of such distinctions.

5

Thinking About Thinking

A democratic society is committed to the dignity of man. The assumption that individual citizens can and should participate in political decision making is integral to the notion of human dignity and is based on a conception of man as an intelligent, rational being. This presupposition of intelligence does not necessarily deny man's non-rationality. Rather, it attests to a faith that the rational rather than the irrational will predominate as a basis for social action.

In addition, there is the expectation that education will expand man's capacity to rely on his intellect in confronting personal and social problems, instead of resorting to mysticism or unquestioned authority. American public schools have long accepted the development of rationality as a legitimate area of concern, and what is often called *critical* or *reflective thinking* has been taken as one of education's primary goals. Social studies educators in particular have seen this as central to their concern with preparing students for citizenship in a democratic society.

Learning by Osmosis?

It has been common for social studies teachers to assume that students will learn new ways of thinking by a process somewhat akin to osmosis. That is, that by studying the works of historians, the student will learn to approach data and think about it as does the historian. This assumption is particularly suspect when one takes into account the great disparities between the content of historical monographs and the over-generalized summation of these in students' textbooks. Of course, it is clearly just as questionable that students will learn the investigatory approaches and methodology of the social scientist by studying his substantive reports — especially in the form in which they arrive in the social studies classroom.

The point is not that substantive knowledge is unimportant, but rather that it alone is not sufficient. For example, in an economics course, students might be taught the concept of scarcity, and then taught that economists believe that the existence of scarcity means that societies must somehow make decisions such as what to produce, how to allocate resources, how to make the most efficient use of the factors of production, and how to divide the goods and services produced. Studying economic ideas in this way, however, is not in itself likely to help the student learn to engage in the hypothesis formulation and testing which underlie the economist's accounts of the society's economic workings. Nor will such study be likely to communicate to students the notion of probabilistic knowledge which is basic to the economist's investigations. The expectation that thought process outcomes will follow from studying the *outcomes* of thought is at best dubious.

Thought and Content

Some educators have recommended that thought process concepts be given an explicit and important place in the social studies curriculum. A common reaction to this position has been the claim that this would mean neglecting the important knowledge, especially historical knowledge,[1] which all men must have as a foundation for intelligent citizenship.

Does the teaching of thought process necessarily interfere with the conveying of information? Shirley H. Engle deals with the relationship between the teaching of facts and the teaching of decision making in the first reading in this section. He contends that decision making should be the focus of social studies instruction, and that this will provide a point of orientation for learning and retaining facts.

Of course, this is not a new idea. John Dewey made the same point early in this century when he attacked the student's position as a learner:

> In schools, those under instruction are too customarily looked upon as acquiring knowledge as theoretical spectators, minds which appropriate knowledge by direct energy of intellect. The very word pupil has almost come to mean one who is engaged not in having fruitful experiences but in absorbing knowledge directly.[2]

Dewey was concerned that the student be engaged in active consideration of problems meaningful to him. He insisted that improvement of instruction necessitated "centering upon the conditions which exact, promote, and test thinking . . . the method of intelligent learning."[3] Dewey was not propounding, as some of his critics have maintained, that information is of no use in the classroom. He argued, as in the brief excerpt from *Democracy and Education* in this section, that involving the student in purposeful thought would not only provide the framework for ordering data, but would require that more resources for seeking information be provided in the classroom.

There is considerable evidence to support the contention that students are more likely to remember information if they use it actively in thinking. Although systematic research on learning in the social studies is scarce, a careful analysis of the results of organizing a two-year, seventh- and eight-grade U.S. history sequence around the analysis of public issues has been reported.[4] During this two-year program, concepts deemed important to the analysis of public issues were taught. Although an over-all coverage of American history was provided, the major portion of time was spent in the discussion and analysis of public issues (e.g., the one created by the Supreme Court's 1954 decision on

---

[1] For an incisive discussion of how to get around the "ground-covering fetish," see Maurice Hunt and Lawrence Metcalf, *Teaching High School Social Studies* (New York: Harper & Row, 1955), pp. 349–352.

[2] John Dewey, *Democracy and Education* (New York: Macmillan, 1961 [paperback edition]), p. 140.

[3] *Ibid.*, p. 153.

[4] Donald W. Oliver and James P. Shaver, *Teaching Public Issues in the High School* (Boston: Houghton Mifflin, 1966). For a summary report, see James P. Shaver and Donald W. Oliver, "Teaching Students to Analyze Public Controversy: A Curriculum Project Report," *Social Education*, 1964, 28, pp. 191–195.

school desegregation). Each issue was, however, set in its historical context. Analysis of test data indicated that at the end of the project period the experimental students not only were better able to apply the analytic concepts to societal issues, but their knowledge of the usual social studies content, as measured by standardized tests, was equal to that of the control students. In fact, closer analysis revealed that the experimental groups scored significantly higher than the other students on test items which measured information that had been studied as part of the textbook coverage of history and also used in the discussion of a public issue. These results held up on test data obtained a year after the students left the experimental program.[5]

The Need for Specificity

As already noted, a number of social studies educators have argued that the teaching of reflective thinking is an important goal. Unfortunately, the proliferation of nebulously stated objectives for the social studies[6] has left reflective thinking as only one of many instructional goals, all indisputably noble, at least at the general level that they are stated. It is doubtful that exhortations to teach students to reflect about societal problems are of much value to the classroom teacher. Such statements are not specific enough to furnish the guidelines that objectives of instruction are supposed to provide for the selection of content and method. In particular, such statements do not answer the question of which intellectual competencies and strategies are helpful in construing and resolving disagreements over public policy issues. This question is crucial to the articulation of an adequate rationale for social studies instruction, and its answer is vital to effective instruction.

Unless the intellectual competencies that the student should be able to exhibit when confronted with an important issue are specifically identified so that instruction can focus on them, the teaching and learning of the competencies will be haphazard, if not accidental. The odds are great that the school will not have a pivotal effect on the concepts used by the individual in thinking about public issues. The social studies teacher has at his disposal only a relatively small proportion of the student's time. In addition, non-school groups, such as the family and the peer group, have powerful influences on the way the student construes his world. If the school's impact on the student's thought processes is to be maximized, the desired intellectual competencies must be defined carefully and taught explicitly.

The importance of defining thinking strategies carefully and organizing the curriculum to teach them is well supported by empirical evidence. Shaver[7] reviewed published research that had investigated the relative effectiveness of different approaches to the teaching of concepts of reflective thinking in secon-

[5] Oliver and Shaver, *Teaching Public Issues in the High School, op. cit.,* Section Three of the Appendix.

[6] See Lawrence E. Metcalf, "Research on Teaching the Social Studies," in N. L. Gage (ed.), *Handbook of Research on Teaching* (Chicago: Rand McNally, 1963), pp. 929–931.

[7] James P. Shaver, "Educational Research and Instruction for Critical Thinking," *Social Education,* 1962, 26, pp. 13–16.

dary school social studies. Though he found that no one method had been proved most effective in achieving this objective, he was able to conclude that:

Probably the most conclusive suggestion supported by the research reviewed here is that we should not expect that our students will learn to think critically as a by-product of the study of the usual social studies content. Instead, each teacher should determine what concepts are essential — e.g., that of relevance — if his students are to perform the intellectual operations deemed necessary to critical thinking — such as, for example, the formulation and evaluation of hypotheses. Each of these should then be taught explicitly to the students. Utilizing what is known about transfer of learning, a further step can be suggested. Situations as similar as possible to those in which the students are to use their competencies should also be set up in the classroom, and the students guided in application of the concepts in this context.[8]

Models of Thinking

We have argued that the teaching of thinking is likely to be more effective if it is done explicitly, and that the teacher should have available a clearly stated and carefully specified model of thinking to guide his instructional behavior. What alternative models of thinking might be used?

One model commonly used in the social studies was proposed by John Dewey. His conceptualization of the steps involved in reflectively solving a problem, as presented in his book *How We Think*, has provided the foundations for a great deal of social studies curriculum work. In the excerpts from *How We Think* included in this section, Dewey discusses the meaning of thinking and then goes on to suggest five phases that a person goes through in meeting a problem reflectively. Some social studies educators have taken the five phases to be *the* five steps in the *scientific method*[9] even though it is unlikely that Dewey intended the schema to be taken in that way. This assumption is crucial because, for many people, reflective thinking has become synonymous with scientific method;[10] and in this age of science, it has not been unusual for some to maintain that scientific method is *the* method appropriate for solving *all* problems.

The prospective or practicing social studies teacher will want to contemplate whether it is adequate, either in conceptualizing what the scientist does or as a basis for social studies instruction, to think of scientific method as a simple set of steps to be followed. The next reading in this section, by George Gaylord Simpson, Professor of Vertebrate Paleontology at Harvard University, indicates

[8] *Ibid.*, p. 16. For more recent research confirming Shaver's conclusions, see the study reported by Oliver and Shaver in *Teaching Public Issues in the High School, op. cit.*

[9] See, for example, Samuel P. McCutchion, George L. Fersh, and Nadine I. Clark, *Goals of Democracy: A Problems Approach* (New York: Macmillan, 1962), pp. 6–7; Joseph I. Arnold and Harland A. Phillippi, *Challenges to American Youth* (Evanston, Ill.: Row, Peterson, 1958), pp. 25–28; William E. Dunwiddie and Horace Kidger, *Problems of Democracy* (Boston: Ginn, 1962), pp. 9–11; J. Oliver Hall and Russell E. Klinger, *American Democracy: Fifty State Edition* (New York: American Book Company, 1961), pp. 11–15.

[10] For example, Lavone A. Hanna, *Challenges for a Free People* (New York: Rand McNally, 1964), p. 2.

that the "simple procedures" notion of science is patently insufficient. Simpson sees scientific method as more a matter of attitude than of procedures. This is illustrated by his definition of scientific truth in terms of the tentativity of knowledge.

B. F. Skinner makes some further suggestions about what science is *not*. Coupled with the Simpson reading, Skinner's account of his own scientific investigations should dispel any notion that scientific method can be easily dissected and described.

These two selections should be read with those in Section 4 in mind: Do the previous selections dealing with the social sciences propose or imply models of scientific inquiry that are divergent from the view of Simpson and Skinner? What are the implications of the Simpson and Skinner views for the teaching of social science methodology as the basis for analyzing public controversy?

The selections by Simpson and Skinner are valuable for their insights into the general nature of the scientific endeavor. They provide the basis for an intellectual stance. However, they give little assistance in deciding upon the particular skills, concepts, and intellectual strategies to be taught in the social studies.

Robert H. Ennis[11] has one set of reflective thinking competencies that has attracted considerable attention. However, he defined *critical thinking* as "the correct assessing of statements," explicitly excluding the consideration of value judgments. This omission brings his treatment of critical thinking into serious question as an adequate model for social studies instruction. Public controversy is fraught with value disputes; most public issues are basically ethical, calling for decisions as to which value or values shall dictate individual or social action. It seems obvious, therefore, that in developing a rationale for social studies education, we must consider the intellectual strategies appropriate to the making of value judgments.

It would be well to ask, however, whether the solution of ethical problems does require different modes of thought or intellectual strategies than does the solution of factual problems. There has been considerable confusion and disagreement over this point. It will be recalled that in Section 1, Charles Beard emphatically made the point that the method of the social sciences is not adequate to the making of value choices unless evaluative criteria are first posited. In this section, Charles L. Stevenson, in his paper "The Nature of Ethical Disagreement," draws a clear distinction between disagreements in *belief* and those in *attitude* involved in ethical disputes. Stevenson also discusses the differing intellectual strategies appropriate to the resolution of disputes over matters of fact as opposed to those over matters of value.

In the next reading, "The Teaching of Thinking," Harold Berlak advances the argument to a more general level. He contends that the use of general thought process models, supposedly applicable to any type of problem, has been a hindrance to the teaching of thinking. Instead, Berlak suggests, models need to be developed with regard to the specific contexts in which it is hoped students will apply them.

[11] Robert H. Ennis, "A Concept of Critical Thinking," *Harvard Educational Review*, 1962, 32, pp. 81–111.

Of course, the context for thought that we have been stressing is that provided by deliberations about public issues. Following the reading by Berlak is an excerpt from *Teaching Public Issues in the High School* by Donald W. Oliver and James P. Shaver that presents a simple model based on the public controversy context. Oliver and Shaver do include value choices as one of the three basic types of problems to be encountered in discourse about public issues. Different strategies are suggested for advancing argumentation, depending on the type of problem being faced.

An adequate model should also take into account the interactions between different strategies in handling public issues. To illustrate: resolving a value conflict may first require that a communication problem be solved by carefully defining terms or that a factual issue in contention be resolved by gathering sufficient evidence. The interrelationships between factual, definitional, and value disputes are discussed further in the book by Oliver and Shaver.[12]

A Comment on Texts and Tests

To this point, our primary concern has been the model of thought that a social studies teacher might adopt in building a rationale for making choices in content and method. Putting such a rationale into effect in the classroom is a paramount task for the teacher. The success of his efforts may be to a large extent contingent on the correspondence between the rationale and the instructional materials available to him for classroom use.

In most school districts, despite an increased interest in audio-video media, the textbook remains the most common instructional material. Some districts have attempted to overcome the shortcomings of the textbook by using several in a single course, the so-called "multi-text" approach. This solution is hardly adequate, since most textbooks exhibit the same inadequacies. For example, Mark Krug has indicated that textbooks generally do not provide controversial settings that might provoke students to involvement in the reflective analysis of public issues.[13] Even with multiple texts available, the teacher will have to seek out textbooks failings and compensate for them with other materials or use them as the basis for analysis and discussion.[14]

Of special concern is the model of thought for dealing with public issues that is evident, either explicitly or implicitly, in the textbook. Are the models adopted by most social studies textbooks sufficient, especially in regard to the value dimension of public controversy? At least one review of textbooks[15] has answered this question in the negative. To the extent that textbooks lack adequate frameworks of reflective thinking, including the neglect of value issues, the great numbers of social studies teachers who must rely heavily on texts have

[12] Oliver and Shaver, *op. cit.*, Chapter 7.
[13] Mark M. Krug, " 'Safe' Textbooks and Citizenship Education," *The School Review*, 1960, 68, pp. 463–480.
[14] For interesting suggestions on the use of textbook inadequacies to encourage thinking, see Maurice Hunt and Lawrence Metcalf, *op. cit.*, 1955, pp. 343–349.
[15] James P. Shaver, "Reflective Thinking, Values, and Social Studies Textbooks," *School Review*, 1965, 73, pp. 226–257.

serious deficiencies to overcome if their teaching is to be structured by an adequately comprehensive model of thinking.

Also of central concern to the social studies teacher, if he is to see his conceptualization of the thought process translated into student learning, will be his testing program. Testing is necessary to assess student learning. It should be just as obvious that tests indicate to the student the types of learning the teacher regards as most important. For example, testing for factual recall will identify for the student what he should study, regardless of the teacher's fine pronouncements concerning learning to think about important issues.

It is easy to say that tests should assess the student's ability to think, but constructing tests that will measure his ability to analyze public issues is an extremely difficult task. The development of valid tests (i.e., ones that directly reflect instructional objectives) has been, and continues to be, a knotty problem for social studies educators. Developing and validating new testing techniques is an educational research problem. Because testing is so important to the accomplishment of curricular goals, test development will be treated briefly in the final section of this book.

Nonrationality and Thinking

In closing this section, it would be well to return to the central concern: the contemplation and articulation of a rationale for the social studies curriculum. The focus of the readings is on decision making and reflective thinking as a central aspect of social studies instruction. Does such an emphasis mean that the affective, non-rational, emotive elements of citizenship should be completely excluded from the curriculum? After completing the readings in Section 5, the reader may wish to return to Donald W. Oliver's selection on individualism in Section 2 with this question in mind.

Responsible, orderly decision making takes place in a context of commitment. If a society is to survive, there must be common emotional bonds among its members. These are the cultural values — or, as the sociologist would call them, the norms — which generally guide the behavior of individuals in the society. In earlier sections, we have borrowed Gunnar Myrdal's term and referred to this non-rational basis for our democratic society as the American Creed. The Creed contains both substantive and procedural values. Our commitment to these norms provides the common language of public debate within the society and serves as a basis for the political system by which major decisions are made and effected.

In Section 2, Oliver examines the relationship of these non-rational elements (what he calls the "projective" level of culture) to the cognitive needs of democracy. And, he proposes specific ways in which the social studies curriculum can handle the seemingly paradoxical need to inculcate cultural values while also teaching analytic skills for contemplating and debating about the policies society should adopt. Re-reading this selection should serve to remind the reader that a conception of the society (or a social theory) is a necessary element in the frame of reference that shapes the curriculum decisions of the social studies teacher.

Decision Making: The Heart of
Social Studies Instruction

Shirley H. Engle

My theme is a very simple one. It is that, in teaching the social studies, we should emphasize decision making as against mere remembering. We should emphasize decision making at two levels: at the level of deciding what a group of descriptive data means, how these data may be summarized or generalized, what principles they suggest; and also decision making at the level of policy determination, which requires a synthesis of facts, principles, and values usually not all found on one side of any question.

In order to make my case, it is useful to draw certain distinctions between the social sciences and the social studies. The social sciences include all of the scholarly, investigative work of historians, political scientists, economists, anthropologists, psychologists, and sociologists, together with such parts of the work of biologists and geographers as relate primarily to human behavior. Closely related fields include philosophy, literature, linguistics, logistics, and statistics. The social studies, including the content of the textbooks, courses of study, and whatever passes in the school for instruction in civic and social affairs, are based on the social sciences but they clearly involve always a selection of and distillation from the social sciences — they encompass only a minor portion of the social sciences.

Selectivity, therefore, is one of the features which distinguishes the social sciences from the social studies. To social science, knowledge is useful for its own sake; all knowledge is of equal worth; there is no concern for immediate usefulness. To the social studies, a central consideration must always be that of determining what knowledge is of most worth. If all of the knowledge of a field of study is to be boiled down into one textbook, what is to be emphasized? If all of the knowledge of the area is to be boiled down into one course of study, what is most important?

There is a more basic distinction to be drawn between the social sciences and the social studies than merely that of selectivity. The impelling purpose of the two is quite different. The orientation of the social scientist is that of research. The more scientific the social scientist, the more specialized becomes his interest, the more consuming becomes his desire to know more and more about less and less, the less concern he shows for broad social problems. He is far more inclined to analyze, dissect, and proliferate than to unite, synthesize, and apply. His absorbing interest is to push back the frontier of dependable knowledge in some limited sector of the social scene.

In marked contrast to the meticulous research orientation of the social sciences, the social studies are centrally concerned with the education of citizens.

From *Social Education*, 1960, 24, pages 301–304, 306 by permission of the National Council for the Social Studies and the author.

The mark of the good citizen is the quality of decisions which he reaches on public and private matters of social concern. The social sciences contribute to the process of decision making by supplying reliable facts and principles upon which to base decisions — they do not supply the decisions ready made. The facts are there for all to see but they do not tell us what to do. Decision making requires more than mere knowledge of facts and principles; it requires a weighing in the balance, a synthesizing of all available information and values. The problems about which citizens must reach decisions are never confronted piecemeal, the facts are seldom clearly all on one side, and values, too, must be taken into consideration. A social problem requires that the citizen put together, from many sources, information and values which the social sciences treat in relative isolation. Thus in the social studies the prevailing motive is synthesis rather than analysis. The social studies begin where the social sciences end. Facts and principles which are the ends in view in the social sciences are merely a means to a further end in the social studies. The goal of the social studies lies not merely in information but in the character of people. The goal is the good citizen.

A good citizen has many facts at his command, but more, he has arrived at some tenable conclusions about public and social affairs. He has achieved a store of sound and socially responsible beliefs and convictions. His beliefs and convictions are sound and responsible because he has had the opportunity to test them against facts and values. In the process of testing his ideas he has greatly increased his fund of factual information and he has become increasingly skillful at intelligent decision making. The development in the mind of students of such a synthesis of facts and values, together with the development of skill in making decisions in the light of numerous and sometimes contrary facts and values, is the special forte of the social studies.

If the purpose of the social studies is to be education for citizenship, if its primary concern is to be the quality of the beliefs and convictions which students come to hold on public questions, and if we are to be concerned with the development of skill at decision making, then there are some things which it becomes imperative that we do in teaching the social studies. I would like to develop briefly some of these imperatives.

We must abandon our use of what I shall call the ground-covering technique, and with it the wholly mistaken notion that to commit information to memory is the same as to gain knowledge. By ground covering I mean the all too familiar technique of learning and holding in memory, enforced by drill, large amounts of more or less isolated descriptive material without pausing in any way, at any time, to speculate as to the meaning or significance of the material, or to consider its relevance and bearing to any general idea, or to consider its applicability to any problem or issue past or present. Even when such material is interesting, and it sometimes is, merely to cover it in this uncritical, matter-of-fact fashion robs the material of its potential for accurate concept formation or generalization which will be useful to students in understanding events and conditions in other times and places in which like data appear. Simply reading and remembering the stories about Indians in our history, no matter how many times repeated, has never insured the development of accurate concepts about Indians or correct generalizations about the relationships between people of divergent cultures and histories. Or, if in our haste to cover ground, we refuse to deal contemplatively and critically with the material we are covering, the student may generalize haphazardly and may, without our help, arrive at totally erroneous conclusions. Thus, it may be said with good reason that the study of Indians frequently does more harm than good, teaching more untruth than truth.

The ground-covering fetish is based on the false notion that remembering is all there is to knowing or the equally false notion that one must be well drilled in the facts before he can begin to think. M. I. Finley, noted British historian, says about ground covering that "a mere telling of individual events in sequence, no matter how accurately done, is just that and nothing else. Such knowledge is meaningless, its mere accumulation a waste of time. Instead, knowledge must lead to understanding. In the field of history this means trying to grasp general ideas about human events. The problem is to move from particular events to the universal; from the concrete events to the underlying patterns and generalities."

Equally fallacious is the background theory of learning, or the notion that we must hold the facts in memory before we are ready to draw conclusions from them or to think about their meaning. This theory is at considerable variance with recognized scientific method and the ways in which careful thinkers approach an intellectual problem. The thinker or scientist frequently engages in speculation or theorizing about possible relationships, from which he deduces tests or possible facts which, if observable, verify his theory. (Some of the great break-throughs in knowledge have come about in this way.) To say that a thinker must know all that he needs to know, let alone hold all this in memory, before engaging in thought is to completely hog-tie his intellectual development. And there is no valid reason in this respect for differentiating between a student trying to understand Indians and an Einstein speculating about the meaning of space.

What happens in our classrooms from too strict an adherence to ground covering is that the number of facts committed to memory is reduced to a relatively small number. These are the so-called basic facts which we learn, and just as promptly forget, over and over again. Thus ground covering actually works to reduce and restrict the quantity of factual information treated in our classes. What is needed instead is a vast multiplication of the quantity of factual material with which students are asked to deal in the context of reaching a reasoned conclusion about some intellectual problem. Such an enrichment of factual background will come about when we turn from our preoccupation with remembering to a more fruitful concern for drawing conclusions from facts or for testing our speculations and ideas about human events with all of the relevant data we are able to collect.

For ground covering, or remembering, we should substitute decision making, which is reflective, speculative, thought provoking, and oriented to the process of reaching conclusions. My thesis is simply this, decision making should afford the structure around which social studies instruction should be organized. The central importance of decision making in the social studies has been cited earlier. The point here is that students are not likely to learn to reach better decisions, that is, grounded and reasoned decisions, except as they receive guided and critically oriented exercise in the decision-making process.

Decision-making opportunities in the social studies classroom may run the entire gamut of difficulty, from very simple situations which take the form merely of posing questions for class consideration which require some thought and a synthesis of information supplied in a single descriptive paragraph to very complex social problems involving questions of public policy or individual behavior. Thus, in studying the Plains Indians in the post-Civil-war period a low level decision could be required by asking which of the following sentences accurately, or most accurately, summarizes the difficulty continually experienced in Indian affairs: (1) The Indians were treated by the settlers as trespassers on land which they (the Indians) had inhabited and claimed as their own for centuries; (2) The Plains Indians were wanderers who knew no fixed abodes and recognized no exclusive right of anyone to own the land; (3) Renegade Indians and white outlaws were at the seat of Indian trouble (this is the Hollywood version of Indian affairs); (4) The handling of Indian affairs by the United States government was characterized by wanton disregard of Indian rights, by treachery, and by broken promises; or (5) The different manner of using the land by the Indians and the whites made agreement between the two impossible. At a higher level of difficulty a decision would be required if one asked, "Do you think General George Crook dealt fairly with the Shoshone chief, Washakie, during the military campaigns to pacify the Plains Indians? What are your grounds?" Or at a still higher level of complexity, there is the question of what should be the policy of the United States toward Indians who contest the sovereignty of the United States.

Some decisions involve essentially matters of fact. For example, suppose we are reading about the building of the transcontinental railroads in the 1870's, 1880's, and 1890's and how the government gave large grants of land and money to the railroad companies to encourage them to build the railroads. We read further that subsequently the railroads, or most of them, went into bankruptcy but also that following their construction the country experienced a great expansion of agricultural and industrial wealth whereby our exports of wheat and corn multiplied tenfold in 20 years, and in the same period the value of our manufacturers' products increased 200 per cent, 180 new factories being built in Philadelphia alone. We have these and many other facts. But the decision rests in concluding what these facts mean. What do they all add up to? Which of the following generalizations accurately summarize these facts? Government subsidization of key industries brings a vast multiplication of other industries under private ownership; private investors will not take the extraordinary risk necessary to start a really new industrial development; one industrial development inevitably leads to other industrial developments; industry in which the government interferes is always inefficient and will fail in the end; private industry can never be expected to provide the transportation facilities needed for an expanding economy; government participation in industry tends to dry up the growth of private industry; industry resulting from government spending is uneconomical and is doomed to fail in the end; if the government had foregone the tax money used to aid the railroads, private individuals would have had money which they would have invested in the railroads. Clearly, the making of decisions among the alternatives listed above is essentially a matter of sorting out and applying facts until a conclusion is reached which honestly and accurately summarizes all facts that are relevant to the problem.

Other decisions, perhaps we should say most decisions, involve values as well as facts. Thus, in dealing with the issue of which of two proposed solutions to the problems of farm surpluses is best, one may conclude, factually, that government support of farm prices leads inevitably to inefficiency in agriculture and to unnecessarily high cost for food and fibre which the farm produces. This much is a factual conclusion. But this does not necessarily get us out of the woods, for one might still prefer government-supported agriculture to an unregulated agriculture because he feared the control of large agricultural corporations (which will almost inevitably follow the removal of governmental restrictions — another factual generalization) more than he fears governmental controls. The latter decision is a value judgment, though one fraught, as are all value decisions, with still further implications which could be grounded factually. For instance, in a hierarchy of values, the *greatest degree of individual freedom* may be the value sought or agreed upon by all involved in the decision. From this premise a factual investigation could be conducted of the relationship between government regulation and individual freedom on the one hand and between corporate control and individual freedom on the other. Thus, though the decision as to value is not in this way resolved, the exact issue over values is clarified by such a factual investigation of the alternatives.

If decision making is to be the focus of social studies instruction, we will need to introduce vastly larger quantities of factual information into our classrooms. Drill to the point of memory on a few basic facts will never suffice. The superficial coverage of one textbook will never be enough. The very moment that a conclusion, such as any of those suggested above, is reached tentatively, the natural demand is for more facts with which to test the conclusion. This means almost surely the introduction of large quantities of supplementary materials, with far too much content to be committed to memory. It means a reversal in the usual attitude on reading habits whereby students will be expected to read larger quantities of materials, to read them more rapidly, and to read them for purposes of getting general ideas or of locating relevant information rather than to read small quantities of material, slowly and laboriously, a few pages each day, for purposes of committing the material to memory. It may mean in the end the abandonment of textbooks and the substitution of numerous, more substantive, more informative, and more exciting books and other materials.

If the quality of decision making is to be the primary concern of social studies instruction, we must take steps to up-grade the quality of intellectual activity in the social studies classroom. Research is demonstrating the disquieting prevalence in many social studies classrooms of what is generously labeled shoddy thinking procedures. In fact, social studies classrooms seem to exhibit a quality of logic far below that exhibited in classrooms in which science, mathematics, or even English is being taught. Admitting the greater difficulty of our content, this is still something about which we cannot be complacent. Among the common errors in logic easily observed in social studies instruction is the acceptance of an assertion as if it were a fact, the confusing of fact with opinion, the validation of the truth of something on authority, the acceptance of a merely plausible explanation for a sufficient explanation, the failure to agree on the meaning of key words (frequently value laden) before engaging in an argument in which the meaning of the word is essential as, for instance, to argue over whether the first Roosevelt was a good or a strong President without first agreeing on a common meaning for "good" and for "strong," and the confusing of questions which must be referred to facts for an answer and those which defer to values for an answer. The persistent practice in our classrooms of errors in logic of the kind mentioned can lead only to intellectual confusion and irresponsibility. If we are really concerned with effective citizenship, we must not only provide the opportunity for decision making but we must see to it that decisions are made in keeping with well known rules of science and logic and that students get practice in making such decisions.

Lastly, if responsible decision making is the end of social studies instruction, we must recognize values formation as a central concern of social studies instruction. Real life decisions are ultimately value decisions. To leave a student unaware of the value assumptions in his decision or to leave him untrained in dealing with value questions is literally to lead an innocent lamb to the slaughter. Such a student could, and he frequently does, return to our fold and say, "But you didn't tell me it was this way." Or he may quickly sink into cynicism or misbelief. The question of what values he should hold probably cannot be settled in the classroom, but values can be dealt with intelligently in the classroom. The nature of the values which people hold can be made explicit, the issues over values can be clarified, and the ends to which holding to a particular value will lead can be established factually to some extent. For instance, it is possible to predict with some accuracy the factual results of valuing segregation over integration in the United States with respect to such matters as economic productivity of the American people, the respect with which America is held abroad, the effect on the efficiency of our educational system, the genetic mixing of the races, etc. Thus, it becomes possible to engage in some appraisal of the value in terms of other values held, as, for instance, world peace, Christian brotherhood, economic security and well being, national unity, the right to choose one's own friends, etc. We can compare and appraise value, to some extent, in an extended hierarchy of values from lower value, such as a preference for having one's hair cut in a segregated barber shop, to higher values, such as the belief that all men should be treated with equal respect.

To duck the question of values is to cut the heart out of decision making. The basic social problem of America today is a problem of value. In simple terms the problem may be stated as to whether we value more the survival of a free America which will require sacrifice for education, for materials of defense, etc., or whether we value more our right as individuals to spend our resources on extra fins for our cars and for all the other gadgets of conspicuous consumptions. It is not impossible to predict the outcome of hewing to either choice. It is not at all certain that our students are being prepared to make the right decision and to make it in time.

My thesis has been a very simple one. It is that quality decision making should be the central concern of social studies instructions. I could cite many renowned people as having essentially supported the position I have here tried to state. Among the ancients these would include Socrates, Plato, and Thucydides, the father of objective history. These would include the great modern philosopher Alfred North Whitehead and such modern critics as the economist

Peter Drucker and President Robert F. Goheen of Princeton. But to quote these would continue the discussion overlong, as I suspect I may have done already. So may I quote instead a simple statement from the noted modern scientist Hans Selye, who has said that "facts from which no conclusions can be drawn are hardly worth knowing."

Thinking and Data

John Dewey

There must be *data* at command to supply the considerations required in dealing with the specific difficulty which has presented itself. Teachers following a "developing" method sometimes tell children to think things out for themselves as if they could spin them out of their own heads. The material of thinking is not thoughts, but actions, facts, events, and the relations of things. In other words, to think effectively one must have had, or now have, experiences which will furnish him resources for coping with the difficulty at hand. A difficulty is an indispensable stimulus to thinking, but not all difficulties call out thinking. Sometimes they overwhelm and submerge and discourage. The perplexing situation must be sufficiently like situations which have already been dealt with so that pupils will have some control of the meanings of handling it. A large part of the art of instruction lies in making the difficulty of new problems large enough to challenge thought, and small enough so that, in addition to the confusion naturally attending the novel elements, there shall be luminous familiar spots from which helpful suggestions may spring.

In one sense, it is a matter of indifference by what psychological means the subject matter for reflection is provided. Memory, observation, reading, communication, are all avenues for supplying data. The relative proportion to be obtained from each is a matter of the specific features of the particular problem in hand. It is foolish to insist upon observation of objects presented to the senses if the student is so familiar with the objects that he could just as well recall the facts independently. It is possible to induce undue and crippling dependence upon sense-presentations. No one can carry around with him a museum of all the things whose properties will assist the conduct of thought. A well-trained mind is one that has a maximum of resources behind it, so to speak, and that is accustomed to go over its past experiences to see what they yield. On the other hand, a quality or relation of even a familiar object may previously have been passed over, and be just the fact that is helpful in dealing with the question. In this case direct observation is called for. The same principle applies to the use to be made of observation on one hand and of reading and "telling" on the other. Direct observation is naturally more vivid and vital. But it has its limitations; and in any case it is a necessary part of education that one should acquire the ability to supplement the narrowness of his immediately personal experiences by utilizing the experiences of others. Excessive reliance upon others for data (whether got from reading or listening) is to be depreciated. Most objectionable of all is the probability that others, the book or the teacher, will supply solutions ready-made, instead of giving material that the student has to adapt and apply to the question in hand for himself.

There is no inconsistency in saying that in schools there is usually both too much and too little information supplied by others. The accumulation and acquisition of information for purposes of reproduction in recitation and examination is made too much of. "Knowledge," in the sense of information, means the working capital, the indispensable resources, of further inquiry; of finding out, or learning, more things. Frequently it is treated as an end itself, and then the goal becomes to heap it up and display it when called for. This static, cold-storage ideal of knowledge is inimical to educative development. It not only lets occasions for thinking go unused, but it swamps thinking. No one could construct a house on ground cluttered with miscellaneous junk. Pupils who have stored their "minds" with all kinds of material which they have never put to intellectual uses are sure to be hampered when they try to think. They have no practice in selecting what is appropriate, and no criterion to go by; everything is on the same dead static level. On the other hand, it is quite open to question whether, if information actually functioned in experience through use in application to the student's own purposes, there would not be need of more varied resources in books, pictures, and talks than are usually at command.

What Is Thinking?

John Dewey

I. Different Meanings of Thought

The Best Way of Thinking

No one can tell another person in any definite way how he *should* think, any more than how he ought to breathe or to have his blood circulate. But the various ways in which men *do* think can be told and can be described in their general features. Some of these ways are better than others; the reasons why they are better can be set forth. The person who understands what the better ways of thinking are and why they are better can, if he will, change his own personal ways until they become more effective; until, that is to say, they do better the work that thinking can do and that other mental operations cannot do so well. The better way of thinking that is to be considered in this book is called reflective thinking: the kind of thinking that consists in turning a subject

From John Dewey, *How We Think*, © 1933, pages 3–16, 106–118. Reprinted by permission of D. C. Heath and Company.

over in the mind and giving it serious and consecutive consideration. Before we take up this main theme, we shall, however, first take note briefly of some other mental processes to which the name *thought* is sometimes given.

The 'Stream of Consciousness'

All the time we are awake and sometimes when we are asleep, something is, as we say, going through our heads. When we are asleep we call that kind of sequence 'dreaming.' We also have daydreams, reveries, castles built in the air, and mental streams that are even more idle and chaotic. To this uncontrolled coursing of ideas through our heads the name of 'thinking' is sometimes given. It is automatic and unregulated. Many a child has attempted to see whether he could not 'stop thinking' — that is, stop this procession of mental states through his mind — and in vain. More of our waking life than most of us would care to admit is whiled away in this inconsequential trifling with mental pictures, random recollections, pleasant but unfounded hopes, flitting, half-developed impressions. Hence it is that he who offers 'a penny for your thoughts' does not expect to drive any great bargain if his offer is taken; he will only find out what happens to be 'going through the mind' and what 'goes' in this fashion rarely leaves much that is worth while behind.

Reflective Thought Is a Chain

In this sense, silly folk and dullards *think*. The story is told of a man in slight repute for intelligence, who, desiring to be chosen selectman in his New England town, addressed a knot of neighbors in this wise: "I hear you don't believe I know enough to hold office. I wish you to understand that I am thinking about something or other most of the time." Now, reflective thought is like this random coursing of things through the mind in that it consists of a succession of things thought of, but it is unlike in that the mere chance occurrence of any chance 'something or other' in an irregular sequence does not suffice. Reflection involves not simply a sequence of ideas, but a *con*-sequence — a consecutive ordering in such a way that each determines the next as its proper outcome, while each outcome in turn leans back on, or refers to, its predecessors. The successive portions of a reflective thought grow out of one another and support one another; they do not come and go in a medley. Each phase is a step from something to something — technically speaking, it is a *term* of thought. Each term leaves a deposit that is utilized in the next term. The stream or flow becomes a train or chain. There are in any reflective thought definite units that are linked together so that there is a sustained movement to a common end.

Thinking Usually Restricted to Things
Not Directly Perceived

The second meaning of thinking limits it to things not sensed or directly perceived, to things *not* seen, heard, touched, smelt, or tasted. We ask the man telling a story if he saw a certain incident happen, and his reply may be, "No, I only thought of it." A note of invention, as distinct from faithful record of observation, is present. Most important in this class are successions of imaginative incidents and episodes that have a certain coherence, hang together on a continuous thread, and thus lie between kaleidoscopic flights of fancy and considerations deliberately employed to establish a conclusion. The imaginative stories poured forth by children possess all degrees of internal congruity; some are disjointed, some are articulated. When connected, they simulate reflective thought; indeed, they usually occur in minds of logical capacity. These imaginative enterprises often precede thinking of the close-knit type and prepare the way for it. In this sense, a thought or idea is a mental picture of something not actually present, and thinking is the succession of such pictures.

Reflective Thinking Aims at a Conclusion

In contrast, reflective thinking has a purpose beyond the entertainment afforded by the train of agreeable mental inventions and pictures. The train must lead somewhere; it must tend to a conclusion that can be substantiated outside the course of the images. A story of a giant may satisfy merely because of the story itself; a reflective conclusion that a giant lived at a certain date and place on the earth would have to have some justification outside of the chain of ideas in order to be a valid or sound conclusion. This contrasting element is probably best conveyed in the ordinary saying: "Think it *out*." The phrase suggests an entanglement to be straightened out, something obscure to be cleared up through the application of thought. There is a goal to be reached, and this end sets a task that controls the sequence of ideas.

Thinking as Practically Synonymous with Believing

A third meaning of thought is practically synonymous with *belief*. "I think it is going to be colder tomorrow," or "I think Hungary is larger than Jugo-Slavia" is equivalent to "I believe so-and-so." When we say, "Men used to think the world was flat," we obviously refer to a belief that was held by our ancestors. This meaning of thought is narrower than those previously mentioned. A belief refers to something beyond itself by which its value is tested; it makes an assertion about some matter of fact or some principle or law. It means that a specified state of fact or law is accepted or rejected, that it is something proper to be affirmed or at least acquiesced in. It is hardly necessary to lay stress upon the importance of belief. It covers all the matters of which we have no sure knowledge and yet which we are sufficiently confident of to act upon and also the matters that we now accept as certainly true, as knowledge, but which nevertheless may be questioned in the future — just as much that passed as knowledge in the past has now passed into the limbo of mere opinion or of error.

There is nothing in the mere fact of thought as identical with belief that reveals whether the belief is well founded or not. Two different men say, "I believe the world is spherical." One man, if challenged, could produce little or no evidence for thinking as he does. It is an idea that he has picked up from others and that he accepts because the idea is generally current, not because he has examined into the matter and not because his own mind has taken any active part in reaching and framing the belief.

Such 'thoughts' grow up unconsciously. They are picked up — we know not how. From obscure sources and by unnoticed channels they insinuate themselves into the mind and become unconsciously a part of our mental furniture. Tradition, instruction, imitation — all of which depend upon authority in some form, or appeal to our own advantage, or fall in with a strong passion — are responsible for them. Such thoughts are prejudices; that is, prejudgments, not conclusions reached as the result of personal mental activity, such as observing, collecting, and examining evidence. Even when they happen to be correct, their correctness is a matter of accident as far as the person who entertains them is concerned.

Reflective Thinking Impels to Inquiry

Thus we are brought again, by way of contrast, to the particular kind of thinking that we are to study in this volume, *reflective thinking*. Thought, in the two first senses mentioned, may be harmful to the mind because it distracts attention from the real world, and because it may be a waste of time. On the other hand, if indulged in judiciously these thoughts may afford genuine enjoyment and also be a source of needed recreation. But in either case they can make no claim to truth; they cannot hold themselves up as something that the mind should accept, assert, and be willing to act upon. They may involve a kind of emotional commitment, but not intellectual and practical commitment. Beliefs, on the other hand, do involve precisely this commitment and consequently sooner or later they demand our investigation to find out upon what grounds they rest. To think of a cloud as a whale or a camel — in the sense of to 'fancy' — does not commit one to the conclusion that the person having the idea would ride the camel or extract oil from the whale. But when Columbus 'thought' the world was round, in the sense of 'believed it to be so,' he and his followers were thereby committed to a series of other beliefs and actions: to beliefs about routes to India, about what would happen if ships traveled far westward on the Atlantic, etc., precisely as thinking that the world was flat had committed those who held it to belief in the impossibility of circumnavigation, and in the limitation of the earth to regions in the small civilized part of it Europeans were already acquainted with, etc.

The earlier thought, belief in the flatness of the earth, had some foundation in evidence; it rested upon what men could see easily within the limits of their vision. But this evidence was not further looked into; it was not checked by considering other evidence; there was no search for new evidence. Ultimately the belief rested on laziness, inertia, custom, absence of courage and energy in investigation. The later belief rests upon careful and extensive study, upon purposeful widening of the area of observation, upon reasoning out the conclusions of alternative conceptions to see what would follow in case one or the other were adopted for belief. As distinct from the first kind of thinking there was an orderly chain of ideas; as distinct from the second, there was a controlling purpose and end; as distinct from the third, there was personal examination, scrutiny, inquiry.

Because Columbus did not accept unhesitatingly the current traditional theory, because he doubted and inquired, he arrived at his thought. Skeptical of what, from long habit, seemed most certain, and credulous of what seemed impossible, he went on thinking until he could produce evidence for both his confidence and his disbelief. Even if his conclusion had finally turned out wrong, it would have been a different sort of belief from those it antagonized, because it was reached by a different method. *Active, persistent, and careful consideration of any belief or supposed form of knowledge in the light of the grounds that support it and the further conclusions to which it tends* constitutes reflective thought. Any one of the first three kinds of thought may elicit this type; but once begun, it includes a conscious and voluntary effort to establish belief upon a firm basis of evidence and rationality.

II. The Central Factor in Thinking

The Suggestion of Something Not Observed

There are, however, no sharp lines of demarcation between the various operations just outlined. The problem of attaining correct habits of reflection would be much easier than it is, did not the different modes of thinking blend insensibly into one another. So far, we have considered rather extreme instances of each kind in order to get the field clearly before us. Let us now reverse this operation; let us consider a rudimentary case of thinking, lying between careful examination of evidence and a mere irresponsible stream of fancies. A man is walking on a warm day. The sky was clear the last time he observed it; but presently he notes, while occupied primarily with other things, that the air is cooler. It occurs to him that it is probably going to rain; looking up, he sees a dark cloud between him and the sun, and he then quickens his steps. What, if anything, in such a situation can be called thought? Neither the act of walking nor the noting of the cold is a thought. Walking is one direction of activity; looking and noting are other modes of activity. The likelihood that it will rain is, however, something *suggested*. The pedestrian *feels* the cold; first he *thinks* of clouds, then he looks and perceives them, and then he thinks of something he does not see: a storm. This *suggested possibility* is the idea, the thought. If it is believed in as a genuine possibility which may occur, it is the kind of thought which falls within the scope of knowledge and which requires reflective consideration.

Up to a certain point there is the same sort of situation as when one who looks up at a cloud is reminded of a human figure and face. Thinking in both of these cases (the cases of belief and of fancy) involves noting or perceiving a fact, followed by something else that is not observed but that is brought to mind, suggested by the thing seen. One thing reminds us, as we say, of the other. Side by side, however, with this factor of agreement in the two cases of suggestion is a factor of marked disagreement. We do not *believe* in the face suggested by the cloud; we do not consider at all the probability of its being a fact. There is no *reflective* thought. The danger of rain, on the contrary, presents itself to us as a genuine possibility — a fact of the same nature as the observed coolness. Put differently, we do not regard the cloud as meaning or indicating a fact, but merely as suggesting it, while we do consider that the coolness may *mean* rain. In the first case, on seeing an object, we just happen, as we say, to think of something else; in the second, we consider the *possibility and nature of the connection between the object seen and the object suggested.* The seen thing is regarded as in some way *the ground or basis of belief* in the suggested thing; it possesses the quality of *evidence.*

The Function of Signifying

This function whereby one thing signifies or indicates another, thus leading us to consider how far the one may be regarded as warrant for belief in the other, is, then, the central factor in all reflective or distinctively intellectual thinking. By calling up various situations to which such terms as *signifies* and *indicates* apply, the student will realize for himself the actual facts denoted. Synonyms for these terms are: points to, tells of, betokens, prognosticates, represents, stands for, implies.[1] We also say one thing portends another, is ominous of another, or a symptom of it, or a key to it, or (if the connection is quite obscure) that it gives a hint, clue, or intimation. Reflection is not identical with the mere fact that one thing indicates, means, another thing. It commences when we begin to inquire into the reliability, the worth, of any particular indication; when we try to test its value and see what guarantee there is that the existing data *really* point to the idea that is suggested in such a way as to *justify* acceptance of the latter.

Reflection Implies Belief on Evidence

Reflection thus implies that something is believed in (or disbelieved in), not on its own direct account, but through something else which stands as witness, evidence, proof, voucher, warrant; that is, as *ground of belief.* At one time, rain is actually felt or directly experienced; at another time, we *infer* that it has rained from the appearance of the grass and trees, or that it is going to rain because of the condition of the air or the state of the barometer. At one time, we see a man (or suppose we do) without any intermediary fact; at another time, we are not quite sure what we see, and hunt for accompanying facts that will serve as signs, indications, tokens of what we are to believe.

Thinking, for the purposes of this inquiry, is accordingly defined as *that operation in which present facts suggest other facts (or truths) in such a way as to induce belief in what is suggested on the ground of real relation in the things themselves,* a relation between what suggests and what is suggested. A cloud *suggests* a weasel or a whale; it does not *mean* the latter, because there is no tie, or bond, in the things themselves between what is seen and what is suggested. Ashes not merely suggest a previous fire, but they signify there has been a fire, because ashes are produced by combustion and, if they are genuine ashes, only by combustion. It is an objective connection, the link in actual things, that makes one thing the ground, warrant, evidence, for believing in something else.

[1] *Implies* is more often used when a principal or general truth brings about belief in some other truth; the other phrases are more frequently used to denote the cases in which a fact or event leads us to believe in some other fact or in a law.

III. Phases of Reflective Thinking

We may carry our account further by noting that *reflective* thinking, in distinction from other operations to which we apply the name of thought, involves (1) a state of doubt, hesitation, perplexity, mental difficulty, in which thinking originates, and (2) an act of searching, hunting, inquiring, to find material that will resolve the doubt, settle and dispose of the perplexity.

The Importance of Uncertainty and of Inquiry

In our illustration, the shock of coolness generated confusion and suspended belief, at least momentarily. Because it was unexpected, it was a shock or an interruption needing to be accounted for, identified, or placed. To say that the abrupt occurrence of the change of temperature constitutes a problem may sound forced and artificial; but if we are willing to extend the meaning of the word *problem* to whatever — no matter how slight and commonplace in character — perplexes and challenges the mind so that it makes belief at all uncertain, there is a genuine problem, or question, involved in an experience of sudden change.

The turning of the head, the lifting of the eyes, the scanning of the heavens, are activities adapted to bring to recognition facts that will answer the question presented by the sudden coolness. The facts as they first presented themselves were perplexing; they suggested, however, clouds. The act of looking was an act to discover whether this suggested explanation held good. It may again seem forced to speak of this looking, almost automatic, as an act of research, or inquiry. But once more, if we are willing to generalize our conceptions of our mental operations to include the trivial and ordinary as well as the technical and recondite, there is no good reason for refusing to give this title to the act of looking. For the result of the act is to bring facts before the mind that enable a person to reach a conclusion on the basis of evidence. In so far, then, as the act of looking was deliberate, was performed with the intention of getting an external basis on which to rest a belief, it exemplifies in an elementary way the operation of hunting, searching, inquiring, involved in any reflective operation.

Another instance, commonplace also, yet not quite so trivial, may enforce this lesson. A man traveling in an unfamiliar region comes to a branching of the road. Having no sure knowledge to fall back upon, he is brought to a standstill of hesitation and suspense. Which road is right? And how shall his perplexity be resolved? There are but two alternatives: he must either blindly and arbitrarily take his course, trusting to luck for the outcome, or he must discover grounds for the conclusion that a given road is right. Any attempt to decide the matter by thinking will involve inquiring into other facts, whether brought to mind by memory, or by further observation, or by both. The perplexed wayfarer must carefully scrutinize what is before him and he must cudgel his memory. He looks for evidence that will support belief in favor of either of the roads — for evidence that will weight down one suggestion. He may climb a tree; he may go first in this direction, then in that, looking, in either case, for signs, clues, indications. He wants something in the nature of a signboard or a map, and *his reflection is aimed at the discovery of facts that will serve this purpose.*

The foregoing illustration may be generalized. Thinking begins in what may fairly enough be called a *forked-road* situation, a situation that is ambiguous, that presents a dilemma, that proposes alternatives. As long as our activity glides smoothly along from one thing to another, or as long as we permit our imagination to entertain fancies at pleasure, there is no call for reflection. Difficulty or obstruction in the way of reaching a belief brings us, however, to a pause. In the suspense of uncertainty, we metaphorically climb a tree; we try to find some standpoint from which we may survey additional facts and, getting a more commanding view of the situation, decide how the facts stand related to one another.

The Regulation of Thinking by Its Purpose

Demand for the solution of a perplexity is the steadying and guiding factor in the entire process of reflection. Where there is no question of a problem to be solved or a difficulty to be surmounted, the course of suggestions flows on at random; we have the first type of thought described. If the stream of suggestions is controlled simply by their emotional congruity, their fitting agreeably into a single picture or story, we have the second type. But a question to be answered, an ambiguity to be resolved, sets up an end and holds the current of ideas to a definite channel. Every suggested conclusion is tested by its reference to this regulating end, by its pertinence to the problem in hand. This need of straightening out a perplexity also controls the kind of inquiry undertaken. A traveler whose end is the most beautiful path will look for other signs and will test suggestions on another basis than if he wishes to discover the way to a given city. *The nature of the problem fixes the end of thought, and the end controls the process of thinking.*

IV. Summary

We may recapitulate by saying that the origin of thinking is some perplexity, confusion, or doubt. Thinking is not a case of spontaneous combustion; it does not occur just on 'general principles.' There is something that occasions and evokes it. General appeals to a child (or to a grown-up) to think, irrespective of the existence in his own experience of some difficulty that troubles him and disturbs his equilibrium, are as futile as advice to lift himself by his boot-straps.

Given a difficulty, the next step is suggestion of some way out — the formation of some tentative plan or project, the entertaining of some theory that will account for the peculiarities in question, the consideration of some solution for the problem. The data at hand cannot supply the solution; they can only suggest it. What, then, are the sources of the suggestion? Clearly, past experience and a fund of relevant knowledge at one's command. If the person has had some acquaintance with similar situations, if he has dealt with material of the same sort before, suggestions more or less apt and helpful will arise. But unless there has been some analogous experience, confusion remains mere confusion. Even when a child (or a grown-up) has a problem, it is wholly futile to urge him to think when he has no prior experiences that involve some of the same conditions.

There may, however, be a state of perplexity and also previous experience out of which suggestions emerge, and yet thinking need not be reflective. For the person may not be sufficiently *critical* about the ideas that occur to him. He may jump at a conclusion without weighing the grounds on which its rests; he may forego or unduly shorten the act of hunting, inquiring; he may take the first 'answer,' or solution, that comes to him because of mental sloth, torpor, impatience to get something settled. One can think reflectively only when one is willing to endure suspense and to undergo the trouble of searching. To many persons both suspense of judgment and intellectual search are disagreeable; they want to get them ended as soon as possible. They cultivate an over-positive and dogmatic habit of mind, or feel perhaps that a condition of doubt will be regarded as evidence of mental inferiority. It is at the point where examination and test enter into investigation that the difference between reflective thought and bad thinking comes in. To be genuinely thoughtful, we must be willing to sustain and protract that state of doubt which is the stimulus to thorough inquiry, so as not to accept an idea or make positive assertion of a belief until justifying reasons have been found.

· ·

The Essential Functions of Reflective Activity

We now have before us the material for the analysis of a complete act of reflective activity. In the preceding chapter we saw that the two limits of every unit of thinking are a perplexed, troubled, or confused situation at the beginning and a cleared-up, unified, resolved situation at the close. The first of these situations may be called *pre*-reflective. It sets the problem to be solved; out of it grows the question that reflection has to answer. In the final situation the doubt has been dispelled; the situation is *post*-reflective; there results a direct experience of mastery, satisfaction, enjoyment. Here, then, are the limits within which reflection falls.

Five Phases, or Aspects, of Reflective Thought

In between, as states of thinking, are (1) *suggestions*, in which the mind leaps forward to a possible solution; (2) an intellectualization of the difficulty or perplexity that has been *felt* (directly experienced) into a *problem* to be solved, a question for which the answer must be sought; (3) the use of one suggestion after another as a leading idea, or *hypothesis*, to initiate and guide observation and other operations in collection of factual material; (4) the mental elaboration of the idea or supposition as an idea or supposition (*reasoning*, in the sense in which reasoning is a part, not the whole of inference); and (5) testing the hypothesis by overt or imaginative action.

We shall now take up the five phases, or functions, one by one.

The First Phase, Suggestion

The most 'natural' thing for anyone to do is to go ahead; that is to say, to *act* overtly. The disturbed and perplexed situation arrests such direct activity temporarily. The tendency to continue *acting* nevertheless persists. It is diverted and takes the form of an idea or a suggestion. The *idea* of what to do when we find ourselves 'in a hole' is a substitute for direct action. It is a vicarious, anticipatory way of acting, a kind of dramatic rehearsal. Were there only one suggestion popping up, we should undoubtedly adopt it at once. But where there are two or more, they collide with one another, maintain the state of suspense, and produce further inquiry. The first suggestion in the instance recently cited was to jump the ditch, but the perception of conditions inhibited that suggestion and led to the occurrence of other ideas.

Some inhibition of *direct* action is necessary to the condition of hesitation and delay that is essential to thinking. Thought is, as it were, conduct turned in upon itself and examining its purpose and its conditions, its resources, aids, and difficulties and obstacles.

The Second Phase, Intellectualization

We have already noted that it is artificial, so far as thinking is concerned, to start with a ready-made problem, a problem made out of whole cloth or arising out of a vacuum. In reality such a 'problem' is simply an assigned *task*. There is not at first a situation *and* a problem, much less just a problem and no situation. There is a troubled, perplexed, trying situation, where the difficulty is, as it were, spread throughout the entire situation, infecting it as a whole. If we knew just what the difficulty was and where it lay, the job of reflection would be much easier than it is. As the saying truly goes, a question well put is half answered. In fact, we know what the problem *exactly* is simultaneously with finding a way out and getting it resolved. Problem and solution stand out *completely* at the same time. Up to that point, our grasp of the problem has been more or less vague and tentative.

A blocked suggestion leads us to reinspect the conditions that confront us. Then our uneasiness, the shock of disturbed activity, gets stated in some degree on the basis of observed conditions, of objects. The width of the ditch, the slipperiness of the banks, not the mere presence of a ditch, is the trouble. The difficulty is getting located and defined; it is becoming a true problem, something intellectual, not just an annoyance at being held up in what we are doing. The person who is suddenly blocked and troubled in what he is doing by the thought of an engagement to keep at a time that is near and a place that is distant has the suggestion of getting there at once. But in order to carry this suggestion into effect, he has to find means of transportation. In order to find them he has to note his present position and its distance from the station, the present time, and the interval at his disposal. Thus the perplexity is more precisely located: just so much ground to cover, so much time to do it in.

The word 'problem' often seems too elaborate and dignified to denote what happens in minor cases of reflection. But in every case where reflective activity ensues, there is a process of *intellectualizing* what at first is merely an *emotional* quality of the whole situation. This conversion is effected by noting more definitely the conditions that constitute the trouble and cause the stoppage of action.

The Third Phase, the Guiding Idea, Hypothesis

The first suggestion occurs spontaneously; it comes to mind automatically; it *springs* up; it "pops," as we have said, "into the mind"; it flashes upon us. There is no direct control of its occurrence; the idea just comes or it does not come; that is all that can be said. There is nothing *intellectual* about its occurrence. The intellectual element consists in *what we do with it*, how we use it, *after* its sudden occurrence as an idea. A controlled use of it is made possible by the state of affairs just described. In the degree in which we define the difficulty (which is effected by stating it in terms of objects), we get a better idea of the kind of solution that is needed. The facts or data set the problem before us, and insight into the problem corrects, modifies, expands the suggestion that originally occurred. In this fashion the suggestion becomes a definite supposition or, stated more technically, a *hypothesis*.

Take the case of a physician examining a patient or a mechanic inspecting a piece of complicated machinery that does not behave properly. There is something wrong, so much is sure. But how to remedy it cannot be told until it is known *what* is wrong. An untrained person is likely to make a wild guess — the suggestion — and then proceed to act upon it in a random way, hoping that by good luck the right thing will be hit upon. So some medicine that appears to have worked before or that a neighbor has recommended is tried. Or the person fusses, monkeys, with the machine, poking here and hammering there on the chance of making the right move. The trained person proceeds in a very different fashion. He *observes* with unusual care, using the methods, the techniques, that the experience of physicians and expert mechanics in general, those familiar with the structure of the organism or the machine, have shown to be helpful in detecting trouble.

The idea of the solution is thus controlled by the diagnosis that has been made. But if the case is at all complicated, the physician or mechanic does not foreclose further thought by assuming that the suggested method of remedy is certainly right. He proceeds to act upon it tentatively rather than decisively. That is, he treats it as a guiding idea, a working hypothesis, and is led by it to make more observations, to collect more facts, so as to see if the *new* material is what the hypothesis calls for. He reasons that *if* the disease is typhoid, *then* certain phenomena will be found; and he looks particularly to see if *just* these conditions are present. Thus both the first and second operations are brought under control; the sense of the problem becomes more adequate and refined and the suggestion ceases to be a *mere* possibility, becoming a *tested* and, if possible, a *measured* probability.

The Fourth Phase, Reasoning (in the Narrower Sense)

Observations pertain to what exists in nature. They constitute the facts, and these facts both regulate the formation of suggestions, ideas, hypotheses, and test their probable value as indications of solutions. The ideas, on the other hand, occur, as we say, in our heads, in our minds. They not only occur there, but are capable, as well, of great development there. Given a fertile suggestion occurring in an experienced, well-informed mind, that mind is capable of elaborating it until there results an idea that is quite different from the one with which the mind started.

For example, the idea of heat [discussed in an] earlier chapter was linked up with what the person already knew about heat — in his case, its expansive force — and this in turn with the contractive tendency of cold, so that the idea of expansion could be used as an explanatory idea, though the mere idea of heat would not have been of any avail. Heat was quite directly suggested by the observed conditions; water was felt to be hot. But only a mind with some prior information about heat would have reasoned that heat meant expansion, and then used the idea of expansion as a working hypothesis. In more complex cases, there are long trains of reasoning in which one idea leads up to another idea known by previous test to be related to it. The stretch of links brought to light by reasoning depends, of course, upon the store of knowledge that the mind is already in possession of. And this depends not only upon the prior experience and special education of the individual who is carrying on the inquiry, but also upon the state of culture and science of the age and place. Reasoning helps extend knowledge, while at the same time it depends upon what is already known and upon the facilities that exist for communicating knowledge and making it a public, open resource.

A physician to-day can develop, by reasoning from his knowledge, the implications of the disease that symptoms suggest to him as probable in a way that would have been impossible even a generation ago; just as, on the other hand, he can carry his observation of symptoms much farther because of improvement in clinical instruments and the technique of their use.

Reasoning has the same effect upon a suggested solution that more intimate and extensive observation has upon the original trouble. Acceptance of a suggestion in its first form is prevented by looking into it more thoroughly. Conjectures that seem plausible at first sight are often found unfit or even absurd when their full consequences are traced out. Even when reasoning out the bearings of a supposition does not lead to its rejection, it develops the idea into a form in which it is more apposite to the problem. Only when, for example, the conjecture that a pole was an index pole had been thought out in its implications could its particular applicability to the case in hand be judged. Suggestions at first seemingly remote and wild are frequently so transformed by being elaborated into what follows from them as to become apt and fruitful. The development of an idea through reasoning helps supply intervening or intermediate terms which link together into a consistent whole elements that at first seemingly conflict with each other, some leading the mind to one inference and others to an opposed one.

Mathematics as Typical Reasoning. Mathematics affords the typical example of how far can be carried the operation of relating ideas to one another, without having to depend upon the observations of the senses. In geometry we start with a few simple conceptions, line, angle, parallel, surfaces formed by lines meeting, etc., and a few principles defining equalities. Knowing something about the equality of angles made by parallel lines when they intersect a straight line, and knowing, by definition, that a perpendicular to a straight line forms two right angles, by means of a combination of these ideas we readily determine that the sum of the interior angles of a triangle is equal to two right angles. By continuing to trace the implications of theorems already demonstrated, the whole subject of plane figures is finally elaborated. The manipulation of algebraic symbols so as to establish a series of equations and other mathematical functions affords an even more striking example of what can be accomplished by developing the relation of ideas to one another.

When the hypothesis indicated by a series of scientific observations and experiments can be stated in mathematical form, that idea can be transformed to almost any extent, until it assumes a form in which a problem can be dealt with most expeditiously and effectively. Much of the accomplishment of physical science depends upon an intervening mathematical elaboration of ideas. It is not the mere presence of measurements in quantitative form that yields scientific knowledge, but that particular kind of mathematical statement which can be developed by reasoning into other and more fruitful forms — a consideration which is fatal to the claim to scientific standing of many educational measurements merely because they have a quantitative form.

The Fifth Phase, Testing the Hypothesis by Action

The concluding phase is some kind of testing by overt action to give *experimental corroboration,* or *verification,* of the conjectural idea. Reasoning shows that *if* the *idea* be adopted, certain consequences follow. So far the conclusion is hypothetical or conditional. If when we look we find present all the conditions demanded by the theory, and if we find the characteristic traits called for by rival alternatives to be lacking, the tendency to believe, to accept, is almost irresistible. Sometimes direct observation furnishes corroboration, as in the case of the pole on the boat. In other cases, . . . experiment is required; that is, *conditions are deliberately arranged in accord with the requirements of an idea or hypothesis to see whether the results theoretically indicated by the idea actually occur.* If it is found that the experimental results agree with the theoretical, or rationally deduced results, and if there is reason to believe that *only* the conditions in question would yield such results, the confirmation is so strong as to induce a conclusion — at least until contrary facts shall indicate the advisability of its revision.

Of course, verification does not always follow. Sometimes consequences show failure to confirm instead of corroboration. The idea in question is refuted by the court of final appeal. But a great advantage of possession of the habit of reflective activity is that failure is not *mere* failure. It is instructive. The person who really thinks learns quite as much from his failures as from his successes. For a failure indicates to the person whose thinking has been involved in it, and who has not come to it by mere blind chance, what further observations should be made. It suggests to him what modifications should be introduced in the hypothesis upon which he has been operating. It either brings to light a new problem or helps to define and clarify the problem on which he has been engaged. Nothing shows the trained thinker better than the use he makes of his errors and mistakes. What merely annoys and discourages a person not while he cannot call them back and must stand their consequences, he gives alert attention to what they teach him about his conduct as well as to the non-intellectual consequences. He makes a problem out of consequences of conduct, looking into the causes from which they probably resulted, especially the causes that lie in his own habits and desires.

In conclusion, we point out that the five phases of reflection that have been described represent only in outline the indispensable traits of reflective thinking. In practice, two of them may telescope, some of them may be passed over hurriedly, and the burden of reaching a conclusion may fall mainly on a single phase, which will then require a seemingly disproportionate development. No set rules can be laid down on such matters. The way they are managed depends upon the intellectual tact and sensitiveness of the individual. When things have come out wrong, it is, however, a wise practice to review the methods by which the unwise decision was reached, and see where the misstep was made.

One Phase May Be Expanded

In complicated cases some of the five phases are so extensive that they include definite subphases within themselves. In this case it is arbitrary whether the minor functions are regarded as parts or are listed as distinct phases. There is nothing especially sacred about the number five. For example, in matters of practical deliberation where the object is to decide what to do, it may be well to undertake a scrutiny of the underlying desires and motives that are operating; that is, instead of asking what ends and means will best satisfy one's wish, one may turn back to the attitudes of which the wish is the expression. It is a matter of indifference whether this search be listed as an independent problem, having its own phases, or as an additional phase in the original problem.

Reference to the Future and to the Past

Again, it has been suggested that reflective thinking involves a look into the future, a forecast, an anticipation, or a prediction, and that this should be listed as a sixth aspect, or phase. As a matter of fact, every intellectual suggestion or idea is anticipatory of some possible future experience, while the final solution gives a definite set toward the future. It is both a record of something accomplished and an assignment of a future method of operation. It helps set up an enduring habit of procedure. When a physician, for example, has diagnosed a case, he usually makes also a *prognosis*, a forecast, of the probable future course of the disease. And not only is his treatment a verification — or the reverse — of the idea or hypothesis about the disease upon which he has proceeded, but the result also affects his treatment of future patients. In some cases, the future reference may be so important as to require special elaboration. In this case, it may be presented as an added, distinct phase. Some of the investigations of an astronomical expedition to watch an eclipse of the sun may be directly intended, for example, to get material bearing on Einstein's theory. But the theory, itself, is so important that its confirmation or refutation will give a decided turn to the future of physical science, and this consideration is likely to be uppermost in the minds of scientists.

Of equal importance is the reference to the *past* involved in reflection. Of course, suggestions are dependent in any case upon one's past experience; they do not arise out of nothing. But while sometimes we go ahead with the suggestion without stopping to go back to the original experience of which it is the fruit, at other times we go consciously over the past experience in considerable detail as part of the process of testing the value of the suggestion.

For example, it occurs to a man to invest in real estate. Then he recalls that a previous investment of this kind turned out unfortunately. He goes over the former case, comparing it bit by bit with the present, to see how far the two cases are alike or unlike. Examination of the past may be the chief and decisive factor in thought. The most valuable reference to the past is likely, however, to come at the time the conclusion is reached. We noted earlier the importance of a final survey to secure a net formulation of the exact result and of the premises upon which it logically depends. This is not only an important part of the process of *testing*, but, as was stated in the earlier discussion, is almost necessary if good habits are to be built up. Ability to *organize* knowledge consists very largely in the habit of reviewing previous facts and ideas and relating them to one another on a new basis; namely, that of the conclusion that has been reached. A certain amount of this operation is included in the testing phase that has been described. But its influence upon the attitude of students is so important that it may be well at times so to emphasize it that it becomes a definite function, or phase, on its own account.

Notes on the Nature of Science by a Biologist

George Gaylord Simpson

There used to be a widespread notion — perhaps it still persists in some quarters — that science is a "method." The method was supposed to be a technique leading to the discovery of facts on specific subjects. The facts were to be given in lecture courses; the technique was to be taught in laboratory sessions. The method was believed to be applicable to a few well-defined subjects clearly labeled "science." Now, of course, practicing scientists, and I hope most teachers, know that although scientific research does favor facts and does use methods and techniques — many different ones — science nevertheless is not a body of facts, not a method, not a technique. Most scientists have long insisted that science *is*, perhaps, or *has*, certainly, a point of view, a systematic orientation, applicable to all material aspects of our world, in everyone's daily activities as well as in the laboratory of a professional scientist.

Attempts at definitions of science have varied from T. H. Huxley's "common sense . . . the necessary mode of working of the human mind" to Norman Campbell's "study of those judgments concerning which universal agreement can be obtained." On the face of them and without such qualifications as their

From *Notes on the Nature of Science*, © 1961, 1962, by Harcourt, Brace & World, Inc. Reprinted by permission of the author.

authors did indeed provide, those definitions can lead to absurdities. Everyone knows that so-called common sense and the working of the human mind have produced an intolerable amount of nonsense, and that above the level of triviality there is hardly any scientific subject on which agreement is literally universal.

Those two inadequate definitions are nevertheless related to the two most important aspects of the scientific attitude. Science is an exploration of the material universe that is, first, orderly and, second, self-testing. This statement is also inadequate and requires some expansion.

The orderliness of science consists in seeking regularities — rationally definable relationships — among the enormously diverse phenomena of the world we live in. It is true, in a sense, that this is a "necessary mode of working of the human mind." Indeed, some such ordering of phenomena, although in extremely varying degrees, is a necessary characteristic of all living organisms. Simultaneous intensification and broadening of that tendency to systematize sensations and perceptions of phenomena have been progressive in many lines of organic evolution. The progression has culminated in man, who in this respect (and some others) is incomparably more advanced than any other species of organisms. Evolution has also built into us a relationship to our environment that obviates much soul-searching and, if I may say so, should correct some futile quibbling by philosophers. Natural selection through some two billion years has ensured that our perceptions are a workable representation of real phenomena and relationships in the world existing outside ourselves. Within certain determinable limits our sensations *have* to tell us truths about external phenomena, and our perceptual analysis and synthesis (and also our statements about them) *have* to correspond with an objective orderliness in nature. Otherwise we would not be here. That is how and why our sense organs and our brains evolved. For example, among the early arboreal primates our ancestors were necessarily those who had the most realistic perception of the law of gravity and the most appropriate reactions to it.

On the more workaday level of the teaching and the practice of science, an important point here is that isolated facts — call them "data" if you like — are meaningless. It is only their generalization and their ordering into principles that give them meaning. It did our ancestors no good merely to think, "Well, well! Ugh fell on the rocks and has quit breathing or moving." They had also somehow to conclude, in no matter how incoherent a way, "Anything that is not supported falls, and if a monkey falls far enough, he dies." In short, simply gathering data does not give meaningful information about the universe and is not science. It is, however, easiest for the teacher to teach, and apparently most congenial to many students to learn, facts, so-called, which may be only verbal labels for things observed but not understood, and to consider rote repetition of those facts as "learning science." Of course you cannot study orderly relationships among phenomena unless the pertinent phenomena have been observed, but no one who only gathers data is in a true sense a scientist. The correct approach to the study of real science is what academic jargon calls the "principles approach."

The development of an organized system of (real or supposed) relationships among phenomena is necessary but not sufficient for a definition of science; it is not confined to science. The same evolutionarily necessitated "mode of working of the human mind" has led to other human activities and bodies of thought, notably the arts, philosophy, and theology. In this respect (however incongruous in other respects), those subjects are related to science and share with science the highest level to which mental processes have yet evolved. The important distinction between science and those other systematizations is that science is self-testing and self-correcting. The testing and correcting are done by means of observations that can be repeated with essentially the same results by normal persons operating by the same methods and with the same approach. That is the sense in which "universal agreement can [in principle] be obtained," and it is not true of the arts, philosophy, theology, or any other nonscientific activities except insofar as they may in fact enter the field of science and become properly subject to its discipline.

Here the essential point of science is respect for objective fact. What is correctly observed *must* be believed. An accepted theory — that is, an inferred relationship among facts — must be sufficient to relate all those facts realistically to each other and there must not be any contradiction by a single valid observation. That, of course, demands diligent search for all pertinent facts, and pertinent facts are those that might contradict the theory. In this respect, the competent scientist does quite the opposite of the popular stereotype of setting out to prove a theory; he seeks to disprove it. If an apparent fact does not fit a hypothesis or theory, then, unless the observation is wrong, the inferred (or postulated) relationship is wrong.

The very concept of "fact" in this context demands a determinable relationship between perception and phenomenon. I have noted the *biological* reason why such relationships are usually reliable. They are not always so, but in this respect, too, science is largely self-correcting. Perception and objective phenomenon are not identical. No objects are red, but some of them have objective attributes that cause us to perceive them as red and we can determine what those attributes are. Unchecked and unaided perceptions cannot always be trusted beyond the point that our ancestors found useful for survival, but we can correct and extend them in ways also made possible by that same evolutionary development. Illusions do not resist rational checking by other means, and our senses are made more acute (for example, by micrometers or microscopes) or extended into other modalities (for example, by translation of radio waves into sound or of electrical potential into a dial reading) by instruments whose scientific significance is just this checking and extension of our perception of reality.

If science is self-correcting and in principle subject to universal agreement, why is not agreement actually universal? That is a question that a scientist must, and a student should, ask. Part of the answer is, of course, mere human weakness: emotional bias, inadequate grasp of pertinent data, failure in logical inference, discrepancy between observation and observed object, and the like. Those factors are eventually eliminated if enough different scientists work over the same problems. Sometimes theories go beyond what is testable, by means now available, at least. Such aspects of theories are, for that reason, not scientific in fact, and the disagreement is in the field of philosophy and not of science. (I am not arguing that scientists should not philosophize; on the contrary, I think it essential that they do so, but they should know when they are doing so.)

The most fundamental reason for disagreement in science is, however, the inherent impossibility of complete certainty. There are here four main factors. First, *one* fact may disprove a theory and not *all* facts can be observed; therefore an investigator cannot completely discard the possibility that a discrepant phenomenon may occur. Second, in any complex situation the data are rarely so complete that only *one* explanation (inferred relationship among the facts) can conceivably be correct. What can actually be established is only a degree of probability. In many instances, indeed, the theories themselves are inherently probabilistic in nature, and that is the third important factor in scientific uncertainty. The reasoning in these instances runs statistically from sample to universe and the inference is a variable range and not a fixed point. Many such theories relate, not to whether a postulate is true or false, but to the frequency with which it is likely to hold good. This being the case, the careful scientist does not speak of "proving" a theory but of obtaining a sufficient degree of confidence in it.

The final factor is that no scientific explanation so far achieved is in the fullest sense of the word *complete*. One may explain an endocrine reaction in terms of molecular chemistry and the molecular chemistry in terms of atomic structure and still be at a loss to explain the atomic structure. Or, in the other direction, one may go from atomic to molecular to physiological properties and still not have explained why or how the atoms came to be in this exceedingly complex, systematically organized state, nor why they should there participate in such activities as, say, bird (or human) courtship, which surely no one could have predicted from the properties of the atoms alone. Such enquiries constantly become more nearly complete in depth as science progresses, but absolute completeness eludes us and perhaps always will.

These, too, are considerations that are often uncomfortable for students and, indeed, for a good many scientists. It would be so much easier to deal with principles, hypotheses, and theories, as well as the data of science, as if they were simply true or false! But the actual nature of scientific endeavor cannot be understood unless its uncertainties and incompletenesses are taken into account.

The concept of "truth" in science is thus quite special. It implies nothing eternal and absolute but only a high degree of confidence after adequate objective self-testing and self-correction. Insofar as they are distinct from science, or are not in fact science, philosophy and theology involve neither objective tests nor corrections. Their "truths" can be regarded as absolute for the very reason that they are not to be tested or corrected, and they are accepted as absolute by different adherents even when they are flatly contradictory. The arts are still less subject to test or correction, and in them "truth" has a still different meaning to the extent that it concerns the subjective personal and not the objective universal. Scientific "truths" are realistically related to the material universe. The other "truths" are not. That is a statement of a difference and not a judgment of relative values.

As for the scope of science, it includes everything known to exist or to happen in the material universe. Since the arts, philosophy, and theology do exist in the material universe, they too are within the scope of science and can properly be studied as psychological, anthropological, and biological phenomena. In biology, they belong in the field of animal behavior. That point of view is not yet common, even among biologists, and I would not now insist on its inclusion in a general biology or general science curriculum. Nonscientists in their other, more mundane affairs, and particularly in Western civilization, have almost unconsciously come to take an increasingly scientific attitude toward the world around them. They do judge its characteristics more and more in relational terms objectively tested and less and less by a superstitious apriorism. In biology the most important post-Darwinian development is less the acceptance of evolution, tremendously important though that is, than the inclusion of *all* the phenomena of life within the field of objective science. I do insist that *that* should be in the curriculum.

A Case History in Scientific Method

B. F. Skinner

It has been said that college teaching is the only profession for which there is no professional training, and it is commonly argued that this is because our graduate schools train scholars and scientists rather than teachers. We are more concerned with the discovery of knowledge than with its dissemination. But can we justify ourselves quite so easily? It is a bold thing to say that we know how to train a man to be a scientist. Scientific thinking is the most complex and probably the most subtle of all human activities. Do we actually know how to shape up such behavior, or do we simply mean that some of the people who attend our graduate schools eventually become scientists?

Except for a laboratory course which acquaints the student with standard apparatus and standard procedures, the only explicit training in scientific method generally received by a young psychologist is a course in statistics — not the introductory course, which is often required of so many kinds of students that it is scarcely scientific at all, but an advanced course which includes "model building," "theory construction," and "experimental design." But it is a mistake to identify scientific practice with the formalized constructions of statistics and scientific method. These disciplines have their place, but it does not coincide with the place of scientific research. They offer a method of science but not, as is so often implied, *the* method. As formal disciplines they rose very late in the history of science, and most of the facts of science have been discovered without their aid. It takes a great deal of skill to fit Faraday with his

From the *American Psychologist*, 1956, *11*, pages 221–233, by permission of the American Psychological Association and the author.

wires and magnets into the picture which statistics gives us of scientific thinking. And most current scientific practice would be equally refractory, especially in the important initial stages. It is no wonder that the laboratory scientist is puzzled and often dismayed when he discovers how his behavior has been reconstructed in the formal analyses of scientific method. He is likely to protest that this is not at all a fair representation of what he does.

But his protest is not likely to be heard. For the prestige of statistics and scientific methodology is enormous. Much of it is borrowed from the high repute of mathematics and logic, but much of it derives from the flourishing state of the art itself. Some statisticians are professional people employed by scientific and commercial enterprises. Some are teachers and pure researchers who give their colleagues the same kind of service for nothing — or at most a note of acknowledgement. Many are zealous people who, with the best of intentions, are anxious to show the nonstatistical scientist how he can do his job more efficiently and assess his results more accurately. There are strong professional societies devoted to the advancement of statistics, and hundreds of technical books and journals are published annually.

Against this, the practicing scientist has very little to offer. He cannot refer the young psychologist to a book which will tell him how to find out all there is to know about a subject matter, how to have the good hunch which will lead him to devise a suitable piece of apparatus, how to develop an efficient experimental routine, how to abandon an unprofitable line of attack, how to move on most rapidly to later stages of his research. The work habits which have become second nature to him have not been formalized by anyone, and he may feel that they possibly never will be. As Richter[1] has pointed out, "Some of the most important discoveries have been made without any plan of research," and "there are researchers who do not work on a verbal plane, who cannot put into words what they are doing."

If we are interested in perpetuating the practices responsible for the present corpus of scientific knowledge, we must keep in mind that some very important parts of the scientific process do not now lend themselves to mathematical, logical, or any other formal treatment. We do not know enough about human behavior to know how the scientist does what he does. Although statisticians and methodologists may seem to tell us, or at least imply, how the mind works — how problems arise, how hypotheses are formed, deductions made, and crucial experiments designed — we as psychologists are in a position to remind them that they do not have methods appropriate to the empirical observation or the functional analysis of such data. These are aspects of human behavior, and no one knows better than we how little can at the moment be said about them.

Some day we shall be better able to express the distinction between empirical analysis and formal reconstruction, for we shall have an alternative account of the behavior of Man Thinking. Such an account will not only plausibly reconstruct what a particular scientist did in any given case, it will permit us to evaluate practices and, I believe, to teach scientific thinking. But that

[1] Richter, C. P. Free research versus design research. *Science*, 1953, 118, 91–93.

day is some little distance in the future. Meanwhile we can only fall back on examples.

Some time ago the director of Project A of the American Psychological Association asked me to describe my activities as a research psychologist. I went through a trunkful of old notes and records and, for my pains, reread some of my earlier publications. This has made me all the more aware of the contrast between the reconstructions of formalized scientific method and at least one case of actual practice. Instead of amplifying the points I have just made by resorting to a generalized account which is not available, I should like to discuss a case history. It is not one of the case histories we should most like to have, but what it lacks in importance is perhaps somewhat offset by accessibility. I therefore ask you to imagine that you are all clinical psychologists — a task which becomes easier and easier as the years go by — while I sit across the desk from you or stretch out upon this comfortable leather couch.

The first thing I can remember happened when I was only twenty-two years old. Shortly after I had graduated from college Bertrand Russell published a series of articles in the old *Dial* magazine on the epistemology of John B. Watson's Behaviorism. I had had no psychology as an undergraduate but I had had a lot of biology, and two of the books which my biology professor had put into my hands were Loeb's *Physiology of the Brain* and the newly published Oxford edition of Pavlov's *Conditioned Reflexes*. And now here was Russell extrapolating the principles of an objective formulation of behavior to the problem of knowledge! Many years later when I told Lord Russell that his articles were responsible for my interest in behavior, he could only exclaim, "Good Heavens! I had always supposed that those articles had demolished Behaviorism!" But at any rate he had taken Watson seriously, and so did I.

When I arrived at Harvard for graduate study the air was not exactly full of behavior, but Walter Hunter was coming in once a week from Clark University to give a seminar, and Fred Keller, also a graduate student, was an expert in both the technical details and the sophistry of Behaviorism. Many a time he saved me as I sank into the quicksands of an amateurish discussion of "What is an image?" or "Where is red?" I soon came into contact with W. J. Crozier, who had studied under Loeb. It had been said of Loeb, and might have been said of Crozier, that he "resented the nervous system." Whether this was true or not, the fact was that both these men talked about animal behavior without mentioning the nervous system and with surprising success. So far as I was concerned, they cancelled out the physiological theorizing of Pavlov and Sherrington and thus clarified what remained of the work of these men as the beginnings of an independent science of behavior. My doctoral thesis was in part an operational analysis of Sherrington's synapse, in which behavioral laws were substituted for supposed states of the central nervous system.

But the part of my thesis at issue here was experimental. So far as I can see, I began simply by looking for lawful processes in the behavior of the intact organism. Pavlov had shown the way; but I could not then, as I cannot now, move without a jolt from salivary reflexes to the important business of the organism in everyday life. Sherrington and Magnus had found order in surgical segments of the organism. Could not something of the same sort be found, to use

Loeb's phrase, in "the organism as a whole"? I had the clue from Pavlov: control your conditions and you will see order.

It is not surprising that my first gadget was a silent release box, operated by compressed air and designed to eliminate disturbances when introducing a rat into an apparatus. I used this first in studying the way a rat adapted to a novel stimulus. I built a soundproofed box containing a specially structured space. A rat was released, pneumatically, at the far end of a darkened tunnel from which it emerged in exploratory fashion into a well-lighted area. To accentuate its progress and to facilitate recording, the tunnel was placed at the top of a flight

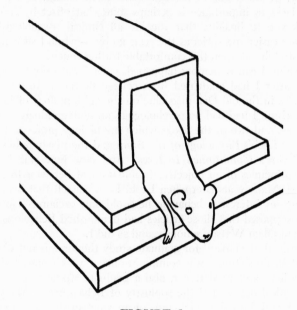

FIGURE 1

of steps, something like a functional Parthenon (Figure 1). The rat would peek out from the tunnel, perhaps glancing suspiciously at the one-way window through which I was watching it, then stretch itself cautiously down the steps. A soft click (carefully calibrated, of course) would cause it to pull back into the tunnel and remain there for some time. But repeated clicks had less and less of an effect. I recorded the rat's advances and retreats by moving a pen back and forth across a moving paper tape.

The major result of this experiment was that some of my rats had babies. I began to watch young rats. I saw them right themselves and crawl about very much like the decerebrate or thalamic cats and rabbits of Magnus. So I set about studying the postural reflexes of young rats. Here was a first principle not formally recognized by scientific methodologists: When you run onto something interesting, drop everything else and study it. I tore up the Parthenon and started over.

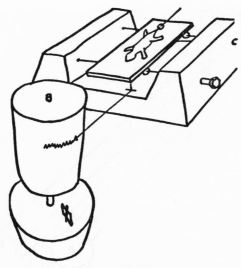

FIGURE 2

If you hold a young rat on one hand and pull it gently by the tail, it will resist you by pulling forward and then, with a sudden sharp spring which usually disengages its tail, it will leap out into space. I decided to study this behavior quantitatively. I built a light platform covered with cloth and mounted it on tightly stretched piano wires (Figure 2). Here was a version of Sherrington's torsion-wire myograph, originally designed to record the isometric contraction of the *tibialis anticus* of a cat, but here adapted to the response of a whole organism. When the tail of the young rat was gently pulled, the rat clung to the cloth floor and tugged forward. By amplifying the fine movements of the platform, it was possible to get a good kymograph record of the tremor in this motion and then, as the pull against the tail was increased, of the desperate spring into the air (Figure 3).

Now, baby rats have very little future, except as adult rats. Their behavior is literally infantile and cannot be usefully extrapolated to everyday life. But if this technique would work with a baby, why not try it on a mature rat? To avoid attaching anything to the rat, it should be possible to record, not a pull against the substrate, but the ballistic thrust exerted as the rat runs forward or suddenly stops in response to my calibrated click. So, invoking the first principle of scientific practice again, I threw away the piano-wire platform, and built a runway, eight feet long. This was constructed of light wood, in the form of a ∪ girder, mounted rigidly on vertical glass plates, the elasticity of which permitted a

FIGURE 3

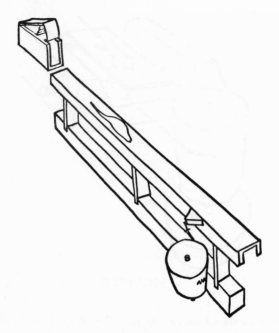

FIGURE 4

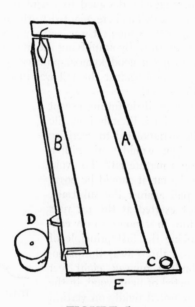

FIGURE 5

very slight longitudinal movement (Figure 4). The runway became the floor of a long tunnel, not shown, at one end of which I placed my soundless release box and at the other end myself, prepared to reinforce the rat for coming down the runway by giving it a bit of wet mash, to sound a click from time to time when it had reached the middle of the runway, and to harvest kymograph records of the vibrations of the substrate.

Now for a second unformalized principle of scientific practice: Some ways of doing research are easier than others. I got tired of carrying the rat back to the other end of the runway. A back alley was therefore added (Figure 5). Now the rat could eat a bit of mash at point C, go down the back alley A, around the end as shown, and back home by runway B. The experimenter at E could collect records from the kymograph at D in comfort. In this way a great many records were made of the forces exerted against the substratum as rats ran down the alley and occasionally stopped dead in their tracks as a click sounded (Figure 6).

There was one annoying detail, however. The rat would often wait an inordinately long time at C before starting down the back alley on the next run. There seemed to be no explanation for this. When I timed these delays with

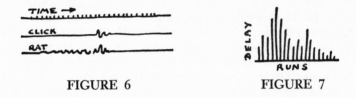

FIGURE 6   FIGURE 7

a stop watch, however, and plotted them, they seemed to show orderly changes (Figure 7). This was, of course, the kind of thing I was looking for. I forgot all about the movements of the substratum and began to run rats for the sake of the delay measurements alone. But there was now no reason why the runway had to be eight feet long and, as the second principle came into play again, I saw no reason why the rat could not deliver its own reinforcement.

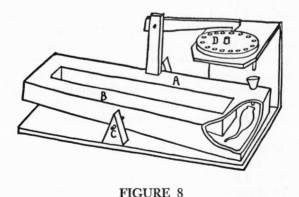

FIGURE 8

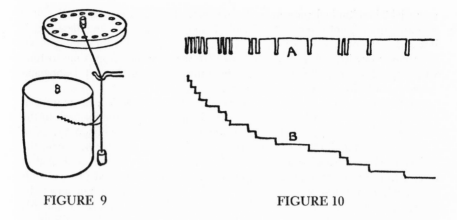

FIGURE 9   FIGURE 10

A new apparatus was built. In Figure 8 we see the rat eating a piece of food just after completing a run. It produced the food by its own action. As it ran down the back alley A to the far end of the rectangular runway, its weight caused the whole runway to tilt slightly on the axis C and this movement turned the wooden disc D, permitting a piece of food in one of the holes around its perimeter to drop through a funnel into a food dish. The food was pearl barley, the only kind I could find in the grocery stores in reasonably uniform pieces. The rat had only to complete its journey by coming down the home stretch B to enjoy its reward. The experimenter was able to enjoy *his* reward at the same time, for he had only to load the magazine, put in a rat, and relax. Each tilt was recorded on a slowly moving kymograph.

A third unformalized principle of scientific practice: Some people are lucky. The disc of wood from which I had fashioned the food magazine was taken from a store room of discarded apparatus. It happened to have a central spindle, which fortunately I had not bothered to cut off. One day it occurred to me that if I wound a string around the spindle and allowed it to unwind as the magazine was emptied (Figure 9), I would get a different kind of record. Instead of a mere report of the up-and-down movement of the runway, as a series of pips as in a polygraph, I would get a *curve*. And I knew that science made great use of curves, although, so far as I could discover, very little of pips on a polygram. The difference between the old type of record at A (Figure 10) and the new at B may not seem great, but as it turned out the curve revealed things in the rate of responding, and in changes in that rate, which would certainly otherwise have been missed. By allowing the string to unwind rather than to wind, I had got my curve in an awkward Cartesian quadrant, but that was easily remedied. Psychologists have adopted cumulative curves only very slowly, but I think it is fair to say that they have become an indispensable tool for certain purposes of analysis.

Eventually, of course, the runway was seen to be unnecessary. The rat could simply reach into a covered tray for pieces of food, and each movement of the cover could operate a solenoid to move a pen one step in a cumulative curve. The first major change in rate observed in this way was due to ingestion. Curves showing how the rate of eating declined with the time of eating comprised the other part of my thesis. But a refinement was needed. The behavior of the rat in pushing open the door was not a normal part of the ingestive behavior of *Rattus rattus*. The act was obviously learned but its status as part of the final performance was not clear. It seemed wise to add an initial conditioned response connected with ingestion in a quite arbitrary way. I chose the first device which came to hand — a horizontal bar or lever placed where it could be conveniently depressed by the rat to close a switch which operated a magnetic magazine. Ingestion curves obtained with this initial response in the chain were found to have the same properties as those without it.

Now, as soon as you begin to complicate an apparatus, you necessarily invoke a fourth principle of scientific practice: Apparatuses sometimes break down. I had only to wait for the food magazine to jam to get an extinction curve. At first I treated this as a defect and hastened to remedy the difficulty. But eventually, of course, I deliberately disconnected the magazine. I can easily recall the excitement of that first complete extinction curve (Figure 11). I had made contact with Pavlov at last! Here was a curve uncorrupted by the physiological process of ingestion. It was an orderly change due to nothing more than a special contingency of reinforcement. It was pure behavior! I am not saying that I would not have got around to extinction curves without a breakdown in the apparatus; Pavlov had given too strong a lead in that direction. But it is still no exaggeration to say that some of the most interesting and surprising results have turned up first because of similar accidents. Foolproof apparatus is no doubt highly desirable, but Charles Ferster and I in recently reviewing the data from a five-year program of research found many occasions to congratulate ourselves on the fallibility of relays and vacuum tubes.

FIGURE 11

I then built four soundproofed ventilated boxes, each containing a lever and a food magazine and supplied with a cumulative recorder, and was on my way to an intensive study of conditioned reflexes in skeletal behavior. I would reinforce every response for several days and then extinguish for a day or two, varying the number of reinforcements, the amount of previous magazine training, and so on.

At this point I made my first use of the deductive method. I had long since given up pearl barley as too unbalanced a diet for steady use. A neighborhood druggist had shown me his pill machine, and I had had one made along the

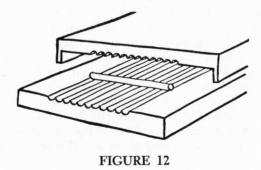

FIGURE 12

same lines (Figure 12). It consisted of a fluted brass bed across which one laid a long cylinder of stiff paste (in my case a MacCollum formula for an adequate rat diet). A similarly fluted cutter was then lowered onto the cylinder and rolled slowly back and forth, converting the paste into about a dozen spherical pellets. These were dried for a day or so before use. The procedure was painstaking and laborious. Eight rats eating a hundred pellets each per day could easily keep up with production. One pleasant Saturday afternoon I surveyed my supply of dry pellets, and, appealing to certain elemental theorems in arithmetic, deduced that unless I spent the rest of that afternoon and evening at the pill machine, the supply would be exhausted by ten-thirty Monday morning.

Since I do not wish to deprecate the hypothetico-deductive method, I am glad to testify here to its usefulness. It led me to apply our second principle of unformalized scientific method and to ask myself why *every* press of the lever had to be reinforced. I was not then aware of what had happened at the Brown laboratories, as Harold Schlosberg later told the story. A graduate student had been given the task of running a cat through a difficult discrimination experiment. One Sunday the student found the supply of cat food exhausted. The stores were closed and so, with a beautiful faith in the frequency-theory of learning, he ran the cat as usual and took it back to its living cage unrewarded. Schlosberg reports that the cat howled its protests continuously for nearly forty-eight hours. Unaware of this I decided to reinforce a response only once every minute and to allow all other responses to go unreinforced. There were two results: (*a*) my supply of pellets lasted almost indefinitely and (*b*) each rat stabilized at a fairly constant rate of responding.

Now, a steady state was something I was familiar with from physical chemistry, and I therefore embarked upon the study of periodic reinforcement. I soon found that the constant rate at which the rat stabilized depended upon how hungry it was. Hungry rat, high rate; less hungry rat, lower rate. At that time I was bothered by the practical problem of controlling food deprivation. I was working half time at the Medical School (on chronaxica of subordination!) and could not maintain a good schedule in working with the rats. The rate of responding under periodic reinforcement suggested a scheme for keeping a rat at a constant level of deprivation. The argument went like this: Suppose you reinforce the rat, not at the end of a given period, but when it has completed the number of responses ordinarily emitted in that period. And suppose you use substantial pellets of food and give the rat continuous access to the lever. Then, except for periods when the rat sleeps, it should operate the lever at a constant rate around the clock. For, whenever it grows slightly hungrier, it will work faster, get food faster, and become less hungry, while whenever it grows slightly less hungry, it will respond at a lower rate, get less food, and grow hungrier. By setting the reinforcement at a given number of responses it should even be possible to hold the rat at any given level of deprivation. I visualized a machine with a dial which one could set to make available, at any time of day or night, a rat in a given state of deprivation. Of course, nothing of the sort happens. This is "fixed-ratio" rather than "fixed-interval" reinforcement and, as I soon found out, it produces a very different type of performance. This is an example of a fifth unformalized principle of scientific practice, but one which has at least been named. Walter Cannon described it with a word invented by Horace Walpole: *serendipity* — the art of finding one thing while looking for something else.

This account of my scientific behavior up to the point at which I published my results in a book called *The Behavior of Organisms* is as exact in letter and spirit as I can now make it. The notes, data, and publications which I have examined do not show that I ever behaved in the manner of Man Thinking as described by John Stuart Mill or John Dewey or in reconstructions of scientific behavior by other philosophers of science. I never faced a Problem which was more than the eternal problem of finding order. I never attacked a problem by constructing a Hypothesis. I never deduced Theorems or submitted them to Experimental Check. So far as I can see, I had no preconceived Model of behavior — certainly not a physiological or mentalistic one, and, I believe, not a conceptual one. The "reflex reserve" was an abortive, though operational, concept which was retracted a year or so after publication in a paper at the Philadelphia meeting of the APA. It lived up to my opinion of theories in general by proving utterly worthless in suggesting further experiments. Of course, I was working on a basic Assumption — that there was order in behavior if I could only discover it — but such an assumption is not to be confused with the hypothesis of deductive theory. It is also true that I exercised a certain Selection of Facts but not because of relevance to theory but because one fact was more orderly than another. If I engaged in Experimental Design at all, it was simply to complete or extend some evidence of order already observed.

. . . .

It is perhaps natural that psychologists should awaken only slowly to the possibility that behavioral processes may be directly observed, or that they should only gradually put the older statistical and theoretical techniques in their proper perspective. But it is time to insist that science does not progress by carefully designed steps called "experiments" each of which has a well-defined beginning and end. Science is a continuous and often a disorderly and accidental process. We shall not do the young psychologist any favor if we agree to reconstruct our practices to fit the pattern demanded by current scientific methodology. What the statistician means by the design of experiments is design which yields the kind of data to which *his* techniques are applicable. He does not mean the behavior of the scientist in his laboratory devising research for his own immediate and possibly inscrutable purposes.

The organism whose behavior is most extensively modified and most completely controlled in research of the sort I have described is the experimenter himself. The point was well made by a cartoonist in the Columbia *Jester* (Figure 17). The caption read: "Boy, have I got this guy conditioned! Every time I press the bar down he drops in a piece of food." The subjects we study reinforce us much more effectively than we reinforce them. I have been telling you simply how I have been conditioned to behave. And of course it is a mistake to argue too much from one case history. My behavior would not have been shaped as it was were it not for personal characteristics which all psychologists fortunately do not share. Freud has had something to say about the motivation

FIGURE 17

of scientists and has given us some insight into the type of person who achieves the fullest satisfaction from precise experimental design and the intricacies of deductive systems. Such a person tends to be more concerned with his success as a scientist than with his subject matter, as is shown by the fact that he often assumes the role of a roving ambassador. If this seems unfair, let me hasten to characterize my own motivation in equally unflattering terms. Several years ago I spent a pleasant summer writing a novel called *Walden Two*. One of the characters, Frazier, said many things which I was not yet ready to say myself. Among them was this:

> I have only one important characteristic, Burris: I'm stubborn. I've had only one idea in my life — a true *idée fixe* . . . to put it as bluntly as possible, the idea of having my own way. "Control" expresses it, I think. The control of human behavior, Burris. In my early experimental days it was a frenzied, selfish desire to dominate. I remember the rage I used to feel when a prediction went awry. I could have shouted at the subjects of my experiments, "Behave, damn you, behave as you ought!" Eventually I realized that the subjects were always right. They always behaved as they ought. It was I who was wrong. I had made a bad prediction.

(In fairness to Frazier and the rest of myself, I want to add his next remark: "And what a strange discovery for a would-be tyrant, that the only effective technique of control is unselfish." Frazier means, of course, positive reinforcement.)

We have no more reason to say that all psychologists should behave as I have behaved than that they should all behave like R. A. Fisher. The scientist, like any organism, is the product of a unique history. The practices which he finds most appropriate will depend in part upon this history. Fortunately, personal idiosyncrasies usually leave a negligible mark on science as public property. They are important only when we are concerned with the encouragement of scientists and the prosecution of research. When we have at last an adequate empirical account of the behavior of Man Thinking, we shall understand all this. Until then, it may be best not to try to fit all scientists into any single mold.

The Nature of Ethical Disagreement

Charles L. Stevenson

1

When people disagree about the value of something — one saying that it is good or right and another that it is bad or wrong — by what methods of argument or inquiry can their disagreement be resolved? Can it be resolved by the methods of science, or does it require methods of some other kind, or is it open to no rational solution at all?

The question must be clarified before it can be answered. And the word that is particularly in need of clarification, as we shall see, is the word "disagreement."

Let us begin by noting that "disagreement" has two broad senses: In the first sense it refers to what I shall call "disagreement in belief." This occurs when Mr. A believes p, when Mr. B believes not-p, or something incompatible with p, and when neither is content to let the belief of the other remain unchallenged. Thus doctors may disagree in belief about the causes of an illness; and friends may disagree in belief about the exact date on which they last met.

In the second sense the word refers to what I shall call "disagreement in attitude." This occurs when Mr. A has a favorable attitude to something, when Mr. B has an unfavorable or less favorable attitude to it, and when neither is content to let the other's attitude remain unchanged. The term "attitude" is here used in much the same sense that R. B. Perry uses "interest"; it designates any psychological disposition of being *for* or *against* something. Hence love and hate are relatively specific kinds of attitudes, as are approval and disapproval, and so on.

This second sense can be illustrated in this way: Two men are planning to have dinner together. One wants to eat at a restaurant that the other doesn't like. Temporarily, then, the men cannot "agree" on where to dine. Their argument may be trivial, and perhaps only half serious; but in any case it represents a disagreement *in attitude*. The men have divergent preferences and each is trying to redirect the preference of the other — though normally, of course, each is willing to revise his own preference in the light of what the other may say.

Further examples are readily found. Mrs. Smith wishes to cultivate only the four hundred; Mr. Smith is loyal to his old poker-playing friends. They accordingly disagree, in attitude, about whom to invite to their party. The progressive mayor wants modern school buildings and large parks; the older citizens are against these "newfangled" ways; so they disagree on civic policy. These cases differ from the one about the restaurant only in that the clash of attitudes is more serious and may lead to more vigorous argument.

From *Facts and Values: Studies in Ethical Analysis*, pages 1–9, by Charles L. Stevenson. Yale University Press, 1963. By permission of the author.

The difference between the two senses of "disagreement" is essentially this: the first involves an opposition of beliefs, both of which cannot be true, and the second involves an opposition of attitudes, both of which cannot be satisfied. Let us apply this distinction to a case that will sharpen it. Mr. A believes that most voters will favor a proposed tax and Mr. B disagrees with him. The disagreement concerns attitudes — those of the voters — but note that A and B are *not* disagreeing in attitude. Their disagreement is *in belief about* attitudes. It is simply a special kind of disagreement in belief, differing from disagreement in belief about head colds only with regard to subject matter. It implies not an opposition of the actual attitudes of the speakers but only of their beliefs about certain attitudes. Disagreement *in* attitude, on the other hand, implies that the very attitudes of the speakers are opposed. A and B may have opposed beliefs about attitudes without having opposed attitudes, just as they may have opposed beliefs about head colds without having opposed head colds. Hence we must not, from the fact that an argument is concerned with attitudes, infer that it necessarily involves disagreement *in* attitude.

2

We may now turn more directly to disagreement about values, with particular reference to normative ethics. When people argue about what is good, do they disagree in belief, or do they disagree in attitude? A long tradition of ethical theorists strongly suggest, whether they always intend to or not, that the disagreement is one *in belief*. Naturalistic theorists, for instance, identify an ethical judgment with some sort of scientific statement, and so make normative ethics a branch of science. Now a scientific argument typically exemplifies disagreement in belief, and if an ethical argument is simply a scientific one, then it too exemplifies disagreement in belief. The usual naturalistic theories of ethics that stress attitudes — such as those of Hume, Westermarck, Perry, Richards, and so many others — stress disagreement in belief no less than the rest. They imply, of course, that disagreement about what is good is disagreement *in belief* about attitudes; but we have seen that that is simply one sort of disagreement in belief, and by no means the same as disagreement *in* attitude. Analyses that stress disagreement *in* attitude are extremely rare.

If ethical arguments, as we encounter them in everyday life, involved disagreement in belief exclusively — whether the beliefs were about attitudes or about something else — then I should have no quarrel with the ordinary sort of naturalistic analysis. Normative judgments could be taken as scientific statements and amenable to the usual scientific proof. But a moment's attention will readily show that disagreement in belief has not the exclusive role that theory has so repeatedly ascribed to it. It must be readily granted that ethical arguments usually involve disagreement in belief; but they *also* involve disagreement in attitude. And the conspicuous role of disagreement in attitude is what we usually take, whether we realize it or not, as the distinguishing feature of ethical arguments. For example:

Suppose that the representative of a union urges that the wage level in a given company ought to be higher — that it is only right that the workers receive more pay. The company representative urges in reply that the workers ought to receive no more than they get. Such an argument clearly represents a disagreement in attitude. The union is *for* higher wages; the company is *against* them, and neither is content to let the other's attitude remain unchanged. *In addition* to this disagreement in attitude, of course, the argument may represent no little disagreement in belief. Perhaps the parties disagree about how much the cost of living has risen and how much the workers are suffering under the present wage scale. Or perhaps they disagree about the company's earnings and the extent to which the company could raise wages and still operate at a profit. Like any typical ethical argument, then, this argument involves both disagreement in attitude and disagreement in belief.

It is easy to see, however, that the disagreement in attitude plays a unifying and predominating role in the argument. This is so in two ways:

In the first place, disagreement in attitude determines what beliefs are *relevant* to the argument. Suppose that the company affirms that the wage scale of fifty years ago was far lower than it is now. The union will immediately urge that this contention, even though true, is irrelevant. And it is irrelevant simply because information about the wage level of fifty years ago, maintained under totally different circumstances, is not likely to affect the present attitudes of either party. To be relevant, any belief that is introduced into the argument must be one that is likely to lead one side or the other to have a different attitude, and so reconcile disagreement in attitude. Attitudes are often functions of beliefs. We often change our attitudes to something when we change our beliefs about it; just as a child ceases to *want* to touch a live coal when he comes to *believe* that it will burn him. Thus in the present argument any beliefs that are at all likely to alter attitudes, such as those about the increasing cost of living or the financial state of the company, will be considered by both sides to be relevant to the argument. Agreement in belief on these matters may lead to agreement in attitude toward the wage scale. But beliefs that are likely to alter the attitudes of neither side will be declared irrelevant. They will have no bearing on the disagreement in attitude, with which both parties are primarily concerned.

In the second place, ethical argument usually terminates when disagreement in attitude terminates, even though a certain amount of disagreement in belief remains. Suppose, for instance, that the company and the union continue to disagree in belief about the increasing cost of living, but that the company, even so, ends by favoring the higher wage scale. The union will then be content to end the argument and will cease to press its point about living costs. It may bring up that point again, in some future argument of the same sort, or in urging the righteousness of its victory to the newspaper columnists; but for the moment the fact that the company has agreed in attitude is sufficient to terminate the argument. On the other hand: suppose that both parties agreed on all beliefs that were introduced into the argument, but even so continued to disagree in attitude. In that case neither party would feel that their dispute had been successfully terminated. They might look for other beliefs that could be introduced into the argument. They might use words to play on each other's emotions. They might agree (in attitude) to submit the case to arbitration, both feeling that a decision, even if strongly adverse to one party or the other, would be preferable to a continued impasse. Or, perhaps, they might abandon hope of settling their dispute by any peaceable means.

In many other cases, of course, men discuss ethical topics without having the strong, uncompromising attitudes that the present example has illustrated. They are often as much concerned with redirecting their own attitudes, in the light of greater knowledge, as with redirecting the attitudes of others. And the attitudes involved are often altruistic rather than selfish. Yet the above example will serve, so long as that is understood, to suggest the nature of ethical disagreement. Both disagreement in attitude and disagreement in belief are involved, but the former predominates in that (1) it determines what sort of disagreement in belief is relevantly disputed in a given ethical argument, and (2) it determines by its continued presence or its resolution whether or not the argument has been settled. We may see further how intimately the two sorts of disagreement are related: since attitudes are often functions of beliefs, an agreement in belief may lead people, as a matter of psychological fact, to agree in attitude.

3

Having discussed disagreement, we may turn to the broad question that was first mentioned, namely: By what methods of argument or inquiry may disagreement about matters of value be resolved?

It will be obvious that to whatever extent an argument involves disagreement in belief, it is open to the usual methods of the sciences. If these methods are the *only* rational methods for supporting beliefs — as I believe to be so, but cannot now take time to discuss — then scientific methods are the only rational methods for resolving the disagreement in *belief* that arguments about values may include.

But if science is granted an undisputed sway in reconciling beliefs, it does not thereby acquire, without qualification, an undisputed sway in reconciling attitudes. We have seen that arguments about values include disagreement in attitude, no less than disagreement in belief, and that in certain ways the disagreement in attitude predominates. By what methods shall the latter sort of disagreement be resolved?

The methods of science are still available for that purpose, but only in an indirect way. Initially, these methods have only to do with establishing agreement in belief. If they serve further to establish agreement in attitude, that will be due simply to the psychological fact that altered beliefs may cause altered attitudes. Hence scientific methods are conclusive in ending arguments about values only to the extent that their success in obtaining agreement in belief will in turn lead to agreement in attitude.

In other words: the extent to which scientific methods can bring about agreement on values depends on the extent to which a commonly accepted body of scientific beliefs would cause us to have a commonly accepted set of attitudes.

How much is the development of science likely to achieve, then, with regard to values? To what extent *would* common beliefs lead to common attitudes? It is, perhaps, a pardonable enthusiasm to *hope* that science will do everything — to hope that in some rosy future, when all men know the consequences of their acts, they will all have common aspirations and live peaceably in complete moral accord. But if we speak not from our enthusiastic hopes but from our present knowledge, the answer must be far less exciting. We usually *do not know*, at the beginning of any argument about values, whether an agreement in belief, scientifically established, will lead to an agreement in attitude or not. It is logically possible, at least, that two men should continue to disagree in attitude even though they had all their beliefs in common, and even though neither had made any logical or inductive error, or omitted any relevant evidence. Differences in temperament, or in early training, or in social status, might make the men retain different attitudes even though both were possessed of the complete scientific truth. Whether this logical possibility is an empirical likelihood I shall not presume to say; but it is unquestionably a possibility that must not be left out of account.

To say that science can always settle arguments about value, we have seen, is to make this assumption: Agreement in attitude will always be consequent upon complete agreement in belief, and science can always bring about the latter. Taken as purely heuristic, this assumption has its usefulness. It leads people to discover the discrepancies in their beliefs and to prolong enlightening argument that *may* lead, as a matter of fact, from commonly accepted beliefs to commonly accepted attitudes. It leads people to reconcile their attitudes in a rational, permanent way, rather than by rhapsody or exhortation. But the assumption is *nothing more*, for present knowledge, than a heuristic maxim. It is wholly without any proper foundation of probability. I conclude, therefore, that scientific methods cannot be guaranteed the definite role in the so-called normative sciences that they may have in the natural sciences. Apart from a heuristic assumption to the contrary, it is possible that the growth of scientific knowledge may leave many disputes about values permanently unsolved. Should these disputes persist, there are nonrational methods for dealing with them, of course, such as impassioned, moving oratory. But the purely intellectual methods of science, and, indeed, *all* methods of reasoning, may be insufficient to settle disputes about values even though they may greatly help to do so.

For the same reasons I conclude that normative ethics is not a branch of any science. It deliberately deals with a type of disagreement that science deliberately avoids. Ethics is not psychology, for instance; for although psychologists may, of course, agree or disagree in belief about attitudes, they need not, as psychologists, be concerned with whether they agree or disagree with one another *in* attitude. Insofar as normative ethics draws from the sciences, in order to change attitudes *via* changing people's beliefs, it *draws* from *all* the sciences; but a moralist's peculiar aim — that of *redirecting* attitudes — is a type of activity, rather than knowledge, and falls within no science. Science may study that activity and may help indirectly to forward it; but is not *identical* with that activity.

4

I can take only a brief space to explain why the ethical terms, such as "good," "wrong," "ought," and so on, are so habitually used to deal with disagreement in attitude. On account of their repeated occurrence in emotional situations they have acquired a strong emotive meaning. This emotive meaning makes them serviceable in initiating changes in a hearer's attitudes. Sheer emotive impact is not likely, under many circumstances, to change attitudes in any permanent way; but it *begins* a process that can then be supported by other means.

There is no occasion for saying that the meaning of ethical terms is *purely* emotive, like that of "alas" or "hurrah." We have seen that ethical *arguments* include many expressions of *belief*, and the rough rules of ordinary language permit us to say that some of these beliefs are expressed by an ethical judgment itself. But the beliefs so expressed are by no means always the same. Ethical terms are notable for their ambiguity, and opponents in an argument may use them in different senses. Sometimes this leads to artificial issues, but it usually does not. So long as one person says "this is good" with emotive praise, and another says "no, it is bad," with emotive condemnation, a disagreement in attitude is manifest. Whether or not the beliefs that these statements express are logically incompatible may not be discovered until later in the argument; but even if they are actually compatible, disagreement in attitude will be preserved by emotive meaning; and this disagreement, so central to ethics, may lead to an argument that is certainly not artificial in its issues so long as it is taken for what it is.

The many theorists who have refused to identify ethical statements with scientific ones have much to be said in their favor. They have seen that ethical judgments mold or alter attitudes, rather than describe them, and they have seen that ethical judgments can be guaranteed no definitive scientific support. But one need not on that account provide ethics with any extramundane, sui generis *subject matter*. The distinguishing features of an ethical judgment can be preserved by a recognition of emotive meaning and disagreement in attitude, rather than by some nonnatural quality — and with far greater intelligibility. If a unique subject matter is *postulated*, as it usually is, to preserve the important distinction between normative ethics and science, it serves no purpose that is not served by the very simple analysis I have here suggested. Unless nonnatural qualities can be defended by positive arguments, rather than as an "only resort" from the acknowledged weakness of ordinary forms of naturalism, they would seem nothing more than the invisible shadows cast by emotive meaning.

The Teaching of Thinking

Harold Berlak

Discussions of the goals of education in workshops and curriculum guides are normally not complete without some mention of the importance of teaching students how to think. While we all indorse this concern for the teaching of thinking, I believe we may question whether the concept of thinking as it ap-

Reprinted from *The School Review*, 1965, vol. 73, pages 1–13 by permission of The University of Chicago Press. Copyright 1965 by the University of Chicago.

pears in the literature of professional education contributes to achievement of this goal. It is commonly accepted in the literature that a set of steps, aspects, or operations subsumed under the labels "critical thinking," "reflective thinking," or "problem-solving," is appropriate for dealing with a wide, if not the entire range of, issues and problems that confront men. I will argue that this "general-aspects" view, for the present at least, is of little value to those engaged in the teaching of thinking. I will propose what I think is a more modest and useful conception of thinking and suggest its implications for teaching.

The General-Aspects View

While critical thinking, reflective thinking, and problem-solving are often not considered to be identical, there appears to be a common assumption that the steps, operations, or aspects named are not context specific, but are applicable to any problem or issue that may confront the learner. This general-aspects view of the thought process, widely accepted among educators, can be found in Dewey as well as in the most recent writings and tests in this area.[1] Probably the most comprehensive statement of a general-aspects position is made by Ennis, who has examined the concept of critical thinking in detail.[2] Since Ennis provides what I believe to be the most scholarly but representative statement of this general-aspects view, I will make special reference to his work.

Ennis takes as his root concept for critical thinking "the correct assessing of statements" (p. 83), and he says that he has examined the literature and selected aspects of critical thinking that are consistent with his basic notion. He simplifies the list and arrives at what he calls twelve aspects or abilities of critical thinking — and three dimensions. I believe his twelve aspects of critical thinking are quite typical:

"(1) Grasping the meaning of a statement; (2) judging whether there is ambiguity in a line of reasoning; (3) judging whether certain statements contradict each other; (4) judging whether a conclusion follows necessarily; (5) judging whether a statement is specific enough; (6) judging whether a statement is actually the application of a certain principle; (7) judging whether an observation statement is reliable; (8) judging whether an inductive conclusion is warranted; (9) judging whether a problem has been identified; (10) judging whether something is an assumption; (11) judging whether a definition is adequate; and (12) judging whether a statement made by an alleged authority is acceptable."

The "dimensions" named by Ennis are as follows:

The *logical dimension*, roughly speaking, covers judging alleged relationships between meanings of words and statements. A person who is competent in this dimension knows what follows from a statement or a group of statements by virtue of their meaning. He particularly knows how to use the logical operators, "all," "some," "not," "and," "if . . . then," "or," "unless," etc. He knows what it is for something to be a member of a class of things. Furthermore, he knows the meaning of the basic terms in the field in which the statement under consideration is made.

The *criterial dimension* covers knowledge of the criteria for judging all statements . . . , except logical criteria, which are covered by the logical dimension.

The *pragmatic dimension* covers the impression of the background purpose on the judgment, and it covers the decision as to whether the statement is good *enough* for the purpose.[3]

First a basic and rather obvious proposition will be stated: *The value of any set of intellectual skills* (Ennis calls them aspects) *rests on whether they have demonstrated value to persons who have dealt successfully with some problem or issue.* This is the "ultimate" test of any set of intellectual operations. If they do not in some way help the learner to deal with issues or to make sense out of his personal life and external reality, the operations are of little value.

Ennis' claims for his list are quite modest — he says (p. 283) that the specification should be considered as "specific ways to avoid the pitfalls in assessment."[4] Nevertheless, assuming that Ennis has identified aspects of critical thought that are of some assistance when a person "correctly assesses statements," the correct assessment of statements cannot be considered as equivalent to the process of engaging in inquiry discourse. A person may know how to cipher, but this certainly is not equivalent to engaging in mathematical inquiry. A person may know grammar and linguistics, but this does not mean he can compose a poem. Ciphering, knowledge of grammar, knowledge of rules of inference, "common pitfalls," and logic *may* be essential to mathematical inquiry, writing, and critical discourse, respectively, but the former are not equivalent to the latter. Ennis may argue, of course, that he prefers to provide a more limited meaning to the term "critical thinking," and the "correct assessment of statements," though limited, is preferable to the usual vague and loose usage of the term. Nevertheless, at some point it must be shown that the aspects selected *are of major importance to persons who are attempting to deal with issues or problems.* Certainly, if a reading expert proposed that knowledge of certain aspects of linguistics is important to the learning of reading, we would expect the proposition to be defended by argument and, if possible, with data. Similarly, if knowledge of the aspects of thinking selected by Ennis or anyone else is of major importance to the process of engaging in critical discourse, then we should expect a justification for selection in terms of argument and data. Ennis does not do this, and rarely does anyone else. In most of the writings in this area, the value of operations is assumed to be prima facie. Hence, it may be of some value to examine arguments for the use of general aspects and to point to some difficulties.

Difficulties with General-Aspects View

On the face of it, a facile case can be made for the significance of many general "aspects." Who, for example, would question the importance of "identifying a problem" to the thought process? The case for importance of such generalized aspects, however, is not at all obvious when we explore the "aspects" in more detail.

Why Use General Aspects?

The first question we will ask is: What are the various domains of experience that an individual may be expected to bring his intellectual abilities to bear on? The following is a brief, tentative list of types of problems.

1. *Personal.* These include everyday problems involving choice of occupation, spouse, child-rearing practices, automobile, and so on.

2. *Social.* These are the social, economic, and political decisions that may be of a personal concern to individuals, but have wider implications for local, national, or international affairs. Voting is one instance, but there are other political choices of various kinds a citizen makes.

3. *Scientific.* Here are included the problems that may face the social and physical scientists in their efforts to explain, describe, categorize, control, or predict phenomena.

4. *Historical.* Included here are the problems faced by historians in describing or explaining past events. It may be that this should not be an independent category. It is separated here because many historians view historical method as something quite distant from the methods of the social and behavioral sciences.

5. *Practical-Professional.* Here are included the problems faced by the physician in treating a patient, the lawyer in winning a case, the teacher in teaching a class, the garage man in repairing an automobile.

6. *Aesthetic.* This is one of the more difficult areas to describe. However, these are the problems that occur whenever aesthetic judgments are rendered and an effort is made to deal with them systematically — or where there is an effort to contribute to the arts.

The foregoing classification is not intended to be exhaustive; nor are the categories independent. However, it does make the point that the domains in which persons are expected to employ intellectual skills and abilities are extraordinarily diverse and complex. Systematic, critical thought related to these problems has occupied the attention of teachers, scholars, scientists, artists, politicians, farmers, housewives, and craftsmen for centuries. Assuming it were possible, a sheer listing of the methods of dealing with "problems" in all these areas, even if restricted to the methods where there is some consensus, would be an enormous task.

Schoolmen have been concerned with teaching students how to handle aspects of these problems for some time. However, if the schools attempted to equip persons to cope with all these domains, they would have an entirely unmanageable task. To teach students the intellectual processes used by the logician, sociologist, statistician, historian, physicist, astronomer, biologist, chemist, plumber, and artist is obviously impossible and probably not desirable. Probably, the most common solution is to attempt to teach students some *generalized structure* or set of operations that would be useful in dealing with problems, ideas, or situations in several, if not all, of the domains. It is usually this general structure or set of operations that educators label "critical thinking," "reflective thinking," or "problem-solving," and this is probably Ennis' and others' strategy when they list basic aspects, dimensions, and operations of critical thinking.

How Much Is Known of the Thought Process?

The listing of a general set of aspects of critical thinking assumes that there is sufficient knowledge to construct such lists. To examine this assumption, a distinction will be drawn between *input* and *output*. Let us say that a person performs operations A, B, C, D, . . . , N, in this order, and the result of his labor is X; we will refer to A, B, C, D, . . . , N, the explicit set of operations or procedures performed, as "input," and X, product of his labor, as "output."[5]

If adequate knowledge were available, one could confidently lay out the input — the recipe, if you will — for doing an experiment, teaching a class, writing an essay, etc.; and, if the recipe were meticulously followed, the desired output would result. Specification of input is commonplace in many areas. We can, for example, lay out the steps for computing a t-test, growing hybrid corn, or building an automobile.

With this distinction in mind, let us reformulate the original question. What is known of the input of complex thinking or problem-solving? Is there sufficient knowledge so that we can lay out imperatives to be followed by the physicist, historian, political scientist, or lawyer when they deal with problems and issues of interest? Most scholars who have studied higher-order mental processes would not presume such knowledge. As Ryle points out in his essay "Thinking," such knowledge simply does not exist.[6] This is not to say that nothing is known by scholars, but only that they are at present unable to formulate either specific or general input strategies.

While examination of the educational literature on problem-solving produces few, if any, instances of attempts to lay down detailed, *explicit input* for thinking, there are attempts to lay out *very general input* (or steps) for reflective or critical thinking. For example, one of the earliest and best known is Dewey's *How We Think*.[7] While Dewey does not argue that his steps are sequential, clearly he has attempted to formulate a generalized model appropriate to most domains of experience.

There are at least two difficulties with this sort of model and its many variations. First, as I have suggested, not enough is known about problem-solving to suggest even general input strategies that are applicable to all domains of experience. Second, the use of general labels tends to overlook the fact that these general aspects are not *unitary* intellectual activities. Problem identification and hypothesis-testing in clinical psychology, in nuclear physics, and in history involve a complex of specific procedures. If a scholar were asked to specify every operation he performs in the course of identifying a problem or testing a hypothesis, he would have a formidable list indeed. How similar are the components of hypothesis-testing in these fields? Does the clinical psychologist "identify a problem" in the same way as does the physicist? Both "identify problems," but certainly there is some doubt as to whether the strategies they employ are similar. To take a second instance, sociologists and historians both "test hypotheses." But there is considerable disagreement among many writers[8] whether the objectivity that some claim is possible in the social sciences is possible in testing hypotheses in history. Some historians talk about "historical facts" as something distinct from what data are considered to be in the other sciences.[9] I am struck more with the diversity and complexity of the approaches used in the various domains of knowledge than with the commonality. It is undeniable that with sufficient study we may find a high enough degree of similarity to justify a general label, but the similarity may be at such a high level of abstraction that it may be more important to pay closer attention to the differences than to the similarities, especially if we expect our students to make some use of the thinking skills we purportedly teach.

Turning to Ennis, we find that he is quite aware of the difficulties of talking about explicit sets of steps or procedures. He avoids some of the apparent difficulties involved in attempts to formulate even general input. As has been noted, his claims are modest; he considers his aspects as a way of helping people to "avoid the pitfalls of assessment." Nevertheless he does not escape the problem of extreme generality. "Judging whether a problem is identified," to take one of his aspects, also involves such a complex of procedures and processes that one again wonders whether the use of the general label is of any assistance in helping people avoid the pitfalls of assessment in the *context* of trying to deal with a *specific* problem in a *given* area.

An Alternative to Use of General Aspects

Before going on to suggest an alternative to our present notions of thinking, I will summarize the argument advanced. The criterion for the value of a set of intellectual skills is that they may be used to deal successfully with problems and issues of interest. It was shown that the "problem areas" in which a person may use his intellectual abilities are exceedingly diverse — so diverse that the use of general steps assumes a knowledge about the thinking process that is simply not available. In addition, while the general lists do use words which are more or less common to inquiry in many areas, for example, hypothesis-testing, assumptions, inference, etc., it is somewhat doubtful that these labels refer to the same set of explicit steps in various domains. A comment by Ryle suggested the basis for the recommendation I will offer. Ryle, in his discussion of the contribution of epistemologists and logicians to our knowledge of thinking, notes that their contribution has been to "give functional descriptions of the various kinds of elements into which *constructed* theories were analyzable. Their eyes were on the connectives, the phrases, the propositions, and the argument of which *published* theories consist."[10] In other words, these scholars have focused on the analysis of the output of successful thought. They have attempted to understand the logical and empirical characteristics of the products of successful inquiry. We do not, at present, have the general theories, principles, or models from which we can make precise predictions, shape pedagogical strategies, write the textbooks that would aid us in teaching thinking effectively. Nevertheless, there are experts in philosophy, history, law, mathematics, scholars as well as men of practical affairs, who have to some degree successfully resolved problems and issues in their areas of interest. From the analyses of their output — not only of their writings but of their discourse, I believe that educators may learn a great deal about intellectual process that can be of substantial value to those interested in the teaching of thinking.

What I am suggesting is that educators rely less on the inadequate general models and focus on studying intellectual process in a *given* area in order to develop output for *that area.* From these *context-specific* models and criteria, educators may develop pedagogical strategies and teaching material that are appropriate for that area.

What sort of pedagogical strategy is likely to follow from this approach? An instance may clarify the implications of this position for teaching. Let us say we are trying to teach a student to write an expository essay. It is not possible to give the student detailed input for successful essay writing. But from an analysis of instances of what are generally conceded to be good[11] essays (i.e., output) educators may be able to identify some criteria or patterns that characterize these essays and perhaps offer some suggestions for input. Now the student writes an essay using the relatively meager input and after the writing is complete applies the output criteria (perhaps with the assistance of a teacher). Through something resembling successive approximation, the student may learn to write a reasonably clear and coherent essay.

It is obvious that the strategy with its emphasis on the learner engaging in the experience, with subsequent or simultaneous evaluation according to a set of criteria or a model, is common in teaching scholars, artists, and artisans complex intellectual, expressive, and manipulative skills. The young musician listens and tries to evaluate the master's output; the student historian prepares a monograph to be criticized by his peers and professor — these are instances of an instructional strategy that capitalizes on the analysis of output.

While this strategy is not novel, I would suggest that it would be novel and of great value if educators who are concerned with the teaching of thinking in a particular domain of experience concentrated on the systematic study of output in particular areas in order to develop *context-specific* models and patterns. Though the models may be skeletal and incomplete, they may serve not as recipes or formulas, but as norms for evaluating and adjusting output of the students as they engage in thinking.

The strategy recommended here was employed in a two-year Cooperative Research Project conducted by the social studies staff of the Harvard Graduate School of Education.[12] A major purpose of the study was to develop a program for teaching junior high school students to engage in the analysis of controversial political issues. A course was built around a set of political issues that have faced Americans throughout their history. Included were historical units on the New Deal and the American Revolution, along with units on desegregation, labor, business competition, the American Indian, and immigration. It became evident that if the investigators were to learn anything of value from the study, they had to study output in the area of political controversy and develop a set of criteria, or some model that could be used in (1) writing texts and cases, (2) constructing evaluation instruments, and (3) developing communicable pedagogical strategies.

The model developed was composed of several simple analytic distinctions, a legal-ethical framework, and patterns of thought. It is based on the investigators' study of adult discourse in the area of political controversy and upon the works of scholars in political science, law, and philosophy. The investigators, operating with this model, which became increasingly explicit and complex as they worked with it, wrote cases and text, and taught seventh- and eighth-grade classes for a two-year period. A rather oversimplified example may clarify how the investigators made use of the model. One of the patterns that appeared to characterize discourse in political issues is the use of hypothetical and real instances which apparently help clarify the conflicting legal-ethical issues and move disputants to a position that takes into account the conflicting principles. This is what may be considered an output criterion. In the preparation of a case study for the use of the students, the investigators "built in" either implicit or explicit reference to conflicting legal-ethical principles. Before entering the classroom the investigators had prepared a set of hypothetical or real instances analogous to the one under consideration. The analogies were for use in the course of discussion with the students. The evaluation instruments for the study were constructed to determine the student's facility in using analogous cases to arrive at position statements. The reliance of the investigators on the pattern derived from the analyses of output was crucial in each of the three tasks. A detailed description of the model, teaching materials, and pedagogical strategies may be found in the report of that study.

There is an essential step in the strategy recommended here that should be underscored. I have said that the value of any set of operations (input or output criteria) depends on whether they can be shown to be of demonstrated value to experts in that area. Thus, if we develop models and patterns, it is the burden of the investigator to demonstrate that the model and the instruments constructed on the basis of the model are valid. The validity problem is, of course, exceedingly complex. Nevertheless, it is not beyond our ingenuity to construct tests of the validity of our models and instruments. This writer in another place reported a study that attempts to check the validity of the model employed in the Harvard study.[13] The study employs factor analysis of an evaluation instrument that was constructed on the basis of the model. In addition, the scores assigned to each subject with use of the instrument were compared to independent judgments rendered by a group of legal scholars and philosophers. It was possible to conclude that the instrument could make discriminations that were related to those made by this group of scholars — thus increasing the investigators' confidence in the model and in the approach recommended in this paper.

Perhaps the use of the terms "critical thinking," "reflective thinking," and "problem-solving," and the traditional set of aspects under these general labels, has lulled us into believing we know a great deal more than we do about the thinking process and how to teach it to students. Whether or not we continue to use these terms is unimportant; however, I believe we must turn our immediate attention from the general imperative "we shall teach thinking" to a careful analysis of the thought process in the various areas of human experience, the construction of models, and a test of their validity.

NOTES

1. Several works in this area are: W. H. Burton, R. B. Kimball, and R. L. Wing, *Education for Effective Thinking* (New York: Appleton-Century-Crofts, 1960); P. L. Dressel and L. B. Mayhew, *General Education: Explorations in Evaluation* (Washington, D.C.: American Council on Education, 1954); E. M. Glaser, *An Experiment in the Development of Critical Thinking* ("Contributions to Education," No. 843 [New York: Teachers College, Columbia University, 1942]); H. G. Hullfish and P. G. Smith, *Reflective Thinking: The Method of Education* (New York: Dodd Mead, 1961); E. R. Smith and R. W. Tyler, *Appraising and Recording Student Progress* ("Adventures in American Education," Vol. III [New York: Harper & Bros., 1942]); and I. Starr, "The Nature of Critical Thinking," in *Skill Development in Social Studies* (33d Yearbook, National Council

for the Social Studies [Washington, D.C.: National Council for the Social Studies, 1963]). Several tests of critical thinking that reflect the general aspects view are *Interpretation of Data Test* (Princeton: Cooperative Test Division, Educational Testing Service, 1950); "Logical Reasoning Test" (Princeton: Cooperative Test Division, Educational Testing Service, 1950); "A Test of Problem Solving" (East Lansing, Michigan: Board of Examiners, Michigan State College, 1953); Progressive Education Association, "Social Problems Test" (Chicago: University of Chicago, 1940); and G. D. Watson and E. M. Glaser, "The Watson-Glaser Critical Thinking Appraisal" (rev. ed.; Yonkers-on-Hudson: World Book Co., 1952).

2. R. H. Ennis, "A Concept of Critical Thinking," *Harvard Educational Review*, XXXII (Winter, 1962), 81–111.

3. *Ibid.*, pp. 84–85.

4. Evaluation of Ennis' work is difficult since he says he has chosen not to justify his root notion of critical thinking. I do not believe that this disclaimer removes from him the burden of demonstrating that the aspects he presents are of major importance to men who attempt to deal with issues or problems.

5. The model is an oversimplification, for in the playing of a violin, e.g., the correct reading of notation, proper bow manipulation, fingering, and so on (the input) are not simply sequenced linear steps but a great many precise operations simultaneously performed.

6. G. Ryle, "Thinking," *Acta Psychologica*, IX (1953), 197–200.

7. J. Dewey, *How We Think* (rev. ed.; Boston: D. C. Heath, 1933). Dewey's steps may be found in the literature in many forms. Virtually all discussions and tests of thinking listed in n. 1 are variations of Dewey's position.

8. See, e.g., C. Beard, "Written History as an Act of Faith"; E. Nagel, "The Logic of Historical Analysis"; M. White, "Can History Be Objective?" reprinted in H. J. Meyerhof (ed.), *The Philosophy of History in Our Time* (New York: Doubleday & Co., 1959). Also see W. H. Wash, *An Introduction to Philosophy of History* (London: Hutchensons University Library, 1951).

9. C. L. Becker, "What Are Historical Facts?" in Meyerhof, *op. cit.*, pp. 203–15.

10. Ryle, *op. cit.*, p. 195. (Italics added.)

11. Agreement does not have to be on what is excellent writing. Agreement may merely be on what is "clear" and "reasonably coherent."

12. D. W. Oliver and J. Shaver with H. Berlak and E. V. Seasholves, *An Analysis of Public Controversy: A Study in Citizenship Education*. U.S. Office of Education, Cooperative Research Project No. 8145. Cambridge: Harvard University Graduate School of Education, 1963. (Mimeographed.)

13. H. Berlak, "The Construct Validity of a Content Analysis System for the Evaluation of Critical Thinking in Political Controversy" (unpublished Ed.D. dissertation, Graduate School of Education, Harvard University, 1963). Parts of this work were delivered in a paper at American Educational Research Association, Chicago, 1963. I wish to acknowledge the criticism and suggestions offered by my teachers at Harvard and my colleagues at the University of California, Santa Barbara.

Selected Analytic Concepts for the
Clarification of Public Issues

Donald W. Oliver and James P. Shaver

It may seem that problems involving human conflict in a democracy are easily resolved. Two people or two groups within a community have an argument over a public issue. Each takes a different position. Who is right? We find out which person is basing his argument on an important value or upon a governmental principle which supports the value. Whoever can rationalize his position in terms of a supporting principle must be right; the other person must be wrong.

There are obviously a number of difficulties with this approach:

1. As most problems which affect the welfare of the American community are discussed, different individuals or groups take different positions. Usually each position can be reasonably supported by important social values.

2. Claiming that a position is supported by an important value or that a position violates some value does not necessarily make the claim true. Such claims must be examined to see exactly how the problem situation is described, as well as the extent to which the description is accurate. Often precise descriptions are not available, so one has difficulty judging the extent to which a value has in fact been violated or is supported.

3. Even when all the facts are clear, people often use differently the words which describe or label values and value-loaded situations. Terms such as *adequate education* and *equal protection* mean different things to different people, although all may be committed to whatever values are described by these labels.

We are likely, then, to encounter problems in analyzing political controversies in our community and nation: One problem involves clarifying which values or legal principles are in conflict and choosing between or among them. A second problem involves clarifying the facts around which the conflict has developed. A third involves clarifying the meanings or uses of words which describe the controversy. As we shall see, there are different strategies for dealing with each problem. It is important, therefore, to distinguish a value problem from a factual problem and a factual problem from a definitional problem. Dealing with political issues usually means resolving disagreements in all these areas. Perhaps we can best illustrate these points, as well as how they might be treated in the classroom, by looking at a concrete incident based on an actual case presented to the Supreme Court.

The Sidewalk Speech

On a raw, windy afternoon in March, a hot-headed, earnest young student named Barry Schwartz was making a speech to a crowd in a small shopping area. The street was in a Negro neighborhood in Poughkeepsie, New York.

From *Teaching Public Issues in the High School*, 1966, pages 88–113. By permission of Houghton Mifflin Company and the authors.

Schwartz stood on a large wooden box on the sidewalk and shouted at the crowd in a high-pitched voice through a loudspeaker system attached to an automobile. He waved his arms, stamped his feet, and once in a while smacked a fist in his palm. He wanted to publicize a meeting of the Young Progressives of America that was to be held that evening. Among other things, Schwartz said,

"The mayor of this city is a champagne-sipping bum; he doesn't care who crushes the Negro people."

"The President of the United States is a bum."

"The Legion of American Veterans is a Nazi Gestapo."

"The Negroes don't have equal rights; they should rise up in arms and fight for their rights."

The crowd listening to Schwartz numbered 75 or 80 people, both Negro and white. It filled the sidewalk and spread out into the street. The people were restless. There was some pushing, shoving, and milling around. Some men picked up bricks and threatened to throw them at Schwartz. Lincoln Frost, who owned a nearby store, was afraid for his plate glass windows, so he phoned the police.

Lieutenant Collins and Sergeant Davis drove up in a squad car to investigate. For a while they just sat in the car and watched. Then one of the women onlookers who thought Schwartz should get a chance came over and said, "What's the matter? You scared? Can't you cops make people behave right?" A big, muscular man nearby turned around and said, "If you cops don't get that guy off his orange crate in two minutes, I'll shove it down his throat." Then he elbowed his way into the crowd until he was very close to Schwartz.

Lieutenant Collins pushed his way after him through the crowd and asked Schwartz to break up the crowd "to prevent it from resulting in a fight." He repeated the suggestion several times. Each time Schwartz ignored the policeman and went on talking. During all this time the crowd was pressing closer around Lieutenant Collins and Schwartz. The muscular man began urging the men near him to "Get Schwartz." Finally, Collins told Schwartz he'd have to arrest him for his own safety, and ordered him to get down from the box.

Schwartz got off the box, but as Collins took him through the crowd to the squad car, he shouted, "What's happening to free speech in this country? I've got a right to say what I think even if the big-wigs don't like it. I've got a right to talk even if some bigots standing around here want me to shut up."

Schwartz was tried and convicted of disorderly conduct and sentenced to thirty days in the county jail. Schwartz appealed the conviction because he said it took away his rights under the First and Fourteenth Amendments of the American Constitution.

In discussing "The Sidewalk Speech" we can ask a number of important questions to clarify the problem. Are any important values being violated? Barry Schwartz claims his freedom of speech is abridged. The Poughkeesie police claim that the peace and order of the neighborhood is threatened. Clearly, there is a conflict over important values. Further questions: Is there any legal basis to support these values? Does the violation of a value in these circumstances also violate a law? And even more important: Does the government have the power under the Constitution to make the law which has allegedly been violated? In this particular case, is there any constitutional protection for freedom of speech? The answer is plain, as Barry Schwartz points out: in the First and Fourteenth Amendments. We might also ask: Does the community have the authority to make laws prohibiting disorderly conduct? Again the answer is surely "yes." We now have a conflict not only between values but also between laws which are designed to protect these values. Although we know that constitutional law is supreme, we also know that the First Amendment does not necessarily protect people from unreasonable use of free speech. Assuming that we want to protect peace and order, then, how is order to be preserved? By arresting the speaker or by restraining those who threaten the speaker with violence. Which course of action is taken depends to a large degree on how "reasonable" use of free speech is defined.

This is not only a definitional and a value problem. It is closely related to an important factual issue: What is a clear and accurate description of the problem situation? The relevant factual questions in "The Sidewalk Speech" center on how much violence actually occurred and to what extent there was an immediate threat of more violence. In this connection the following factual questions might be important:

How large was the crowd?
To what extent did the crowd obstruct traffic or pedestrians?
To what extent was there "pushing, shoving, and milling around"?
How many people actually threatened Schwartz?
How serious were their intentions?
How many policemen were available to keep order?

Analyzing a case such as "The Sidewalk Speech" is a complicated business. We must identify the different kinds of problems involved: value conflicts, legal and constitutional problems, factual problems, problems regarding the interpretation or definition of value, and problems regarding the definition of terms used in the factual description. While this process of analysis is a creative endeavor, and will be done differently by different individuals, there are, we believe, concepts which might generally be useful as guidelines.

It is important to note, however, that in teaching, the objective of analyzing such a case is not simply to impart conceptual abstractions; more particularly it is to teach the ability to shift alternately from conceptual analysis to the testing ground for the validity and adequacy of the analysis — the concrete facts in the case itself. With such a goal, the "case method" is a powerful tool. Instead of being provided with pre-analyzed material which he then applies to new situations, the student is engaged in a process that allows him latitude in testing the utility of alternative conceptual systems. Cases, then, are not simply a means of *illustrating* and *teaching* concepts; they provide the grounds by which general statements about public policy can be generated and tested. The classroom discussion that follows a case will of necessity be dialectical and controversial in the type of curriculum we suggest — no one conception of a case is necessarily the "right" one. This does not preclude the idea that there are *principles of analysis*, which the teacher should have in mind, that give such discussion focus and direction in raising appropriate questions. The following sections lay out some of these principles. Again, the fact that they are made explicit does not mean they should necessarily be taught as final principles. They do, however, provide guidelines for the testing of questions which inevitably arise in the attempt to come to general principles of public policy and public conduct.

Analyzing Three Types of Disagreement and Strategies for Their Resolution

It is important at the outset to note that although we often will discuss controversies over definition, value, and fact as though they were different and distinct types of problems, they are closely related. Our purpose in this section is to describe certain distinctions between these types of problems and various strategies for dealing with them. In Chapter Seven we will try to show the interrelationships among these problems as one attempts to deal with complex social issues.

Definitional Problems

A basic problem in discussions of public controversy involves the ambiguous or confusing use of words or symbols. It is important, therefore, that words have reasonably common meanings for those taking part in a discussion. Without such common understanding, discussions are likely to be frustrating, fruitless, or even needless.

There are two main aspects to defining or describing how words are to be used. The first is ascertaining how a word is actually being used in the discussion, i.e., what meaning it has for the participants. The second is determining what the most useful definition of a word is when it becomes clear that there is disagreement over its meaning. Also related to the problem of definition, and an important element of it, is the issue of clarification. Arguments over classification, for example, can often be settled or clarified by careful definition of the class name.

Two Types of Definition. In clarifying and resolving definitional disputes it is probably useful to distinguish between two types of definitional operation: defining by example and defining by the use of general criteria. Suppose, for instance, that a creature from another planet landed in our backyard and there were severe problems of communication. If it appeared to be an intelligent being that could speak, we might want to talk to it. As a start, we might point to ourselves and say "man" (or "woman") and then point to it and say "creature," thus quickly reaching some common understanding of what to call or label each other. With a little practice, the creature could probably look at any adult human and say "man." Communicating what is meant by a term through pointing at or enumerating examples of persons, objects, actions, or any specific referent might be called a *pointing definition* or *definition by example.*

Although it is possible to create or "invent" a word-referent relationship (scientists and advertisers do it all the time), most of us communicate with labels which are learned within a highly structured cultural framework, and which are intricately woven into a complex system of meaning. When we try to define by citing examples, therefore, we are probably relating the example to an implied system of classification. Thus the effort to define one word usually involves us in the clarification of class names, and soon becomes a question of distinguishing between two classes which overlap in meaning. In these situations general criteria by which a class can be defined are ordinarily used to clarify or resolve definitional disagreement.

To illustrate the development of such a disagreement, consider the following example. Suppose we defined "democratic country" by referring to the United States, the United Kingdom, France, and Belgium. A fellow discussant, however, asks why we include Belgium and do not include the Soviet Union. We reply that the answer is simple: Belgium is a democratic country and the Soviet Union is not. He disagrees, claiming that the Soviet Union is a democracy and Belgium is a dictatorship. At this point the pointing definition has broken down.

In order to determine more precisely how we are disagreeing over the term *democratic country*, we may list specific characteristics, or *criteria*, that distinguish those countries we consider democratic from those we consider non-democratic. For example, we say a democratic country is one which (1) has a constitution that provides certain basic rights for all the people and (2) elects directly or indirectly the major officers of government. Such an attempt to delineate the appropriate uses of a word by listing the distinguishing characteristics or criteria of its referents may be called a *criterial definition*.

The Resolution of Definitional Disagreements. The initial problem, of course, is determining whether or not a term is being used in a discussion in more than one way; the second problem is how a common meaning can be established for the participants in the discussion. This is a matter of inquiry into the *facts of meaning* for the individuals involved and usually boils down to determining what shall be the "correct" usage of a word. In definitional disagreements, it is important to remember first that the "correct" relationship between a label or term and the thing for which it stands is a matter of convention. There is no "natural" relationship between a word and its referent. Using the word *boys* to label young male humans and *girls* to label young female humans, for example, is based simply on the need for common symbolic meaning if communication is to take place. We could just as well change the convention, reverse the terms, and call a young male human a girl and a young female human a boy. (This, of course, assumes agreement plus adequate dissemination of the change so that confusion would not result. It also ignores the fact that people become emotionally attached to symbol-referent relationships, tend to see them as real, and resist usages which are "unnatural," i.e., unfamiliar.) What the example points up is that a definition can be changed whenever people can be persuaded that a different example, in the case of a pointing definition, or a different set of criteria would appropriately define the word.

Since convention is the basis for definition, one approach to definitional controversy is an appeal to popular or common usage. This may entail research designed to find out how most people use the word. Since most people have neither the time nor the resources to engage in such projects, the dictionary fills the gap as an authority on word usage. If the definition found there serves as a common ground for discussion, the purpose is fulfilled. However, one must be cautious not to assume that all people will use the word as it is defined in the dictionary. Dictionary definitions are often outdated. Moreover, dictionaries sometimes do not contain words which have been in use a relatively short period of time. Or dictionary definitions may be inadequate because they are only exemplary or pointing in character, because they are circular, or because they are not complete or specific enough to meet the needs of the particular argument.

To cope with uncertainties arising from deficiencies in dictionaries, *stipulation* is often used to resolve definitional problems. The discussants spell out, or stipulate, the meaning which the word is to have in their discussion, preferably by listing agreed-upon criteria. Here again, the danger is that the definition will be assumed to be adequate outside of the specific discussion context — which, in fact, it may be. It is also essential to keep the criteria in mind as the discussion progresses because definitions can shift very subtly and imperceptibly.

The use of stipulation may well involve the process of translation for some discussants. If, for example, it is agreed that for the purposes of discussion an essential criterion of the term *democratic society* is that there is public ownership of property, any participant who is not accustomed to using the term in this way must translate it to encompass this meaning whenever the words are used in this particular discussion. It is easy to see how a shift in the standards of translation could result, causing confusion or misunderstanding.

Perhaps the most important problem in resolving definitional disputes occurs when there is disagreement over classification. Let's look again at the case of the "democratic country." Two criteria were stated having to do with the existence of a constitution and the election of officials. We have suggested that recourse to convention or stipulation is in order if there is disagreement over the correctness of these criteria. But suppose the discussants agree on the criteria but one participant still insists that the Soviet Union is a democratic country, i.e., should be classified as a democratic country, because it has a constitution and elections. To this claim the reply might well be, "In the Soviet Union there is a constitution, but it does not *in fact* restrain the government and prevent it from trampling on important rights of the people; there are elections, but they are 'rigged' by the government and do not *in fact* allow the people to freely express their will." Obviously our criteria must have greater specificity. A democratic country is one which (1) has a constitution that guarantees important rights to all the people and that is respected and obeyed by the government and (2) has elections in which the people can express their wishes freely without fear of intimidation. Before actually getting to the problem of determining whether or not the Soviet Union conforms to these criteria, we may yet have to define key terms and phrases such as *respect for basic rights* and *free elections*. The process of definition involves specifying the criteria which define the class and determining whether or not referents commonly included in the class conform to the criteria and therefore whether or not the criteria are useful and adequate. The next problem of classification, once the category definitions are agreed upon, is to determine whether the controversial referent (in our example, the Soviet Union) has the characteristics implied by the class. And this is fundamentally a matter of testing factual claims — in this case gathering evidence to determine whether or not in fact constitutional restraints and free elections are part of the Soviet Union's political system.

Ideological or Value-Laden Class Names in Political Controversy. One of the major difficulties in discussing broad public issues is the extent to which labels or terms are used which stand for broad political or ideological positions. For example, we can place the following situations in a single value class.

A strong boy fighting with a weak boy.

A teacher keeping one boy after school and not keeping another boy after school, when both boys were caught breaking the same rule.

One man being allowed to vote and a second not being allowed to vote, when both have the same qualifications.

Two men making the same amount of money but one paying half of it in taxes, the other paying a quarter of it in taxes.

All of these situations can be described as violating one value position — equal treatment. We have classed them together because they evidence one characteristic — inequality. The process of putting objects or events into broad value classes and giving them a common label goes on all the time and is apparently a necessary element of political debate. As we have pointed out, however, it is not so natural to consider carefully the criteria according to which some objects or events are included in a class and others are excluded.

The use of class names is especially dangerous in that it leads toward hasty generalizations. We may see a man giving a speech criticizing the United States and classify him as "red" or Communist. Putting him in this class means that we will make certain assumptions about many of his political views. If the speech is the only information on which the classification is based, we may jump to unwarranted conclusions. General terms such as *Communist*, which are common in political arguments, are difficult to define and are often used for their emotional appeal rather than to convey a specific message. We often hear someone referred to as conservative, reactionary, liberal, left-wing, subversive, yet we rarely hear a careful definition of these terms.

We might define a Communist, for example, as one who (1) believes in the teachings of Karl Marx, (2) goes to Communist party meetings, and (3) works for world domination by Russia, China, or any country friendly to Russia or China. If these were our criteria, a person would have to meet all three to be classified as a Communist. The fact that a person believed in the teachings of Karl Marx would not be enough; we might call him a Marxist, but not a Communist. The fact that someone had gone to Communist party meetings would not give us sufficient information to classify him as a Communist; an FBI undercover agent or a curious college student might go to meetings of the Communist party.

Liberal is another ambiguous term commonly used in politics. Some men are described as liberals because they believe that the federal government should take greater leadership and spend more money to improve the general welfare of the people in all the states: through better education, more dams for public power, public aid to people for medical care. Others are called liberals because of their strong commitment to civil liberties for minority groups: voting rights for Negroes, the right of free speech for Communists. The label thus has two quite different meanings. How do we then classify a person who believes in greater federal leadership in welfare spending but who expresses no concern about the loss of civil liberties by minority groups?

The Emotional Component of Words. One of the most widely discussed aspects of controversy analysis is the emotional impact of language. A sample of the literature on this subject is instructive. The following remarks are taken from *How Do You Talk About People?* by Irving Lee:

> A story is told about the way a Greek communist newspaper reported some remarks of Paul Porter, made at a banquet in Macedonia while on an economic mission. He said, "It is indeed a pleasure to be here tonight with you good citizens of Greece. You Greeks and we Americans have very much in common. We like to eat. We like to drink. And we like to sit around and talk." The newspaper said, "Ambassador Porter said that we are just like Americans, gluttons, drunkards, and gossips."
>
> It is one of the commonplaces of studies in semantics that a number of words may refer to the same thing though each may imply strikingly different attitudes to it. As Sam Weller said, "When a poor fellow takes a piece of goods from a shop, it is called theft, but if a wealthy lady does the same thing, it is called monomania." It has been recently observed that "the rich are alcoholics and the poor are drunks." We learn rather quickly to reserve some words for use when things are considered pleasant and desirable and others for the contrary. If you wished to express approval of someone, would you not be likely to choose the former of the following pairs? Strength of purpose — pigheadedness, generous — spendthrift, zealot — fanatic, patriot — chauvinist, progressive — new-fangled, supporter of free enterprise — capitalist.
>
> A language will include terms which can point to things as well as convey the speaker's attitude toward them. This is relevant to our concern with evaluation, because so many people seem prone to judge others in accordance with the attitudes which accompany the words they apply to them. They not only choose words which by custom come to reflect their positive or negative notions but they are in turn influenced to look at people or things in terms of the notions implied by the terms which are used.[1]

The point is simply that political terms have strong emotional loadings and are especially difficult to define and use. Faced with such words in a discussion, we should remember to keep our thoughts on the accuracy of the description or on the criteria which define the words, not on the feelings they may summon.

To summarize: In this section we have discussed definitional problems and the problem of communication in a political controversy. We noted first that it is essential to determine whether the same words have different meanings for participants involved in a discussion, and whether different words are actually being used to suggest the same referent. If it is suspected that a disagreement has a definitional basis, communication can be clarified either by determining how the word is commonly used, i.e., what the social conventions are, or by stipulating the meaning which is to be applied to the word for the purposes of the specific discussion.

A second and related type of problem often occurs during controversies over public policy. It involves disagreement about the proper classification of an object, action, or person. The resolution of arguments over classification may entail one or more of the following steps: (1) determining what the proper class definition shall be if there is disagreement over the appropriateness or relevance of one or more of the criteria, (2) greater specification if it is found that there is disagreement or confusion over the meanings of specific words used in the criteria, and (3) inquiry into the factual description of the particular example being classified to determine whether its characteristics meet appropriate criteria.

It was also noted that because political labels are frequently used loosely one must be alert to their ambiguity and vagueness, especially when the label carries a strong emotional loading which will affect one's attitudes toward the object being classified.

Value Problems

Since we have already talked a great deal about value problems, the statements in this section are, in part, summaries of what has gone before. The act of valuing involves classifying objects or actions as "good" or "bad," "right" or "wrong." Values are those actions or objects that are valued. When we say due process is a value, we mean that to us actions or procedures labeled *due process* are good.

Personal Preferences, Aesthetic Judgments, and Social Values. Suppose we noted the following terms: *the music of Beethoven, blue neckties, equal voting rights.* If these are considered values, the phrase *is good* or *are good* is implied after each term. Intuitively, we know there is something quite different about asserting that blue neckties are good and that equal voting rights are good. Probably the most useful way to describe the distinction is in terms of the number of people our value judgment may affect and the extent to which each person may be affected. It is difficult to imagine the community's suffering any severe injury if people do not value blue neckties. This is not the case with such values as free speech and voting rights.

Values which are *not* significant enough to become the subject of general community or governmental concern we will call personal preferences. The problem of controversy over personal preference will not be dealt with here. (This is not to suggest that liking blondes rather than brunettes is not important. It is simply that such preferences are just as well left as private matters.)

Values which involve artistic taste or judgments of beauty, i.e., aesthetics, will also not be discussed. Again, they are indeed important to individuals. Unlike personal preferences, however, they are often the subject of wide discussion and social controversy.

The values with which we are mainly concerned are those political and social values — e.g., personal freedom, equality and justice, general welfare, and peace and order — which were discussed earlier. They are appropriate for discussion in a public school because they are the major concepts used by our government and private groups to justify public policies and decisions.

Values and Decisions. A value judgment suggests not only that something has been judged good or bad but also that a person will act on the basis of this judgment. A social value judgment, moreover, suggests that all people should act on the basis of the judgment. Likewise, suggested actions or decisions imply the support of a value judgment. That is, value judgments suggest decisions; decisions imply the support of value judgments. For example:

Value Judgment		Decision
Equal educational opportunity is good	Suggests that	Negroes should be given just as good instruction in the public schools as whites
A peaceful community is good	Suggests that	We should have an adequate police force
Free speech is good	Suggests that	We shouldn't pass laws censoring Communist literature

Decisions or policy stands describe the actions one is likely to support or carry out. Decisions can be justified by predicting that certain consequences will occur or that other consequences will be avoided if a decision is carried out. This assumes that everyone agrees on the goodness or badness of the consequences. Decisions can also be justified by demonstrating that important social values will be violated if the decision is not made.

Disagreements which center on whether or not a predicted consequence will occur as a result of a decision can often be resolved by gathering factual information and evidence to support one's prediction. Disagreements over whether or not the consequences themselves are good or bad must first be dealt with by referring both the consequences and the decisions back to important social values. For example:

Decision	Specific Consequence
We should arrest people who make Communist-sounding speeches because	these people will spread Communist ideas

If the person who gives this argument is confronted with evidence that arresting people who make Communist-sounding speeches does not prevent the spread of Communist ideas it weakens his position. But if he produces evidence that such arrests do in fact halt the spread of Communist ideas, someone might say, "That is bad. We should have as many people as possible know about Communist ideas. We should have a free market place of ideas."

At this point in a value disagreement, the people disagreeing can refer back to more basic social values that each wants to preserve in the community. For example:

	Decision	Social Value
Mr. Smith might say:	We should jail people who talk in favor of Communism because . . .	such talk threatens the safety of the community.

Mr. Jones might say: We should let everyone
speak on any subject he
pleases, as long as he
does not use lies to dam-
age people's reputations,
because . . . .   free speech is an essential
ingredient of personal
freedom.

Justifying decisions by asserting that they tend to support or violate basic social values forces us into the problem of value conflict. A single decision may be defended on the grounds that it preserves one social value and at the same time denounced because it violates another. In the example above, censorship of Communist speeches was defended on the grounds that it preserved peace and order and denounced on the grounds that it abridged free speech.

Confrontation between these controversial points of view, however, depends upon the assumption that there is at least *some truth* to the implied claims of consequences behind each person's value position. For example, the person who stresses the importance of peace and order assumes that Communist speeches will lead to violence and disorder and to a general weakening of important societal values. If we found upon careful investigation that there was very little chance that Communist speeches and publications would lead to violence, disorder, and the deterioration of important values, there would be no value conflict. Censorship would be seen as simply bad. If, on the other hand, we found that in several countries where Communists were given freedom of speech there was a loss of respect for law and individual freedom resulting in riots, or even revolutions, we might seriously consider some censorship on the grounds that it would help preserve a lawful society. We can see, therefore, that value conflicts may disappear when the factual assumptions behind each value position are tested.

But suppose we test the factual assumptions behind each value position and find that for a given situation any reasonable decision will lead to the violation of at least one important value. For example:

Situation	*Alternative Decisions*
The Amish, a religious group in Pennsylvania, believe that the government should not provide citizens with old-age pensions. It is part of their religious conviction that each person should take care of his own family in sickness and in old age.	1. The government can force the Amish to pay their social security taxes, which will never benefit them, and which violate their religious convictions; *or*
	2. The government can exempt the Amish from the tax and violate equal protection under the law, i.e., everyone but the Amish will be required to pay the tax.
There is a national emergency. The North Korean Communists have invaded South Korea. President Truman wants to call up several military reserve units. Many of the men in these units served three and four years in the armed forces during World War II.	1. The President can call up the troops in the reserve units and have a better-trained defense force to protect the national security; *or*

Their lives were disrupted once by war, and now they will be disrupted again. But the President needs troops.

2. The President can draft young men who have never served their country, and give all young citizens more equal treatment.

Let us assume that in these situations (and in many like them) there is a genuine value conflict, one that does not disappear when the facts are in. No simple solution exists. One cannot resolve the conflict by saying that the answer is only a matter of opinion. Public policy is at stake, and a wrong decision may affect the future of the nation. One cannot resolve it by simply saying it is a matter of definition, using the right words to describe the situation. No matter how the situation is described, there is, in some sense, a violation of fairness or justice. One cannot solve the problem by saying "Get more evidence." The evidence indicates more and more clearly that some people's rights are going to be violated in the interests of the community.

In confronting this issue we must accept the fact that there is no "correct" or "right" solution. We must create or accept that policy which least violates our concept of human dignity and which least violates any of the social values that promote human dignity. The purpose of analyzing political problems of this type is to lead to a decision which will minimize the violation of important values, not to pretend that no conflict between these values exists.

Importance of Reflective Analysis. In general, value problems are at the center of political and social disagreements. In a community which is concerned with maintaining a balance between governmental actions that benefit the community and governmental actions that protect the freedom of each individual, every one of us has an obligation to weigh in our own minds the wisdom of proposed governmental action and make a decision in terms of its benefit to the dignity of each individual. To surrender this obligation to influence governmental actions through carefully thought-out decisions can lead to loss of the freedoms that are most important to us all.

Factual Problems

We have discussed some concepts related to both definitional problems and value problems. In this section we will take up disagreements over fact — what we will call *claims*. In political argument the center of a controversy is usually a disagreement over conflicting values: Which value is more closely associated with human dignity or rational consent? Whether or not there actually is a value conflict often depends upon the accuracy of factual information. The accuracy of factual information in an argument over public decisions is important in at least two ways:

1. While a decision itself is based on the elements in a situation which each person thinks are good and bad, right and wrong, and cannot be "proved" true or false, the decision very soon leads to certain implied factual considerations. For example, the statement "Voting rights of Negroes in the South are violated" implies certain facts. This is quite a different statement from "Negroes should have full voting rights," which does not say whether or not Negroes have these rights. Thus, it is important to establish the facts suggested by the claim that a value has been violated before assuming that a value conflict exists. After a

careful investigation of the facts all may agree that there is no value conflict at all.

2. In a political controversy people make factual predictions to support a value position. For example, it is often stated that a social security program guaranteeing unemployment assistance and old-age pensions will weaken the initiative and self-reliance of workers; or that high personal income taxes weaken the initiative of business and professional people because most of what they earn will be taken in taxes by the government. Although often such arguments are put forward by people who favor private property rights over efforts of the government to provide for the general welfare, the arguments themselves depend upon the reliability of specific factual claims, not upon the validity of one's values. The dispute is not over whether property rights or taxes are good but rather over whether or not governmental action will, in fact, lead to certain undesirable consequences: a lazy and irresponsible work force.

Determining the Reliability of Factual Claims. It is important to distinguish among *conclusions* drawn from specific observations of events, the *observations* themselves, and the *events* observed. An event may be defined as a happening or a state of affairs in the world around us. All knowledge, as we define knowledge, depends upon the observation and description of these events. The raw material of an event consists of living things, objects, and actions. When we describe events we are actually describing our perception of events. We never know *for sure* what the exact nature of an event is. We know only what our senses have told our brain and what our brain has interpreted the event to mean. These general interpretations of specific observations we are here calling *conclusions*. The distinction between factual observation and conclusion is well illustrated by the following anecdote.

> President Eliot of Harvard enjoyed telling the story of an experience he once had, illustrating proper caution in drawing a conclusion. When he entered a crowded New York restaurant, he handed his hat to the doorman. As he came out he was astonished to see the doorman promptly pick his hat out of the hundreds there and hand it to him. In his surprise he asked, "How did you know that was my hat?" "I didn't know that was your hat, sir," was the answer, "Why then," asked Mr. Eliot, "did you hand it to me?" Very courteously the doorman replied, "Because you handed it to me, sir."[2]

When a factual conclusion is questioned, we usually defend it in two ways. First, we try to show that specific observations tend to support the more general conclusion. Second, we try to show that other facts fit into a logical pattern if the conclusion under question is also assumed to be true.

For example, suppose we make the claim

> Workers who belong to labor unions are better off than workers who have no such affiliation.

First we must settle the definitional problem of what "better off" means. Suppose we agree that "better off" is defined in such terms as wages, working conditions, vacation pay, sick leave, pension funds, and job security. The first way we might support the statement is to look at more specific claims. We might find that

1. Truck drivers in the Teamsters Union get 45 per cent higher wages than non-union truck drivers.
2. Construction workers in Georgia are paid less than construction workers in New York City. The construction workers in Georgia are largely unorganized, while the construction workers in New York City almost all belong to unions.

The greater number of specific claims we can identify which tend to support the conclusion we are trying to prove, the more reliable the conclusion becomes.

A second way to support the claim is to relate it to other general facts which are accepted as true. For example, we might cite a dramatic rise in wages paid to unskilled factory workers between the years 1935 and 1940, knowing that this was the period when many unskilled factory workers joined unions. These facts would be consistent with the conclusion that union workers are better off than non-union workers. (Note that this does *not* prove that joining unions was the cause of higher wages.) In general, then, we back our factual conclusions by giving specific information which supports the general conclusion under dispute and by showing that the conclusion is logically related to other facts.

Specific claims are descriptive statements about events occurring at a particular time in a particular place. "Franklin Roosevelt died in 1945." "The United States dropped two atomic bombs on Japan in August 1945." While the exact time or place may not be stated, these are examples of specific claims. There is, however, another kind of claim which is not tied to a particular time and place. For example:

1. Negroes are not as intelligent as whites.
2. Depressions occur when corporations refuse to increase the wages of workers to keep pace with increase in production efficiency.

These claims describe or summarize events which allegedly occur consistently and predictably. They are general claims or *generalizations*. Generalizations tend to be confirmed when we find specific examples to support them. In the generalizations listed above we would

1. Look at individual Negroes and whites, or look at groups of Negroes and whites, to find out whether or not Negroes were *generally* as intelligent as whites.
2. Compare periods in our history in which production efficiency increased rapidly and wages remained the same, and see whether such periods were followed by depressions.

Generalizations are a particular kind of conclusion arrived at by looking at a number of instances of a type of event. Note that they not only summarize a number of specific claims or facts but imply that, because particular types of events have been observed in the past, evidence gathered in the future will probably support the general conclusion already reached. In this sense, all generalizations are predictions. In checking whether or not a generalization is sound, it is important to evaluate the number and reliability of specific instances or specific facts which tend to support the generalization.

We commonly call generalizations, as well as specific claims, *facts*. As has just been pointed out, whether or not a generalization, like a specific claim, is a fact depends upon the reliability and quantity of evidence supporting it. *Evidence* is defined here as any statement that can be used to support the truth or reliability of another statement. Thus, evidence can be specific or general. It is likely, however, to be more specific than the statement it supports.

For example, the general conclusion "The United States is the richest nation in the world" can be supported by many "facts." These facts can be generalizations or general conclusions: The United States produces more cars than any other nation; the United States produces more wheat than any other nation; and so on. Each general statement can then be supported by a more specific statement. Thus we can build a general-to-specific chain of evidence:

The United States is the richest nation in the world [because]

It produces more cars per capita than any other nation [which is confirmed by the fact that]

The United States produced five million cars last year and this was more than the number produced by all other nations combined [which is confirmed by figures recently released by]

The United States Department of Commerce indicating the number of cars produced in the United States and abroad.

Each more specific statement could be considered "evidence" supporting the statement above it. When generalizations are questioned, we try to back them with more specific generalizations, statistics, or reliable sources.

Statistics. A statistic is a numerical estimate based on a count of several events that have been observed. It summarizes a number of observations. Some statistical statements are not generalizations because they refer to specific observations that have already been made and assume nothing about the nature of future observations. However, some statistical statements are generalizations because, while they may be based on a specific enumeration of events, they go on to a general inference or prediction. For example, we might look at the rate of economic growth of the Soviet Union and that of the United States in terms of specific statistics. A summary of these observations would be a descriptive statistic. If we went on to conclude that the Soviet Union has, in general, a higher rate of economic growth than the United States, this would be an inference, or generalization, based on the statistic.

Sources. When a specific claim, a generalization, or a statistic is questioned, we often try to prove its reliability by identifying where we obtained the information, i.e., its source. The following types of sources are convenient labels to begin to describe sources and test their reliability.

1. *Intuition as a source of evidence.* Intuition is often called "common sense." Someone supports a statement by saying, "It's common sense." If pressed, he may go on to explain, "Well, I just know that it is true." Many claims we believe to be true are based on intuitive evidence. Intuition is, as a rule, a poor source of evidence because it offers no way of proving to other people that our claim is a fact and that their claim is false. When there is a factual disagreement, it is usually best to look beyond intuition and seek other sources of evidence.

Intuition is, however, related to two other types of evidence which we shall discuss. In the first place, intuitions are often based on experiences the person has had. So a statement that "I just have a feeling that the Chinese people will never be able to revolt against the Communists" may actually have some implicit factual basis; i.e., there may be observational data sufficient to warrant a reasonable "hunch." Or if the person said that it was just "common sense" that such a revolution would not take place now, he may actually have based this statement on some historical data with which he is familiar. In this case it would be important to move to the evaluation of those data. If one had to make a choice between relying on intuition supported by no experiences or information and intuition rooted in some concrete evidence even though not thoroughly substantiated by it, the latter would certainly provide a firmer ground for action.

It should also be recognized that some intuitions are more "respectable" than others because of specific past experiences an individual has had or because he seems to have particularly valid insights about some things. For example, we would probably give Ambassador Thompson's "hunch" about how the Russians would react to a specific treaty proposal a great deal of weight even though his judgment was based only on a "hunch." So, while in general we should apply rigorous standards of proof to intuitively based claims, we should at the same time recognize that an intuitional statement by a person with some competence in the field under consideration, even though not substantiated by concrete evidence, is probably a better basis for a decision than no evidence at all.

2. *Authority as a source of evidence.* The claim is made by a history student that "Germany was defeated in World War II." When we ask him how he knows, he says, "My history book says so." Someone makes the claim that there has been a revolution in a Latin-American country. He says he knows it is true because he read it in yesterday's *New York Times.* Often a person faced with the problem of proving a claim points to someone else who has made the claim. The "someones" are usually people, like the author of a history book or a *New York Times* reporter, who are supposed to know more than we do about a given claim. In other words, these are people who we believe are reliable authorities.

What makes an authority reliable? The following questions can be used to gather evidence of reliability:

a. Is the authority a firsthand observer of the events about which he tells? Did the newspaper reporter, for instance, actually witness the Latin-American revolution?

b. If the authority is not a firsthand observer, does he state who told him the claims he is repeating?

Different people may present contradictory reports, even though they have read or heard the same piece of information. It is important, therefore, to know the original source from which each person got his information so that we can find out what it really said. Because we cannot check testimony unless we know where to find it, most reliable authorities indicate the source of their information.

c. Is the authority an expert on the subject about which he is writing? How much training and experience has he had in his field?

Someone may report that Brazil is becoming a Communist country. This testimony may very probably require knowledge about Communism, knowledge about the leaders of Brazil and its history and tradition. Before believing the claim that Brazil is becoming a Communist country, we must be convinced that the man who made the claim has the necessary knowledge to make accurate observations on the subject. When an authority is reporting an observation for which technical knowledge is necessary, it is important to obtain information about his technical competence.

d. Is there any information about the authority that would lead us to believe that he has a personal bias or prejudice?

If the officer of a corporation is asked whether high corporation taxes are slowing the growth of business, he will almost certainly answer "yes." If asked why, he will give a number of very good reasons. It is possible that he has given a fair view of the situation and that corporations are actually overtaxed. It is also possible, however, that he favors corporations because he runs one, and has built a set of reasons to justify his own biases.

The word *bias* indicates that a strong personal feeling about the goodness or badness of a person, action, or object may interfere with the evaluation of truth or falsity of a related claim or set of claims. People do not usually admit that they have biases or prejudices. They prefer to think that they believe certain claims because they are actually true.

A person who has no personal "interest" in a subject under discussion is often referred to as "disinterested." He does not have money, property, or his reputation at stake in the outcome of an issue. Because he has no personal interests involved, he has no obvious reason to be biased for or against the claim under question. The corporation officer would not be disinterested about taxes because his living depends on running a corporation profitably, which in turn may depend on convincing us (or the government) that corporations are being overtaxed.

An authority can, however, have a personal interest in an issue and still make reliable claims. Many reporters, like the southern Negro who makes a statement on race relations, have a personal interest in what they report. The way to evaluate the testimony of any reporter who we suspect has a personal interest in an issue is to attempt to assess whether his interest prevents him from giving accurate testimony. We can determine this by asking other questions about the authority's account.

e. Does the authority contradict himself at any point?

Does the authority give a careful, consistent argument? For example, the corporation officer may claim that corporations are being "taxed broke" and then in another setting boast about the high dividends paid to the stockholders.

f. Are the claims supported by other authorities?

The southern Negro claims there is discrimination in the South. If other authorities familiar with the South agree with him, we would tend to accept the Negro's claim.

These are only a few of the more important questions we may ask about authorities to help us judge their reliability. It should also be noted here that people sometimes look for symbols of authority which may have little to do with the question of whether or not a person is competent. Some of these questionable symbols are suggested below:

Many children and young people believe that *being an adult* makes a person an authority. We commonly assume that the older we get, the more we know.

People sometimes try to prove claims by saying that an older person "told me so." Older people obviously have limited knowledge, and, in fact, often disagree with one another.

Some people believe anything they read. A *claim in print* — black print on white paper — seems to cast a magic spell of seeming truth. Yet it is almost as easy to make false or exaggerated claims on paper as it is by word of mouth. It is just a little more expensive.

Many people believe that because a man has *status* — because he is *important* in the eyes of the community — he is a reliable authority on all subjects. Businessmen, political leaders, doctors, television stars, and people with a great deal of money have high status. We often believe what they say, whether or not they are expert on the subject about which they are making claims.

3. *Personal observation as a source of evidence.* A third source of evidence is direct personal observation. While in some situations it is one of the best types of evidence, it does have important limitations, especially in the study of political controversy, where one often cannot prove things by personal observations. In evaluating historical evidence, it is impossible to set up a demonstration that enables us to see firsthand exactly what happened in some earlier period. For this reason, in issues of public policy which depend largely on historical knowledge we try to prove things more often by use of authorities than by use of personal observation and demonstration.

Another difficulty is the tendency to see what we wish to see or hear what we wish to hear, selecting and remembering those aspects of an experience which are most consonant with our previous experience and background.

4. *Proof by analogy.* Frequently the lengthy process of carefully evaluating evidence in the effort to support a claim is bypassed in favor of a much simpler method — proof by analogy. Someone claims, for example, that a constitution is necessary to run a government. Instead of gathering evidence to show that his claim is true, he simply says, "A written constitution is as necessary to a government as a rulebook is to an orderly game of football." We know that a complicated game like football would be very confusing without a rulebook. We know that government is complicated too. We are likely to accept the claim that government and football are alike in requiring a written constitution or a rulebook because they are alike in being complicated. We might then conclude that memory or informal customs can't be depended on to solve disputes in government any more than in football. A comparison is made between something simple or familiar and something more abstract or complex.

Analogies can, however, be misleading. Although two objects, acts, or situations may be analogous in certain ways, they may be different in other important ways. A football rulebook spells things out in great detail. A constitution tends to be more general. If our Constitution, written almost 200 years ago, had been very specific, it would be out of date today and perhaps have been cast aside long since. Constitutional amendments are much more difficult to make than changes in a football rulebook and have more serious consequences for the community. In these respects a constitution is very different from a football rulebook. The person comparing two similar objects or situations in an effort to prove a point, therefore, must be careful to notice the ways in which they are different as well as the ways in which they are alike.

Sampling: How Much Evidence Do We Need? We have talked about the need for distinguishing between conclusions and evidence, or specific observations which are given to support them. A further point is that the accuracy and reliability of conclusions based on specific claims depend not only on the *truth* of the specific claims upon which the conclusion is based but also upon the *number* and *type* of events actually observed. In other words, we have to be concerned not only with the *reliability* of our evidence but also with the *amount* of evidence. The process of selecting and observing facts which may support a particular generalization or conclusion is called *sampling*. There are two important considerations to keep in mind in evaluating the sample of evidence supporting a conclusion. (1) The sample must be large enough to justify the generalization or conclusion. If we assert that "the average labor union member is dissatisfied with his labor leaders," it is better to have asked 1000 members than to have asked 10. (2) The sample must be representative of the types of events about which conclusions are to be drawn. To conclude that union members are dissatisfied with their leaders, the evidence should be based on the sampling of a variety of different kinds of unions in a variety of different kinds of industries. Some labor unions, for example, are made up mainly of unskilled workers. Others are mostly for skilled workers. Still others are organized on an industry-wide basis, like those of the steel and rubber workers, and include both skilled and unskilled workers. If a classification such as "skilled" versus "unskilled" might be related to the type of leadership a union has, or to whether or not the worker might be dissatisfied with this leadership, we would want to be certain that the sample of workers included a representative number of workers who belonged to both kinds of unions.

Telling How Sure We Are That Factual Statements Are Reliable. Whether or not a claim is actually true depends upon the quality and quantity of evidence supporting it. Because evidence is always limited, we never know for sure whether a claim is absolutely correct or absolutely false. And since there is always some degree of doubt about the truth or falsity of a claim, we need some way to express the degree of certainty we feel in making a factual statement.

When there is a great deal of evidence to support a claim, it is usually called a *fact*. In our terms, a fact is a claim that can be proved beyond reasonable doubt, e.g., Abraham Lincoln was elected President in 1860. This does not mean that the statement is absolutely true; it may still be possible to cast doubt on its reliability. However, for all intents and purposes, we can treat it as true. Specific claims are more likely to be true beyond reasonable doubt than are conclusions.

In many cases there is scarcity of evidence supporting a claim, or some contradictory evidence. The history of labor unions shows, for example, that they usually have helped workers, although there is also some evidence that unions have damaged the workers' interests. When most of the evidence available indicates that a statement like "Labor unions help workers" is true, we can say that a statement is *probably true*.

When the great preponderance of evidence indicates that a statement is not true, the statement can be called *false beyond reasonable doubt*. This also is a fact, if in a negative sense.

When most of the evidence indicates that a statement is false, we might say that the statement is *probably false*.

Some statements cannot be thought of in any of these terms because the evidence is too scanty or because what evidence is available is too contradictory. When such situations arise, we can consider the statements *doubtful* or *controversial*. It is sometimes important, however, not to accept doubtful or controversial statements as they stand, but rather to deal with statements at a lower level of generality which may be susceptible of proof with additional evidence. For example, in arguments over the race problem in America, a common issue raised is whether or not there is a genetic basis for intellectual differences between Negroes and whites. The evidence on this issue is so cloudy that almost any statement one can make is, at best, controversial. It is well established, however, that in general the white performs better than the Negro on intelligence tests and measures of academic achievement. This fact may itself require clarification and qualification quite apart from the question of whether one can adequately deal with the more general question of innate intellectual differences.

While the language one uses in describing certainty of knowledge may seem trivial, this often seems to be a point on which arguments become stalemated. The simple true-false dichotomy sets a requirement that, in many cases, is unattainable. What is suggested here is a rhetoric allowing for degrees of provisional truth.

Loaded Statements: The Thin Line Between Value Judgments and Factual Claims. We have already discussed the problem of loaded definitions and labels. The general problem of affectively toned language is even more difficult to deal with when considered in the context of total statements. The fact of the matter is that value judgments and claims are seldom clearly separated in statements. More often values and preferences are woven into factual claims, which are then commonly called loaded statements.

Two questions can always be asked about any loaded statement: (1) Does the statement contain an accurate descriptive claim? and (2) Do we agree or disagree with the value or preference that the statement expresses? Let's ask these two questions of the following statement: "The President spends more time vacationing than he does taking care of public business." This can be treated as a claim and subjected to a factual test, or we can simply react to the implied value judgment. In answering the two questions about this statement, we may find that (a) we like the President even though he plays golf more than he attends to public business (we accept the accuracy of the facts but we disagree with the preference expressed); (b) or we dislike the President even though he spends most of his time attending to public business (we agree with the preference expressed but we do not accept the accuracy of the facts); (c) or we like the President and know that he spends most of his time attending to public business (we disagree with the preference and do not accept the accuracy of the facts expressed); (d) or we dislike the President because he spends more time vacationing than he does attending to public business (we accept the accuracy of the facts and agree with the preference expressed). The point is that we must be careful to analyze both the feelings and the claims expressed in a loaded statement, for, although our values may differ from those implied in the loaded statement, we may be forced to agree that the facts are correct.

Sometimes it is possible to change a few key words and thereby change the value-loading implied in the statement even though the facts expressed remain the same. For example, a person might say, "Through radical and reckless spending on socialistic schemes our state is now on the verge of bankruptcy and financial disaster." Or he might say, "In our effort to provide state funds to give a decent standard of living to the sick, the needy, and the disabled we have spent much money, and new sources of revenue are now needed to keep our state solvent." From a factual point of view, both statements may be saying pretty much the same thing. However, the feelings expressed by the two statements are quite different.

It is important that we understand clearly why we are attacking or defending a statement. Are we doing it on the basis of its factual meaning or on the basis of its value implication? Unless the basis of attack is clear, we may end up defending a factual claim simply because it "sounds good" rather than because it can be supported by evidence.

Conclusion

We have now talked about three different kinds of disagreement: disagreement over the use or meaning of words, disagreement over the relative importance of certain principles of social and political conduct, and disagreement over the accuracy or plausibility of certain events in the world around us. A controversial discussion may embrace disagreements falling into one or more types, and the relationship between them may be subtle and complex. Categorizing disagreements in this way is a useful initial step in the analysis of political discussion, since the appropriateness of one's approach to the controversy depends upon seeing the specific nature of the conflict. Intense discussions over the value of fallout shelters during the summer and fall of 1961 illustrate this point very well. The following questions were commonly raised: (1) After an atomic war, would life be worth living in the midst of what was left? (2) Would a shelter program actually decrease or increase the likelihood of war? (3) Does a man have the right to lock his neighbor out of his shelter to protect his own family?

The initial strategies for dealing with these three questions might be quite different. In the first question a great deal hinges on the definition of two terms: *worth living* and *what was left*. The second term (*what was left*) can immediately be translated into a factual issue whereas the first term (*worth living*) explicitly presents a value issue. The second question is clearly a factual one. The third, however, is again a value question. Discussions commonly raised these important questions but failed to deal with them systematically. Each antagonist tended to dwell on those issues he intuitively felt favored his side of the argument; he refused to deal with the issues which tended to operate against him. If one is aware of the fact that discussion becomes more fruitful when individuals go beyond the initial statement of issues to the question of an appropriate strategy for resolution, the process of rational consent may hopefully be carried out with greater intelligence. This chapter has sought to provide a framework with which sources of disagreement may be conceptualized as well as to suggest strategies by which different types of controversy may be clarified or resolved.

REFERENCES

1. Irving Lee. *How Do You Talk About People?* (New York: Anti-Defamation League of B'nai B'rith, 1956), p. 18.
2. Walter B. Cannon, *The Way of an Investigator* (New York: W. W. Norton & Company, Inc., 1945), p. 337, quoted in Lee *op. cit.*, p. 13.

FURTHER READING FOR SECTION 5

Ennis, Robert H. "A Concept of Critical Thinking," *Harvard Educational Review*, 1962, 32, pp. 81–111.

In this article, Ennis attempts a simplified description of the dimensions of critical thinking. It is often cited and might well help the teacher to decide on the dimensions of critical thinking to be taught. Note, however the absence of any treatment of value judgments.

Hunt, Maurice P., and Lawrence E. Metcalf. *Teaching High School Social Studies.* New York: Harper, 1955.

This textbook is of overall value to the social studies teacher because of its careful presentation of the rationale underlying a curricular position favoring reflective thinking. Chapter 17 presents a discussion of ways to teach for reflective thinking while still meeting the superficial demands of content, "ground-covering" oriented schools.

Larrabee, Harold A. *Reliable Knowledge*, rev. ed. Boston: Houghton Mifflin, 1964.

This book is something of a standard on critical thinking. It is very readable and covers a good cross-section of problems in knowledge verification. It does not treat value issues.

Shaver, James P. "Reflective Thinking, Values, and Social Studies Textbooks," *School Review*, 1965, 73, pp. 226–257.

How adequate is the treatment of reflective thinking in social studies texts? This article is a critical review in the context of concepts needed to think about public issues. It will be helpful to the teacher who wishes to determine the adequacy of the textbooks he uses.

Stevenson, Charles L. *Ethics and Language.* New Haven, Conn.: Yale University Press, 1944. *Facts and Values.* New Haven, Conn.: Yale University Press, 1963.

These scholarly discussions of the problems of ethical analysis have been hailed as outstanding. Neither book is easy to read, especially the first, but both are well worth the effort for a teacher looking for an incisive treatment of ethics that goes beyond the notion that the final solution to an ethical problem is to check the consequences of different actions.

6

Research in Social Studies
Instruction

Whether or not the field of education is classified as a science (or a discipline) is of little import to most social studies teachers. It is of some importance, however, that the possibilities of studying education scientifically be stressed. Educators must recognize that empirical research can be conducted on questions which are significant to the teaching of social studies. This is not to say that all studies in education must be scientific; philosophical and logical analysis are appropriate and necessary for many questions. Nor would we deny that a great deal of what has passed for research in education has been so poorly done that it hardly merits the label *science*.

Educational Research: Problems and Criticisms

Educational research still has far to go, and this is especially true of research in the teaching of the social studies. One indication of the state of the field is McPhie's annotated list of doctoral dissertations in social studies education between 1934 and 1962.[1] As Metcalf has noted,[2] graduate studies are likely to reflect the research interests and methods of professors of social studies education and so should provide some evidence of the state of knowledge in the field. Yet Metcalf concluded that the dissertations listed by McPhie contributed little to the building or clarification of any theory for social studies instruction.

> Dissertations have resulted in teaching manuals, course outlines, trend identification, status studies which are soon out of date, surveys of local peculiarities, controlled experiments of dubious design, historical studies, and textbook analysis. Many studies are local and dated in nature, and no attempt has been made to relate them to the larger, abiding questions in teaching the social studies.[3]

Educational research is undoubtedly lacking in many respects, but criticism should take into account the many practical and theoretical difficulties with which this sort of research is fraught. For example, controlling the variables that impinge on an educational setting in order to come up with nice "clean" answers is extremely difficult, especially as compared to physical science and

[1] Walter E. McPhie, *Dissertations in Social Studies Education: A Comprehensive Guide* (Washington: National Council for the Social Studies, 1964).
[2] Lawrence E. Metcalf, "Research on Teaching the Social Studies," in N. L. Gage (ed.), *Handbook of Research on Teaching* (Chicago: Rand McNally, 1963), p. 931.
[3] *Ibid.*

some behavioral science research. Nevertheless, the many constraints do not necessarily preclude the conduct of rigorous and illuminating educational research. In fact, much of the careless and trivial research in education undoubtedly reflects the fact that the researchers have lacked the rigorous research orientation and training that are prerequisites to grappling with the many problems involved in carrying out quality investigations which might ultimately be of benefit to ongoing educational institutions.

In addition, researchers in education have not developed strategies and techniques for attacking many of the peculiar difficulties of educational research. Models for experimentation that have long standing in the biological and physical sciences are rarely directly applicable to classroom research. Students cannot be easily subjected to experimental treatments which might prove harmful to them or violate their individual rights. Moreover, the complexity of human learning and of the situations in which it occurs makes it nearly impossible to insure that "key" variables have not been overlooked and left uncontrolled. Also, measurement is basic to any science, and the problems of measuring complex educational outcomes still baffle educational researchers. However, new research strategies and techniques are being developed[4] along with new tests and testing techniques, and educational research can be expected to make new and valuable contributions in the years to come. This section will treat a few interesting developments to date.

In judging the products of educational research (and other behavioral science research), it is important to recall that empirical research in education is a relatively recent phenomenon, in contrast, for example, with the over three hundred years of empirical work in physics. We do not intend to write an apologia for poor research. Yet the fact that quantitative educational research dates back only to the early part of this century has a bearing on the unproductiveness for which this research has been criticized. As recently as the 1920's, the major emphasis in educational research was on test construction and on gathering descriptive data about schools and students.[5] This may have been a necessary developmental stage, but descriptive studies provide little knowledge about teaching and the learning process. Research in which relevant variables are controlled (called *experimentation*) and hypotheses are tested is more likely to provide useful knowledge about learning than are descriptive studies — especially when information is sought about complex matters such as the contingencies involved in teaching students to apply analytical skills to social issues. Central to the building of sound knowledge on any one topic, but generally absent from educational research, is a large number of carefully designed and executed studies in which hypotheses are accepted, rejected, or reformulated and retested.

Research in instruction is just beginning to produce the accumulation of knowledge which is necessary to assist educators in devising educational programs. It would be an exaggeration to say that educational research up to the late 1960's has contributed a great deal to our understanding of classroom learning. Except in a few limited areas, there is as yet too little cumulative

[4] See, for example, the chapters on research design and on research techniques in N. L. Gage (ed.), *Handbook of Research on Teaching, ibid.*

[5] See, e.g., Walter R. Borg, *Educational Research: An Introduction* (New York: David McKay, 1963), Chapter 1.

research to yield a substantial body of knowledge upon which to base educational practice.

What does all of this have to do with the classroom teacher? It would be absurd to advocate that each classroom teacher become a sophisticated educational researcher. At the same time, however, it is important that each teacher be aware of the state of the knowledge upon which classroom instructional decisions must be based. Although the teacher may not always be competent to judge the technical adequacy of educational research, it will be increasingly important in the years to come that he be sufficiently literate to make some judgments about research in his field. Certainly, he must be cautious of accepting instructional suggestions just because the claim is made that they are "based on research."

Research on Teaching

The teacher may select his content or method for a number of reasons, including his judgment of their efficacy for his ends or because of what he considers his own instructional strengths to be. The readings and commentary in previous sections have been concerned primarily with the problems of establishing an adequate rationale for the curriculum. The selection of content and method on the basis of a rationale is to some extent a matter of logic. Once a rationale is clarified and goals set, criteria for the selection of content can be derived from the rationale and goals, and content and methods selected as they relate to the criteria. However, curriculum development has too long proceeded as if selection were only a matter of logical correspondence between goals on the one hand and content and method on the other. The question of the correspondence between curriculum and goals is also empirical: Do the content and method of instruction accomplish the goals? Or, does *this* set of content or *this* organization of content accomplish the goals better than another? In other words, the curriculum (including both content and method) should be judged by its impact on students.

For example, there is much that is intuitively attractive about the proposition that social studies courses should be organized around the structures of social science disciplines as identified by social scientists. The vision of knowledge unfolding in logical order with a resultant increment in psychological meaning for the student is appealing. Yet should the way the scientist orders the concepts of his field determine the order in which social knowledge is taught to the student? Perhaps an ordering of concepts based on their relevance to the discussion of public issues or other topics will be more effective. Or a combined approach utilizing both the scientist's ordering and an ordering based on issues or topics may be the most effective for insuring that the student will learn the concepts, retain them, and later see their relevance and application to issues facing himself and the society.

Though the focus in previous sections has been on the rationale for social studies instruction, there have been several references to research. Studies have been cited that indicate that (1) concepts of "reflective thinking" should be identified and taught explicitly and (2) focusing on the analysis of public issues in the classroom will not necessarily mean a decrement in the learning of the usual social studies content. Nevertheless, many urgent questions about content selection and organization and about teaching still lack research answers.

What, for example, does research tell us about the types of teacher or teaching which are most effective — that is, most likely to bring about desired pupil learning? Is the "democratic" teacher likely to be more successful than the "autocrat"? The answer seems clear on a common sense basis, and instructors of methods courses have emphasized the importance of "democratic" teacher behavior. After an exhaustive review of the research dealing with the democratic-autocratic or teacher-centered versus learner-centered dimension of teaching behavior, Anderson concluded that:

> To summarize the educational research reviewed in this article, eleven studies have reported greater learning for learner-centered groups, thirteen have shown no difference, and eight have found teacher-centered methods superior to learner-centered. It should be noted that while some investigations have reported a statistically significant difference favoring one method or other, it is doubtful if any of these differences are of practical or social significance.[6]

The problem is not just that we know little about the effects of democratic versus autocratic behavior,[7] but that we know little about teacher effectiveness in general. In the first reading in this section, Donald M. Medley and Harold E. Mitzel review the unproductive research which has attempted to estimate a teacher's efficiency on the basis of ratings by supervisors. They comment generally on the state of knowledge about teacher effectiveness, indicate some approaches to future research that may prove productive, and end on a note of hopeful optimism about future possibilities.

Measurement Problems in Research on Teaching

Among the areas presenting tremendous deficiencies yet to be overcome in educational research, measurement is foremost. The efforts of researchers and teachers in the social studies suffer alike from the lack of valid tests for assessing instructional outcomes. The use of standardized tests may seem to be the answer to this problem. However, standardized tests are designed to measure knowledge likely to be learned by students across the nation; too often the test items are not relevant to the instructional objectives of a specific curriculum.

In addition, standardized tests are especially inadequate for the measurement of the students' ability to analyze societal issues. Several criticisms have been leveled at the validity of published tests of "critical thinking."[8] It is claimed,

---

[6] Richard C. Anderson, "Learning in Discussions: A Resume of the Authoritarian-Democratic Studies," *Harvard Educational Review*, 1959, 29, p. 201.

[7] The seminal studies of Lewin, Lippitt, and White (Kurt Lewin, Ronald Lippitt, and Robert White, "Patterns of Aggressive Behavior in Experimentally Created 'Social Climates,'" *Journal of Social Psychology*, 1939, 10, pp. 271–299) indicated that the type of group leadership can affect productivity. But, as Anderson's review indicates, a general instructional effect has not been established.

[8] For a comprehensive discussion of the validity of published tests of critical thinking, see Harold Berlak, "The New Curricula and the Measurement of Thinking," *Educational Forum* 1965, 30, pp. 303–311. For a synopsis of these criticisms, see James P. Shaver and Donald W. Oliver, "Teaching Students to Analyze Public Controversy: A Curriculum Project Report," *Social Education*, 1964, 28, p. 193.

for example, that the multiple-choice, paper-and-pencil format is unrealistic, for people do not make decisions about controversial matters while sitting at a desk selecting answers from a number of responses already structured and written out. Criticisms of this sort are undoubtedly as applicable to most of the tests developed by teachers for classroom use as they are to published tests. Testing techniques that break from the restrictions of the paper-and-pencil setting are sorely needed if research in social studies education is to come up with findings of educational significance, and if teachers are to have a meaningful basis for evaluating pupils and, concurrently, their own teaching.

The development of better measurement methods by researchers should produce techniques that can be used by the classroom teacher. One recent development which appears promising is the technique of *systematic content analysis* of small-group discussions. In one use of this technique, students are given a case involving a public issue to discuss and their discourse is analyzed to determine whether or not the concepts and intellectual strategies supposedly taught by the curriculum were in fact used. To carry out the analysis, the discussion is broken up into "units of talk" (e.g., each simple sentence might be considered a unit), and these units classified into categories based on the objectives of instruction.

Discussions of the types of paper-and-pencil tests commonly used in the classroom can be easily found in other books; however, because the content analysis of discussions is a relatively recent development of educational and behavioral research, discussions of this technique as a tool for assessing learning are not readily available. For that reason we have included the reading, "Evaluating the Jurisprudential Approach to the Social Studies," by Oliver and Shaver. The sections of the reading that deal with technical matters, such as statistical estimates of reliability, have been deleted. The remaining material indicates how a set of categories for analyzing discussions was derived from a specific social studies curriculum rationale. Some implications for teachers are also suggested. It is not intended that the approach presented in the reading be taken as the definitive answer to assessment problems. It is hoped, however, that it will encourage social studies teachers to think about and try promising new methods of testing.

We have intended to emphasize that even if valid measures of learning were available, much remains to be done in the study of teaching methods and content selection and organization. The reading by Medley and Mitzel indicates how little we know to date about the effect of the teacher's behavior on learning. It is evident, though, that no one method is likely to be appropriate for all objectives or for all students. For example, some students may like the self-regulation and the proscribed constraints of programed instruction; others may find the format restrictive and boring. Programed instruction has been compared to other instructional methods, but traditional research designs in which the effects of one method are compared against those of another, or in which the learning of students taught by an "experimental" method is compared to that of "control" students who are in the regular curriculum, do not get at questions about varying effects on different types of students. Recent developments in research design and statistics[9] are providing new avenues of investiga-

[9] See Chapters 4 and 5 of Gage (ed.), *Handbook of Research on Teaching, op. cit.*

tion, and the cutting edge of research into teaching methodology at this point is the investigation of the differential effects that particular methods have on students who bring different personality characteristics[10] and social and educational backgrounds to the classroom.

What Lies Ahead?

The prospects for the future are brighter. Educational researchers are being trained at a higher rate and new research and statistical techniques are being developed under the impetus of the recent national allocations of resources to educational research. However, the first general federal support of research in education was the Cooperative Research Act of 1954. In the 1964 fiscal year, only $3.50 out of every $1000 of federal research and development funds went to education. In the 1965 fiscal year, sixteen million dollars was spent on federally sponsored cooperative research, as compared with about eight *billion* dollars for defense research and development. All educational research and development accounted for only seventy-two million dollars, *less than two-fifths of one per cent* of national educational expenditures at a time when many industries invest as much as ten per cent of annual expenditures in research and development.[11] It is little wonder that past research has been scattered and limited. It is to be hoped, however, that the niggardly past has been but a prologue to an increase in research that will build the needed systematic knowledge about education in general, and about teaching the social studies in particular.

Even with the increased tempo of research activity, the pace at which firm knowledge is produced will seem slow to the practitioner. Five, ten, even fifteen years is a comparatively short time for complex research activity which aims to reach conclusions about teaching and learning that are sufficiently verified to serve as a firm basis for classroom decisions. In the meantime, the social studies teacher will need to evaluate his content and methods as critically as possible in his non-research setting, keeping in mind the lack of finality of our knowledge about teaching. He will often need to function on the basis of his hunches and those of his experienced colleagues in the schools and universities.

Special efforts must also be made to keep abreast of new curriculum developments and the state of knowledge about teaching and learning. This is crucial if the rationale upon which the teacher bases his curricular decisions is to be adequate. The difficulties of keeping up to date are so great in this period of expanding knowledge that individuals cannot be expected to do so alone. School systems must develop deliberate policies of information gathering and dissemination, along with plans and policies for systematic and effective implementation. But the role of the individual teacher will remain central. Teachers must be willing to accept and respond to promising educational in-

[10] See Oliver and Shaver, *Teaching Public Issues in the High School*, *op. cit.*, Section Five of the Appendix, for a discussion of the effect of student personality and for the presentation of one of the few published research efforts in this area.

[11] Philip H. Des Marais, *The Elementary and Secondary Act of 1965*, U.S. Department of Health, Education and Welfare (Washington: Government Printing Office, May 1965), p. 18.

novations, while maintaining an attitude of healthy skepticism toward proposals for change. The demands are heavy. To meet them, educators will often have to rely upon the advice of individuals who have both research competence and knowledge of the complexities underlying curricular decisions in the social studies. The use of expert advice, however, should not deter teachers from demanding research evidence concerning the effects that new programs have on students. One consequence of the teacher's increased research literacy may well be the abandonment of many of the current shibboleths of social studies education. Above all, however, the teacher's curricular decisions should be rational and intelligent, grounded not just in the research evidence at hand, but in the careful consideration of the meaning of democracy and the role of the social studies in general education.

The Scientific Study of Teacher Behavior

Donald M. Medley and Harold E. Mitzel

The research we have been doing in the division of teacher education of The City University of New York comes from the tradition of educational rather than psychological research. We decided to study classroom behavior not in order to test or develop any theory of behavior (although we may yet come to that), but in order to find out what the graduates of our teacher education program were doing in their classrooms. We wanted to find out what patterns of classroom behavior were characteristic of those graduates who were effective teachers, in the fond hope of relating effective behaviors of graduates to something in the training we had given them.

In attacking this problem, we have made use of at least five assumptions (that we are aware of). We have assumed, first of all, that *the most promising approach is a quantitative approach.* To us it seems obvious that the modern method of science is quantitative in nature. The tremendous contributions to knowledge made by the physical sciences seem to us to be the direct result of the success physicists have had in quantifying the aspects of physical phenomena relevant to their problems. Newton's laws of motion could neither have been formulated nor verified without the mass of measurement data in the areas of mechanics and astronomy which were available to him; nor could Einstein's theory have been formulated on the basis of the data available to Newton; his more inclusive theory had to wait on improvements in instrumentation and the amassing of quantitative data utilizing those improvements. It is our contention that no general theory of classroom behavior can be formulated until ways of

Reprinted with the permission of the Publisher from Arno A. Bellack, editor, *Theory and Research in Teaching* (New York: Teachers College Press, 1963). © 1963 by Teachers College, Columbia University.

quantifying classroom behaviors have been developed, and a large body of measurements of behaviors using these methods has been assembled. The fact that the phenomena we study are vastly more complex than the phenomena of physics make the employment of the quantitative method all the more necessary.

We have also assumed that in order to learn anything about classroom behavior *it is necessary to study behavior in the classroom;* we have *not* assumed (as many psychologists seem to assume) that it is possible to learn something about classroom behavior by studying laboratory behavior; or that much can be found out about how pupils learn by studying how college students, apes, or white mice learn. We have not found it necessary to assume the existence of laws of learning which are uniform across subjects, learning tasks, learning environments, and species. We have eschewed research, the findings of which are applicable to the classroom only through analogy.

We have tried to avoid any use of analogous reasoning except, perhaps, in the generation of hypotheses to be tested. We take the position that a conclusion drawn from a specific study may be applied only to other teachers, pupils, or classes which could be drawn at random from a population of teachers, pupils, or classes which could also contain the teachers, pupils, or classes studied. While it is not always easy to decide whether two subjects could come from the same population, it is sometimes easy to tell when two subjects could *not*. It seems obvious, for example, that a pupil and a mouse, or a psychological laboratory and a third-grade classroom, or a tachistoscope and a kindergarten teacher, could not both be simple random samples from single populations of pupils, classrooms, or teachers — or of mice, laboratories, or tachistoscopes, for that matter.

A third basic assumption we have made is that any effect the teacher has on the pupils is mediated by some overt behavior on the teacher's part. If the behavior takes place in the classroom, *it is therefore capable of being seen or heard by a properly trained observer.* If this assumption is not tenable, then the task of studying teachers' classroom behavior by the objective scientific method must be regarded as impossible.

We further assume that *each behavior a teacher exhibits has a purpose* (conscious or unconscious), and may be effective in achieving that purpose to a greater or less degree. The competence of a teacher is defined as the average success of all of his behaviors in achieving their intended effects. Strictly speaking, we cannot assess the competence of a particular teacher unless we know what effects he is seeking to achieve. We can, however, measure certain effects of his behavior and see which of his behaviors are followed by effects in which we are interested. If this information were made known to the teacher, he could presumably modify his behavior and increase his competence. There are as many ways of being effective as there are effects to be produced; the competent teacher is able to select those modes of behavior which will produce the effects he intends to produce. As research workers, we have studied effectiveness, rather than competence. Let someone else wrestle with the problem of teacher competence, since it involves value judgments which we do not regard as part of the province of science.

Our fourth assumption is that *what the teacher does is an important factor in determining what the pupil learns.* We do not rule out the pupil's capacity, maturation, or school and neighborhood environment as important factors; we hold that teacher behavior is also important, and have chosen to study it.

Finally, I suppose we have also assumed that, once effective patterns of teacher behavior have been identified, it will be possible to teach education students how to exhibit them. At least we have hoped that this is true. If, as some investigators seem to believe, teacher behaviors are manifestations of teacher personality characteristics not likely to be affected by college courses, then the problem of staffing the schools is a selection problem rather than a training problem. We choose to assume that teachers could learn to behave more effectively without undergoing any basic personality change, if only we knew enough about effective behavior to teach them how.

The development of a science of effective teacher behavior is almost certainly the most urgent research problem that faces the profession today. If teaching is not a science, then it must be an art — that is, a skill possessed only by teachers who either were born that way, or have been lucky enough to stumble on its secrets by chance. Without definite knowledge of the nature of effective teaching, it is impossible either to identify and recruit those young people born with this talent, or to make successful teachers out of young people born without it.

To form an estimate of the present state of the science of teacher behavior, it is only necessary to perform the following simple experiment: Think of the one principle or rule of teaching behavior which to you seems least open to question — the one which you would pass on to a beginning teacher with the greatest certainty that it would be useful to him. Then consider the nature of the evidence on which that principle is based. Is it based on a series of carefully controlled research studies which have demonstrated its validity beyond reasonable doubt? Or is the principle accepted because it agrees with modern educational philosophy? Or does the evidence rest on successful personal experiences of teachers who believe in the principle and try to follow it?

The fact is that very few of the things teachers do in classrooms today are done because they have been demonstrated scientifically to be effective ways of behaving. An honest appraisal of the content of teacher training would reveal that it does not resemble the rigorous quantitative set of laws which form the substance of the training of architects or engineers as much as it resembles the treasured store of traditions passed on by one witch doctor to another. No doubt the principles followed by teachers have more validity than those followed by the witch doctor, but both are based on the same kind of evidence. Indeed, many educators openly express the conviction that teaching is a mysterious, almost magical process which nobody understands or can hope to understand thoroughly. Possibly much of this lore is perfectly true — we are not yet in a position to advocate that any of it be thrown out. But progress comparable to that seen in the physical sciences can only be achieved when teaching becomes a science.

Scientifically based knowledge of the nature of effective teacher behavior must be sought in studies attempting to relate teacher behavior to teacher effectiveness; if the quantitative scientific method is to be used, each such study must obviously incorporate objective measurements of both types of variables. Domas and Tiedeman [20] have listed over a thousand investigations related to teacher competence; although many of them do not attempt to relate behavior and effectiveness, there are a number of studies which do. Why have these studies contributed so little to the science of effective behavior?

Aside from the fact that practically nobody reads these old studies any more, there are two cogent reasons why their impact has been so slight. First or all, the vast majority of the research in teacher effectiveness that has been done must be discarded as irrelevant because the criteria of effectiveness used have been invalid. Second, an even larger part of the research must be rejected because it has failed to incorporate any objective measures of teacher behavior. Mitzel and Gross [44], in a critical review of attempts to measure teacher effectiveness, found only about twenty studies which used measures which met their criteria; Medley and Mitzel [41], in a similar review of studies of teacher behavior, also found only some twenty studies which incorporated objective measures of behavior. There is not much overlap between the two lists, so it seems safe to say that the serious student of effective teacher behavior would need to consult only about forty research reports among the hundreds that have been done to have read all of those which are germane to his purpose.

The question of why so much of the research in teacher effectiveness has not led to usable results will be discussed in terms of two problems: the problem of measuring teacher effectiveness and the problem of measuring teacher behavior.

The Problem of Measuring Teacher Effectiveness

It is widely agreed [see, for example, 13, 1, 46] that the ultimate criterion of teacher effectiveness must be based on changes in pupils. Intermediate criteria must be shown to be relevant, that is, correlated with the ultimate criterion. There are many factors which make it difficult to measure a teacher's effectiveness in producing changes in pupil behaviors. Some of the difficulties are philosophical or definitional in nature and relate to the selection of which changes are to be measured. These problems call for a willingness on the part of the research worker to take a stand (somewhere out on a limb, usually). Some have to do with the removal of influences on pupil growth other than the teacher's behavior; such problems call for familiarity with the proper procedures for analyzing data. None of these problems are insurmountable. And none of them can be solved by abandoning the attempt to measure pupil growth entirely. Yet the attempt has been abandoned in at least 90 per cent of the studies of teacher effectiveness done up to now. In almost every research study in the area, some unvalidated intermediate criterion in the form of judgments or ratings of teacher effectiveness has been used instead of a direct measure of the effects on pupils of the teachers studied.

There is no misconception more deeply rooted in the mind of modern man — layman and professional educator alike — than the notion that it is possible to recognize a good teacher by watching him teach.

Research in teacher effectiveness began with studies in which large numbers of laymen were asked to recall great teachers they had once had, and to tell the investigator what characteristics made them great. The investigator would then classify and summarize these characteristics and publish some sort of a list. Later researchers refined this method by asking only people qualified as experts, a large part of whose *expertise* must have consisted in familiarity with these very same lists, to identify the effective teachers. The final refinement was to have the experts rate teachers' possession of qualities which according to these same lists, were characteristic of effective teachers. Nowhere in this circular process was there any verification of the assumption that teachers originally judged to be more effective were actually producing greater changes in pupils than teachers identified as less effective.

Recently there have been a few studies which do compare judgments of teacher effectiveness (made by experts) and actual measurements of changes in pupils. Typical conclusions drawn from such studies are:

Teacher rating scales . . . are only slightly related to the observed pupil growth [32].

Correlations between supervisors' ratings and the two measures of growth . . . [were] + .133 and + .067 [42].

. . . evaluations based on . . . supervisors' ratings and those based on measures of pupil growth and achievement were not significantly correlated [6].

. . . supervisory ratings here provided are invalid [as measures of pupil gain] [37].

. . . supervisory ratings . . . seem to lack reliability and validity [as measures of pupil gain] [35].

The criterion of pupil change apparently measures something different than that measured by teacher ratings [30].

The three criteria . . . [pupil gain, pupil evaluations, and a composite of five supervisory ratings] are not related to a greater degree than can be attributed to chance [39].

Whatever pupil gain measures in relation to teaching ability it is not emphasized in supervisory ratings [36a].

Employers' ratings of teaching ability are not related to pupil gains in information [16].

These results may be interpreted as implying that a teacher whose pupils learn almost nothing from him is just about as likely to be rated highly effective as one whose pupils learn a great deal. A characteristic highly correlated with "effectiveness" as judged by a supervisor or other trained person is no more likely to be correlated with measured effectiveness than any other. It is in this sense that studies of effectiveness using judgments of effectiveness as criteria are irrelevant.

Perhaps an outline of what is involved in the measurement of teacher effectiveness will suggest why ratings of effectiveness lack validity. The first step in measuring a teacher's effectiveness is to test his pupils with an achievement test or battery of tests at the beginning and end of a term. Often an aptitude test and a personality test or adjustment inventory are also administered at the beginning of the term. The final achievement score of each individual pupil is then adjusted (by the technique known as analysis of covariance) to make due allowance for any influence that each pupil's aptitude, previous learning, and personality or adjustment (as measured by the tests) may have on his final achievement score. Finally, the mean of these adjusted scores of all pupils in each teacher's class is compared with similar means of classes of other teachers (with further adjustments for effects of school and community differences if the classes are in different schools). It is then possible to make statements about the relative effectiveness of the teachers which are called measures of teacher effectiveness.

Would it seem reasonable to ask even the most experienced supervisor to visit a teacher, watch him teach a while, and then judge his effect on even a single pupil — that is, predict the score that pupil would get at the end of the term, making proper allowances for the scores he would get at the beginning of the term? The use of a judgmental criterion would seem to ask the judge to do just this, not for one, but for every pupil in the class, to estimate the mean of all these adjusted scores, and then to compare that mean (with allowances for school and community influences) with similar means for other teachers he may not even have observed.

The belief that an observer can judge a teacher's effectiveness must be based on the idea that by noting the extent to which the teacher behaves in ways known to be effective (or ineffective), the observer can form a judgment of the effect the teacher will probably have on pupils. In other words, the validity of judgmental criteria of teacher effectiveness depends on the assumption that the science of teacher behavior already exists, and studies using such criteria can hardly be expected to contribute much to the birth of the science.

The Problem of Measuring Teacher Behavior

When we speak of an effective teacher behavior we do not mean to imply that the behavior was necessarily effective in achieving the teacher's purpose; we judge effectiveness of a behavior in terms of the outcomes we choose to study. This implies the assumption that *the effect of a behavior may not depend on the purpose of the teacher.* Behaviors identical in every respect except the teacher's purpose should have identical effects on the pupils, since the pupils are unaware of the purpose of the teacher so long as it is not manifested externally. What the teacher needs to know to achieve competence is what the probable effect of each behavior is, so that he can exhibit those behaviors which will achieve his purposes most efficiently.

Two behaviors are seldom identical in all observable respects. What would seem to be the same behavior can be quite different in impact according to who exhibits it. This is what the poet had in mind when he characterized the behavior of his mistress by observing that,

> Her very frowns are fairer far
> Than smiles of other maidens are.

The setting or situation in which a behavior occurs also alters its effect. There is a time and a place for everything. Moreover, when a particular teacher does a particular thing at a particular time, it does not necessarily have the same effect on all thirty of his pupils. These three points may be summarized under the heading of the problem of heterogeneity of effects of behavior. If a given behavior had the same effect on every pupil every time it occurred, our task would be simple. It does not and it is not.

. . . .

The Present Status of the Science

Workable systems for recording at least some aspects of behavior have been in existence almost as long as research in teacher effectiveness has been going on. But it was not until after World War II that studies using objective measurements of classroom behavior began to appear in any number. At Wisconsin, a number of investigations (many of which involved direct observation of teachers) appeared [for example, 32, 35, 37, 39], following lines laid down by Barr [11]. At Illinois, H. H. Anderson and his associates [3, 4, 5], working in the context of child psychology, developed objective measures of emotional climate in nursery and elementary schools. Also at Illinois, but more in the tradition of curriculum research along the lines of Wrightstone's earlier work [61], Cornell and his associates [19] measured differences in classroom behavior in schools of various types in communities of various sizes.

Techniques for the measurement of classroom behavior have been further refined in the past decade or so. Classroom climate is probably the one dimension that has been most successfully measured, the initial work of H. H. Anderson having been advanced by Withall [58], Mitzel and Rabinowitz [45], and Flanders [23]. In our own work we [43] combined the Withall technique with modifications of the Cornell instrument into an instrument called the Observation Schedule and Record (or OScAR) on which three practically orthogonal dimensions of behavior could be scored: Emotional Climate, Verbal Emphasis, Social Organization. Conspicuously absent, however, was any dimension or set of dimensions related to the organization of the content of instruction and the flow of ideas in the lesson. Progress toward the development of dimensions in this area is provided in the work of Muriel Wright and Virginia Proctor [60] in mathematics classes, and that of B. O. Smith [55] in classes in various high school subjects.

The behaviors of teachers while they teach and pupils while they learn are beginning to become objectively quantifiable. Better measures of at least some of the changes in pupil behavior which represent the effects of teacher behavior than have ever been available before are provided by several achievement batteries developed in the forties and fifties. The potentialities which inhere in modern statistical methods for teasing out relationships between behaviors and effects, despite the many irrelevant factors which tend to mask them, are beginning to be realized and exploited; this is, of course, greatly facilitated by modern high-speed computers. Are we on the verge of a major breakthrough in the science of teacher behavior?

BIBLIOGRAPHY

1. Ackerman, Walter I. "Teacher Competence and Pupil Change," *Harvard Educational Review*, Vol. 24 (1954), pp. 227–239.
3. Anderson, Harold H., and Brewer, Helen M. *Studies of Teachers' Classroom Personalities, I: Dominative and Socially Integrative Behavior of Kindergarten Teachers.* Applied Psychology Monographs, 1945, No. 6.
4. Anderson, Harold H., and Brewer, Joseph E. *Studies of Teachers' Classroom Personalities, II: Effects of Teachers' Dominative and Integrative*

Contacts on Children's Classroom Behavior. Applied Psychology Monographs, 1946, No. 8.

5. Anderson, Harold H., Brewer, Joseph E., and Reed, Mary Frances. *Studies of Teachers' Classroom Personalities, III: Follow-up Studies of the Effects of Dominative and Integrative Contacts on Children's Behavior.* Applied Psychology Monographs, 1946, No. 11.

6. Anderson, H. M. "A Study of Certain Criteria of Teacher Effectiveness," *Journal of Experimental Education*, Vol. 23 (1954), pp. 41–71.

11. Barr, A. S. *Characteristic Differences in the Teaching Performance of Good and Poor Teachers of the Social Studies.* Bloomington, Ill.: Public School Publishing Co., 1929.

13. Barr, A. S., Bechdolt, B. V., Coxe, W. W., Gage, N. L., Orleans, J. S., Remmers, H. H., and Ryans, D. G. "Report of the Committee on Criteria of Teacher Effectiveness," *Review of Educational Research*, Vol. 22 (1952), pp. 238–263.

16. Brookover, W. B. "The Relation of Social Factors to Teaching Ability," *Journal of Experimental Education*, Vol. 13 (1945), pp. 191–205.

19. Cornell, F. G., Lindvall, C. M., and Saupe, J. L. *An Exploratory Measurement of Individualities of School and Classrooms.* Urbana, Ill.: College of Education, University of Illinois, Bureau of Educational Research, 1952.

20. Domas, S. J., and Tiedeman, D. V. "Teacher Competence: An Annotated Bibliography," *Journal of Experimental Education*, Vol. 19 (1950), pp. 101–218.

23. Flanders, Ned A. *Teacher Influence, Pupil Attitudes, and Achievement: Studies in Interaction Analysis.* U.S. Office of Education Cooperative Research Project, No. 397. Minneapolis: University of Minnesota, 1960. (Mimeographed.)

30. Gotham, R. E. "Personality and Teaching Efficiency," *Journal of Experimental Education*, Vol. 14 (1945), pp. 157–165.

32. Hellfritsch, A. G. "A Factor Analysis of Teacher Abilities," *Journal of Experimental Education*, Vol. 14 (1945), pp. 166–199.

35. Jayne, C. D. "A Study of the Relationship Between Teaching Procedures and Educational Outcomes," *Journal of Experimental Education*, Vol. 14 (1945), pp. 101–134.

36a. Jones, R. D. "The Predicting of Teaching Efficiency from Objective Measures," *Journal of Experimental Education*, Vol. 15 (1946), pp. 85–99.

37. LaDuke, C. V. "The Measurement of Teaching Ability: Study No. 3," *Journal of Experimental Education*, Vol. 14 (1945), pp. 75–100.

39. Lins, L. J. "The Prediction of Teaching Efficiency," *Journal of Experimental Education*, Vol. 15 (1946), pp. 2–60.

41. Medley, D. M., and Mitzel, H. E. "Measuring Classroom Behavior by Systematic Observation," in N. L. Gage(Ed.), *Handbook of Research on Teaching.* Chicago: Rand McNally & Co., 1963.

42. Medley, D. M., and Mitzel, H. E. "Some Behavioral Correlates of Teacher Effectiveness," *Journal of Educational Psychology*, Vol. 50 (1959), pp. 239–246.

43. Medley, Donald M., and Mitzel, Harold E. "A Technique for Measuring Classroom Behavior," *Journal of Educational Psychology*, Vol. 49 (April 1958), pp. 86–92.

44. Mitzel, H. E., and Gross, Cecily. "The Development of Pupil Growth Criteria in Studies of Teacher Effectiveness," *Educational Research Bulletin*, Vol. 37 (1958), pp. 178–187 and 205–215.

45. Mitzel, Harold E., and Rabinowitz, William. "Assessing Social-Emotional Climate in the Classroom by Withall's Technique," *Psychological Monographs, General and Applied*, Vol. 67, No. 18, Whole No. 368 (1953), pp. 1–19.

46. Morsh, S. E., and Wilder, Eleanor W. "Identifying the Effective Instructor: A Review of the Quantitative Studies, 1900–1952," *USAF Personnel Training Research Center Research Bulletin* (1954), No. AFPTRC-TR-54-44.

55. Smith, B. Othanel, and Associates. *A Study of the Logic of Teaching: A Report on the First Phase of a Five-Year Research Project*. U.S. Office of Education Cooperative Research Project, No. 258 (7257). Urbana, Ill.: University of Illinois, 1960.

58. Withall, John. "The Development of a Technique for the Measurement of Social-Emotional Climate in Classrooms," *Journal of Experimental Education*, Vol. 17 (March 1949), pp. 347–361.

60. Wright, E., Wright, Muriel J., and Proctor, V. H. *Systematic Observation of Verbal Interaction as a Method of Comparing Mathematics Lessons*. U.S. Office of Education Cooperative Research Project, No. 816. St. Louis: Washington University, 1961.

61. Wrightstone, J. Wayne. *Appraisal of New Practices in Selected Public Schools*. New York: Bureau of Publications, Teachers College, Columbia University, 1935.

Evaluating the Jurisprudential Approach to the Social Studies

Donald W. Oliver and James P. Shaver

Reflective morality is the term used by Dewey to indicate an intellectual process by which men in a democratic society might deal with and resolve political and social problems. In another article,[1] we called our own efforts to teach such a process of reflection the "jurisprudential" approach to instruction. We stated that a jurisprudential curriculum would focus upon a series of related questions:

1. What is an adequate description of the objective situation which causes an ethical controversy or dispute?

From *The High School Journal*, 1962, 46, pages 53–60, 61–63, by permission of the University of North Carolina Press and the authors.

[1] Donald W. Oliver. "Educating Citizens for Responsible Individualism, 1960–1980." In Franklin Patterson (ed.), *Citizenship and a Free Society: Education for the Future*. Washington, D.C.: National Council for the Social Studies, 30th Yearbook, 1960, Chapter 11. [See pages 97–120.]

2. To what extent is the controversial situation so pressing that the government can justifiably use its coercive power to restrict personal liberty in the interests of the community?
3. To what extent do the rights we wish to restrict by law have Constitutional guarantees?
4. To what extent do specific checks and restrictions within the American Constitutional system adequately reduce or unreasonably restrict governmental power?

In a jurisprudential approach to instruction, we suggested, certain concepts and their application should be taught. These included:

1. Concepts which describe the basic values of American society, as well as the consent system designed to maintain and support these values. These include such values as personal freedom and personal privacy (e.g. speech, conscience, contract and property), equal opportunity, equal protection under law, peace and order, a concern for the general welfare and progress of the community, and concern for the welfare of each individual, i.e., brotherhood and charity.[2]
2. Concepts related to the intellectual process by which ethical and empirical disputes can be more intelligently handled. These concepts would include the distinction between definitional, empirical, and normative problems as well as the proof process by which problems can best be handled.[3]
3. Concepts from the social sciences which give the person a more adequate means of describing and handling descriptions of social phenomena, e.g., "culture" and "social class."

We must confess that there is nothing very new in these objectives. They are commonly described and espoused under the term "critical" or "reflective" thinking or the "problems approach." The works of Dewey and Tufts,[4] Raup et al.,[5] and Hunt and Metcalf[6] are each landmarks in social education clarifying and reinforcing this point of view. We have done two things, however, on which we should like to comment. We have developed a two year curriculum specifically designed to teach "reflective morality." (We realize that most curricula have as one of their aims the teaching of "critical thinking." However, this outcome is usually anticipated as a by-product of some more central objective, such as "teaching American history.") Second, we have attempted to translate the objectives of jurisprudential teaching into specific learning out-

[2] See, for example, Gunnar Myrdal on the American Creed in An American Dilemma. New York: Harper & Brothers, 1944.

[3] See, for example: Max Black. Critical Thinking: An Introduction to Logic and Scientific Method. (2nd ed.) New York: Prentice-Hall, 1952; M. R. Cohen and Ernest Nagel. An Introduction to Logic and Scientific Method. New York: Harcourt, Brace & Co., 1934; and, C. L. Stevenson. Ethics and Language. New Haven: Yale University Press, 1944.

[4] John Dewey and James H. Tufts. Ethics. New York: H. Holt & Co.: 1908.

[5] R. B. Raup, G. E. Axtelle, K. D. Benne, and B. O. Smith. The Improvement of Practical Intelligence. New York: Harper & Brothers, 1950.

[6] Maurice P. Hunt and Lawrence E. Metcalf. Teaching High School Social Studies. New York: Harper & Brothers, 1955.

comes which can be described and identified more precisely. It is this latter effort that we shall describe briefly in this paper. Before doing so, however, we should clarify two points. First, we make no pretense that these outcomes constitute an exhaustive inventory of reflective thinking concepts or skills. Second, they are not general critical or reflective thinking outcomes in the sense that they apply to any content; we are concerned only with their appropriateness in teaching students how to deal with political controversy within the framework of the Western political tradition.

Operational Objectives of a Jurisprudential Social Studies Curriculum

A student should be able to:

1. Deal with political controversy at a general analytic level and relate his analysis to specific issues and concrete cases. For example, in a case involving the arrest of a sidewalk orator, the students should see that certain general values are involved, e.g. freedom of speech, the peace and safety of the community, and the property rights of nearby shoppers. If the orator is said to be creating a disturbance, the student should see that the term "disturbance" is a relatively vague one which creates definitional problems. He should see that the assertion about the speech causing a disturbance requires greater specification. Thinking about a particular case in terms of such issues as defining "disturbance" and "free speech" we think, allows the student to deal with the case at two levels: he identifies general problems inherent in this kind of case, and then places the facts of this case within the context of these more general problems.
2. Identify inconsistencies and conflicts between two or more values, empirical statements, or definitions.
3. Deal with inconsistencies and conflicts between values by identifying an array of situations in which the inconsistent or conflicting values are presented in varying degrees of favorableness or unfavorableness in order to delineate at what point he should support one value as against the other. For example, we might support free speech over peace and order if the only danger involved was a sidewalk disturbance. We might however, reverse our position if such speeches were inflaming riots or an insurrection.
4. Deal with inconsistencies and conflicts between empirical statements by seeking and evaluating specific evidence to support the statements.
5. Deal with the inconsistent or ambiguous use of words by seeking evidence concerning how the words are most commonly used, or how the concepts which the words label may be most accurately described.
6. Distinguish between those factual claims which are relevant to the central value issues in a controversy and those claims which bear little or no relationship to the value.

The level of specificity with which these operations are stated above, we think, makes the problem of assessing a student's ability to perform any of them less difficult than assessing whether or not a student has learned to use some general process called "critical thinking" or "problem solving." Even with generality and ambiguity reduced, however, many problems of measurement remain.

The Assessment of Learning Outcomes

We have tried a number of ways of translating these learning outcomes into measurable units. All start at the same point. We ask the student to read and analyze, either by himself or in a group, a controversial political situation — a controversial case. In one approach, we then give the student specific statements in the argument, either in written or oral form, and ask him what function they serve. Do they, for example, transform the case into a more general problem, or continue to deal with it as an isolated instance of personal conflict? A second approach is to take statements made in the argument, and ask the student to rebut them. This can be done either with open-ended questions, or by presenting series of five or six rebuts from which he is to choose the best and/or the worst.

The approach we have found the most promising, however, is the systematic analysis and categorization of statements made in oral discussions. Some advantages to this approach are obvious. The oral discussion is a more natural situation in which to ascertain the analytical skills of the students. (How many students write about political questions after they leave school?) The oral discussion also provides the student with less structure than objective pencil-and-paper tests. In critical thinking tests of the latter type, for example, the student is commonly presented with a message, parts of which are abstracted for analysis. He is then asked to deal only with these parts in his response, which is already restricted by a multiple choice set. The student thus has a very narrow range of behavior within which he can choose. In the open discussion, however, he must select relevant parts of the controversial case and the ensuing discussion with which to deal. He is thus forced to select from a much broader range of alternative responses which he must create for himself.

This last "advantage" of systematic content analysis is, of course, also its greatest difficulty. Because there is such a wide range of alternative responses which the student can make, all types of responses must be anticipated so that they can be evaluated and scored. Instead of a simple key to a test, the scorer finds himself with a long and complex manual in which hundreds of types of responses may be described and classified. Because of this complexity, scoring is difficult, requiring a long training period. Furthermore the scoring process itself is less reliable.

As an example of the systematic content analysis approach, we should like to present a set of categories we have worked out and used to evaluate the student's ability to handle controversial political issues.

Synopsis of a Content Analysis System for Scoring the Student's Ability to Analyze and Resolve Political Controversy

Although the following discussion may seem somewhat technical, the reader should understand that because content analysis attempts to deal with "free communication," many problems occur which are simply avoided in a pre-structured test. Nor can we deal here with all the problems of an approach to the evaluation of reflective thinking based on content analysis. It is hoped, however, that we might communicate both the advantages as well as the complexities of this approach in the short space available.

Systematic analysis of interaction, as we use the methodology, involves analyzing ongoing interaction into discrete units which are then categorized. There are three important considerations in carrying out this categorization:

(1) Into what size units will the total train of interaction be broken?
(2) What is the frame of reference of the scorer?
(3) What is the specific nature of the categories used to describe the interaction?

Theoretically, units can range in size from entire meetings or discussions to particular segments of the discussion which may be defined in terms of time, a completed verbal interchange, or according to some linguistic convention. We have defined our unit as a single item of thought. Linguistically, this is most commonly a simple or complex sentence or the independent clauses of compound sentences. There are, however, some exceptions to this convention which bring us back to the more general rule of a single item of thought. For example, if a case is presented which is to be compared to the original case under discussion, it is scored as a single unit even though it may consist of several sentences. Also, sources of evidence, although they are embedded in simple sentences, are scored separately. ("The New York Times reported that federal troops were used to restore order at Central High School," would be scored as two units.)

In determining the frame of reference of the scorer a major consideration is how much of the discussion the observer should take into account in classifying a particular act. Since our system uses two scoring systems superimposed on each other, it also uses two contexts: one for what we call static categories; the other for dynamic categories. The dynamic system (see Chart 1) consists of categories which require the scorer to deal with a context beyond the statement being categorized. This may include one or several other sentences. Scoring in these categories is determined by relationships among statements. The static categories (see Chart 2) theoretically can be scored without taking into account any context beyond the scorable unit. Every unit of behavior is scored in a static category. Dynamic operations are scored only when they are identified. Thus, when a dynamic operation is scored, a double categorization of the same unit occurs.

There are some exceptions, however, to this distinction between static and dynamic categories. The category "relevance," for example, is a dynamic category, but it is scored as if it were static because the assertion or questioning of relevance usually contains an obvious cue within the statement itself, and because there is no static category which can be appropriately scored with it.

Posture of the Speaker

"Posture" refers to the attitude of the speaker toward the statement he is making. Put another way, posture indicates the function which that statement is performing for the speaker. We have identified and used four postures: declarative statements; interrogative statements; statements which question or express doubt about a prior statement (often in either the declarative or interrogative form, but with an overtone of argumentative intent); and, statements which express self-doubt (as, for example, uncertainty as to the validity of a claim which has been or is going to be made by the speaker). The posture of the speaker is scored with a symbol within the space provided on a scoring sheet for the appropriate static category.

Orientation of the Speaker to the Discussion:
Analysis versus Persuasion

We also distinguish and score whether or not the speaker is trying to persuade other group members that his position in the argument is correct, or whether he is attempting to stay "outside" the argument and simply analyze how the group might construe the issues in the case. For example, "That person should not have been allowed to speak because avoiding a riot is more important than his right to speak," is scored as persuasive. The statement, "The problem here is that the principles of freedom of speech and peace and order are both involved in the situation and we must decide which value should be given greater weight in this instance," is scored an analytical.

Validity and Reliability

Initially, of course, using the system to categorize statements in a discussion results in an abstract cognitive description of the discussion. This description must be translated into a quantitative score by determining which categories seem valuable from the point of view of our objectives, and then counting the frequency with which the units are scored in these categories. This selection of valued categories is essentially a question of validity. Thus far the system appears to have not only intuitive or face validity, but it also reflects the effect of increased training in reflective thinking. We plan to carry out procedures by which validity can be more firmly established, however. Presently, we feel that the following categories have value for a discussion involving political controversy.

Static Categories:

General Value Judgments and *General Legal Claims* are valued because they allow the student to deal with the controversial case at a more abstract and general level.

Specific Factual Claims and *Sources* are valued because they are most commonly used to support more general claims. They are most often associated with the empirical proof process.

Definitional Claims are valued because they tend to be used to give greater precision to the various positions in the argument.

Clarification is *not* valued, since it involves mainly statements which repeat something already said. When the student clarifies by drawing finer distinctions between positions or terms in the argument, it is scored as a *Definitional Claim.*

Case is valued because, by definition, it is an attempt to expose the point at which an individual will reverse his position, given an array of similar situations to judge. It is essentially part of a defining operation.

Relevance is valued because it indicates that the student is attempting to deal with the relationship between a particular statement and some larger facet of the total argument.

Dynamic Categories:

For obvious reasons, all three dynamic categories are valued. They have been selected for scoring precisely because we think they are important.

Orientation to Discussion:

The analytic orientation to the discussion is valued because it tends to indicate that the student is attempting to stand back from the immediate persuasive aspects of the argument and provide a more impartial framework by which to deal with the controversy.

It should be noted that these valued acts are not simply a product of *a priori* guessing about what acts operate to produce the most intelligent discussion. In arriving at our present position, we have listened to many discussions and done a good deal of cutting and fitting to make our quantitative scores consistent with our intuitive judgments about what behavior is actually valuable. Although validity is based mainly on the casual subjective judgments of scorers, we have done more systematic work to establish whether or not the subtleties of language can be reliably scored with these gross categories.

. . . .

Conclusion

The translation of the objectives of the jurisprudential approach into specific learning outcomes which can be measured with a set of categories such as described in this article presents, we believe, unusual possibilities for curricular evaluation. Because learning outcomes can then be measured in a situation less structured than paper-and-pencil tests and approaching much more closely the circumstances in which the desired concepts will later be applied, the evaluation of educational objectives takes on greater meaning and validity. Our reliability data suggest the feasibility of this approach to assessment both in experimentation and classroom teaching. It should be noted, too, that just as a teacher might during any one period of time teach for only one or a few of the concepts included in the category set, so might the set be modified to include fewer categories in order to simplify scoring.

There is no denying the impracticability of the system for the day to day needs of the average classroom. Teachers, in general, have neither the research competence nor the time to learn and use such a complex system. Ultimately, however, the more complex instrument might be used to establish the validity of simpler category systems, or even of pencil-and-paper tests. There is little doubt in our minds that present methods of measurement which attempt to assess the process of reflective thinking with a series of fragmented multiple choice items show insufficient respect for the subtlety and complexity of this competence. It is our conviction that measurement programs will become more significant to teachers and research people when evaluation begins with a recognition of the complexity of the phenomena they are attempting to describe and assess.

Chart 1 — Dynamic Categories

Conflict-Consistency: Statements that indicate explicitly or implicitly that the speaker is aware of a real or possible inconsistency within his own or another speaker's position.

Specification and *Generalization:* Specification occurs when the speaker gives a specific statement to illustrate or support a more general statement. Generalization occurs when the speaker draws a more general conclusion from one or more specific statements already given.

Example of specification: "Desegregation is not going well. Only 7% of the Negro children in the South are now going to integrated schools after seven years of illegal segregation." The second sentence would be scored as the static operation "specific claim" and the dynamic operation "specification."

Example of a generalization: "After World War II, Russia captured the countries of eastern Europe, helped China to become a Communist nation, and tried its best to take over Greece and Turkey. Russia is the greatest imperialistic nation the world has ever known." Statement two would be scored as a static operation "general claim," and a dynamic operation "generalization."

Qualifying: A statement which deals with an implicit or explicit inconsistency or conflict by pointing out under what general circumstances an exception to a general principle is allowable or possible we score as a qualifying act.

Example: Mr. A: Our civil liberties are our most precious asset. To try and restrict them for any citizen is un-American.

Mr. B: If you had been in Germany in the early 1930's, would you have restricted some of the civil liberties granted Hitler when he was conducting mass hate meetings?

Mr. A: I very well might have. I would say that civil liberties should be restricted, however, only when the government which is pledged to protect them is in real danger from an undemocratic and brutal force, which would destroy all civil liberties.

Mr. A's modified position would be scored as static operation "general value judgment," and dynamic operation "qualification."

Chart 2 — Static Categories

General Value Judgments: Statements in which the speaker expresses a preference for a person, object or position in the argument in terms of a general social or legal value, such as: personal privacy, property, contract, speech, religion, general welfare of the group, equality, justice, brotherhood, due process, consent and representation. "Mr. Kohler certainly should have the right to run his property and to make contracts with his workers without union interference."

Specific Value Judgments: Statements in which the speaker expresses a preference for a person, object or position in the argument in terms of the specific case under discussion. "I think Mr. Kohler should have met the demands of the United Auto Workers."

General Legal Claim: Statements in which the speaker asserts that someone has a legal right to do something, expressed in terms of a general legal principle, such as: rule of law, due process, equal protection under the law, constitutional restraints, etc. "He has a right to a fair trial under the United States Constitution."

Specific Legal Claim: Statements in which the speaker asserts that someone has a legal right to do something, but does not give a legal principle as a basis for the right. "Mr. Kohler has a right to fire any worker he wants."

General Factual Claims: Casual, descriptive, or predictive generalizations. "Negroes are just as intelligent as whites."

Specific Factual Claims: Statements describing specific events delineated in time and space. "The first attempt at integration in Little Rock was on September 4, 1957."

Source: A statement or part of a statement describing the source on which a claim, definition or value judgment is based. "Emergency is defined this way in *Webster's New International Dictionary.*"

Definitional Claim: A statement about how a word or phrase is defined or should be defined. It is also a statement of analysis by which several meanings of a single word might be distinguished. "An emergency occurs when one or more people are in danger of being injured or losing their lives and property."

Clarification: A statement in which the speaker communicates something already stated in order to focus the discussion. It may include simple repetition, in that saying something again may emphasize or clarify a person's position.

Case: A set of statements which describes specific real or hypothetical situations analogous to the one under discussion. Its main purpose is to elaborate the range of situations to which one might apply a value judgment. "Suppose Negroes and whites were given schools of equal quality, teachers of equal quality, books and educational facilities of equal quality: Would Negro schools still be inferior to white schools?"

Relevance: A statement which explicitly deals with the way a statement or group of statements is related to the total argument. "I don't see what that statement has to do with the discussion."

Debate Strategy: Ad hominem or other remarks which explicitly discuss the tactics being used by the opponent. "You're just trying to confuse me."

Task Problem: Procedural: A statement directed at controlling the immediate interpersonal situation, and which assumes that everyone in the discussion is trying to do a conscientious job. "Let's take a vote." "Let's give everyone a chance to talk."

Task Problem: Deviance Control: A statement directed at controlling the immediate interpersonal situation, and assuming that one or more people are violating group norms. "Get back in your seat and sit down." "You don't have to shout."

FURTHER READING FOR SECTION 6

Gross, R. E., and W. V. Badger. "Social Studies," in C. W. Harris (ed.), *Encyclopedia of Educational Research*, 3rd ed. New York: Macmillan, 1960. Pp. 1296–1319.

A rather complete survey of a broad range of topics related to the social studies curriculum. By reading the Gross and Badger chapters in conjunction with the more up-to-date annual reviews of research in *Social Education* and Lawrence E. Metcalf's chapter, "Research on Teaching the Social Studies," in the *Handbook of Research on Teaching* (edited by N. L. Gage, Chicago: Rand McNally, 1963), the student can obtain a comprehensive view of research in the social studies field.

Harrison, Sylvia E., and Robert J. Solomon. "Review of Research in the Teaching of Social Studies: 1960–1963," *Social Education*, 1964, 28, pp. 277–292. Harrison, Sylvia E., and Robert J. Solomon. "Review of Research in the Teaching of Social Studies: 1964," *Social Education*, 1965, 29, pp. 281–290, 298. Cox, C. Benjamin, Emily S. Girault, and Lawrence E. Metcalf. "Review of Research in Social Studies: 1965," *Social Education*, 1966, 30, pp. 348–350. Girault, Emily S., and C. Benjamin Cox. "Review of Research in Social Studies: 1966," *Social Education*, 1967, 31, pp. 388–396, 404.

These exhaustive reviews, an annual feature in *Social Education*, the journal of the National Council for the Social Studies, are excellent for reports of research on social studies carried out in recent years.

Massialas, Byron G., and C. Benjamin Cox. *Inquiry in Social Studies.* New York: McGraw-Hill, 1966.

Chapter 3 is a quite comprehensive review of research on reflective thinking. It includes references to research on the relation of open-closed mindedness to critical thinking.

Oliver, Donald W., and James P. Shaver. *Teaching Public Issues in the High School.* Boston: Houghton Mifflin, 1966.

The Appendix of this book reports the results of testing a curriculum based on the rationale presented in the body of the book. It completes a unique presentation in one book of a rationale for a curriculum, the outline of the curriculum, and the results of a careful research program to test the curriculum.